CO-ATE-262

The Mental Health Industry: A Cultural Phenomenon *by Peter A. Magaro, Robert Gripp, David McDowell, and Ivan W. Miller III*

Nonverbal Communication: The State of the Art *by Robert G. Harper, Arthur N. Weins, and Joseph D. Matarazzo*

Alcoholism and Treatment *by David J. Armor, J. Michael Polich, and Harriet B. Stambul*

A Biodevelopmental Approach to Clinical Child Psychology: Cognitive Controls and Cognitive Control Theory *by Sebastiano Santostefano*

Handbook of Infant Development *edited by Joy D. Osofsky*

Understanding the Rape Victim: A Synthesis of Research Findings *by Sedelle Katz and Mary Ann Mazur*

Childhood Pathology and Later Adjustment: The Question of Prediction *by Loretta K. Cass and Carolyn B. Thomas*

Intelligent Testing with the WISC-R *by Alan S. Kaufman*

Adaptation in Schizophrenia: The Theory of Segmental Set *by David Shakow*

Psychotherapy: An Eclectic Approach *by Sol L. Garfield*

Handbook of Minimal Brain Dysfunctions *edited by Herbert E. Rie and Ellen D. Rie*

Handbook of Behavioral Interventions: A Clinical Guide *edited by Alan Goldstein and Edna B. Foa*

Art Psychotherapy *by Harriet Wadeson*

Handbook of Adolescent Psychology *edited by Joseph Adelson*

Psychotherapy Supervision: Theory, Research and Practice *edited by Allen K. Hess*

Psychology and Psychiatry in Courts and Corrections: Controversy and Change *by Ellsworth A. Fersch, Jr.*

Restricted Environmental Stimulation: Research and Clinical Applications *by Peter Suedfeld*

Personal Construct Psychology: Psychotherapy and Personality *edited by Alvin W. Landfield and Larry M. Leitner*

Mothers, Grandmothers, and Daughters: Personality and Child Care in Three-Generation Families *by Bertram J. Cohler and Henry U. Grunebaum*

Further Explorations in Personality *edited by A.I. Rabin, Joel Aronoff, Andrew M. Barclay, and Robert A. Zucker*

Hypnosis and Relaxation: Modern Verification of an Old Equation *by William E. Edmonston, Jr.*

Handbook of Clinical Behavior Therapy *edited by Samuel M. Turner, Karen S. Calhoun, and Henry E. Adams*

Handbook of Clinical Neuropsychology *edited by Susan B. Filskov and Thomas J. Boll*

The Course of Alcoholism: Four Years After Treatment *by J. Michael Polich, David J. Armor, and Harriet B. Braiker*

Handbook of Innovative Psychotherapies *edited by Raymond J. Corsini*

The Role of the Father in Child Development (Second Edition) *edited by Michael E. Lamb*

Behavioral Medicine: Clinical Applications *by Susan S. Pinkerton, Howard Hughes, and W.W. Wenrich*

Handbook for the Practice of Pediatric Psychology *edited by June M. Tuma*

Change Through Interaction: Social Psychological Processes of Counseling and Psychotherapy *by Stanley R. Strong and Charles D. Claiborn*

Drugs and Behavior (Second Edition) *by Fred Leavitt*

Handbook of Research Methods in Clinical Psychology *edited by Philip C. Kendall and James N. Butcher*

A Social Psychology of Developing Adults *by Thomas O. Blank*

Women in the Middle Years: Current Knowledge and Directions for Research and Policy *edited by Janet Zollinger Giele*

Loneliness: A Sourcebook of Current Theory, Research and Therapy *edited by Letitia Anne Peplau and Daniel Perlman*

(*continued on back*)

TREATMENT OF FAMILY VIOLENCE

Treatment of Family Violence

A SOURCEBOOK

Edited by

ROBERT T. AMMERMAN
Western Pennsylvania School for Blind Children

MICHEL HERSEN
University of Pittsburgh School of Medicine

A WILEY-INTERSCIENCE PUBLICATION

JOHN WILEY & SONS

New York • Chichester • Brisbane • Toronto • Singapore

From Robert to His Mother
From Michel to Vicki, Jonathan, and Nathanial

Library of Congress Cataloging in Publication Data

Treatment of family violence : a sourcebook / [edited by] Robert T.
   Ammerman, Michel Hersen.
      p.   cm.
   Includes bibliographical references.
   ISBN 0-471-61023-2
   1. Family violence--United States.   2. Problem families-
-Counseling of--United States.   3. Family social work--United
States.   I. Ammerman, Robert T.   II. Hersen, Michel.
HQ809.3.U5T74   1989   89-39492
362.82'92--dc20

Printed in the United States of America

10   9   8   7   6   5   4   3   2   1

Contributors

Robert T. Ammerman, PhD
Supervisor, Department of
  Research and Clinical
  Psychology
Western Pennsylvania School for
  Blind Children
Pittsburgh, Pennsylvania

Judith V. Becker, PhD
Professor of Psychiatry
Sexual Behavior Clinic
New York Psychiatric Institute
New York, New York

Marla R. Brassard, PhD
Director, Office for the Study of
  the Psychological Rights of the
  Child
Counseling and Educational
  Psychology
University of
  Massachusetts–Amherst
Amherst, Massachusetts

Jeannette Smith Christopher, MA
Graduate Student of Clinical
  Psychology
Department of Psychology
West Virginia University
Morgantown, West Virginia

Loren P. Conaway, MA
Graduate Student of Clinical
  Psychology
Department of Psychology
West Virginia University
Morgantown, West Virginia

Jon R. Conte, PhD
Associate Professor and Associate
  Dean
The School of Social Service
  Administration
The University of Chicago
Chicago, Illinois

Deborah Daro, DSW
Director, Center on Child Abuse
  Prevention Research
National Committee for Prevention
  of Child Abuse
Chicago, Illinois

Robert Geffner, PhD
Director, Family Violence
  Research Program
University of Texas at Tyler
Tyler, Texas

Christine R. Hanneke, PhD
Research Associate
Opinion Research Division
Fleishman-Hillard Research
St. Louis, Missouri

David J. Hansen, PhD
Assistant Professor
Department of Psychology
West Virginia University
Morgantown, West Virginia

Stuart N. Hart, PhD
Director, Office for the Study of
  the Psychological Rights of the
  Child
Counseling and Educational
  Psychology
Indiana University-Purdue
  University at Indianapolis
Indianapolis, Indiana

Ann P. Hazzard, PhD
Assistant Professor of Pediatrics
  and Psychiatry
Emory University School of
  Medicine
Atlanta, Georgia

Michel Hersen, PhD
Professor of Psychiatry and
  Psychology
Western Psychiatric Institute and
  Clinic
University of Pittsburgh School of
  Medicine
Pittsburgh, Pennsylvania

Gerald T. Hotaling, PhD
Research Scientist
Family Research Laboratory
University of New Hampshire
Durham, New Hampshire

Meg S. Kaplan, PhD
Research Scientist/Therapist
Sexual Behavior Clinic
New York Psychiatric Institute
New York, New York

Paula K. Lundberg-Love, PhD
Associate Professor of Psychology
Associate Director of Family
  Violence Research Program
University of Texas at Tyler
Tyler, Texas

Roland D. Maiuro, PhD
Assistant Professor of Psychiatry
  and Behavioral Sciences
Harborview Mental Health Center
University of Washington
School of Medicine
Seattle, Washington

Robert S. Marin, MD
Assistant Professor of Psychiatry
Western Psychiatric Institute and
  Clinic
University of Pittsburgh School of
  Medicine
Pittsburgh, Pennsylvania

Richard K. Morycz, PhD
Assistant Professor of Psychiatry
  and Medicine
Western Psychiatric Institute and
  Clinic
University of Pittsburgh School of
  Medicine
Pittsburgh, Pennsylvania

Mildred Daley Pagelow, PhD
Adjunct Research Professor
Department of Sociology
California State University,
  Fullerton
Fullerton, California

Karl A. Pillemer, PhD
Assistant Professor of Sociology
  and Research Associate
Family Research Laboratory
University of New Hampshire
Durham, New Hampshire

Patricia A. Resick, PhD
Professor, Department of
    Psychology
University of Missouri–St. Louis
St. Louis, Missouri

Alan Rosenbaum, PhD
Associate Professor in Psychiatry
University of Massachusetts
Medical School
Worcester, Massachusetts

Mindy S. Rosenberg, PhD
Visiting Assistant Professor of
    Psychology
University of California–Berkeley
Berkeley, California

B.B. Robbie Rossman, PhD
Clinical and Research Associate
    and Senior Lecturer
Department of Psychology
University of Denver
Denver, Colorado

Robert F. Schilling, PhD
Assistant Professor
The Columbia University School of
    Social Work
New York, New York

Nancy M. Shields, PhD
Assistant Dean
Evening College and Department of
    Sociology
University of Missouri–St. Louis
St. Louis, Missouri

David B. Sugarman, PhD
Research Associate
Family Research Laboratory
University of New Hampshire
Durham, New Hampshire

J. Jill Suitor, PhD
Assistant Professor of Sociology
Fordham University
New York, New York
Research Assistant
Family Research Laboratory
University of New Hampshire
Durham, New Hampshire

Rosalie S. Wolf, PhD
Associate Professor of Psychology
University of Massachusetts
    Medical Center
Worcester, Massachusetts

Series Preface

This series of books is addressed to behavioral scientists interested in the nature of human personality. Its scope should prove pertinent to personality theorists and researchers as well as to clinicians concerned with applying an understanding of personality processes to the amelioration of emotional difficulties in living. To this end, the series provides a scholarly integration of theoretical formulations, empirical data, and practical recommendations.

Six major aspects of studying and learning about human personality can be designated: personality theory, personality structure and dynamics, personality development, personality assessment, personality change, and personality adjustment. In exploring these aspects of personality, the books in the series discuss a number of distinct but related subject areas: the nature and implications of various theories of personality; personality characteristics that account for consistencies and variations in human behavior; the emergence of personality processes in children and adolescents; the use of interviewing and testing procedures to evaluate individual differences in personality; efforts to modify personality styles through psychotherapy, counseling, behavior therapy, and other methods of influence; and patterns of abnormal personality functioning that impair individual competence.

IRVING B. WEINER

University of South Florida
Tampa, Florida

Preface

Considerable public and professional attention has recently focused on the alarmingly high incidence of family violence. Indeed, intrafamilial abuse and neglect are much more prevalent than previously believed, and many experts contend that numerous cases are undetected each year because of limited service resources and impediments to identification of maltreatment. Moreover, additional populations of maltreated individuals are only now being recognized. These include children who observe interparental abuse, mistreated elders, adult survivors of child sexual abuse, and victims of psychological mistreatment.

Initial research efforts in the area of family violence concentrated on the delineation of causative factors implicated in the etiology of maltreatment. In particular, the contribution of societal variables (e.g., poverty, crowding, educational underachievement) was emphasized. In the 1970s, however, understanding of the development of family violence broadened to include individual and dyadic characteristics in addition to societal factors. Concurrently, there was a dramatic growth of interest in the treatment and prevention of maltreatment. Thus, by the early 1980s, a number of research studies and position papers appeared evaluating specific remedial intervention programs and suggesting guidelines for treatment of both perpetrators and victims. Although the need for continued empirical research remains, a significant body of data has accrued outlining appropriate interventions for the various forms of family violence.

The purpose of *Treatment of Family Violence: A Sourcebook,* therefore, is to examine closely the current status of treatment approaches for families engaged in abuse or neglect. Each of the chapters critically examines the features of the various types of family violence, the interventions developed to remediate or prevent maltreatment, and future directions that research might take in these areas. Specifically, the book is divided into five parts. In Part One, Introduction, clinical issues typically encountered in treating family violence are discussed. Part Two, Treatment of Victims, reviews interventions with victims of child maltreatment, spouse abuse, elder abuse, and marital rape, as well as interventions with child witnesses of marital abuse and adult survivors of incest. Treatment programs for perpetrators of child physical abuse, child sexual abuse, spouse abuse, and elder abuse are outlined in Part Three, Perpetrators of Maltreatment. In Part Four, Prevention of Family Violence, important new developments in the prevention of family violence are presented for child physical abuse, child sexual abuse, spouse abuse, and elder abuse. Finally, current empirical efforts are evaluated and recommendations for future research priorities are discussed in Part Five, Future Directions in Research.

A number of individuals have assisted us in developing this volume, and we greatly appreciate their patience and dedication. First, we thank the contributors to this volume for being willing to share their expertise and knowledge. Second, we gratefully acknowledge the technical assistance provided by Mary Anne Frederick, Mary Jo Horgan, Jenifer McKelvey, Louise B. Moore, and Mary H. Newell. Third, we thank Edward W. Gondolf for his gracious suggestions during the early stages of developing our outline for the book. Finally, we are indebted to our editor, Herb Reich, for his unlimited patience and valuable advice in bringing this sourcebook to fruition.

ROBERT T. AMMERMAN
MICHEL HERSEN

Pittsburgh, Pennsylvania
March 1990

Contents

PART THREE   PERPETRATORS OF MALTREATMENT

PART FOUR   PREVENTION OF FAMILY VIOLENCE

PART FIVE   FUTURE DIRECTIONS IN RESEARCH

TREATMENT OF FAMILY VIOLENCE

PART ONE

Introduction

CHAPTER 1

Issues in the Assessment and Treatment of Family Violence

ROBERT T. AMMERMAN AND MICHEL HERSEN

INTRODUCTION

The recent growth in interest in family violence is both welcome and long overdue. Since the early 1960s, increased attention has focused on the previously ignored area of domestic maltreatment of children and adults. Yet, contemporary studies document the pervasiveness of domestic violence in general, and abuse and neglect in particular. For example, the American Humane Association (1984) reports that there were 929,310 cases of child abuse and neglect in 1982, a rise of 123% since 1976. Moreover, many authors believe that numerous instances of child abuse and neglect go undetected and that these figures are underestimates of the true incidence of child maltreatment. Spouse abuse also occurs at alarmingly high rates. The projected incidence of wife battering ranges from 3.8%, or about 0.8 million women annually (Straus, Gelles, & Steinmetz, 1980), to as high as 16% (Hornung, McCullough, & Sugimoto, 1981). Elder mistreatment has been estimated to occur in 32 individuals per 1000 over the age of 65 (Pillemer & Finkelhor, 1988). Taken together, these data point toward the increased awareness of maltreatment among professionals and the public, as well as a possible actual increase in some forms of family violence relative to past generations. Gelles and Straus (1987), using information from telephone interviews, further highlight the widespread incidence of intrafamily physical violence, although they note a reported decrease in violence between 1975 and 1985.

The initial decades of family violence research primarily concentrated on identifying the causative variables in maltreatment. In particular, sociological

Preparation of this chapter was facilitated in part by a grant from the National Institute on Disabilities and Rehabilitation Research, U.S. Department of Education (No. G008720109), and a grant from the Vira I. Heinz Endowment. However, the opinions reflected herein do not necessarily reflect the position of policy of the U.S. Department of Education or the Vira I. Heinz Endowment, and no official endorsement should be inferred. The authors wish to thank Mary Jo Horgan for her assistance in preparation of the manuscript.

explanations provided the most compelling account for the etiology of abuse and neglect. Thus, efforts concentrated on these societal factors (e.g., poverty, educational disadvantage, prolonged exposure to stress) that may engender violence within families. In addition, much work was devoted to the medical and legal crises typically associated with domestic assault. These include the provision of emergency medical care for victims and the responses by the police, protective services, and courts to issues of victim safety and perpetrator disposition. Only recently, however, have efforts been directed toward the implementation and empirical evaluation of treatment approaches in family violence. There are two reasons for this new development:

1. An influx of professionals primarily interested in treatment (e.g., psychologists, psychiatrists, social workers) has occurred on a large scale only during the past decade. It is natural that their research interests should center on remediation and treatment.

2. Research delineating the role of individual and dyadic characteristics, in addition to societal factors as contributors to abuse and neglect, has underscored the utility of psychologically based therapeutic techniques in the treatment and prevention of domestic violence.

Because interest in the treatment of abuse and neglect is relatively nascent, few empirically controlled evaluation studies of specific interventions have been conducted. In addition, there has been an uneven evolution of research in this area. Thus, treatment efforts with perpetrators of child maltreatment are more fully developed than those with child victims (see Ammerman, 1989), whereas in the area of spouse abuse interventions with abusers have just recently been investigated relative to work with their victims (Gondolf, 1987). Furthermore, a number of newly recognized maltreated populations have come to the attention of professionals. These include abused and neglected elderly persons, psychologically mistreated children and adults, and child witnesses of family violence. As more is learned about these recently identified groups, treatment outcome studies should show a corresponding growth.

Despite these considerations, the field as a whole has matured enough to permit initial recommendations for treatment. Indeed, several features common to most types of family violence warrant close attention by clinicians. These consist of (a) intergenerational transmission of violence, (b) the prevalence of skills deficits in psychosocial functioning exhibited by perpetrators of maltreatment, (c) deviant interactional processes in violent dyads and family systems, and (d) the pervasive short- and long-term negative consequences of violence in victims. In addition, family violence cases usually present the clinician with impediments to identification and assessment, as well as a variety of complexities in case management. The remainder of this chapter will be devoted to a review of the aforementioned features and a general discussion of the issues faced by clinicians in assessing and treating families engaged in intervention.

CLINICAL FEATURES IN FAMILY VIOLENCE

To a large degree, research concerning the different types of family violence has been conducted separately and independently. Accordingly, treatment investigations often have lagged behind developments in other areas of study. There are, however, a number of elements that are common to domestic violence (see Burgess & Draper, 1988). These frequently encountered clinical features, in turn, form the basis for many of the treatment efforts currently practiced (Gondolf, 1987; Kelly, 1983). Thus, although the unique elements of one form of maltreatment versus another may dictate alternative intervention strategies, commonalties in the etiology and presentation of family violence suggest common modes of treatment.

Prior Experience of Maltreatment

Perhaps the most consistent finding in family violence research is that perpetrators of abuse and neglect are likely to have been themselves abused or neglected as children (Gelles, 1987). This phenomenon has been extensively examined in the area of child abuse. Although estimates of the intergenerational transmission of child abuse range from 18% to 90% depending on different methodological approaches, Kaufman and Zigler (1987) conclude that approximately 30% of abused children grow up to be abusive parents. Similar findings have been reported for spouse abuse, in which a significant proportion of wife batterers were abused as children (Kalmuss, 1984), and sexual abuse, where as many as 85% of child molesters were sexually exploited during childhood (Groth, 1982). Comparatively lesser attention has been focused on elder abuse until recently, and although there is some suggestion that those who mistreat elders were abused as children, researchers are wary to endorse such a relationship at this time (see Breckman & Adelman, 1988). Perhaps an even more robust finding is the positive relationship between witnessing violence as a child and engaging in maltreatment as an adult (Hotaling & Sugarman, 1986).

The preceding findings demonstrate the importance of past experience in the development of maltreatment. The processes that contribute to intergenerational transmission are unclear, although several explanations are likely. O'Leary (1988), for example, has argued that the experience of violent mistreatment in childhood provides a maladaptive learning experience for conflict resolution in adulthood. Thus, early modeling of such inappropriate strategies increases the likelihood that they will be used later in life. It also is probable that many perpetrators of adult maltreatment experienced pervasive disruptions in normal development as a function of child maltreatment, resulting in deficits in emotional regulation, impulse control, and social skill. Still another theory highlights the importance of social influences on the practice of violence and points toward the cultural acceptance and even promotion of the use of physical means to express anger and carry out discipline. Each of these explanations contributes to intergenerational transmission in some way. Furthermore, clinicians must attend to the possibility that past maltreatment has at least partly contributed to current incidents of family violence.

Skills Deficits

Another consistent finding in the literature is the pervasive skills deficits exhibited by perpetrators of mistreatment. For example, Wolfe (1987) summarized findings from a variety of studies and concludes that child-abusive parents exhibit deficits in frustration tolerance, appropriate expression of anger, social competence, and parenting skills. Likewise, neglectful parents have been noted to lack competency in a variety of areas involving parenting. Deficits in a number of specific skills also have been implicated in spouse abuse. These consist of poor impulse control, inadequate expression of anger, and lack of assertion (Rosenbaum & O'Leary, 1981).

It is unlikely that lack of specific skills per se directly causes family violence. The absence of such skills, however, may be a necessary, albeit insufficient, condition for the development of abuse or neglect. In either case, these behavioral deficits clearly must be addressed in treatment. Of course, a number of personality factors differentiate maltreating from non-maltreating individuals. For example, parents who abuse children often report low self-esteem and moderate depressive symptoms. Spouse abusers typically have defective self-images, adopt rigid sex-role identities, and experience low self-esteem. It is important to address all these areas in treatment. Skills deficits, however, are excellent treatment targets, in that they lend themselves to objective assessment techniques and respond to direct intervention approaches. In fact, with child abuse and neglect, empirical treatment evaluations have primarily emphasized competency-based interventions (Kelly, 1983) that appear to be effective (see Ammerman, 1989).

Interactional Dysfunction

For the most part, etiological models of maltreatment have directed attention to the role of the perpetrator in family violence. This is quite understandable given that abuse and neglect are characterized by the commission or omission of specific acts on the part of the perpetrator. Recent studies, however, have highlighted the interactive nature of and the processes implicated in abuse. It is now widely acknowledged that characteristics of the perpetrator, victim, and situational context combine to increase the likelihood of abuse. For example, Starr (1988) and Wolfe (1987) offer models describing the complex interplay of societal (e.g., underprivileged, economic hardship), parental (e.g., poor coping skills, inadequate knowledge of child development), and child (e.g., oppositionality, noncompliance) characteristics in the emergence of child abuse.

An increasingly large body of evidence has accrued identifying the interactional elements that can escalate conflict as well as more general dysfunction in family violence. In child maltreatment, parent–child interactions have been observed to be largely negative in nature relative to nonmaltreating families. Although maltreating dyads do not exhibit a greater number of negative interactions relative to nonmaltreating peers, a greater proportion of the interactions are negative. Furthermore, Reid, Patterson, and Loeber (1982) document mutual interchanges of poor management techniques and defiance in abusive mother–child pairs that can escalate conflict to the point of physical violence. Interactional deficits also have been noted in cases of spouse abuse. Indeed, current evidence points toward the mutual escalation of violence between the spouse abuser and his victim during conflict situations (O'Leary et al., 1989).

The aforementioned findings highlight the need to examine family violence from a system perspective. Until recently, attention was almost exclusively focused on the perpetrator as the sole agent of abuse and neglect. Although the perpetrator clearly holds the responsibility for the act of mistreatment, it is vital that the context in which abuse and neglect takes place be considered before implementing an intervention. This is the reason that so many practitioners now emphasize the importance of treating each member of the family. Also, it is sometimes possible to treat the dyad or family *as a unit,* although safety concerns may augur against this approach.

The Impact of Trauma on Victims

The focus of clinical attention has differentially shifted in the various types of maltreatment. In the area of child abuse and neglect, the greater proportion of treatment outcome studies have been devoted to remediation of perpetrators (e.g., Wolfe & Sandler, 1981). Although a good deal of assessment research has been conducted on the child victims of maltreatment, only recently have interventions been proposed (Fantuzzo et al., 1988) and evaluated. In the area of spouse abuse, on the other hand, the pattern is reversed. Initial efforts and recommendations in the field emphasized the treatment of battered wives. Efforts directed toward interventions with spouse abusers are quite recent. At this juncture in the field, however, there is now widespread agreement that the sequelae of maltreatment in children and adults are both pervasive and deleterious. Likewise, a large body of evidence has been amassed that indicates the long-term negative effects of child physical abuse (see Ammerman, Cassisi, Hersen, & Van Hasselt, 1986), child sexual abuse (see Browne & Finkelhor, 1986), and wife abuse (see Dutton, 1988). For this reason, it is imperative that clinicians and researchers attend to both the short- and long-term needs of victims following discovery of maltreatment.

The first concern for victims of maltreatment is safety from further abuse or neglect. To this end, child protective services are mandated to ensure the welfare of children, shelters provide battered women with an escape from potentially life-threatening abusive situations, and civil and criminal courts permit legal interventions as a means of protection. Of course, much has been written about the limitations of these programs and the need for increased staff and governmental support. They remain, however, the first line of intervention with victims of maltreatment.

The short- and long-term consequences of abuse and neglect require therapeutic treatment. The immediate effects of trauma are widespread and debilitating. Although some victims develop posttraumatic stress disorder, others display symptoms that are more diffuse and diagnostically elusive. Fear, hypervigilence, anxiety, and somatic complaints are often noted in the case of physical abuse, in both children and adults. The short-term effects of neglect are less understood, but can include withdrawal and dysphoria. Child sexual abuse also leads to fear and general psychosocial maladjustment, as well as inappropriate sex play and/or masturbation. Victims of maltreatment typically feel powerless and obviously are not in control of their own environments. A supportive therapeutic setting is a requirement for maltreated persons, in addition to specific interventions targeted at existing clinical symptoms.

The long-term consequences of maltreatment are only now being elucidated and described. It is becoming clear that the negative impact of abuse and neglect is insidious, particularly in the area of sexual abuse (see Browne & Finkelhor, 1986). As previously mentioned, there is a relatively high likelihood that maltreated children will become maltreating parents in adulthood. Similarly, a large proportion of battered wives report being abused as children or at least witnessing violent acts between family members. Preliminary data also indicate continued psychosocial maladjustment in adult victims maltreated as children, and in adult victims of violence long after abusive incidents have ceased. Victims with a history of past maltreatment have largely been ignored until recently; clinical efforts devoted to this population are warranted and require greater empirical investigation.

ISSUES IN THE ASSESSMENT OF FAMILY VIOLENCE

Assessment is the hallmark of well-planned interventions. Information gathered from assessment approaches should guide the development and course of treatment. Unfortunately, clinical assessment in family violence has received scant attention relative to other areas in the field. There are two reasons for this state of affairs:

1. The delay of interest in treatment of victims and perpetrators has coincided with a similar neglect of clinical assessment. Thus, although assessment techniques designed specifically to address research issues abound, relatively little is available for the practicing clinician. There is no doubt that our understanding will improve as the field continues to develop.

2. The lack of well-developed assessment approaches is inherent in the nature of maltreatment. Abuse and neglect are, by and large, private and socially undesirable events. Violent or neglectful behavior is rarely exhibited in the office, and it is unwise and unethical to elicit such behavior in simulated conditions in the clinic or laboratory. As a result, information about maltreatment depends on the victims and perpetrator's self-reports, which are often susceptible to error, distortion, and confabulation. This dilemma, in combination with the more general disagreement in the field regarding exactly what constitutes abuse and neglect, impedes the assessment process and limits the type and quantity of information that can be gathered.

Despite these concerns, it is possible to offer several guidelines for assessment in family violence. The multiple etiological influences and causative pathways contributing to abuse and neglect make it critical to conduct an assessment of multiple levels of functioning. These include such areas as psychopathology, global functioning, family communication and adjustment, and social functioning. In addition, each type of maltreatment requires particular investigation. For example, child abusers must be examined in terms of parenting skills and knowledge of child development. Both child abusers and spouse abusers require an assessment of anger and impulse control. Although maltreaters and victims are unlikely to exhibit deficits or difficulties in all of the areas assessed, the heterogeneity of family violence necessitates such a comprehensive and broadly based assessment strategy.

There are three sources of information in the assessment process: (a) the clinical interview, (b) psychometric measures, and (c) observation. The clinical interview is the most important facet of the assessment. The clinical interview is the most informative assessment technique currently available. Data should be gathered regarding a variety of areas of individual and family functioning, including psychopathology, conflict resolution, and communication processes. Although domestic violence typically is symptomatic of more global family disturbance, it is imperative that the clinician delineate details regarding the specific incidents of abuse and mistreatment. Especially important in this regard are precipitating factors to violent interactions. Indeed, the first task of the clinician in treatment is to prevent further occurrences of physical violence, and such information is necessary in treatment planning.

Psychometric assessment in family violence comprises a multimodel evaluation utilizing numerous and diverse instruments. Few measures have been developed specifically for the assessment of family violence. Rather, a variety of instruments have been borrowed from other areas to examine constructs related to maltreatment (e.g., stress, anger responsivity, psychopathology). At this point in time, strategies for the psychometric assessment of family violence are largely determined by the areas of need identified in the clinical interview. Refinement of the psychometric assessment process is a major goal for future research.

Behavioral observation, on the other hand, has emerged primarily as a research assessment approach. A variety of complex and cumbersome coding systems to examine family interactions are currently available but are difficult to implement in clinical settings. Nonetheless, home or in-office observations frequently are recommended in order to more fully assess patterns of family interaction and communication.

ISSUES IN THE TREATMENT OF FAMILY VIOLENCE

There are three goals in the treatment of domestic violence: (a) stopping current incidents of mistreatment, (b) preventing recurrence of mistreatment, and (c) remediating the concomitant individual and family dysfunctions that characterize abusive and neglectful families. Embedded within these goals are related clinical issues involving frequent contacts with other professionals from the legal, child protective, and medical systems. The clinician entrusted with the care of families engaging in abuse and neglect must be a case manager par excellence, coordinating the various professionals involved in working with the family. Indeed, treating the abusive or neglectful family is one of the most difficult and challenging tasks a clinician will ever face.

Case Management

Because domestic violence consists of one or more family members endangering the welfare of others, the legal system is involved in many cases of family maltreatment. This is especially true in child abuse and neglect, in which clinicians are required by law in most states to report suspected instances of child maltreatment to protective service authorities. In cases of severe maltreatment of children, criminal justice systems also will become involved. Likewise, spouse abuse or elder abuse cases often come to the attention of the police prior to clinician involvement. These organizations have considerable leeway in the disposition of families engaged in maltreatment, and some of their decisions may compete with and contradict the recommendations of clinicians. Thus, clinicians must be adroit in balancing the interests of other professionals who may have their own priorities in dealing with the case and may not fully understand or appreciate the needs of the family and its individual members from a treatment perspective.

However, the importance of the legal and protective service systems in intervening with domestic violence should not be underestimated. The safety of the victim is the single most important consideration in treating abusive or neglectful families. The legal and protective service organizations are mandated to take actions to ensure that child and adult victims are not in immediate danger of mistreatment. Although understaffing, lack of sufficient resources, and varied levels of experience with family violence impede this process and have led to widespread criticism of these systems, disposition of perpetrators and protection of victims still constitute the critical first step of intervention. In addition, it is probable that law enforcement officials will be the first to be made aware of physically violent families, particularly in cases of spouse abuse. It is imperative that clinicians work closely with law enforcers so that, in addition to ensuring public safety, they will make the appropriate referrals to treatment services.

Physicians and other medical personnel are other likely first contacts for families engaged in abuse or neglect. This is especially true in cases involving more severe instances of maltreatment, in which injuries to victims necessitate medical attention. Emergency physicians now consider recognition of abuse and neglect a vital component of medical assessments. Moreover, the growing awareness of family violence in general has underscored the importance of psychosocial interventions in the remediation of abuse and neglect, as well as the role of the medical professions in referring families to clinicians.

Victim advocates make up one more group that the clinician must work with. Advocacy groups provide numerous services to victims of family violence, including shelters, legal advice, and financial assistance. Some organizations even offer counseling services. The clinician must carefully balance the goals of advocacy groups with the clinical needs of the family. Often these will be complementary, although disagreement between organizations and the clinician may arise. Dissension, however, does not serve the needs of the family and prolongs the road to recovery for victims and perpetrators alike.

Treatment Options

The first decision in treatment is to determine the family members most in need of intervention. Typically each family member will display psychosocial difficulties that require attention. The victim will exhibit the scars of mistreatment, the perpetrator must learn to control aggressive impulses, and observers (e.g., children, siblings) will also need help. In some cases, the family must be seen together, whereas in other cases various combinations of couples and individual treatment are in order. Unfortunately, there are few data to guide the clinician in delineating the target(s) of treatment. Clinical judgment must be based on probability of success and victim safety. In many instances, it is desirable for family members to see separate clinicians.

Another consideration in providing treatment is the implementation of individual versus group treatment formats. Group interventions are very common in the area of family violence, comprising victim support groups for battered wives, parenting groups for abusive parents, groups for battering men, and group therapy programs for sexually abused children. Such formats offer the support and shared experiences of fellow victims or perpetrators and are especially cost-effective in light of the limited resources available for treatment. Individual treatment, on the other hand, permits specific interventions designed to meet the unique needs of the client. This may be particularly valuable with clients who present with more severe psychopathology, such as major depression or posttraumatic stress disorder. Once again, clinical judgment is required to select the appropriate treatment format.

Because research on the treatment of family violence has only recently emerged, it is impossible to make specific recommendations regarding the utility of strategies based on theoretical orientations. In general, treatment approaches differ in their emphasis on psychodynamic processes or competency-based interventions. Those that concentrate on psychodynamic processes dictate the identification and working through of dysfunctional intrapsychic mechanisms. Such interventions are especially suited for victims of mistreatment, given the consistent finding of low self-esteem and depressive symptoms among abused children and battered women. Competency-based interventions, on the other hand, target skills deficits for remediation and utilize behavioral methods to teach parenting skills, assertion, anger control, and stress reduction. These approaches have received some empirical support, especially in the treatment of child abusers (see Ammerman, 1989), and are now being applied to victims of child mistreatment (Fantuzzo et al., 1988). Furthermore, data confirming the existence of skills deficits in spouse abusers suggest that competency-based programs may be useful interventions for this population.

Neither psychodynamic nor competency-based interventions are fully sufficient treatments in family violence. The complexity of clinical presentations of both victims and perpetrators necessitates a broad and comprehensive program utilizing multiple treatment components. There are many pathways that lead to abuse and neglect; likewise, a variety of therapeutic techniques are needed to fully address the heterogeneous presentations of families engaged in maltreatment.

SUMMARY AND FUTURE DIRECTIONS

Preliminary efforts in the treatment of family violence show considerable promise. Etiologic factors are more clearly elucidated, and common features among types of maltreatment have been delineated. At the same time, recently developed interventions address the multiple areas of dysfunction displayed by families who engage in mistreatment. Continued research will greatly enhance the ability of professionals to (a) select the appropriate treatment for each family, and (b) provide the most cost-effective intervention approach(es).

Several treatment issues, however, remain inadequately explored. For example, greater attention must be directed toward the victim of family violence. This is particularly important in child physical and sexual abuse, where proportionately more effort has been applied to perpetrators of maltreatment. Treatment of victims of spouse assault, however, also requires increased scrutiny. As evidence accrues indicating that victims suffer short- *and* long-term negative consequences from abuse and neglect, the need for treatment at various levels of development is evident.

REFERENCES

American Humane Association. (1984). *Highlights of official child neglect and abuse reporting 1982.* Denver, CO: Author.

Ammerman, R. T. (1989). Child abuse and neglect. In M. Hersen (Ed.), *Innovations in child behavior therapy* (pp. 353–394). New York: Springer.

Ammerman, R. T., Cassisi, J. E., Hersen, M., & Van Hasselt, V. B. (1986). Consequences of physical abuse and neglect in children. *Clinical Psychology Review, 6,* 291–310.

Breckman, R. S., & Adelman, R. D. (1988). *Strategies for helping victims of elder mistreatment.* Newbury Park, CA: Sage.

Browne, A., & Finkelhor, D. (1986). Impact of child sexual abuse: A review of the research. *Psychological Bulletin, 99,* 66–77.

Burgess, R. L., & Draper, P. (1988). A biosocial theory of family violence: The role of natural selection, ecological instability, and coercive interpersonal contingencies. In L. Ohlin & M. H. Tonry (Eds.), *Crime and justice—an annual review of research: Family violence* (pp. 59–116). Chicago: University of Chicago Press.

Dutton, D. G. (1988). Profiling of wife assaulters: Preliminary evidence for a trimodal analysis. *Violence and Victims, 3,* 5–29.

Fantuzzo, J. W., Jurecic, L., Stovall, A., Hightower, A. D., Goins, C., & Schachtel, D. (1988). Effects of adult and peer social initiations on the social behavior of withdrawn, maltreated preschool children. *Journal of Consulting and Clinical Psychology, 56,* 34–39.

Gelles, R. J. (1987). The family and its role in the abuse of children. *Psychiatric Annals, 17,* 229–232.

Gelles, R. J., & Straus, M. A. (1987). Is violence toward children increasing? A comparison of 1975 and 1985 national survey rates. *Journal of Interpersonal Violence, 2,* 212–222.

Gondolf, E. W. (1987). Changing men who batter: A developmental model for integrated intervention. *Journal of Family Violence, 2,* 335–349.

Groth, A. N. (1982). The incest offender. In S.M. Sgroi (Ed.), *Handbook of clinical intervention in child sexual abuse* (pp. 215–240). Lexington, MA: Lexington Books.

Hornung, C. A., McCullough, B. C., & Sugimoto, T. (1981). Status relationships in marriage: Risk factors in spouse abuse. *Journal of Marriage and the Family, 42,* 675–692.

Hotaling, G. T., & Sugarman, D. (1986). An analysis of risk markers in husband to wife violence: The current state of knowledge. *Violence and Victims, 1,* 101–124.

Kalmuss, D. (1984). The intergenerational transmission of marital aggression. *Journal of Marriage and the Family, 46,* 11–19.

Kaufman, J., & Zigler, E. (1987). Do abusive children become abusive parents? *American Journal of Orthopsychiatry, 57,* 186–192.

Kelly, J. A. (1983). *Treating child abusive families: Intervention based on skills-training principles.* New York: Plenum.

O'Leary, K. D. (1988). Physical aggression between spouses: A social learning theory perspective. In V. B. Van Hasselt, R. L. Morrison, A. S. Bellack, & M. Hersen (Eds.), *Handbook of family violence* (pp. 31–55). New York: Plenum.

O'Leary, K. D., Barling, J., Arias, I., Rosenbaum, A., Malone, J., & Tyree, A. (1989). Prevalence and stability of spousal aggression: A longitudinal analysis. *Journal of Consulting and Clinical Psychology, 57,* 263–268.

Pillemer, K., & Finkelhor, D. (1988). Prevalence of elder abuse: A random sample survey. *Gerontologist, 28,* 51–57.

Reid, J. B., Patterson, G. R., & Loeber, R. (1982). The abused child: Victim, instigator, or innocent bystander? *Nebraska Symposium on Motivation, 29,* 47–68.

Rosenbaum, A., & O'Leary, D. K. (1981). Marital violence: Characteristics of abusive couples. *Journal of Consulting and Clinical Psychology, 49,* 63–71.

Starr, R. H., Jr. (1988). Physical abuse of children. In V. B. Van Hasselt, R. L. Morrison, A. S. Bellack, & M. Hersen (Eds.), *Handbook of family violence* (pp. 119–155). New York: Plenum.

Straus, M. A., Gelles, R. J., & Steinmetz, S. K. (1980). *Behind closed doors: Violence in the American family.* Garden City, NY: Anchor Books.

Wolfe, D. A. (1987). *Child abuse: Implications for child development and psychopathology.* Newbury Park, CA: Sage.

Wolfe, D. A., & Sandler, J. (1981). Training abusive parents in effective child management. *Behavior Modification, 5,* 320–335.

PART TWO

Treatment of Victims

CHAPTER 2

Victims of Child Physical Abuse

DAVID J. HANSEN, LOREN P. CONAWAY, AND JEANETTE SMITH CHRISTOPHER

INTRODUCTION

Throughout history, children often have been treated with incredible cruelty and have received little protection from such treatment. In a famous case of maltreatment in 1874, for example, Mary Ellen Wilson's rescue from starvation and beatings was aided by Henry Bergh, the founder of the Society for Prevention of Cruelty to Animals (Bremner, 1971; Walker, Bonner, & Kaufman, 1988). Several months later the attorney hired by Bergh started the Society for Prevention of Cruelty to Children. Unfortunately, widespread societal concern over child abuse as a significant problem dates back to only the 1950s and 1960s (Williams, 1983; Wolfe, 1988). In recent decades, protection efforts for abused children have steadily increased, perhaps because of frequent and intense attention from diverse sectors of society—the media, the general public, the professional community, and legislators.

Although the "battered child syndrome" was identified by Kempe well over two decades ago (Kempe, Silverman, Steele, Droegenmueller, & Silver, 1962), the treatment of physically abused children has received surprisingly little attention. In fact, the paucity of adequately controlled research focusing on maltreated children is disappointing given the prevalence and severity of physical abuse. Attention has been primarily on the parent as the perpetrator of the act, and this narrow viewpoint has been at the expense of the child victims.

This chapter examines the research literature and clinical issues regarding child victims of physical abuse by parents. Potential consequences of maltreatment, and assessment and treatment procedures for abused children are discussed. Directions for clinical treatment and research are also presented.

Definitions

Discriminating between types of maltreatment is important because the topography of each type is quite different. Patterns of maltreatment are inflicted in dissimilar ways, may be triggered by different conditions, and may result in dissimilar consequences. Operational, practical definitions have been difficult to develop because of problems in specifying what is excessive discipline or inappropriate treatment of children.

Physical abuse has been defined as an act of commission by the parent(s) and is characterized by the infliction of overt physical violence (Kelly, 1983; Wolfe, 1988). It usually occurs in discrete, low-frequency episodes and is often accompanied by frustration and anger toward the child (Kelly). Physical abuse may include beating, squeezing, burning, lacerating, suffocating, binding, poisoning, exposing to excessive heat or cold, subjecting to sensory overload (e.g., excessive light, sound, stench, aversive taste), or preventing sleep (Williams, 1983).

Child neglect involves maltreatment through acts of omission by the parent(s), such as failing to meet the child's physical, nutritional, medical, and emotional needs (Kelly, 1983). Sexual abuse includes sexual intrusion (e.g., penile penetration—oral, anal, or genital), genital contact, or other acts such as exposure or fondling of breasts, or buttocks (National Center on Child Abuse and Neglect, 1988). Forced or coerced contact and contact with a much older person (e.g., 5 or more years) are considered sexual abuse. Psychological maltreatment, which is even more difficult to define, is receiving increased attention. Garbarino, Guttman, and Seeley (1986) define psychological maltreatment as "a concerted attack by an adult on a child's development of self and social competence, a *pattern* of psychically destructive behavior" (p. 8). This maltreatment often accompanies other types of abuse and may take five forms: rejecting, isolating, terrorizing, ignoring, and corrupting (Garbarino et al., 1986).

It is essential for professionals to be familiar with the statutes in their state that define child abuse and mandatory reporting. Definitions in state statutes vary significantly in terms of specificity (Edwards & Gil, 1986). Identifying, reporting, and intervening for child abuse involve many statutory and judicial requirements, policies, and procedures that can complicate and even compromise the activities of professionals. These factors contribute to the varied and often conflicting roles of professionals working with abused children and abusive parents. Information on state laws and procedures are available from local child protective services (CPS) offices.

Etiology of Abuse

Although a detailed review of potential causes of physical abuse is beyond the scope of this chapter, a brief review is important for understanding the abused child's environment (see reviews by Kelly, 1983; Spinetta & Rigler, 1972; Wolfe, 1988). Early conceptualizations proposed that child abuse results from severe parental psychopathology (cf. Spinetta & Rigler, 1972; Steele & Pollock, 1974). However, it is estimated that as few as 5% to 10%

of abusing parents evidence significant psychopathology and can be diagnosed as psychotic, schizophrenic, or sociopathic (Kelly, 1983).

Learning clearly plays an important role in the etiology of aggressive behavior (Bandura, 1973). Because parents serve as role models for their children, abusive parents might be imitating the child-rearing techniques demonstrated by their parents. Many abusive parents do report a history of abuse, but most parents abused as children are not abusive (Kempe & Helfer, 1972; Silver, Dublin, & Lourie, 1969; Wasserman, 1967). Possibly as few as 15% of abused children become abusive parents (Wolfe, 1988).

Many abuse incidents may be seen as the result of complex maladaptive interactions that are influenced by parental skills or knowledge deficits and other stress factors (Kelly, 1983; Wolfe, Kaufman, Aragona, & Sandler, 1981). Skills deficits may be found in areas such as child-management and parent–child interaction (Burgess & Conger, 1978; Trickett & Kuczynski, 1986), anger and stress control (Wolfe, Fairbank, Kelly, & Bradlyn, 1983), or problem-solving deficits (Azar, Robinson, Hekimian, & Twentyman, 1984; Hansen, Pallotta, Tishelman, Conaway, & MacMillan, in press). Investigators also have found that abusive parents may have unrealistic expectations and distorted perceptions of child behavior, or may make problematic attributions regarding the causes of child behavior (e.g., Azar et al., 1984; Azar & Rohrbeck, 1986; Bauer & Twentyman, 1985; Larrance & Twentyman, 1983).

Physically abusive mothers may exhibit an overall lower rate of interactions and display fewer positive behaviors and more negative behaviors toward their children than do nonmaltreating parents (Burgess & Conger, 1978; Lahey, Conger, Atkeson, & Treiber, 1984). Abusive parents' inability to effectively control child behavior may lead to coercive cycles (i.e., negative reinforcement traps), involving increases both in the parent's use of aversive control techniques and in child noncompliance and coercive behaviors (Burgess & Richardson, 1984; Patterson, 1982). Trickett and Kuczynski (1986) found that physically abusive parents used more punishment (e.g., verbal, physical, response cost) than nonabusive parents, who relied more on reasoning and simple commands. Abusive parents were also more angry and disgusted after discipline and used punishment as the primary type of discipline, regardless of the misbehavior.

Environmental factors that may influence the likelihood of abuse include financial, employment, housing, and interpersonal problems, and parental social isolation (Garbarino & Crouter, 1978; Kelly, 1983; Spinetta & Rigler, 1972). Many abusive parents may be socially isolated or "insular," with relatively few close friends or sources of emotional support, small social networks, and relatively high frequencies of negative interactions and contacts with helping agencies (Salzinger, Kaplan, & Artemyeff, 1983; Wahler, 1980). Parental social isolation may lead to feelings of being trapped, decreased coping and support resources, and increased probability of abuse.

Insularity also has been related to increased child behavior problems, poor parent–child interactions, and poor maintenance of parent-training effects (Wahler, 1980).

Specific child behaviors or characteristics may increase the risk of a child's being abused (Frodi, 1981; Wolfe, 1988). For example, some investigators found an increased incidence of abuse among low birth weight and premature infants (Faranoff, Kennell, & Klaus, 1972; Herrenkohl & Herrenkohl, 1979); although other evidence indicates that low birth weight and prematurity are not risk factors for abuse (Leventhal, 1981; Shearman, Evans, Boyle, Cuddy, & Norman, 1983). Abused and neglected infants have also been shown to exhibit distorted affect, which may interfere with parent–child interactions and elicit negative responses on the part of parents (Gaensbauer & Sands, 1979). A variety of other child characteristics (to be discussed later) are correlated with abuse and are often assumed to be consequences of mal-treatment, but they may also play a role in its occurrence (e.g., aggression, noncompliance, developmental delays).

EPIDEMIOLOGY

Differences in definitions of maltreatment have made obtaining reliable data regarding incidence and prevalence difficult. In the most recent and extensive study, the National Center on Child Abuse and Neglect (NCCAN) conducted the second national incidence study of child abuse and neglect, utilizing a national probability sample of 29 counties (NCCAN, 1988). The results dra-matically describe the extent of the problem. In 1986, approximately 5.7 children per 1,000 (for a total of 358,300 children) were physically abused in the United States. In fact, it was estimated that 0.02 per 1,000 (or 1,100 children) died from maltreatment in 1986. There was a 63% increase in physical abuse from 1980 to 1986 (NCCAN, 1988). It is unclear, however, whether that figure reflects an actual increase in incidence or is a result of growing public awareness and increased reporting.

The NCCAN (1988) study found that, unlike sexual abuse, physical abuse was equally common for male and female children in the sample. The study also indicated that, as the abused children grew older, they were abused more frequently. Children in families with four or more children were sig-nificantly more likely to be abused than children in smaller families. County status (urban versus rural) was not related to maltreatment.

Children from lower income families (i.e., less than $15,000 per year) have been found to be four times more likely to be physically abused than children from higher income families (i.e., $15,000 or more) (NCCAN, 1988). A strong relationship between low socioeconomic status and child abuse has been both assumed and questioned (Kelly, 1983; Pelton, 1978). Abuse has also been identified in more advantaged families, and the socioeconomic distri-bution of reported abuse may not accurately reflect the actual occurrence among the classes (Steele & Pollock, 1974; Straus, 1980). Statistics may reflect reporting bias because individuals of lower socioeconomic status may simply be more available to public and protective scrutiny.

CONSEQUENCES OF PHYSICAL ABUSE

Physical abuse may be related to a variety of detrimental consequences (cf. Ammerman, Cassisi, Hersen, & Van Hasselt, 1986; Conaway & Hansen, 1989; Lamphear, 1985). In attempting to determine consequences of physical abuse, most studies have assessed the behavior of children after abuse has occurred. Unless the children are observed both before and after abuse, the so-called "consequences" of abuse can usually only be viewed as characteristics of those children.

Physical Injuries

An estimated 1,000 to 5,000 children may be killed each year by their parents (NCCAN, 1988; Newberger, 1982). Additionally, a variety of injuries result from child physical abuse. These include skeletal injuries (McHenry, Girdany, & Elmer, 1963) and neurological and ocular damage (Smith, 1975). As many as 1.5% of substantiated cases of abuse and neglect are victims of burns (Newberger, 1982). Approximately 2.5 children per 1,000 (or 160,000 children) are seriously injured or impaired by abuse and neglect (e.g., loss of consciousness, interrupted breathing, broken bones, third-degree burns; NCCAN, 1988). The most common signs of abuse may be bruises, lacerations, and contusions (Kelly, 1983). Physical abuse may also take the shape of gastric or intestinal perforations and intestinal obstructions resulting from trauma to the abdomen (Kempe, 1971). Over 60% of all abuse fatalities and over 50% of all cases of permanent disability occur among children under 2 years of age, primarily from head injuries (Newberger, 1982).

Developmental and Educational Characteristics

An important, initial study by Elmer and Gregg (1967) found that physically abused children received lower than average scores on standardized measures of intelligence. These results have been supported by a variety of investigations (Hoffman-Plotkin & Twentyman, 1984; Perry, Doran, & Wells, 1983; Salzinger, Kaplan, Pelcovitz, Samit, & Krieger, 1984). Additionally, investigators have found an increased incidence of developmental delays (Allen & Wasserman, 1985; Parish, Myers, Brandner, & Templin, 1985), mental retardation (Morse, Sahler, & Friedman, 1970), and a higher percentage of special educational placements (Kline, 1977) among physically abused children. Parish et al. found that 83% of 53 abused children exhibited moderate to marked developmental delays, the greatest deficits being in fine motor and language skills. Abused infants exhibit evidence of communication disorders more often than nonabused infants (Allen & Wasserman). Developmental and educational differences may be due to lower cognitive skills and may also be a result of a chaotic lifestyle, including decreased school attendance and acquisition of behaviors that are adaptive for survival within the family but are incompatible with learning (Martin & Rodeheffer, 1976; Salzinger et al., 1984).

Behavior Problems

Abused children may be more likely to exhibit aggressive behavior than nonabused children, because aggression is modeled in the home as a means of controlling others' behavior. Several studies have utilized anecdotal case reports and archival data to indicate physically abused children are aggressive (e.g., Kent, 1976; Kline, 1977; Silver et al., 1969). Other investigations have used direct observation procedures to compare aggressive behavior exhibited by abused children with that exhibited by peers. George and Main (1979) found that physically abused children exhibited more aggression toward, and more avoidance of friendly overtures from both peers and caregivers than children from stressed, nonabusive families. Investigators have also compared the behavior of physically abused and neglected children. Compared with neglected and nonabused children, abused children have been observed to be more aggressive toward therapists (Reidy, 1977) and peers (Hoffman-Plotkin & Twentyman, 1984). Furthermore, Bousha and Twentyman (1984) used direct observation but found that both abused and neglected children were more aggressive toward their mothers than nonabused peers. Hoffman-Plotkin and Twentyman found that parents and teachers rated both abused and neglected children as more aggressive than peers. Reid, Kavanagh, and Baldwin (1987) noted no significant differences in direct observation of interactions between abused children and their peers but found that parents of abused children rated their children as more aggressive than peers. Discrepancy between parental ratings and direct observation may result, in part, from abusive parents' distorted perceptions or unrealistic expectations of child behavior (e.g., Azar et al., 1984; Azar & Rohrbeck, 1986; Bauer & Twentyman, 1985).

Abused children have been rated as exhibiting more externalizing behavior problems (e.g., aggressiveness, hyperactivity, delinquency) than nonabused control children (Mash, Johnston, & Kovitz, 1983; Jaffe, Wolfe, Wilson, & Zak, 1986). Additionally, some investigators have found that physically abused children are less compliant than peers (Kent, 1976; Trickett & Kuczynski, 1986), whereas others report no differences between physically abused children and their peers (Hoffman-Plotkin & Twentyman, 1984; Mash et al., 1983). Moreover, data indicate that physically abused children display a variety of other behavior problems more frequently than peers, including enuresis, temper tantrums, and distractibility (Egeland, Sroufe, & Erickson, 1983; Jaffe et al., 1986; Martin & Beezley, 1977; Wolfe & Mosk, 1983).

Social and Emotional Adjustment

Investigators have also assessed "social skills" or "social competence." Unfortunately, selection of target behaviors is rarely based on a demonstrated relationship with socially competent functioning. Several studies relying solely on parent or teacher ratings of child behavior indicate that there are no differences between abused, neglected, and nonabused children in terms of social skills and social competence (Egeland et al., 1983; Jaffe et al., 1986; Perry et al., 1983). Other investigations noted that abusive parents rated their children as less socially competent than did parents of nonabused children (Salzinger et al., 1984; Wolfe & Mosk, 1983). Additionally, Kravic (1987) found that although parents of abused children rated their children as less socially competent than did parents of nonabused children, there were no differences when compared with ratings by parents of "troubled" nonabused children.

Investigations have also focused on the quality and content of both peer and family interactions. Friedman and Morse (1974) found no differences between maltreated and nonmaltreated children's relationships with siblings and peers; other studies, however, have indicated that physically abused children have more difficulties with social relationships than nonabused children but do not differ from neglected peers (Kent, 1976; Kline, 1977). Likewise, direct observational data have yielded conflicting results. Physically abused children have been observed to engage in fewer social interactions and less prosocial behavior, and to express fewer positive emotions and concern toward peers and adults (Bousha & Twentyman, 1984; George & Main, 1979; Hoffman-Plotkin & Twentyman, 1984; Main & George, 1985). Physically abused children also exhibit more difficulties entering new peer groups than nonmaltreated peers (Howes & Espinosa, 1985). Conversely, other investigations using direct observation found no differences in physically abused children's interactions with peers and adults as compared to nonabused children (e.g., Bradley, Caldwell, Fitzgerald, Morgan, & Rock, 1986; Reid et al., 1987).

Abused children have been rated as exhibiting more internalizing problems (e.g., depression, anxiety, somatic complaints) than nonabused control children (e.g., Jaffe et al., 1986; Mash et al., 1983). Physically abused children may exhibit a variety of other emotional problems, including low self-esteem, negative affect, impaired impulse control, separation difficulties, poor body image, withdrawal, and difficulty establishing trust (Egeland et al., 1983; Hjorth & Harway, 1981; Kinard, 1982). Research has also demonstrated that abused children may have attachment problems. For instance, using the Ainsworth Strange Situation assessment, Lyons-Ruth, Connell, Zoll, and

Stahl (1987) found that maltreated infants showed more avoidance and resistance to their mothers than nonmaltreated parent–child dyads.

Child maltreatment may be related to later psychopathology (Bryer, Nelson, Miller, & Krol, 1987). Abuse histories have been related to the development of multiple personalities (Coons, 1986; Wilbur, 1984) and affective disorders (Kashani, Shekim, Burk, & Beck, 1987).

Coping with Maltreatment

Deficits in social interactions and peer and family relationships, as well as excesses in aggressive behavior and emotional problems, suggest deficits in coping strategies and resources; yet, there is little information on the processes by which abused children may cope with maltreatment or other problems. However, the processes children use to cope with divorce (e.g., Kurdek, 1986), and interparental conflict and background anger (e.g., Cummings, 1987) have been investigated. Findings from these studies may provide insight to coping strategies employed by children who experience traumatic events.

Lazarus and Folkman (1984) defined coping as "constantly changing cognitive and behavioral efforts to manage specific external and/or internal demands that are appraised as taxing or exceeding the resources of the person" (p. 141). Adaptive coping resources include problem-solving skills and problem-focused coping, social support, and social skills (Compas, 1987; Compas, Malcarne, & Fondacaro, 1988; Kurdek, 1986; Lazarus & Folkman, 1984). Problem-focused strategies are efforts to change the source of stress, whereas less effective emotion-focused efforts are intended to regulate the emotional states associated with the stress (Compas et al.; Lazarus & Folkman). An important basis for problem-solving and adaptive coping is a sense of efficacy or control over the environment (Kurdek, 1986). For instance, Weisz, Weiss, Wasserman, and Rintoul (1987) found that perceived incompetence and uncertainty about control of contingencies were related to depression in clinic-referred youth. In addition, Compas et al. have shown that use of problem-focused coping is negatively related to emotional/behavioral problems, whereas emotion-focused coping is positively correlated with such problems.

Activities that provide social support include assisting during emotional distress, sharing responsibilities, providing advice or material aid, and teaching skills. Support from the family is important in helping children cope with stress (Asarnow, Carlson, & Guthrie, 1987), and the family is less likely to be supportive when the stressor is maltreatment by parents.

Recent research has demonstrated that abusive and neglectful parents may be deficient in the coping resources of problem-solving skills and social support (e.g., Azar et al., 1984; Hansen et al., in press, Salzinger et al., 1983). Because appropriate strategies are not taught or modeled, it seems even more probable that maltreated children may also exhibit coping deficits.

Implications for Treatment

The literature suggests that the consequences of physical maltreatment on children vary significantly. A variety of factors may help negate or exacerbate the effects, including age of the child when abused, severity and type of abuse, the child's coping abilities and resources, and response to the abuse incidents by the abuser and others in the environment. In addition, as the child develops, the expression of the consequences of abuse may vary. Information regarding the characteristics displayed frequently by abused children is useful for anticipating areas in which these children might encounter difficulties. Intervention to decrease or prevent development of maladaptive behaviors, or improve coping resources, might begin as soon as maltreatment is detected.

TREATMENT

The treatment of physically abused children often is complicated by problems with definition and identification, family patterns and interactions, environmental resources, cultural differences, and motivation or compliance. Procedures for the treatment of physically abused children will be presented within the framework or context of these difficulties.

Intervention with abused children can take place in a variety of modalities—while the child is living with the abusive parent (if risk has not been deemed severe enough for removal), living with a nonabusive parent or other relative, or living in a foster care placement. Intervention may also occur during a child's attendance at a day-care or school setting. Interventions may focus on the child or the whole family, may have varied orientation such as traditional psychotherapy, skills training, or operant procedures, and may use a group or individual approach.

It is important to note that victims of physical abuse often are removed from the home. This may lead to placement in a temporary foster care situation, or in more severe instances, termination of parental rights and placement in an adoptive home. The use, outcome, and problems of foster care placements are not well understood. Lawder, Poulin, and Andrews (1986) studied 185 children who had been placed in foster care 5 years previously. Time in foster care was variable: 47% spent less than 6 months in foster care, 23.3% spent between 6 months and 2 years, 11.9% spent between 2 years and 5 years, and 17.8% remained in foster care after 5 years. The majority (61.7%) of the children were returned to their parents or extended family members within 5 years.

Issues unique to the child and family's culture or subculture must be considered by service providers. Many cultural factors may have substantial impact on the assessment and treatment of abuse, such as reluctance to report, variations in what is considered abuse and how to respond, family loyalty that interferes with appropriate response, and interventions that may not be viewed as relevant, helpful, or desirable (Edwards & Gil, 1986; Long, 1986). In addition, victims and those who report abuse may have to live near or regularly see the abuser. In one case, a man in a rural area who reported an incident of physical abuse did not remain anonymous as authorities had promised and was subsequently beaten and harassed by relatives of the abusive mother (Long).

Relevant assessment and treatment approaches are described in this chapter. Treatment may be designed to prevent recurrence of abuse and negative consequences of abuse. Because there is a shortage of intervention research with abused children, more general investigations and resources from the literature will also be emphasized. Readers are encouraged to consult general texts on child assessment (e.g., Mash & Terdal, 1988) or treatment (e.g., Morris & Kratochwill, 1983; Ross, 1981) in conjunction with the literature outlined in the following sections.

Assessment Issues and Procedures

A thorough assessment is a necessity, particularly when the child remains in the home. This may include collecting information to validate the occurrence of maltreatment (e.g., for the court or child protective services), but it is usually to identify target areas for intervention and monitor progress throughout treatment. A scientist-practitioner approach to assessment and intervention is always important, but the empirical selection and evaluation of treatment procedures is especially helpful and comforting when under the scrutiny of the court and child protective services.

Considering that specific child behaviors may precipitate abuse and may result in varied negative consequences, assessments of developmental, intellectual, educational, emotional, social, or behavioral functioning are necessary. The clinician must select the assessment techniques that are likely to be the most relevant to the abused child's and abusive family's areas of need.

Frequently, by the time a therapist has the first session with an abusive family, legal, medical, and social service personnel have already been involved with the case. Therefore, the child and family may be hesitant to discuss issues with an additional professional. Children may have had to describe the incident(s) to many other adults, and parents or relatives may have made the child feel guilty, threatening that their family will be torn apart or that a parent will be jailed (Walker et al., 1988). It is important to approach both the parent and child in a warm and supportive manner, without condoning abusive behavior, and develop rapport before trying to conduct assessments.

A functional analytic perspective is helpful for conducting a complete, treatment-relevant assessment. Antecedents of the abuse may include specific child behaviors, developmental problems, conflict between parents, unrealistic expectations or problematic attributions regarding child behavior, or other stressors or interaction problems. There may be many positive consequences for abusive behavior; for example, abusive behavior may remove an aversive event (e.g., noncompliance and tantruming). It may bring praise or approval to the abusive parent from others who perceive the actions as being appropriately firm disciplinary procedures. Another possible consequence is that the parent is hurting the spouse's preferred child. The absence of negative consequences may further contribute to continued abuse.

A clinical interview is an essential procedure, especially if the purpose of assessment is to document and describe the maltreatment. Therapists must be aware, however, that this validation may interfere with cooperation and rapport needed for intervention. The child may be interviewed regarding circumstances surrounding abuse episodes and other problems, as well as his or her strengths and interests. Questions concerning parental characteristics, discipline techniques, and extent and quality of parent–child interactions can be addressed during an interview with the abused child. It also is important to investigate the occurrence of other types of maltreatment.

A detailed developmental history often is required, and a formal developmental evaluation of intellectual, perceptual motor abilities, and speech may be indicated. The Vineland Adaptive Behavior Scales-Revised (Sparrow, Balla, Cicchetti, 1984), which measures communication, self-care, and cognitive development, is helpful in this regard. This criterion-referenced instrument is particularly useful because parental responses can be compared to actual child behavior. The Denver Developmental Screening Test (Frankenburg, Dodds, Fandal, Kazuk, & Cohrs, 1975), which provides information concerning physical, motor, perceptual, and cognitive development, may be appropriate. Because academic and learning difficulties can be problematic, an achievement test such as the Wide Range Achievement Test-Revised (Jastak & Wilkinson, 1984), or an intelligence test such as the Wechsler Intelligence Scale for Children-Revised (Wechsler, 1974), is important. Teacher reports and school records (e.g., grades, standardized test scores), or more specific tests of learning disability, may provide additional information about developmental functioning. A neurological assessment or neuropsychological battery such as the Luria-Nebraska (Golden, Hammeke, & Purisch, 1985) may be indicated when a child shows signs of organicity or a learning disability.

The abused child's behavioral strengths and deficits can be assessed in a number of modalities. Direct observation, particularly in naturalistic settings, is sometimes less contaminated by abusive parent's perceptions than are rating scales. People who know the child has an abuse history may also have inaccurate perceptions of the child's adjustment and functioning (e.g., teachers or foster parents may overinterpret normal misbehaviors as representing underlying emotional conflict). Although direct observation often is expensive and time consuming, it provides the most accurate evaluation of the behaviors of interest. Observation can examine relatively typical child behavior, appropriate and inappropriate child behaviors, avoidant behaviors (e.g., withdrawing or flinching when parent nears), and approach behaviors

(Wolfe, 1988). Systematic procedures and coding systems may be helpful; for example, parent–child interactions may be observed by using procedures such as the Dyadic Parent–Child Interaction Coding System (Robinson & Eyberg, 1981).

Behavior rating scales such as the Child Behavior Checklist and Profile (CBCL; Achenbach & Edelbrock, 1983) and the Eyberg Child Behavior Inventory (Eyberg & Ross, 1978) are well-validated instruments for identifying problem areas. Children who are suspected of being hyperactive may also be evaluated with rating scales such as the Conner's scales for parents and teachers (Conners, 1969, 1970). An additional benefit of rating scales is that they may be completed by both parents and teachers to assess differences in behavior across situations.

Assessment of social interactions and competence may be necessary. Interactions with both peers and adults are required. Among the procedures useful for this purpose, are direct observation, sociometrics and peer ratings, teacher ratings, and self-report (cf. Hops & Greenwood, 1988). The social competence scale of the CBCL or other rating scales may be helpful screening devices.

Measures may be needed to assess the child's emotional functioning. Children who show signs of depression could complete an inventory such as the Children's Depression Inventory (Kovacs & Beck, 1977). Fear and anxiety problems can be assessed using instruments such as the Children's Manifest Anxiety Scale-Revised (Reynolds & Richmond, 1978), State-Trait Anxiety Scale for Children (Speilberger, 1973), or Fear Survey Schedule for Children-Revised (Ollendick, 1983).

It is impossible to conduct a thorough assessment without involving others in the child's environment. When the abused child continues to live with the abusive parent, the assessment of the child's parents is of primary importance. Direct observation of the parent–child interactions often is an integral component of a thorough assessment, and the parents are additionally involved in completing forms concerning the child's behavior and development. Moreover, it is useful to assess the social context in which the family lives (Kelly, 1983; Walker et al., 1988). This may include the parents' work history, the socioeconomic status, and the family's social support network. Parents may be assessed on areas such as child management skills, knowledge and expectations of child development and behavior, anger and stress control, intelligence, emotional sensitivity, and problem-solving skills for coping with familial, social, and economic stressors (see Chapter 10; and reviews by Kelly, 1983; Wolfe, 1988).

Intervention Approaches

Traditional Psychotherapy

Psychotherapy with a psychoanalytic, attachment theory or more eclectic orientation has been recommended for abused children. Play therapy and more verbal, insight-oriented therapy are common procedures to achieve catharsis, labeling of feelings, corrective emotional experiences, development of internal structure, and "working through" (cf. Freedheim & Russ, 1983). Ney (1987) described a seven-stage "natural sequence of events" in the treatment of abused children. If the sequence is not completed, it may result in the "unfinished business" evidenced by abused children who become abusive parents. The stages are as follows:

1. Realizing they are victims
2. Protesting against their maltreatment
3. Dealing with the guilt of their involvement
4. Working through despair by mourning the loss of years of their childhood
5. Reevaluating present relationships
6. Reconciling with members of their family who have abused them; and
7. Reconstructing their lives and using what they learned from their experience for the benefit of themselves and others

Ney also points out that abused children may engage in a number of defense processes, such as apathy, guilt, depression, revenge, rebellion, and identification with the aggressor.

Crenshaw, Rudy, Triemer, and Zingaro (1986) stress that "breaking the silence" regarding abuse is a major step in psychotherapy with physically and sexually abused children. In addition, a warm, accepting, and trusting relationship with the therapist is needed to provide the child with a "corrective emotional experience that promotes the healing of the injured sense of trust" (p. 34). Techniques such as making a "This Is Your Life" book, using child narration during doll play, and telling stories about victims of abuse are used to allow enough emotional distance to facilitate disclosure. Crenshaw et al. report that their child patients initially denied maltreatment, but after therapy for periods as long as 2 years, they finally admitted and described the maltreatment. Unfortunately, there is no empirical support for the widely supported notion that it is important for a child's adjustment to disclose and discuss the details of abuse.

Weinbach and Curtiss (1986) criticize the indiscriminate practice of making child abuse victims aware of their victimization. Although it might be a necessity for some cases, such a disclosure may serve little or no purpose in others and may even be dysfunctional and potentially harmful. Weinbach and Curtiss provide several suggestions regarding making the victim aware of abuse:

1. Youth at risk for continued abuse may need to be aware that the aggression is legally defined as abuse.
2. In all cases that involve sexual abuse, increased awareness appears desirable.

3. If the youth is from a violent subculture where such behavior seems the norm, then awareness is desirable.

4. A tactful, critical, but not judgmental, approach is best for discussing abuse.

5. If abuse is no longer a threat, it may not be appropriate to bring abuse into conscious awareness and "undercut ego defenses" that may be adaptive.

6. Making a youth aware of abuse may be damaging to self-esteem or self-image as a result of being labeled a "victim" or being implicated as a cause of the problems.

7. Terms such as "child abuse" may be substituted with less emotional terms such as "excessive physical discipline."

8. Bringing abuse into awareness is only appropriate when it is judged to be therapeutic.

Attachment may be another therapy issue because deficiencies in abused children's attachment to maltreating caretakers has been demonstrated (e.g., Lyons-Ruth et al., 1987). Frazier and Levine (1983) describe "reattachment therapy," the goal of which is to eliminate developmental and attachment disturbances associated with abuse in young children. In the first phase, attachment substitution, the therapist creates a warm, accepting, and permissive environment, and stimulates attachment bonding by gratifying some of the child's needs. In the second phase, attachment inducement, the therapist works with the child to improve physical appearance to facilitate parental attachment (e.g., clean the child's face, fix hair, refer for services), reinforce attachment-eliciting behaviors (e.g., looking, smiling, laughing), decrease clinging behavior, and eliminate behaviors that frequently preceded abuse. Green (1976) cautions that parents of abused children in psychotherapy may feel threatened and may experience a great deal of jealousy and competitiveness with therapists who may be perceived as trying to preempt their parental role. Parents may attempt to interrupt therapy when the child develops an attachment to the therapist.

Although various authors have recommended such psychotherapy techniques with abused children, conclusions have been based on informal, clinical case studies (e.g., Crenshaw et al., 1986; Frazier & Levine, 1983; Ney, 1987). Theoretical and empirical support and evaluation are notably absent. The impact of these approaches on the child's adjustment and coping, family functioning, and prevention of further abuse is unknown. Other concerns about psychotherapy-based treatment of abused children are evident. These approaches generally require cooperation from the child, significant communication skills, and time-intensive and lengthy intervention. An additional concern is that traditional forms of counseling and therapy are considered least effective with clients who are members of minority and lower socioeconomic groups (Edwards & Gil, 1986).

Intervention with Parents and Caretakers

The primary focus of the literature on physical abuse of children has been on parents—the perpetrators. If the abuse is not so extreme as to permanently remove the child from the home, then it is critically important to intervene immediately with the parent(s) to prevent further maltreatment. Intervention with abusive parents is critical to reduce the likelihood of further maltreatment, and such intervention may also be important for improving the abused child's social, emotional, behavioral, and academic functioning. Intervention with foster parents or other caretakers may also be indicated.

Treatments for abusive parents, with a goal of improving the children's behavior, have been evaluated (see Chapter 10; Kelly, 1983; Wolfe et al., 1981). For example, Wolfe and Sandler (1981) used parent training and contingent reinforcement of parents' use of trained skills with three abusive mothers and their children. A family interaction coding system was used to record parent and child behaviors in the home. Total aversive behaviors of parents and children were significantly reduced, and child compliance was significantly improved. Similarly, Wolfe, Sandler, and Kaufman (1981) used parent training and self-control training with eight abusive families. Significant improvements as compared with a wait-list control were found at a 10-week follow-up for number and intensity of child behavior problems as measured by the Eyberg Child Behavior Inventory (Eyberg & Ross, 1978), and for the parents' child management skills as measured by home observations and caseworker ratings.

A wide range of interventions with parents may be appropriate. In addition to parent training to improve parent–child interactions, increase compliance, and decrease aggression, procedures may be necessary for problems such as enuresis, encopresis, stealing, lying, tantruming, and so forth. Contingent reinforcement and praise, as well as approaches such as time-out, response cost, extinction, and differential reinforcement of other behavior (DRO), may be needed (cf. Gelfand & Hartmann, 1984).

Social Skills Intervention

As discussed earlier, a variety of literature suggests that physically abused children are more likely than nonabused peers to have social interaction deficits (cf. Conaway & Hansen, 1989). Although research is desperately needed regarding intervention to remediate the social deficits of abused children, there is an extensive literature on social skills interventions with other child and adolescent populations (see Hansen, Watson-Perczel, & Christopher, 1989; Matson & Ollendick, 1988).

Intervention approaches can vary significantly depending on the nature of the deficit and problems. Operant approaches may be used, such as positive adult attention or contingency management to increase positive peer interactions or reduce aggressive, negative behaviors (Morris & Kratochwill, 1983; Ross, 1981). Office-based training of specific social behaviors or "skills" may also be conducted (e.g., Combs & Lahey, 1981; Hansen, St. Lawrence, & Christoff, 1988), which includes both social skills and problem-solving training (e.g., Plienis et al., 1987). Skills-training procedures normally are utilized: The therapist provides rationale and instruction for the skills being trained and models the skill performance; the trainee rehearses the skill; and the therapist provides corrective feedback and reinforcement.

Peer-mediated approaches also have been utilized. Socially successful peers, for example, can be instructed to initiate and maintain interactions with a target child (e.g., Guevremont, MacMillan, Shawchuck, & Hansen, 1989; Sisson, Van Hasselt, Hersen, & Strain, 1985), or peers can be trained to provide feedback regarding cooperative and aggressive behaviors (e.g., Grieger, Kauffman, & Grieger, 1976). Moreover, combination skills training and peer-mediated approaches have been used (Bierman & Furman, 1984).

In a recent investigation, Fantuzzo et al. (1988) compared adult and peer social-initiation interventions with a no-initiation control condition on the social behavior of withdrawn, maltreated (physically abused or neglected) preschool children. Results supported the effectiveness of the peer-initiation intervention for increasing positive verbal and motor social behaviors observed in treatment and generalization settings. The peer-initiation intervention also reduced problem behaviors at school as measured by teacher ratings.

Howes and Espinosa (1985) emphasized the importance of the social experience and social support network provided by day-care settings, and the social support missing from the family environment of abused children. They found that in newly formed groups in a clinic setting, abused children were less socially competent and expressed less positive emotion than normal children. Abused and normal children in well-established groups in day-care settings were comparable in peer interaction and expression of positive emotion and were more competent than abused and clinic children in newly formed groups. Normal children had similar interactions in either group.

Problem-Solving Training

Research has documented the problem-solving deficiencies of abusive parents (Azar et al., 1984; Hansen et al., in press), as well as aggressive, impulsive, emotionally disturbed and behavior-problem children and adolescents (D'Zurilla, 1986; Tisdelle & St. Lawrence, 1986). To date, research has not specifically identified abused children as a population with deficient problem-solving abilities. Yet, there are clear rationales for providing problem-solving training to maltreated children, including avoidance or elimination of problem situations and behaviors that may precipitate abuse, improvement of interactions with family and peers, and improvement of general coping strategies.

Problem-solving interventions generally use skills-training procedures and follow a multistep model, such as teaching the individual to (a) recognize and constructively approach problematic situations; (b) identify the problem and select an appropriate goal; (c) generate multiple potential solutions; (d) evaluate the alternative solutions and select the "best" solution; (e) develop a detailed, sequential, realistic plan to implement the solution; (f) implement the plan; and (g) evaluate effectiveness of the actions and respecify the problem and goal as needed (D'Zurilla, 1986). Research has documented the effectiveness of problem-solving training for aggression and interpersonal problems in childhood and adolescence (e.g., Kazdin, Esveldt-Dawson, French, & Unis, 1987; Tisdelle & St. Lawrence, 1988), but further work is needed to determine its impact on actual behavior and adjustment, and its effectiveness with abused children.

Relaxation Approaches

Resesarch suggests that abused children may have an excess of both externalizing symptoms (e.g., aggression) and internalizing symptoms (e.g., anxiety, withdrawal) (cf. Ammerman et al., 1986; Wolfe, 1988). As a result, relaxation training may be an appropriate treatment. Specific research with abused children has not been conducted, but the application of relaxation training with children has been evaluated for problems ranging from fears to psychosomatic problems (Morris & Kratochwill, 1983; Ross, 1981; Wielkiewicz, 1986).

The relaxation procedures utilized depend on a variety of factors, including therapist training and preference, type of problem, and age and functioning of the child. Progressive muscle relaxation (PMR) is probably the most common relaxation technique with adults and adolescents; it seems most applicable for older children and adolescents. Generally, as many as 16 muscle groups are systematically tensed then relaxed. Excellent guides for conducting PMR are available (e.g., Bernstein & Borkovec, 1973). With children, minor changes may be needed, such as shorter sessions if attention span is a problem, or additional instruction if learning the relaxation process is slower. Often a relaxation tape is provided for client practice sessions at home. Although providing a tape seems logical and even essential for children; its effectiveness remains to be empirically determined.

Teaching deep-breathing techniques may be appropriate and practical with some abused children. The child is taught diaphragmatic breathing by gradually inhaling enough to expand the stomach while holding his/her hands on the stomach to feel the expansion. The child then gradually releases the air and repeats the process several times until relaxed. With young children, a related technique is to ask the children to imagine that they are a balloon or tire that must be filled up; after they fill up the balloon, they are asked to let the air out slowly between the lips or teeth (Walker et al., 1988).

Imagery can be a useful relaxation strategy for adolescents and some older children. Usually clients are helped to choose a scene that is relaxing. Some therapists (and children) prefer scenes that are active, such as riding horseback or walking in the woods; others prefer a less active approach, such as lying on a beach or in the woods. Therapists guide the child through the scene, encouraging them to use their senses—to experience the sights, sounds, smells, and tactile or movement sensations. A related process with children is the "Magic Carpet" approach, in which the child is instructed to imagine riding a safe magic carpet that can go anywhere the child wishes (Walker et al., 1988).

If specific fears or phobias are present, procedures such as systematic desensitization, exposure, or modeling may be needed along with relaxation training. For desensitization approaches, in vivo methods are likely to be more appropriate and effective for children than imaginal methods (Morris & Kratochwill, 1983; Ross, 1981).

Anger-Control Training

The literature suggests that abuse victims may have aggression and anger problems (see reviews by Ammerman et al., 1986; Conaway & Hansen, in press; Wolfe, 1988). This is not surprising given that an abusive parent is a poor model of anger-control skills.

Feindler and Ecton (1986) have developed a practical resource for conducting anger-control training with adolescents. The approach involves several components, including education about anger and its effects, and self-assessment, relaxation, and assertiveness training. Self-instruction training, with cognitive restructuring and thought stopping, and problem-solving training also are taught. Skills-training procedures and frequent homework assignments are utilized. Research has supported the effectiveness of this approach with aggressive and delinquent children and adolescents (Feindler & Ecton, 1986; Feindler, Ecton, Kingsley, & Dubey, 1986). Empirical efforts, however, have not specifically examined anger-control training with abused youth.

Self-Instruction Training

Self-instruction training has shown some potential at improving the academic and behavioral functioning of hyperactive, impulsive, and disruptive children (cf. Morris & Kratochwill, 1983; Ross, 1981), and it may be a useful intervention for abused children as well (Walker et al., 1988). Self-instruction training involves teaching the child to ask questions about the problem at hand, giving feedback about performance, and providing reinforcement and corrective feedback (Meichenbaum, 1977). A typical sequence involves (a) trainer performance of a task while asking questions and providing self-instructions and self-evaluations aloud, (b) child imitation of the trainer's performance of task and overt self-instruction, (c) trainer modeling of self-instruction in a whisper, (d) child imitation of whispered performance, (e) trainer modeling of covert self-instruction, and (f) child imitation of the trainer's performance (Meichenbaum & Goodman, 1971).

Remediating Developmental Delays

Developmental delays, such as language and intellectual deficits, are commonly associated with abused infants and children (e.g., Elmer & Gregg, 1967; Perry et al., 1983), and this may be a direct result of the maltreating environment. For example, Dietrich, Starr, and Kaplan (1980) demonstrated that abusive mothers provided less stimulation (e.g., tactile, auditory, and vestibular) than nonabusive control mothers. Specific individualized intervention may be required for abused children who exhibit developmental delays. Referrals for service include speech therapists, specialized preschools for developmentally delayed children, special-education placement and services, and agencies such as the Easter Seal Society.

Parish et al. (1985) evaluated the effectiveness of a family-oriented, Family Development Center Program on the developmental milestones of abused children. The program included a "therapy-group-interaction" for the parents and a daily preschool class and occasional field trips for the children. Fine motor and language skills were significantly delayed for the group as a whole and showed the most improvement following intervention. Fifty-three children were tested, and 42 showed significant developmental skill gains.

Family Therapy

Research has documented the interaction problems of abusive families (Burgess & Conger, 1978; Burgess & Richardson, 1984) and has emphasized the role of marital discord as an influential factor in the occurrence of physical abuse (Kelly, 1983; Lutzker, 1984; Walker et al., 1988). A family therapy perspective may view maltreatment of a child as the result of problematic interaction and communication patterns among family members. Families can be viewed as systems that strive to maintain a certain balance or homeostasis, and a family member may become a focus of problems to maintain the systems' balance. A child in such a situation might exhibit problem behaviors that elicit abuse to prevent the father from abusing the mother and to keep the family from dissolving (Walker et al., 1988).

A variety of family approaches have been developed that may be appropriate for abusive families (Walker et al., 1988). The strategic approach (Haley, 1984) suggests that presenting symptoms metaphorically represent some other problems, that may, in turn, stem from unbalanced or incongruent hierarchies (e.g., one parent has more power). Interventions frequently involve rebalancing the hierarchy. A structural approach focuses on the structural aspects of the family, including alliances and coalitions, and intergenerational boundaries (Minuchin & Fishman, 1981). A structural explanation for abuse might focus on disengagement (underinvolvement) of the father and enmeshment (overinvolvement) of the mother and son. A mother may precipitate the child's acting out; such behavior requires the father's presence at home for discipline; that situation then increases the father's involvement in the family while also increasing the probability of physical abuse (Walker et al., 1988). Intervention may involve eliciting problem behaviors during a session and reframing or directing behavior change, or it may focus on conflict resolution and the use of paradox.

A behavioral family therapy approach emphasizes personal, behavioral, and situational factors and might include identification of skill deficits and unrealistic expectations, as well as responses to stressors (Stuart, 1980; Walker et al., 1988). Intervention may involve problem-solving, negotiation, communication training, contracting, and activity structuring.

Alexander and Parsons (1982) emphasize examining the function of problems in regulating relationships within the family (functional family therapy). A number of overall goals are developed, including clarifying the meaning of each family member's behavior and descriptions, establishing an interdependent relationship among family members, creating an atmosphere conducive to change, and assigning homework to facilitate change. The therapist uses several techniques that focus on relationships, such as asking questions, making comments on the impact of behavior and feelings, offering interpretations, identifying sequences of behavior, stopping and starting interactions, and interrelating feelings, thoughts, and behavior. Some techniques that change the meaning of descriptions and behavior are nonblaming and relabeling, overtly discussing the implications of symptom removal, changing the impact or context of the symptom, and shifting the focus from one problem or person to another. Communication skills are emphasized, such as brevity, "I" statements, directness, presentation of alternatives, congruence, concreteness and behavioral specificity, feedback, impact statements, and active listening. Several helpful "technical aids" for facilitating change are contingency contracting, token economies, time-out, charts and graphs, note and message centers, notes from school, and relaxation. The importance of understanding and overcoming resistance to change and intervention also is emphasized (Alexander & Parsons, 1982; Dale & Davies, 1985).

Dale and Davies (1985) highlight the importance of a "wider systems view" in intervention with abusive families. They view the family as part of a context of several wider systems (i.e., family, therapeutic, multidisciplinary treatment team, interagency, and family–agency systems). They suggest that the community and professional agencies may play a "pathological role" and unintentionally maintain abuse. For instance, at the interagency level there may be "conflicts and rivalries, alliances, scapegoats and power struggles interweaving through patterns of overt and covert communication" (pp. 451–452). Dale and Davies report that utilization of a wider systems approach has been effective for the majority of families served by their child protection team. Maladaptive patterns and structure, communication problems, and resistance must be overcome to eliminate maltreatment.

School Intervention

Abused children are more likely than nonabused children to have academic, intellectual, and behavioral difficulties. Thus, a common site of intervention with abused children is the school, preschool, or day-care setting. Many interventions already described are relevant with school problems (e.g., social and problem-solving skills training). In addition, consultation and cooperation with the child's teacher may be needed. Interventions such as contingent reinforcement of homework completion or on-task behavior may be necessary. The professional assists with developing intervention and co-operation between parent and teacher. See Wielkiewicz (1986) for a helpful introduction to behavior management in schools.

Pharmacological Intervention

Another potential, but last resort, type of treatment of abused children is pharmacological intervention. This may be particularly relevant if the child has a diagnosis of attention deficit-hyperactivity disorder (ADHD) and may be receiving stimulant medication. Although effects are variable, stimulants have resulted in improvements in sustained attention, concentration, impulse control, disruptive behavior, compliance, independent play, and social responsiveness (Barkley, 1983). Improved attention and on-task behavior may be related to gains in specific measures of academic achievement for some children (Pelham, Bender, Caddell, Booth, & Moorer, 1985).

Drug therapy has also been utilized for a variety of other problems. Research has provided initial support for the use of antidepressants (e.g., imipramine) with some depressed children, but further evaluation is clearly needed (Campbell, Green, Perry, & Anderson, 1983). Research also has supported use of imipramine with some enuretic children, but relapse is common and psychological treatments are generally preferred (Campbell et al., 1983). In addition, neuroleptics or major tranquilizers (such as chlorpromazine or haloperidol) have been used for children. Positive findings are variable, but there is some support for the effectiveness of neuroleptics with psychoses, severe aggressive behavior, tics, and Tourette's disorder (Campbell et al.).

Several serious, negative side effects have been attributed to use of medication for psychological and behavioral problems in children (Barkley, 1983; Campbell et al., 1983). Thus the decision to prescribe medications must be made carefully and after other treatments have been tried and evaluated. Drug treatment with abused children has not been specifically evaluated.

General Treatment Issues

A variety of general issues are relevant for the treatment of abused children. For interventions designed to prevent recurrence of abuse or negative consequences of a dysfunctional, maltreating environment, the importance of generalization (e.g., to other settings, behaviors) and maintenance of treatment effects is clear. Therapists must actively program and assess generalization and not simply hope that generalization will occur (Stokes & Baer, 1977). Procedures that may facilitate generalization include teaching behaviors that naturally elicit reinforcement, utilizing varied trainers and training stimuli, teaching a variety of responses, and employing indiscriminable contingencies such as delayed reinforcement (Gelfand & Hartmann, 1984; Stokes & Baer, 1977). Making the training environment as similar as possible to the generalization setting, and reinforcing the occurrence of generalization responses also are recommended. Fading the intervention gradually and providing booster sessions as needed facilitate maintenance. Further, it is important to verify that significant others in the environment will tolerate the procedures and behavior change.

A multidisciplinary approach to the assessment and treatment of physically abused children and families has been widely advocated and adopted (Hochstadt & Harwicke, 1985). In this approach the professionals involved (e.g., medical, psychological, social, educational, legal) meet to develop a complete evaluation and treatment plan. Few studies have examined the effectiveness of this approach. Hochstadt and Harwicke found that during one year following evaluation, a large percentage of a multidisciplinary team's recommendations for service were followed in a sample of 180 children. Rivara (1985) collected data from a multidisciplinary team and child protective services records on 71 abused children under 2 years old and reported a "sobering picture" for the prognosis for abused children and their families. For example, despite supervision by CPS workers, only one third of the families complied with recommendations to obtain counseling and parent training. In addition, there was no relationship between compliance with treatment and incidence of further abuse. A criticism of most multidisciplinary programs is the failure to reach out to many of these dysfunctional families and provide services in an environmentally and culturally relevant manner.

A general intervention problem with abusive families is compliance with assessment and treatment procedures. Therapists must be sensitive to the factors that may contribute to noncompliance, such as insufficient or unclear instructions, lack of client skills to perform the assignment, and competing contingencies that may reinforce noncompliance or punish compliance. Other problems include lack of relevance according to the client's perception of what is needed, a negative therapy history, rapport or conflict problems, lack of motivation to change, or problematic attributions or cognitions. Therapists may need to do a functional analysis of compliance and noncompliance, arrange antecedents to enhance compliance, and place contingencies on compliance.

"Project 12-Ways," a model treatment program developed by Lutzker and his colleagues for child-abusive and neglectful families, is an example of integration of many of the preceding treatment issues and procedures and an attempt to provide relevant, effective intervention (Lutzker, 1984). It is an "ecobehavioral" approach that provides in vivo intervention (e.g., in homes, schools). Intervention services include parent–child training in child-management skills, child behavior, and parent–child interactions; stress-reduction skills training for parental stress and anxiety; assertiveness training for parents; self-control training for parents; basic skills training for children lagging in developmental skills (e.g., toilet training, bicycle riding); leisure-time training for families; marital counseling; alcohol treatment referral; social support groups for parents; job procurement training; money management training; health maintenance, nutrition, and hygiene training; home safety training; multiple-setting behavior management training (e.g., home, day-care, school); and prevention services for unwed mothers. A number of treatment and program evaluations have supported the effectiveness of Project 12-Ways (Lutzker, 1984; Lutzker & Rice, 1984).

Another treatment issue is that abused children may have low self-esteem and poor self-image as a result of their negative life experiences and learning history (Egeland et al., 1983; Walker et al., 1988). Certainly many of the preceding procedures should impact the child's view of him- or herself through improved family and peer relations and interactions, improved academic and behavioral adjustment, and enhanced self-control and problem-solving abilities.

Prevention of the occurrence of abuse should be a primary goal of the professional community, and research is providing hope that significant efforts can decrease child abuse (see Chapter 14; Helfer, 1982; Wolfe, Edwards, Manion, & Koverola, 1988). Tertiary prevention is aimed at preventing future abuse in families who have had previous instances of abuse, or at preventing negative consequences of abuse. This includes the treatment procedures described in the preceding sections of this chapter. Primary prevention focuses on populations of people who may or may not be at risk, interventions to enhance parent and child competencies and interaction, and increased awareness of abuse (Rosenberg & Reppucci, 1985).

Secondary prevention targets groups at risk for abuse. As discussed earlier, research indicates that abused children often exhibit many different deficits and problems, and varied parental problems and deficits may be associated with abuse. Thus, a wide range and large number of children and families might be considered "at risk." High-risk families can be screened during the hospital maternity stay and when the child enters school. However, Schmitt (1980) cautions against waiting until the child enters school, as abuse may have already occurred in two thirds of the abusive cases. The likelihood of many false positives within a high-risk group can be costly in time and effort; yet relative to the cost of false negatives or failure to prevent abuse, the cost of false positives may be worthwhile. Wolfe et al. (1988) identified high-risk families on the basis of the age of the parent and child, major problems with parenting, and scores within the "at risk" range on the Child Abuse Potential Inventory (CAPI; Milner, 1986). Results indicated that subjects in a behavioral parent-training group showed significant reduction of child behavior problems and parenting risk as measured by the CAPI. In addition, caseworkers rated parents more favorably with regard to risk of maltreatment and ability to manage their families.

SUMMARY AND FUTURE DIRECTIONS

Because of the widespread and serious nature of physically abusive home environments there are many potential consequences of abuse, and a wide range of treatment procedures may be needed with abused children. These procedures were described, from operant and parent-training approaches to more traditional psychotherapy techniques. Intervention may involve the child, the abusing or nonabusing parent, foster parents, peers, or teachers, and treatment may focus on the victim, the abuser, and the environment.

There is much empirical support for many of the assessment and treatment approaches with children in general (cf. Gelfand & Hartmann, 1984; Morris & Kratochwill, 1983; Ross, 1981), although not specifically with abused populations. Assessment and interventions with physically abused children, as well as the consequences of abuse, are clearly important areas for investigation. Processes for coping with the immediate stresses of abuse incidents and the longer term effects of maltreating, dysfunctional environments also need examination.

Research Issues

Methodological problems are frequently present in research with maltreated children (Conaway & Hansen, in press). A number of issues regarding subject selection are relatively specific to research in the area of child abuse. Problems in the literature include failure to (a) differentiate between abuse and neglect, (b) confirm allegations of maltreatment, (c) determine the frequency and severity of abuse, (d) establish the time elapsed since the last reported abuse incident, and (e) determine whether maladaptive child behaviors are present before the occurrence of abuse or are a consequence of abuse.

As with other types of investigations, it is important to consider the age range and sex of subjects in order to keep them within similar developmental levels. Assessment of other variables, such as determining if maltreating parents are substance abusers or display deviant behaviors other than abuse (e.g., psychopathology), is necessary because inclusion of subjects exposed to different types of parental aberrant behavior may confound the results.

Group-design investigations often fail to report having matched groups on potentially important demographic characteristics, such as socioeconomic status. Clinical samples provide useful comparison subjects, such as nonabusive families with child behavior problems, child-management deficits, or parent–child conflict. Because a number of studies have indicated a correlation between interparental conflict, children's emotions, and behavior problems such as aggression (Emery, 1982), interparental conflict should be controlled in studies assessing the characteristics of abused children. Controlling for recent divorce or separation also is important, as the child may experience stress until the family stabilizes (Kurdek, 1986).

Much research with maltreated children must be interpreted with caution because investigators often fail to collect data systematically or to use measures with known psychometric properties. Many investigations depend almost exclusively on parental report or ratings of child behavior, but parental report may be unreliable. Research has shown that some maltreating parents have problematic expectations or attributions regarding children's behavior (e.g., Azar et al., 1984; Azar & Rohrbeck, 1986; Larrance & Twentyman, 1983) and, thus, may not provide accurate reports.

Conclusion

Although much work remains to be done, the literature indicates that physically abused children are more likely than their nonabused peers to exhibit problems with adjustment, development, and behavior. Clearly a need exists for more extensive development and evaluation of intervention procedures to remediate or prevent the problems of abused children. It is unfortunate that there is very little empirical investigation of treatment procedures specifically implemented with physically abused children. Because maltreated children may have a more dysfunctional and aggressive environment, less parental support and participation in treatment, and a variety of negative consequences of abuse, such specific evaluations of interventions are necessary. Given that much has already been learned with regard to treating children and conducting research on intervention and assessment, this knowledge must be utilized to the benefit of physically abused children. Until research demonstrates otherwise, clinicians may base selection and implementation of procedures on the available literature and systematic evaluation of treatment effects.

REFERENCES

Achenbach, T. M., & Edelbrock, C. S. (1983). *Manual for the Child Behavior Checklist and Revised Child Behavior Profile*. Burlington, VT: Queen City Printers.

Alexander, J., & Parsons, B. V. (1982). *Functional family therapy*. Monterey, CA: Brooks/Cole.

Allen, R., & Wasserman, G. A. (1985). Origins of language delay in abused infants. *Child Abuse and Neglect, 9,* 335–390.

Ammerman, R. T., Cassisi, J. E., Hersen, M., & Van Hasselt, V. B. (1986). Consequences of physical abuse and neglect in children. *Clinical Psychology Review, 6,* 291–310.

Asarnow, J. R., Carlson, G. A., & Guthrie, D. (1987). Coping strategies, self-perceptions, hopelessness, and perceived family environments in depressed and suicidal children. *Journal of Consulting and Clinical Psychology, 55,* 361–366.

Azar, S. T., Robinson, D. R., Hekimian, E., & Twentyman, C. T. (1984). Unrealistic expectations and problem-solving ability in maltreating and comparison mothers. *Journal of Consulting and Clinical Psychology, 52,* 687–691.

Azar, S. T., & Rohrbeck, C. A. (1986). Child abuse and unrealistic expectations: Further validation of the Parent Opinion Questionnaire. *Journal of Consulting and Clinical Psychology, 54,* 867–868.

Bandura, A. (1973). *Aggression: A social learning analysis.* Englewood Cliffs, NJ: Prentice-Hall.

Barkley, R. A. (1983). Hyperactivity. In R. J. Morris & T. R. Kratochwill (Eds.), *The practice of child therapy* (pp. 87–112). Elmsford, NJ: Pergamon.

Bauer, W. D., & Twentyman, C. T. (1985). Abusing, neglectful, and comparison mothers' responses to child-related and non-child-related stressors. *Journal of Consulting and Clinical Psychology, 53,* 335–343.

Bernstein, D., & Borkovec, T. (1973). *Progressive relaxation training: A manual for the helping profession.* Champaign, IL: Research Press.

Bierman, K. L., & Furman, W. (1984). The effects of social skills training and peer involvement on the social adjustment of preadolescents. *Child Development, 55,* 151–162.

Bousha, D. M., & Twentyman, C. T. (1984). Mother–child interactional style in abuse, neglect, and control groups: Naturalistic observations in the home. *Journal of Abnormal Psychology, 93,* 106–114.

Bradley, R. H., Caldwell, B. M., Fitzgerald, J. A., Morgan, A. G., & Rock, S. L. (1986). Experiences in day care and social competence among maltreated children. *Child Abuse and Neglect, 10,* 181–189.

Bremner, R. H. (1971). *Children and youth in America: A documentary history. Vol. II: 1866–1932.* Cambridge, MA: Harvard University Press.

Bryer, J. B., Nelson, B. A., Miller, J. B., & Krol, P. A. (1987). Child sexual and physical abuse as factors in adult psychiatric illness. *American Journal of Psychiatry, 144,* 1426–1430.

Burgess, R. L., & Conger, R. D. (1978). Family interaction in abusive, neglectful, and normal families. *Child Development, 49,* 1163–1173.

Burgess, R. L., & Richardson, R. A. (1984). Coercive interpersonal contingencies as a determinant of child maltreatment. In R. F. Dangel & R. A. Polster (Eds.), *Parent training: Foundations of research and practice* (pp. 239–259). New York: Guilford.

Campbell, M., Green, W. H., Perry, R., & Anderson, L. T. (1983). Pharmacotherapy. In C. E. Walker & M. C. Roberts (Eds.), *Handbook of clinical psychology* (pp. 1109–1130). New York: Wiley.

Combs, M. S., & Lahey, B. B. (1981). A cognitive skills training program: Evaluation with young children. *Behavior Modification, 5,* 39–60.

Compas, B. E. (1987). Coping with stress during childhood and adolescence. *Psychological Bulletin, 10,* 393–403.

Compas, B. E., Malcarne, V. L., & Fondacaro, K. M. (1988). Coping with stressful events in older children and young adolescents. *Journal of Consulting and Clinical Psychology, 56,* 405–411.

Conaway, L. P., & Hansen, D. J. (1989). Social behavior of physically abused and neglected children: A critical review with implications for research and intervention. *Clinical Psychology Review, 9,* 627–652.

Conners, C. K. (1969). A teacher rating scale for use in drug studies with children. *American Journal of Psychiatry, 126,* 884–888.

Conners, C. K. (1970). Symptom patterns in hyperkinetic, neurotic, and normal children. *Child Development, 41,* 667–682.

Coons, P. M. (1986). Child abuse and multiple personality disorder: Review of the literature and suggestions for treatment. *Child Abuse and Neglect, 10,* 455–462.

Crenshaw, D. A., Rudy, C., Trimmer, D., & Zingaro, J. (1986). Psychotherapy with abused children: Breaking the silent bond. *Residential Group Care and Treatment, 3,* 25–38.

Cummings, E. M. (1987). Coping with background anger in early childhood. *Child Development, 58,* 976–984.

Dale, P., & Davies, M. (1985). A model of intervention in child-abusing families: A wider systems view. *Child Abuse and Neglect, 9,* 449–455.

Dietrich, K. N., Starr, R. H., & Kaplan, M. G. (1980). Maternal stimulation and care of abused infants. In T. M. Field, S. Goldberg, D. Stern, & A. M. Sostek (Eds.), *High-risk infants and children: Adult and peer interactions* (pp. 25–41). New York: Academic Press.

D'Zurilla, T. J. (1986). *Problem-solving therapy: A social competence approach to clinical intervention.* New York: Springer.

Edwards, D. L., & Gil, E. G. (1986). *Breaking the cycle: Assessment and treatment of child abuse and neglect.* Los Angeles: Association for Advanced Training.

Egeland, B., Sroufe, L. A., & Erickson, M. (1983). The developmental consequences of different patterns of maltreatment. *Child Abuse and Neglect, 7,* 459–469.

Elmer, E., & Gregg, G. S. (1967). Developmental characteristics of abused children. *Pediatrics, 40,* 596–602.

Emery, R. E. (1982). Interparental conflict and the children of discord and divorce. *Psychological Bulletin, 92,* 310–330.

Eyberg, S., & Ross, A. (1978). Assessment of child behavior problems: The validation of a new inventory. *Journal of Clinical Child Psychology, 7,* 113–116.

Fantuzzo, J. W., Jurecic, L., Stovall, A., Hightower, A. D., Goins, C., & Schachtel, D. (1988). Effects of adult and peer social initiations on the social behavior of withdrawn, maltreated preschool children. *Journal of Consulting and Clinical Psychology, 56,* 34–39.

Faranoff, A. A., Kennell, J. H., & Klaus, M. H. (1972). Follow-up of low birth weight infants: The predictive value of maternal visiting patterns. *Pediatrics, 49,* 287–290.

Feindler, E. L., & Ecton, R. B. (1986). *Adolescent anger control: Cognitive-behavioral techniques.* Elmsford, NY: Pergamon.

Feindler, E. L., Ecton, R. B., Kingsley, D., & Dubey, D. (1986). Group anger control training for institutionalized psychiatric male adolescents. *Behavior Therapy, 17,* 109–123.

Frankenburg, W. K., Dodds, J. B., Fandal, A. W., Kazuk, E., & Cohrs, M. (1975). *The Denver Developmental Screening Test* (rev. ed.). Denver: Ladoca Project and Publishing Foundation.

Frazier, D., & Levine, E. (1983). Reattachment therapy: Intervention with the very young physically abused child. *Psychotherapy: Theory, Research and Practice, 20*, 90–100.

Freedheim, D. K., & Russ, S. R. (1983). Psychotherapy with children. In C. E. Walker & M. C. Roberts (Eds.), *Handbook of clinical child psychology* (pp. 978–994). New York: Wiley.

Friedman, S. B., & Morse, C. W. (1974). Child abuse: A five-year follow-up of early case findings in the emergency department. *Pediatrics, 54*, 404–410.

Frodi, A. M. (1981). Contribution of infant characteristics to child abuse. *American Journal of Mental Deficiency, 4*, 314–349.

Gaensbauer, T. J., & Sands, K. (1979). Distorted affective communications in abused/neglected infants and their potential impact on caretakers. *Journal of the American Academy of Child Psychiatry, 18*, 236–250.

Garbarino, J., & Crouter, A. (1978). Defining the community context for parent–child relations: The correlates of child maltreatment. *Child Development, 49*, 604–616.

Garbarino, J., Guttman, E., & Seeley, J. W. (1986). *The psychologically battered child: Strategies for identification, assessment, and intervention.* San Francisco: Jossey-Bass.

Gelfand, D. M., & Hartmann, D. P. (1984). *Child behavior analysis and therapy* (2nd ed.). Elmsford, NY: Pergamon.

George, C., & Main, M. (1979). Social interactions of young abused children: Approach, avoidance, and aggression. *Child Development, 50*, 306–318.

Golden, C. J., Hammeke, T. A., & Purisch, A. D. (1985). *The Luria-Nebraska Neuropsychological Battery.* Los Angeles: Western Psychological Services.

Green, A. H. (1976). A psychodynamic approach to the study and treatment of child-abusing parents. *Journal of the American Academy of Child Psychiatry, 15*, 414–419.

Grieger, T., Kauffman, J. M., & Grieger, R. M. (1976). Effects of peer reporting on cooperative play and aggression in kindergarten children. *Journal of School Psychology, 14*, 307–313.

Guevremont, D. C., MacMillan, V. M., Shawchuck, C. R., & Hansen, D. J. (1989). A peer-mediated intervention with clinic-referred socially isolated girls: Generalization, maintenance, and social validation. *Behavior Modification, 13*, 32–50.

Haley, J. (1984). *Ordeal Therapy.* San Francisco: Jossey-Bass.

Hansen, D. J., Pallotta, G. M., Tishelman, A. C., Conaway, L. P., & MacMillan, V. M. (in press). Parental problem-solving skills and child behavior problems in abusive, neglectful, clinic, and community families. *Journal of Family Violence.*

Hansen, D. J., St. Lawrence, J. S., & Christoff, K. A. (1989). Group conversational-skills training with inpatient children and adolescents: Social validation, generalization, and maintenance. *Behavior Modification, 13*, 4–31.

Hansen, D. J., Watson-Perczel, M., & Christopher, J. S. (1989). Clinical issues in social-skills training with adolescents. *Clinical Psychology Review, 9*, 365–391.

Helfer, R. E. (1982). A review of the literature on the prevention of child abuse and neglect. *Child Abuse and Neglect, 6*, 251–261.

Herrenkohl, E. C., & Herrenkohl, R. C. (1979). A comparison of abused children and their nonabused siblings. *Journal of the American Academy of Child Psychiatry, 18*, 260–269.

Hjorth, C. W., & Harway, M. (1981). The body-image of physically abused and normal adolescents. *Journal of Clinical Psychology, 37,* 863–866.

Hochstadt, N. J., & Harwicke, N. J. (1985). How effective is the multidisciplinary approach? A follow-up study. *Child Abuse and Neglect, 9,* 365–372.

Hoffman-Plotkin, D., & Twentyman, C. T. (1984). A multimodal assessment of behavioral and cognitive deficits in abused and neglected preschoolers. *Child Development, 55,* 794–802.

Hops, H., & Greenwood, C. R. (1988). Social skill deficits. In E. J. Mash & L. G. Terdal (Eds.), *Behavioral assessment of childhood disorders* (2nd ed.) (pp. 263–314). New York: Guilford.

Howes, C., & Espinosa, M. P. (1985). The consequences of child abuse for the formation of relationships with peers. *Child Abuse and Neglect, 9,* 397–404.

Jaffe, P., Wolfe, D., Wilson, S., & Zak, L. (1986). Similarities in behavioral and social maladjustment among child victims and witnesses to family violence. *American Journal of Orthopsychiatry, 56,* 142–146.

Jastak, S., & Wilkinson, G. S. (1984). *Wide Range Achievement Test-Revised.* Wilmington, DE: Jastak Associates.

Kashani, J. H., Shekim, W. O., Burk, J. P., & Beck, N. C. (1987). Abuse as a predictor of psychopathology in children and adolescents. *Journal of Clinical Child Psychology, 16,* 43–50.

Kazdin, A. E., Esveldt-Dawson, K., French, N. H., & Unis, A. S. (1987). Problem-solving skills training and relationship therapy in the treatment of antisocial child behavior. *Journal of Consulting and Clinical Psychology, 55,* 76–85.

Kelly, J. A. (1983). *Treating child-abusive families: Intervention based on skills-training principles.* New York: Plenum.

Kempe, C. H. (1971). Pediatric implication of the battered baby syndrome. *Archives of Diseases in Childhood, 46,* 28–37.

Kempe, C. H., & Helfer, R. H. (1972). *Helping the battered child and his family.* Philadelphia: Lippincott.

Kempe, C. H., Silverman, F., Steele, B., Droegenmuller, W., & Silver, H. (1962). The battered child syndrome. *Journal of the American Medical Association, 181,* 17–24.

Kent, J. T. (1976). A follow-up study of abused children. *Journal of Pediatric Psychology, 2,* 25–31.

Kinard, E. M. (1982). Experiencing child abuse: Effects on emotional adjustment. *American Journal of Orthopsychiatry, 52,* 82–91.

Kline, D. F. (1977). Educational and psychological problems of abused children. *Child Abuse and Neglect, 1,* 301–307.

Kovacs, M., & Beck, A. T. (1977). An empirical-clinical approach toward a definition of childhood depression. In J. G. Schulterbrandt & A. Raskin (Eds.), *Depression in childhood: Diagnosis, treatment and conceptual models* (pp. 1–25). New York: Raven Press.

Kravic, J. N. (1987). Behavior problems and social competence of clinic-referred abused children. *Journal of Family Violence, 2,* 111–120.

Kurdek, L. A. (1986). Children's reasoning about parental divorce. In R. D. Ashmore & D. M. Brodzinsky (Eds.), *Thinking about the family: Views of parents and children* (pp. 233–276). Hillsdale, NJ: Erlbaum.

Lahey, B. B., Conger, R. D., Atkeson, B. M., & Treiber, F. A. (1984). Parenting behavior and emotional status of physically abusive mothers. *Journal of Consulting and Clinical Psychology, 52,* 1062–1071.

Lamphear, V. S. (1985). The impact of maltreatment on children's psychosocial adjustment: A review of the research. *Child Abuse and Neglect, 9,* 251–263.

Larrance, D. T., & Twentyman, C. T. (1983). Maternal attributions and child abuse. *Journal of Abnormal Psychology, 92,* 449–457.

Lawder, E. A., Poulin, J. E., & Andrews, R. G. (1986). A study of 185 foster children 5 years after placement. *Child Welfare, 65,* 241–251.

Lazarus, R. S., & Folkman, S. (1984). *Stress, appraisal and coping.* New York: Springer.

Leventhal, J. M. (1981). Risk factors for child abuse: Methodologic standards in case-control studies. *Pediatrics, 68,* 684–690.

Long, K. A. (1986). Cultural considerations in the assessment and treatment of intrafamilial abuse. *American Journal of Orthopsychiatry, 56,* 131–136.

Lutzker, J. R. (1984). Project 12-Ways: Treating child abuse and neglect from an ecobehavioral perspective. In R. F. Dangel & R. A. Polster (Eds.), *Parent training: Foundations of research and practice* (pp. 260–291). New York: Guilford.

Lutzker, J. R., & Rice, J. M. (1984). Project 12-Ways: Measuring outcome of a large in-home service for treatment and prevention of child abuse and neglect. *Child Abuse and Neglect, 8,* 519–524.

Lyons-Ruth, K., Connell, D. B., Zoll, D., & Stahl, J. (1987). Infants at social risk: Relations among infant maltreatment, maternal behavior, and infant attachment behavior. *Developmental Psychology, 23,* 223–232.

Main, M., & George, C. (1985). Responses of abused and disadvantaged toddlers to distress in agemates: A study in the daycare setting. *Developmental Psychology, 21,* 407–412.

Martin, H. P., & Beezley, P. (1977). Behavioral observations of abused children. *Developmental Medicine and Child Neurology, 19,* 373–387.

Martin, H. P., & Rodeheffer, M. A. (1976). The psychological impact of abuse on children. *Journal of Pediatric Psychology, 1,* 12–15.

Mash, E. J., Johnston, C., & Kovitz, K. (1983). A comparison of the mother-child interactions of physically abused children during play and task situations. *Journal of Clinical Child Psychology, 12,* 337–346.

Mash, E. J., & Terdal, L. G. (Eds.). (1988). *Behavioral assessment of childhood disorders* (2nd ed.). New York: Guilford.

Matson, J. L., & Ollendick, T. H. (1988). *Enhancing children's social skills: Assessment and training.* Elmsford, NY: Pergamon.

McHenry, M., Girdany, B. R., & Elmer, E. (1963). Suspected trauma with multiple skeletal injuries during infancy and childhood. *Pediatrics, 31,* 903–908.

Meichenbaum, D. (1977). *Cognitive behavior modification: An integrative approach.* New York: Plenum.

Meichenbaum, D., & Goodman, J. (1971). Training impulsive children to talk to themselves: A means of developing self-control. *Journal of Abnormal Psychology, 77,* 115–126.

Milner, J. S. (1986). *The Child Abuse Potential Inventory: Manual* (2nd ed.). Webster, NC: PSYTEC.

Minuchin, S., & Fishman, H. C. (1981). *Family therapy techniques.* Cambridge, MA: Harvard University Press.

Morris, R. J., & Kratochwill, T. R. (Eds.). (1983). *The practice of child therapy.* Elmsford, NY: Pergamon.

Morse, C. W., Sahler, O. J. Z., & Friedman, S. B. (1970). A three-year follow-up study of abused and neglected children. *American Journal of Diseases of Children, 20,* 439–446.

National Center on Child Abuse and Neglect. (1988). *Study of national incidence and prevalence of child abuse and neglect: 1988.* Washington, DC: U.S. Department of Health and Human Services.

Newberger, E. H. (1982). *Child abuse.* Boston: Little, Brown.

Ney, P. G. (1987). The treatment of abused children: The natural sequence of events. *American Journal of Psychotherapy, 41,* 391–401.

Ollendick, T. H. (1983). Reliability and validity of the Revised Fear Survey Schedule for Children. *Behaviour Research and Therapy, 21,* 685–692.

Parish, R. A., Myers, P. A., Brandner, A., & Templin, K. H. (1985). Developmental milestones in abused children, and their improvement with a family-oriented approach to the treatment of child abuse. *Child Abuse and Neglect, 9,* 245–250.

Patterson, G. R. (1982). *Coercive family processes.* Eugene, OR: Castalia.

Pelham, W. E., Bender, M. E., Caddell, J., Booth, S., & Moorer, S. H. (1985). Methylphenidate and children with attention deficit disorder: Dose effects on classroom academic and social behavior. *Archives of General Psychiatry, 42,* 948–952.

Pelton, L. H. (1978). Child abuse and neglect: The myth of classlessness. *American Journal of Orthopsychiatry, 48,* 608–617.

Perry, M. A., Doran, L. D., & Wells, E. A. (1983). Developmental and behavioral characteristics of the physically abused child. *Journal of Clinical Child Psychology, 12,* 320–324.

Plienis, A. J., Hansen, D. J., Ford, F., Smith, S., Stark, L. J., & Kelly, J. A. (1987). Behavioral small group training to improve the social skills of emotionally-disordered adolescents. *Behavior Therapy, 18,* 17–32.

Reid, J. B., Kavanagh, K., & Baldwin, D. V. (1987). Abusive parents' perceptions of child problem behaviors: An example of parental bias. *Journal of Abnormal Child Psychology, 15,* 457–466.

Reidy, T. J. (1977). The aggressive characteristics of abused and neglected children. *Journal of Clinical Psychology, 33,* 1140–1145.

Reynolds, C. R., & Richmond, B. O. (1978). What I think and feel: A revised measure of children's manifest anxiety. *Journal of Abnormal Child Psychology, 6,* 271–280.

Rivara, F. P. (1985). Physical abuse in children under two: A study of therapeutic outcomes. *Child Abuse and Neglect, 9,* 81–87.

Robinson, E. A., & Eyberg, S. M. (1981). The Dyadic Parent-Child Interaction Coding System: Standardization and validation. *Journal of Consulting and Clinical Psychology, 49,* 245–250.

Rosenberg, M. S., & Reppucci, N. D. (1985). Primary prevention of child abuse. *Journal of Consulting and Clinical Psychology, 53*, 576–585.

Ross, A. O. (1981). *Child behavior therapy*. New York: Wiley.

Salzinger, S., Kaplan, K., & Artemyeff, C. (1983). Mothers' personal social networks and child maltreatment. *Journal of Abnormal Psychology, 92*, 68–76.

Salzinger, S., Kaplan, S., Pelcovitz, D., Samit, C., & Krieger, R. (1984). Parent and teacher assessment of children's behavior in child maltreating families. *Journal of the American Academy of Child Psychiatry, 23*, 458–464.

Schmitt, B. D. (1980). The prevention of child abuse and neglect: A review of the literature with recommendations for application. *Child Abuse and Neglect, 4*, 171–177.

Shearman, J. K., Evans, C. E., Boyle, M. H., Cuddy, L. J., & Norman, G. (1983). Maternal and infant characteristics in abuse: A case control study. *The Journal of Family Practice, 16*, 289–293.

Silver, L. B., Dublin, C. C., & Lourie, R. S. (1969). Does violence breed violence? Contributions from a study of the child abuse syndrome. *American Journal of Psychiatry, 126*, 404–407.

Sisson, L. A., Van Hasselt, V. B., Hersen, M., & Strain, P. S. (1985). Peer interventions: Increasing social behaviors in multihandicapped children. *Behavior Modification, 9*, 293–321.

Smith, S. M. (1975). *The battered child syndrome*. London: Butterworths.

Sparrow, S. S., Balla, D. A., & Cicchetti, D. V. (1984). *Vineland Adaptive Behavior Scales (Revised)*. Circle Pines, MN: American Guidance Services.

Spielberger, C. D. (1973). *State-Trait Anxiety Inventory for Children*. Palo Alto, CA: Consulting Psychological Press.

Spinetta, J. J., & Rigler, D. (1972). The child-abusing parent: A psychological review. *Psychological Bulletin, 77*, 296–304.

Steele, B. F., & Pollock, C. B. (1974). A psychiatric study of parents who abuse infants and small children. In R. E. Helfer & C. H. Kempe (Eds.), *The battered child* (2nd ed., pp. 3–21). Chicago: University of Chicago Press.

Stokes, T. F., & Baer, D. M. (1977). An implicit technology of generalization. *Journal of Applied Behavior Analysis, 10*, 349–368.

Straus, M. A. (1980). Stress and physical child abuse. *Child Abuse and Neglect, 4*, 75–88.

Stuart, R. (1980). *Helping couples change: A social learning approach to marital therapy*. New York: Guilford.

Tisdelle, D. A., & St. Lawrence, J. S. (1986). Interpersonal problem-solving competency: Review and critique of the literature. *Clinical Psychology Review, 6*, 337–356.

Tisdelle, D. A., & St. Lawrence, J. S. (1988). Adolescent interpersonal problem-solving skill training: Social validation and generalization. *Behavior Therapy, 19*, 171–182.

Trickett, P. K., & Kuczynski, L. (1986). Children's misbehaviors and parental discipline strategies in abusive and nonabusive families. *Developmental Psychology, 22*, 115–123.

Wahler, R. G. (1980). The insular mother: Her problem in parent-child treatment. *Journal of Applied Behavior Analysis, 13,* 207–219.

Walker, C. E., Bonner, B. L., & Kaufman, K. L. (1988). *The physically and sexually abused child: Evaluation and treatment.* New York: Pergamon.

Wasserman, S. (1967). The abused parent of the abused child. *Children, 14,* 175–179.

Wechsler, D. (1974). *Wechsler Intelligence Scale for Children-Revised.* New York: Psychological Corp.

Weinbach, R. W., & Curtiss, C. R. (1986). Making child abuse victims aware of their victimization: A treatment issue. *Child Welfare, 65,* 337–346.

Weisz, J. R., Weiss, B., Wasserman, A. A., & Rintoul, B. (1987). Control-related beliefs and depression among clinic-referred children and adolescents. *Journal of Abnormal Psychology, 96,* 58–63.

Wielkiewicz, R. M. (1986). *Behavior management in the schools: Principles and procedures.* Elmsford, NY: Pergamon.

Wilbur, C. (1984). Multiple personality and child abuse. *Psychiatric Clinics of North America, 7,* 3–7.

Williams, G. J. R. (1983). Child abuse. In C. E. Walker & M. C. Roberts (Eds.), *Handbook of clinical child psychology* (pp. 1219–1248). New York: Wiley.

Wolfe, D. A. (1988). Child abuse and neglect. In E. J. Mash & L. G. Terdal (Eds.), *Behavioral assessment of childhood disorders* (pp. 627–669). New York: Guilford.

Wolfe, D. A., Edwards, B., Manion, I., & Koverola, C. (1988). Early intervention for parents at risk of child abuse and neglect: A preliminary investigation. *Journal of Consulting and Clinical Psychology, 56,* 40–47.

Wolfe, D. A., Fairbank, J. A., Kelly, J. A., & Bradlyn, A. S. (1983). Child abusive parents' physiological responses to stressful and non-stressful behavior in children. *Behavioral Assessment, 5,* 363–371.

Wolfe, D., Kaufman, K. A., Aragona, J., & Sandler, J. (1981). *The child management program for abusive parents.* Winter Park, FL: Anna Publishing.

Wolfe, D. A., & Mosk, M. D. (1983). Behavioral comparisons of children from abusive and distressed families. *Journal of Consulting and Clinical Psychology, 51,* 702–708.

Wolfe, D. A., & Sandler, J. (1981). Training abusive parents in effective child management. *Behavior Modification, 5,* 135–148.

Wolfe, D. A., Sandler, J., & Kaufman, K. A. (1981). A competency-based parent training program for child abusers. *Journal of Consulting and Clinical Psychology, 49,* 633–640.

CHAPTER 3

Victims of Child Sexual Abuse

JON R. CONTE

INTRODUCTION

Mental health professionals have been aware of the sexual abuse of children by older persons since at least the late 1890s. At that time, Freud first postulated a connection between "hysterical" illness in 18 of his adult patients and their reports of childhood sexual experiences with adults (see Masson, 1984). Although there has been periodic mention of this phenomenon in the professional literature since Freud, it is only recently that sexual abuse of children has received major professional attention.

Much of this attention has been focused on legal aspects of these cases (Whitcomb, Shapiro, & Stellwagen, 1985), how to prevent abuse (Conte, Wolf, & Smith, 1989; Nelson & Clark, 1986), the incidence of abuse in the general population (Russell, 1984, 1986) or in special populations (Finkelhor, 1986), treatment of sexual offenders (Greer & Stuart, 1983), initial medical and mental health handling of abused children and their families (Burgess, Groth, Holstrom, & Sgroi, 1978; Sgroi, 1982), and other issues that do not deal directly with the mental health treatment of the sexually abused child. It is only very recently that substantial attention has been directed toward the treatment of sexually abused children.

The infancy of research and professional experience in the mental health treatment of sexually abused children requires that professionals approach sexually abused children with great care. Little is known about the effects of various therapeutic interventions. There is considerable disagreement about how sexual abuse should be viewed as a mental health problem, what treatment approaches are indicated, how treatment should be structured, how treatment of child victims should be coordinated with treatment of other family members, and many other issues that influence intervention processes with abused children.

Although most therapists believe that their interventions are, in fact, effective, both the psychotherapy research literature (e.g., Lambert, Shapiro, & Bergin, 1986) and clinical experience suggest that clients can be and are harmed by misdirected or inappropriate interventions. Unsuccessful therapy may result from a number of other factors (e.g., inadequate client motivation, poor therapist–client match, lack of environmental support), but it also can occur because of inappropriate treatment.

This caveat is offered to the reader as an introduction both to the state of professional knowledge on the treatment of sexually abused children and to this chapter. In the following pages, care will be taken to differentiate statements that are supported by research from those based on clinical experience. Furthermore, the reader is advised to approach all material, but especially that resulting from clinical experience, with the caution that is appropriate for unsubstantiated and potentially powerful information.

This chapter will review (a) the epidemiology of child and sexual abuse, (b) the consequences of abuse, (c) prevailing models for understanding the effects of abuse, and (d) issues, problems, and common therapeutic issues that arise when treating sexually abused children. The chapter is intended to further the dialogue among those engaged in the treatment of sexually abused children toward the end that, in time, more specific, empirically validated treatment models will become available.

EPIDEMIOLOGY

Statistics describing the increased reports of child sexual abuse to state child protection agencies or the prevalence of child sexual abuse in society often are cited as indications of the seriousness of this problem. The use of reports to mandated state agencies, however, is believed to be quite problematic in identifying the incidence of child sexual abuse. For example, underreporting of abuse appears to occur because many state agencies are overwhelmed with reports and thus may encourage their refusal (e.g., if the abuse took place long ago or if the offender does not fall under the agency's legal mandate). Moreover, it is not always clear if incidence figures are derived from all reports or only those that are subsequently substantiated or found to be credible. This is particularly important because the rate of substantiated reports of child sexual abuse varies from state to state.

In a comprehensive and thoughtful review of studies on the incidence and prevalence of child sexual abuse, Peters, Wyatt, and Finkelhor (1986) report that estimates of the prevalence range from 6% to 62% for females, and from 3% to 31% for males. As they point out, a number of factors may account for this variation among studies, including use of different definitions of abuse, employment of different samples (e.g., college students or the general population) or methods (e.g., data collection made in person vs. by telephone), or utilization of a varying number of questions to elicit information about abuse experiences.

Clinical reports are helpful in alerting mental health professionals to the high incidence of sexual abuse in specific clinical populations. These include clinical studies on sexually abused children that have found indications of depression, guilt, learning difficulties, sexual promiscuity, runaway behavior, somatic complaints, and changes in behavior (Kolko, Moser, & Weldy, 1988), hysterical seizures (Goodwin, Simms, & Bergman, 1979; Gross, 1979), phobias, nightmares, and compulsive rituals (Weiss, Rogers, Darwin, & Dutton, 1955), and self-destructive or suicidal behavior (Carroll, Schaffer, Spensley, & Abramowitz, 1980; de Young, 1982; Yorukoglu & Kemph, 1966).

From an epidemiological perspective, these findings suggest several points for the mental health professional. Child sexual abuse is a relatively common experience in childhood. Whether it is 6% or 62% of females and 3% or 31% of males, many children are exposed to sexual abuse. Histories of childhood sexual abuse appear to be common in clients who seek out mental health professionals. Many victims may not seek service and abuse may not be the only factor that brings victims to treatment, but it is becoming increasingly clear that many clients do have such histories. An understanding of how abuse affects victims and skills in treating these effects are essential for the mental health professional engaged today in direct services to clients.

Children who are referred to the mental health professional for possible sexual abuse come for a variety of reasons. An increasing amount of mental health time is devoted to substantiating the allegation of abuse. Another professional or a child's parent may suspect abuse because of something the child said (e.g., "he put his peepee up inside me") or something that was observed (e.g., an adult pulling up his pants when leaving a child's room, or a child engaging in sexual play with stuffed animals). Often child victims will be seeing a professional for other reasons (e.g., behavior problems), and the abuse will have not been diagnosed. On occasion, a parent will take a child to a therapist, indicating that he or she was abused at about the same age and wanting the therapist to determine if the child also has been abused.

The epidemiological data suggest that sexual abuse of children is a significant problem of childhood and that certain common behavioral and emotional problems, although not exclusively associated with abuse, are present in many abused children. When such problems are present, the professional should not rule out sexual abuse. If the child, child's parent, or other professional gives some indication that abuse may be present, further assessment is indicated. When a referral is made specifically for sexual abuse, it is still prudent for the professional to confirm what took place and what effects it may have had on the child. This is necessary because the original determination that the child was abused may not be accurate. Moreover, if it is accurate, the professional requires such information in order to plan treatment.

CONSEQUENCES OF SEXUAL ABUSE

There is a large body of literature dealing with the effects of sexual abuse on children (see reviews by Browne & Finkelhor, 1986; Conte, 1985). Until recently, much of this literature consisted of anecdotal reports using relatively small clinic samples. Generally, these are studies of unknown representatives, typically with small sample sizes, that consist of subjects who are identified because they have mental health problems, and which most often lack measurement or group comparisons (see Conte, 1985). These methodological problems limit the usefulness of this literature in understanding the effects of sexual abuse on children or adults abused as children for several reasons. Because the sample is defined in terms of a specific problem other than sexual maltreatment, and comparison groups are typically absent, it is not known how many abused subjects do not exhibit that specific problem. In addition, factors other than the abuse may account for the development of mental health problems. In some cases, the clinical presentation, although important for the subjects in the report, may be a rare effect of abuse. Nevertheless, clinical observations of sexually abused children indicate a variety of behavioral and emotional difficulties.

Recent research, on the other hand, has employed more specific measures of psychological functioning and some form of control group. These studies, in turn, have helped reveal differences in psychological functioning between children who have been sexually abused and those who have not. For example, Gomez-Schwartz, Horowitz, and Sauzier (1985) compared 156 sexually abused children to the norms provided with the Louisville Behavior Checklist (LBC). Results indicated that, for preschool children ($n = 30$), sexually abused children were rated more pathological than the normative group on 9 of the 16 behavioral dimensions of the LBC (infantile aggression, aggression, sensitivity, fear, inhibition, immaturity, cognitive disability, prosocial deficit, and neurotic behavior). However, comparison of these abused children to the norms for a group of children receiving mental health services revealed that abused children exhibited less overall pathology and fewer specific difficulties than the norms derived from clinically referred children. School-age sexually abused children ($n = 58$), on the other hand, exhibited significantly more pathology on every dimension of the LBC (infantile aggression, hyperactivity, antisocial behavior, aggression, social withdrawal, sensitivity, fear, inhibition, academic disability, immaturity, learning disability, normal irritability, neurotic behavior, psychotic behavior, somatic behavior, and prosocial deficits [lack of socially valued interpersonal skills]). School-age sexually abused children exhibited less problematic functioning on 11 of 16 LBC dimensions (infantile aggression, hyperactivity, antisocial behavior, aggression, social withdrawal, sensitivity, inhibition, immaturity, normal irritability, psychotic behavior, and somatic behavior) than other children in mental health treatment. It should be noted that comparison of samples to standardized norms can be quite problematic because it often is not known in what ways the sample significantly varies from the sample used to develop the norms.

Several recent studies have employed comparison groups. For example, Conte and Schuerman (1987) compared a sample of 369 sexual abuse victims aged 4 to 17 years with a community comparison group of 318 children who had not been abused. On a 110-item parent-completed behavior checklist (Child Behavior Profile [CBP]), sexually abused children were found to display significantly deviant scores on 12 dimensions (concentration problems, aggression, withdrawal, somatic complaints, character personality style [e.g., nice or pleasant disposition, too anxious to please], antisocial behavior, nervous/emotional problems, depression, behavioral regression, body image/self-esteem problems, fear, and symptoms of posttraumatic stress).

In another study, Gale, Thompson, Moran, and Sack (1988) reviewed medical records of 202 children of whom 37 were sexually abused, 35 physically abused, and 130 nonabused (children referred for emotional and behavioral problems) seen between 1982 and 1984 at a child and family community mental health clinic. Significant differences were found in the proportion of the subsamples exhibiting inappropriate sexual behavior (51% of the sexual abuse group and less than 5% of the other two groups). Moreover, the sexual abuse group exhibited less noncompliance than the abuse group (62% for the sexual abuse group vs. 79% for the abused and 88% for the nonabused group). No significant differences were found between groups for depression, anxiety, withdrawal, antisocial aggressive, affective disorder, and psychosomatic complaints. As the authors point out, some of the children in the nonabused group may be undiagnosed abuse victims. Whatever the case, they do appear to represent some kind of a nonspecific clinical sample and the results of this record review suggest that few clinical symptoms are associated solely with sexual abuse.

Rimsza, Berg, and Locke (1988) examined 368 children and adolescents receiving medical evaluations in Maricopa County, Arizona, comparing 72 sexually abused children to a matched control group of general clinic child patients. Results indicated that sexually abused children were more likely to report symptoms of muscle tension, gastrointestinal and genitourinary difficulties, emotional reactions, runaway behavior, and other behavior problems. Differences for school problems and early pregnancy, however, were not significant.

Friedrich (1988) summarizes data collected over a 4-year period on 155 cases (3–12-year-old children) from his consultation, supervisory, and private practice using the Child Behavior Profile (Revised) (CBCR). In a study of a group of sexually abused boys ($N = 20$) and a comparison group ($N = 23$) of conduct disorder boys, the only significant differences were that the conduct disorder boys were more aggressive and more externalizing and the sexually abused boys were significantly more likely to exhibit sex problems (e.g., behaves like opposite sex and plays with own sex organs in public). In a second study, nonabused children ($M = 67$), a psychiatric outpatient group of children ($n = 58$), and a group of sexually abused children ($n = 72$) were compared and contrasted. Significant differences were found on four of the CBCR dimensions (hyperactivity, aggression, sex items, and externalization). For each of these descriptions of behavior, the sexually abused children reflected scores between the nonabused and psychiatric outpatient groups, except for sex items, in which the sexually abused children exhibited significantly more problematic functioning than the other groups.

Kolko et al. (1988) report the results of a study of psychiatrically hospitalized sexually ($N = 29$) and physically ($N = 52$) abused children. Children were assessed on a 26-item Sexual Abuse Symptom Checklist (SASC) measuring child functioning in four domains (home routines/relationships, behavioral and affective reactions, physical/sexual behavior, and school behavior). The SASC was administered to the child's parent or guardian by the unit nurse practitioner. A factor analysis of the SASC yielded six factors: sexual activity, fear/mistrust, unhappiness/escape, conduct problems, school apathy/neglect, and withdrawal/poor appetite. Sexually abused hospitalized children were found to exhibit significantly more sexual activity, fear/mistrust, and withdrawal/poor appetite relative to their physically abused peers.

The aforementioned studies examining the effects of sexual abuse on children point to several conclusions. Sexually abused children display a variety of negative social, emotional, and physical sequelae relative to children who are not known to have been abused, and those who are identified as problematic (e.g., those who seek outpatient mental health treatment). It is unclear, however, the extent to which psychopathology in sexually abused children is specific to sexual abuse or to childhood trauma in general. The identification of effects specific to sexual abuse, physical abuse, and other types of childhood trauma is of considerable practical importance as it is likely to direct intervention (see Summary and Future Directions). There are several methodological limitations of research in this area; although typical in applied research, they somewhat limit the generalizability of findings. For example, investigators have employed different measures of effects as well as different control groups. Despite these discrepancies, there is considerable agreement that abuse is associated with a variety of negative effects.

There are a number of other problems with much of the existing research on the effects of sexual abuse as they relate to recommendations for treatment. As Berliner and Wheeler (1987) point out, much of the existing research has been atheoretical or lacked conceptualization of effects or diagnostic relevance likely to be helpful in treatment. The listings of symptoms or aspects of child functioning influenced by abuse are not helpful to the clinician unless such groupings lead to implications for treatment. At present, such implications have not been well developed.

Another problem is that reported groupings of symptoms vary considerably in terms of behavioral specificity. Many studies describe behaviors in abstract terms (e.g., externalizing behavior or behavioral regression). In addition, although most of the reviewed investigations provide descriptive information regarding the clinical presentation of sexually abused children, few data are available examining the etiological processes involved. For example, Conte and Schuerman (1987) and Conte, Berliner, and Schuerman (1986) report that sexually abused children are significantly more likely to be described as having concentration problems than their nonabused peers. What is not clear is the reason for this problem. Indeed, the two possible causal dynamics have potentially quite different treatment responses. Thus, one explanation could be that abused children experience flashbacks of the abuse and are preoccupied with reexperiencing the abuse. Another explanation, however, is that during the abuse children learn to be dissociative and then exhibit that response in nonabuse situations.

Conceptual Models of the Sequelae of Sexual Abuse

A number of conceptual models have been offered that help the clinician understand the effects of sexual abuse on children. Although a comprehensive review of each of these is not possible here, it is important for the reader to keep these models in mind in subsequent sections of this chapter.

Posttraumatic stress disorder (PTSD) is a popular framework for thinking about trauma and its effects on the victim. The essential features of PTSD are (a) the existence of a stressor (sexual abuse) that evokes significant symptoms of distress in most persons; (b) a reexperiencing of the trauma through recurrent, intrusive thoughts or images of the event, dreams of the event, or a sudden acting or feeling as if the event were taking place; and (c) a numbing of responsiveness to or reduced involvement (e.g., feeling detached or estranged from those around one) with the external world beginning sometime after the trauma. In addition, at least two of the following symptoms are present: sleep disturbance, hyperalertness or exaggerated startle response, guilt about surviving, memory impairment or trouble concentrating, avoidance of activities that trigger memories of the event, or an intensification of symptoms by exposure to a situation that triggers or resembles the event (American Psychiatric Association, 1987).

As Goodwin (1983) has pointed out, many of the symptoms of abused children are consistent with PTSD (e.g., fear and startle responses, reenactment of the trauma, sleep disturbances, signs of guilt and depression). Clinical experience suggests that some sexually abused children present symptoms consistent with a PTSD diagnosis whereas others do not. Reenactment of the trauma may be found in play with toys or other children. Some children develop abuse-associated fears (e.g., fear of men, fear of the place(s) where abuse occurred), and some are easily startled. As previously suggested, it is unclear why so many abused children exhibit concentration problems, but it is thought that some of these children may often reexperience the sexual abuse.

An information-processing model for understanding the effects of sexual abuse has been proposed by Burgess and her colleagues (Burgess & Grant, 1988). This model is quite similar to PTSD and other anxiety-processing models. According to this formulation, a specific trauma or stressor (sexual abuse) produces anxiety. The child then employs defensive coping operations (e.g., dissociation, denial, or reenactment) to cope with anxiety. Trauma learning may take place in which the child "learns" to use anxiety reduction mechanisms (e.g., dissociation) in nonabuse situations or at nonabusive times. Some of these may involve a reenactment of the abuse (e.g., through play) or the use of the new behavior (e.g., dissociation) at highly anxious times for the child (e.g., when the child is reminded of the abuse). The encapsulation of the trauma may be effective if the trauma produces no negative symptoms (e.g., reenactment of the abuse or dissociation), or is ineffective, in which case the child is symptomatic.

Based on work with several different samples, Burgess and her colleagues (Burgess & Grant, 1988; Burgess, Hartman, McCausland, & Powers, 1984) have observed common response patterns or posttrauma outcomes. These include (a) integrated, in which the trauma is adequately processed and the child masters the anxiety; (b) anxious, in which the symptoms (e.g., behavioral acting out, depression) indicate that the child is coping poorly with anxiety associated with abuse; and (c) avoidant, in which the child's anxiety is suppressed (e.g., child runs away, child refuses to talk about or otherwise deal with the abuse).

A learning paradigm is offered by Wheeler and Berliner (1988) who suggest that anxiety plays a key role in the development of abuse effects through classical conditioning. In this paradigm, neutral stimuli (e.g., a known and trusted adult) become associated with painful or aversive stimuli (e.g., sexual behavior, threats, or physical coercion). This leads to conditioning of maladaptive social behaviors, beliefs, and attitudes that children learn from the abuse context.

Browne and Finkelhor (1986) propose a quite different formulation involving four traumagenic dynamics of sexual abuse: traumatic sexualization, betrayal, powerlessness, and stigmatization. Each of these factors describes an inherent aspect of child sexual abuse hypothesized to be associated with its effects. For example, betrayal consists of several ingredients in which the child's vulnerability and trust are manipulated, the child's well-being is ignored, the child does not receive support or protection, and the child's expectation that others will provide care and protection is violated. This dynamic produces psychological impacts such as grief, depression, anger, impaired ability to judge trustworthiness of others, and mistrust of others.

Finkelhor (1988) has been quite critical of the application of PTSD to sexual abuse, suggesting that (a) not all symptoms of sexual abuse fit within the PTSD theory, (b) it does not accurately fit the experience of all victims, and (c) it does "not truly present a theory that explains how the dynamics of sexual abuse lead to the symptoms" (p. 350). Other problems noted by Finkelhor are that the emphasis in PTSD theory is on intrusive imagery, and yet many victims do not appear to have this component. Moreover, many of the symptoms of PTSD consist of affective disturbances, yet many victims also display negative behavioral and cognitive effects.

Although these points are well taken, there are a number of problems with the traumagenic dynamics model as well. This model is described as an "eclectic but comprehensive model that suggests a variety of different dynamics to account for the variety of different types of symptoms" (Finkelhor, 1988, p. 354). Although the four trauma-producing dynamics have an elegant parsimony, no current research has documented that these are in fact consequences of victimization. Clinical experience suggests that victims vary considerably on the extent to which these dynamics may be present. Indeed, not all victims have experienced all dynamics as salient aspects of their abuse.

Some victims appear to be most affected by dynamics subsumed within these four broad dynamics. For example, for some victims the physical force employed by the offender seems to be the paramount source of pain, anxiety, and trauma. Coercion is viewed as one of the dynamics of powerlessness within the model, but it is not clear whether the trauma-producing dynamic is the victim's sense of powerlessness or the pain from the physical force. Subsuming coercion within a larger and more abstract framework places less emphasis on what is more salient to the victim.

The psychological impacts associated with the four traumagenic factors may themselves produce trauma. For example, anxiety, fear, isolation, guilt, shame, and confusion about sexual identity are likely to be directly responsible for many of the symptoms associated with abuse. Conte (1985) has postulated that sexual abuse might best be considered as consisting of first- and second-order sources of trauma or impact. First-order factors consist of those directly derived from sexual abuse. They include the specific actions of offenders to gain sexual access to the victim, the sexual behavior, and actions taken by the offender to maintain the victim's silence (e.g., emotional or psychological threat, force or threat of force, bribes). Second-order sources of trauma result from the victim's processing the first-order events and may become trauma-producing in their own right. For example, threats and force may create fear. Some victims develop fears specific to the abuse (e.g., fear of the offender, fear of the place where the abuse took place) and others more generalized fear (e.g., men or places similar to the abuse location [e.g., parks, old buildings]). Other children may view their compliance with the abuse, or compliance induced by threat, bribes, or meeting emotional needs, as evidence of their complicity. In time, this may lead to guilt which, in turn, is associated with additional problems or symptoms (e.g., self-blame, concept of self as bad).

Although the traumagenic factor model is quite helpful to the clinician in underscoring that sexual abuse may be associated with a variety of symptoms and contain elements that may vary across cases and produce trauma, the model does not direct treatment. This formulation, as well as PTSD and the learning model proposed by Berliner and Wheeler (1987), calls attention to several concepts that can suggest treatment targets. These include sexual abuse as anxiety, adaptive and maladaptive coping, and sexual abuse as a learning situation.

Sexual Abuse and Anxiety

Having a sexual experience with an adult produces anxiety with which the child must cope. Moreover, sexual abuse consists of a large number of components (e.g., what sexual act is performed, who does it, what threats or other verbal statements accompany the abuse, how the child feels about the abuse). Depending on the specific nature of the abuse and the child's psychological makeup, these characteristics may produce more or less anxiety. The child victim somehow has to deal with the anxiety produced by the sexual experience.

Berliner and Wheeler (1987) note that a good deal of treatment of child victims involves addressing anxiety. How the specific anxiety is dealt with depends on how the child expresses it. Indeed, clinical experience suggests that many child victims cope with the anxiety through denial and repression. Such children are seen as reluctant to talk about the abuse. In extreme cases, these children may recant or deny that they ever said the abuse took place. The clinical challenge in these cases is to encourage expression of the anxiety so that the child is able to talk about the abuse. Other children may express the anxiety through specific behavioral responses. For example, some children will exhibit fears or somatic complaints that are believed to result from acute anxiety. So that the abuse experiences no longer produce such anxiety such children have to be helped to cope through rituals (e.g., bedtime prayers, arranging the light and furniture in their rooms to detect movement) that make them feel safe; repeated storytelling or play in which abuse themes are retold or reenacted until they no longer produce anxiety; or desensitization, in which exposure to abuse stimuli in a relaxed state removes the anxiety-producing nature of the abuse experience.

Adaptive and Maladaptive Coping

Little is currently known about how coping styles are developed or what specific coping strategies are associated with problematic functioning in childhood or later in adult life. Many clinicians have suggested that some strategies may be successful in coping with the anxiety during sexual abuse, but when exhibited at nonabuse times they become problematic. For example, it is speculated that some children learn to separate from the experience of abuse by pretending that it is not happening or imagining that they are somewhere else. This coping effort makes it possible not to feel or be aware of the abuse while it is taking place. This is believed to be the origin of the tendency toward dissociation noted in adults abused as children (Briere & Runtz, 1988).

The clinician must be aware that little is known about how coping styles mediate the effects of sexual abuse. In fact, there has been a great deal of debate about this issue among clinicians. For example, Lamb (1986) has argued that telling abused children that they are not responsible for the maltreatment removes the only sense of control that a child may have in a sexual abuse experience. If this is true, such a strategy may be associated with an increase in symptomatology.

Clinical experience indicates that, in some cases, a child's sense that there is something left to do if the abuse becomes "bad enough" (e.g., run away, tell the teacher) provides a sense of power over events surrounding the abuse. For example, a child may make a decision to tell others about her abuse because she fears that her mother will not be able to handle the information. She decides to continue to go with the offender, knowing that she will be abused but also thinking that if she can no longer tolerate the abuse, she will tell her teacher or run away. Her silence thereby "protects" her mother. Later in life, the adult may recall the decision to comply with the abuse, but will no longer recall her youthful thinking process in which she was protecting her mother. This, in turn, may lead to feelings of duplicity and increased guilt because she did not tell and thereby is responsible for her own abuse.

The preceding clinical hypothesis illustrates how coping styles as a result of sexual abuse in childhood may lead to negative effects that can have further deleterious consequences over the course of the victim's development. Until more is known about the relationship between specific coping strategies and subsequent functioning, the clinician should be aware of the importance of how the victim copes with the anxiety of the abuse. If this coping strategy is maladaptive at the time the child is being seen by the therapist or becomes so later in life, the clinician should intervene.

Sexual Abuse and Learning

If nothing else, sexual abuse is an experience in which the child victim learns new behaviors. Many of these behaviors (e.g., sexual behavior, including masturbation to reduce anxiety; the use of power to coerce a smaller person; the keeping of secrets from adults) are ones that the child may not otherwise have learned or would not have learned until considerably later in life. Both overt behaviors (e.g., masturbation) and cognitions (e.g., beliefs about power, attitudes regarding the use of other people for one's own needs, an understanding about how safe the world is) appear to be learned from sexual abuse experiences in childhood.

Clinicians are divided on whether the behavioral effects of sexual abuse can be targeted directly in treatment or as symptoms of internal dynamics. Illustrative of this disagreement is how to conceptualize masturbation, a common reaction to sexual abuse. Behaviorally oriented therapists view masturbation as a behavior that the sexually abused child learns from sexual contact. Because it is self-reinforcing, the child is likely to exhibit the behavior for some time. In an effort to avoid making the child uncomfortable with sexual behavior, treatment may focus on helping the child learn the settings (e.g., bedroom) and times (e.g., at night) when the behavior is considered appropriate. The contrary view is that masturbation reflects a replay of the trauma or a behavioral expression of the trauma. Over time, as treatment focuses on the therapeutic expression of the trauma (e.g., through play or art therapy), the abuse loses its capacity to produce anxiety, and the behavior should decrease in frequency.

It is likely that many behaviors associated with sexual abuse reflect both a learned component and the victim's psychological or emotional processing of the abuse. For example, masturbation may be both a pleasing (self-reinforcing) behavior that the child has learned and one that the child has come to associate with a reduction in anxiety. When the child is anxious (e.g., is having memories of the abuse), he or she may be more likely to exhibit the behavior. Treatment may be concerned with altering the conditions of occurrence (frequency, time, or location) of the behavior as well as changing the stimulus events (e.g., memories of the abuse) associated with its occurrence.

It also is increasingly clear that many of the behavior problems stemming from sexual abuse can be secondarily reinforced. For example, the aggressive behavior of some victims may be reinforced because it is effective in controlling a victim's environment (see Patterson, 1976). Likewise, dissociation may be negatively reinforced because it reduces the pain of experiencing the abuse or reexperiencing it through flashbacks.

TREATMENT OF THE CHILD VICTIM OF SEXUAL ABUSE

Issues Encountered in Clinical Interventions with Sexually Abused Children

To date there are no evaluations of alternative treatment approaches with sexually abused children. There exist no treatment outcome studies. Nor are there many case studies that describe in detail the utilization of various treatment techniques or approaches. Therefore, it is premature to describe what forms of treatment are most effective for sexually abused children. Clinical experience, however, does suggest some principles that may form the basis of treatment of the sexual abuse victim. These are outlined in the following sections.

Working with the Child's Support System

Virtually all therapy with children involves work with the child's parent(s) and other support persons (e.g., extended family, teachers). Mental health professionals have long recognized that gains obtained in individual therapy with children may be obscured or obviated if conditions in the child's home and social environment are not supportive. Models of therapy vary in how they prescribe working with the child's social environment. Some approaches involve providing adults with individual or couples therapy, or consulting with adults about the child's needs and problems.

Sexual abuse of a child is an assault on the adults who care for and love the child. Regardless of whether the offender is a family member, a family friend or acquaintance, or a stranger, sexual assault of a child has a profound effect on caregivers. If nothing else, the family experiences the pain associated with something terribly unpleasant happening to a loved one. Depending on the specifics of the case, other effects also can be exhibited. In some instances, where the parent was abused as a child, the child's abuse can reopen old emotional issues. Adults vary in the degree to which they feel guilty for not protecting the child, feel angry at the child or offender, are emotionally able to handle the trauma, or are willing to deal with the implications of sexual abuse. Given the often highly sensationalized accounts of victimization in the mass media (e.g., victims grow up to be prostitutes, women who murder their mates, or drug addicts), parents often feel that the child is forever "damaged" by the abuse. Some parents come to view the child as a "monster" or as having a deviant personality that is currently dormant. Other parents seem to underestimate the significance of what has happened to the child. This type of parent is apt to use the culturally prescribed method for dealing with an unpleasant event, which is not to talk about it and "keep a stiff upper lip," as a rationale for not keeping the child in therapy and for not talking with the child about the abuse.

In cases where the offender is a family member, special issues come into play. Mothers often are financially and emotionally dependant on incest offenders. This, in turn, can cloud the decisions they have to make about future protection and support of their children.

Interventions Involving Parents

Although the literature has frequently described mothers who conspire with fathers in the abuse, data suggest that most mothers take actions to protect their children when they learn of the maltreatment (Conte & Berliner, 1981). Nevertheless, clinical experience supports the notion that the response of adults to sexual abuse varies dramatically. This variation becomes a key issue for the child victim for a number of reasons. It is generally recognized that parent or caregiver participation is key in getting children to their mental health appointments. More critically, it appears that the child's relationship with supportive adults and siblings is among the more powerful factors associated with recovery (Conte & Schuerman, 1988). Current research has not adequately identified specifically how this support assists recovery, or what actions or words constitute support. Key factors implicated in the recovery of sexually abused children include (a) the family members' acceptance and acknowledgment of the child's abuse; (b) family members' care, attention, and affirmation of the child disclosure (which may communicate to the child that he/she is not changed by the abuse, can rely on the family, and will be safe in the future); and (c) communication that life will again be "normal."

Treatment of child victims requires assessing the degree to which victimization has had or is likely to have an ongoing negative impact on members of the child's family. This consists of examining the capacity of family members to be helpful to the child and identifying historical or current elements that impair the family members' ability to be supportive. Treatment of family members involves crisis intervention during the early part of disclosure; individual or couples treatment focusing on unresolved or new issues that may surface in supportive psychotherapy, law enforcement, or medicine; and psychoeducational efforts to help family members learn about sexual abuse and how to be helpful to the member of their family who has been abused. In many cases, the professional serves as an advocate with other systems to ensure that the family and child are appropriately treated. For example, many families require social services and financial or other resources (e.g., food stamps, vouchers for treatment, transportation) to enable them to help the child victim.

The Focus of Treatment

Therapists who work with sexually abused children must recognize the complexity and, at times, competing interests involved in treatment. Each member of the family may exhibit negative emotional reactions to the abuse and its disclosure. A child's mother and the offender may be alcoholic or drug dependent. A victim, his/her siblings, and the mother may feel guilty and strongly ambivalent regarding the offender and disclosure of the abuse. A victim may be angry at a mother who did not respond to the victim's efforts to disclose mistreatment, whereas the mother may be angry that the victim did not report the abuse more directly or sooner. A victim may be angry at siblings who wish to remain in contact with the offender. On the other hand, the victim may feel guilty if he or she was unsuccessful in protecting them from the offender, or ambivalent that siblings were not abused as well. Siblings, in turn, may feel guilty for not protecting their sister or brother, relieved that they were spared the abuse, and yet jealous of the special attention and privileges that the victim received from the offender to maintain silence. Although these issues are frequently more pronounced in incest cases, virtually all families in which a child has been sexually abused face one or more of them. The degree to which each issue is a significant factor in a case varies considerably.

In many instances, a number of these problems demand attention at the same time, and frequently several members of the family have competing needs for therapeutic attention. Indeed, family members can become so absorbed in their own pain that they become less available to each other. There are a variety of ways to approach the complexity of therapeutic work with sexually abused children and their families. Some clinicians propose that multiple therapists be assigned to the case so that each family member receives individual treatment. Other programs use specialized programs or sequences of treatment to deal with offenders, victims, and family members in combination or as a group. Some argue that a single therapist can provide adequate services in those cases in which it is critical to keep the therapy focused on key treatment goals.

Which of these alternatives is in fact the best is unclear. The level of therapeutic intervention is, in part, dependent on etiological influences for a given case. For example, family models view sexual use of a child as a family problem in which each member of the family contributes to its origin and maintenance. Some approaches to family therapy conceptualize the problem of sexual use of a child as primarily an expression of a problem between the married partners. Using this formulation, treatment focuses more on the relationship between the incest victim's parents than on the victim or on the relationship between mother and victim. In using this intervention strategy, however, the victim's recovery or strengthening the mother–child relationship in order to provide a future source of protection for the victim may be overlooked.

Of course, it also is possible to employ family perspectives that give equal attention to repairing the relationship between the marital couple and the mother–victim dyad, while helping the victim recover from the trauma of incestuous abuse. Maintaining the focus of treatment requires that the therapist explicitly understand the goals of treatment, recognize the extent to which those goals originate in models of treatment, and work within the complexities of the emotional and psychological lives of the victim and his/her family to help the client(s) achieve treatment goals.

Characteristics of Sexual Abuse

It is important that the therapist identify the specific elements of sexual abuse to which the child victim has been exposed. As previously indicated, the aspects of sexual abuse or trauma that lead to specific outcomes are unclear and an understanding of what the child has been exposed to is extremely helpful to the therapist in assessment and treatment planning. In assessment, such knowledge helps direct the therapist toward the kinds of experiences, feelings, perceptions, and reactions the child may have had related to the abuse. In treatment, this information helps the therapist understand the kinds of corrective interventions the victim may need.

Sexual abuse consists of specific actions that the offender employs to engage a victim and maintain that victim in an abusive situation, as well as particular sexual behaviors and practices. The elements of sexual abuse that make up these actions include manipulation of the child (e.g., psychologically separating the child from his or her mother), coercion (e.g., using adult authority or size differential), force (e.g., physically restraining the victim or showing a weapon), threats (e.g., "If you tell, I will kill your mother," "I will go to jail"), and virtually every kind of sexual behavior. The sexual interactions may involve only the offender and child, or additional victims and/or offenders may participate. In some cases, photographs, movies, or videos of other abuse are made by the offender(s).

The environmental and social context in which the abuse takes place also is crucial for treatment planning. Environments associated with the abuse often elicit anxiety or other strong negative emotions in the victim. For example, some victims may come to feel anxious, insecure, and depressed in their own bedrooms. Some victims report that the abuse destroys the sense of family and happiness associated with the family and home, and that this is more troubling than the sexual behavior itself. Victims may be abused because (a) they were left in the care of an offender, (b) an offender had access to them when no one was available to protect the victim, and/or (c) adults in their lives were unable or unwilling to protect them. Victims especially younger children, may be unable because of developmental limitations or psychological reaction to the trauma (e.g., use of repression as a coping strategy) to describe many of these elements. Consequently, the therapist should try to obtain as much information as possible from significant others in the child's life, from referral and police or child protection reports, and from other sources (see also Encouraging Expression, later in this chapter). Information concerning the characteristics and the environmental and social context of the abuse alerts the therapist to aspects of the child's experience that may be used in developing appropriate interventions.

Symptom Versus Dynamic Focus

There is considerable dispute over the extent to which interventions with sexually abused children should emphasize treatment of specific symptoms (e.g., fearfulness or sexualized play) or the dynamics of victimization (e.g., psychological trauma, the victim's sense of having been betrayed). As outlined earlier, current theoretical explanations of the effects of sexual abuse direct attention to both internal dynamics and symptoms believed to result from mistreatment. Whether the therapist targets the internal dynamics or the symptoms directly can vary depending on the theoretical model used or the specific target in need of intervention. In situations where the relationship between an internal process and symptom is clearly delineated (e.g., the symptom appears to be directly elicited by a dynamic process), intervention directed toward the dynamic may be most efficient. In cases where it is unclear what internal processes elicit the symptom, or no eliciting process can be readily identified, or in cases where the symptom appears to be maintained by environmental or other consequences, it often is more expedient to target the symptom directly.

Until an empirically derived therapeutic outcome literature is available that identifies the types of treatments or techniques most effective with sexual abuse, interventions directed toward both internal dynamic processes and specific symptoms are warranted. Within such a perspective, the therapist's task is to identify symptoms or problems and to determine what internal psychological processes elicit or maintain the problem, what environmental processes or situations maintain the symptom, and to decide whether interventions should be directed toward internal, environmental, or a combination of internal and environmental factors.

The following cases illustrate the advantages of considering both environmental and internal cases for behavior in treatment.

CASE EXAMPLE 1

Shawn, a 7-year-old male victim of sexual abuse by an adolescent male, appeared to have few emotional or psychological reactions to the abuse, with the exception of increasingly obstinate (argumentative and noncompliant) and defiant behavior directed toward his parents. A careful family assessment revealed that, immediately after disclosure of the abuse, Shawn's parents became "overly protective and indulgent" toward Shawn. As they began to return to their normal way of relating to their son, his behavior changed. Shawn received considerable attention for misbehavior. The parents were encouraged to provide attention and special family outings when Shawn had maintained cooperative behavior, and his behavior quickly returned to a predisclosure pattern. This environmental intervention appears to have been successful over the long term.

CASE EXAMPLE 2

Liz, a 5-year-old incest victim, presented with considerable regressive behavior (e.g., clinging to mother when left at the day-care center, refusing to go to bed, and complaining of stomach aches) and periodic masturbation. Liz's father voluntarily left the family home and Liz was seen weekly in individual therapy. Although Liz's play was oriented toward games (e.g., Candyland) and was symbolically unremarkable, the therapist and Liz talked about how much the sexual abuse (digital penetration) had hurt, that Mom didn't know what Daddy had been doing, and that now Mommy knew and would not let it happen again. A joint session with Liz and her mother reaffirmed that her mother was glad that Liz had disclosed the abuse and that her mother would not permit its recurrence. Symptoms subsided quickly over a period of a month. The therapist's efforts to give voice to the pain the sexual abuse had caused and to make Liz feel safe from future pain by telling her and then having the mother repeat that she would protect her daughter, appeared to be responsible for reducing the symptoms.

Encouraging Expression

An important aspect of treatment, especially during the beginning phases, is encouraging the victim to talk about the abuse and give expression to the thoughts, feelings, and beliefs that may be associated with maltreatment.

Although the ease with which children talk about the abuse and abuse-related details varies between children, it is quite common for victimized children to be reluctant to disclose details of the abuse. Sexually abused children often talk about the abuse for brief periods during treatment and then try to divert the therapist to other topics, or only partially describe the abuse and abuse context (e.g., by minimizing details), or otherwise avoid or reduce the amount of time in treatment directly devoted to the abuse.

There are many reasons for this tendency in children. Some children will have successfully repressed the experience from current awareness. Others find the material quite anxiety provoking and try to avoid anxiety arousal by reducing discussion of the material. Still other children will be protective of the adult (especially family members) and reveal other portions of what happened. Finally, some children are developmentally unable to provide full details or may have been unaware of many aspects of what took place.

Some therapists believe that a sexually abused child's nonverbal behavior (e.g., change in affect, protective body language, or a general decrease in responsiveness) when asked about certain aspects of the abuse can be used to gauge the therapeutic importance of the material to the child. In other cases, it is not always clear if the child's unwillingness or inability to talk about certain material is because that material is not relevant to the child, or because the child has successfully coped with the information. It is necessary to make every effort to have the child talk about abuse and abuse-related events so that the therapist can determine whether continued probing is necessary.

It should be noted that the therapist walks a fine line between encouraging expression and trying to force a child to reveal information that the child is reluctant to talk about. The therapist must be aware that being coercive may cause considerable distress in the child. Indeed, it is unlikely that a child will be forthcoming under conditions of force. On the other hand, it also is unlikely that child will express anxiety-causing material unless the therapist encourages such revelations.

This encouragement can come from initial efforts to get the child talking about anything (e.g., favorite games or toys) and to engage the child in other relationship-building activities, moving gradually to aspects of abuse. It comes more directly from efforts by therapists to communicate their understanding of what the child has been through, and their ability to handle anything that the child may say. Efforts should be made not to imply to the child that the therapist already knows what the victim has experienced, what it felt like, or what the child should feel, because these may be wrong for any given child and they tend to discourage expression.

Asking the child about certain aspects of the experience can elicit relevant material. With younger children, the availability of play materials (e.g., doll family figures, children's books about sexual abuse) can help elicit material. Victim treatment groups can be quite useful because children can hear their peers describe similar experiences and situations. As a general approach, it is useful for the therapist to indicate that talking about what happened is important for the child, but how much is said at any one time and when the child says it is under the control of the child.

The therapist also must realize that some children will not discuss in any detail the abuse or abuse-related events. In such cases, the therapist may try to address key issues of abuse and set the stage for the child's subsequent recovery and growth. The clinician's broad aim at a number of issues without clearly knowing the salient issues for a particular child is only appropriate when the child has been unwilling or unable to identify the important issues for the therapist and is intended to provide the child with new information, new perspectives, or an increased understanding about the abuse and the abuse-related context. It is hoped that these will be useful to the child in recovery and growth that will take place without the direct involvement of the therapist.

Some of the children's books (Chetin, 1977; Polese, 1985; Winston-Hillier, 1986) about sexually abused children and their experiences can serve this broad intervention strategy. No currently available book deals with all the possible issues, and not all children will respond to books. Consequently, the therapist has to demonstrate understanding about the nature of sexual abuse and the specific information about the case, and select from the range of possible issues those that may be salient for a given child. In some cases, children will begin to respond to the therapist's statements by self-disclosure, whereas others will be more resistant.

The Child's Understanding of Abuse

The cognitive effects of sexual abuse are not well understood at present. For some time, it has been suggested that victimization is an assault on the "assumptive world" of the victim (Janoff-Bulman & Freizo, 1983). It is likely that children strive to make sense out of their victimization by developing attitudes, beliefs, and values, although the specific cognitions resulting from abuse have yet to be empirically identified. Given the powerful impact of sexual abuse, it is probable that sexual abuse provides influential experiences that teach children maladaptive ways in viewing the world. Indeed, a number of lessons might be learned from the experience, including the following: Being bigger than someone makes it possible to hurt the smaller person; bad things must only happen to bad people; sex is something that more powerful people do to less powerful people; and people close to you eventually hurt you.

Cognitions derived from sexual abuse will vary according to the child's specific experiences as well as developmental level. Children's cognitions develop over time. Some cognitions may not be formed as much at the time of the abuse as later in development when certain developmentally critical issues arise. For example, the young child does not necessarily form beliefs about sexual behavior, power in relationships, or self as a sexual object.

These attitudes may form later in development and can be influenced by sexual abuse and abuse-related experiences. It is important to identify and alter dysfunctional cognitions resulting from victimization. The lessons or values, attitudes, and beliefs that children learn from abuse include those that deal with relationships, power, sexuality, and their self-concepts. To the extent that they are able, children should be encouraged to express what they have learned about these aspects of life. The therapist should provide alternative "lessons" or ideas to counteract negative and inaccurate beliefs. To this end, the therapist can talk with the victim about such issues as why the abuse took place (i.e., why me?), why adults are concerned when an older person has sex with a younger person, who was responsible for the abuse, and what power differentials in relationships allow more powerful persons to do. These ideas may offset what the child has learned from the sexual abuse experience and provide adaptive cognitions prior to the development of maladaptive ones later in life.

Sexual Abuse Prevention

Current efforts to prevent sexual victimization of children involve teaching children that there are different kinds of touch (e.g., good touch/bad touch), that they should not keep secrets about "bad" touches, that they have a right to control access to their own bodies, that they can say "no" to adults, and that they should tell an adult if someone tries to or has touched the private parts of their bodies (Conte, Rosen, & Saperstein, 1986).

Abused children, perhaps even more than children who have not been abused, should have access to prevention concepts and skills. Abused children have already been the victims of deliberate grooming efforts of offenders (see Conte et al., 1989) in which they have been manipulated or coerced into sexual contact. In about 70% of cases the abuse has occurred more than one time (Russell, 1986). Even if they have tried to tell someone about the abuse, in many cases their disclosure was disguised.

Although it is not clear at present if all children are at equal risk for sexual abuse, or why some children tell after the first incident of abuse and others do not, abused children may benefit from prevention concepts and skills. To date, there has been little discussion about how current prevention concepts and skills need to be modified for the special needs of children who have already been abused. Several modifications are likely. For example, prevention concepts and skills will have to be presented in a way that does increase the victim's guilt at failure to disclose the previous abuse. Prevention concepts will also have to help children understand why they did not report before they did (or how to report more effectively) and that even though their experience may seem to have taught them to the contrary, they really can control access to their own bodies.

An abused child who has been badly treated by professionals (e.g., has not been believed, has been removed from the home, or has watched the family undergo harmful experiences) may be less likely to report abuse in the future. Therapists can help increase the likelihood that children will report subsequent abuse by helping the child identify the "good" things that have happened, even though mostly "bad" things have taken place. Given the current capacity of intervention by child protection and justice system personnel to discount the feelings of victims or to expose victims to painful processes (e.g., removal of the child from home or dismissing charges against an offender because the child witness is young), the task of increasing the likelihood that a victim will report again is an extremely difficult one.

SUMMARY AND FUTURE DIRECTIONS

Research

Research on the effects of sexual abuse is becoming increasingly sophisticated, employing multiple measures of child functioning and comparison groups. It is too early in the development of this research to determine the usefulness of existing measures in future research with sexually abused children. Findings from a number of studies demonstrating that sexually abused children fall between scores on many of these measures for samples of nonabused children and psychiatrically impaired children are of limited clinical utility. More critically, the global nature of many of the domains of existing measures leaves the clinician with an understanding that sexual abuse appears to affect child functioning but witih little direction for intervention.

Future research is quite likely to develop or refine existing measures of sexual abuse and its consequences. Promising in this regard is the work reported by Kolko et al. (1988) on the Child Sexual Abuse Symptom Checklist or Friedrich's (1988) development of sexual behavior items for the Child Behavior Profile. In time it is likely that research will be conducted linking specific appropriate treatments with specific behavioral and emotional effects of sexual abuse. However, outcome research will not be possible until measures of the effects of sexual abuse have been developed that are sufficiently specific and sensitive enough to assess change over the relatively short time periods characteristic of most therapy with children.

The use of comparison groups of physically abused or other maltreated children is likely to continue, and future research should be helpful in understanding if there are effects specific to each type of abuse or to childhood trauma in general. The construction of comparison groups where histories of abuse or other childhood trauma have been carefully examined will be quite important in understanding the development of mental health problems in childhood. For example, it may well be that many children in psychiatrically impaired comparison groups (especially in studies employing published norms for these groups where it has not been possible for the researchers to screen subjects) are in fact victims of childhood maltreatment.

The other biological, environmental, and experiential factors associated with childhood pathology, as well as their relationship to child sexual abuse, are likely to become more clear in research over the next decade.

It is also likely that future research will detect what is trauma producing about abuse and what factors influence variation in the impact of abuse. A number of investigators (Browne & Finkelhor, 1986; Wyatt & Powell, 1988) have examined factors associated with variation in the effects of sexual abuse. Much of this work has focused on aspects of the abuse (e.g., relationship between the offender and victim or the duration and type of sexual behavior) or the child victim (e.g., age, gender). Although understanding what aspects of the abuse and the abuse-context are associated with variation in the effects of sexual abuse can be helpful in identifying children who are at highest risk for the most extreme reaction to victimization (e.g., children who have been abused over the longer duration), such information has limited utility from a clinical perspective. Little can be done to alter who abused the child, what behaviors the child was exposed to, or over what time period the child was abused.

It would, however, be clinically meaningful to elucidate factors that mediate the effects of abuse, especially those factors that can be targeted for intervention by the therapist. For example, it would be quite helpful to know what actions of significant others in the child's environment (e.g., family members or teachers) constitute support that mediates the effects of sexual abuse (Conte & Schuerman, 1987). Interventions could then be developed to help significant others be more helpful to victims, and therapies could be devised that aid in the victim recovery process. It would also be helpful to understand the child perceptions, beliefs, coping strategies, or other processes associated with variation of effects so that these could be successfully targeted for intervention by the mental health professional. It is clear that future research will seek to identify these psychological and environmental processes.

Clinical Practice

In part, future directions in clinical practice will be set by advances in research on the effects of sexual abuse, factors associated with variations of effects, and outcome evaluations of treatment programs and therapeutic techniques. This is as it should be in knowledge-based professions such as social work, psychology, psychiatry, and other helping professions. Two other major factors will set the future direction for practice in this area: social policy and clinical practice itself.

Social policy regarding victims of sexual assault as articulated in state law, policy, and procedure and as implemented at social service, medical, mental health, and law enforcement intervention levels is fragmented, contradictory, and often ambivalent. Considerable attention has been directed toward initial investigation and legal processing of child sexual abuse cases.

Often it appears that prosecution of those who sexually abuse children is a more important goal than treatment of child victims. Certainly, the increasing number of disclosures of child maltreatment, especially sexual abuse, and the decreasing support for public social services have placed a considerable amount of pressure on child protection departments that find the demands to investigate taking preference over the responsibility to treat these cases.

Representative data are unavailable describing the therapy experiences of child victims, but preliminary data confirm that few victims receive adequate therapy. For example, in a follow-up study of 198 sexually abused children, Conte and Berliner (1988) report that although 82% of children receive some counseling, the average number of months of counseling was 3.6 (probably less than 12 sessions). In most states where state funding is dedicated to victim treatment, it is reserved for incest victims only. Some state victim compensation funds have been used to support treatment programs, but it is not currently known how many victims are helped by these funds.

Popular opinion favors criminal prosecution of adult offenders. Many communities appear to favor alternative dispositions for incest offenders but the availability of such programs (e.g., treatment as a condition of probation) or the number of offenders receiving each kind of legal outcome (e.g., acquittal, probation, incarceration) is unknown. Clinical experience suggests that most offenders do not see the inside of courtrooms and few receive incarceration as an outcome. What happens to offenders is important to the treatment of victims. Untreated or unsuccessfully treated offenders are believed to be a risk for their victims and other children who may be victimized by them in the future. Adversarial courtroom practices that harm or cause pain to victims and fail to help the offender change his/her behavior do little for the victim or society. In the case of incest victims, interventions that disrupt family life, fail to alter the family and other conditions associated with the incestuous abuse, and leave victims just about as they were prior to disclosure, are of no use to victims, their families, or society.

Formulation of social policy is obviously a complex process involving the public, elected officials, and professionals. Crucial in the policy process will be efforts to articulate social goals balancing society's interest in protection from sexual offenders and treatment of child victims. In the effort to articulate such a set of goals and supporting rationales, the clinician with knowledge about the factors that produce sexual offenders, the ways in which offenders can be successfully treated, and the costs of sexual abuse to society and to individuals (e.g., in health and mental health problems) can have a key role. As much as anyone in society, the clinician with direct contact with victims can help articulate and advocate for the needs and concerns of victims.

Clinical practice is undergoing rapid and dramatic change. These changes are likely to have considerable impact on therapy with victims of sexual abuse. In the final section of this chapter it is possible only to highlight these changes. Among the most dramatic changes in mental health are ongoing efforts to make practice more accountable. Efforts by state regulatory agencies, insurance companies, and professional associations are increasingly limiting or placing other boundaries on clinical practice. The number of sessions of therapy that are reimbursable, qualifications of the therapist, the type of supervision or consultation deemed appropriate, the extent of continuing professional education required to maintain a license, and other matters (e.g., type of record keeping), are aspects of practice that will have implications for the treatment of sexually abused children. The therapist specializing in victim treatment will have to both be aware of these changing requirements and exercise leadership in assuring that these matters are directed, in part, to the needs of child victims (e.g., by having continuing education requirements cover treatment of victims or mandating that consultation be available from experts on treatment of child victims).

In general, mental health practice is becoming increasingly specialized. This trend is likely to continue in the sexual abuse field as the knowledge-informing practice becomes increasingly complex and specialized. In the near future, it is unlikely that the same practitioner will treat victims, offenders, and family units. This will increase the complexity of practice because several therapists will have to coordinate and share information. This activity, like so much of the case management and system intervention (e.g., child protection or court) work, is rarely reimbursed. The mental health professional who treats victims will have to find feasible and responsible ways of meeting the coordination and other system-oriented needs of these cases.

At the same time, as practice is becoming more specialized, the knowledge base supporting practice is becoming more complex. Treatment of child victims of sexual abuse currently can draw on knowledge from child development, children's attribution theory, emotional disorders of childhood, stress and coping, social support, general child psychotherapy, and a host of other knowledge areas. This rapid growth of knowledge and the need for keeping pace with such current advances in the field place considerable responsibility on the therapist. Pressure on professional journals, continuing education experiences, and professional associations will be great as they seek to meet the knowledge needs of therapists working with victimized children.

Finally, it is likely that there will be a continuing effort to link therapists who work with child victims and those who work with adult victims of childhood trauma. What is trauma producing about different types of childhood events (e.g., physical abuse, sexual abuse, family disruption due to substance abuse, or major illness of parents), what effects are specific to each type of trauma and which (if any) are a function of trauma in general, what factors mediate these effects, and how the effects can be treated are some of the questions requiring collaboration among therapists of child and adult victims.

The therapist working with child victims is in a field of practice with considerable ambiguity and unknowns and with much potential. It is this tension between what is unknown, what needs to be known, and the potential to be quite helpful to large numbers of victims that makes practice in this area so important and meaningful.

REFERENCES

American Psychiatric Association. (1987). *Diagnostic and statistical manual of mental disorders* (DSM-III-R; 3rd. ed.-rev.). Washington, DC: Author.

Berliner, L., & Wheeler, J. R. (1987). Treating the effects of sexual abuse on children. *Journal of Interpersonal Violence, 2,* 415–434.

Briere, J., & Runtz, M. (1988). Symptomatology associated with childhood sexual victimization in a nonclinical adult sample. *Child Abuse and Neglect, 12,* 51–59.

Browne, A., & Finkelhor, D. (1986). Initial and long-term effects: A review of the research. In D. Finkelhor (Ed.), *A sourcebook on child sexual abuse* (pp. 143–179). Beverly Hills, CA: Sage.

Burgess, A. W., & Grant, C. A. (1988). *Children traumatized in sex rings.* (Monograph). Washington, DC: National Care for Missing and Exploited Children.

Burgess, A. W., Groth, A. N., Holstrom, L. L., & Sgroi, S. M. (1978). *Sexual assault of children and adolescents.* Lexington, MA: Lexington Books.

Burgess, A. W., Hartman, C. R., McCausland, M. P., & Powers, P. (1984). Response patterns in children and adolescents exploited through sex rings and pornography. *American Journal of Psychiatry, 141,* 656–662.

Carroll, J., Schaffer, C., Spensley, J., & Abramowitz, S. I. (1980). Family experience of self-mutilating patients. *American Journal of Psychiatry, 137,* 852–853.

Chetin, H. (1977). *Frances Ann speaks out: My father raped me.* Berkeley, CA: New Seed.

Conte, J. R. (1985). The effects of sexual abuse on children. A critique and suggestions for future research. *Victimology, 10,* 110–130.

Conte, J. R., & Berliner, L. (1981). Sexual abuse of children: Implications for practice. *Social Casework, 61,* 601–606.

Conte, J. R., & Berliner, L. (1988). *What happens after disclosure* (unpublished manuscript). Available from first author at the University of Chicago, 969 East 60th Street, Chicago, IL 60637.

Conte, J. R., Berliner, L., & Schuerman, J. R. (1986). *The impact of sexual abuse on children: Final report.* Available from first author at the University of Chicago, 969 East 60th Street, Chicago, IL 60637.

Conte, J. R., Rosen, C., & Saperstein, L. (1986). An analysis of programs to prevent the sexual victimization of young children. *Journal of Primary Prevention, 6,* 141–155.

Conte, J. R., & Schuerman, J. R. (1987). Factors associated with an increased impact of child sexual abuse. *Child Abuse and Neglect, 11,* 201–211.

Conte, J. R., & Schuerman, J. R. (1988). The effects of sexual abuse on children:

A multidimensional view. In G. E. Wyatt & G. J. Powell (Eds.), *Lasting effects of child sexual abuse* (pp. 157–170). Newbury Park, CA: Sage.

Conte, J. R., Wolf, S., & Smith, T. (1989). What sexual offenders tell us about prevention. *Child Abuse and Neglect, 13,* 293–302.

de Young, M. (1982). Self-injurious behavior in incest victims: A research note. *Child Welfare, 61,* 577–584.

Finkelhor, D. (1986). *A sourcebook on child sexual abuse.* Beverly Hills, CA: Sage.

Finkelhor, D. (1988). The trauma of child sexual abuse: Two models. In G. E. Wyatt & G. J. Powell (Eds.), *Lasting effects of child sexual abuse* (pp. 171–191). Newbury Park, CA: Sage.

Friedrich, W. N. (1988). Behavior problems in sexually abused children: An adaptational perspective. In G. E. Wyatt & G. J. Powell (Eds.), *Lasting effects of child sexual abuse* (pp. 171–191). Newbury Park, CA: Sage.

Gale, J., Thompson, R. J., Moran, T., & Sack, W. H. (1988). Sexual abuse in young children: Its clinical presentations and characteristic patterns. *Child Abuse and Neglect, 12,* 163–170.

Gomez-Schwartz, B., Horowitz, J. M., & Sauzier, M. (1985). Severity of emotional distress among sexually abused preschool, school-age, and adolescent children. *Hospital and Community Psychiatry, 36,* 503–512.

Goodwin, J. (1983, October). *Posttraumatic symptoms in abused children.* Paper presented at the 11th annual Friends Hospital Clinical Conference, "Mental Illness: The Impact of Psychic Trauma," Philadelphia, PA.

Goodwin, J., Simms, M., & Bergman, R. (1979). Hysterical seizures: A sequel to incest. *American Journal of Orthopsychiatry, 49,* 698–703.

Greer, J. G., & Stuart, I. R. (Eds.). (1983). *The sexual aggressor: Current perspectives on treatment.* New York: Van Nostrand Reinhold.

Gross, M. (1979). Incestuous rape: A cause for hysterical seizures in four adolescent girls. *American Journal of Orthopsychiatry, 49,* 704–708.

Janoff-Bulman, R., & Freizo, I. (1983). A theoretical perspective for understanding response to victimization. *Journal of Social Issues, 39,* 1–17.

Kolko, D. J., Moser, J. T., & Weldy, S. R. (1988). Behavioral/emotional indicators of sexual abuse in child psychiatric inpatients: A controlled comparison with physical abuse. *Child Abuse and Neglect, 12,* 529–541.

Lamb, S. (1986). Treating sexually abused children: Issues of blame and responsibility. *American Journal of Orthopsychiatry, 56,* 303–307.

Lambert, M. J., Shapiro, D. A., & Bergin, A. E. (1986). The effectiveness of psychotherapy. In S. L. Garfield & A. E. Bergin (Eds.), *Handbook of psychotherapy and behavior change* (pp. 157–212). New York: Wiley.

Masson, J. M. (1984). *The assault on the truth: Freud's suppression of the seduction theory.* New York: Farrar, Strauss, & Giroux.

Nelson, M., & Clark, K. (1986). *The educator's guide to preventing child sexual abuse.* Santa Cruz, CA: Network.

Patterson, G. R. (1976). The aggressive child: Victim and architect of a coercive system. In E. J. Mash, L. A., Hamerlynck, & L. C. Handy (Eds.), *Behavior modification and families* (pp. 267–366). New York: Brunner/Mazel.

Peters, S. D., Wyatt, G. E., & Finkelhor, D. (1986). Prevalence. In D. Finkelhor (Ed.), *A sourcebook on child sexual abuse* (pp. 15–59). Beverly Hills, CA: Sage.

Polese, C. (1985). *Promise not to tell*. New York: Human Sciences.

Rimsza, M. E., Berg, M. D., & Locke, C. (1988). Sexual abuse: Somatic and emotional reactions. *Child Abuse and Neglect, 12,* 201–208.

Russell, D. E. H. (1984). *Sexual exploitation: Rape, child sexual abuse, and workplace harassment*. Beverly Hills, CA: Sage.

Russell, D. E. H. (1986). *The secret trauma: Incest in the lives of girls and women*. New York: Basic Books.

Sgroi, S. M. (1982). *Handbook of clinical intervention in child sexual abuse*. Lexington, MA: Lexington Books.

Weiss, J., Rogers, E., Darwin, M. R., & Dutton, C. E. (1955). A study of girl sex victims. *Psychiatric Quarterly, 29,* 1–27.

Wheeler, J. R., & Berliner, L. (1988). Treating the effects of sexual abuse on children. In G. E. Wyatt & G. J. Powell (Eds.), *Lasting effects of child sexual abuse* (pp. 227–247). Newbury Park, CA: Sage.

Whitcomb, D., Shapiro, E. R., & Stellwagen, L. D. (1985). *When the victim is a child: Issues for judges and prosecutors* (Contract No. J-LEAA-011-81). Washington, DC: National Institute of Justice.

Winston-Hillier, R. (1986). *Some secrets are for sharing*. Denver: M.A.C.

Wyatt, G. E., & Powell, G. J. (Eds.). (1988). *Lasting effects of child sexual abuse*. Newbury Park, CA: Sage.

Yorukoglu, A., & Kemph, J. P. (1966). Children not severely damaged by incest with a parent. *Journal of the American Academy of Child Psychiatry, 55,* 111–124.

CHAPTER 4

Psychological Maltreatment of Children

STUART N. HART AND MARLA R. BRASSARD

INTRODUCTION

Psychological maltreatment (i.e., emotional abuse and neglect) may be more destructive than other forms of child abuse and neglect, is probably more prevalent, and contains key elements essential to revealing the nature of child maltreatment in general. In a recent review of the state of knowledge for psychological maltreatment we felt justified in concluding:

> Psychological maltreatment is arguably the core issue in child maltreatment. The concept clarifies the dynamics that underlie the destructive power of all forms of child abuse and neglect. In addition, it incorporates individual cases, as well as institutional and cultural practices, that would otherwise be ignored. Most important, there is mounting evidence that psychological maltreatment per se is associated with the development of the severest forms of behavior disorders and developmental delays in children. (Hart & Brassard, 1987a, p. 164)

Though a strong argument can be presented to encourage recognition of the seriousness of psychological maltreatment, it is given relatively little attention by the public and professions and tends not to be dealt with directly in research and intervention. The information in this chapter clarifying the nature of psychological maltreatment and the most promising directions for correcting and preventing it is presented in three sections: Epidemiology, Consequences, and Treatment.

EPIDEMIOLOGY

Forms and Types

Psychological maltreatment has been given many names (e.g., emotional abuse and neglect, mental injury, verbal abuse). The term *psychological maltreatment* best subsumes all affective and cognitive aspects of child maltreatment and, therefore, has been recommended for use (Brassard, Germain, & Hart, 1987; Garbarino, Guttman, & Seeley, 1986, Hart & Brassard, 1987b). The various forms and types of psychological maltreatment generally may be classified under one or more of the following broad categories: verbal and emotional assault, passive and passive-aggressive inattention to needs, prevention or punishment of development of self-esteem and interpersonal skills, interference with development of personal autonomy and integrity, and impairment of the victim's ability to function within an expected range of performance (see Hart & Brassard, 1987a, for references). These broad categories and more specific attempts at description or definition developed prior to 1983 were found to be inadequate for purposes of research, policy, and intervention by specialists in these areas. As an example, there is widespread agreement that rejection is a form of psychological maltreatment. Its destructive power has been recognized regardless of the culture in which it occurs (Hart, 1988; Rohner & Rohner, 1980). And yet, it has not been defined in operational terms that are considered to be adequate, and its many forms suggest it may be better to place it within other categories (Hart, 1988; Hart & Brassard, 1986; Office for the Study of the Psychological Rights of the Child, 1986).

Definitions

New and stronger efforts to deal with psychological maltreatment were encouraged in 1983 as the result of the International Conference on Psychological Abuse of Children and Youth conducted by the Office for the Study of the Psychological Rights of the Child, in Indianapolis. The conference produced the following working definition:

> Psychological maltreatment of children and youth consists of acts of omission and commission which are judged by community standards and professional expertise to be psychologically damaging. Such acts are committed by individuals, singly or collectively, who by their characteristics (e.g., age, status, knowledge, organizational form) are in a position of differential power that renders a child vulnerable. Such acts damage immediately or ultimately the behavioral, cognitive, affective, or physical functioning of the child. Examples of psychological maltreatment include acts of rejecting, terrorizing, isolating, exploiting, and mis-socializing. (p. 2)

A broad level of support has been expressed for this generic definition; it and the other products of the conference appear to have produced renewed interest in the topic (Garrison, 1987; Melton & Davidson, 1987; Rosenberg, 1987). This interest has appropriately focused on the need to identify and operationally define the major acts of psychological maltreatment.

Psychological maltreatment acts are currently the subject of research to produce operational definitions embodying unambiguous and tested standards for application (Hart & Brassard, 1986), the lack of which has been the major stumbling block to previous psychological maltreatment work. Preliminary results from this research indicate that the following act categories, presented here with broad definitions and selected examples, can be transformed to operational status.

Spurning. To refuse to acknowledge the presence or worth; to throw away or treat as useless, unsatisfactory; to reduce from a higher level to lower rank or degree; to depreciate or devalue another's thoughts or feelings. Examples include treating a child differently from siblings or peers in ways suggesting a dislike for the child; calling a child "stupid"; labeling as inferior; publicly humiliating.

Terrorizing. To impress with terror (a state or instance of extreme fear, violent dread, fright); to coerce by intimidation; to place or threaten to place a child in a chaotic or unsafe environment. Examples include threatening to physically hurt, abandon or kill; forcing a child to observe violence (verbal or physical) directed toward loved ones; leaving a child unattended in frightening circumstances.

Isolating. To confine; to place unreasonable limitations on opportunities for normal contact with people and freedom of movement within the child's environment. Examples include locking in a closet or, for an extended period of time, in a room alone; refusing to allow interactions or relationships with peers or adults outside the family.

Corrupting/Exploiting. To render antisocial or malsocialized; to socialize in a manner in conflict with prevailing moral standards; to use basely for one's own advantage or profit; to influence a child's development in a manner that serves the interests of the perpetrator and not the natural healthy tendencies of the child. Examples include keeping a child at home in the role of a servant or surrogate parent in lieu of school attendance; encouraging or allowing a child to participate in sexual contact with an adult or in the production of pornography.

Denying Emotional Responsiveness. To fail to provide the sensitive, responsive care necessary to facilitate healthy social-emotional development; to be detached and uninvolved; to interact only when necessary; to ignore the child's legitimate mental health needs. Examples include ignoring a child's attempt to interact; handling a child mechanistically, that is, without physical and verbal signs of interest and affection such as eye contact, hugs, stroking, kisses, and talk.

A wide range of researchers recently have focused their work on quite similar sets of act categories (Baily & Baily, 1986; Brassard et al., 1987; Garbarino, Guttman, & Seeley, 1986; Hart, Gelardo, & Brassard, 1986; Office for the Study of the Psychological Rights of the Child, 1986). A set of categories of particular heuristic value was established by the National

TABLE 4.1. NCCAN and OSPRC Psychological Maltreatment Act Categories

	Spurning	Terrorizing	Isolating	Corrupting/ Exploiting	Denying Emotional Responsiveness
Abuse					
Close Confinement Tortuous restriction of movement, as by tying a child's arms or legs together or binding a child to a chair, bed, or other object, or confining a child to an enclosed area (such as threats of beating, sexual assault, abandonment, etc.).		P	P		
Verbal or Emotional Assault Habitual patterns of belittling, denigrating, scapegoating, or other nonphysical forms of overtly hostile or rejecting treatment, as well as threats of other forms of maltreatment (such as threats of beating, sexual assault, abandonment, etc.).	P	S		S	
Other or Unknown Abuse Overtly punitive, exploitative, or abusive treatment other than those specified under other forms of abuse, or unspecified abusive treatment. This form includes attempted or potential physical or sexual assault, deliberate withholding of food, shelter, sleep, or other necessities as a form of punishment, economic exploitation, and unspecified abusive actions.	S	P		S	
Neglect					
Inadequate Nurturance/Affection Marked inattention to the child's needs for affection, emotional support, attention, or competence.	S		S		P

Chronic/Extreme Spouse Abuse Chronic or extreme spouse abuse or other domestic violence in the child's presence.		S	P
Permitted Maladaptive Behavior Encouragement or permitting of other maladaptive behavior (e.g., severe assaultiveness, chronic delinquency) under circumstances where the parent/guardian had reason to be aware of the existence and seriousness of the problem but did not attempt to intervene.	S	P	S
Refusal of Psychological Care Refusal to allow needed and available treatment for a child's emotional or behavioral impairment or problem in accord with competent professional recommendation.	P	S	
Delay in Psychological Care Failure to seek or provide needed treatment for a child's emotional or behavioral impairment or problem which any reasonable layman would have recognized as needing professional psychological attention (e.g., severe depression, suicide attempt).	P	S	
Other Emotional Neglect Other inattention to the child's developmental/emotional needs not classifiable under any of the above forms of emotional neglect (e.g., markedly overprotective restrictions which foster immaturity or emotional overdependence, chronically applying expectations clearly inappropriate in relation to the child's age or level of development, etc.).	P		
Permitted Drug and Alcohol Abuse Encouragement or permitting of drug or alcohol use by the child: cases of the child's drug/alcohol use were included here if it appeared that the parent/guardian had been informed of the problem and had not attempted to intervene.	S	P	S

Note. Adapted from National Center on Child Abuse and Neglect (NCCAN), 1988. P = primary; S = secondary.

Center on Child Abuse and Neglect (NCCAN) (1988) for application in its national incidence studies conducted in 1980 and 1986. For comparison purposes those categories are presented in Table 4.1 to indicate logical relationships with the set being researched by Hart and Brassard (1986).

Theoretical Perspectives on the Nature of Psychological Maltreatment

The nature of psychological maltreatment has been postulated from several different but compatible perspectives. Hart, Germain, and Brassard (1987) and Gil (1987) theorize that psychological maltreatment derives its power by virtue of being an attack on basic psychological need fulfillment. Psychological maltreatment, from this perspective, creates negative stress, which in turn produces various levels and types of distortion in the individual's functioning, according to the influence of intervening variables. The maltreatment experience influences the victim's functioning toward deviancy in mildly to severely maladaptive forms. This position, although speculative and as yet unproven, has been recognized for its explanatory power in the work of others (Lourie & Stefano, 1978; Maslow, 1970; Montagu, 1970).

Among other theoretical positions that may help to explain the nature of psychological maltreatment are the coercion, the organizational, and the prisoner of war models. The coercion model, constructed by Patterson (1982, 1986), postulates chains of actions and reactions among parents and children that stimulate progressively higher levels of destructiveness in the quality and quantity of aversive behavior. The organizational model gives primary importance to critical issues within developmental psychosocial stages. It predicts that when these issues (e.g., attachment, autonomy) are dealt with unsuccessfully, development is distorted or retarded. The organizational model is based on the work of Erikson (1963) and Bowlby (1973, 1980, 1982) and has been refined and applied in child maltreatment work by Sroufe, Egeland, and their associates (Cicchetti & Braunwald, 1984; Erickson, Sroufe, & Egeland, 1985; Sroufe, 1979). The prisoner of war (POW) model is based on the posttraumatic stress disorder explanation of dysfunctional psychological reactions to encounters with highly stressful and violent experiences, such as physical attack and natural disasters. Posttraumatic stress disorder has been suggested to be the primary mechanism for explaining the maladaptively deviant functioning of victims of child abuse (Benedek, 1985). Under this view, family dynamics in severe cases of psychological maltreatment place the child in a position similar to, but more devastating than, that of a POW (Turgi & Hart, 1988). The victim of psychological maltreatment as a captive unable to avoid psychologically destructive conditions of degradation, terrorization, severe unpredictability, and isolation develops survival behaviors that under other conditions would be considered antisocial, aberrant, and self-destructive. In contrast to the POW, the child victim of severe, continuing psychological maltreatment (a) does not have the benefit of previously healthy interpersonal experiences to guide reality testing and perspective taking, (b) is passing through critical developmental stages powerfully affected by maltreatment, (c) does not have recourse to the understandable cognitive explanation of aversive treatment by an enemy, and (d) is encouraged to deny and repress justifiable feelings of hate and anger (Turgi & Hart, 1988).

Ecological Perspectives

Ecological perspectives should be incorporated in psychological maltreatment work in combination with the application of appropriate major theoretical orientations. Ecological models help to clarify the manner in which psychological maltreatment pervades human experience beyond the individual level of interactions, to the family, neighborhood, subculture, community, and culture (Bronfenbrenner, 1979; Garbarino, 1977; Valentine, Freeman, Acuff, & Andreas, 1985). Maltreatment perpetrated directly and indirectly, in the forms of racial and ethnic prejudice, and sanctioned violence expressed in the home, society, and child-rearing institutions, as well as through the media, are examples. Table 4.2 presents psychological maltreatment conditions representative of three points along a continuum of levels of directness in attacks on individuals. The examples exhibit a variety of human ecological system levels.

Table 4.2 and the generic definition previously presented indicate it is not only parents who perpetrate maltreatment. Schools, for example, which are the second most influential child-rearing institution in our society, perpetrate

TABLE 4.2. Psychological Maltreatment: A Continuum of Direct to Indirect Forms

	Levels of Directness	
Less Direct		More Direct
Destructive Perspectives and Practices	Inescapable Negative Conditions in Child's Immediate Environment	Direct and Personal Attacks on Child
Presentation of excessive violence and distortions of reality through public media	Making child captive audience to violence or chaos in lives of significant adults	Publicly humiliating child Terrorizing child with threats of extreme violence
Institutionalized restricting of reinforcements to very limited range of talents	Modeling of substance abuse by significant adults	Repeatedly making child scapegoat for personal difficulties
Cultural disrespect for competencies of young people	Teaching child racial/sexual stereotypes that degrade others	
Societal disinterest in impediments to relationships between people of different ages		

psychological maltreatment directly and indirectly through widespread personnel and institutional practices. Such customary actions include discipline and control through fear and intimidation; low quantity and quality of human interaction; limited opportunities to develop competencies and self-worth; encouragement to be dependent; and denial of opportunities for healthy risk taking (see Hart, Brassard, & Germain; 1987; Hart, 1987a, 1987b, for extensive coverage).

Incidence

Estimates of the incidence of psychological maltreatment in the United States from state reports and research projections, in their most conservative formulations, have suggested that approximately 200,000 to 300,000 cases occur per year (American Humane Association, 1987; NCCAN, 1981, 1988). The National Center on Child Abuse and Neglect has conducted two of the best designed studies of incidence and prevalence of child abuse and neglect. A discussion of some of the characteristics, findings, and implications of the studies should be useful as a background for prevention and correction considerations.

The Center (NCCAN, 1981, 1988) collected data concerning cases of child maltreatment recognized and reported to the study by community professionals in a national probability study of 29 counties throughout the United States. Local Child Protective Services (CPS) staff and key personnel in a variety of other agencies, such as schools, hospitals, police departments, and juvenile probation centers, were respondents. This allowed for a comparison of findings by CPS and by other agencies likely to be confronted with evidence of child maltreatment. Cases reported were compared to operational definitions, including standards of seriousness, victim characteristics, and perpetrator characteristics. The NCCAN emotional maltreatment definitions presented earlier (Table 4.1) were applied. In the 1980 and 1986 studies emotional maltreatment was counted if (a) the act of omission or commission fit definitional criteria, was purposive and avoidable, and occurred during the study period; (b) the victim was less than 18 years of age at the time of maltreatment and was a noninstitutionalized dependent of parent(s)/parent-substitute(s); and (c) the child suffered demonstrable harm as a result of the maltreatment. In addition, a second set of statistics was gathered during the 1986 study to include cases for which demonstrable harm was *not* in evidence but CPS or non-CPS professionals judged the child's health or well-being to have been seriously endangered by the maltreatment reported. Table 4.3 presents NCCAN findings of incidence for the general categories of physical, sexual, and emotional maltreatment, and Table 4.4 presents findings for all subcategories of psychological maltreatment. These tables include data for 1980 and 1986 and for the application of both original and revised definitions.

TABLE 4.3. Incidence of Major Forms of Child Maltreatment

| | Original Definitions | | | | | | 1986 Revised Definitions | |
| | 1980 | | 1986 | | 1980–1986 | | | |
	Totals[a]	(Rates)[b]	Totals[a]	(Rates)[b]	Totals[a]	(Rates)[b]	Totals[a]	(Rates)[b]
Categories of Abuse								
Physical	199,100	(3.10)	311,200	(4.90)	112,100	(1.80)	358,300	(5.70)
Sexual	42,900	(0.70)	138,000	(2.20)	95,100*	(1.50)*	155,900	(2.50)[c]
Emotional	132,700	(2.10)	174,400	(2.80)	41,700	(0.70)	211,100	(3.40)
Categories of Neglect								
Physical	103,600	(1.60)	182,100	(2.90)	+78,500	(1.30)	571,600	(9.10)
Emotional	56,900	(0.90)	52,200	(0.80)	−4,700	(−0.1)	223,100	(3.50)
Educational	174,000	(2.70)	291,100	(4.60)	+117,100	(+1.9)	292,100	(4.60)

Note. Adapted from National Center on Child Abuse and Neglect (NCCAN), 1988.
[a]Total numbers of children rounded to the nearest 100; not adjusted by population totals.
[b]Per 1,000 children in the population.
[c]Includes teenage perpetrators.
*The 1986 and 1980 incidence rates differed significantly at the $p < .05$ level.

TABLE 4.4. Incidence of Psychological Maltreatment

| | Original Definitions | | | | | | 1986 Revised Definitions | |
| | 1980 | | 1986 | | 1980–1986 Difference | | | |
	Totals[a]	(Rates)[b]	Totals[a]	(Rates)[b]	Totals[a]	(Rates)[b]	Totals[a]	(Rates)[b]
Emotional Neglect								
Close confinement	3,200	(0.05)	8,700	(0.14)	5,500	(0.08)	11,100	(0.18)
Verbal or emotional assault	115,200	(0.18)	120,800	(0.19)	5,600	(0.10)	144,300	(2.30)
Other unknown abuse	18,300	(0.30)	51,700	(0.80)	33,400*	(0.50)*	63,200	(1.00)
Total	132,700	(2.10)	174,400	(2.80)	41,700	(0.70)	211,100	(3.40)
Emotional Abuse								
Inadequate nurturance/affection }	24,900	(0.40)	5,000	(0.10)	−19,900*	(−0.3)*	48,500	(0.80)
Spouse abuse							27,100	(0.40)
Permitted drug and alcohol abuse }	13,400	(0.20)	16,800	(0.30)	+3,400	(+0.1)	44,900	(0.70)
Permitted other maladaptive behavior							24,200	(0.40)
Refused psychological care }							24,000	(0.40)
Delay in psychological care }	19,200	(0.30)	31,200	(0.50)	+12,000	(+0.2)	25,700	(0.40)
Other emotional neglect							57,600	(0.90)
Total	56,900	(0.90)	52,200	(0.80)	−4,700	(−0.1)	223,100	(3.50)

Note. Adapted from National Center on Child Abuse and Neglect (NCCAN), 1988.

[a]Total numbers of children rounded to the nearest 100; not adjusted by population totals.

[b]Per 1,000 children in the population.

*The difference in rate of incidence between 1986 and 1980 were significant at the $p < .05$ level.

According to the NCCAN data, the incidence of countable cases of total maltreatment by its original definitions increased significantly (68%) between 1980 and 1986, with the only reliable difference and the greatest increase in abuse (74%) being that which was attributable specifically to physical and sexual abuse. This increase was judged to be the result of greater sensitivity and recognition rather than increases in occurrence. Incidence for the expanded definitions was much higher than for original definitions, with the majority of cases for maltreatment in general representing neglect (68%) and fewer than half representing abuse (43%).

Results for emotional abuse and neglect did not produce statistically significant differences under the original definitions for the two periods. However, among increases in incidence caused by applying the expanded definitions in contrast to the original definitions, the largest one within the neglect categories of maltreatment was for emotional neglect (37%), and the second largest within abuse categories was for emotional abuse (21%, exceeded by physical abuse at 23%). This suggests that professional opinions regarding endangerment are particularly important in identifying emotional maltreatment.

Within the emotional maltreatment categories of both sets of definitional standards the following findings appear important:

"Verbal or emotional assault" had the highest incidence rate for emotional abuse (68% of countable children).

"Other or unknown abuse" showed a significant increase (167%) under original definitions between 1980 and 1986.

Original definition findings for 1986 identified the combined categories of refusal of or delay in obtaining psychological care and "other emotional neglect" as the most frequently occurring subcategory of emotional neglect.

The least frequently occurring subcategory of emotional neglect under original definitions, and the only one displaying a significant drop between 1980 and 1986, was that which combined "inadequate nurturance/affection" and "spouse abuse."

The most frequently occurring forms of emotional abuse under revised definitions were the "other emotional neglect" (9 per 10,000) and "inadequate nurturance/affection" (8 per 10,000) categories.

Among the possible interpretations of these findings are the following:

"Verbal or emotional assault" is the most visible and well-publicized form of emotional abuse and would be expected to show high incidence (see later coverage of media focus on this category).

Under "other or unknown abuse" sensitivity to attempted or potential physical or sexual assault has very probably increased similarly to its extant forms, thereby increasing incidence for this category.

Increased reporting of refusal of or delay in obtaining psychological care may have been supported by society's increased concern for medical neglect.

The relatively high incidence rates for "other emotional neglect" and "inadequate nurturance/affection" under revised definitions, especially in comparison to findings under original definitions, suggest again the importance of the endangerment criteria in establishing the potential for harm for infants and young children.

These recent NCCAN findings regarding incidence of emotional maltreatment, like others that have preceded them (American Humane Association, 1987; NCCAN, 1981), justifiably may be considered somewhat inaccurate and probably far below the level of actual occurrence. NCCAN figures do not account for all child abuse and neglect because the agency (a) uses relatively conservative definitions, (b) has not gathered information other than from CPS and non-CPS professional or investigatory agencies likely to identify child maltreatment (e.g., parents, other members of families, neighbors), and (c) has no way of knowing how many cases have not come to the attention of anyone who would recognize them (NCCAN, 1988, pp. x–xi). Specific to psychological maltreatment, NCCAN estimates are inadequate because cases of emotional maltreatment that accompany other forms of maltreatment and are not known to produce negative consequences verifiably unique to their contribution are not counted. That is, NCCAN excludes from its count acts of emotional maltreatment falling in categories such as sexual abuse (the majority of which is purely emotional maltreatment), achieved physical assault (for which the major destructive ingredient is probably emotional maltreatment in most cases), and "inattention to special educational need." The latter, a subcategory of educational neglect, is a form of refusing or delaying psychological care in many if not most instances. Data gathered annually by other sources are also inadequate, because most state statutes do not define emotional maltreatment, those that do define it use a variety of nonequivalent definitions, and state and local CPS systems/personnel differ widely in their application of standards (Brassard et al., 1987; Corson & Davidson, 1987). Under these conditions, it is clear that the true extent of psychological maltreatment is not known. It is logical to assume that incidence of psychological maltreatment, where it accompanies other forms of maltreatment or stands alone, exceeds the 1.5 million cases recorded by NCCAN for 1986 and the 2 million cases per year of child maltreatment recorded by the American Humane Association (1987).

Mediating Variables Influencing Occurrence and Impact

For child maltreatment, in all its general and specific forms, the manner and degree to which correlated factors influence likelihood to maltreat, to be maltreated, and to be influenced by maltreatment are not known. Factors previously found to be correlated with maltreatment include specific care-taker characteristics (e.g., aggression, history of abuse, unmet basic psy-chological needs, poor coping skills); caretaker or family characteristics (e.g., economic and marital stress, lack of social support, social isolation, and extremes of family privacy); and aberrant child characteristics or be-haviors (e.g., physical or intellectual handicaps, difficult temperaments). Under a broad ecological perspective, additional factors such as media prior-ities, societal perspective on the value of children, child management/ socialization practices, and sanctioned violence must be included. These characteristics have not been investigated to determine the specific causal mechanisms by which they influence maltreatment conditions. It is important to recognize that there are families with maladjusted parents living under conditions of social stress whose lives parallel those of abusive families and yet who do not perpetrate maltreatment. There are children with charac-teristics similar to those of maltreated children who do not elicit maltreat-ment, and there are children living under high levels of psychological stress who do not exhibit the unhealthy development expected of them. Ample evidence exists for the need to give priority to clarifying mediating variables.

Relative to the state of knowledge about child maltreatment in general, the recent incidence study by NCCAN provides additional evidence. Re-garding child characteristics, females experienced more abuse than males, particularly because of greater likelihood of being sexually abused. Females were more likely to experience "probable" injury or impairment compared to males. Under the original definitions, maltreatment incidence increased with age for both abuse and neglect (across all subcategories of abuse, while limited to the educational neglect category under neglect), and under ex-panded definitions physical abuse and educational and emotional neglect correlated with age. Fatalities were more likely to occur for younger children, and moderate injuries were more prevalent among older children. Race and ethnicity were unrelated to incidence of maltreatment. Regarding family characteristics, low family income (below $15,000 per year) was strongly related to higher incidence (i.e., 5 times as likely for maltreatment overall and for emotional maltreatment under original definitions; 7 times more likely for maltreatment overall and 4–5 times more likely for emotional maltreat-ment under revised definitions). All forms of injury/impairment were more likely for victims in the low income range. Regarding county type, the county metropolitan status, "metrostatus," was not reliably related to incidence according to any measure of severity but was related to size of increases from 1980 to 1986, with urban counties showing the greatest increases.

More specific to psychological maltreatment, the following perspectives from research and expert opinion regarding mediating factors are instructive. Egeland and Erickson (1987) conclude from their work with psychological maltreatment that the unmet emotional needs of caretaker-perpetrators may be a critical causative variable and that denying emotional responsiveness to a child and ignoring a child's need for intimate human interaction are the most destructive forms of abuse and neglect short of killing or permanently maiming the child. Child development research indicates that children do not initially elicit psychological maltreatment but are its victims as the result of the spillover of problems and conflicts of adults (Herrenkohl, Herrenkohl, & Egolf, 1983). Moreover, children learn maladjustive behavior from a rejecting parent as early as the 1st to 3rd year of life (Main & Goldwyn, 1984). Erickson and Egeland (1987) and Montagu (1970) have presented research and opinion evidence indicating that maltreatment early in the life cycle may have a stronger and longer lasting negative effect on the child than that which occurs later and that the appropriateness of caretaker behaviors must be judged in its relevance to the particular period of child development. Research on "stress resistant" or "invulnerable" children suggests that those who are psychologically maltreated but who have had one or more of their basic psychological needs sufficiently met may be able to develop in a healthy manner (Anthony & Cohler, 1987; Garmezy, 1987; Werner, 1985). However, such potential may not be realized under conditions of poverty (Egeland & Farber, 1987). Additionally, the importance of the meaning given to maltreatment through the subjective perspective of the victim has been indicated to be potentially of critical importance (Hart, 1988; Hart & Brassard, 1987b; Navarre, 1987).

CONSEQUENCES

Direct and severe forms of psychological maltreatment appear to produce emotional and behavioral problems for children (Hart, Germain, & Brassard, 1987). Currently available evidence strongly associates psychological maltreatment with a wide range of destructive child outcomes. Empirical cause and effect evidence, although sparse, does exist for a small sample of children whose parents were verbally abusive and hostile and/or provided psychologically unavailable caretaking. These children, subjects in a prospective longitudinal research project, have displayed serious social, emotional, and learning problems beyond other general effects of their environments (Egeland & Erickson, 1987; Egeland, Sroufe, & Erickson, 1983).

Where little empirical research evidence exists, it is possible to take direction from expert opinion (frequently based on case study and correlational findings) and the available empirical evidence. At the national level, expert opinion endorsed by the American Humane Association (Wald, 1961) and NCCAN (Broadhurst, 1984) has presented the following list of possible negative consequences of psychological maltreatment: habit disorders, conduct disorders, neurotic traits, psychoneurotic reactions, behavior extremes, overly adaptive behaviors, lags in development, and attempted suicide (see Hart, Brassard, & Germain, 1987, p. 10, for further clarification).

A special form of organized expert opinion exists in the work of state agencies that have attempted to develop standards of evidence to apply in cases of suspected psychological maltreatment. Virginia and Mississippi have provided leadership in this regard (Corson & Davidson, 1987). The following list is a composite of the child outcomes identified by those states as providing evidence of mental abuse and mental neglect: excessive need for sucking; rocking; feeding and sleeping problems; excessive, age-inappropriate, or unrealistic fears; enuresis; excessive masturbation; stuttering; intense symbiotic relationships; functional or social retardation; functional/organic disorders such as failure-to-thrive syndrome and psychosocial dwarfism; inability to form trusting and mutual relationships; apathy; lethargy; depression; low self-esteem; self-denial; impaired memory; difficulty in concentrating; mental confusion and disorientation; psychological numbing; pseudomaturity; poor school performance; runaway behavior; stubborn or defiant activity; poor peer relationships; extensive denial; suicide threats or behavior; property destruction; and violent behavior toward others (Mississippi Department of Public Welfare, 1984, pp. 5, 8; Virginia Department of Social Services, 1985, pp. 6c, 6d; see Brassard et al., 1987, for further information).

At a somewhat higher level of evidence, Hart, Germain, and Brassard (1987) have organized a list of negative consequences of psychological maltreatment revealed by clinical case studies, and in some cases by correlational and empirical cause-and-effect research. The list includes poor appetite; lying and stealing; encopresis and enuresis; low self-esteem or negative self-concept; emotional instability or emotional maladjustment; reduced emotional responsiveness; inability to become independent; incompetence and/or underachievement; inability to trust others; depression; prostitution; failure to thrive; withdrawal; suicide; aggression; and homicide (see original source for extensive references). Recently, evidence has been accumulating that suggests that children and adults "without a conscience," psychopaths, and serial murderers are produced through psychological neglect (particularly those denied emotional responsiveness, bonding, and attachment) and psychological abuse (Hickey, 1988; Magid & McKelvey, 1988).

Maladaptive deviancy, represented by items and subsets of this broad array of negative conditions, is widely recognized as the probable consequence of psychological maltreatment. However, not enough is yet known about the cause-and-effect relationships that exist between psychological maltreatment and negative child outcomes to produce consensus-based standards for decision making. Interventions would find stronger support if recognized, research-established, conceptual structures were available to clarify cause and effect relationships. The probable child outcomes of psychological maltreatment, in individual and patterned form, are subsumable under psychiatric disorder constructs (American Psychiatric Association, 1987), and it has been suggested that these standards be refined so that they will be more clearly applicable to this problem area (Corwin, 1985; Hyman, 1985). In contrast, standards for the "seriously emotionally disturbed" in the Education for All Handicapped Act (Public Law 94-142) have been suggested to be particularly pertinent to understanding and communicating the consequences of psychological maltreatment because (a) they tend to be behaviorally oriented, (b) they are not encumbered by esoteric language, and (c) a wealth of experience is developing regarding their meanings and applications through widespread national use in the public schools (Hart, Germain, & Brassard, 1987). The standard categories of this act are:

1. An inability to learn which cannot be explained by intellectual, sensory, or health factors
2. An inability to build or maintain satisfactory interpersonal relationships with peers or teachers
3. Inappropriate types of behavior or feelings under normal circumstances
4. A general pervasive mood of unhappiness or depression
5. A tendency to develop physical symptoms or fears associated with personal or school problems

Hart, Germain, and Brassard (1987, pp. 12–14) have organized findings from empirical studies relevant to psychological maltreatment into the "seriously emotionally disturbed" symptoms categories. Even though relatively few such studies have been conducted, evidence has already accrued validating the relevance of the second, third, and fourth categories. Research is now being conducted by Egeland and associates (1983) and by Hart and Brassard (1986) to develop operational definitions of emotional maltreatment; it shows promise for producing data that will validate the first and fifth categories as well. However, empirical research on psychological maltreatment is in its very early stages, and much work needs to be done to clarify cause-and-effect relationships and the nature and influence of mediating variables.

TREATMENT: CORRECTION AND PREVENTION

Expert opinion has argued that comprehensive programs of correction and prevention should be implemented and that prevention should be given priority status because it has the greatest potential for producing long-term major improvements (Brassard et al., 1987; Hart & Brassard, 1987b; National Committee for Prevention of Child Abuse, 1987a). As indicated previously, psychological maltreatment pervades the human experience. It exists in subtle to blatant and direct to indirect forms that are channeled through (a) face-to-face interactions between people (e.g., publicly humiliating a child), (b) inescapable negative conditions in the child's immediate environment (e.g., being captive audience to violence or chaos in the lives of adults), and (c) destructive perspectives and practices encouraged by the culture and its institutions (e.g., cultural disrespect for the competencies of young and old people). Some instances of maltreatment are so grossly excessive and offensive in form as to engender public support for involuntary intervention in family affairs where adequate standards of evidence exist. However, adequate standards of evidence do not exist for most of these situations, and they represent the minority of psychological maltreatment conditions. Probably most psychological maltreatment involves more subtle and less conspicuous acts that may also produce grave accumulated effects. These acts are not likely to be the targets of coercive involuntary intervention by social services and would probably prove quite resistant to the short-term "crisis intervention" strategies generally applied to problems in the United States (Hart, 1987b). Appreciation of these points may lead to an understanding that it is not just the qualitatively different "others" who perpetrate maltreatment, but something many of "us" may have experienced, perpetrated, or allowed. Therefore, it is a problem to be targeted for major prevention efforts as well as correction efforts.

Prerequisites for Effective Treatment

Correction and prevention efforts that will have substantial impact on psychological maltreatment must be supported by operational definitions, standards for decision making, awareness, and public support, clarification of variables mediating risk for occurrence and impact, and more promising treatment strategies. Some progress is being made.

Operational Definitions and Standards for Decision Making

Operational definitions must be produced that will have both research and expert-opinion support beyond what currently exists. Hart and Brassard (1986) have just completed a 2-year research project to accomplish the first major stage in producing empirically derived definitions. The major acts of maltreatment, presented in an earlier section of this chapter, have been translated into paper and pencil questionnaire form, incorporating child management vignettes, and into an observational system for coding mother–child interactions. Early results from this project indicate that these instruments show promise for discriminating between maltreatment and nonmaltreatment conditions. The operational definitions being produced are strongly compatible with those previously derived through expert opinion (Baily & Baily, 1986; NCCAN, 1981, 1988). Operational definitions, when available, will help bring resolution to problems inherent in the development of standards for decision making or determination of justifiable evidence for intervention.

Standards of Evidence

Three basic positions, somewhat in conflict, are currently proposed for the nature of evidence necessary to support intervention where conditions of psychological maltreatment are found or suspected to exist. They require the following conditions: (a) Serious negative child outcomes must exist and be clearly tied to verified maltreatment acts—the most conservative position and generally supported by the legal establishment (American Bar Association, 1980); (b) maltreatment acts at high levels of seriousness exist that are judged by experts to endanger the well-being of the child—a position supported by a broad base of human service workers (Baily & Baily, 1986) and by the revised standards of the National Center on Child Abuse and Neglect (NCCAN, 1988); and (c) child outcomes in the form of serious maladaptive deviancy exist that may be attributable to maltreatment—a position proposed by policy and research leadership (Hart, 1987c). Although progress is being made, the present state of knowledge does not supply sufficiently clear and generally supported standards for decision making for any of these positions, with the possible exception of the last one (see Corson & Davidson, 1987; Hart, Germain, & Brassard, 1987; Melton & Corson, 1987; Melton & Davidson, 1987; Melton & Thompson, 1987, for extensive coverage of issues).

Awareness and Public Support

Support for intervention with psychological maltreatment must be enhanced by an awareness of its existence, forms, and impact. Many examples of progress exist. Psychological maltreatment has been targeted for national prevention activities in the form of awareness campaigns (National Committee for Prevention of Child Abuse, 1987b). The nature of psychological maltreatment is being communicated at a variety of levels of sophistication through various media to a wide range of publics. Theme issues of scholarly journals describe research and expert opinion (*American Psychologist*, 1987; *School Psychology Review*, 1987). State-of-knowlege books are available for academics and practitioners (Brassard, Germain, & Hart, 1987; Garbarino, Guttmann, & Seeley, 1986). Videotapes and support materials have been prepared that are appropriate for public television, community agency, and parent/professional educational uses (Garbarino & Merrow, 1986; NEWIST, 1987). Booklets are available presenting concise overviews (Garbarino & Garbarino, 1986), in easy reading form for parents and practitioners (Brassard & Hart, 1987), and in comic book form for children (Marvel Comics, 1988). And public information television spots and posters are available for dissemination (National Committee for Prevention of Child Abuse, 1987b).

Treatment activities, particularly those prevention oriented, will require support from influential publics who sufficiently understand the insidious, pervading, and powerfully destructive nature of psychological maltreatment. Such a requirement argues for the development and application of strong public awareness programs. Effectiveness of the awareness activities cited should be tested, and the results should be applied to developing refinements and expanded versions.

Clarification of Mediating Variables

In an earlier section, information was presented regarding the present state of knowledge for mediating variables that may influence the occurrence or impact of psychological maltreatment. At this time relatively little is known with certainty regarding the wide variety of conditions speculated to be of influence. More research is needed, requiring that the operational definitions, standards, and public/professional interest encouraged above be in place to support pursuit of well-defined questions regarding mediating variables. For the present, treatment must be based on what little is known about maltreatment in general and psychological maltreatment specifically.

Available knowledge appears to support the following position. Treatment programs should be developed to cover and cut across the human ecological levels at which maltreatment originates or is expressed (e.g., individual, family, community, society). Three categories of content areas for treatment subsume most of the desired strategies: (a) basic psychological needs fulfillment, (b) knowledge and skills development, and (c) negative stress reduction. Within these categories, strategies should be constructed to deal directly with problems strongly associated with child maltreatment (i.e., dysfunctional parenting, child vulnerability, and societal stressors) (Belsky, 1984; Bittner & Newberger, 1982; Egeland & Erickson, 1987; Garbarino, 1977; Smith, 1984; Starr, 1979; Turgi & Hart, 1988).

Treatment Strategies

Treatment, herein, means subjection to some agent, which is the meaning attached to it in science (Random House, 1963). Correction and prevention will refer to processes whereby conditions associated with, causing, or resulting from psychological maltreatment are subjected to an agent to influence those conditions.

In general, very little progress has been made in developing and applying effective correction and prevention strategies for child abuse and neglect (Rosenberg & Reppucci, 1985; Smith, 1984; Starr, 1979). Although a great deal of attention has been focused recently on child sexual abuse in the United States, correction and prevention efforts specific to that area have shown little promise (Brassard & McNeill, 1987; G. Melton, personal communication, August 31, 1987, New York). Psychological maltreatment correction and prevention work has barely begun. Major hindrances to progress in treatment, in addition to the lack of operational definitions, decision-making standards, and public awareness discussed earlier, exist in the following areas: (a) general lack of understanding of psychological maltreatment, (b) cultural preference for crisis-oriented correction over prevention, (c) competition for limited child service resources, (d) hesitancy to intrude in family life, and (e) fear that efforts to help will do more harm than good (Hart & Brassard, 1987b).

Treatment strategies may be considered to fall on a continuum ranging from *primary prevention*—aimed at the general population without concern for levels of risk, and meant to reduce the likelihood that anyone will maltreat, be the victim of, or suffer significant negative consequences as a result of maltreatment—through *secondary prevention*—aimed at segments of the population exhibiting identifiable levels of risk for maltreatment, as determined by the quantity, quality, and interaction of measurable risk factors (e.g., caretaker abused as a child, financial stress, history of aggression). Secondary prevention efforts are strategies to reduce the likelihood that maltreatment will occur or be destructive. "Tertiary prevention," better labeled "correction," is aimed at those people or conditions who/which have perpetrated maltreatment and those who have been victims of maltreatment, with the intention of overcoming or reducing the negative influences of previous maltreatment experiences while reducing the likelihood of future maltreatment.

The perspectives on correction and prevention to be presented in the next two subsections fall within and cut across points on this treatment continuum. The majority of the strategies are supported only by their logically derived opposition to associates of maltreatment, whereas some are supported by expert opinion, case study, or empirical research. The strategies target the adult caretaker, the family, and the child to achieve a reduction in psychological maltreatment and its negative child outcomes. Examples applicable at various ecological levels are included.

Correction

Parent/Caregiver Level

Much of the research on intervention programs with maltreating families suggests that they are very difficult to treat and that often professional efforts are unsuccessful. Cohn and Daro recently (1987) reviewed the findings of the four major multiyear evaluation studies funded by the National Center on Child Abuse and Neglect of the effectiveness of treatment approaches with maltreating families. The authors concluded that "child abuse and neglect continue despite early, thoughtful, and often costly intervention" (p. 440). They noted that programs focusing on improved parental functioning (e.g., lay counseling and parent evaluation), parents who sexually abuse, and interventions with children have shown the most success. Relatively ineffective are programs attempting to halt and reduce the likelihood of more severe cases of physical abuse, neglect, and psychological maltreatment; 33% or more parents maltreated their children during treatment and over 50% were judged by staff as likely to mistreat following termination from the program.

The designs of the programs evaluated were flawed by lack of random assignment of families to treatment condition (multiple comparison groups were used) and a reliance on staff ratings as outcome measures. If anything, these methodological constraints might increase the number of families rated as treatment successes. Given that the review is referring to model demonstration projects, representing the best treatment currently available, these findings are disheartening.

Certain factors were related to more successful outcomes: (a) comprehensive treatment programs that addressed the practical needs of the families as well as their interpersonal issues, and (b) length of time in treatment (7–18 months may be optimal). Cohn and Daro's recommendations were to (a) institute a major redistribution of child protection and treatment resources to prevention, (b) provide comprehensive services to all members of maltreating families when providing treatment, and (c) apply intensive resources in the initial months of treatment.

In addition to the family support and casework services traditionally applied, theoretically guided treatment approaches based on social learning/behavior theory, psychoanalytically influenced theories, and family systems theory have also been developed and to some extent tested. Social learning theory or behavioral analysis models focus on critical antecedents, important events in the history of the parent or development of the child, the nature of the maltreating act, consequences that may maintain the behavior, and the context—familial, community, and larger social system—in which the abuse occurs (Wolfe, 1987). Research based on this model has been very promising in the area of building parenting skills, although few studies have conducted follow-up assessments for longer than a few months after treatment ended (see Goldstein, Keller, & Erné, 1985; Wolfe, 1987). In the two studies that did follow up over 1 to 2 years (Christopherson et al., 1976; Lutzer, 1983), treatment effects appeared to continue. Social learning approaches also appear to be successful in improving parents' control of anger and interpersonal skills. There is some evidence that such skills training approaches may be most successful in a group format (Goldstein, Keller, & Erné, 1985).

Psychoanalytically influenced researchers have also developed treatment approaches that have been applied to maltreating or high-risk parents. Models arising from this theoretical framework assume that a particularly critical caregiver function is to provide the context that enables the child to develop a model of interpersonal relationships and to learn what to expect of the other and of the self in relationships. The research generated by this model has tied patterns of caregiving (hostile, rejecting, psychologically unavailable care giving) to impaired child competence at successive stages and the development of psychopathology. It has also demonstrated a relationship between a mother's emotional and environmental resources and her competence in parenting (Egeland & Farber, 1984) and between a mother's childhood history of adequate or abusive care (as assessed retrospectively) and the quality and pattern of care she gives her children (Egeland, Jacobvitz, & Papatola, 1987; Main & Goldwyn, 1984; Sroufe, Jacobvitz, Mangelsdorf, DeAngelo, & Ward, 1985).

Consequently, the treatment approaches developed from this perspective stress the importance of developing a long-term (at least a year) therapeutic relationship with the maltreating parent (usually the mother). Such a relationship provides the parent with an opportunity to learn new ways of relating to another individual, work through some of the psychological trauma from the parent's childhood that may serve as barrier to providing a nurturant relationship with the child, and then work on additional social skills that are important in successful functioning as an adult and parent in our society.

Fraiberg's (1983) clinical infant mental health program developed in Michigan and the University of Minnesota's STEEP Project (Erickson, 1988) are two examples of intervention projects that appear to be successful in treating maltreating mothers from this approach. However, a critical evaluation of their effectiveness is not yet available.

Family Level

Maltreating families are dysfunctional families. Although they exhibit difficulties similar to those of other client families and require many of the same approaches and interventions, their problems are often more severe and multidimensional (Faller, 1985). As a result of their similarity to other client families, few family system researchers have examined the treatment of the abusive families per se. Several family theorists have proposed treatment models for abusive families from a family system theory perspective (Alexander, 1985; Kaufman, 1988). From this theoretical approach child abuse should not be viewed as an end in itself but as a complex behavioral pattern symptomatic of a family in distress. It is not an isolated phenomenon, but part of a more general pattern of parent–child interaction that can only be understood in the context of the family system. Treating child abuse is not just a matter of fighting the symptom by blaming the abusive parent for victimizing the child, but requires thorough examination to determine which patterns of family interaction generate, maintain, and perpetuate the abusive behavior. As in other dysfunctional families, the abusive family may display symptom formation in family members other than the identified "victim." Symptom formation may also be apparent in multiple family crises, structural disorganization, and impaired communication and problem-solving skills.

Family systems theory has not produced research on abusive families in support of its model. However, family therapy may be considered a promising treatment approach compared with both no treatment and alternative treatment controls, if one generalizes from the success of family treatment of parent–child conflict (see Hazelrigg, Cooper, & Borduin, 1987, for a recent review).

Child Level

There is a large and growing literature documenting the long-standing and serious damage children suffer as a result of maltreatment (Brassard et al.,

1987; Mann & McDermott, 1983). Thus, abused children require special handling. They have not had important psychological needs met by significant adults. This maltreatment is related to cognitive deficits, problems with aggression and self-control, and maladaptive peer relationships. In addition, abused children are perceived by mothers and teachers to be less socially and academically competent (Brassard & Gelardo, 1987; Erickson & Egeland, 1987). Some of these children seem to encourage people to dislike them (Gelardo & Brassard, 1987; Sroufe, 1983), and some are irritatingly clingy and needy.

Because child maltreatment is usually seen as a symptom of parental dysfunction, most interventions have focused on changing parents or the home environment rather than on direct treatment of children (cases where a child is removed from the home and provided with treatment would be the exception). This approach rarely relieves the child's emotional response to the maltreatment and leaves the child vulnerable to repeating the pattern with his or her own children (Mann & McDermott, 1983).

Therapeutic work with children in general is still in its infancy (Kazdin, 1988), but some promising models and findings suggest that this is a fruitful area for exploration. Play therapy (see Mann & McDermott, 1983), developmental therapy (Ivey, 1987), and group therapy for children (Cohn & Daro, 1987) are several models that merit further evaluation.

Prevention

Although the strategies outlined below are organized in categories targeting adult caretakers and children, it will be apparent that many of them are applicable to both populations, separately and together as a family, that they could be pursued at any of several ecological levels, and that helping professionals could choose to pursue their adoption/application at one or several of those ecological levels.

Targeting the Adult Caretaker to Reduce Maltreatment

Strategies to reduce the likelihood that adult caretakers will psychologically maltreat children are organized in three categories: basic psychological needs fulfillment, development of knowledge and skills for parenting, and reduction of negative stress. Simple self-explanatory lists of strategy options will be presented, followed by a brief discussion of some strategies that have special support or are good examples for multiecological level pursuit by helping professionals.

Basic Psychological Needs Fulfillment

Establish love and belonging as a child, friend, spouse, co-worker
Ensure development of practical competencies and opportunities for meaningful work

Teach people strategies to meet their basic needs through direct instruction and modeling

Establish responsible human need fulfillment as the primary goal of society

Establish a positive ideology of the child in society

Involve adults and children in health promotion programs

Development of Knowledge and Skills for Parenting

Establish child development and parenting as basics in education

Provide hands-on training in child care in schools, churches, and community

Offer education to at-risk adults dealing with critical periods (e.g., marriage, pregnancy, childbirth)

Provide concrete rewards for participation in ongoing parenting/child development education (e.g., tax incentives, released time from work, child-care respite)

Emphasize development of self-esteem and prosocial behavior competencies through instruction in home, church, school, and community

Model prosocial behaviors and good parenting practices in popular media

Reduction of Negative Stress

Encourage dependable extended family/social support networks

Provide home-visitor services to all families

Provide stress-management training as community and employment benefits

Provide child care at places of employment

Provide concrete support for good parenting (e.g., paid leave from employment for either parent during the first 2 years of a child's life) (Hart, 1987d)

Many other strategies that might be effective could be added to this list. Most of the items identified have so far achieved only face validity by virtue of being in opposition to factors associated with maltreatment. Research is needed to investigate their effectiveness. Some of these strategies presently have more than face validity support and, therefore, justify early application. The home-visitor model, for example, has been shown to have genuine promise for preventing maltreatment (see Rosenberg & Reppucci, 1985, for review). Currently being tested is an expanded and refined version of this model that incorporates personal relationship counseling, home visits, and the development of a social support and practical issues problem-solving group for new mothers at risk to maltreat. The first year of this project has produced promising results (M. Erickson, personal communication, April 7, 1988, Chicago). Additionally, based on the accumulated results from the longitudinal prospective research on child maltreatment conducted by Egeland and associates (Egeland & Erickson, 1987), support exists for programs targeting high-risk mothers prior to the birth of their first child. These programs are intended to meet the mother's unmet emotional needs, increase sensitivity to her child's cues, increase understanding of child development, and increase contact with social, emotional, and physical support for child rearing.

Many opportunities exist to exert influence toward prevention. An individual practitioner might decide to apply a comprehensive health promotion perspective. In so doing he or she could (a) offer health promotion education or counseling, applying the full range or any set of wellness or self-regulation model elements (e.g., fitness, nutrition, stress management, problem solving, values-based decision making, prosocial behavior, social support) to individual parents; (b) contribute to these programs at a community health center; or (c) lobby for the inclusion of such a program under community services, through employee benefits, or as a part of health insurance. If the practitioner were to emphasize increasing the understanding and application of child development knowledge he or she might (a) teach specific parents constructive child management skills (e.g., Parent Effectiveness Training, Gordon, 1970; Piagetian cognitive and moral development strategies, Kamii, 1984), (b) help local community agencies (e.g., schools, churches, health centers) develop and offer parent education programs, and (c) lobby for education nationally and locally to establish child development and parenting as educational basics for all young people.

Targeting the Child to Reduce Vulnerability

Strategies for reducing the vulnerability of children to maltreatment and its impact are organized into three categories: basic psychological needs fulfillment, development of knowledge and skills necessary to meet needs and counter adversity, and reduction of negative stress.

Basic Psychological Needs Fulfillment

Establish bonding patterns between newborn and parent(s) before they leave hospital

Establish love and belonging as child, sibling, friend, and student

Assure low child-to-adult ratios in child care and education

Ensure the development of practical competencies and opportunities for meaningful work in home and school

Make basic psychological need fulfillment and achievement of responsible autonomy the major goals of child development in home/school/community

Establish protector-mentor persons in home/school/community for at-risk children

Development of Knowledge and Skills to Meet Needs and Counter Adversity

Develop ability to communicate feelings and needs to caring adults and peers

Prepare children to meet own needs and to assert personal rights

Teach children prosocial behaviors and skills/attitudes necessary to elicit and provide social support

Develop ability to delay gratification

Develop practical judgment, problem solving, critical thinking, and responsible decision making

Develop special talents and potentials

Provide stress-management training

Reduction of Negative Stress

Provide home-visitor services to newborns and family

Offer child development screening and prescriptions to families at all critical development stages

Provide stress-management, respite, social support and personal development programs to at-risk parents

Train child-care workers and educators to identify and support at-risk children

Encourage intergenerational relations in home/school/community

Establish after-school learning/leisure centers for children of working parents (Hart, 1987d).

At the present time most strategies targeting the child are primarily supported by face validity, as was the case for those targeting adults. Strategies and conditions having additional support include fulfilling basic need for love and belonging (Glasser, 1965; Maslow, 1970; for review of research support see Montagu, 1970); family cohesion and stability (see Garmezy, 1987, for review of research); establishment of dependable adult mentor-mediator relationships (Feuerstein & Hoffman, 1982; Henricksen, 1982); development of cognitive and social competencies (Garmezy, 1987; Rutter, 1985); raising socioeconomic status and intellectual functioning (Garmezy, 1987).

A helping professional might become involved in efforts to produce any of the conditions just cited. If emphasis were to be given to programs that would help children get off to a good start in their first hours and years, a practitioner might provide maternity ward services to help new mothers and their children successfully relate to and bond with each other; offer child development evaluation and prescriptive services through a local free clinic or low-cost consortium of professional services; or lobby to gain support for low child-to-adult ratios in child-care centers and to provide home-visitor services for all first-time mothers. If efforts were focused on enabling children to provide early warning regarding a pattern of care that tended toward maltreatment, one could train child-care workers to help children develop the ability to communicate their feelings, needs, and concerns to caring adults; encourage media producers and sponsors to include self-protection information in children's television programs; or establish outreach programs from community agencies (e.g., churches, health centers, recreation centers) to families to reduce family and child isolation. If long-term basic psychological need fulfillment were the priority chosen by a helping professional, he or she might develop or distribute self-instructional programs to parents to guide self-esteem building for their children; educate parents to recognize and properly interpret the needs of children through the cues they provide; or lobby for child rearing priority in homes and schools to be devoted to "Mega-Skills" achievement (e.g., confidence, motivation, responsibility, initiative, problem solving, prosocial behavior; see Glasser, 1965; Rich, 1988).

Critical Position of a Positive Ideology and Community Structure

Genuine progress in the treatment of psychological maltreatment can be stimulated through a wide variety of direct and indirect approaches meant ultimately to serve the general population, those at risk, and those being maltreated. There are two conditions that are particularly critical to assuring substantive support for treatment programs: the establishment of a consensus-supported positive ideology of children and of community organizational structures to facilitate community action.

The establishment of a "positive ideology of children," a perspective that values children in their own right and not solely for the manner in which they can meet the needs of others, may be essential to the development and long-term support of comprehensive treatment programs. Currently, children's rights usually compete with and defer to parental rights, family rights (usually meaning parental rights), and property rights (Hart & Brassard, 1987b). The high value stated for children rings hollow when compared to the low allocation of resources to their welfare (Gil, 1987; Hyman, 1987). A broadly supported positive ideology of children does not exist in our country or any other, according to Melton (1983).

A positive ideology of children is fundamental to the major societal changes necessary to reduce child maltreatment, according to many social scientists (Gil, 1987; Hart & Brassard, 1987b; Melton, 1983). Because strong consensus support for a positive ideology of children has not existed, child development knowledge guiding caretakers toward positive practices has never achieved high levels of application. It is equally unlikely that sustained and rigorous treatment programs will be mounted on the basis of threats of negative consequences for children alone. Although the establishment of a clear and strong positive values orientation toward children may appear to be an overwhelming job, progress can be made toward the goal. Any progress made can support efforts to combat psychological maltreatment. Our colleagues might help groups of parents, and lay or professional publics with whom they work, to achieve a point of view about children that will guide their behavior; they might lobby collectively for state and national laws and regulations that will express a positive view of children; they might initially work within their own professional organizations to develop a positive ideology of children to guide lobbying and practice efforts. Guidance and support exist for such efforts. The United Nations' Declaration of the Rights of the Child (1973), the Declaration of the Psychological Rights of the Child produced by psychologists (Catterall, 1979), and the articles of the proposed United Nations Convention on the Rights of the Child (UNICEF, 1988) provide direction for the essential ingredients of an ideology. Hart (1989) has recommended that an ideology include three major themes—developmental goals, autonomy, social responsibility, and self-actualization. In the same source, specific encouragement and direction have been given to school psychology to pursue this work.

Effective application of a positive ideology of children, and of the many strategies for treatment that could fall under its umbrella, must have the support of local leadership as well as a coordination and implementation base. We recommend the formation of "child development councils" at the local community level to carry out these functions. Such councils should be organized as the rallying point for all the major child development interests of a community, cutting across and integrating correction, prevention, and health promotion. They should be structures widely representative of community interests and resources with participation by education, mental health, medical, social service, religious, political, business, parent, and youth groups. Though some of these entities by themselves have been and will continue to be strong, positive influences for good child development programs, in isolation none has been capable of providing or stimulating the breadth of programs needed, and some embody unfortunate negative stigmatizing power. Therefore, the council should not be organized under or housed in an existing agency, which might suggest superior influence. Instead, it should be a collaborative freestanding entity. A council of this nature could serve a wide variety of purposes. It could (a) provide the leadership base that would guide the community toward commitment to a positive ideology of children; (b) design, direct, and coordinate child health promotion programs at the home, school, and community agency level; (c) design and direct communitywide early warning systems for children at risk; (d) apply nonstigmatizing leverage to enlist child caretakers in programs to reduce risk; and (e) support follow-through on corrective programs. Councils such as this have been tested and found effective for narrower purposes of child abuse and neglect (Hart, Brassard, & Germain, 1987; McClare, 1983). The model has been recommended as the preferred organizational structure to direct and coordinate cooperative child development programs within school communities (Hart, Brassard, & Germain, 1987). More recently, child development councils, as described here, have been recognized as a critical need for advancing the broader purposes of child health promotion within communities (Indiana Department of Mental Health, 1988).

SUMMARY AND FUTURE DIRECTIONS

Psychological maltreatment is a major problem and the core issue in child abuse and neglect. It is probable that the elements most critical to understanding and combating all child abuse and neglect are integral to psychological maltreatment and will be sufficiently revealed only as it is clarified. Five major types of psychological maltreatment are currently recognized: spurning, terrorizing, isolating, corrupting/exploiting, and denying emotional responsiveness. Recorded incidence rates are only rough approximations. It is likely that the incidence of psychological maltreatment would far exceed the 2 million cases per year estimated for all child abuse and neglect if consideration were given to (a) both its pure, discrete forms and forms combined with other types of maltreatment; and (b) cases of both established and threatened negative consequences. Psychological maltreatment, of sufficient power and/or consistency, appears to produce maladaptive deviancy for victims that is seriously destructive to quality of life for the victims, those with whom they have contact, and society in general. In fact, its subtle-and-mild to dramatic-and-powerful forms may accumulate to produce the majority of serious emotional and behavioral problems. The destructive power of psychological maltreatment has been explained as resulting from its essential nature as an attack on basic psychological need fulfillment.

The status of psychological maltreatment is in an embryonic stage. Acceptance of a broad generic definition has occurred, and the major acts have been identified. However, operational definitions and standards for decision making, although now being researched, have yet to be achieved. Substantial progress in the exploration of causes, mediating variables, and effects must await developments in these areas. Even at this early stage in knowledge development specific to psychological maltreatment, promising directions for treatment exist that are supported by findings and perspectives within other child maltreatment and child development knowledge bases.

Treatment recommendations, both corrective and preventive, have been identified to target parents/caretakers, families, and children. Suggestions have been given for the development and application of treatment strategies within and across a wide range of human ecological system levels. So far, few corrective treatments have proven effective in dealing with child abuse and neglect. The most promising corrective models are those that (a) comprehensively address the practical needs of families, including interpersonal and emotional needs of all family members, (b) emphasize social learning/behavioral analysis models, and (c) apply intensive resources in the initial months of treatment and assure extended follow-through. Prevention has been recognized as having much greater potential than correction for reducing psychological maltreatment and its destructive consequences. Among the many preventive strategies deserving emphasis are expanded and refined versions of the home-visitor model; prosocial skills development; child development monitoring and support services; parenting education and support services; stress-management, wellness, and self-regulation programs.

Many opportunities present themselves for combating psychological maltreatment. To realize their potential, certain prerequisites must be achieved: establishment of operational definitions, decision-making standards, and standards of evidence; clarification of mediating variables; and heightening of public awareness and support. These are goals deserving the concerted and coordinated efforts of researchers, practitioners, and policy experts. However, achievement of these goals will not assure the changes required to improve human conditions critical in their relationship to psychological maltreatment unless two additional goals also are attained: (a) a positive ideology of children to provide basic societal direction and support for good child rearing; and (b) community organizational structures to act as local leadership, coordination, and implementation bases for prevention and correction. Progress in these areas will be difficult, but not impossible. This combined set of goals should stand as the agenda for work in the immediate future.

REFERENCES

Alexander, P. C. (1985). A systems theory conceptualization of incest. *Family Process, 24,* 79–88.

American Bar Association Juvenile Justice Standards Project/Institute of Judicial Administration (not officially approved by the ABA). (1980). *Standard relating to abuse and neglect* (Standard 2.1c). Cambridge, MA: Ballinger.

American Humane Association. (1987). *Highlights of official child neglect and abuse reporting 1985.* Denver, CO: Author.

American Psychiatric Association. (1987). *Diagnostic and statistical manual of mental disorders* (DSM-III-R; 3rd ed.-rev.) Washington, DC: Author.

American Psychologist. (1987). Psychology in the public forum. *42,* 157–175.

Anthony, E. J., & Cohler, B. (Eds.). (1987). *The invulnerable child.* NY: Guilford.

Baily, F. T., & Baily, W. H. (1986). *Operational definitions of child emotional maltreatment.* Augusta, MA: Maine Department of Social Services.

Belsky, J. (1984). The determinants of parenting: A process model. *Child Development, 55,* 83–96.

Benedek, E. P. (1985). Children and psychic trauma: A brief review of contemporary thinking. In S. Eth & R. S. Pynoos (Eds.), *Posttraumatic stress disorder in children* (pp.1–16). Washington, DC: American Psychiatric Association.

Bittner, S., & Newberger, E. H. (1982). Child abuse: Current issues of etiology, diagnosis, and treatment. In J. Henning (Ed.), *The rights of children: Legal and psychological perspectives* (pp. 64–98). Springfield, IL: Charles C Thomas.

Bowlby, J. (1973). *Attachment and loss: Vol. 2. Separation.* New York: Basic Books.

Bowlby, J. (1980). *Attachment and loss: Vol. 3. Loss, sadness, and depression.* New York: Basic Books.

Bowlby, J. (1982). *Attachment and loss: Vol. 1. Attachment* (2nd ed.). New York: Basic Books.

Brassard, M. R., & Gelardo, M. S. (1987). Psychological maltreatment: The unifying construct in child abuse and neglect. *School Psychology Review, 16*, 127–136.

Brassard, M. R., Germain, R., & Hart, S. N. (Eds.). (1987). *Psychological maltreatment of children and youth.* Elmsford, NY: Pergamon.

Brassard, M. R., & Hart, S. N. (1987). *Emotional abuse: Words can hurt.* Chicago: National Committee for Prevention of Child Abuse.

Brassard, M. R., & McNeill, L. (1987). Child sexual abuse. In M. R. Brassard, R. Germain, & S. N. Hart (Eds.), *Psychological maltreatment of children and youth* (pp. 69–88). Elmsford, NY: Pergamon.

Broadhurst, D. D. (1984). *The educator's role in the prevention and treatment of child abuse and neglect.* Washington, DC: National Center on Child Abuse and Neglect, U.S. Department of Health and Human Services.

Bronfenbrenner, U. (1979). *The ecology of human development: Experiments by nature and design.* Cambridge, MA: Harvard.

Catterall, C. (1979). Children's psychological rights. *School Psychology International, 1*, 6–7.

Christopherson, E. R., Kuehn, B. S., Grinstead, J. B., Barhard, J. D., Rainey, S. K., & Kuchn, F. E., (1976). A family training program for abuse and neglect families. *Journal of Pediatric Psychology, 1*, 90–94.

Cicchetti, D., & Braunwald, K. G. (1984). An organizational approach to the study of emotional development in maltreated infants. *Infant Mental Health Journal, 5*, 172–183.

Cohn, A. H., & Daro, D. (1987). Is treatment too late: What ten years of evaluative research tell us. *Child Abuse and Neglect, 11*, 433–442.

Corson, J., & Davidson, H. A. (1987). Emotional abuse and the law. In M. R. Brassard, R. Germain, & S. N. Hart (Eds.), *The psychological maltreatment of children and youth* (pp. 185–202). Elmsford, NY: Pergamon.

Corwin, D. (1985). *The sexually abused child disorder.* Paper presented at the National Summit Conference on Diagnosing Child Sexual Abuse, Los Angeles.

Egeland, B., & Erickson, M. (1987). Psychologically unavailable caregiving. In M. R. Brassard, R. Germain, & S. N. Hart (Eds.), *Psychological maltreatment of children and youth* (pp. 110–120). Elmsford, NY: Pergamon.

Egeland, B., & Farber, E. (1984). Infant–mother attachment: Factors related to development and change over time. *Child Development, 55*, 753–771.

Egeland, B., & Farber, E. (1987). Invulnerability among abused and neglected children. In E. J. Anthony & B. Kohler (Eds.), *The invulnerable child* (pp. 253–288). New York: Guilford.

Egeland, B., Jacobvitz, D., & Papatola, K. (1987). Intergenerational continuity of parental abuse. In J. Lancaster & R. Gelles (Eds.), *Biosocial aspects of child abuse*. San Francisco: Jossey-Bass.

Egeland, B., Sroufe, L. A., & Erickson, M. (1983). The developmental consequence of different patterns of maltreatment. *Child Abuse and Neglect, 7*, 459–469.

Erickson, M. F. (1988, April). *School psychology in preschool settings*. Paper presented at the annual meeting of the National Association of School Psychologists, Chicago, IL.

Erickson, M. F., & Egeland, E. (1987). A developmental; view of the psychological consequences of maltreatment. *School Psychology Review, 16*, 156–168.

Erickson, M. F., Sroufe, L. A., & Egeland, B. (1985). The relationship between quality of attachment and behavior problems in a high-risk sample. In I. Bretherton & E. Waters (Eds.), Growing points of attachment theory and research (pp. 147–166). *Monographs of the Society for Research in Child Development, 50* (1–2, Serial No. 209).

Erikson, E. (1963). *Childhood and society* (2nd ed.). New York: Norton.

Faller, K. C. (1985). Unanticipated problems in the United States child protection system. *Child Abuse and Neglect, 9*, 63–69.

Feuerstein, R., & Hoffman, M. B. (1982). Intergenerational conflict of rights: Cultural imposition and self-realization. *Viewpoints in Teaching and Learning, 58*, 44–63.

Fraiberg, S. (Ed.). (1983). *Clinical studies in infant mental health: The first year of life*. New York: Basic Books.

Garbarino, J. (1977). The human ecology of child maltreatment. *Journal of Marriage and the Family, 39*, 721–736.

Garbarino, J., & Garbarino, A. C. (1986). *Emotional maltreatment of children*. Chicago: National Committee for Prevention of Child Abuse.

Garbarino, J., Guttmann, E., & Seeley, J. (1986). *The psychologically battered child: Strategies for identification, assessment and intervention*. San Francisco: Jossey-Bass.

Garbarino, J., & Merrow, J. (1985). *Psychological maltreatment of children: Assault on the psyche* [videotape]. University Park: Pennsylvania State University.

Garmezy, N. (1987). Stress, competence, and development: Continuities in the study of schizophrenic adults, children vulnerable to psychopathology, and the search for stress-resistant children. *American Journal of Orthopsychiatry, 57*, 159–174.

Garrison, E. G. (1987). Psychological maltreatment of children: An emerging focus for inquiry and concern. *American Psychologist, 42*, 157–159.

Gelardo M., & Brassard, M. (1987, April). *An ecological comparison of the psychological characteristics of physically abused primary grade children and matched classmates*. Paper presented at the biennial meeting of the Society for Research in Child Development, Baltimore.

Gil, D. G. (1987). Maltreatment as a function of the structure of social systems. In M. R. Brassard, R. Germain, & S. N. Hart (Eds.), *Psychological maltreatment of children and youth* (pp. 159–170). Elmsford, NY: Pergamon.

Glasser, W. (1965). *Reality therapy*. New York: Harper & Row.

Goldstein, A., Keller, H., & Erné, D. (1985). *Treating child abusive families*. Champaign, IL: Research Press.

Gordon, T. (1970). *Parent effectiveness training: PET*. New York: Plume.

Hart, S. N. (1987a). Psychological maltreatment in schooling. *School Psychology Review, 16*, 169–180.

Hart, S. N. (1987b). *Psychological maltreatment in schools through personnel and institutional practices*. Paper presented at the annual meeting of the American Psychological Association, New York.

Hart, S. N. (1987c). Mental health neglect. In M. R. Brassard, R. Germain, & S. N. Hart (Eds.), *Psychological maltreatment of children and youth* (pp. 269–270). Elmsford, NY: Pergamon.

Hart, S. N. (1987d). Guides for preventing psychological maltreatment and its effects. In *But names can hurt forever* [study guide to accompany videotape program] (pp. 13–14, 21–22). Green Bay, WI: NEWIST.

Hart, S. N. (1988). Psychological maltreatment: Emphasis on prevention. *School Psychology International, 9*, 243–255.

Hart, S. N. (1989). NASP at thirty: A vision for children. *School Psychology Review, 18*, 221–224.

Hart, S. N., & Brassard, M. (1986). *Developing and validating operationally defined measures of emotional maltreatment: A multimodal study of the relationships between caretaker behaviors and child characteristics across three developmental levels*: (Grant No. DHHS 90CA1216-01). Washington, DC: Department of Health and Human Services and the National Center on Child Abuse and Neglect.

Hart, S. N., & Brassard, M. R. (1987a). A major threat to children's mental health: Psychological maltreatment. *American Psychologist, 41*, 160–165.

Hart, S. N., & Brassard, M. R. (1987b). Psychological maltreatment: Integration and summary. In M. R. Brassard, R. Germain, & S. N. Hart (Eds.), *Psychological maltreatment of children and youth* (pp. 254–266). Elmsford, NY: Pergamon.

Hart, S. N., Brassard, M. R., & Germain, R. (1987). Psychological maltreatment and education/schooling. In M. R. Brassard, R. Germain, & S. N. Hart (Eds.), *Psychological maltreatment of children and youth* (pp. 217–242) Elmsford, NY: Pergamon.

Hart, S. N., Gelardo, M. S., & Brassard, M. R. (1986). Psychological maltreatment. In J. Jacobsen (Ed.), *Psychiatric sequelae of child abuse* (pp. 133–168). Springfield, IL: Charles C Thomas.

Hart, S. N., Germain, R., & Brassard, M. R. (1987). The challenge: To better understand and combat the psychological maltreatment of children and youth. In M. R. Brassard, R. Germain, & S. N. Hart (Eds.), *Psychological maltreatment of children and youth* (pp. 3–24). Elmsford, NY: Pergamon.

Hazelrigg, M., Cooper, H. M., & Borduin, C. M. (1987). Evaluating the effectiveness of family therapies: An integrative review and analysis. *Psychological Bulletin, 101*, 428–442.

Henricksen, B. (1982). *Your money or your life*. Aberdeen University Press.

Herrenkohl, R. C., Herrenkohl, E. C., & Egolf, B. P. (1983). Circumstances surrounding the occurrence of child maltreatment. *Journal of Consulting and Clinical Psychology, 51*, 424–431.

Hickey, E. (in press). *Serial murderers and their victims*.

Hyman, I. A. (1985, September). *Psychological abuse in the schools: A school psychologist's perspective*. Paper presented at the annual meeting of the American Psychological Association, Los Angeles.

Hyman, I. A. (1987). Psychological correlates of corporal punishment. In M. R. Brassard, R. Germain, & S. N. Hart (Eds.), *Psychological maltreatment of children and youth* (pp. 59–68). Elmsford, NY: Pergamon.

Indiana Department of Mental Health (1988, Nov. 17). *Minutes of Prevention Task Force*. Indianapolis: Author.

Ivey, A. (1987). *Developmental therapy*. San Francisco: Jossey-Bass.

Kamii, C. (1984, February). Autonomy: The aim of education envisioned by Piaget. *Phi Delta Kappan*, pp. 410–415.

Kaufman, K. (1988). *Child abuse assessment from a systemic perspective*. Unpublished paper obtainable from the author, Children's Hospital, Department of Pediatrics, Ohio State University, Columbus, Ohio 43210.

Kazdin, A. (1988). *Child psychotherapy: Developing and identifying effective treatments*. Elmsford, NY: Pergamon.

Lourie, M. D., & Stefano, L. (1978). On defining emotional abuse. Child abuse and neglect: Issues in innovation and implementation. In *Proceedings of the Second Annual National Conference on Child Abuse and Neglect*. Washington, DC: Government Printing Office.

Lutzker, J. R. (1984). Project 12-Ways: Treating child abuse and neglect from an ecobehavioral perspective. In R. F. Dangel & R. A. Polster (Eds.), *Parent training: Foundations of research and practice* (pp. 260–297). New York: Guilford.

Magid, K., & McKelvey, C. A. (1988). *High risk: Children without a conscience*. New York: Bantam Books.

Main, M., & Goldwyn, R. (1984). Predicting rejection of her infant from mother's representation of her own experience: Implications for the abused-abusing intergenerational cycle. *Child Abuse and Neglect, 8,* 203–217.

Mann, E., & McDermott, Jr., J. F. (1983). Play therapy for victims of child abuse and neglect. In C. Schaefer & K. O'Connor (Eds.), *Handbook of play therapy* (pp. 283–307). New York: Wiley.

Marvel Comics. (1988). *Amazing Spiderman on emotional abuse*. Chicago: National Committee for Prevention of Child Abuse.

Maslow, A. (1970). *A theory of human motivation*. New York: Harper & Row.

McClare, G. (1983). The management of child abuse and neglect cases in schools: The Toronto model. *Child Abuse and Neglect, 7,* 83–89.

Melton, G. B. (1983). *Child advocacy: Psychological issues and interventions*. New York: Plenum.

Melton, G. B., & Corson, J. (1987). Psychological maltreatment and the schools: Problems of law and professional responsibility. *School Psychology Review, 16,* 188–194.

Melton, G. B., & Davidson, H. A. (1987). Child protection and society: When should the state intervene? *American Psychologist, 42,* 172–175.

Melton, G. B., & Thompson, R. A. (1987). Legislative approaches to psychological maltreatment: A social policy analysis. In M. R. Brassard, R. Germain, & S. N. Hart (Eds.), *The psychological maltreatment of children and youth* (pp. 203–216). Elmsford, NY: Pergamon.

Miller, A. (1983). *For their own good.* New York: Free Press.

Mississippi Department of Public Welfare. (1984). *Definitions of child abuse and neglect with guidelines.* Mississippi: Author.

Montagu, A. (1970, May). A scientist looks at love. *Phi Delta Kappan,* pp. 463–467.

National Center on Child Abuse and Neglect. (1981). *Executive summary: National study of the incidence and severity of child abuse and neglect.* Washington, DC: Author.

National Center on Child Abuse and Neglect. (1988). *Study findings: Study of national incidence and prevalence of child abuse and neglect: 1988.* Washington, DC: Author.

National Committee for Prevention of Child Abuse (1987a). *NCPCA fact sheet no. 7: Emotional child abuse.* Chicago: Author.

National Committee for Prevention of Child Abuse (1987b). *Child abuse campaign (magazine ads).* Chicago: Author.

Navarre, L. (1987). Psychological maltreatment: The core component of child abuse and neglect. In M. R. Brassard, R. Germain, & S. N. Hart (Eds.), *The psychological maltreatment of children and youth* (pp. 45–58). Elmsford, NY: Pergamon.

NEWIST (1987). *But names can hurt forever.* (Videotape program and use guide). Green Bay, WI: Northeastern Wisconsin In-School Telecommunications.

Office for the Study of the Psychological Rights of the Child. (1983, October). Abuse of children and youth. In *Proceedings of the International Conference on Psychological Abuse of Children and Youth.* Indiana University: Indianapolis.

Office for the Study of the Psychological Rights of the Child. (1986, February). *Minutes of the national advisory board meeting.* Indianapolis: Author.

Patterson, G. R. (1982). *Coercive family process.* Eugene, OR: Castalia.

Patterson, G. R. (1986). Performance models for antisocial boys. *American Psychologist, 41,* 432–444.

Public Law 94-142. (1975). *The Education for All Handicapped Children Act.*

Random House. (1967). *The American college dictionary.* NY: Author.

Rich, D. (1988). *Megaskills.* Boston: Houghton Mifflin.

Rohner, R. P., & Rohner, E. C. (1980). Antecedents and consequences of parental rejection: A theory of emotional abuse. *Child Abuse and Neglect, 4,* 189–198.

Rosenberg, M. S. (1987). New directions for research on the psychological maltreatment of children. *American Psychologist, 42,* 166–171.

Rosenberg, M. S., & Reppucci, N. D. (1985). Primary prevention of child abuse. *Journal of Consulting and Clinical Psychology, 53,* 576–585.

Rutter, M. (1985). Resilience in the face of adversity: Protective factors and resistance to psychiatric disorder. *British Journal of Psychiatry, 147,* 598–611.

School Psychology Review. (1987). Mini-theme issue: Psychological maltreatment of children. *16,* 126–211.

Smith, S. L. (1984, June). Significant research findings in the etiology of child abuse. *Social Casework: The Journal of Contemporary Social Work,* 337–346.

Sroufe, L. A. (1979). The coherence of individual development. *American Psychologist, 34,* 834–841.

Sroufe, L. A. (1983). Infant–caregiver attachment and patterns of adaptation in preschool: The roots of maladaption and competence. In M. Perlmutter (Ed.), *The Minnesota symposium on child psychology* (Vol. 16, pp. 41–83). Hillsdale, NJ: Erlbaum.

Sroufe, L. A., Jacobvitz, D., Mangelsdorf, S., DeAngelo, E., & Ward, M. J. (1985). Generational boundary dissolution between mothers and their preschool children. *Child Development, 56,* 317–325.

Starr, R. H. (1979). Child abuse. *American Psychologist, 34,* 872–878.

Turgi, P., & Hart, S. N. (1988). Psychological maltreatment meaning and prevention. In O. C. S. Tzeng & J. J. Jacobsen (Eds.), *Sourcebook for child abuse and neglect* (pp. 287–317). Springfield, IL: Charles C Thomas.

UNICEF (1988). *The proposed UN convention on the rights of the child: Info-paper 2.* New York: Author.

United Nations. (1973). *Declaration of the rights of the child: United Nations Resolution 1386.* New York: Author.

Valentine, D. P., Freeman, M. L., Acuff, S., & Andreas, T. (1985). Abuse and neglect: Identifying and helping school children at risk. *School Social Work Journal, 9,* 83–89.

Virginia Department of Social Services. (1985). *Protective services,* Vol. VII, Sec. III, Chap. A, pp. 6b, 6d. Richmond: Author.

Wald, M. (1961). *Protective services and emotional neglect.* Denver: American Humane Association.

Werner, E. E. (1985, May). *Longitudinal studies of vulnerability and resiliency among early adolescents.* Paper presented at the Symposium on Biological and Behavioral Research in Early Adolescence, meeting of the American Association for the Advancement of Science, Los Angeles.

Wolfe, D. A. (1987). *Child abuse: Implications for child development and psychopathology.* San Francisco, CA: Sage.

CHAPTER 5

Victims of Spouse Abuse

ROBERT GEFFNER AND MILDRED DALEY PAGELOW

INTRODUCTION

In the context of this chapter, spouse abuse refers to a pattern of behavior in a relationship by which one person victimizes the other. Abuse can take many forms: physical, sexual, verbal, and/or psychological. It can also refer to intense and continuous degradation or intimidation for the purpose of controlling the actions or behavior of the other person, or placing that other person in fear of serious bodily injury to self or another. This type of domestic violence has most frequently been discussed as woman-battering or wife abuse because in most cases of spouse abuse the violence is directed at the woman (Dobash & Dobash, 1979; Pagelow, 1981a; Walker, 1979). The gender-neutral term "spouse" used here refers to persons who are married, formerly married, cohabitant, former cohabitant, or who have had an intimate relationship with another.

In order to treat spouse abuse, it is very important for helping professionals to distinguish between the presenting problems or symptoms of clients/patients and the occurrence of spouse abuse that may underly the cause (Hilberman & Munson, 1978; Pagelow, 1984). Although it is critical to identify spouse abuse as a causal factor before intervention can be effective, both victims and abusers often minimize or deny the violence. Therapists sometimes find themselves faced with a declared goal of family conciliation and later discover that one party is using overt or covert intimidation to control the other partner. Sometimes "helpers" join the "conspiracy of silence" and minimize or deny indications of family violence. This is especially true when the person treating the individual or couple has no prior training or knowledge of spouse abuse.

It is imperative, therefore, for the professional to determine whether abuse has occurred in the relationship before designing a treatment plan. The first section of this chapter describes the epidemiology and etiology of spouse abuse. Following that is a delineation of the possible consequences of spouse abuse (psychological, medical, and legal), including the negative effects from inappropriate treatment or lack of intervention. Treatment options are then addressed, consisting of both practical considerations and therapeutic modalities. The chapter ends with a summary and suggestions for future directions in treating and reducing spouse abuse.

EPIDEMIOLOGY

Spouse abuse is now widely recognized as a major epidemic because, directly and indirectly, it affects such a great number of people. Depending on the particular study, it is estimated that spouse abuse occurs at least once in 20% to 30% of families (Stark & Flitcraft, 1988; Straus & Gelles, 1986). In addition, Stark and Flitcraft (1988) reported that nearly 20% of women who go to hospital emergency rooms for medical treatment have been battered, and Helton (1986) found that almost 25% of pregnant women in relationships have been abused. These statistics clearly underscore the prevalence and severity of the problem.

For many years, it was assumed that abusers were merely sadistic men who enjoyed beating their wives and that battered women were masochistic and did not want to escape the violence. However, these beliefs are now recognized as myths, even though many people still tend to look for simplistic, single-factor solutions and try to blame the victim. A common question still asked by the public is "Why does she stay?" Various levels of analysis have been used to try to determine the roots of spouse abuse and to explain the dynamics of the gradual conditioning process.

For example, one approach has been to focus on the personality characteristics of the batterers and their victims (Geffner, Jordan, Hicks, & Cook, 1985; Hamberger & Hastings, 1986). Another approach has studied the marital and family relationships (Caesar, 1988; Geffner, 1987; Margolin, 1988). Still other researchers have suggested that the important origins of spouse abuse are at the cultural or societal level and must include stereotyping and patriarchal values (Dobash & Dobash, 1979; Pagelow, 1984). Unfortunately, the roots of spouse abuse are still unclear, but a combination of the above factors probably is necessary to account for this type of violence.

Recent research has attempted to determine the risk factors involved in spouse abuse so that treatment and prevention strategies can be developed. The greatest risk factor, according to these studies, is having witnessed parental violence as a child (Hotaling & Sugarman, 1986). Other vulnerability factors, according to Stark and Flitcraft (1988), are social isolation, alcohol use, status differences between partners, low self-esteem, and pregnancy. These findings do not specifically indicate the causes of spouse abuse, but the more factors that are present in a relationship, the more likely it is that violence will occur.

Research has also found many similar characteristics when comparing male batterers to battered females. These include low self-esteem, aggressiveness, hostility, depression, lack of communication, lack of assertiveness,

social isolation, impulsiveness, stereotyped views of sex roles, use of alcohol, and a history of abuse in the family of origin (Douglas & Colantuano,
1987; Geffner et al., 1985; Hamberger & Hastings, 1986). It should again be
noted, however, that this research does not specify the causes for these
characteristics. It is quite possible that being battered for many years promotes characteristics in the victims that are similar to the ones exhibited by
the abusers. Because research has not yet studied abusers or their victims
prior to the abuse, the reasons for such similarities are unknown.

Violence does not necessarily begin after marriage. Indeed, intimidation
and verbal abuse can begin during dating relationships and escalate over the
years (Makepeace, 1984; Stets & Pirog-Good, 1987). It again appears that
the best prediction of the severity and duration of abuse in relationships is
the early exposure to violence during childhood. This intergenerational transmission of violence is an important aspect of spouse abuse and therefore
must be dealt with in treatment. It is also relevant when addressing the
consequences of spouse abuse.

CONSEQUENCES OF SPOUSE ABUSE

No one in a violent family escapes harm when spouse abuse occurs. The
primary victim, of course, is the spouse who is beaten or terrorized, but
regardless of age, the children who share residence with such a couple are
also victims. Finally, the abuser himself is harmed by what he is doing to
those nearest and, usually, dearest to him. In this respect, one might consider
that all those involved become victims in some way or another. As stated
earlier, many abusers were the victims or witnesses of parental violence
during their childhood.

As long as the spouse abuse continues without intervention, severe consequences are almost sure to follow. Because other chapters focus on the
abusers (Chapter 12) and on the children who witness interparental violence
(Chapter 8), this chapter largely restricts discussion of the consequences to
the wives of violent spouses. It should be noted that battered husbands
exhibit similar dynamics and consequences, but they make up only 10% or
less of the abused population (Pagelow, 1985). Therefore, this chapter often
refers to the battered spouse as the wife because this is the most prevalent
situation. In any case, the consequences of spouse abuse for the victim can
be psychological, medical, or legal.

Psychological Consequences

On an emotional level, the spouse who is being abused suffers a constant
deterioration of self-confidence and a simultaneous increase in fear and confusion. Batterers contribute to the loss of self-confidence by verbally deni-
grating battered women. The victims gradually accept the negative infor-

mation as part of their own self-images because of a lack of positive feedback from outside support systems (Dobash & Dobash, 1979; Dutton, 1988; Pagelow, 1981a).

Many victims make repeated efforts to obtain outside assistance, and some are successful (Bowker, 1983; Gondolf & Fisher, 1988; Pagelow, 1981b). Other victims meet with failure in their attempts, or they are blamed for their situation; they gradually develop a sense of hopelessness and help-lessness. Walker (1984) discovered that two out of three battered women she surveyed saw no way out of their situations, and she related this to the "learned helplessness" of animals in studies conducted by Seligman (1975). Walker's idea of the "battered woman syndrome" is that the victims grad-ually become immobilized by fear, they no longer believe that they have other options, and they therefore stay in the situation coping the best they can. This gradual conditioning process of helpless and hopeless feelings is one of the main reasons that battered spouses stay in their abusive rela-tionships longer than many outside people expect.

Less frequently discussed in the literature is the phenomenon commonly referred to as the "Stockholm Syndrome," or sometimes as the "Patty Hearst Syndrome" (NiCarthy, 1983; Ochberg, 1980; Pagelow, 1984). It has most frequently been noted in the behavior and attitudes of hostages and prisoners of war, but the process is similar to the phenomenon that develops in the lives of battered spouses. The syndrome occurs when victims who are isolated, extremely mistreated, and fearful for their lives begin to develop positive feelings toward their captors and overlook or minimize negative features. The victims become totally helpless, confined people and begin to believe that everything they need and want depends on the whims of others. Even the slightest favor (or lessening of their pain or punishment) is seen as a "gift" from their captors, to whom they are grateful (Pagelow, 1984).

Symonds (1975) stated that battered wives are "brainwashed by terror," and NiCarthy (1983) noted that occasional and unpredictable favors be-stowed by abusers provide intermittent reinforcement. NiCarthy (1983) stated that:

> These techniques of emotional abuse are similar to those which have been used to control prisoners of war. . . . As stated in a report published by Am-nesty International, these techniques induce "dependency, dread and debil-ity." To the extent that a person is victimized by these techniques, she or he tends to become immobilized by the belief that she or he *is* trapped, *cannot* escape. (pp. 117–118)

A survey of battered women revealed that the most commonly mentioned reason given for staying with abusers after repeated battering was *fear* (Pagelow, 1981a). Such women fear not only for their own safety, but for the safety of their children whose lives have also been threatened by their fathers; or they fear that the men will take the children away from them.

Many do not reveal the abuse to friends and family because they know that their spouses' explosive anger and jealousy can endanger the lives of others. Sometimes they fear for the health and welfare of the abusers themselves, concerned that they will "fall apart" or commit suicide if they leave (NiCarthy, 1983). Their fears may seem exaggerated or to be generated by hysteria rather than reality, and sometimes they have developed a fear so great that they believe their abusers are almost omnipotent. These fears should not be ignored. If anyone knows an abuser's capability for violence, it is his victim, and if her fears are shown later to be unrealistic, it is still better to have erred on the side of safety than to have taken chances with the lives of victims, their children, and others who try to assist them.

In addition to fear, the battered women examined by Pagelow (1981a) also reported helplessness, confusion, isolation, depression, and humiliation, as well as guilt and feelings of failure. These emotional responses often lead to somatic complaints and may contribute to the development of life-threatening illnesses. Many contemporary mental health professionals diagnose this type of trauma-induced behavioral and emotional reaction as post-traumatic stress disorder. This may be one of the reasons that so many abused women report a variety of mental health problems, including depression, anxiety, stress-induced illnesses, and suicide attempts.

Stark and Flitcraft (1988) contend that battering accounts for one in every four suicide attempts by all women and half of all suicide attempts by black women. Researchers have found that suicide has been seriously considered by almost half of their samples, and many victims admit they made at least one attempt at some point during the abuse history (Pagelow, 1981b). A hospital study found that 12% of the women at risk for abuse had been treated for at least one suicide attempt (Stark, et al., 1981). Among female patients seeking emergency services after attempted suicide, 29% were battered. Almost half of them were battered the same day they made their suicide attempts, and almost three out of four attempted suicide within 6 months of an abusive incident. Stark et al. (1981) conclude: "Thus battering should be regarded as frequent precipitant of female suicide attempts, and conversely, women who attempt suicide are likely to have a history of domestic violence" (p. 20). Accurate statistics on suicides by battered women are difficult to obtain because of the inconsistent way many deaths are recorded, but there is no doubt that many suicide attempts are successful.

Medical Consequences

It is estimated that injuries due to domestic violence result in at least $10 million in medical bills yearly in the United States (Esposito, 1986). It also has been estimated that battering is the most common source of injury to women (Stark & Flitcraft, 1988). Furthermore, battering is significantly associated with alcoholism and substance abuse. In October 1985, the office of the Surgeon General of the United States sponsored a workshop on violence and public health. The work group assigned to the topic of the evaluation and treatment of spouse abuse produced a list of recommendations with preliminary remarks that included this statement: "Spouse abuse is a crime perpetrated primarily against women, often causing them serious injury and premature death and affecting the psychological development of their children and of other family members" (U.S. Department of Health and Human Services, 1986, p. 71).

Campbell (1987) and Stark et al. (1981) state that medical personnel tend to overlook most cases of woman-battering (only correctly diagnosing 1 battered woman out of 25), and they argue that improvement in the medical response is urgently needed to combat the battering syndrome. Recently, Surgeon General Koop reported to the media that over 2 million women were battered each year, and that physicians must do a better job of recognizing and referring these victims for treatment.

Another recent study found that only 5% of female trauma patients were identified as battered following the usual medical treatment, but 30% of these type of patients were identified as battered by emergency room staff once they asked basic questions concerning the injuries (McLeer & Anwar, 1989). The women were merely asked in a brief protocol how their injuries occurred and whether someone was responsible for them. Evidence is growing that health care professionals and the health care system are trying to improve their record. Indeed, model protocols and training manuals for hospital staff and health care professionals have already been produced (Esposito, 1986; Varvaro & Cotman, 1986).

Medical professionals are also likely to encounter pregnant battered women, and these women are more likely to have a pregnancy terminated by abortion or miscarriage when they are injured (Stark et al., 1981). Estimates are that 23% to 45% of battered women are beaten during pregnancy (Helton, 1986). Pagelow (1981a) noted that many women who were battered during pregnancy reported occurrences of stillbirths, miscarriages, brain-damaged children, birth defects, and chronic illnesses, as well as other physical and emotional handicaps. Obviously, the physical consequences of battering pregnant women are extremely serious, both to the women and their unborn children.

That the abuse during pregnancy among battered women is so high is not surprising in light of the observation made by Finkelhor (1983), who notes that the most common pattern of family violence involves the most powerful abusing the least powerful. Pregnant women are particularly vulnerable to physical attack, and some wives are battered *only* when they are pregnant (Pagelow, 1984). To help in identification of pregnant patients who have been battered, a basic protocol and an educational module were developed for use by health care providers (McFarlane, Anderson, & Helton, 1987). This booklet offers assessment and intervention strategies and education materials to help alert the public and at-risk women.

Marital rape is another type of physical and psychological trauma, and one that often is overlooked. Among rape victims, half of all rapes to women over 30 are part of the battering syndrome (Stark et al., 1981). An untold number of rapes by spouses remain undetected among victims who seek medical services for other physical complaints. As Russell (1982) has clearly established, women are much more reluctant to reveal rape by their spouses than to disclose physical abuse. Among studies of battered women, reports indicate a high incidence of marital rape (Bowker, 1983; Shields & Hanneke, 1983), and many of these women are raped more than once (Pagelow, 1988).

Researchers who study marital rape point out that these occurrences are not merely "lovers' quarrels" or "bedroom spats" but often are extremely violent and brutal (Finkelhor & Yllo, 1985). Despite the high incidence of rape among battered women, most of the protocols designed for medical professionals make little or no mention of the possibility that the patient may have been sexually assaulted *as well as* physically beaten. Oversight of rape or sexual assault can lead to serious consequences for victims because of incomplete or inadequate treatment plans.

Legal Consequences

Most spouse abuse researchers have found that the violence tends to increase in frequency and intensity over time. Without intervention, this can sometimes lead to homicide of the victim, the abuser, or both. Likewise, children may be physically involved in family violence. Although 1 out of every 10 murdered men is a husband killed by his wife, 1 out of every 3 murdered women is a wife killed by her husband (Browne, 1987; Esposito, 1986). However, many more men than women are murdered in general, most often by other men. In 1980, the majority of victims of spouse murders were wives (Flanagan & McLeod, 1983).

Browne's (1987) comprehensive study of battered women who kill their abusers found that the differences between the women who kill and those who do not are related to the actions of their abusers, not to the victims. Battered wives were more likely to make the fatal attempt to free themselves and their children from their abusers based on the following elements: (a) frequency of abuse and severity of injury, (b) frequency of sexual assaults (c) husband's drug use, (d) husband's threats to kill, and (e) wife's threats to commit suicide.

A few battered wives who kill are found not guilty, as in the much-publicized Francene Hughes case involving the wife's immolation of her alcoholic ex-husband (McNulty, 1980). In some other cases, the charges are dismissed, but there often is a public outcry that wives are being given a "license to kill" (Mitchell, 1978). Of the large population of abused wives, those who murder or attempt to murder are relatively rare.

More often, battered women turn to the legal system for protection from their abusers, but not always with success. Indeed, Browne (1987) presents a case concerning a woman who obtained a court restraining order after her husband locked her in their apartment without a telephone, beat and choked her, and threatened to kill her. The judge scolded the woman for wasting taxpayers' money by taking up the court's time when it had "more serious matters" (p. 170) to contend with. The judge also ridiculed her request for police escort when she went back to the apartment to pack some clothes. He told her to "just go there and act as an adult" (p. 170). A few months later the batterer met his wife at the bus stop as she returned from work, maced her mother who was there to meet her daughter, and shot his wife in the abdomen when she tried to escape. He dragged her into his car and sped away; her body was found the following day. In another case, a judge would not administer a stiffer prison sentence to a man who shot his wife five times in the face at close range and killed her. The judge stated that the woman had deceived her husband by being "extremely loving and caring" up to the morning that she secretly left the family home to proceed with a divorce (Browne, 1987).

Battered wives also turn to the legal system for divorce as their solution to freedom from abuse. However, as increasing numbers of them are finding, many abusive husbands quickly learn to use the system to maintain control over their victims. More states are adopting "no-fault" divorce laws, eliminating the need to obtain evidence of fault by the other party, but along with no-fault has grown the idea of joint custody and parental rights. Many caring fathers are seriously concerned about maintaining close relationships with their children after divorce, and joint custody appears to work very well when both parents desire this arrangement. However, abusive men have also used the court's concern for parental contact after divorce to their own advantage.

California was the first state to institute mediation for all divorcing parents who come to court without an agreement for custody and visitation, and other states are quickly following suit. In some states, couples are offered, but not mandated to use, mediation services, whereas other states mandate mediation but make exceptions for certain circumstances such as a history of spousal violence. California, however, mandates mediation and makes no exceptions other than for investigation of child abuse allegations. Some legislators and many judges believe that spouse abuse has no relevance to the issue of parental fitness. Even murder of a spouse is sometimes deemed totally irrelevant in deciding parental rights.

A basic premise of mediation is that the parties are relatively equal in bargaining power and capable of reaching a workable agreement that is in the best interests of their children. However, the power imbalance may be too great at times to be balanced by even the most skilled mediator, and, in many cases, the mediator is not even aware of the couples' turbulent histories. These people are processed through the system like everyone else because *both* victims and abusers are unlikely to talk about the violence and, if confronted, tend to minimize or deny the abuse. In one case a wife, ordered into mediation with her abusive husband, had previously obtained an order of protection. The couple met with mediators who apparently were unaware of court documents alleging wife abuse, child abuse, child snatching, and threats to kill her. One mediator even urged the wife to "date" her abuser. The abusive husband eventually persuaded his wife to relinquish custody of their older two sons to him, with the endorsement of the mediator. However, later, in a fit of rage and revenge, he shot all three boys and himself (Brodeur & Downey, 1987).

Thus, a battered wife who decides to break away from her violent husband through legal separation or divorce often has a dilemma: The family court system may provide the justification and methods for the abuser to continue to maintain his control over her through their children or finances. If a battered spouse turned to helping professionals earlier without obtaining effective intervention, or if professionals in the helping services did not previously identify her problem as stemming from being battered by her spouse, it may be unlikely that she will be able to convince her attorney or the court that she requires special protection from her abusive spouse as she goes through the system and afterward. She, or her children, or all of them may be subject to continuing years of emotional and physical abuse.

TREATMENT FOR THE BATTERED SPOUSE

The foregoing should make it clear why it is vital for helping professionals to identify battered spouses, regardless of whether they openly acknowledge that their problems emanate from spouse abuse. To misdiagnose their problem could mean inappropriate treatment, and this could have potentially disastrous effects.

The concept of *treatment* can mean different things. To a sociologist, trained to focus primarily on societal influences, with the individual as an important but lesser part of the clinical picture, treatment generally means addressing social and economic issues. To a psychologist, trained to focus primarily on the individual or the relationship, with his or her immediate environment as an important but lesser part of the picture, treatment generally consists of assisting individuals to use their inner resources to cope with and improve their situation. Treatment for battered spouses is best accomplished by a combination of sociological and psychological solutions, balanced to meet individual needs. The first step, however, is to identify victims of spouse abuse.

Identification of Victims of Spouse Abuse

Bearing in mind that both victims and their abusers are likely to minimize or deny the occurrence of spousal violence, professionals need to draw upon their training, experience, and their observational skills to make accurate assessments. The first clues may or may not be visible in the appearance or outward behavior of the clients. Victims often appear to be incompetent, unsure (much more so in the abuser's presence), edgy, indirect, nervous, depressed, brittle, and humorless. On the other hand, abusers often appear "normal," competent, smiling, and charming. At the other extreme, abusers may present themselves as pathetic and helpless victims, and in these cases, the victim may appear to play a mothering role. Battered women can be educated and of upper socioeconomic status; race, class, and educational level are not determining factors.

The initial interviews are very important in this process. At least one interview with each spouse should be conducted in private, but if one party resists or objects to the other being seen alone, this should be duly noted. It is very important, even in marital or conjoint therapy, to have at least one private session with each person because research evidence clearly indicates that abusers tend to provide significantly different information from that provided by the abused even when both admit to the violence (O'Leary & Arias, 1988; Rosenbaum & O'Leary, 1981). It is also very important to determine the level of intimidation that may be taking place and how free the battered spouse may be to express her feelings and opinions.

Medical professionals may have a greater opportunity to observe whether a husband is a "steamroller." This is indicated when his attitude is antagonistic to the system, and he complains that all others (except the interviewer) are inept and incompetent. The steamroller tries to build a partnership to enlist the interviewer's assistance in expediting the assessment process.

There should be certain items on an assessment checklist that, in combination, raise "red flags" for the interviewer. Some items in the couple's history are especially crucial. For example, were they very young at the time of their marriage? Was there a premarital pregnancy? Was the wife *both* young and pregnant at the time of marriage? Were there any children living in the home not biologically related to both parties? Even more specifically, did the woman bring into this relationship a child fathered by another man?

The history of the individual or couple should include items about both their present relationship and their families of origin. Have the couple changed locations or residences frequently? Are there any indicators of alcohol or drug abuse, present or past? Did either of them come from alcohol-abusing homes? The interviewer should probe to learn if either of them was physically, sexually, or emotionally abused in childhood. Is there a history of violence in the families of origin of either husband or wife? If so, was the violence directed at the child or children, or was the violence directed at one parent by the other? Children are much more likely to model their same-sex parents; thus, boys whose fathers beat their mothers are more likely to become wife abusers than boys raised in homes without parental violence (Hotaling & Sugarman, 1986; Pagelow, 1984).

The interviewer can learn much by watching and listening to the couple during joint interviews. For example, pay attention to body language—watch for eye contact, reactions indicating possible fear rather than ordinary nervousness, and avoidant posture. Listen for "permission" words between them. Does either party talk about men and women exclusively in terms of traditional stereotypes? Are these terms negative about the other sex? Be alert for indicators of jealousy pointing to possessiveness, immaturity, or low self-esteem.

Trained interviewers should be able to discover how important decisions are reached in the family, especially concerning financial matters. Yet they should be aware that the person who writes the checks does not necessarily have decision-making powers; sometimes the controlling spouse merely delegates the check-writing and accounting duties to the other. An important fact is whether all their bank accounts and credit cards are in one or both their names. The roles of each spouse should also be explored to determine domination and subservience. Details concerning how each spouse spends time at home—their respective chores, responsibilities, and decision-making powers—provide indications of possible rigid role restrictions suggestive of potential abuse.

Another vital question is whether the family is socially isolated. The interviewer should determine the geographic distance from the closest friends and relatives of each spouse, and how often visits occur. Often relatives and friends of victims are unwelcome in abusive homes because they might detect some subtle signs of abuse.

Physical abuse often is preceded by psychological abuse. An abuser may begin by intimidation, such as punching holes in walls with his fist or destroying or disposing of some property owned or at least valued by the partner. Always inquire whether a pet or other animals have been hurt or poisoned. The interviewer should keep these characteristics in mind in searching for evidence of spousal violence.

When clients come to a professional for individual, marriage, or family counseling, it is relatively easy to include the preceding questions, as well as questions concerning the couple's ideal husband–wife relationship. If the projected image is impossibly idealistic or rigid, this can be an important clue, especially if the more extreme version is presented by the husband. Does either spouse, especially the suspected abuser, seem to have an extreme degree of religiosity? This can be another potential red flag concerning rigidity and possible abuse.

Finally, if there are any children, the interviewer should seek information about them. Are there any indications that the children are dysfunctional without an adequate explanation? Examples are school failure, behavioral problems, aggressiveness, depression, eating disorders, minor illness, or somatic complaints. Are any of the children bed wetters, sleepwalkers, or fire setters? Do the children display extremes in behavior (e.g., overly fearful or overly aggressive)? Does any child assume a parental role in the family by waiting on the parents or caring for younger siblings?

When the professional has an opportunity to meet privately with a spouse suspected of being abused but who has not yet admitted being victimized, there are some questions that should be posed either directly or indirectly, depending on the degree of therapeutic alliance that has been built. The main goal is to assess her safety. Such questions include:

Do you feel safer when I talk with you alone?

Has your spouse ever threatened to harm you?

Has he ever deliberately hurt you?

Do you believe that your spouse ever hit a former spouse or lover?

Does your spouse treat his parents roughly or disrespectfully?

Has he ever hit his parents, brothers, or sisters?

Have you been attacked or blamed when your spouse got angry?

Are you afraid of your spouse's temper?

Do you usually give in to settle arguments?

Has your spouse ever deliberately hurt or killed a pet?

Have you felt free to invite your family or friends to visit you or your home?

Does your spouse listen in when you're talking on the phone?

Has your mail been opened before you receive it?

Do you select your own clothes?

Does your spouse insist on going everywhere with you?

Is your spouse suspicious of your every move?

Has your spouse accused you of being unfaithful?

Is your spouse an extremely jealous person?

Are your spouse's problems usually blamed on you or others?

When drinking, does your spouse get rough or violent?

Has your spouse ever forced you to have sex even though you did not want to?

Does your spouse have a "Dr. Jekyll and Mr. Hyde" personality?

Have you ever called, or thought of calling, the police because you feared an argument was getting out of control?

Have your neighbors or friends ever called the police?

If the police were called, was your spouse arrested or given a citation?

Are your children scared when your spouse is angry?

Does your spouse ever threaten to take the children where you cannot find them? Has this ever occurred?

In some cases, an abused spouse will adamantly refuse to admit or discuss the abuse, even after the sensitized professional has used these techniques skillfully and found sufficient reason to be convinced of the client's victimization. Once trust is established, the client will begin to communicate more openly, but until then, denial need not impede the development and initiation of a successful treatment program. It is far better that the professional make a false positive identification of abuse than to err in the direction of non-detection and inadequate or even misdirected treatment.

Sociological Approaches to the Treatment of Battered Spouses

Using a sociological viewpoint, victims of spousal violence are seen as people who *have* problems. This approach rejects the medical model, in which victims of spousal violence are viewed as people who *are* the problem. Indeed, the first and initially very popular explanation proposed to account for family violence was the *individual psychopathology*, or medical model, view. Shortly after the "discovery" of child abuse, the notion was advanced that parents who abused their children were depraved persons suffering some sort of mental illness. Early researchers struggled to locate individual characteristics of abusers that set them apart from normal people, who did not abuse their children, but this was to no avail. This belief was also applied to spouse abuse, in which the focus was on individual pathology rather than on social problems.

The danger in accepting the medical model to explain spouse abuse and formulate a treatment strategy is that it tends to blame the victim and excuse the abuser. If the fault lies within the victim, then the victim must be "cured" to stop the violence. An extension of the medical model has been the proposal that the *masochistic personality* diagnosis be revised to include battering victims. However, the spouse abuse evaluation and treatment work group at the Surgeon General's Workshop, as well as many clinicians and researchers, oppose the proposed new psychiatric diagnosis of masochistic personality disorder for victims of spouse abuse. They argue that this diagnosis is both victim blaming and pejorative (U.S. Department of Health and Human Services, 1986).

From a sociological viewpoint, spouse abuse is a social problem, rather than one of individual pathology. Without doubt victims, after years of psychological and physical abuse, need and can benefit from certain types of psychotherapy. Many suffer from impaired levels of self-esteem, dependency, depression, and a lack of assertiveness.

The treatment for spouse abuse necessarily must include and be directed at the abusers, not just their victims. Treatment approaches for the abusers are presented in another chapter (see Chapter 12). The battered spouse can benefit from assistance on two levels to avoid further victimization: the intrapsychic and the social. The psychological aspects of treatment will be addressed in the next section. This section focuses on the social needs of the victims and suggests ways to meet these needs. Based on our own research and a review of the literature, however, some pressing social needs must be met to assist battering victims.

Professionals in all helping services must become sensitized to the indications of spouse abuse and knowledgeable about ways to effectively deal with it. There should be constant awareness of the tendency to blame the victims. Law enforcement officers must respond to domestic crimes with the same training and dedication that they use when approaching other types of crimes. The entire criminal justice system, including police officers, prosecutors, and the judiciary, should receive intense, specialized training concerning spouse abuse. Violent lawbreakers should be treated as such, whether their victims are intimate partners or strangers. Child protective service workers and other social workers must begin to look beyond the identified victims of family violence and become aware that many of the mothers of abused or neglected children are themselves victims of violence in the family. Economic assistance for women, improved child care and health services, and more shelters for battered women are urgently needed.

From a social viewpoint, a major factor in treating spouse abuse must be to change the societal stereotypes of male and female sex roles that allow the acceptance and perpetuation of violence. The lessening of social approval of domestic violence and the reduction of family isolation must occur if there is to be a long-term reduction in spouse abuse. Therefore, these ideas must be incorporated into our educational system at early grade levels so that the cycle of intergenerational transmission of violence can be stopped.

Psychological Approaches to the Treatment of Battered Spouses

The psychological treatment for battering has involved four perspectives, each dependent on different theoretical orientations. Originally, battered women sought help from shelters to protect them and their children; there they usually received individual counseling from an advocacy standpoint. Group and support therapy for battered women became another avenue of treatment. This, too, originated in shelters and was later adopted by other mental health professionals. As groups for battered women began spreading, practitioners realized that the focus of violence needed to be on the batterer (see Chapter 12). Therefore, group treatment programs for batterers were developed (Adams & McCormick, 1982; Ganley, 1981; Hamberger & Hastings, 1988). In recent years, two additional approaches have been utilized in the treatment of battering: "parallel" groups for the batterers and battered women that are conducted concurrently but separately, and conjoint therapy that involves the husband and wife in treatment.

The individual treatment of battered women in a shelter or similar setting has primarily focused on empowering the victim, reducing social isolation, providing social advocacy, reducing dependence, increasing assertiveness, and improving self-esteem (NiCarthy, 1986; Pagelow, 1984; Rouse, 1986; Walker, 1984). The main concern is to remove the victim from the violent home and eliminate contact with the abuser in order to maintain her safety. For many women, this is quite successful in empowering them, but it does not deal directly with the cause of the abusive behavior (i.e., the batterer). Even if the battered women obtains a divorce and leaves the abusive environment, as many abused women do, the batterer often proceeds to find another woman to abuse. A caution has also been raised concerning the possible danger of training abused wives to be assertive without providing suitable interventions for the abusers (O'Leary, Curley, Rosenbaum, & Clarke, 1985).

In addition, many shelters now realize that although they help substantial numbers of battered women, nearly half still return to their abusive environments, often being battered again. Sometimes they return because the abuser has agreed to seek counseling (Gondolf & Fisher, 1988). Interviews with battered women reveal that many do not want their marriages to end, that they love their husbands, but want to stop the abuse (Sedlak, 1988). A number of programs offer self-help support groups for battered and formerly battered women (Campbell, 1986; NiCarthy, 1986). A modified 12-step program taken from some of the ideas of Alcoholics Anonymous has recently been developed for battered and formerly battered women's groups, and a treatment manual has been published that describes the program (Franks, Geffner, Laney, McGaughey, & Mantooth, 1988).

However, the problem still remains for those women who want to stay in their relationships, but without violence or intimidation. Prior treatment efforts emphasized anger-management training with violent spouses to prevent further incidents of battering. A weakness of many programs that focus on anger management for men who batter, however, is that they do not deal with all the many other problems that exacerbate the battering, nor do they focus on the verbal abuse and intimidation (Gondolf & Russell, 1986). Therefore, two additional approaches for treating spouse abuse have been developed.

With the use of parallel groups, the batterer and the battered woman are treated in separate but coordinated programs (Douglas, 1987; Ganley, 1981). In addition to the usual techniques that would be used in the men's groups for anger management and in the women's groups for assertiveness, this approach allows the therapists to deal with relationship issues by combining the groups at times. This is an important feature because it allows direct therapy contact with both the abuser and the abused as they confront important issues including violence. Role-play interactions in a nonviolent, nonintimidating atmosphere can verify the abuser's reports of improvement and changes in behavior.

The final approach takes the preceding ideas a step further. This method involves the treatment of the batterer and victim conjointly, either as an individual couple or in couple groups (Geffner, Mantooth, Franks, & Rao,

1989; Geller & Wasserstrom, 1984; Harris, 1986). This strategy has probably been the most controversial because those opposed to it believe that the woman may be placed in danger and that the full responsibility for the violence is not placed upon the batterer (e.g., Willbach, 1989). These are legitimate concerns; it is very important for the batterer to assume full responsibility for his actions and to realize that there is *no excuse* for hitting his partner. It is crucial that the batterer and victim recognize and accept the ideas that violence is a choice and that it is a learned response that can be unlearned in most cases. An exploration of the violence in the family compared to other environments, such as work, can usually make the point that the batterer decides when to be violent.

Safety precautions must be clearly explained to both partners so that options are available for the woman and definite consequences are established for the man (sometimes this must be monitored by the criminal justice system and courts). These should be emphasized and consistently enforced. Nonviolence contracts are often used, and they do seem to have impact during the initial "honeymoon" period of treatment (Rosenbaum & O'Leary, 1986). The goal is to eliminate violence and intimidation while also attempting to improve the entire relationship for those couples who desire this option. It is often believed that an abuser will not volunteer for treatment and will not want to change behaviors. However, more programs are reporting that some batterers do volunteer for treatment. These men state that they do not want to abuse their spouses but that they do not know how to stop. In addition, fear of loss of their relationship is a powerful motivation for both batterers and their spouses, and this can often be used to maintain the batterer in treatment if it is reinforced by the spouse and therapist.

The conjoint therapy approach utilizes some aspects of family systems theory as well as communication techniques. It focuses in part on the family of origin because that is where much of the violence seems to originate. It should be noted that the concept of *blame* is often eliminated from this treatment approach and the concept of *responsibility* is used instead. This distinction is important because it removes the therapist as a punitive judge while enabling him/her to emphasize that violence is unacceptable behavior and the sole responsibility of the abuser. It should also be noted that this approach is not appropriate for all battering couples. It usually will not be successful if there is little motivation for change or if the batterer falls into the category of extreme psychopathology (i.e., he is violent in general, not just at home, and is violent even when there has been no interaction with his spouse).

In general, cognitive-behavioral and psychoeducational techniques are often used in conjunction with the family systems and communication theories. It is recommended that a male-female cotherapist team, if possible, conduct this type of conjoint therapy with abusive couples. Many of the conjoint programs begin with anger management and behavioral techniques to defuse the situation, use nonviolence contracts and other safety precautions, and then shift to psychoeducational methods for self-esteem enhancement, assertiveness, and communication. As the attitudes and behavior change, more emphasis is placed on the dynamics of the relationship, including sex-role stereotypes, power issues, problem-solving strategies, and intimacy issues. Utilization of multiple resources are often included, such as separate treatment programs for alcohol or substance abuse, and additional support groups for batterers and for battered women (Geffner et al., 1989). Concurrent treatment for substance abuse appears to be quite important for successful therapy.

Specific Techniques for Treating the Battered Spouse

It is critical to determine the lethality of the batterer before beginning any treatment. The use of alcohol, severe violence over a long time period, sexual abuse, and high stress level are a few of the warning signs for potentially severe violence (Harris, 1986; Rosenbaum & O'Leary, 1986). Intake interviews must be conducted separately to determine possible lethality as well as the actual motivation of the male and/or female to be in treatment. A thorough history of the violence should be taken from both partners if possible, but any discrepancies should be weighted in the battered spouse's favor. It is very important not to minimize the potential danger or the denial and to refer to the battering and hitting directly, without using euphemistic terms.

Most programs that treat spouse abuse will then focus on anger management and the right to live in an abuse-free atmosphere. Desensitization techniques to lower stress levels may also be appropriate. Power and control issues are quite important at this point, because this is one of the major issues in abusive relationships. Increasing assertiveness and independence are very important for the overall self-esteem of the battered spouse, and this is usually emphasized in therapy. However, merely teaching the victim to be assertive without emphasizing the ramifications and the ways to protect herself can be dangerous if the batterer is not also in treatment. Helping the battered spouse realize her own strengths and assets is often needed to offset the strong dependency and worthlessness feelings that have been conditioned as part of the battering cycle.

Overcoming the victim's fear is often the most difficult barrier at this point because it may be quite realistic. This helplessness also maintains the low levels of self-esteem. Thus, cognitive reframing is often a good technique to help the battered spouse realize that she is not to blame, that violence is not normal, and that she has a right to meet her needs. Substantial role playing is used at this time in conjunction with social advocacy and a support network in order for her to overcome her feelings of helplessness. To help reduce "irrational beliefs" concerning the self-blame and guilt often experienced by the battered spouse and to emphasize that relationships do not have to be violent, rational-emotive techniques are often employed (Ellis &

Harper, 1975). Role playing is again an excellent way to practice new responses and to help the victim become empowered. The therapist can also use this approach to model appropriate skills.

Conflict resolution and communication techniques are further emphasized so that alternative, more productive options to violence are available. Being able to recognize, label, and express feelings is important to avoid minimization or denial. The first step is for victims to learn to understand the nature of their own feelings; next, they must learn to listen to others. Being able to resolve disputes systematically is usually lacking in abusive families. In addition, many battered spouses come to believe that violence, intimacy, love, sex, and affection are intermingled. In fact, the intermittent reinforcement of affection following abusive incidents often maintains the cycle of violence in battered spouses (Walker, 1979).

Various manuals have been published in recent years to provide more detailed information concerning the treatment of battered women (e.g., Foreman & Frederick, 1984; McEvoy & Brookings, 1986; Sinclair, 1985), and one provides specific techniques that could be used with battered women as well as with couples conjointly (Mantooth, Geffner, Franks, & Patrick, 1987). It is important to emphasize again that professionals treating battered spouses should be fully aware of the ramifications of their techniques and should be well trained in working with this type of violence.

SUMMARY AND FUTURE DIRECTIONS

Spouse abuse has finally been recognized as a major domestic crime because it affects so many families directly or indirectly. The consequences, if appropriate intervention is not implemented, are almost always serious to the victims as well as to their children. Unfortunately, the tragedy of spouse abuse is too often seen in newspaper accounts of battered women and their children who have been killed by the batterers. The criminal justice system is not yet consistently fair in the treatment of battered women, and even the granting of a divorce may not end the intimidation and control by many batterers. However, treatment approaches are available for battered spouses and batterers either independently or conjointly.

This chapter has presented the main issues involved in spouse abuse, the consequences to the victims, and the various types of treatment approaches currently employed. It is hoped that more programs will be developed and that more mental health, medical, criminal justice, and social service professionals will obtain training and expertise in spouse abuse so that victims can be properly identified and treated. Unless this problem is dealt with at both individual and societal levels, it will be impossible to end the intergenerational transmission of domestic violence. Education is extremely important, especially for young children who may be witnesses of abuse in their homes, because research indicates that such childhood experiences are significantly associated with later battering or with being a victim of such abuse.

Unfortunately, a lack of cooperation often exists among the types of agencies and professionals who are involved with spouse abuse, and there is too much "in-fighting" concerning particular methods for treating this problem. Professionals need to unite, no matter what the specialty or field, so that interdisciplinary cooperation can begin to make a dent in this epidemic. To accomplish this, it is necessary to treat the victims and the abusers, using empirical methods to find the techniques that work best.

Research concerning the effectiveness of treatment programs is still in the nascent stage. Future investigative efforts need to focus on controlled outcome studies so that those techniques that are most effective in treating victims of abuse can be more fully developed and expanded. For example, recent research suggests that there are subtypes of batterers, and there may even be subtypes of victims. It would not be surprising, therefore, if different techniques may be needed depending on the type of batterer and victim, whether they want to change individually or together, whether they want to remain in the relationship, and the severity and duration of abuse. Examples of programs that seem to have successfully used a multidisciplinary approach for treatment of batterers, battered spouses, and violent couples include the Domestic Abuse Project in Minneapolis, the Harborview Hospital Project in Seattle, and the Family Violence Research and Treatment Program in Tyler, Texas.

The long-term solution to spouse abuse must eventually come from educational and societal interventions, however. Spouse abuse will not stop until domination and abuse are no longer socially accepted. The problem will not end until *all* men, women, and children can live in peace without violence, without the threat of violence, and without intimidation in their own homes.

REFERENCES

Adams, D. C., & McCormick, A. J. (1982). Men unlearning violence: A group approach based upon the collective model. In M. Roy (Ed.), *The abusing partner: An analysis of domestic battering* (pp. 170–197). New York: Van Nostrand.

Bowker, L. H. (1983). *Beating wife-beating.* Lexington, MA: Lexington Books.

Brodeur, N., & Downey, C. (1987, August 18). Father shoots 3 sons, killing 1, then takes his own life in south county. *Orange County Register*, A1–A2.

Browne, A. (1987). *When battered women kill.* New York: Free Press.

Caesar, P. L. (1988). Exposure to violence in the families-of-origin among wife abusers and maritally nonviolent men. *Violence and Victims, 3*, 49–63.

Campbell, J. C. (1986). A survivor group for battered women. *Advances in Nursing Science, 8*, 13–20.

Campbell, J. C. (1987). The second national nursing conference on violence against women. *Response to the Victimization of Women, 10,* 27–29.

Dobash, R. E., & Dobash, R. P. (1979). *Violence against wives.* New York: Free Press.

Douglas, M. A. (1987, August). A parallel treatment program for batterers and victims: Treatment effectiveness. In R. Geffner (Chair), *Applying recent family psychology research: Practical suggestions for the clinician.* Symposium presented at the annual meeting of the American Psychological Association, New York.

Douglas, M. A., & Colantuano, A. (1987, June). *Cluster analysis of MMPI scores among battered women.* Paper presented at 3rd National Conference for Family Violence Researchers, Durham, NH.

Dutton, D. G. (1988). *The domestic assault of women: Psychological and criminal justice perspectives.* Boston, MA: Allyn & Bacon.

Ellis, A., & Harper, R. A. (1975). *A new guide to rational living.* North Hollywood, CA: Wilshire Book Co.

Esposito, C. N. (1986). *Domestic violence: A guide for emergency medical treatment.* Trenton, NJ: Domestic Violence Prevention Program, New Jersey Department of Community Affairs.

Finkelhor, D. (1983). Common features of family abuse. In D. Finkelhor, R. J. Gelles, G. T. Hotaling, & M. A. Straus (Eds.), *The dark side of families: Current family violence research* (pp. 17–28). Beverly Hills, CA: Sage.

Finkelhor, D., & Yllo, K. (1985). *License to rape.* New York: Holt, Rinehart & Winston.

Flanagan, T. J., & McLeod, M. (Eds.). (1983). *Sourcebook of criminal justice statistics: 1982.* Department of Justice, Bureau of Justice Statistics. Washington, DC: Government Printing Office.

Foreman, R., & Frederick, M. (1984). *Domestic violence: A training manual for mental health professionals.* Saratoga, CA: R & E Publishers.

Franks, D., Geffner, R., Laney, N., McGaughey, L., & Mantooth, C. (1988). *Help end abusive relationship tendencies (HEART): A personal growth program manual for battered and formerly battered women.* Tyler: University of Texas at Tyler Press.

Ganley, A. (1981). *Court-mandated counseling for men who batter.* Washington, DC: Center for Women Policy Studies.

Geffner, R. (1987, June). *A systemic approach to wife abuse: Implications for systems therapies.* Invited plenary paper presented at the annual meeting of the American Family Therapy Association, Chicago.

Geffner, R. A., Jordan, K., Hicks, D., & Cook, S. K. (1985, August). Psychological characteristics of violent couples. In R. A. Geffner (Chair), *Violent couples: Current research and new directions for family psychologists.* Symposium conducted at the annual meeting of the American Psychological Association, Los Angeles.

Geffner, R., Mantooth, C., Franks, D., & Rao, L. (1989). A psychoeducational, conjoint therapy approach to reducing family violence. In P. L. Caesar & L. K. Hamberger (Eds.), *Therapeutic interventions with batterers: Theory and practice* (pp. 103–133). New York: Springer.

Geller, J. A., & Wasserstrom, J. (1984). Conjoint therapy for the treatment of domestic violence. In A. R. Roberts (Ed.), *Battered women and their families: Intervention strategies and treatment programs* (pp. 383–48). New York: Springer.

Gondolf, E. W., & Fisher, E. R. (1988). *Battered women as survivors.* Lexington MA.: Lexington Books.

Gondolf, E. W., & Russell, D. M. (1986). The case against anger control treatment programs for batterers. *Response, 9*, 2–5.

Hamberger, L. K., & Hastings, J. (1986). Personality correlates of men who abuse their partners: A cross-validation study. *Journal of Family Violence, 1*, 323–345.

Hamberger, L. K., & Hastings, J. (1988). Skills training for treatment of spouse abusers: An outcome study. *Journal of Family Violence, 3*, 121–130.

Harris, J. (1986). Counseling violent couples using Walker's model. *Psychotherapy, 23*, 613–621.

Helton, A. (1986). The pregnant battered woman. *Response to the Victimization of Women and Children, 9*, 22–23.

Hilberman, E., & Munson, D. (1978). Sixty battered women. *Victimology, 2*, 460–470.

Hotaling, G. T., & Sugarman, D. B. (1986). An analysis of risk markers in husband to wife violence: The current state of knowledge. *Violence and Victims, 1*, 101–124.

Makepeace, J. M. (1984, August). *The severity of courtship violence injuries and precautionary measures.* Paper presented at the 2nd National Conference for Family Violence Researchers, Durham, NH.

Mantooth, C. M., Geffner, R., Franks, D., & Patrick, J. (1987). *Family preservation: A treatment manual for reducing couple violence.* Tyler: University of Texas at Tyler Press.

Margolin, G. (1988). Interpersonal and intrapersonal factors associated with marital violence. In G. T. Hotaling, D. Finkelhor, J. T. Kirkpatrick, & M. A. Straus (Eds.), *Family abuse and its consequences: New directions in research* (pp. 203–217). Beverly Hills, CA: Sage.

McEvoy, A. W., & Brookings, J. B. (1986). *Helping battered women.* Holmes Beach, FL: Learning Publications.

McFarlane, J., Anderson, E. T., & Helton, A. (1987). Response to battering during pregnancy: An educational program. *Response to the Victimization of Women and Children, 10*, 25–27.

McLeer, S. V., & Anwar, R. (1989). A study of battered women presenting in an emergency department. *American Journal of Public Health, 79*, 65–66.

McNulty, F. (1980). *The burning bed.* New York: Harcourt, Brace, Jovanovich.

Mitchell, M. H. (1978). Does wife abuse justify homicide? *Wayne Law Review, 24*, 1705–1731.

NiCarthy, G. (1983). Addictive love and abuse: A course for teen-aged women. In S. Davidson (Ed.), *The second mile: Contemporary approaches in counseling young women* (pp. 115–159). Tucson, AZ: New Directions for Women.

NiCarthy, G. (1986). *Getting free: A handbook for women in abusive relationships.* New York: Seal Press.

Ochberg, F. M. (1980). Victims of Terrorism. *Journal of Clinical Psychiatry, 41*, 72–74.

O'Leary, K. D., & Arias, I. (1988). Assessing agreement of reports of spouse abuse.

In G. T. Hotaling, D. Finkelhor, J. T. Kirkpatrick, & M. A. Straus (Eds.), *Family abuse and its consequences: New directions in research* (pp. 218–227). Beverly Hills, CA: Sage.

O'Leary, K. D., Curley, A., Rosenbaum, A., & Clarke, C. (1985). Assertion training for abused wives: A potentially hazardous treatment. *Journal of Marital and Family Therapy, 11*, 319–322.

Pagelow, M. D. (1981a). *Woman-battering: Victims and their experiences.* Beverly Hills, CA: Sage.

Pagelow, M. D. (1981b). Secondary battering and alternatives of female victims to spouse abuse. In L. H. Bowker (Ed.), *Women and crime in America* (pp. 277–300). New York: Macmillan.

Pagelow, M. D. (1984). *Family violence.* New York: Praeger.

Pagelow, M. D. (1985). The "battered husband syndrome?" Social problem or much ado about nothing? In N. Johnson (Ed.), *Marital violence* (pp. 172–195). London: Routledge & Kegan Paul.

Pagelow, M. D. (1988). Marital rape. In V. B. Van Hasselt, R. L. Morrison, A. S. Bellack, & M. Hersen (Eds.), *Handbook of family violence* (pp. 207–232). New York: Plenum.

Rosenbaum, A., & O'Leary, K. D. (1981). Marital violence: Characteristics of the abusive couples. *Journal of Consulting and Clinical Psychology, 49*, 63–71.

Rosenbaum, A., & O'Leary, K. D. (1986). Treatment of marital violence. In N. Jacobson & A. Gurman (Eds.), *Clinical handbook of marital therapy* (pp. 385–405). New York: Guilford.

Rouse, L. P. (1986). *You are not alone.* Holmes Beach, FL: Learning Publications.

Russell, D. E. H. (1982). *Rape in marriage.* New York: Macmillan.

Sedlak, A. J. (1988). Prevention of wife abuse. In V. B. Van Hasselt, R. L. Morrison, A. S. Bellack, & M. Hersen (Eds.), *Handbook of family violence* (pp. 457–481). New York: Plenum.

Seligman, M. P. (1975). *Helplessness: On depression, development, and death.* San Francisco: W. H. Freeman.

Shields, N. M., & Hanneke, C. R. (1983). Battered wives' reactions to marital rape. In D. Finkelhor, R. J. Gelles, G. T. Hotaling, & M. A. Straus (Eds.), *The dark side of families* (pp. 17–28). Beverly Hills, CA: Sage.

Sinclair, D. (1985). *Understanding wife assault: A training manual for counselors and advocates.* Toronto: Ontario Ministry of Community and Social Services, Family Violence Program.

Stark, E., & Flitcraft, A. (1988). Violence among intimates: An epidemiological review. In V. B. Van Hasselt, R. L. Morrison, A. S. Bellack, & M. Hersen (Eds.), *Handbook of family violence* (pp. 293–317). New York: Plenum.

Stark, E., Flitcraft, A., Zuckerman, D., Grey, A., Robison, J., & Frazier, W. (1981). *Wife abuse in the medical setting: An introduction for health personnel.* Rockville, MD: National Clearinghouse on Domestic Violence.

Stets, J. E., & Pirog-Good, M. A. (1987). Violence in dating relationships. *Social Psychology Quarterly, 50*, 237–246.

Straus, M. A., & Gelles, R. J. (1986). Societal change and change in family violence from 1975 to 1985 as revealed by two national surveys. *Journal of Marriage and the Family, 48*, 465–479.

Symonds, M. (1975). Victims of violence: Psychological effects and aftereffects. *American Journal of Psychoanalysis, 355*, 19–26.

U.S. Department of Health and Human Services (1986). *Surgeon General's workshop on violence and public health report.* Washington, DC: Government Printing Office.

Varvaro, F. F., & Cotman, P. G. (1986). *Domestic violence: A focus on emergency room care of abused women.* Pittsburgh, PA: Women's Center & Shelter of Greater Pittsburgh.

Walker, L. E. (1979). *The battered woman.* New York: Harper & Row.

Walker, L. E. (1984). *The battered woman syndrome.* New York: Springer.

Willbach, D. (1989). Ethics and family therapy: The case management of family violence. *Journal of Marital & Family Therapy, 15*, 43–52.

CHAPTER 6

Victims of Elder Abuse

ROBERT S. MARIN AND RICHARD K. MORYCZ

INTRODUCTION

At first glance, one would think that the facts of elder abuse would resemble those of other forms of family violence. Physical injury, psychological pain, and personal exploitation occur in all and present the same irony of family members suffering at the hands of the persons who care most about them. It would not be surprising to find the explanations of elder abuse in the same places as for other forms of family violence—in a history of conflictual relationships between the victim and perpetrator of abuse, in a pattern of family violence during childhood now perpetuated in later life, or in the deviant personality of the perpetrator of abuse. However, over the past 10 years, as the study of family violence has turned to the elderly, investigators have discovered that the facts of elder abuse differ in important ways from these expected patterns. Moreover, it is evident that the explanations for elder abuse and, presumably, the treatments will prove to be different as well.

In retrospect, the differences are not surprising because the context of elder abuse is so different from that of children or younger adults. In each, one encounters conflict between spouses or between parents and children. However, the setting of elder abuse is the ending, not the beginning, of a relationship. Many dilemmas that arise in treating elder abuse derive from this fact. For example, a frail, aged mother may reject living in a seniors' residence so that she can remain home with her retarded, but abusive, son because she believes he will be unable to function without her. Or, because of his own dependency fears, a husband rejects in-home services for the proper care for his demented wife, whom he hits in frustration when she refuses medicine or food. Or, finally, a professional feels obliged to remove an abused elder from the home, knowing that there will be no recourse to prevent the children from appropriating the elder's belongings. Elder abuse thus occurs in relationships strained by problems of later life: illness, disability, dependence, and death.

Whatever the facts of elder abuse, their interpretation will be influenced by society's perceptions of the elderly. Too strong an association of frailty with aging may cause professionals to overlook that a debilitated, but still demanding, father may provoke his dependent son's verbal attacks. Similarly, if professionals fail to see that a demented elder is still in possession of his values or sense of dignity despite being rendered incompetent by memory loss they may be too quick to take a paternalistic role in making decisions on his behalf. Because of culturally determined perceptions of the elderly, it has been suggested (Sengstock & Hwalek, 1987) that relative to the abusers of children, there is a greater inclination to prejudge the abuser of the older person, to ascribe actions to greed or perversity, and not to see the mistreatment as a reaction to natural pressures or emotional provocation. Indeed, the offensive circumstances of elder abuse may sometimes make it difficult for practitioners to view the perpetrator of abuse as deserving treatment (Quinn & Tomita, 1986). The extent to which this arises from agist beliefs, valid ethical distinctions, or countertransference varies from case to case.

Heterogeneity, it is sometimes said, is a hallmark of the elderly. Certainly, it is relevant in trying to characterize the circumstances and thus the treatment of abused elders. Given this notion of heterogeneity, it is an oddity of the literature in this area that investigators seemed for some time to have sought a single profile of the abused elder that would somehow explain the occurrence of elder abuse. In fairness, the simplification undoubtedly reflected an attempt by the initial investigators of elder abuse (Hudson & Johnson, 1986) to provide hypotheses that would give order and direction to further studies. And that indeed has happened. Over the past 10 years, the depiction of the abused elder—as a frail, impaired, and dependent elderly woman in her middle 70s—has undergone considerable differentiation. In the process, some of the expected heterogeneity of elder abuse is becoming evident.

A variety of other general principles of aging would help to clarify the context of elder abuse. Finances, living arrangements, and functional capacity are just a few. Some additional considerations will be evident in this chapter's discussion of the epidemiology, consequences, and treatment of elder abuse.

EPIDEMIOLOGY

Definitions

Defining elder abuse is a prerequisite for studying its epidemiology. In addition to their use for researchers and clinicians, definitions are important in the legal setting. Many states have passed laws that provide definitions for different types of elder mistreatment. These definitions are intended to facilitate the detection, reporting, and treatment of mistreated elders. However, as Valentine and Cash (1986) note: "From a legal standpoint, the task of defining elder maltreatment is the difficult task of defining where and what form of maltreatment is considered excessive abuse, neglect, and violating the rights of the elder" (p. 19).

Defining elder abuse should be a simple matter. Abuse would exist whenever an elderly person is deliberately subjected to mistreatment by another person. As with most endeavors, however, attempts to study phenomena that seem self-evident prove unexpectedly difficult. Certainly this has been the case for elder abuse. Interpreting the epidemiological literature is impeded by definitions that often are vague, concrete, circular, or inconsistent (Hudson, 1986; Johnson, 1986). As an illustration, the definition just cited is vague and general. If abuse is defined as deliberate mistreatment by another, then elder abuse would have to include instances of adult children who treat their elderly parents impolitely, or all the forms of crime committed against the elderly. This definition of abuse would be difficult to use because in many situations it is difficult to determine whether the mistreatment was intentional. Conversely, if there was gross mistreatment that was not intended as such, would one then say that abuse had not occurred? Another problem with this definition is that it does not help clarify the relationship of abuse to neglect. Some (Douglass, Hickey, & Noel, 1980), but not all (Fulmer & Ashley, 1986) have considered neglect to be part of abuse. The issue of neglect is further complicated by the requirement for "mistreatment by another." Because the early literature indicated that self-neglect and self-abuse are common, there has been a reluctance to exclude them from studies of elder abuse, although, again, there are opinions on both sides of the argument (Johnson, 1986; Lau & Kosberg, 1979).

Consensus positions on the definition of elder abuse have not yet been developed. With the growing activity in the area, researchers will undoubtedly attempt this in the near future. As a starting point for defining terms, we suggest defining elder abuse and neglect as instances of the general category of mistreatment. This approach, proposed by Johnson (1986), defines mistreatment as:

> A state of self or other inflicted suffering unnecessary to the maintenance of the quality of life of the older person . . . identified by one or more behavioral manifestations characterized physical, psychological, sociological . . . measured by determining the intensity and density of behavioral manifestations . . . and treated whether the cause is the result of passive neglect, active neglect, passive abuse, or active abuse. (p. 180)

This definition is of value in several ways. As noted, the concept of elder mistreatment serves as a superordinate category for classifying individual cases (e.g., as abuse, neglect, crimes against the elderly). There are then three dimensions on which to classify individual cases. The first is in terms of the manifestation of the abuse as psychological, physical, social, or financial (see Table 6.1). The second is in terms of the action that caused the mistreatment. Abuse denotes acts of commission whereas neglect denotes acts of omission. The third asks whether the acts in question were carried out with intention to produce suffering. If the answer is yes, then it is a case of active abuse or active neglect. If not, it is passive abuse or passive neglect.

These distinctions are helpful in practice as well as in principle. An agitated older person may be tied to a chair to prevent falling or wandering out of doors. This may be done with the best of intentions by a truly concerned nurse who has 10 other patients under her care in a nursing home. Or, it may be done so that a homebound caregiver can convince herself that it is safe to leave the home for a few hours to visit a friend. In either case, however, the situation probably represents an instance of elder mistreatment that warrants intervention. Johnson (1986) argues that the professional's appraisal of the caregiver's judgment and intentions will influence the interventions recommended and also is likely to influence their acceptability to the caregiver. The key point, however, is that these appraisals should alter the conclusion that mistreatment has occurred and that intervention is needed. The interested reader is encouraged to consult Johnson's illuminating discussion of the function and structure of definitions and their application to the problem of elder abuse. In this chapter, the discussion will be limited to instances of mistreatment inflicted by others. Because self-neglect probably constitutes a substantial fraction of elder mistreatment cases, the reader should be cognizant of this fact. On the other hand, many of the principles of treatment discussed later to such cases also apply.

Etiology

Professionals involved in the treatment of elder abuse invariably consider some notion of etiology in determining a course of treatment for a new client. Is mistreatment due to the demands placed on the caregiver by the client's physical or psychiatric status? Is the caregiver disposed to physical or psychological abuse because of his or her personality or relationship to the client? Does the household suffer from lack of physical appurtenances, financial supports, or in-home services? These are but a few of the many possibilities to consider in working out an individual treatment plan.

Research on the etiology of elder abuse and neglect has primarily focused on the validity of three models of elder mistreatment (O'Malley & Fulmer, 1988; Phillips, 1986; Pillemer, 1985). The *psychopathological model,* or the model of intraindividual dynamics, maintains that persons who inflict abuse on older persons have deviant personalities. The *sociological model* views abuse as a consequence of social learning. One version, which emphasizes intergenerational transmission of violence, predicts that those who mistreat elders were themselves abused as children or were witness to the abuse of elders. Somewhat surprisingly, research to date has found little support for this explanation of elder mistreatment (Pillemer, 1986). Another version of

Table 6.1. The Extrinsic Definition of Elder Mistreatment (Behavioral Manifestations)

Physical	Psychological	Sociological	Legal
I. Medical Health Maltreatment (medication/care) • absence • excessiveness • irregularity • improperness • inadequacy • duplication • refusal	I. Humiliation • shaming • blaming • ridicule	I. Isolation • involuntary withdrawal from social interactions • voluntary withdrawal from social interaction • inadequate supervision • improper supervision • inadequate social support	I. Material Exploitation • misuse of money • misuse of property • misuse of possessions • misuse of insurance • blocking access to money • blocking access to property • blocking access to possessions • blocking access to insurance
II. Bodily Impairment • malnutrition • dehydration • emaciation • poor hygiene • drug addiction • sleep/rest disturbance • unexplained fatigue • hypo/hyperthermia • improper ventilation • failure to thrive	II. Harrassment • name calling • intimidation • threats • instilling fear • shouting	II. Role Confusion • role conflict • role dispersion • role inversion • role dissolution	II. Exploitation of Person • denial of rights to self-determination of competent elderly • denial of rights to self-determination of incompetent elderly • involuntary servitude

III. Bodily Assaults
- burns
- abrasions
- bruises
- fractures
- dislocations
- welts
- wounds
- rashes
- sores
- sprains
- internal injuries
- suicidal behavior
- sexual assaults
- physical restraint

III. Manipulation
- information withheld
- falsified information
- unreasonable dependence
- interference with decision making

III. Life-style Incompatibility
- lack of privacy
- household disorganization
- unsafe environment
- poor allocation of space
- abandonment

III. Theft
- stealing money
- stealing property
- stealing possessions
- stealing insurance
- extortion of property
- extortion of possessions
- extortion of insurance

Note. From Tanya Johnson, ''Critical Issues in the Definition of Elder Mistreatment,'' by Tanya Johnson, in *ELDER ABUSE: Conflict in the Family*, K.A. Pillemer and R.S. Wolf, eds. Copyright 1986 by Auburn House Publishing Company, an imprint of Greenwood Publishing Group, Inc., Dover, MA. Reprinted with permission.

the sociological model focuses on the relationship between the perpetrator and the victim of abuse, considering their interaction in the past and present and also the family dynamics that provide the context for that interaction. The *dependency or stress model* maintains that functional dependency, arising either from physical or psychological impairment, leads to frustration or resentment and eventually to mistreatment of elders. A variation of this model attempts to predict elder mistreatment by examining the balance or reciprocity between gains and losses experienced in the relationship (George, 1986). An alternative is to view such helping behavior as part of a normative commitment to provide care to loved ones without expectation of reward. Mistreatment would arise in this model when the threshold for such unconditional helping behavior is exceeded (George, 1986). A third variation proposes that the abusive caregiver feels powerless in relationship to the victim and the mistreatment is a response to that sense of powerlessness (Finkelhor, 1983; Pillemer, 1986).

The modest research that has been accomplished to date has led investigators to recast concepts of the etiology of elder mistreatment in a number of ways. The earlier studies of elder mistreatment (Beachler, 1979; Hudson & Johnson, 1986; Lau & Kosberg, 1979; O'Malley, et al., 1979), which used samples of convenience obtained from service agency registries, suggested, as previously noted, that the typical victim was a woman in her 70s who suffered from mental or physical impairments affecting her capacity to perform daily living tasks (O'Malley, Everitt, O'Malley, & Campion, 1983). Her functional impairments were a source of stress for the caregiver, and her frailties left her relatively defenseless. It was assumed that the abuser was motivated by deviant personality or greed and was not primarily concerned with the welfare of the victim.

Such depictions have prompted some to suggest that the literature on abuse and neglect has painted a far less sympathetic view of these problems in the elderly than in children or younger adults (Sengstock & Hwalek, 1987). With little question this literature supports the sometimes agist view of the elderly as disabled, dependent, and demanding. A quite different appraisal of elder abuse arises when elder mistreatment is viewed in the context of the burgeoning literature on the family and its place in caregiving to the elderly. Families provide the vast majority of home care to the elderly in need (Shanas, 1980). Functional disability is found in 20% to 45% of the elderly, depending on the criteria used. Among persons 70 or older, the rates reach well over 50% (Soldo & Myllylaoma, 1983). But, at any time, only 5% of those over 65 years of age are institutionalized, which leaves the vast majority of disabled elderly to be cared for at home. Furthermore, the position of the family as caregiver is changing. As the mean age of the population rises, as the number of very old increases, and as social forces (e.g., lower birth rate, more women in the work force, increased rates of divorce and remarriage) complicate family caregiving patterns, the demands on families for caregiving will increase as well.

It is not surprising, therefore, that most cases of elder mistreatment occur within families. There is little doubt that providing care to an impaired older person may affect the caregiver's emotional state, living pattern, health, and social relationships (Morycz, 1985). Sengstock and Hwalek (1987) maintain that caregiver burden has not received adequate attention as a risk factor in elder abuse.

Recent research on elder mistreatment supports the relevance of caregiving issues but calls on professionals to differentiate their thinking about etiology according to the type of mistreatment in question. Regarding the abuser (see Chapter 13), it has not been possible to document the stereotype of the abuser as motivated by deviant personality or greed. On the other hand, there is considerable reason to suspect that alcohol abuse is a predictor of elder abuse and neglect (Pillemer, 1986) and that psychiatric disorders are more prevalent among abusers. Wolf (1986) found that 31% of elder abusers reported a history of psychiatric illness and 43% had substance abuse problems. Both observations suggest that the perpetrator of abuse frequently has psychiatric problems that may be amenable to treatment. Furthermore, this association of psychiatric disorders with the perpetrators of mistreatment seems particularly valid for cases of physical abuse and, perhaps to a lesser extent, psychological abuse. Also, in these types of abuse, but not in neglect or material abuse cases, there often is a history of a long-standing disturbance in the relationship between the victim and perpetrator (Wolf, Godkin, & Pillemer, 1984).

It could be argued that this finding of increased psychiatric disorders among the perpetrators of elder mistreatment is simply a variation on the original, if crude, version of the psychopathological model of elder mistreatment. The *dependency/stress* model of elder mistreatment has taken two unexpected turns, however, as investigators have looked more carefully at the relationship between the participants in such cases. The original hypothesis that abuse was a reaction to the victim's dependency arose from descriptive studies of cases identified by agencies involved in elder mistreatment. Examining the hypothesis in controlled studies and using more narrowly defined samples of victims, however, led to an unexpected finding: abused elderly are not more impaired than elderly controls (Phillips, 1983) and, in some respects, may be less impaired (Pillemer, 1986). The second and even more remarkable finding, which has now been reported by several investigators in this area, is that perpetrators of elder mistreatment are dependent on their victims, at least financially (Hwalek, Sengstock, & Lawrence, 1986; Pillemer, 1986; Wolf et al., 1984), and possibly with respect to housing, household repair, and transportation as well (Pillemer, 1986).

This revision of the dependency/stress model needs cautious interpretation. First, Pillemer's study (1986) dealt only with cases of physical abuse, which limits the generalizability of this finding. Furthermore, in this study the assessment of abuser's dependency on the victim was based on the victim's appraisal of the relationship. Data on the *abuser's* perception of the relationship was not included. In addition, though, it should be noted that in looking for factors that predict elder abuse, there is a risk of misinterpreting data obtained from control groups. In the studies just cited, the comparable levels of functional capacity shown by abused and nonabused elderly have been interpreted to suggest that functional dependency of the victim is not a major risk factor for elder abuse (Pillemer, 1986). However, the studies in question used control groups drawn from caseloads of the agencies from which the abuse victims were drawn. Therefore, the functional status of the controls was probably not representative of all elderly. A more precise interpretation of such a controlled comparison is that given two groups of comparably impaired elderly, variables other than functional dependency will be predictive of abuse. But this is a different statement from the assertion that functional impairment of the victim is unrelated to abuse. A test of this hypothesis would entail comparing abuse rates in samples that *differ* in level of impairment. For example, it would be appropriate to use a control group of normal elderly persons. More generally, the pursuit of "critical risk factors" may be misleading. Findings need to be viewed in the context of the variables that have, in effect, been incorporated into the methodology of a study. Simply put, evaluation of etiological models involves evaluating the relative weights of multiple variables. Talking about critical factors invites the inference that there is one factor or variable that should be sufficient to predict elder mistreatment. However, there is a dearth of multivariate statistical analyses in the literature dealing with risk factors for elder mistreatment (see, however, the multivariate study of Phillips, 1983). Furthermore, once such variables are found to discriminate between abuse and nonabuse cases, it will be necessary to demonstrate that they actually have a "dose-response" relationship to the index of abuse that is used. In other words, if the measurement of mistreatment is objectified so that it can be treated as a dimension having intensity and density attributes (Johnson, 1986), it would be important to show that the severity of mistreatment can be predicted, in a multivariate fashion, by the weight of the different variables that are of etiological importance.

This current research suggests a complex relationship between the proposed models to explain elder abuse and neglect. Characteristics of the perpetrator and the victim, their association over time, and the social circumstances in which they live seem to vary according to the type and manifestation of abuse. As summarized by Wolf (1986), elder neglect seems most closely to fit what used to be considered the typical profile of elder mistreatment. Victims of neglect seem most likely to have physical or mental problems that render them dependent on a caregiver. As a correlate of these factors, they tend to be older and female. Neglect victims are more likely to live by themselves and to have a smaller support system (Pillemer & Finkelhor, 1988; Wolf, 1986).

Psychological abuse cases are marked by psychiatric disorders in the victim and perpetrator and, presumably as a correlate of this fact, a history of conflictual interpersonal relationships. In contrast to neglect cases, victims of psychological abuse are relatively self-sufficient and unimpaired in terms of their cognitive abilities and physical health. Cases of physical abuse are marked by emotional disturbance and dependency on the part of the perpetrator, complicated again by a history of disturbed relationships between victim and perpetrator.

Cases of material abuse fit a different pattern than other types of mistreatment. Here the important factors are that the perpetrator is a distant relative or nonrelative, not emotionally or otherwise closely involved with caregiving, and that victims of material abuse seem to accrue vulnerability through their social isolation.

Rates of Abuse and Neglect

Until recently, estimates of the rates of elder abuse and neglect were based on data from cases already identified by social service agencies or other organizations formally involved in the treatment of these conditions. Because such detected cases are unlikely to provide accurate measures of the rates or profiles of abuse, estimates of the actual situation required investigators to deal with many unknowns in extrapolating to the population as a whole. Predictably, the estimates of prevalence rates ranged widely, from figures of around 1% (Gioglio & Blakemore, 1983) to as high as 10% (Steinmetz, 1981). The 1981 report of the Select Committee on Aging (U.S. House of Representatives, 1981, 1985) maintained that abuse was widespread and underreported, affecting an estimated 4% of those over 65.

Many factors contribute to the variability in the rates and types of reported elder mistreatment. Problems in definition have already been discussed. Relying on agencies for identifying cases has obvious artifacts as well. Previous random sample studies were limited by either low response rates (Block & Sinnott, 1979) or small sample size (Gioglio & Blakemore, 1983). Thus, the study of elder mistreatment has taken an important step forward in the recently completed study conducted by Pillemer and Finkelhor (1988) at the University of New Hampshire Family Violence Research Program. Based on a stratified random sample study of 2020 community-elders in Boston who were interviewed either by telephone or in person, it was estimated that some form of elder mistreatment (physical violence, verbal aggression, or neglect) was present in 3.2% of the elderly population. This rate is slightly higher than the upper bound of the confidence interval found in the study of Gioglio and Blakemore, but it is relatively close to the 4% figure often cited (U.S. House of Representatives, 1981, 1985).

Finally, there is the question of the relative rates of different types of elder mistreatment. This is particularly unsure ground because inconsistencies in definition have immediate effects on the rates found. Some impressions can be gathered from the existing literature, keeping in mind that problems of definition, reliance on reported cases, and a paucity of population-based studies again mean that conclusions will change considerably in the coming years.

Most instances of elder mistreatment are recurrent (Boydston & McNairn, 1981; O'Malley et al., 1979). Reports on the most common forms of elder mistreatment vary. Many have found that neglect is the most common form, occurring in 60% to 65% of cases (Block, 1983; Douglass et al., 1980; Rounds, 1985; Valentine & Cash, 1986). However, some have found psychological (Block & Sinnott, 1979; Hageboeck & Brandt, 1981) or physical abuse (Lau & Kosberg, 1979) the most frequent. Financial exploitation and, particularly, violation of rights are less common forms of elder mistreatment, although exceptions have been found (Gioglio & Blakemore, 1983). In the population-based study of Pillemer and Finkelhor (1988), the rates for the three types of mistreatment surveyed were 2.0% for physical violence, 1.1% for chronic verbal aggression, and a strikingly low 0.4% for neglect, although the latter may reflect restrictive definitions and procedures for identifying neglect (L. Phillips, personal communication, January 1989).

Although uncertainty remains regarding the rates of elder mistreatment overall or in terms of its subtypes, it can be said with reasonable certainty that elder mistreatment occurs in all racial, ethnic, and socioeconomic groups (Steuer & Austin, 1980), perhaps with equal rates for each (Pillemer & Finkelhor, 1988). Men (Pennsylvania Department of Aging, 1982), women (Steinmetz, 1983), and adult children (Sengstock & Laing, 1982) all may be the perpetrators of elder mistreatment. However, it has been suggested (Finkelhor, 1983) that when the probability of mistreatment is corrected for by the amount of time the perpetrator of abuse spends with the victim, men are considerably more likely than women to be responsible for elder mistreatment. In the study of Pillemer and Finkelhor (1988), perpetrators of abuse turned out more often to be spouses than children or unrelated individuals. In either case, in the vast majority of occurrences those who mistreat elders are members of the victim's family and, in fact, usually live with the victim (Pillemer, 1985).

Pillemer and Finkelhor (1988) found nearly equal numbers of men and women in their sample of victims, which is an exception to the rule that women far outnumber men in convenience samples. This exception is even more dramatic, though, when the absolute numbers are converted to probabilities by adjusting for the number of men and women in the population. When this is done, the risk of abuse for men was twice that for women (5.1% vs. 2.3%). On the other hand, the severity of the mistreatment tends to be greater for women, which may explain the higher risks reported for women in samples drawn from agency registries. In other words, women may be more likely to come to the attention of social agencies because they have been more severely injured (Pillemer & Finkelhor, 1988).

CONSEQUENCES

There is little information regarding the long-term consequences of elder abuse. In fact, information is still limited regarding the immediate consequences of elder abuse. Available information is primarily concerned with the physical and, to a lesser extent, with the psychological state of victims. Even less is known about the consequences of abuse on the abuser, although some useful information can be garnered by viewing the problem in terms of caregiver strain.

The physical injuries sustained by abuse victims (see Table 6.1) may be internal or external, mental or physical, temporary or permanent. Bruises, burns, abrasions, lacerations, fractures, and contractures are all seen. The patterns of these physical injuries may be symptomatic of the method of physical abuse. For example, wrist or leg abrasions may reflect the use of restraints. Decubitus sores may be a symptom of confinement or a complication of medical deterioration, which itself may be symptomatic of neglect. Sores on the skin often reflect blunt trauma but may be difficult to distinguish from burns. Loss of hair or scalp discoloration from subcutaneous bleeding may be caused by hair pulling (Rathbone-McCuan & Voyles, 1982).

Medical or psychiatric problems resulting from mistreatment are even more likely to be overlooked. The consequences of neglect are particularly likely to manifest themselves in this way. Thus, failure of a caregiver to ensure adequate hydration, nutrition, or compliance with medical treatments may result in physical deterioration. Perpetrators may dispense with these symptoms by attributing them to medical disease. More subtle evidences of mental or physical deterioration, such as weakness, malaise, lack of energy, apathy, depression, or cognitive impairment are susceptible to the more insidious attribution that they are the result of aging itself. Using aging as an explanation represents double jeopardy for the client because it implies not only that treatment is unnecessary, but that there is really no problem.

The psychological state of the victim may be understandably altered by abuse or neglect and may provide clues to their existence. Perhaps the most useful general principle is that virtually all psychiatric symptoms may represent sequelae of mistreatment. Cognitive, perceptual, or emotional symptoms of any sort may be present, including frank delusions or hallucinations. The sensory deprivation associated with severe neglect may itself be responsible for such psychotic changes. Thus, psychiatric symptoms may indicate some diagnosable psychiatric disorder that has been instigated or aggravated by the conditions of mistreatment. Either the stress of mistreatment or the neglect of needed treatment may be the responsible mechanism. Realizing that mistreatment can precipitate psychiatric disorders avoids the fallacy of concluding that abuse and neglect have not occurred because the symptoms in question are caused by some condition that one assumes cannot be a response to external stressors.

Psychiatric symptoms may also reflect whatever personal meanings the victim attaches to the prospect of intervention. Victims of abuse may anticipate an episode of physical abuse after a visit from an outsider (Quinn & Tomita, 1986). As a result, their behavior in the presence of the professional may be marked by fear. It is important not to mistake this fear, or associated symptoms such as reticence, withdrawal, avoidance, or disorganization for aging or mental illness (Rathbone-McCuan & Voyles, 1982).

The consequences of abuse and neglect on the perpetrator have received little attention. The literature on caregiver burden suggests that, for at least some abusers, the circumstances that have led to abuse have taken their toll on the abuser as well. The dependency/stress model, in fact, is based on this notion. The aged need assistance when they no longer are able to carry out activities of daily living. This includes not only self-care tasks, such as bathing or dressing, but also instrumental activities, such as preparing meals, taking medication appropriately, or handling finances. These problems are particularly important in dementing diseases, such as Alzheimer's disease, or in conditions associated with marked motor impairments, such as Parkinson's disease or arthritis. When an older family member becomes ill or disabled, the modified extended family is usually the first resource for emotional support, crisis intervention, social support, and community linkages (Shanas, 1980). However, the cognitive, behavioral, and functional impairments produced by dementia and other conditions create considerable stress on caregiving relatives. Thus, the consequences of abuse on the caregiver include these changes: (a) emotional state, including feelings of depression, anger, embarrassment, loneliness, guilt, or anxiety; (b) living patterns, such as reduced privacy, decreased socialization, or disruption in household routine; (c) relationships of the elder with other family members or friends; and (d) physical health of the caregiver, including both real or imagined illnesses (Coppel, Burton, Becker, & Fiore, 1985; George & Gwyther, 1986; Snyder & Keefe, 1985). Spouse caregivers often find that all of their other outside roles shrink to that of caregiver; children and other relatives often have to deal with too many roles (or roles that compete or conflict). In any case, role exhaustion appears to be the end point of role strain due to overload, conflict, or constriction (Morycz, 1985). Many families collapse under the strain, and this may be a major factor in the decision to institutionalize (Morycz, 1985; Ross & Kedward, 1977; Tobin & Kulys, 1981). Support to the family is therefore crucial in maintaining the older individual in the community (Zarit, Reeves, & Bach-Peterson, 1980). If this support is inadequate, however, the same interventions that prevent institutionalization may increase the risk of abuse because they continue the exposure of the elder victim to the burdened caregiver.

TREATMENT

In principle, the treatment of elder abuse is straightforward. After a comprehensive assessment that attends to the medical, psychological, and socioenvironmental dimensions of the victim and the suspected abuser, one optimizes the medical and psychiatric status of the victim and introduces those clinical, interpersonal, legal, financial, and community interventions that will alleviate or terminate those conditions and stressors that maintain abuse. In the process, priority is given to the values and rights of the victim.

In practice, of course, there are many obstacles to accomplishing this task. It may be difficult to obtain the needed information from clients themselves or from third parties, who may be neighbors, relatives, or social agencies (Powell & Berg, 1987). Even if the necessary information is obtainable, it may be impossible to secure the cooperation of the victim and perpetrator in the proposed treatment program. Or, even if the content of an effective treatment is obvious, there may be obstacles deriving from the values of either the client or the professional that constitute insurmountable ethical dilemmas (Matlaw & Mayer, 1986; Quinn, 1985). Finally, treatment may falter because the needed resources are unavailable—either they do not exist or bureaucratic requirements make them inaccessible (Faulkner, 1982). Thus, in practice, numerous factors interact to determine the content and outcome of treatment (Phillips & Rempusheski, 1985).

Keeping these complexities in mind, the treatment of elder abuse may be divided into three overlapping stages: identification, assessment, and management or intervention (Hudson, 1986). Case identification entails establishing procedures for receiving and responding to referrals and for carrying out preliminary steps in gathering and organizing data that will be of use at the initial contact. Assessment focuses on establishing a relationship with the caregiver and victim and then gathering, through the process of interviewing, observing, and recording, the further data on which to base diagnosis and interventions. This should include gathering collateral data from neighbors or other agencies. One of the goals of assessment is detection: that is, the determination that mistreatment is actually occurring. In almost all states, there are mandatory reporting laws to facilitate detection (Salend, Kane, Satz, & Pynoos, 1984; Traxler, 1986). However, numerous practical, legal, and ethical problems are involved in mandating the reporting of suspected cases (Faulkner, 1982). Furthermore, policy differences from state to state complicate the interaction between detection and reporting. Professionals who provide care or services to the elderly are urged to familiarize themselves with the regulations that affect their responsibilities. The third stage of treatment is the management, or intervention, phase. It consists of those actions carried out to alleviate suffering or injury and to prevent further mistreatment. The object of these interventions includes the victim and the caregiver at a minimum. Other members of the family and support system may also be included.

Assessment

The methods and goals involved in the assessment and treatment of abuse and neglect will vary to some extent with the discipline of the professional (Crouse, Cobb, Harris, Kopecky, & Poertner, 1981). Ideally, the assessment of elder abuse and neglect is carried out by a multidisciplinary team of professionals (Council on Scientific Affairs, 1987). Usually this requires implementation through a hospital setting (Carr et al., 1986) although, in principle, collaborative efforts of concerned organizations within a single community may facilitate this process (Lau, 1986). Professionals who are not primarily involved in elder abuse probably face the greatest challenge: to be cognizant of the possibility of elder mistreatment, to suspect it based on subtle or indirect cues, and to initiate the clinical, social, and legal steps that may be needed for proper intervention. Clinicians who detect cases in their own practices may have the advantage of an existing relationship with the suspected victim or perpetrator. They are saved, therefore, the problem of establishing a relationship that can serve as the basis for further care. This very advantage, however, places the clinician's objectivity at stake. There are few clinicians who will not be prone to rationalize suggestive evidence in a way that denies the possibility of abuse (Rathbone-McCuan & Voyles, 1982). Furthermore, when a professional, trusting relationship exists, clinicians will have to press themselves doubly hard so that they do not compromise their evaluation out of fear of losing their client's affection, respect, or patronage.

Regardless of the setting in which one detects elder mistreatment, assessment entails a combination of objectivity and intuition. A relatively fixed protocol must be followed to obtain the information necessary to guide management (Anderson & Thobaben, 1984; Fulmer & Wetle, 1986; Sengstock, Hwalek, & Moshier, 1986). At the same time, a variety of intangible impressions, based on observing one's own emotional responses and the process of the interviews with client and caregiver, are important in developing an optimal assessment and treatment plan. Proper management of suspected cases of elder abuse requires careful attention to both the process and content of this information gathering.

With regard to the content of assessment, the general recommendation is that professionals employ a formal assessment outline or schedule specifying the types of information that must be gathered. The content areas of such an assessment tool should permit a characterization of the circumstances of mistreatment in terms of the psychological, social, medical functional, financial, and legal circumstances of the victim and perpetrator (Sengstock & Hwalek, 1987). Care is needed in choosing an instrument for this purpose because, until recently, those available overrepresented risk factor information, ignored some kinds of abuse, and required little information concerning actual evidence of abuse or neglect (Sengstock & Hwalek, 1987). Several fairly new assessment devices (Fulmer & Wetle, 1986; Sengstock et al., 1986) may represent improvements in these areas by (a) incorporating information from multiple sources or multiple visits, (b) systematically inquiring about a more complete range of types of abuse and neglect, (c) relying on both direct and indirect indicators of mistreatment, and (d) attempting to document intentionality (Sengstock et al., 1986).

Information gathered in the identification stage permits reconstruction of the events and concerns that led to the assessment itself. This would include the individuals or agencies involved in making the initial referral. The con-

ditions under which referral was actually initiated may provide useful indicators of elder mistreatment. For example, was the client's condition first
reported by a concerned neighbor instead of a family member? Did the
patient first present to an emergency room unaccompanied by an appropriate
caregiver or demonstrating signs of inadequate medical care (Quinn & Tomita, 1986)?

When the client is first seen, the basic elements of a clinical assessment
should be carried out. If the client is seen in a medical setting, this will
include a full medical examination. Even when this is not the case, in-home
medical evaluation by a visiting nurse or physician should be planned. However, any professional involved in the evaluation of elder mistreatment should
have sufficient clinical skills to perform a formal assessment of mental status,
including an appropriate profile of cognitive capacity (Folstein, Folstein, &
McHugh, 1975), an assessment of functional capacity (Lawton, 1976), and
an evaluation of the patient's general medical status. The mental status
should include a description of the patient's general behavior, speech, mood
and affect, thought content, insight, and judgment. Standardized assessment
tools for evaluating functional capacity and cognitive capacity (Kane &
Kane, 1981) are preferred to unstructured descriptive assessment (Quinn &
Tomita, 1986; Rathbone-McCuan & Voyles, 1982; Tomita, 1982). The professional should be skilled at recognizing evidence of dehydration and malnutrition or other frank signs of medical debility. Visible signs of injury
should be documented carefully, including drawings and measurements or,
when appropriate, photographs.

The foregoing information will be of general use in determining that the
client's health and well-being are compromised. It also plays a crucial role
in helping the professional determine the patient's competence to make
decisions on his/her own behalf. This will be of particular importance in the
management phase if the client is unwilling to take actions that would, by
conventional standards, seem to be in his or her own best interest.

More specific to the assessment of mistreatment is the inquiry into the
victim's appraisal of the situation. Does he/she report having been the target
of specific acts such as hitting, shoving, burning, insults, ridicule, confinement, deprivation of food or medical care (see Table 6.1)? In what ways is
the victim dependent on his/her caregiver? Does the victim need emotional
support? Is there financial dependency, impaired self-care ability, or limited
mobility? Does he/she rationalize the mistreatment and, if so, what explanations are used to justify the perpetrator's behavior? If there are discrete
episodes of abuse, can the victim identify his/her own specific behaviors or,
perhaps, other circumstances (e.g., alcohol consumption by the perpetrator)
that serve as precipitants? What actions have been taken or contemplated
to change the situation? What are the anticipated advantages and disadvantages of interventions that might be undertaken with outside assistance?

Turning from the content to the process of assessment, there is probably
no step more stressful in the management of elder abuse than the profes-

sional's first contact with the alleged perpetrator and victim of elder abuse. Particularly when such contact occurs at the individual's home, real jeopardy exists for the professional. Quinn and Tomita (1986) provide numerous recommendations for the management of this first contact. They also provide leads to a broader literature concerning such approaches as crisis intervention, negotiation, and persuasion techniques. The interested reader is urged to read their lengthier, highly informative discussion. Much of the remainder of this section is drawn from their presentation.

Quinn and Tomita (1986) advise the professional to be prepared with a range of approaches because the first contact with the clients may vary from a desperate desire for as much help as possible to a total and, perhaps, threatening refusal to allow even the briefest discussion. Therefore, considerable preparation is called for prior to making the first visit to a client's home. If other agencies have been involved in the case, their reports should be reviewed. Talking directly to the previous caseworkers may be highly useful in identifying possible pitfalls or key pieces of information. The preceding caseworker may remain involved, at least for the purpose of accompanying the professional to the first meeting.

Regardless of the referral route, arrangements for the initial contact should be made in advance, by talking directly to the victim. Telephone messages or written requests can go astray easily. Upon arrival at the client's home, it may be difficult to secure the cooperation of caregiver or possible victim. Access can often be obtained simply through a competent and friendly professional demeanor, combined with a statement of one's desire to obtain information that will be of potential use to both the caregiver and care recipient.

Faced with a client who does not agree to any assessment at all, professionals have a range of approaches at their disposal. The best one will depend on the particulars of each case. Their common goal is to shift a conflict situation to a treatment situation. One approach is to offer incentives. The professional can suggest specific potential benefits, indicate the possibility of being an advocate to the caregiver, express concern for the needs of the victim or the caregiver, or offer emotional support by alluding to the likely burden experienced by the caregiver (Goodwin, 1985). More direct appeals to power or authority may be needed in other situations. Professionals can refer to their own obligations to fulfill duties mandated by social or legal institutions. One can also allude to involving police or other legal authorities.

Quinn and Tomita (1986) further urge the professional to interview the victim first and to ensure that this interview take place in private. The privacy of the interview situation should be made clear to the elderly client. This may alleviate fears of discovery or retribution. Equally important, it prevents the caregiver from eliminating inconsistencies in information that will serve later as important clues to the existence of abuse.

Often the victim will be reluctant to talk candidly about abuse or neglect. When there is incongruity between the victim's words and other facts (e.g., affective evidence of fearfulness or blatant evidence of poor living conditions or physical neglect; Rathbone-McCuan & Goodstein, 1985), the professional is at risk of impugning the candor or integrity of either victim or caregiver. Such discrepancies may also prompt suspicions of dishonesty, collusion, or withholding. However, such conclusions go beyond the facts and emotionalize the professional's judgments (Quinn & Tomita, 1986; Rathbone-McCuan & Voyles, 1982). It is preferable simply to keep track of these findings and to follow up on them as part of further assessment.

In the initial evaluation, it is crucial to carry out a careful search for physical or observational data that suggest abuse or neglect. The physical condition of the victim and his/her living circumstances must be carefully evaluated. The victim or caregiver may suggest that physical problems, such as bruises, dehydration, or poor vision, are due to unavoidable falls, poor physician care, or aging processes. At this stage, however, these interpretations are of secondary importance, except for elucidating the judgment and problem-solving capacities of the caregiver or recipient. Rather, the focus is on observing and documenting the concrete facts of the situation. As suggested already, verbal descriptions, body maps, and photographs facilitate the process of documentation.

The next step in the assessment phase is the interview of the suspected perpetrator. The plan to do so should be shared with the client and should include explicit reassurance regarding the confidentiality of the information that has already been shared. If the victim is apprehensive, it may be helpful to give an example of what one actually might say to the caregiver. This will allay the client's fantasies that the professional may unwittingly undermine the confidences that have been shared. For example, one might say:

> I'm going to tell your son something like this. "Your mother and I have been talking about ways in which I might be of help to her. Because you are so closely involved in her day-to-day care, I wouldn't want to make any plans without getting your description of what her needs are and what you think should be done to help her."

The interview of the caregiver should take place immediately after the client interview. Assumptions about the caregiver's role—either positive or negative—should be avoided. This makes for a more effective demeanor with the caregiver—objective, concerned, open-minded—and also is consistent with the goals of this phase of the evaluation: to gather all information from which a diagnosis and formulation will later be developed. It is easy to be misled by one's emotional response. Caregivers who describe numerous stresses and losses and underscore their good intentions are likely to elicit sympathy. A caregiver who seems formal or dispassionate may elicit suspiciousness or anger, particularly if the client is obviously in poor health. Although both of these reactions may be valid, they can shift the professional's expectations in misleading ways. When feeling sympathetic, there is the risk of failing to identify evidence that the well-intended caregiver is also benefiting financially from the relationship. One might, for example, feel guilty about reviewing financial records that would show excessive expenditures. When feeling angry at a guarded caregiver, one may mistake personality traits of guardedness for intention to harm and thereby fail to gather the information that would document efficient use of limited resources or the existence of multiple stressors for which this guarded caregiver is reluctant to seek help.

From a strategic standpoint, it is easier to elicit the caregiver's cooperation by making the victim's well-being the focus of evaluation. Thus, questions may deal with descriptions of the client's behavior, emotions, medical needs, or functional capacity. In order to shift the focus to the caregiver, further questions may then address the way the client deals with the caregiver. What happens when the client needs help with walking, washing, and eating? Potentially accusatory questions should be couched in terms that, again, are client-focused and are supportive of the caregiver's role. For example, "There obviously are times when your mother needs more help than you can provide. Whom do you turn to then?" When it is clear that the caregiver is defensive about an issue, it may be helpful to embed the issue of concern in a statement that does not require an explicit acknowledgment of the problem at first. For a caregiver who is reluctant to acknowledge anger, one might say, "Obviously, you have a huge responsibility in caring for your wife. But you're only human. What do you do to deal with those moments of frustration that come when she won't do what she needs to?"

It is hoped that some degree of trust and candor exists when the time comes to ask questions about specific acts. Most questions can still be asked with implied support. For example, "Can you help me understand how your mother became so _____ [bruised, dehydrated, malnourished]?" Even questions about specific acts can be implicitly supportive to some extent, such as "Have you ever felt so frustrated that you felt like hitting her . . . or may have done so?"

Another approach for introducing sensitive topics is to offer the caregiver a list of some of the varied reactions that people in his predicament sometimes experience. Some will be readily endorsed, others not. The listener's response will be informative in two ways. They may endorse one reaction explicitly; this may entail an acknowledgment of one problem or excessive denial of another. In addition, there may be a nonverbal change (e.g., in facial expression or eye gaze) that the professional can use as a gauge of what is actually happening at home.

Management and Interventions

Management of elder abuse is determined by the results of assessment, the discipline and goals of the professional responsible for care, and the strengths and resources of the client, including his or her family and community.

Because of the breadth of problems and possible interventions, it is desirable, as noted earlier, to use a multidisciplinary approach in treatment (Ambrogi & London, 1985; Carr et al., 1986; Council on Scientific Affairs, 1987). When this is done, one individual should be identified as the case coordinator or case manager to ensure that there is continuity and integration of services. In most instances, this individual will also serve as the primary therapist or clinician.

Approach to Treatment

Before starting treatment, it is advisable to develop a formulation of the case that identifies the nature (abuse, neglect, or some other form of mistreatment) and severity of the case, the manifestations of mistreatment (psychological, physical, neglect), the risk factors for continued mistreatment, and the characteristics of the victim or abuser that determine his or her willingness and competence to accept treatment. Care should be taken to note strengths or potentials that exist on the part of victim, abuser, extended family, or the community that can be harnessed in order to improve the likelihood of success. The formulation and, therefore, the treatment plan, will evolve as time goes on because much important information will be gathered only after several weeks or months of contact (O'Malley et al., 1983).

Of immediate importance in considering treatment options is to determine the urgency of the case and the competence of the victim. Abuse and neglect cases may represent crises because of imminent medical, financial, or legal problems. In such situations, the professional must be prepared to act rapidly to arrange immediate hospitalization, protection of material resources, or separation of victim and perpetrator, either through emergency placement of the victim or through legal measures. The matter of competency will interact with each of these considerations when the victim disagrees with the professional's judgment that mistreatment is occurring or requires intervention. Competency also is important if the victim must execute legal or financial arrangements. Therefore, at an early point in the assessment process, it is prudent to make a preliminary judgment as to the client's competency to protect his or her own rights and interests and, in particular, to refuse treatment (Quinn & Tomita, 1986; Roth, Meisel, & Lidz, 1977).

In the beginning stages of treatment, it is helpful to distinguish between short-term and long-term treatment goals (Quinn & Tomita, 1986). Top priority must be given, of course, to terminating abusive acts and to safeguarding victims, their property, or their rights when there is immediate danger. Even when one is involved in individual or family-oriented psychotherapy, it is important to make it clear to all involved that, whatever else may be accomplished, the prevention of further mistreatment is a first priority (Quinn & Tomita, 1986; Rathbone-McCuan & Voyles, 1982).

With short-term treatments, the major goals are to terminate abusive acts, provide appropriate medical or psychiatric treatment for clinical problems, and to provide both the victim and caregiver with the personal or community supports that will reduce caregiver strain or mutual dependency. In short-term treatments, it is important to establish a trusting relationship with the clients, but one should not seek or expect those additional qualities that can only be developed with extended treatment programs. Short-term treatment will also be more concerned with identifying concrete behaviors that serve either as provocations or rewards for abuse. Once identified, the professional attempts to educate both the victim and the caregiver as to the impact of these behaviors and to provide alternate responses at the critical times so that provocative behaviors are less likely to occur (Quinn & Tomita, 1986). Another approach is to determine the purpose or reward of the abusive behavior for the abuser. For example, the abuser may report that after an abusive episode, "At least I have a few hours to myself," or "I have a chance to talk to my friends without being interrupted all the time." Whatever the outcome of abuse identified in this way, helping the abuser find other ways of obtaining needs may be effective in decreasing the frequency of further episodes. Simply knowing that a responsible individual from outside the family is monitoring or poised to act upon further incidents will often serve as a restraint on the perpetrator (L. Phillips, personal communication, January 1989).

In long-term treatment situations, one continues those actions that realize the goals of short-term treatment. Now, however, there is opportunity to address risk factors for abuse that are long-standing characteristics of the victim, the perpetrator, or the family system that includes them. A long-term treatment program offers greater opportunity to develop trust and familiarity. These, in turn, enable the professional to address attitudinal or characterological resistances to treatment. For example, the victim who overvalues loyalty to the abuser may have an opportunity to reevaluate priorities so that he/she can contemplate legal steps to gain protection from further abuse. Victims who feel guilty because of their dependency and, therefore, undeserving of better treatment, may be able to acquire a more positive sense of entitlement. Or, in a family where an abused mother is fearful of living elsewhere because she thinks her retarded son will be unable to manage independently, the professional may be able to aid both by working with the son to acquire social supports or vocational skills that will reassure the mother about her son's future.

Methods of Treatment

CLINICAL SKILLS.   General clinical skills help professionals develop a relationship in which they are seen as a concerned, competent source of knowledge and assistance, capable of dealing empathically with interpersonal conflict or emotional turmoil, while remaining prepared to take actions or positions that will end the abusive behavior. Ensuring proper diagnosis and management of psychiatric disorders, especially depression, is an essential part of treating abuse and neglect.

PROVIDING INFORMATION OR EDUCATION.   This method can serve diverse needs or problems. It is particularly effective for those clients who agree that there is a problem warranting treatment. For the victim who wants help but is unaware that it is available, providing information about the availability of in-home services, alternative living arrangements, or legal steps that can be taken to protect property may be helpful. Knowledge of the availability of in-home services, respite care, or senior companions may be equally useful for the caregiver. For the burdened caregiver it may be helpful to know that the behaviors presented by a mentally impaired parent are expectable symptoms of a dementing disease. Education of the caregiver can also include specific suggestions on the management of such difficult behaviors as wandering, nocturnal disruption, screaming, or suspiciousness (Zarit, Anthony, & Boutselis, 1987). Thus, both information and education can be vehicles for *acquiring new skills* that are useful to the caregiver in managing his or her own situation. Such skills may range from the caregiver's learning new ways to help an elder victim bathe or walk, to arranging, without a professional's help, for in-home services or respite care at appropriate intervals.

ACCURATE LABELING OF BEHAVIORS AND THEIR CONSEQUENCES.   This aspect of providing information deserves emphasis for those cases in which denial, ignorance, or impaired judgment prevent clients from recognizing the dangers of continued mistreatment. Making such labels useful requires that victims or perpetrators learn to think and talk differently about their situation. The professional should plan to repeat such important information periodically.

COUNSELING OR PSYCHOTHERAPY STRATEGIES.   Such strategies come into play when the victim or perpetrator presents behaviors, attitudes, or beliefs that are risk factors for mistreatment and does not recognize or effectively deal with them as such. Thus, some of these counseling issues will overlap in content with the agenda of educational approaches (e.g., helping a victim relabel mistreatment as abuse so that it is no longer viewed as a normative part of aging). More complicated agendas arise in dealing with characterological or attitudinal issues that have been prized as virtues throughout much of one's life but which now serve as immediate impediments to accepting treatment. For example, elders with lifelong tendencies to meet adversity stoically or to regard unpleasant emotions as private are unlikely to participate in treatment. Unflagging loyalty to family members may equally stand in the way of treatment. So, too, can an exaggerated sense of responsibility that can translate itself into an overvaluing of control or a tendency to blame one's self for everything (Kosberg, 1988). In undertaking treatment for such issues, it is helpful to have at hand more than one approach to psychotherapy. Family and group therapies have been used in the treatment of elder abuse (Goodwin, 1985; Quinn & Tomita, 1986). It also may be helpful to use family (Anderson & Stewart, 1983) or strategic approaches (Fisch, Weakland, & Segal, 1982) that have been developed for difficult cases.

As an illustration of a strategic approach, consider an elderly mother of a psychologically dependent, but verbally abusive, son. How might one work with the mother if her son has denied abuse and she is unwilling to set limits on him directly? She rationalizes his behavior by saying that pressuring him to stop the abuse or to get a job would exacerbate the insecurities he already feels because of his inability to leave home. She may believe that the best way to help him is to give him a model of strength and independence. "He needs me to be strong," she asserts. The result, however, is that she reinforces the abuse because her tolerance really entails a good deal of helpless pleading during and after the abusive episodes. Telling her to assert herself will only make her feel more guilty and helpless, thus making her a more inviting target for her son's sense of powerlessness and dependency. In such a situation, a paradoxical instruction, if used judiciously, may help her to harness real power. Thus, instead of convincing her to take the abuse more seriously and do something directly to stop her son, it may be more fruitful to encourage her, in effect, to act less concerned. One might do this by reframing the periods of verbal abuse as opportunities to model her own well-honed capacity for being strong and independent. She can be told that because her son has so many problems in this area that she has to bend over backward to show how she can tolerate his abuse without signs of weakness. Probably she just has not been strong enough. Therefore, she can be instructed to demonstrate her strength and independence by giving no sign of emotional reaction at all to the abuse; in fact, she should go about her own business with seeming indifference and might do well to take up new tasks in the midst of the episode, perhaps turning on the television or going into another room to take care of a chore. If not disabled, she might go out to shop, perhaps even inviting her son to join her, where he will likely be further constrained from continuing the abuse. Of course, the use of such paradoxical procedures should be based on careful clinical judgment and expertise.

KNOWLEDGE OF THE LEGAL SYSTEM.   Familiarity with the legal system is an important part of the management of elder mistreatment. There is a wide range of legal actions that the professional may recommend or initiate on behalf of the victim of abuse or neglect (Quinn & Tomita, 1986; Sengstock & Barrett, 1986). The basic principle in protecting the older client is to recommend the legal action that entails the least possible infringement on the victim's rights. In many situations the professional will need to take actions that protect the victim's rights or property. In other situations the goal is to help meet financial or legal responsibilities and, while so doing, to minimize loss of rights. In addition, knowledge of the legal system will permit the professional to discover situations in which a family member or even an unrelated individual has already taken legal actions that jeopardize

TABLE 6.2.   Range of Community Service Options for Illustrative Problems

Problem	Options
Social isolation of victim	Telephone contacts
	Friendly visitor/senior companion
	Day care
	Volunteer work
	Support group
	Change of living arrangements to group living environment
Financial exploitation	Direct deposit of checks
	Representative payee
	Termination of exploitative power of attorney or guardianship
	Establishment of appropriate power of attorney or guardian
Caregiver strain due to excessive contact between victim and caregiver	Involvement of neighbors or extended family
	Home companion or friendly visitor
	Day-care program for victim
	Temporary change in living arrangements (e.g., respite care)
	Permanent change in living arrangements

either the victim's rights or assets. With a minimum of legal effort, for example, a friend or acquaintance may acquire power of attorney for writing checks. Another means for obtaining access to the victim's assets is for the perpetrator to become the joint owner of some part of the victim's property. A related variation is to become the joint recipient of checks sent to the victim. In any of these situations, the key step for the professional is to know that it is necessary to evaluate the victim's financial documents and speak to the banks or other institutions that either provide or receive the resources in question. Once any such infringement is suspected, the professional will need to involve a protective service agency, which can collaborate in evaluating the actions of the perpetrator and in setting up a power of attorney, trust, or guardianship protecting the client's assets.

INVOLVEMENT OF COMMUNITY SERVICES.   The use of diverse community resources can help in dealing with the legal, social, or functional problems related to treatment of elder abuse (Kinderknecht, 1986). The actual mechanism for involving them will depend on the discipline of the professional. Agencies or professionals routinely involved in the treatment of elder abuse will have existing links to the many community services that are needed. Others will need to develop them (Quinn & Tomita, 1986). In either case the overall aim is to develop an effective network of the resources that may be necessary for treatment. Knowledge of the extent and limitations of these resources is necessary for optimal treatment planning and requires familiarity with the laws, regulations, and entitlements that govern the client's actions and opportunities.

The community services included in a particular case will depend on the results of assessment. Usually, there will be a range of options available for any problem (see Table 6.2). The option chosen will be determined by the client's needs and preferences. Cost will be an important factor. And, as in the case of legal actions, the aim will be to find the least restrictive alternative for the victim or caregiver.

SUMMARY AND FUTURE DIRECTIONS

Research carried out in the past 10 years demonstrates that elder abuse and neglect are widespread in American society. Despite the many uncertainties that still exist, investigators have had considerable success in defining variables that need to be evaluated in trying to understand etiology and in developing appropriate treatments. However, there are both conceptual and practical problems that stand in the way of progress. Future studies will have to focus on the interaction of demographic variables, dependency, functional ability, and psychiatric disorders in furthering understanding of the factors that contribute to abuse and neglect (Hudson, 1986; Phillips, 1986). Further knowledge of etiological considerations will influence treatment. Moreover, there is a pressing need for empirically controlled treatment outcome studies with abused or neglected elderly persons. Until such research is conducted, recommendations for interventions will be based on clinical speculations and anecdotal sources. However, progress is equally impeded by the lack of policy and funding to support the complex process of reporting, detection, assessment, and intervention that comprises the treatment of elder abuse (Ambrogi & London, 1985). After the quantum jump in public awareness that occurred in the wake of the first published reports of elder maltreatment, congressional efforts to provide expanded research and treatment have fallen off. This is a cause of continuing concern (Callahan, 1988). However, individual states and communities have gradually developed sensitivity to the problem. Almost all states now have legislation addressing the problems of elder abuse and neglect (Salend et al., 1984; Traxler, 1986). Although much is wanting in these initiatives, they do represent steps in the right direction.

REFERENCES

Ambrogi, D., & London, C. (1985). Elderly abuse laws. Their implications for caregivers. *Generations, 10,* 37–39.

Anderson, C. M., & Stewart, S. (1983). *Mastering resistance: A practical guide to family therapy.* New York: Guilford.

Anderson, L., & Thobaben, M. (1984). Clients in crisis. When should the nurse step in? *Journal of Gerontological Nursing, 10,* 6–10.

Beachler, M. A. (1979). Mistreatment of elderly persons in the domestic setting. Unpublished manuscript, Brasoria County, Texas.

Block, M. D. (1983). Abuse of the elderly. In S. H. Kadish (Ed.), *Encyclopedia of crime and justice* (pp. 1635–1637). New York: Free Press.

Block, M. R., & Sinnott, J. D. (1979). The battered elderly syndrome: An exploratory study. College Park: Center on Aging, University of Maryland.

Boydston, L. S., & McNairn, J. A. (1981). Elder abuse by adult caretakers: An exploratory study. In *Physical and financial abuse of the elderly* (pp. 135–136). Publication No. 97-297, U.S. House of Representative Select Committee on Aging, Washington, DC: U.S. Government Printing Office.

Callahan, J. J. (1988). Elder abuse: Some questions for policy-makers. *The Gerontologist, 28,* 453–458.

Carr, K., Dix, G., Fulmer, T., Kavesh, W., Kravitz, L., Matlaw, J., Mayer, J., Minaker, K., Shapiro, M., Street, S., Wetle, T., & Zarle, N. (1986). An elder abuse assessment team in an acute hospital setting. *Gerontologist, 26,* 115–118.

Coppel, D. B., Burton, C., Becker, J., & Fiore, J. (1985). Relationships of cognitions associated with coping reactions to depression in spousal caregivers of Alzheimer's disease patients. *Cognitive Therapy and Research, 9,* 253–266.

Council on Scientific Affairs (1987). Elder abuse and neglect. *Journal of the American Medical Association, 257,* 966–971.

Crouse, J. S., Cobb, D. C., Harris, B. B., Kopecky, F. J., & Poertner, J. (1981). Abuse and neglect of the elderly in Illinois: Incidence and characteristics, legislation and policy recommendations. Unpublished manuscript, Illinois Department on Aging, Springfield, IL.

Douglass, R. L., Hickey, T., & Noel, C. (1980). A study of the elderly and other vulnerable adults. Unpublished manuscript, University of Michigan, Ann Arbor.

Faulkner, L. R. (1982). Mandating the reporting of suspected cases of elder abuse: An inappropriate, ineffective, and agist response to the abuse of older adults. *Family Law Quarterly, 15,* 69–91.

Finkelhor, D., (1983). Common features of family abuse. In D. Finkelhor, R. Geeles, G. Hotaling, & M. Strauss (Eds.), *The dark side of families: Current family violence research,* Beverly Hills, CA: Sage.

Fisch, R., Weakland, J. H., & Segal, L. (1982). *The tactic of change.* San Francisco: Jossey-Bass.

Folstein, M. F., Folstein, S. E., & McHugh, P. R. (1975). Mini-mental state: A practical method for grading the mental state of patient for the clinician. *Journal of Psychiatric Research, 12,* 189–198.

Fulmer, T., & Ashley, J. (1986). Neglect: What part of abuse? *Pride Institute Journal of Long-Term Home Health Care, 5,* 14–18.

Fulmer, T., & Wetle, T. (1986). Elder abuse screening and intervention. *Nurse Practitioner, 11,* 33–38.

George, L. K. (1986). Caregiver burden: Conflict between norms of reciprocity and solidarity. In K. A. Pillemer, & R. S. Wolf (Eds.), *Elder abuse: Conflict in the family* (pp. 67–92). Dover, MA: Auburn House.

George, L. K., & Gwyther, L. (1986). Caregiver well-being: A multi-dimensional examination of family caregivers of demented adults. *Gerontologist, 26,* 253–259.

Gioglio, G. R., & Blakemore, P. (1983). Elder abuse in New Jersey: The knowledge and experience of abuse among older New Jerseyans. Unpublished manuscript, Department of Human Services, Trenton, NJ.

Goodwin, J. (1985). Family violence: Principles of intervention and prevention. *Hospital and Community, 36,* 1074–1079.

Hageboeck, H., & Brandt, K. (1981). Characteristics of elderly abuse. Iowa City: University of Iowa Gerontology Center.

Hudson, M. (1986). Elder mistreatment: Current research. In K. A. Pillemer & R. S. Wolf (Eds.), *Elder abuse conflict in the family* (pp. 125–165). Dover, MA: Auburn House.

Hudson, M., & Johnson, T. (1986). Elder abuse and neglect: A review of the literature. In C. Eisdorfer (Ed.), *Annual review of gerontology and geriatrics* (Vol. 6). New York: Springer.

Hwalek, M., Sengstock, M., & Lawrence, R. (1986). Assessing the probability of abuse of the elderly. *Journal of Applied Gerontology, 5,* 153–173.

Johnson, T. (1986). Critical issues in the definition of elder mistreatment. In K. A. Pillemer & R. S. Wolf (Eds.), *Elder abuse conflict in the family* (pp. 167–196). Dover, MA: Auburn House.

Kane, R. L., & Kane, R. A. (1981). *Assessing the elderly: A practical guide to measurement.* Lexington, MA: Lexington Books.

Kinderknecht, C. H. (1986). In home social work with abused or neglected elderly: An experiential guide to assessment and treatment. *Journal of Gerontological Social Work, 9,* 29–41.

Kosberg, J. I. (1988). Preventing elder abuse: An identification of high-risk factors prior to placement decisions. *Gerontologist, 28,* 43–50.

Lau, E. (1986). Inpatient geropsychiatry in the network of elder abuse services. In M. Galbraith (Ed.), *Elder abuse: Perspectives on an emerging crisis. Convergence in aging* (Vol. 3, pp. 65–80). Kansas City KS: Mid-American Congress on Aging.

Lau, E., & Kosberg, J. I. (1979). Abuse of the elderly by informal care providers. *Aging, 229-301,* 10–15.

Lawton, M. P. (1976). Assessing the competence of older people. In D. P. Kent, R. Kastenbaum, & S. Sherwood (Eds.), *Research planning action for the elderly* (pp. 122–143). New York: Behavioral Publications.

Matlaw, J. R., & Mayer, J. B. (1986). Elder abuse: Ethical and practical dilemmas for social work. *Health and Social Work, 11,* 85–94.

Morycz, R. K. (1985). Caregiving strain and the desire to institutionalize family members with Alzheimer's disease. *Research on Aging, 7,* 329–361.

O'Malley, H., Bergman, J., Seagars, H., Perax, R., Mitchell, V., & Kruepfel, G. (1979). Elder abuse in Massachusetts: A survey of professionals and paraprofessionals. Boston: Legal Research and Services for the Elderly.

O'Malley, T. A., Everitt, D. E., O'Malley, H. C., & Campion, E. W. (1983). Identifying and preventing family-mediated abuse and neglect of elderly persons. *Annals of Internal Medicine, 98,* 998–1005.

O'Malley, T. A., & Fulmer, T. T. (1988). Abuse, neglect, and inadequate care. In J. W. Rowe & R. W. Besdine (Eds.), *Geriatric medicine* (2nd ed.). Boston: Little, Brown.

Pennsylvania Department of Aging, Bureau of Advocacy. (1982). Elder abuse in Pennsylvania. Harrisburg: Author.

Phillips, L. R. (1983). Abuse and neglect of the frail elderly at home: An exploration of theoretical relationships. *Journal of Advanced Nursing, 8,* 379–392.

Phillips, L. R. (1986). Theoretical explanations of elder abuse: Competing hypotheses and unresolved issues. In K. A. Pillemer & R. S. Wolf (Eds.), *Elder abuse conflict in the family* (pp. 197–217). Dover, MA: Auburn House.

Phillips, L. R., & Rempusheski, V. F. (1985). A decision-making model for diagnosing and intervening in elder abuse and neglect. *Nursing Research, 34,* 134–139.

Pillemer, K. (1985). The dangers of dependency: New findings on domestic violence against the elderly. *Social Problems, 33,* 146–158.

Pillemer, K. (1986). Risk factors in elder abuse: Results from a case-control study. In K. A. Pillemer & R. S. Wolf (Eds.), *Elder abuse conflict in the family* (pp. 239–263). Dover, MA: Auburn House.

Pillemer, K., & Finkelhor, D. (1988). The prevalence of elder abuse: A random sample survey. *Gerontologist, 28,* 51–57.

Powell, S., & Berg, R. C. (1987). When the elderly are abused: Characteristics and intervention. *Educational Gerontology, 13,* 71–83.

Quinn, M. (1985). Elder abuse and neglect raise new dilemmas. *Generations, Quarterly Journal of the American Society on Aging, 10,* 22–25.

Quinn, M., & Tomita, S. (1986). *Elder abuse in neglect: Causes, diagnosis, and intervention strategies.* New York: Springer.

Rathbone-McCuan, E., & Goodstein, R. K. (1985). Elder abuse: Clinical considerations. *Psychiatric Annals, 15,* 331–339.

Rathbone-McCuan, E., & Voyles, B. (1982). Case detection of abused elderly parents. *American Journal of Psychiatry, 139,* 189–192.

Ross, H., & Kedward, H. (1977). Psychiatric hospital admissions from the community and institutions. *Journal of Gerontology, 32,* 420–427.

Roth, L. H., Meisel, A., & Lidz, C. W. (1977). Tests of competency to consent to treatment. *American Journal of Psychiatry, 134,* 279–283.

Rounds, L. (1982). A study of select environmental variables associated with non-institutional settings where there is abuse or neglect of the elderly. Unpublished doctoral dissertation, University of Texas, Austin.

Salend, E., Kane, R. A., Satz, M., & Pynoos, J. (1984). Elder abuse reporting: Limitations of statutes. *Gerontologist, 24,* 61–67.

Sengstock, M., & Barrett, S. (1986). Elderly victims of family abuse, neglect, and maltreatment. Can legal assistance help? *Journal of Gerontological Social Work, 2,* 43–61.

Sengstock, M., & Hwalek, M. (1987). A review and analysis of measures for the identification of elder abuse. *Journal of Gerontological Social Work, 10,* 21–36.

Sengstock, M., Hwaleck, M., & Moshier, S. (1986). A comprehensive index for assessing abuse and neglect of the elderly. In M. Galbraith (Ed.), *Elder abuse: Perspectives on an emerging crisis. Convergence in aging* (Vol. 3, p. 41–64). Kansas City, KS: Mid-America Congress on Aging.

Sengstock, M., & Laing, J. (1982). Identifying and characterizing elder abuse. Detroit: Institute of Gerontology, Wayne State University.

Shanas, E. (1980). Older people and their families: The new pioneers. *Journal of Marriage and the Family, 42,* 9–15.

Snyder, B., & Keefe, K. (1985). The unmet needs of family caregivers of frail and disabled adults. *Social Work in Health Care, 10,* 1–14.

Soldo, B., & Myllylaoma, J. (1983). Caregivers who live with dependent elderly. *Gerontologist, 23,* 605–611.

Steinmetz, S. (1981). Elder abuse. *Aging, 315-316,* 6–10.

Steinmetz, S. (1983). Dependency, stress, and violence between middle-aged caregivers and their elderly parents. In J. L. Kosburg (Ed.), *Abuse and maltreatment of the elderly* (pp. 134–149). Littleton, MA: John Wright—P.S.G.

Steuer, J., & Austin, E. (1980). Family abuse of the elderly. *Journal of the American Geriatrics Society, 28,* 372–376.

Tobin, S., & Kulys, R. (1981). The family and the institutionalization of the elderly. *Journal of Social Issues, 37,* 145–157.

Tomita, S. (1982). Detection and treatment of elder abuse and neglect: A protocol for health care professionals. *Physical Therapy and Occupational Therapy in Geriatrics, 2,* 37–51.

Traxler, A. (1986). Elder abuse laws: A survey of state statutes. In M. Galbraith (Ed.), *Elder abuse: Perspectives on an emerging crisis. Convergence in aging* (Vol. 3, p. 139–167). Kansas City, KS: Mid-America Congress on Aging.

U.S. House of Representatives. (1981). Elder abuse: An examination of a hidden problem. Select Committee on Aging, 97th Congress Committee. Publication No. 97-277. Washington, DC: U.S. Government Printing Office.

U.S. House of Representatives. (1985). Elder abuse: Select Committee on Aging, 99th Congress Committee. Publication No. 99-516. Washington, DC: U.S. Government Printing Office.

Valentine, D., & Cash, T. (1986). A definitional discussion of elder maltreatment. *Journal of Gerontological Social Work, 9,* 17–28.

Wolf, R. (1986). Major findings from three model projects on elderly abuse. In K. A. Pillemer & R. S. Wolf (Eds.), *Elder abuse conflict in the family* (pp. 218–238). Dover, MA: Auburn House.

Wolf, R., Godkin, M., & Pillemer, K. (1984). *Elder abuse and neglect: Final report from three model projects.* Wooster: University Center on Aging, University of Massachusetts Medical Center.

Zarit, S. H., Anthony, C. R., & Boutselis, M. (1987). Interventions with caregivers of demented patients: A comparison of two approaches. *Psychology and Aging, 2,* 225–232.

Zarit, S. H., Reeves, K., & Bach-Peterson, J. (1980). Relatives of the impaired elderly: Correlates of feelings of burden. *Gerontologist, 20,* 649–655.

CHAPTER 7

Victims of Marital Rape

NANCY M. SHIELDS, PATRICIA A. RESICK, AND CHRISTINE R. HANNEKE

INTRODUCTION

Marital rape has recently gained recognition as an area worthy of scientific investigation. This interest in marital rape has developed out of the research findings on battered women and on nonmarital (i.e., stranger, date, and acquaintance) rape. Most available research on marital rape is limited; its primary focus has been on simply establishing the existence of marital rape, with only a minor focus on its causes and consequences. Estimates of the prevalence of marital rape are limited by the lack of representative samples on which to base estimates. From a clinical perspective, the treatment of marital rape victims is essentially an unexplored frontier.

The lack of systematic analysis of the marital rape experience may be attributed to historical legal definitions, definitions and perceptions of marital rape victims and society in general, and lack of uniform definitions of marital rape among social science researchers. Until recently, there has been no legal basis for defining forced sex between spouses as rape. In fact, laws prohibiting forced sex between married persons still do not exist in many states. The lack of legal definitions reflects the perceptions of many members of our society, including victims and perpetrators, who do not believe that it is possible for a husband to rape his wife. Finally, social scientists have contributed to the confusion by defining marital rape in various ways, such as unwanted sexual experiences of any kind, sexual experiences involving the use or threat of force, and unwanted sexual intercourse only.

EPIDEMIOLOGY

Several different types of studies are available that provide estimates of the prevalence of marital rape. One kind of study is focused on the prevalence

The research presented in this chapter was supported by a grant, "Victim Reaction to Rape and Battering," from the National Institute of Mental Health, National Center for the Prevention and Control of Rape (No. 5R0 1MH37102-02).

of marital rape among victims of nonsexual family violence. For example, Prescott and Letko (1977) found that 32% of 44 women responding to an advertisement in *Ms.* magazine had experienced marital rape. Frieze (1983) found that 34% of 137 battered women in her study in the Pittsburgh area had experienced marital rape. Shields and Hanneke (1983) found that 46% of battered women in their St. Louis sample had experienced both marital rape and battering. Finally, Walker (1984) found that 59% of battered women in her study were also marital rape victims. According to these studies of battered women, between 32% and 59% of these women are also victims of marital rape.

There have also been a few studies that have based prevalence rates on samples of the general population, although not all these studies have used random sampling. Finkelhor and Yllo (1982) found that 6% of 133 clients at a family planning clinic had experienced marital rape. Doron (1980) found that of 612 respondents to a newspaper survey in New Jersey, 7% were victims of marital rape, 4% had been victims of sexual violence only, 3% were victims of marital rape and battering, and another 14% were victims of battering but not sexual violence. Lewis (1984) found that of 78 women seeking counseling for marital or relationship problems, 10% had experienced marital rape in the previous 12 months. One person had experienced rape only, 7.7% had experienced marital rape and battering, and 12.8% battering only. Hanneke, Shields, and McCall (1986) used a variety of case finding methods to identify victims of marital violence. Of the 307 respondents in the sample, 69% were nonvictims, 1% victims of rape only, 8% victims of rape and battering, and 22% victims of battering only.

Other studies have employed random sampling. Russell (1982) studied a probability sample of 644 women in the San Francisco area. She found that of the women who had ever been married, 14% had experienced marital rape. Four percent were victims of rape only, 10% were victims of rape and battering, and 12% were victims of battering only. As part of a general telephone survey of victimization of women, Kilpatrick et al. (1987) found that of all assault victims, 8% of the assailants were husbands. Of all rape victims, 9% had been raped by their husbands. Finkelhor and Yllo (1985) studied a random sample of mothers of school-age children in the Boston area. They found that of 323 respondents, 10% had experienced forced sex. Accordingly, estimates of the prevalence of marital rape in the general population range from around 6% to 14%.

Another group of studies have focused on rape victims rather than victims of battering. For example, Koss, Dinero, and Seibel (1988) studied rape among a representative sample of female college students. Of all the rape victims who were identified ($N = 489$), 9% had been raped by family members, including husbands. George and Winfield-Laird (1986) report on a large sample of rape victims ($N = 3146$) in the Piedmont area of North Carolina. They found that 20% of all sexual assaults involved husbands as assailants, and in 6% of the assaults lovers were identified as the assailants.

A survey of all these various types of studies suggests that marital rape occurs at a significant level among married women in the general population and that many battered women are also in fact victims of marital rape. In addition, studies of different types of sexual assault indicate that a significant proportion of assailants of sexual assault are actually family intimates.

Many of the studies that have been described are flawed by the lack of representative samples as well as other methodological limitations. Furthermore, for the most part these studies do not go beyond attempting to establish simple prevalence rates. Unfortunately, more sophisticated epidemiologic studies of marital rape face many of the same difficulties as similar studies of nonmarital rape. George and Winfield-Laird (1986) have described the difficulties encountered by rape researchers in attempting to identify risk factors and describe population characteristics of rape victims when prevalence rates are low (for statistical purposes). As they point out, "It does not seem likely that the resources will be available to support a large number of population-based studies of the size that would be required to perform the kinds of multivariate analyses desperately needed in the field" (p. 72). It seems likely that marital rape researchers interested in epidemiologic analysis will face similar problems.

CONSEQUENCES

There has been very little research on the consequences of marital rape. Three studies have examined the psychological consequences using an interview format (Finkelhor & Yllo, 1985; Frieze, 1983) and have found diverse reactions to victimization. Finkelhor and Yllo (1985) report that feelings of betrayal, anger, and humiliation are common. They also note that fear reactions may be long term with a general inability to trust others. Sexual dysfunctions also appeared to be common reactions.

Russell (1982) found similar psychological consequences of marital rape. Her respondents reported an increase in negative feelings toward their husbands, as well as negative feelings toward men in general. A decrease in the quality of the marital relationship, and sometimes divorce, were reported. Respondents also reported an increase in negative feelings toward themselves. Worry, fear, anxiety, depression, and anger were psychological responses to victimization. Like Finkelhor and Yllo (1985), Russell (1982) also found a generalized mistrust of others among victims of marital rape. Marital rape also appeared to produce negative sexual feelings and negatively affected victims' perceptions of their own sexuality.

Frieze (1983) classified and coded emotional reactions of marital rape victims into four categories: self-blame, no allocation of blame (depression, concern, surprise, etc.), blame of the husband, and positive affect. The majority of marital rape victims reported anger and blame of the husband. However, those women who were raped often by their husbands were more likely to blame themselves (20%) than those who were raped only once (6%). Battered women who were raped were more likely to seek help from friends, family, religious sources, and social service agencies than those who were battered but not raped. The battered and raped women were also more likely to call police (62%), press legal charges (59%), and carry out a separation or divorce (49%) than those who were not raped but were battered (45%, 33%, and 35% respectively). A regression analysis to determine the reactions most related to marital rape indicated that trying to leave the husband was the most likely reaction of those who had been raped.

Kilpatrick et al. (1987) conducted an assessment, including a standardized interview with female crime victims who had been identified through a random telephone survey. By this means they were able to compare stranger, marital, and date rape situations. They found no differences among the three groups on the three types of mental health problems they examined: major depressive episode, social phobia, and sexual dysfunction.

Although the interview studies give indications of probable reactions, standardized scales are needed to determine the extent to which the reported reactions actually exceed those found in the nonvictimized, nonmarital rape, or battered population. Two studies have used standardized scales of symptomatology.

Koss et al. (1988) conducted a national survey of college students on the prevalence of rape. They also gave the participants the Trait Anxiety Scale, the Beck Depression Inventory, and several Likert-type questions regarding sexual satisfaction, trust, and intimacy. They found that acquaintance rapes were rated as less violent than stranger rapes, except when they were perpetrated by a husband or family member. When all of the types of acquaintance rape were collapsed and compared to stranger rape victims, there were no differences in symptoms. When the acquaintance groups were divided into nonromantic, casual date, steady date, or spouse/family, there were no differences on the symptom measures of depression, anxiety, or sexual satisfaction. The only difference between these groups of acquaintance rape victims was on relationship quality. Women who were raped by husbands or family members had lower ratings of relationship quality than other groups of acquaintance rape victims. Unfortunately, because marital rape was collapsed with incest, the effect of marital rape per se on functioning was not determined.

The primary thrust of the research to be presented in the remainder of this section is based on a project by the present authors on the consequences of marital rape and battering. During the primary data collection phase of the project, 142 interviews were conducted by two of the authors. The subjects included women who had experienced marital rape only (5), battering only (48), marital rape and battering (44), and a group of comparable nonvictims (45). Because there were so few, the respondents who had experienced marital rape only were later dropped from statistical analyses. All respondents were recruited from shelters for battered or homeless women, self-help groups and programs, and social service agencies, by advertising and "snowballing." Of the respondents 56% were black and 44% were white. They ranged in age from 17 to 63 years, and the average age was 31.4. Seventy-one percent of the respondents had been married to their partners, and 29% had cohabited. Seventy-four percent of the respondents were separated from their partners at the time of the interview, but most had been separated for less than a year. The average number of years of education was 12.2.

Sexual violence was defined by a panel of experts as *moderate* or *severe* sexual violence that had occurred on two or more occasions. Moderate or severe sexual violence was defined by 17 specific sexual behaviors that were engaged in as a result of force or threat of force. Similarly, physical abuse was defined by the panel as *moderate* or *severe* nonsexual violence, which had occurred on two or more occasions. Moderate and severe physical abuse included 11 specific nonsexually violent behaviors. "Battered only" victims were women who had experienced physical abuse but not sexual violence in their most recent marital/cohabiting relationship, and "raped and battered" victims were women who had experienced both sexual violence and physical abuse in their most recent relationships. There were no differences in the severity of physical abuse experienced between the raped and battered and battered only groups.

Tennessee Self-Concept Scale

The Tennessee Self-Concept Scale (TSCS) was used to measure current self-concept, which was conceptualized as a consequence of victimization. Researchers of battered women (Hilberman, 1980; Pagelow, 1984; Walker, 1979) and marital rape victims (Shields & Hanneke, 1983) have all suggested that victimization results in lowering a woman's self-esteem. Based on these previous findings, we hypothesized that the raped and battered women would have the lowest self-esteem, because they had experienced both physical abuse and sexual violence in their marital relationships, followed by the battered only women who had experienced only physical abuse in their relationships. It was predicted that nonvictims would have the highest levels of self-esteem because they had experienced no violence in their relationships.

The TSCS consists of 100 items that measure various aspects of self-concept. Ten of these items constitute a "lie" scale, and the remaining 90 items constitute the subscales of Identity, Self-Satisfaction, Behavior, Physical Self, Moral-Ethical Self, Personal Self, Family Self, and Social Self. Norms for the general population are available.

The Identity subscale describes how the individual sees herself. The raped and battered and battered only groups scored close to one another on this subscale, and the nonvictims scored close to the norm mean. The nonvictims scored significantly higher than both victim groups but not significantly higher than the norm. Accordingly, the victims had more negative feelings about who they were than did the nonvictims or the norm group.

The Behavior subscale measures the woman's perception of her own behavior or how she acts. All three groups scored significantly lower than the norm group, with the raped and battered group scoring the lowest. The raped and battered group was significantly different from the battered only group and the nonvictim group. The women in the raped and battered group were the least pleased with their behavior and the nonvictims were most pleased, but not as pleased as the norm group.

The Moral-Ethical subscale describes an individual's feeling of how good or bad she is as a person, her moral worth, and her relationship to God. On this subscale, the nonvictims scored slightly above the norm mean, the battered only group close to the norm mean, and the raped and battered group lower than the norm. However, scores were not significantly different from the norm for any of the groups. Nonvictims were significantly higher than the raped and battered group.

The Personal Self subscale measures an individual's sense of personal worth (i.e., feelings of adequacy and evaluation of personality). On this subscale, none of the groups were significantly different from the norm. The raped and battered group scored significantly lower than the battered only group and the nonvictim group.

The Family Self subscale measures an individual's perception of her worth, value, and adequacy as a family member. All three groups of respondents scored significantly lower than the norm, with the raped and battered group scoring the lowest. All three groups were significantly different from one another. All three groups felt inadequate as family members when compared with the norm.

The three groups did not differ from one another on three subscales: Self-Satisfaction, Social Self, and Physical Self. In addition, none of the groups had scores significantly different from the norm on the Social Self and Physical Self subscales. However, all three groups were significantly lower than the norm on Physical Self, the subscale that measures a person's perception of her body, physical appearance, physical skills, and sexuality.

In summary, it appears that victims have lower self-esteem in general than nonvictims or the norm group. Overall, marital rape study respondents were satisfied with their self-concepts relative to relationships with other people, but not in relation to family members. Raped and battered victims displayed significantly lower self-esteem than battered only victims on the subscales of Behavior, Personal Self, and Family Self.

Modified Fear Survey

The Modified Fear Survey (MFS) was developed by Kilpatrick, Veronen, and Resick (1979a) in order to assess fear reactions in sexual assault victims. The MFS has been revised by Resick, Veronen, Calhoun, Kilpatrick, and

Atkeson (1984) and currently consists of 62 items that can be broken down into eight subscales: Fear of Vulnerable Situations, Classical Fears, Sexual Fears, Social Evaluation and Failure, Medical Fears, Agoraphobia, Fear of Noise, and Fear of Weapons.

Fear and anxiety have been shown to be reactions to stranger rape (Kilpatrick et al., 1979a, 1979b) and have been hypothesized to be possible reactions to battering (Dobash & Dobash, 1979; Hilberman & Munson, 1977–1978) and marital rape (Russell, 1980). The MFS was used to measure fear and anxiety levels because of its proven effectiveness in measuring fear and anxiety of stranger rape victims. It was predicted that the raped and battered victims would exhibit higher levels of fear and anxiety than the battered only group and the nonvictim group. Again, we anticipated that the nonvictims would exhibit the lowest levels of fear and anxiety, with battered only women scoring between the raped and battered and the nonvictim groups.

As predicted, the raped and battered group scored higher than the other two groups on all subscales, except Medical Fears. There were no significant differences among the three groups regarding medical fears. Raped and battered victims scored significantly higher than both the battered only group and nonvictims on Fear of Vulnerable Situations, Classical Fears, and Agoraphobia. The battered only women were not significantly different from the nonvictims on these variables. This suggests that marital sexual and non-sexual violence in combination have a greater impact on producing phobias, including agoraphobia and fear of vulnerable situations, than does physical abuse alone. The nonvictims were significantly different from both victim groups, in that they scored lower on the Fear of Failure and the Fear of Weapons subscales. This suggests that marital victimization in general increases fear of these items. All three groups were significantly different from one another on the Sexual Fears subscale, with the raped and battered group being the most fearful and the comparison group the least fearful. This implies that physical abuse alone significantly increases fear levels over nonvictims, but the addition of sexual violence increases fear levels even more.

Derogotis Brief Symptom Inventory

Depression and somatic complaints have been found to be reactions to battering (Gelles, 1974; Hilberman & Munson, 1977) and marital rape (Finkelhor & Yllo, 1985). The Brief Symptom Index (BSI: Derogotis & Spencer, 1982) was chosen for use because of reliability and the availability of published norms. We anticipated that the raped and battered group would exhibit the highest levels of depression and somatic complaints and anxiety-related problems, followed by the battered only group, and finally the nonvictims. It was expected that the scores of the comparison group would approximate the scores of a normal population, or be only slightly elevated.

The BSI consists of 53 items designed to measure the psychological symptom patterns of individuals on nine primary symptom dimensions: Physical

Somatization, Obsessive-Compulsiveness, Interpersonal Sensitivity, Depression, Anxiety, Hostility, Phobic Anxiety, Paranoid Ideation, and Psychoticism. There are also three global indices (two of which will be discussed) that are helpful in the overall assessment of an individual's psychological status. The BSI is the brief form of the Symptom Checklist-90-Revised (SCL-90-R), and measures the same nine dimensions and global indices (Derogotis & Spencer, 1982).

According to Derogotis and Spencer (1982), a "General Severity Index" score (the mean score over all 53 items) of 63 or greater is indicative of a positive diagnosis. When GSI scores were examined, both the raped and battered and the battered only groups scored over the cutoff point, and therefore appear to have been experiencing clinical levels of psychological distress. The nonvictims scored below the cutoff. Examining the individual dimensions, one finds that the raped and battered group scored over the cutoff point on all nine subscales; the battered only group scored over the cutoff on all subscales except Physical Somatization. The comparison group scored below the cutoff on all subscales except one, Anxiety.

When between-group comparisons were made, the raped and battered group scored significantly higher than both the battered only group and the nonvictims on the Somatization subscale. On the Obsessive-Compulsiveness subscale, all three groups were significantly different from one another, with the raped and battered group displaying the highest levels of compulsive behavior. The same pattern was observed for the Interpersonal Sensitivity, Hostility, Paranoid Ideation, Psychoticism, and Depression subscales. On the Anxiety and Phobic Anxiety subscales, nonvictims scored significantly lower than either victim group.

Sexual Functioning Assessment

In order to determine if sexual and nonsexual violence have an effect on sexual functioning, respondents were asked seven questions about their sexual behavior and sexual functioning in the year prior to the interview. Disruption of sexual functioning has been hypothesized to be a reaction to battering, as manifested by withholding sex (Gayford, 1975) and loss of interest in sex (Dobash & Dobash, 1979; Hirsch, 1981). Disrupted sexual functioning has also been suggested as a response to marital rape (Shields & Hanneke, 1983). It was anticipated that the marital rape victims would be experiencing more sexual functioning problems than either the battered only group or the nonvictims.

Of the three groups, the raped and battered victims were the least likely to have enjoyed sex during the year prior to the interview. The two victim groups were also less likely to be orgasmic than the comparison group. The raped and battered group was the least likely of all the groups to be interested in sex or to enjoy sex. Comparing the three groups overall, the raped and battered group was the most sexually dysfunctional, then the battered only group, and finally the comparison group. These results suggest that any type of physical violence will negatively affect the victim's sexual functioning in the marital relationship, but that experiencing sexual violence leads to the most dysfunction.

Revised Michigan Alcohol Screening Test

The use of alcohol for depression has been hypothesized to be a reaction to battering (Frieze & Knoble, 1980; Hirsch, 1981) and to marital rape (Shields & Hanneke, 1983). A slightly revised version of the Michigan Alcohol Screening Test (MAST) was used to measure alcohol abuse because it has been demonstrated to be an easily administered and understood scale and because comparison groups are available (Moore, 1971, 1972; Selzer, Vinokur, & Van Rooijen, 1975). The MAST is a 25-item self-administered questionnaire designed to screen respondents for possible alcoholism. The MAST was also revised to assess drug use. It was anticipated that the raped and battered women would have the most problems with alcohol, followed by the battered only group, and that nonvictims would have the fewest alcohol problems.

In fact, the three study groups were not significantly different from one another in their use of alcohol. When compared with a group of known alcoholics and a group of nonalcoholics, all respondents were more similar to the nonalcoholics than to the alcoholics. Similarly, there were no significant differences between groups in their use of drugs. None of the groups displayed a high level of drug use. These are important findings, because there has been a general tendency to assume that alcohol problems exist among battered women (Martin, 1978). However, to our knowledge, this is the first research to use a standardized, reliable measure of alcohol abuse and to compare alcohol use of battered women with norms and comparison groups.

Borderline Personality

The exploratory phase of the research project and clinical psychological research (Resick, 1982) led us to hypothesize that symptoms of borderline personality would be more common among victims than nonvictims. Based on the description of factors indicative of possible borderline personality in the *Diagnostic and Statistical Manual of Mental Disorders* of the American Psychiatric Association (DMS-III, 1980), a 14-item scale was designed to measure the eight characteristics listed there. The scale included six response categories ranging from *strongly agree* to *strongly disagree*. Two summary scores were computed. One consisted of a mean score over all items. The second score consisted of the number of positive responses (i.e., agree slightly to strongly agree) to five or more of the eight characteristics listed as characteristics in DMS-III. This score is the criterion given in DMS-III for a positive diagnosis of borderline personality.

Using the mean scores only, all three groups were significantly different from one another. The raped and battered group scored the highest, followed by the battered only group, and then the nonvictims. In contrast, using the scoring method advised by DMS-III, there were no significant differences between groups. However, because this is, to our knowledge, the first systematic measurement of borderline personality among battered women, the mean differences among the three groups suggest a promising new direction for further research.

Comparison with the Robins Epidemologic Catchment Area Study

We were able to compare the responses of the marital rape study groups on specific items with responses of women who were part of a study of the general population in the St. Louis area (L. Robins, personal communication, January 1984). During 1981–1983, the Epidemologic Catchment Area Study was conducted in the St. Louis area by Dr. Lee Robins of Washington University. A purpose of the study was to investigate the physical, psychological, and emotional well-being of individuals in the area. Although many of the same variables were measured, in general the Catchment Area Study used more elaborate questioning techniques. The study involved interviews with over 3500 people. For current purposes, the relevant Catchment Area Study subsample consists of 686 women. All were over 17 and were married or cohabiting at the time of the interview.

Analysis of the data revealed that all three groups in the marital rape study had more problems with nightmares, anxiety attacks, depression, weight loss, sleep problems, feelings of worthlessness, feelings of hopelessness about life, and difficulty concentrating than women in the Catchment Area Study. The women in the Catchment Area Study had fewer problems than the nonvictims in the marital rape study, who had fewer problems than the battered only group, who, in turn, had fewer problems than the raped and battered group.

For problems with headaches, the percentages for nonvictims and battered only women are very comparable to the overall percentage for women in the Catchment Area Study. However, when headaches were due to emotional stress, all marital rape study respondents had more problems than respondents in the Catchment Area Study. Raped and battered women had more headaches due to emotional stress than any other group.

Concerning stomach problems, nonvictims were less likely than victims of either type to have stomach problems. Battered only respondents and Catchment Area Study respondents were about equally likely to have stomach problems. Again, more of the raped and battered women had stomach problems than any other group.

The nonvictims in the marital rape study were significantly less likely than either victim group to be bothered by crowds, public transportation, closed spaces, and strangers. They were significantly different from the raped and battered group in that they were also less likely to be bothered by being alone. The raped and battered group was significantly more likely than either of the other groups to be bothered by insects, animals, and medical fears. In general, the nonvictims were least likely to be bothered by phobias, and the raped and battered women were most likely to be bothered. When only the percentages of women who were bothered "very much" were examined, the nonvictims scored about the same as the women in the Catchment Area Study.

In general, it appears that women in the marital rape study were more traumatized than a random sample of women in the St. Louis area. All marital rape study groups were more likely to have had stress-related problems than women in the Catchment Area Study. In general, the women in the Catchment Area Study had the fewest problems, then the nonvictims in the marital rape study, then the battered group, and finally the raped and battered group.

IMPLICATIONS FOR TREATMENT

When you are raped by a stranger you have to live with a frightening memory. When you are raped by your husband, you have to live with your rapist. (Finkelhor & Yllo, 1985, p. 138)

Given the high prevalence of marital rape and the severe effects that have been found in this and preceding studies (Finkelhor & Yllo, 1985; Frieze, 1983; Russell, 1982), the lack of clinical literature on this topic is alarming. Marital rape is a frequent occurrence, and those who are raped and battered suffer significantly more than those who are battered but not raped. At this point there has been no research on treatment of marital rape victims, and only one article has discussed treatment issues (Weingourt, 1985). This void in the literature may reflect the problem of identification and labeling and the lack of recognition of the event as a crime. It may also reflect cultural attitudes that, if a woman has had sex with a man before, it is not traumatic if sex is forced on occasion. However, in fact, both Koss et al. (1988) and Russell (1982) have found that rape by a husband is equal to or worse than rape by a stranger with regard to impact.

The first therapeutic issue is one of identification and labeling. Because it is likely that many of these women will not have labeled their experience as rape or are too embarrassed to bring up the topic in therapy, the onus for identification is on the therapist. Because such events are not identified as crimes in many states, neither therapists nor clients may consciously label such experiences as rape. It is important that therapists take the first step in identification of these unacknowledged victims. Otherwise the victim of marital rape may be experiencing a trauma reaction, depression, and sexual dysfunctions yet have no way of formulating and understanding her experience or reactions, nor of eliciting social support.

Treatment of a woman* who has been in a physically or emotionally abusive relationship should always include assessment of sexual abuse, not by asking if the woman was raped, but by asking about unwanted sexual experiences and the use of force. The therapist should also ask about the frequency of forced sexual intercourse, if it was accompanied by threats or violence, and the woman's reactions during the assault, to assess the perceived life-threatening nature of the event(s). Recent research indicates that the level of anxiety and the extent of perceived life threat during crime is predictive of severity of reactions following crime (Resick, 1988).

The psychological impact of marital rape should be assessed. Based on the more extensive literature on rape victims in general and the limited marital rape literature, the most likely reactions are posttraumatic stress disorder (PTSD), including intrusive recollections, avoidance, and anxiety; depression, anger, self-blame/low self-esteem; sexual dysfunctions and sexual avoidance; and problems with trust in interpersonal relationships. The cognitive impact, how the client interprets the event, should also be assessed.

It is unlikely that issues and treatment of *symptoms* of marital rape will be the focus of therapy in an intact relationship. In an intact marriage, the woman is living under the threat of unpredictable violence or rape, and it is unrealistic to expect to treat fear, anxiety, or depression in such a situation. Anxiety is a realistic reaction to ongoing danger. Once such an act of power and degradation has occurred in a relationship, it is probably unrealistic to believe that trust in that partner can be completely reestablished. Even if the woman eventually felt comfortable with her spouse in other ways, sexual intimacy and fulfillment require a level of relaxation, vulnerability, and trust that would be difficult to attain after such a betrayal.

Therefore, it is unlikely that reactions to marital rape can be adequately treated until the woman has successfully extricated herself from the relationship. Frieze (1983) found that victims of marital rape were more likely to blame their husbands (and to be outraged) than to blame themselves. However, she found that victims who had been raped repeatedly were more likely to blame themselves than those who had been raped only once. Those who stay in the relationship despite repeated violence may have come to believe that at least on some level they are to blame for the violence and have total responsibility to make the marriage work. Therapy at this juncture will need to focus on helping the woman to accept the reality of the relationship and that she cannot take full responsibility for the marriage. She

---

*This chapter focuses on individual treatment of the victim of marital rape. It is unlikely that the perpetrating husband will admit to marital rape or to agree to treatment. If a woman seeks therapy after she has entered another relationship, it may be helpful to conduct couples therapy with the woman and her new, nonabusive partner. However, couples therapy is not recommended until both partners have had individual therapy to deal with their separate reactions to the rape(s) and to provide education to the partners about the reasons for and likely course of symptoms.

cannot make her husband change if he does not want to and she cannot totally prevent violence.

Victims of marital rape and abuse sometimes believe that if they keep trying harder they can make it work (i.e., the husband will change) or at least that they can "stick it out" because they believe that divorce would reflect their own failure. Emotional and physical abuse go hand in hand. Victim-blame is the way in which the perpetrator justifies his violence. In these cases it is very likely that the husband, for the duration of the marriage, has been telling the abuse victim that all problems are the wife's fault and that such events as rape are caused by her lack of responsiveness or failure as a sexual partner.

As the therapist listens to the client's recounting of various abusive events and her causal interpretation of those events, she/he will need to help the client to reevaluate her role if she is engaging in undue self-blame or has unrealistic expectations about her ability to "fix" her partner. The impact of such incidents on the victim should be explored. Traumatic forced sex should be labeled as rape in a matter-of-fact manner. The therapist's job is not to push the client out of the relationship but to help her separate the reality of the relationship from the fantasy of what she has wanted it to be. The client will need to determine the actual probability of achieving those goals with this particular partner. The therapist must also address the client's safety needs in a pragmatic manner with emergency phone numbers and escape routes.

If the relationship has been terminated recently because of rape or a combination of rape and other abuse, therapy may again need to focus first on issues other than the impact of the trauma, such as financial security and safety. Interpersonal issues and treatment of symptoms are likely to take a back seat until these more basic needs are met. Therapists sometimes wonder why battered and raped women deny reactions or are very symptomatic but seem unmotivated to work on symptom reduction. A reexamination of Maslow's hierarchy of needs may be in order. Emotional reactions to traumatic events are sometimes delayed and could be conceptualized as a luxury if basic survival and safety needs are not met. If a woman believes that her husband is going to appear at any time to kill or attack her physically or sexually, she is unlikely to practice relaxation or "let down her guard" in other ways. If she suddenly finds herself the sole support of herself and her children on an inadequate income, a client is likely to focus all of her energy and attention on these more basic issues. Therapy at this point consists of support, training in problem solving, and agency referrals. It is also the phase when trust in the therapist is established.

When it is possible to begin to deal with symptom reduction, therapies that have been demonstrated effective in the treatment of PTSD and depression with rape victims may prove quite helpful. Several types of cognitive and behavioral therapies have been demonstrated to be effective, with none as yet proving to be a superior mode of treatment. Treatments that have been demonstrated to be effective for rape are stress inoculation (Olasov & Foa, 1987; Resick, Jordan, Girelli, Hutter, & Marhoefer-Dvorak, 1988; Veronen & Kilpatrick, 1983), systematic desensitization (Frank et al., 1988; Wolff, 1977), cognitive therapy (Frank et al., 1988), and assertion training (Resick et al., 1988).

As proposed in either the information-processing model of PTSD symptom development (Foa, Steketee, & Olasov, 1989) or two-factor behavioral theory, which consists of classical conditioning and operant avoidance (Holmes & St. Lawrence, 1983; Kilpatrick et al., 1979b), all of the treatments listed earlier may serve two functions. One is to expose clients to conditional fear cues that may trigger flashbacks, anxiety, or other symptoms, in a safe environment with no negative consequences. Such exposure to fear-inducing stimuli results in extinction/desensitization of the fear and anxiety responses. Another function of these therapies is to modify negative appraisals and facilitate more adaptive emotional processing and acceptance of the event. Successful emotional processing should reduce the intrusive recollections of the event that are the hallmark of PTSD (Foa & Kozak, 1986; Foa, Olasov, & Steketee, 1987).

Treatment of sexual dysfunctions in rape victims has been studied by Becker and Skinner (1983, 1984) using the two-factor theory as a basis. That is, sexual dysfunctions develop as a result of pairing sexual activity with fear. Consequently, Becker and Skinner's sexual dysfunction treatment program is a systematic and comprehensive approach to reduce anxiety and increase sexual pleasure. Results of the program appear promising.

In addition to fear and anxiety reactions, other issues may need to be addressed in therapy. Trust might be defined as the belief that one will come to no harm at the hands of another. Trust is an issue that is likely to emerge in therapy with those who have been raped in intimate relationships. Although Koss (1988) found no difference between stranger and nonfamily-acquaintance rape victims in relationship satisfaction, including trust, those who were raped by family members, including husbands, had greater problems with relationship satisfaction. Because rape in an intimate relationship destroys the very basis for intimacy (i.e., trust), there may be a great deal of reluctance on the part of the marital rape victim to risk exposure to further violence by trusting another person and developing an intimate relationship. Avoidance of intimacy is likely to be pervasive and long-lasting.

The therapist could address such loss of trust as a learned fear much like other learned fears and treat it with the therapy techniques listed earlier, with some type of graduated exposure in relationships that are appraised unlikely to be dangerous. For those women who view trust as an either-or phenomenon, some cognitive restructuring may be helpful, such as having them view it on a continuum in which people earn trust a bit at a time.

Finally, issues of self-esteem will need to be addressed in therapy. Cognitive techniques that help the client examine her attributions regarding victimization and modify self-defeating beliefs may prove beneficial. These techniques should also be helpful in the treatment of depressive symptoms that are likely to occur following marital rape. Just as the victim of marital rape may lose trust in other people, she may also lose trust in herself (i.e., in her ability to choose safe relationships or make decisions). It may be helpful for the therapist to explore these issues and to help the client develop problem-solving strategies to restore confidence in herself.

SUMMARY AND FUTURE DIRECTIONS

The research presented in this chapter suggests that marital rape is both a significant problem and a problem that tends to go undiagnosed in therapy. Women who are raped as well as physically abused in other ways have significantly more problems than those who are physically abused but not raped. It appears that clinicians need to be more alert to the possibility of marital rape when treating women with marital problems of all kinds, especially victims of battering.

Several therapies have been systematically evaluated concerning their success with rape victims (i.e., victims of nonmarital rape). Although the results are suggestive of the kinds of therapies that might be effective with victims of marital rape, they still need to be explored and formally evaluated. At this point, it is not known whether therapies that have been successful with rape victims will generalize to marital rape victims or if treatments need to be designed specifically for marital rape victims.

The psychological impact of marital rape has been investigated two ways: by comparing marital rape victims who are also battered (as is most often the case) with battered women who have not been raped or with rape victims who are not married to the perpetrator. From the limited research that has been conducted, those women who are both raped and battered fare worse than those who are battered but not raped. However, no differences have been found between marital rape victims and nonmarital rape victims. If one can extrapolate from these findings, a dubious undertaking given the differences in sample selection and methodology, it would appear that marital rape victims might be more like rape victims than like battered women in terms of psychological impact. However, without a study comparing all of these groups with appropriate methodology and sufficient sample sizes, this hypothesis is mere conjecture.

Among the most tentative, yet interesting, findings of our research are the findings regarding the presence of symptoms of borderline personality among victims of marital rape. Although victims did not display enough symptoms to warrant a positive diagnosis, they did display significantly more symptoms than the group of battered women or the comparison group. This finding suggests the possibility that symptoms of borderline personality may actually be a consequence of marital rape. This is a possibility that should be explored by further research. Furthermore, the findings of the research on marital rape conducted thus far are a clear indication that more research on *all* aspects of marital rape is needed. The sparse research is disquieting considering the prevalence and apparent impact on victims.

REFERENCES

American Psychiatric Association. (1980). *Diagnostic and statistical manual of mental disorders* (DSM-III; 3rd ed.). Washington, DC: Author.

Becker, J. V., & Skinner, L. J. (1983). Assessment and treatment of victims of rape-related sexual dysfunctions. *The Clinical Psychologist, 36,* 102–105.

Becker, J. V., & Skinner, L. J. (1984). Behavioral treatment of sexual dysfunctions in sexual assault survivors. In I. Stuart & J. Greer (Eds.), *Victims of sexual aggression* (pp. 211–234). New York: Van Nostrand Reinhold.

Derogotis, L. R., & Spencer, P. M. (1982). *The brief symptom inventory (BSI): Administration, scoring and procedures manual—1.* Towson: MD.: Clinical Psychometric Research.

Dobash, R. E., & Dobash, R. (1979). *Violence against wives.* New York: Free Press.

Doron, J. (1980, August). *Conflict and violence in intimate relationships: Focus on marital rape.* Paper presented at the annual meeting of American Sociological Association, New York.

Finkelhor, D., & Yllo, K. (1982). Forced sex in marriage: A preliminary research report. *Crime & Delinquency, 28,* 459–478.

Finkelhor, D., & Yllo, K. (1985). *License to rape: Sexual abuse of wives.* New York: Holt, Rinehart, & Winston.

Foa, E. B., & Kozak, M. J. (1986). Emotional processing of fear: Exposure to corrective information. *Psychological Bulletin, 99,* 20–35.

Foa, E. B., Olasov, B., & Steketee, G. S. (1987, September). *Treatment of rape victims.* Paper presented at the NIMH conference, State of the Art Workshop on Victims of Sexual Assault, Charleston, SC.

Foa, E. B., Steketee, G. S., & Olasov, B. (1989). Behavioral cognitive conceptualizations of post-traumatic stress disorder. *Behavior Therapy, 20,* 155–176.

Frank, E., Anderson, B., Stewart, B. D., Dancu, C., Hughes, C., & West, D. (1988). Efficacy of cognitive behavior therapy and systematic desensitization in the treatment of rape trauma. *Behavior Therapy, 19,* 403–420.

Frieze, I. H. (1983). Investigating the causes and consequences of marital rape. *Signs: Journal of Women in Culture and Society, 8,* 532–553.

Frieze, I. H., & Knoble, J. (1980). *The effects of alcohol on marital violence.* Paper presented at the annual meeting of the American Psychological Association, Montreal, Canada.

Gayford, J. J. (1975). Wife battering: A preliminary survey of 100 cases. *British Medical Journal, 25,* 194–197.

Gelles, R. (1974). *The violent home.* Beverly Hills, CA. Sage.

George, L. K., & Winfield-Laird, I. (1986). *Sexual assault: Prevalence and mental health consequences.* A final report submitted to the National Institute of Mental health for supplemental funding to the Duke University Epidemiologic Catchment Area Program.

Hanneke, C. R., Shields, N. M., & McCall, G. J. (1986). Assessing the prevalence of marital rape. *Journal of Interpersonal Violence. 1,* 350–362.

Hilberman, E. (1980).Overview: The wife beater's wife reconsidered. *American Journal of Psychiatry, 137,* 1336–1347.

Hilberman, E., & Munson, K. (1977–1978). Sixty battered women. *Victimology, 2,* 460–471.

Hirsch, M. (1981). *Women and violence.* New York: Van Nostrand Reinhold.

Holmes, M. R., & St. Lawrence, J. (1983). Treatment of rape-induced trauma: Proposed behavioral conceptualization and review of the literature. *Clinical Psychology Review, 3,* 417–433.

Kilpatrick, D. G., Veronen, L. J., & Resick, P. A. (1979a). Assessment of the aftermath of rape: Changing patterns of fear. *Journal of Behavioral Assessment, 1,* 133–148.

Kilpatrick, D. G., Veronen, L. J., & Resick, P. A. (1979b). The aftermath of rape: Recent empirical findings. *American Journal of Orthopsychiatry, 49,* 658–669.

Kilpatrick, D. G., Veronen, L. J., Saunders, B. E., Best, C. L., Amick-McMullan, A., & Paduhovich, J. (1987). *The psychological impact of crime: A study of randomly surveyed crime victims.* Final report submitted to the National Institute of Justice, Grant No. 84-IJ-CX-0039.

Koss, M. P., Dinero, T. E., & Seibel, C. A. (1988). Stranger and acquaintance rape: Are there differences in the victim's experience? *Psychology of Women Quarterly, 12,* 1–24.

Lewis, B. Y. (1984, August). *Wife abuse and marital rape in a clinical population.* Paper presented at the Second Family Violence Research Conference, University of New Hampshire, Durham.

Martin, J. P. (Ed.) (1978). *Violence and the family.* Chicestor, England: Wiley.

Moore, R. A. (1971). The prevalence of alcoholism in a community general hospital. *American Journal of Psychiatry, 128,* 638–639.

Moore, R. A. (1972). The diagnosis of alcoholism in a psychiatric hospital: A trial of the Michigan Alcoholism Screening Test (MAST). *American Journal of Psychiatry, 128,* 1565–1569.

Olasov, B., & Foa, E. (1987, July). *The treatment of post-traumatic stress disorder in sexual assault survivors using stress inoculation training (SIT).* Paper presented at the Third World Congress of Victimology, San Francisco.

Pagelow, M. D. (1984). *Family violence.* New York: Praeger.

Prescott, S., & Letko, C. (1977). Battered women: A social psychological perspective. In M. Roy (Ed.), *Battered women.* New York: Van Nostrand Reinhold.

Resick, P. A. (1982, November). *Therapeutic considerations in working with a grown incest and rape victim: A case study.* Paper presented at the Association for the Advancement of Behavior Therapy, Los Angeles.

Resick, P. A. (1988). *Reactions of female and male victims of rape or robbery.* Final report submitted to the National Institute of Justice, Grant No. 85-IJ-CX-0042.

Resick, P. A., Jordan, C. G., Girelli, S. A., Hutter, C. K., & Marhoefer-Dvorak, S. (1988). A comparative outcome study of behavioral group therapy for sexual assault victims. *Behavior Therapy, 19,* 385–401.

Resick, P. A., Veronen, L. J., Calhoun, K. S., Kilpatrick, D. G., & Atkeson, B. M. (1986). Assessment of fear reactions in sexual assault victims: A factor analytic study of the Veronen-Kilpatrick Modified Fear Survey. *Behavioral Assessment, 8,* 271–283.

Russell, D. (1980, August). *The prevalence and impact of marital rape in San Francisco.* Paper presented at the annual meeting of the American Sociological Association, New York.

Russell, D. (1982). *Rape in marriage.* New York: Macmillan.

Selzer, M. L., Vinokur, A., & Van Rooijen, L. (1975). A self-administered Short Michigan Alcoholism Screening Test (SMAST): The quest for a new diagnostic instrument. *American Journal of Psychiatry, 127,* 1653–1658.

Shields, N. M., & Hanneke, C. R. (1983). Battered wives' reactions to marital rape. In D. Finkelhor, R. J. Gelles, G. T. Hotaling, & M. A. Straus (Eds.), *The dark side of families: Current family violence research* (pp. 132–148). Beverly Hills, CA: Sage.

Veronen, L. J., & Kilpatrick, D. G. (1983). Stress management for rape victims. In D. Meichenbaum & M. E. Jaremko (Eds.), *Stress reduction and prevention.* New York: Plenum.

Walker, L. E. (1979). *The battered woman.* New York: Harper & Row.

Walker, L. E. (1984). *The battered woman syndrome.* New York: Springer.

Weingourt, R. (1985). Wife rape: Barriers to identification and treatment. *American Journal of Psychotherapy, 39,* 187–192.

Wolff, R. (1977). Systematic desensitization and negative practice to alter the after effects of a rape attempt. *Journal of Behavior Therapy and Experimental Psychiatry, 8,* 423–425.

CHAPTER 8

The Child Witness to Marital Violence

MINDY S. ROSENBERG AND B. B. ROBBIE ROSSMAN

INTRODUCTION

The topic of family violence has received unprecedented attention from researchers, mental health professionals, and the media over the last decade and particularly during the past 5 years. Different aspects of family violence have been identified for study and treatment strategies have been developed for such areas as child physical abuse and neglect, child sexual abuse, child psychological maltreatment, and marital violence. Children who witness their parents' violence have only recently been targeted as a unique population warranting research and clinical attention. These are children who may be the sole witnesses to acts of physical and psychological violence between their parents (or between parent and intimate partner), including repeated beatings, mental degradation, assaults with guns and knives, threats of suicide and homicide, and destruction of property. These children are at risk for developing a range of behavioral and emotional problems as a result of growing up in a violent home, even if they themselves are not maltreated. Within this population, however, there may also be children who are victims of other forms of abuse and/or neglect.

Clinical and research interest in child witnesses to marital violence emerged from several directions. First, shelters for victims of domestic violence have long recognized that many children of battered women needed clinical attention and began to develop children's programs once their general operation funding was secure and battered women's services were developed and running smoothly (Carlson, 1984). Because the shelter movement across the United States gained momentum in the mid-to-late 1970s and early 1980s (Martin, 1981), children's programs in shelters tend to be a fairly recent phenomenon. A second avenue of concern for child witnesses originated during the late 1970s when protective service workers, public health nurses, and other mental health professionals felt helpless in situations where they

Preparation of this work was supported in part by a grant awarded to both authors from the National Institute of Mental Health (No. MH41051).

could not intervene legally to protect children who witnessed extreme incidents of marital violence, unless there also was evidence of child physical abuse or neglect. Most states at that time did not include the concept of psychological maltreatment in their child protection statutes. Since then, many have argued for increased legal and clinical attention to children who may fall under the category of psychological maltreatment, although considerable debate surrounds the definition and inclusion of this concept in child protection proceedings (see Brassard, Germain, & Hart, 1987; Rosenberg, 1987a).

Finally, the inclusion of posttraumatic stress disorder (PTSD) in the third and revised editions of the *Diagnostic and Statistical Manual of Mental Disorders* (American Psychiatric Association, 1980, 1987) has directed attention to the constellation of psychological effects that can emerge following an event outside the range of usual human experience. Characteristic symptoms include recurrent and intrusive reexperience of the event; emotional numbing; avoidance of thoughts, feelings, or activities associated with the event; and persistent symptoms of increased arousal (American Psychiatric Association, 1987). Although traumatized adults formed the initial sample groups in studies of PTSD, recent investigations have been concerned with the development of this disorder in children who have experienced such stressors as war, natural disasters (e.g., earthquakes, fires), and human-induced disasters (Eth & Pynoos, 1985). Children who witness extreme marital violence (i.e., serious injury or murder) are included under the latter category and are considered at risk for developing PTSD.

This chapter reviews the current research and clinical literature on child witnesses to marital violence. It begins with a discussion of the known epidemiology of the problem, followed by research findings on the psychological effects of witnessing violence on children. Next is a review of treatment strategies used in crisis intervention, group and individual therapy, and parenting interventions. The chapter ends with a discussion about future research and treatment directions.

EPIDEMIOLOGY

Unfortunately, there are no epidemiological studies on the incidence or prevalence of children who witness marital violence. Geffner, Rosenbaum, and Hughes (1988) suggest that large-scale national probability sample surveys similar to the ones conducted by Straus and colleagues (Straus & Gelles, 1986; Straus, Gelles, & Steinmetz, 1980) would provide the field with basic information about the extent of witnessing experiences for children and the demographic variables associated with these experiences, such as family composition, socioeconomic indicators, religious background, child gender and age, frequency and intensity of violence witnessed, and various types of violence witnessed (e.g., physical, psychological) and experienced.

Current estimates of the number of children exposed to marital violence typically come from two sources. First are extrapolations based on the Straus et al. (1980) national survey data of spouse and child violence in 2143 families. By using Straus's conclusion that approximately 3 million American families experience at least one serious violent incident yearly (i.e., defined as one likely to cause physical injury, such as punching, kicking, or using a weapon) between spouses or nonmarried cohabitating persons, and assuming an average of two children per family in the 55% of violent families that contained a child between the ages of 3 and 17, Carlson (1984) projected that a minimum of 3.3 million children yearly are at risk for exposure to marital violence. The Straus et al. data base did not include families with children under the age of 3 or divorced families where violence continues between ex-spouses who maintain contact for purposes of child visitation. Carlson, therefore, feels that her estimate is a gross underrepresentation of the actual number of children exposed to marital violence. Although the 1985 survey replication with 3520 families suggests that the overall couple violence rate declined from 160 per thousand families in 1975 to 158 per thousand families in 1985 (Straus & Gelles, 1986), a similar-sized estimate of children who may witness their parents' violence is likely.

A second, more circumscribed, source of data about children's exposure to marital violence could potentially come from research studies on the children themselves. One drawback in obtaining basic information about frequency and intensity of violence witnessed by children is that, typically, researchers in this area assume that children witness marital violence if it is present in their home, without actually asking the children what they saw or heard. This assumption is held even when researchers use a standardized measure such as the Conflict Tactics Scale (Straus, 1979) to document specific violent behaviors between spouses (e.g., Brown, Pelcovitz, & Kaplan, 1983; Wolfe, Jaffe, Wilson, & Zak, 1985). Rosenberg (1984) addressed this methodological problem by adding the question, ''How often did your child see this?'' following each behavior listed in the Conflict Tactics Scale, and used this revised scale to obtain empirical information about 5- to 8-year-old children from mothers' self-reports. The sample was composed of two groups: mothers and children who resided temporarily in battered women's shelters and mothers and children who were not exposed to marital violence. In addition, Rosenberg also interviewed and tape-recorded the responses of these children about their experiences when their parents fought. Children's reports of witnessing their parents' violence generally supported their mothers' reports, although mothers were able to provide more detailed information, in terms of frequency and intensity, than were children (as expected). The important finding was that despite one or both parents' intentions to shield children from violent behavior, nearly all such incidents were seen and/or heard by the children. However, in some situations, mothers believed the children slept through the arguments and beatings, whereas the children described listening to these incidents as they remained in their bedrooms, too frightened to leave. Because there can be discrepancies in parent and child reports of violence, it is important to document what was actually witnessed by the child (i.e., what was seen and heard), in order to represent more accurately the child's experience and to determine statistically how this type of experience relates to other aspects of family life and the child's psychological functioning.

CONSEQUENCES OF WITNESSING MARITAL VIOLENCE ON CHILDREN

There is a small, slowly emerging literature on the effects of witnessing violence on children's psychological development. Initially, this literature was limited to clinical descriptions of children's behavioral and emotional problems elicited primarily from children in battered women's shelters or who accompanied their mothers to emergency rooms (see Goodman & Rosenberg, 1987, for a review). Although criticisms concerning research design and measurement continue to abound (e.g., Geffner, Rosenbaum, & Hughes, 1988), recent studies have improved methodologically by including appropriate comparison groups and standardized measures, and by tapping a wider range of domains where children may display dysfunctional as well as adaptive behavior. These studies represent beginning efforts to document the effects of witnessing marital violence on children's behavior, cognitive and social problem-solving abilities, and coping and emotional functioning.

Behavioral Functioning

In studies that investigate child witnesses' behavioral functioning, researchers typically ask mothers to complete a child behavior checklist to obtain an indication of child adjustment. Rarely is additional information sought from an "objective" source such as a teacher, day-care worker or neighbor, and it is unlikely that behavioral observations are catalogued and coded. Thus, much of researchers' knowledge about child witnesses' behavior is based on maternal perceptions of their children. Because many of these mothers are in the midst of their own personal crisis when they complete the questionnaire (i.e, recently experienced a battering, left their husband, and moved to a shelter), these perceptions may be uniquely biased.

Overall, studies on children's behavior suggest that child witnesses are at greater risk for both externalizing and internalizing behavioral problems in contrast to children from nonviolent families, although the results across studies are not always consistent for type of problem, gender, and age (see Goodman & Rosenberg, 1987). One relatively consistent finding, however, is that not all child witnesses are similarly affected by witnessing violence, and the sample is clearly a heterogeneous one. Moreover, there is some indication that witnessing violence per se may not be the only, or even the most critical, factor in predicting child adjustment. For example, Wolfe et al. (1985) found that approximately 25% of children in their violent sample were reported to experience behavioral problems in the clinical range of severity, with boys' scores more elevated than girls' scores. Those children who fell in the clinical range of behavioral distress were more likely to have been exposed to higher frequency and intensity of physical violence, and their mothers reported more negative life events during the past year in comparison with children who were in the behaviorally adjusted range. Approaching the problem of children's behavior from a slightly different perspective, Jouriles, Barling, and O'Leary (1986) found that witnessing marital violence was not related significantly to child behavior problems. However, witnessing violence was associated with parent–child aggression, and parental aggression toward children was associated with a range of child problems, including attention problems, anxiety-withdrawal, motor excess, and conduct problems.

In our own research, we found that child witnesses to marital violence who reside temporarily in shelters are perceived by their mothers as significantly more aggressive and hyperactive than children from discordant couples or satisfactorily married couples. Child witnesses who continue to live with their parents' ongoing violence are reported to experience significantly more somatic complaints than children in any of the other groups. It appears that children in the latter group are expressing their internalized distress quietly rather than calling attention to themselves by acting-out behaviors. These symptoms may also be a safe way to elicit parental attention and reassurance in an unpredictable situation engendered by continued marital violence (Rosenberg, 1988; Rossman, 1988).

Cognitive and Social Problem-Solving Abilities

Professionals who come in contact with child witnesses around academically oriented tasks (i.e., reading, writing) tend to note that some children have difficulty concentrating on the material, are easily frustrated and distracted, achieve below their grade level in school, and attempt to avoid tasks that require sustained attention. Other child witnesses are better able to focus their attention, tend to do quite well in school, and appear to welcome academic involvement as a diversion to their life at home. Despite these clinical reports of heterogeneous cognitive effects from the stress of marital violence, empirical attention to cognitive factors is virtually absent in the child witness literature, with a few exceptions noted in the following paragraphs.

Westra and Martin (1981) conducted one of the earliest studies on the cognitive abilities of children of battered women by comparing the functioning of twenty 2½- to 8-year-old children to standardized norms on the McCarthy Scale of Children's Abilities. Child witnesses to marital violence and child victims were not differentiated. As predicted, children of battered women scored significantly lower than a standardized population on the verbal, quantitative, motor, and general cognitive index of the McCarthy measure. Although neurological examinations revealed normal functioning, these children also evidenced a number of medical problems, including prematurity and/or low birthweight, speech articulation and hearing difficulties, serious accidents, and incidents of physical abuse. Because child victims and child witnesses were not separated, it is impossible to draw conclusions about the specific effects of either experience on children's cognitive functioning or the possibility that children of one group were overrepresented in reported medical problems.

One aspect of cognitive functioning that has received empirical attention in the child witness population is social problem-solving abilities. There is ample evidence from social learning theory to predict that children who witness their parents' violent and otherwise nonconstructive means of resolving interpersonal conflict will have frequent opportunities to observe, acquire, and produce similar behaviors in response to their own interpersonal problems (Bandura, 1973). Similarly, shelter staff who work with child witnesses typically identify "problem-solving abilities" as an important area for intervention based on their clinical experience and acceptance of social learning principles to explain violent behavior. There have been two empirical studies that offer tentative support for the idea that children's social problem-solving abilities are affected by witnessing their parents' violence.

In the first study, Rosenberg (1984) investigated the social problem-solving abilities of children aged 5 to 8 years who witnessed their parents' violence but were not themselves abused, compared with children from nonviolent families. She used the Social Problem Situation Analysis Measure (SPSAM), a paper-and-pencil measure that tapped a range of social-cognitive skills and problem resolution strategies in three situations involving peer conflict (e.g., a child wanting to use another child's paintbrush; a child wanting to play in a group ball game) and one situation where a child witnesses a parental argument (Elias, Larcen, Zlotlow & Chinsky, 1978). Children from violent homes who witnessed relatively high levels of violence (i.e., many types and high frequency of violent behavior) differed from those who witnessed relatively less violence in two important ways. First, they did less well on a submeasure of interpersonal sensitivity, which meant they had greater difficulty identifying the problem situations and understanding the thoughts and feelings of those involved. Second, they tended to choose either passive (e.g., wishing for something to change, resolution by another's action) or aggressive (e.g., use of physical force) strategies to resolve interpersonal conflict and were less likely to choose assertive strategies (e.g., direct discussion, mutual compromise). The finding that their responses revolved around a passive-aggressive dimension suggests that these children have ready access to problem resolution strategies similar to the strategies clinicians find with male batterers, that is, the difficulty in responding assertively to their wives and the ease in using passive or aggressive solutions to interpersonal conflict (Dutton, 1988; Sonkin, Martin, & Walker, 1985).

In an elaboration of Rosenberg's study, Groisser (1986) investigated the effects of negative affect (i.e., anger) on child witnesses' social-cognitive skills. She adapted the SPSAM methodology to include videotapes of a child witnessing parent and peer conflict in two affect conditions (mild and strong anger), and presented these videotapes to children aged 6 to 12 years from violent and nonviolent families. Every attempt was made to separate child victims from child witnesses in the violent group and to screen for battering and child abuse in the comparison group. Several important findings emerged. First, in contrast to children from nonviolent families, child witnesses were less skillful in resolving interpersonal problems when faced with obstacles to their initial solution. Here is another indication that child witnesses lack a reservoir of effective problem-resolution strategies and become stymied after their first efforts. Second, children's observation of parental conflict resolution strategies was related to their own choice of strategies in the peer conflict videotapes. Children who witnessed greater levels of their parents' violence gave fewer constructive (e.g., direct discussion, assertive action, compromise) and more nonconstructive (e.g., verbal or physical aggression, passive resolution) strategies to resolve incidents of peer conflict, regardless of affect level. Choice of nonconstructive problem-resolution strategies was associated with greater behavioral problems and fewer social competencies as perceived by mothers, whereas children who chose constructive problem resolution strategies were perceived as having fewer behavioral problems. Finally, children who witnessed greater levels of spousal reasoning generated more alternative solutions to resolving peer conflict and were perceived by their mothers as more socially competent.

The effects of anger on children's problem-solving skills emerged most clearly on the submeasure of interpersonal sensitivity. As in Rosenberg's findings (1984), there was a trend for children from violent families to perform less well on this submeasure in contrast to children from nonviolent homes. However, child witnesses performed significantly better on this submeasure when viewing videotapes of parental conflict in the strong anger condition than they did in the other three conditions (parent-mild, peer-mild, and peer-strong anger). Groisser (1986) hypothesized that children from violent families may be desensitized to all but the most extreme instances of anger, having had greater exposure to high levels of conflict and aggression in their everyday lives than children from nonviolent families, necessitating a more powerful demonstration of anger to activate problem-solving abilities. An alternative, although not mutually exclusive, explanation is that for the child witness, angry parental arguments may portend future violence, which may necessitate the child's active, protective response toward the victim of abuse, typically his or her mother (e.g., calling a neighbor or the police, trying to break up a fight). Therefore, the child needs to be "ready" psychologically to intervene on the parent's behalf. This result is also reminiscent of the finding that abused children are often vigilant to environmental cues as an adaptive way of protecting themselves from additional physical harm (see Aber & Cicchetti, 1985).

In summary, there is tentative evidence to suggest that children's observation of their parents' violence affects their own abilities to solve interpersonal conflict, as measured by paper-and-pencil measures and reactions to videotaped scenarios of parent and peer conflict. Although considerably more research is needed to explicate the effects of witnessing parental violence on children's cognitive functioning, initial findings indicate that the domain of social problem-solving abilities may represent an important arena for treatment and ultimately, prevention efforts.

Coping and Emotional Functioning

Because research on children's coping has only recently emerged as a topic of interest among child clinical and developmental theorists (see Compas, 1987 for a review), it is not surprising that research on coping processes specific to child witnesses has received scant empirical attention. Having a greater understanding of the ways in which child witnesses attempt to deal with the myriad of issues that are faced as a result of observing their parents' violence, and the differential effectiveness of these coping strategies, would provide an important direction for treatment. Information reviewed in this section, therefore, will focus first on theoretical issues about children's coping in general, followed by recent clinical and research findings specific to child witnesses of violence.

For purposes of this discussion, coping can be conceptualized as children's cognitive and behavioral efforts to manage external and/or internal events that are potentially harmful to the child (Lazarus & Folkman, 1984). In the case of child witnesses, the external events may include the actual violence between parents and the potential for the child to be physically injured during the battering incidents. The internal events may include management of overwhelming emotions such as anxiety, fear, confusion, and anger during and after the violence. These coping efforts are goal directed in their intent to reduce threat to physical or psychological well-being. They may include strategies at lower levels of consciousness such as classic defense mechanisms and/or readily conscious strategies that are well-learned, automatic behaviors and are easily observable and reportable. Coping efforts need not be successful in reducing threat to be considered "coping" as long as they represent attempts to manage threat resulting from the stressor.

What are the threats for children inherent in marital violence? Because marital violence can be characterized as a multithreat stressor, a child may, over the course of one or many incidents, experience threats such as these: (a) a parent's physical danger and, possibly, a parent's death; (b) personal physical injury; (c) feelings of helplessness about intervening to stop the violence; (d) family dissolution; and (e) loss of self-esteem if the child is somehow implicated in the conflict. The importance of thinking about marital violence as a multithreat stressor becomes clear when researchers attempt to study child witnesses' coping efforts, because it is necessary to specify exactly what the child is coping with (e.g., events that may require problem-solving skills; emotional dilemmas that may require the ability to soothe oneself and seek out comfort and support). This distinction between problem- and emotion-focused coping was introduced initially by Folkman and Lazarus (1980) to describe dimensions of adult coping and later by Compas (1987) to describe child and adolescent coping efforts, and it is applicable to the context of marital violence. During an incident of marital violence and its aftermath, it would be difficult to find a single coping behavior that would be responsive to diverse threats. Therefore, it might appear most adaptive for children to develop an effective repertoire of coping strategies including both problem- and emotion-focused strategies.

A second consideration in recognizing marital violence as a multithreat stressor is that multiple threats, whether they occur within one event or across multiple occurrences of that event, are considered more damaging psychologically than individual incidents or single-threat stressors (Rutter, 1983). Thus, the stress associated with marital violence for children should be especially severe and would require considerable mobilization of coping resources.

Clinical descriptions and empirical studies of children's coping with a multiplicity of traumatic events have begun to emerge in the psychiatric and psychological literatures, including, but not limited to such occurrences as attacks on children by their psychotic parents (Anthony, 1986); earthquakes (Galante & Foa, 1986); physical abuse (Green, 1985); the nuclear accident at Three Mile Island (Handford et al., 1986); war (Kinzie, Sack, Angell, Manson & Ruth, 1986); and Terr's classic work on a school-bus kidnapping in Chowchilla, California (1979, 1983). Attention to children's coping processes and the identification of factors that contribute to adaptive and maladaptive outcomes are apparent in these initial studies of children who have been victimized as well as who have been observers of others' victimization.

The work of Pynoos and Eth brings a noteworthy contribution to the descriptive literature on child witnesses' coping processes. In their clinical work with children who have witnessed extreme violence (e.g., murder, rape, suicide, aggravated assault), Pynoos and Eth (1986) noted four common defensive strategies used by preadolescent children to modulate their anxiety shortly after the traumatic event. When the child witnesses were asked to draw a picture and tell a story, some children reversed the violent outcome of their story and provided a more acceptable ending as a way of coping with their painful reality. Pynoos and Eth refer to this strategy as "denial-in-fantasy." A second group of children inhibited spontaneous thought and avoided associations to the traumatic event by disregarding potentially important aspects of their picture or fantasy. Children in the third group were unable to distance themselves from the trauma by engaging in fantasy and drew the actual scene of the event, accompanied by an unemotional account of what occurred. A fourth group of children were described as in a "constant state of anxious arousal." Their preoccupation with feelings of vulnerability and thoughts of future danger preempted discussion of the recent event.

Empirical efforts to identify the coping strategies of child witnesses and the links between coping and children's psychological outcomes are beginning to extend these clinical findings. The initial findings from our collaborative research on child witnesses (Rosenberg, 1988; Rossman, 1988) will be presented, after describing our research design in some detail. The intent of this work was to investigate children's coping strategies and their beliefs about control in situations of parental violence and discord as they related to child outcome, including measures of children's self-perceptions, distress, and adaptive and problem behaviors. In contrast to previous research, the children participating in this study came from families placed at different points along the continuum of marital violence and discord, which allowed for more refined comparisons than those provided by a violent versus control group design. Ninety-four mother–child pairs were interviewed, with children ranging in age from 6 to 13 years. Participants were divided into four groups based on a combination of scores from two screening instruments designed to measure marital aggression (physical and verbal) and marital satisfaction. These groups included mother–child pairs from the following marital situations:

1. Violent couples, where mothers and children resided temporarily at a shelter for victims of domestic violence ("violent-shelter")
2. Violent couples, where mothers and children lived in their own homes ("violent-home")
3. Discordant couples ("discordant")
4. Nonviolent, nondiscordant couples ("satisfactory")

A measure of the extent to which children witnessed marital violence and discord was obtained from interviews with their mothers.

As part of the assessment protocol, children were asked to endorse their preferred coping strategies when feeling negative affect in general, without identifying the specific situations that elicited these feelings. These strategies included both problem- and emotion-focused items that constitute five subscales from the Child Perceived Coping Questionnaire (Rossman, 1986): Use of Parents, Use of Peers/Self, Distraction/Avoidance, Emote, and Self-soothe. Problem-oriented use of others for coping is emphasized with use of parents, peers, and self. Distraction/avoidance strategies represent attempts to divert or withdraw from the stressor or the negative affect resulting from the stressor. Emote and self-soothe strategies are considered attempts at emotion regulation, where emoting includes such behaviors as crying and biting nails, and self-soothing involves distancing and self-calming messages and behaviors. Denial of negative affect was also assessed as an avoidant, emotion regulation strategy.

Children in the violent-home and discordant groups endorsed greater use of parents for coping with negative feelings than children in either the violent-shelter or satisfactory groups. Higher endorsement of parents may represent more urgent attempts by children in these groups to gain parental attention, support, and reassurance. These attempts may be prompted by distress from the continued marital violence and discord. In fact, mothers in the violent-home group reported their children to evidence the highest level of somatic complaints compared to children in the other groups, which further supports the idea that children who witness continued marital violence are perceived to experience significant internal distress.

It is all the more noteworthy that children witnessing continued marital violence and discord endorse relatively high levels of parental use for coping when one compares these results with the developmental expectation for latency-age children in general. In a sample of "normal" 6- to 12-year-old children from nonviolent families, Rossman (1986) found that girls' reliance on parents for coping typically decreases over the latency-age period while latency-age boys consistently report low levels of parental use for coping. Children in this age range are expected to rely increasingly on their peers for support, and on their own developing sense of self (Harter, 1983; Hartup, 1983). In our sample, children's endorsement of use of peer/self for coping was positively and significantly related to their judgments of self-worth and positive views of their social and physical competence, as well as their behavioral conduct.

A negative relationship emerged between level of marital violence and discord and children's endorsement of items reflecting denial of negative affect, such that as marital violence and discord increased, children's denial of negative affect decreased. It appears that children who witness their parents' consistent and extreme violence have great difficulty denying their negative and distressed feelings, which is actually a realistic response to overwhelming stress. Whereas the expected negative relationship between denial of painful affect and anxiety emerged for children in the discordant and satisfactory groups (i.e., "a little denial is a good thing"), no such relationship emerged for children in either violent group. Perhaps the consistency and severity of marital violence precludes child witnesses from using denial to reduce their anxiety. Our finding is not to be confused with Pynoos and Eth's (1986) clinical report that some children cope initially with trauma by "denial in fantasy," because the two research teams appear to be studying different aspects of denial (i.e., denial of the event outcome versus denial of negative affect), observed child witnesses at different time points (i.e., after the traumatic incident vs. after multiple incidents of ongoing violence), and used different methods to elicit information (i.e., picture drawing vs. self-report questionnaire).

Across the entire sample of children, we found that endorsement of emote coping strategies (e.g., biting nails, crying) was related strongly to children's negative psychological outcomes, including higher anxiety; lower perceptions of self-worth; lower perceptions of social, athletic, and physical competence; negative perceptions of behavioral conduct; and self-blame (i.e., making internal attributions) for failure experiences in school and with peers.

The preceding findings begin to identify strategies used by child witnesses to cope with negative affect in general. But what strategies do children use to cope specifically with parental violence and discord? Clinical interviews with child witnesses suggest that differences in their perceptions of control over their parents' and their own behavior may mediate psychological functioning. For example, children who recognize that they had little or no control over their parents' behavior during a parental argument or violent episode but felt they could control their own behavior appeared to be doing "better" psychologically (i.e., behavioral, academic, and social adjustment) than children who felt they could control their parents' actions. Findings in the divorce literature (e.g., Wallerstein & Kelly, 1980) lend tentative support for this idea by suggesting that children who hold unrealistic beliefs about their responsibility for the divorce or their ability to influence their divorcing parents have poorer adjustment than children who recognize their parents' responsibility for the divorce and feel unable to control the outcome. In addition, literature on adult coping identifies the sense of personal control as an important mediator of stress (see Thompson, 1981). Consistent with these findings, we hypothesized that children who believed themselves in control of their own thoughts and behavior during parental conflict and violence, but not those of their parents, should show better adjustment. Children who believe in their personal control may feel a sense of mastery or security. But children who feel they can control their parents' conflicts are placing themselves in an unrealistic position and are likely to see their control attempts fail. When this happens, children may react by feeling anxious, and incompetent, and/or may display problematic behavioral and adaptive functioning.

Based on Thompson's (1981) typology of control beliefs and interview data collected from children of violent and nonviolent families, we devised a self-report questionnaire to assess the extent to which children believed they had behavioral and cognitive control over themselves and their parents when their parents fought. Examples of the control items are the following: cognitive control over self, as in thinking about other things when parents fight; cognitive control over parent, as in praying hard enough to stop parents from fighting; behavioral control over self, as in protecting oneself when parents fight; behavioral control over parent, as in keeping parents from fighting before they begin.

No unique pattern of control beliefs was found for children of violent versus nonviolent parents. As a general finding, children from shelters tended to hold the lowest beliefs of control about their own and their parents' behavior and cognitions, whereas children in the satisfactory group held the highest control beliefs. However, the variability within each group suggested that group membership was not synonymous with a specific pattern of control beliefs.

The data were then analyzed to assess the potential mediating effects of control beliefs on children's psychological functioning by dividing the sample into those children who had relatively high and those who had relatively low control beliefs. Children who believed they had control over their own thoughts and behavior during their parents' fights were less anxious, had lower reports of delinquent behaviors as measured by a behavioral checklist, and perceived themselves more positively in terms of their behavioral and social competence, and sense of self-worth. The sense of empowerment appears to be very useful for these children. When control over self and control over parent beliefs were considered together, children with higher control beliefs in both domains evidenced fewer problem behaviors than children in the other groups. Thus, our initial hypothesis was only partially supported. The belief of control over self does appear important for children's positive psychological functioning, but children who do well may also hold the belief that they can influence their parents during incidents of conflict and violence. However, the importance of control beliefs about the self is illustrated by findings about children who had the poorest psychological outcomes. These were children who believed they had control over their parents' thoughts and behavior but little or no control over their own. This particular combination of beliefs may characterize children who in some sense, feel the most powerless. Children who hold this pattern of beliefs have the highest depression scores, display low adaptive functioning, and evidence many behavioral problems, including aggression.

In summary, the emerging empirical literature on children who witness their parents' violence is beginning to document the negative effects that such experiences can have on children's psychological development. Child witnesses to marital violence are at greater risk for developing a range of both internalizing (e.g., somatic complaints) and externalizing (e.g., aggression) behavioral problems, for learning nonconstructive ways of resolving interpersonal conflicts, and for tending to experience themselves as less efficacious when faced with negative emotions or, not surprisingly, their parents' violence. The next section is a review of a variety of treatment strategies designed to intervene with child witnesses and address some of the difficulties they experience.

TREATMENT RECOMMENDATIONS

Unfortunately, the empirical literature on the efficacy of various treatments for child witnesses is sorely lacking, and, with one or two exceptions, there are no systematic treatment studies available. Although many battered women's shelters have developed a variety of innovative interventions to use with children and their mothers, the strategies are typically passed on by word of mouth, at local and national conferences, but rarely are subjected to systematic analysis within an experimental framework. Hence, researchers know very little about the types of interventions that work with these children. Moreover, basic descriptions of innovative clinical efforts rarely are published and disseminated to a larger professional audience, so it is very difficult to obtain detailed information about strategies that are currently in use with this population. Consequently, the information discussed here is compiled from several sources: (a) our combined clinical experience of working with multiple shelters in several states, (b) the available treatment literature on child witnesses, and (c) treatment suggestions based on the recent empirical research reviewed in the previous section. Treatment will be discussed first in terms of crisis intervention strategies, followed by issues to consider in group, individual (child), and familial (i.e., parenting, parent–child) interventions.

Crisis Intervention Strategies

It is often difficult to make a clear distinction between the concepts of *stress* and *crisis* in the case of domestic violence. Some battered women and children describe their typical familial lives as filled with tension and stress, interspersed by the crisis of a battering incident. Others have likened the experience of witnessing violence and being battered to "living in a war zone," or being in a state of "continual crisis." The diagnosis of posttraumatic stress disorder may be given to those battered women and children who display the characteristic cognitive, affective, and physiological symptoms that follow a serious threat to one's life or physical integrity, or the witnessing of someone's serious injury or death as a result of physical violence (Douglas, 1987; Eth & Pynoos, 1985).

Both stress and crisis refer to "a condition that disrupts former adaptation and involves states in which there is threat capable of overwhelming the coping resources of the individual" (Korchin, 1976, p. 502). What appears important to the development of a crisis state is the psychological meaning attributed to the event (e.g., to lose trust in adult emotional and physical restraint), the social setting in which the event occurred (e.g., family), whether the event is linked symbolically to earlier stressors that resulted in increased vulnerability (e.g., witnessing recurrent threats and incidents of violence that relate to children's increased anxiety and depression), and the individual's personality and coping resources (Korchin, 1976). From this perspective, it is likely that child witnesses would be in a crisis state when they come to the attention of shelter staff or mental health professionals.

Crisis intervention theory postulates that people are most amenable to change (either positive or negative) when they are in disequilibrium (i.e., crisis; Caplan, 1961). In those battered women's shelters with children's programs, staff members can do several things to help child witnesses in crisis. First, children may have their own orientation to the shelter program, typically in an individual session with a children's worker. Many shelters have developed a welcome coloring book that describes why children and their mothers come to shelters, feelings children may have, what to expect at the shelter, and shelter rules (e.g., no hitting). Some child workers may use the coloring book as a focus for their individual or group sessions with children. At this point, the initial crisis intervention goals are to provide immediate, active direction to the children, assure the children that they and their mothers are safe, and convey support and an expectation that the crisis will be handled. Later on in the children's stay, additional crisis intervention goals (i.e., focused problem solving, improvement of self-esteem, and the development of adaptive coping strategies) can be addressed in group or individual sessions.

In cases of escalating marital violence where the lethality factor is high (Browne, 1987; Sonkin, Martin, & Walker, 1985), it is not uncommon for children to witness the more extreme acts of violence such as marital rape, parental suicide, and parental murder, in addition to witnessing previous incidents of aggravated assault. In their work with children who have witnessed extreme violence, Pynoos and Eth (1986) developed an interview protocol designed to engage children between the ages of 3 to 16 years in discussion about the traumatic event shortly after its occurrence; it can be thought of as a crisis or early intervention tool. Their interview format deserves special attention, because it is conceptually articulate and is a clinically helpful guide in the initial work with traumatized children.

The interview format consists of three stages: opening, trauma, and closing. During the opening stage, the interviewer greets the child and establishes the focus for the interview by making a statement that expresses the desire to understand what it was like for the child to have experienced what she or he did. The child is then asked to draw a picture of something that she or he can tell a story about and is encouraged by the interviewer to elaborate on the story and the drawing. The clinical assumption behind the drawing task is that the violent event continues to remain active and intrusive in the child's mind and will be represented somewhere in the story. The interviewer's task is to identify the traumatic references and the strategies children may use to cope with their anxiety that mask or distort these references (i.e., denial-in-fantasy, inhibition of spontaneous thought, inability to fantasize, constant anxious arousal).

The second stage begins by the interviewer's linking some aspect of the drawing or story directly to the trauma, which facilitates the child's emotional connection to the event, permits the subsequent emotional release, and allows the reconstruction process (i.e., reliving the experience) to begin. The authors identify several critical aspects of the reconstruction process, including (a) encouraging the child to verbalize what happened; (b) focusing on the central violent action witnessed by the child and elaborating on the child's sensory experience of the event; (c) discovering whether the child has given traumatic meaning to a particular detail that may suggest identification with the victim, perpetrator, or protector with the immediate goal of helping the child differentiate him/herself from the victim or perpetrator; (d) asking the child to disclose the worst moment; and (e) helping the child recall and unburden him/herself of the visual image of physical mutilation.

After the reconstruction process is completed, the authors describe several psychological issues necessary for the child to confront in order to begin actively coping with the traumatic experience. Because the violence was human-perpetrated, children first need to explore the issues of whom they hold accountable for the act, their understanding of the motive, and ideas about how it might have been prevented. Child witnesses to family violence may have particular difficulty assigning responsibility because of their strong, and often conflicted feelings for both parents. For example, some children may believe that their father is wrong to beat their mother but hold their mother responsible for refusing to obey his orders.

To counter the helplessness that these children often feel, it is important to explore children's "inner plans of action" that serve to reverse the situation outcome. Children may develop cognitive action plans that attempt to alter the precipitating events, to undo the violent act, to reverse the lethal consequences, or to gain safe retaliation (Pynoos & Eth, 1986). Exploration of these plans through verbal discussion, drawing, or play may indicate to what extent the child feels personally responsible for the event. Revealing their feelings about punishment or retaliation against the offender may be a relief for some children. Once retaliation is addressed, children may fear that the offender will return to hurt them, and they should be informed and reassured to the contrary. Children may also be concerned about their own impulse control and wonder whether they will behave aggressively when angry. Research findings on child witnesses' behavior, problem-solving strategies, and perceptions of their conduct suggest that this fear is a realistic one and may need additional attention in the form of a brief or longer term treatment. At this point in the interview, it is appropriate for children to discuss previous traumatic experiences, traumatic dreams, describe concerns they may have about future interpersonal relationships, and address the current stresses resulting from the traumatic event (e.g., media coverage, school changes, placement outside the family).

In the final stage of the interview, closure, the tasks are to (a) help the child review and summarize the session; (b) acknowledge the child's realistic fears about their own safety during the event; (c) discuss the expected course of traumatic reactions over time (e.g., bad dreams that will lessen in time, being startled at hearing loud noises) and suggest that the child share these reactions with trusted adults; (d) acknowledge the child's courage, either regarding some behavior performed during the event or his/her willingness to talk about painful issues during the interview; (e) elicit the child's feelings about the interview, discussing what was helpful, not helpful, and most difficult, and what made the child feel better to talk about; and (f) say good-by, emphasizing the interviewer's availability for future contact if needed (e.g., anniversary reactions), and provide the child with a professional card listing phone number and address should the child (or parent/guardian) wish to make future contact.

Pynoos and Eth's (1986) child interview highlights several important issues when considering crisis intervention work with child witnesses to family violence. First, by focusing on the traumatic event with the help of a clinically skilled guide, children will be able to link their emotional experience to the event rather than develop strategies to ward off overwhelming emotion. Because it is common for battered women and their partners to minimize or deny the extent and psychological impact of violence (Douglas, 1987; Sonkin et al., 1985), child witnesses may not have the opportunity to share their emotional experience with their parents, and extended family members may or may not be aware of the violence or know how to respond. Furthermore, family members may share a similar belief with some mental health professionals who question whether focusing on the traumatic event might further upset an already vulnerable child (Pynoos & Eth, 1986). Based on their extensive clinical experience with traumatized children, Pynoos and Eth report that open discussion of the trauma appears to reduce children's anxiety, with many children appearing less alienated and emotionally detached.

Second, the process of gaining mastery over the traumatic experience(s) begins by involving the child in active description, drawing, or play in a partial attempt to offset the passive witness role. Interviewers are also encouraged to explore children's cognitive action plans that serve to counter the child's helplessness. These ideas are reminiscent of previously reviewed research findings suggesting that children who feel more in control of their own thoughts and behaviors during their parents' fights report less anxiety and hold more positive perceptions of their competence.

The strategies advocated by Pynoos and Eth (1986) represent an important contribution to the field of crisis/early intervention with child witnesses to violence, in that they offer a clinical road map through some of the issues that these children face in the aftermath of violence. A next step would be to empirically test these ideas with the hope of learning even more about the process of mastering trauma for children.

Group Intervention

Group intervention with child witnesses represents one of the most commonly used treatment modalities in shelters for victims of domestic violence. More recently, mental health clinics and professionals who treat child witnesses recognize that the group format is particularly suited for use with this population. Group interventions are frequently used with children who have experienced a range of different problems related to family violence, including physical abuse, sexual abuse, substance abuse, and the effects of living with alcoholic or drug-addicted parents. Specific descriptions of group interventions with child witnesses are few, although some do exist in the literature.

Alessi and Hearn (1984) provide an excellent description of a fairly typical approach to group treatment for children in shelters and offer the reader strategies to overcome the obstacles inherent in working with this particular population (i.e., limited space and staff, transient nature of the population, wide age range of children). Their groups are limited to children aged 8 to 16 years and are designed according to the following goals: (a) Provide children with support through the crisis period, (b) help children identify and express feelings, (c) teach children problem-solving skills, and (d) help children learn healthy coping behaviors. Treatment is time limited (6 sessions) and pragmatic, and emphasizes the child's strengths and potential rather than deficits. Each session has a different focus and includes participatory exercises, discussion and sharing, and homework assignments. Topics for the six sessions are

1. Identifying and expressing feelings
2. Violence
3. Unhealthy ways to solve problems
4. Healthy ways to solve problems
5. Sex, love, and sexuality
6. Termination and saying good-by

During the last session, the children complete a written program evaluation, the results of which were not included in the chapter.

Jaffe, Wilson, and Wolfe (1986a) organized a pilot group therapy program for children who witnessed extensive marital violence and were recent shelter residents. Group sessions were held for 1½ hours over a period of 10 weeks and focused on the following issues:

1. Identifying feelings
2. Dealing with one's own anger
3. Prevention of child abuse and acquiring basic safety skills
4. Identifying and using social supports
5. Social competence and self-concept
6. Dealing with feelings of responsibility for violence in the family
7. Coping with wishes about the family and dealing with repeated separations or uncertainty about future plans
8. Exploring sexual stereotypes and myths about men and women

Eighteen boys and girls were assigned to two groups of 9 children based on age: 8- to 10-year-olds and 11- to 13-year-olds. Pre- and postgroup interviews were conducted to assess the impact of the group on children's attitudes and skill development. Of the mothers interviewed, 93% perceived that their children enjoyed the group, 62% felt that their children learned something from participating, and 33% felt that the group led to a significant behavior change in their children. Interviews with the children revealed several pre-post improvements in practical skills and attitudes toward violence. After the intervention, more children could identify appropriate strategies for handling emergency situations (73% at post-test vs. 44% at pretest) and were able to identify two or more positive things about themselves (85% vs. 53%); also fewer children condoned the use of violence by men toward women, women toward men, or parents toward children. In a second study comparing child witnesses who received the group intervention with wait-list controls, Jaffe, Wilson, and Wolfe (1986b) found that group participants showed significant improvement in measures of overall adjustment, school behavior, and school performance according to mother and self-report, thereby supporting and extending their initial findings. However, as with many of the child sexual abuse prevention programs, it still remains to be proven whether children can maintain their newly acquired knowledge and skills over time and can use what they have learned if there are future incidents of their parents' violence or if they are physically abused (i.e., call 911 for help, tell someone about their abuse).

The group intervention models described by Alessi and Hearn (1984) and Jaffe et al. (1986a, 1986b) are frequently adopted models for child witnesses, with some variations in discussion topics, organizational structure, and emphasis of information. For example, some shelters organize groups for children of all ages including preschool children (e.g., see Hughes, 1986), and parent–toddler groups to enhance the quality of interaction between battered women and their young children. One particularly innovative shelter in Charlottesville, Virginia (S.H.E.: Shelter for Help in Emergency) has developed a creative, engaging puppet show and accompanying curriculum to teach nonviolent problem-solving skills to children in their shelter. Because S.H.E. also has a firm commitment to preventive intervention in domestic violence, staff members routinely take their show to elementary, junior high, and high schools in the surrounding communities to discuss problem-solving skills with a wider audience. Other shelters (e.g., Gateway Shelter, Aurora, Colorado, and Alternatives to Family Violence, Commerce City, Colorado) have developed extensive long-term group services so that children and mothers can continue to take advantage of the shelter's "outclient" program once they leave the residential program.

It is important to note that, in general, topics chosen for group intervention are usually derived from clinical experience with child witnesses or based on "face valid" notions about what would be helpful. As more researchers investigate the psychological problems associated with witnessing family violence, their findings will help to inform clinical service. For example, learning nonviolent problem-solving strategies is often included as a primary topic of importance in group work, yet it would be helpful to identify more specifically the problem-solving deficits exhibited by child witnesses and thereby increase the potency of the intervention. Additionally, professionals who work with this population can offer researchers many challenging clinical issues to be addressed by empirical study.

Individual Interventions

Each of the issues covered in the sections on crisis intervention and group treatment can serve as a focus of attention in individual child therapy, and therefore, will not be reviewed again here. However, one issue in particular, the development of appropriate social problem-solving skills, deserves special emphasis because both research and clinical data suggest the importance of including this topic when planning interventions with child witnesses. The reader is referred to Rosenberg (1987b) for a detailed discussion of assessment and intervention strategies with children of battered women.

Although empowerment is a common theme in the treatment of adult victims of domestic violence, it has not received as much attention in work with child victims or child witnesses. Our research suggests that more emphasis needs to be placed on understanding children's perceptions of control in regard to parental fighting, and helping children develop realistic ways to assert personal control over their own thoughts and behavior. Pynoos and Eth's (1986) work also supports the idea that children make a variety of psychological attempts to regain their lost sense of control through developing inner plans of action and unconscious fantasies (including fantasies of aggression and retaliation) that attempt to alter the event outcome. Both findings underscore the importance of understanding children's cognitions about the trauma (or series of traumatic events), of linking their emotional reactions with their cognitions, and of helping children realistically appraise what happens during a battering incident and what their attributions are about their role in that event.

For therapists working with child witnesses, it is necessary to consider the child's age, cognitive ability, and level of ego development in planning interventions because these variables will influence the child's experience of violence, coping abilities, and understanding of responsibility (Pynoos & Eth, 1986; Shirk, 1988). For example, if one therapeutic goal is to teach nonaggressive strategies to solve interpersonal conflict, a young child may need to be taught to inhibit aggressive responses such as grabbing or hitting and to substitute nonaggressive responses such as asking or sharing. Problem-solving information would need to be collapsed into fewer steps. The use of puppets to demonstrate conflict situations and problem resolution strategies would be a good medium through which elementary-school-age children could learn information, particularly if demonstrations were followed up with discussion and behavioral rehearsal of newly acquired skills. As children approach adolescence and begin to assess means–ends relationships and others' intentions, an intervention might include developing conflict resolution skills as well as helping youth to evaluate others' intentions, to use cues for understanding interpersonal conflict and to predict the social consequences of various behaviors.

A second example of the need to be sensitive to developmental issues comes from Selman's (1980) work about developmental changes in children's understanding of conflict. From early childhood to early adolescence, children are thought to move through three stages in understanding conflict. For young children (preschoolers) conflict is understood in terms of its immediate consequences for the child, and the child's goal is to defend his or her possessions or rights. This is a fairly egocentric perspective. Slightly older children (early elementary-school-age) begin to have some appreciation of the psychological effects of conflict but only for one person. Bilateral understanding of conflict is demonstrated in children aged 8 to 14 years. For these children, bilateral agreement about the resolution of the conflict is important, and their behaviors are based on the goal of establishing and maintaining good relationships. Therefore, in planning an intervention around problem solving and conflict resolution, the focus for young children might be to highlight the immediate rewards of nonaggression, but for older children one could emphasize the importance of developing these skills for attracting and keeping friends. Researchers could also use Selman's theoretical ideas to determine whether a similar developmental pattern occurs for children who have witnessed extensive adult conflict and have had limited opportunity to see conflict resolved constructively.

It would appear that for children to continue gaining mastery over their experience with violence, they need the support and understanding of their family and other trusted adults in their immediate environment. Child witnesses to parental violence and parental murder may face additional stress by being placed outside the nuclear family in relatives' homes or in foster care. These types of placements may result from situations where one parent is arrested for murdering the other, a parent is hospitalized for physical or psychological problems stemming from the violence, or a child protection agency finds neither parent able to provide appropriate care. Relatives may have strong opinions about who is "right" or "wrong" in the marital relationship, and children may be put in an emotionally destructive bind. Thus, a crucial role for professionals who work with child witnesses is to include the relevant family members in treatment and to develop and maintain alliances with appropriate school and social service personnel.

Familial Interventions

The most common type of "familial" intervention for child witnesses can be found in shelters for battered women and usually involves only one member of the family: the mother. Such interventions typically present information in a group format (although individual sessions also occur), and include discussions on learning normal child development, improving parent–child relationships and parenting skills, understanding children's emotional needs, identifying how positive and negative relationship patterns in the family of origin may be repeated in the nuclear family, recognizing the effects of witnessing marital violence on children, understanding health and medical issues, and helping mothers teach safety precautions to their children (Hughes, 1986).

Although the need for empirical studies on the parenting practices of battered women has been noted (Rosenberg, 1985), there has been little systematic investigation of the issue. One exception is the work of Jouriles, Barling, and O'Leary (1986), who found that witnessing marital violence was associated with parent–child aggression, and it was the parents' aggressive behavior that was related to children's behavioral problems. Clinical observations of battered women's interactions with their children suggest that parenting abilities vary widely. Discipline appears to be particularly difficult for these mothers and tends to elicit inconsistent and/or extremes of reaction from overly strict and controlling behavior on the one hand to overly permissive and laissez-faire behavior on the other. Some mothers feel guilty about setting limits on their children's behavior and argue, "My children have been through enough and do not need any additional frustration." Other mothers want to make sure that their children do not grow up "wild, like their fathers," and attempt to quell the first indication of disobedience. As mentioned in the section on behavioral problems, child witnesses display both externalizing (i.e., aggressive and delinquent behavior) and internalizing behaviors (i.e., depression, psychosomatic complaints). Mothers typically have a more difficult time finding solutions to their children's acting-out behaviors. These and other discipline problems can be addressed in group or individual sessions through role-playing, discussion, and in vivo parent–child interaction sessions, where the therapist attempts to change nonconstructive behavioral patterns as they occur between mother and child.

A second issue that often confronts professionals working with battered women is the quality of the parent–child relationship and its effects on children's psychological functioning. In some families, the presence of violence in the marital relationship may be associated with certain compensations in the mother–child relationship. It is not uncommon, for example, to see a young child in the role of confidante, providing support and advice to a mother who is isolated from her own support system and relies on her child for emotional guidance (Giberson & Rosenberg, 1985). Other scenarios also may occur, such as mothers who are emotionally unavailable to their children due to the stress of the violence or their own feelings of helplessness and depression, or mothers who scapegoat the children as one way of relieving tension in the marital relationship. Furthermore, coalitions between one parent and child against the other parent are likely and tend to leave children confused and angry. In general, there is less clinical information available about the quality of father–child relationships in maritally violent families. Giberson (1986) found that fathers and sons in violent families tended to perceive their relationships as more conflictual than did fathers and sons in nonviolent families. She also found that the more violence children observed between their parents, the more conflictual they perceived their relationship with their mothers. Clearly, the study of parent–child relationships in families where marital violence occurs would provide critical information for the development of treatment strategies designed to improve parenting practices and parent–child relationships.

A current debate in the clinical literature involves the question of which treatment modality (e.g., individual, couples, or family therapy) is most effective in intervening with battered women, abusive men, and their children. One approach, as exemplified by Sonkin et al. (1985), suggests that men seek treatment, preferably group therapy, to confront their violence and learn alternative ways of expressing anger. Battered women are encouraged to participate in their own treatment, and if the couple wishes to continue working on their relationship, they do so after the man gains control over his violent behavior and the woman feels safe enough to express her feelings in the couple therapy. Family therapy, to address a range of family problems, including problems with children, also may occur once the couple has made some progress on their own issues. An alternative perspective, as exemplified by Neidig and Friedman (1984), takes an interpersonal approach to understanding and treating marital violence and intervenes directly with the couple. The latter perspective has been soundly criticized by feminist scholars (e.g., Bograd, 1984), who reject the idea of applying traditional systemic thinking to the problem of marital violence. Extending this line of reasoning to include children raises the question of whether to prescribe family treatment when working with child witnesses. For families where the man's violence has not been addressed successfully in group or individual therapy, family therapy would be premature and potentially dangerous for the woman and their children. Therapists need to consider such issues as the likelihood that the violence is under control, the children's degree of safety in expressing their thoughts and feelings, and the pros and cons of adopting a family systems perspective with a particular family before automatically recommending its use.

SUMMARY AND FUTURE DIRECTIONS

After reviewing the available research and clinical literature on child witnesses to marital violence, it is clear that this is an understudied population of children who present a tremendous challenge to the researcher and clinician. There are several general areas to consider for future research and treatment directions. First, the field lacks basic incidence and prevalence information about child witnesses as well as information about the interrelationship between witnessing violence and experiencing other forms of child abuse and neglect. At this point, there is only a rough estimate about the numbers of child witnesses based on extrapolation from national survey data on marital violence, and no data are available about children witnessing violence in extended families (e.g., aunts and uncles).

A second research direction concerns the type of question posed about child witnesses. A typical research strategy is to ask what general effects witnessing violence has on children and to give children and mothers an array of measures to complete. Because child witnesses tend to be a heterogeneous population, it might be more fruitful to identify variables that mediate children's psychological outcome, rather than to assume that all children will be equally affected by witnessing violence. These variables might be child related, such as gender, temperament, or intelligence; adult related, such as the absence of individual psychopathology; family related, such as the quality of the parent–child relationship or parenting practices; and/or environmentally related, such as the availability of crisis intervention and follow-up services for children and parents.

Third, it is rare to find a published evaluation (or even an unpublished, systematic evaluation) of treatment strategies that have been tried with child witnesses and their parents. Many shelters have children's programs, and other mental health facilities treat this population of children. It is important for those professionals working with child witnesses to let others know about their treatment efforts and to determine empirically whether their treatment strategies are effective. It is becoming increasingly common for shelters to work with college and university faculty to recruit student volunteers for shelter programs and to allow students and faculty access to battered women and children for research purposes. Systematic description and evaluation of treatment strategies is a necessary next step in learning how best to intervene with child witnesses and their parents.

In conclusion, professionals are just beginning to understand the effects of witnessing marital violence on children, as well as the problems such experiences pose in treating these children. This is an area where researchers and clinicians would do best to work together in charting the course of children's short- and long-term reactions to marital violence, and in developing strategies to help these children achieve a meaningful understanding and resolution of their familial experience.

REFERENCES

Aber, J. L., III, & Cicchetti, D. (1985). The socio-emotional development of maltreated children: An empirical and theoretical analysis. In H. Fitzgerald, B. Lester, & M. Yogman (Eds.), *Theory and research in behavioral pediatrics* (Vol. 2). New York: Plenum.

Alessi, J. J., & Hearn, K. (1984). Group treatment of children in shelters for battered women. In A. R. Roberts (Ed.), *Battered women and their families: Intervention strategies and treatment programs* (pp. 49–61). New York: Springer.

American Psychiatric Association. (1980). *Diagnostic and statistical manual of mental disorders* (DSM III; 3rd ed.). Washington, DC: Author.

American Psychiatric Association. (1987). *Diagnostic and statistical manual of mental disorders* (DSM-III-R; 3rd ed.-rev.). Washington, DC: Author.

Anthony, E. J. (1986). Terrorizing attacks on children by psychotic parents. *Journal of the American Academy of Child Psychiatry, 25,* 326–335.

Bandura, A. (1973). *Aggression: A social learning theory analysis.* Englewood Cliffs, NJ: Prentice-Hall.

Bograd, M. (1984). Family systems approaches to wife battering: A feminist critique. *American Journal of Orthopsychiatry, 54,* 558–567.

Brassard, M. R., Germain, R., & Hart, S. N. (Eds.). (1987). *Psychological maltreatment of children and youth.* New York: Pergamon.

Brown, A. J., Pelcovitz, D., & Kaplan, S. (1983, August). *Child witnesses of family violence: A study of psychological correlates.* Paper presented at the annual meeting of the American Psychological Association, Anaheim, CA.

Browne, A. (1987). *When battered women kill.* New York: Free Press.

Caplan, G. (1961). *An approach to community mental health.* London: Tavistock.

Carlson, B. E. (1984). Children's observations of interparental violence. In A. R. Roberts (Ed.), *Battered women and their families: Intervention strategies and treatment programs* (pp. 147–167). New York: Springer.

Compas, B. E. (1987). Coping with stress during childhood and adolescence. *Psychological Bulletin, 101,* 393–403.

Douglas, M. A. (1987). The battered women's syndrome. In D. J. Sonkin (Ed.), *Domestic violence on trial: Psychological and legal dimensions of family violence* (pp. 39–54). New York: Springer.

Dutton, D. G. (1988). *The domestic assault of women: Psychological and criminal justice perspectives.* Boston, MA: Allyn & Bacon.

Elias, M. J., Larcen, S. W., Zlotlow, S. F., & Chinsky, J. M. (1978, September). *An innovative measure of children's cognitions in problematic interpersonal situations.* Paper presented at the annual meeting of the American Psychological Association, Toronto, Canada.

Eth, S., & Pynoos, R. S. (Eds.). (1985). *Post-traumatic stress disorder in children.* Washington, DC: American Psychiatric Press.

Folkman, S., & Lazarus, R. S. (1980). An analysis of coping in a middle-aged community sample. *Journal of Health and Social Behavior, 21,* 219–239.

Galante, R., & Foa, D. (1986). An epidemiological study of psychic trauma and treatment effectiveness for children after a natural disaster. *Journal of the American Academy of Child Psychiatry, 25,* 357–363.

Geffner, R., Rosenbaum, A., & Hughes, H. (1988). Research issues concerning family violence. In V. B. Van Hasselt, R. L. Morrison, A. S. Bellack, & M. Hersen (Eds.), *Handbook of family violence* (pp. 457–481). New York: Plenum.

Giberson, R. (1986). *Parental functioning as a mediating mechanism between spousal violence and child adjustment.* Unpublished master's thesis. University of Denver, Denver, CO.

Giberson, R., & Rosenberg, M. S. (1985, August). Child witnesses to spousal violence: A family systems approach. Paper presented as part of the *Symposium on Mediating Factors in Children's Adjustment to Family Violence,* at the annual meeting of the American Psychological Association, Los Angeles.

Goodman, G. S., & Rosenberg, M. S. (1987). The child witness to family violence. In D. J. Sonkin (Ed.), *Domestic violence on trial: Psychological and legal dimensions of family violence* (pp. 97–126). New York: Springer.

Green, A. H. (1985). Children traumatized by physical abuse. In S. Eth & R. S. Pynoos (Eds.), *Post-traumatic stress disorder in children* (pp. 135–154). Washington, DC: American Psychiatric Press.

Groisser, D. (1986). *Child witness to interpersonal violence: Social problem solving skills and behavioral adjustment.* Unpublished master's thesis. University of Denver, Denver, CO.

Handford, H. A., Dickerson, S., Mattison, R. E., Humphrey, F. J., Bagnato, S., Bixler, E. O., & Kales, J. D. (1986). Child and parent reaction to the Three Mile Island nuclear accident. *Journal of the American Academy of Child Psychiatry, 25,* 346–356.

Harter, S. (1983). Developmental perspectives on the self-system. In E. Mavis Hetherington (Ed.), *Socialization, personality, and social development.* (Vol. 4, pp. 275–385). New York: Wiley.

Hartup, W. W. (1983). Peer relations. In E. Mavis Hetherington (Ed.), *Socialization, personality, and social development.* (Vol. 4, pp. 103–196). New York: Wiley.

Hughes, H. M. (1986, August). Child-focused intervention in shelters. Paper presented as part of the *Symposium on New Approaches to Treating Family Violence,* at the annual meeting of the American Psychological Association, Washington, DC.

Jaffe, P., Wilson, S., & Wolfe, D. A. (1986a). Promoting changes in attitudes and understanding of conflict resolution among child witnesses of family violence. *Canadian Journal of Behavioral Science, 18,* 356–366.

Jaffe, P., Wilson, S., & Wolfe, D. A. (1986b, August). Impact of group counseling for child witnesses to wife battering. Paper presented as part of the *Symposium on Children in Shelters for Battered Women,* at the annual meeting of the American Psychological Association, Washington, DC.

Jouriles, E. N., Barling, J., & O'Leary, K. D. (1987). Predicting child behavior problems in maritally violent families. *Journal of Abnormal Child Psychology, 15,* 165–173.

Kinzie, J. D., Sack, W. H., Angell, R. H., Manson, S., & Rath, B. (1986). The psychiatric effects of massive trauma on Cambodian children. *Journal of the American Academy of Child Psychiatry, 25,* 370–376.

Korchin, S. J. (1976). *Modern clinical psychology: Principles of intervention in the clinic and the community.* New York: Basic Books.

Lazarus, R. S., & Folkman, S. (1984). Coping and adaptation. In W. D. Gentry (Ed.), *The handbook of behavioral medicine.* New York: Guilford.

Martin, D. (1981). *Battered wives.* San Francisco: Volcano Press.

Neidig, P. H., & Friedman, D. H. (1984). *Spouse abuse: A treatment program for couples.* Champaign, Il: Research Press.

Pynoos, R. S., & Eth, S. (1986). Witness to violence: The child interview. *Journal of the American Academy of Child Psychiatry, 25*, 306–319.

Rosenberg, M. S. (1984). *The impact of witnessing interparental violence on children's behavior, perceived competence, and social problem-solving abilities.* Unpublished doctoral dissertation. University of Virginia, Charlottesville.

Rosenberg, M. S. (1985, August). Mother-child relationship quality mediating psychological adjustment of child witnesses. Paper presented as part of the *Symposium on Mediating Factors in Children's Adjustment to Family Violence,* at the annual meeting of the American Psychological Association, Los Angeles.

Rosenberg, M. S. (1987a). New directions for research on the psychological maltreatment of children. *American Psychologist, 42,* 166–171.

Rosenberg, M. S. (1987b). Children of battered women: The effects of witnessing violence on their social problem-solving abilities. *Behavior Therapist, 4,* 85–89.

Rosenberg, M. S. (1988). *Children of violent parents: Child coping and control.* Final report submitted to the National Institute of Mental Health (Grant No. MH41051).

Rossman, B. B. R. (1986, April). *Child and parent perceptions of child distressing events and coping behaviors.* Paper presented at the meeting of the Rocky Mountain Psychological Association, Denver, CO.

Rossman, B. B. R. (1988). *Family violence: Child control and coping—The Denver sample.* Final report for subcontract project No. 5-32962 submitted to the National Institute of Mental Health (Grant No. MH41051).

Rutter, M. (1983). Stress, coping, and development. In N. Garmezy & M. Rutter (Eds.), *Stress, coping, and development in children.* New York: McGraw-Hill.

Selman, R. (1980). *The growth of interpersonal understanding: Developmental and clinical analyses.* New York: Academic Press.

Shirk, S. R. (Ed.). (1988). *Cognitive development and child psychotherapy.* New York: Plenum.

Sonkin, D. J., Martin, D., & Walker, L. E. A. (1985). *The male batterer: A treatment approach.* New York: Springer.

Straus, M. A. (1979). Measuring intrafamily conflict and violence: The conflict tactics scales. *Journal of Marriage and the Family, 41,* 75–88.

Straus, M. A., & Gelles, R. J. (1986). Societal change and change in family violence from 1975 to 1985 as revealed by two national surveys. *Journal of Marriage and the Family, 48,* 465–479.

Straus, M. A., Gelles, R. J., & Steinmetz, S. K. (1980). *Behind closed doors: Violence in the American family.* New York: Doubleday/Anchor.

Terr, L. (1979). Children of Chowchilla: A study of psychic trauma. *Psychoanalytic Study of the Child, 34,* 547–623.

Terr, L. (1983). Chowchilla revisited: The effects of psychic trauma four years after a school-bus kidnapping. *American Journal of Psychiatry, 140,* 1542–1550.

Thompson, S. C. (1981). Will it hurt less if I could control it? A complex answer to a simple question. *Psychological Bulletin, 90,* 89–101.

Wallerstein, J. S., & Kelly, J. B. (1980). *Surviving the break-up.* New York: Basic Books.

Westra, B. & Martin, H. P. (1981). Children of battered women. *Maternal-Child Nursing Journal, 10,* 41–54.

Wolfe, D. A., Jaffe, P., Wilson, S., & Zak, L. (1985). Children of battered women: The relation of child behavior to family violence and maternal stress. *Journal of Consulting and Clinical Psychology, 53,* 657–665.

CHAPTER 9

Adult Survivors of Incest

PAULA K. LUNDBERG-LOVE

INTRODUCTION

Historically, for many people, the word *incest* has conjured up images of an act committed by a deviant individual somewhere in the backwoods. Or it was considered a rarity that occurred only in lower class, dysfunctional families. When incest did occur, people typically attributed blame to a cold, neglectful, absent mother or an overly seductive daughter. However, during the past decade these myths have been soundly debunked. Early anecdotal and clinical reports (Allen, 1982; Armstrong, 1982; Herman, 1981; Meiselman, 1978) suggested that incest was far more common than previously thought. It was usually nonviolent but coerced; its onset and termination were often prepubertal; sexual activity typically escalated over time and could include a spectrum of behaviors. Also, the oldest female child seemed to be at greatest risk for incestuous abuse. Furthermore, practitioners have identified a variety of sequelae that occur subsequent to incestuous abuse. These can include depression, anxiety disorders, substance abuse, sexual dysfunction, eating disorders, dissociative disorders, somatization disorders, and the tendency to experience revictimization in other relationships, both within and outside the family. As a result, increasing numbers of women who were abused incestuously are seeking treatment to resolve the many issues that stem from their abuse. The purpose of this chapter is to describe the epidemiology and consequences of incestuous abuse, to discuss the present approaches to the treatment of incest survivors, and to suggest possible directions for future research and treatment studies in this area.

Throughout this chapter adults who were victims of incestuous abuse will be termed *incest survivors* as opposed to *victims*. Russell (1986) has said

I would like to thank Sherry Rhodes, Connie Schreiber, Debbie Anderson, and Linda Fleming for their assistance in the preparation of this manuscript as well as the University of Texas at Tyler and the Hogg Foundation for their financial support of this work. I am also greatly indebted to all the incest survivor clients who have graciously afforded me the opportunity to accompany them on their paths to recovery. Their courage and strength inspired this chapter and so I dedicate it to them.

that the term *incest survivor* suggests that "merely to have survived incestuous abuse is a remarkable achievement" and that "the term 'victim' may be alienating to those individuals who experienced less severe forms of abuse" (p. 14). However, during five years' experience in treating adults who were childhood victims of incestuous abuse, therapists participating in the Family Violence Research and Treatment Program (FVRTP) at the University of Texas at Tyler have repeatedly heard from these victims that they prefer being called survivors. Regardless of the degree of severity of their abuse, they *do* feel that having survived the abuse *is* a remarkable achievement. Because this chapter is dedicated to the nearly 100 women who have received treatment at the FVRTP and because this treatment approach emphasizes empowerment, the term *incest survivor* will be used throughout this chapter. Also, incestuous abuse is primarily perpetrated by males against female children (Finkelhor, 1986; Russell, 1986); this discussion, therefore, will include treatment approaches designed for female incest survivors. Although I do not mean to minimize the experiences of male survivors, scant data currently exist concerning treatment of male incest survivors.

EPIDEMIOLOGY

Estimations of the prevalence of incest vary depending on the characteristics of the source. Values derived from official statistics tend to underestimate the prevalence of violence against women in general (Koss, 1985). Incest is no exception (Russell, 1986). Indeed, were it not for the work of particular feminists (Herman, 1981; Meiselman, 1978; Russell, 1984, 1986; Wyatt, 1985) and some courageous survivors (Allen, 1982; Armstrong, 1982; Brady, 1979), knowledge regarding incest might have derived solely from the works of Freud (1953) and Kinsey (Kinsey, Pomeroy, Martin, & Gebhard, 1953).

The Kinsey (Kinsey et al., 1953) data suggest that 2% to 3% of the women in their study were sexually abused by a male relative before the age of 14 years. These results led the Kinsey team to conclude that there were too few incest cases to warrant any further data analysis other than to comment on the low frequency. Given what researchers now know about incest survivors' strong reluctance to disclose their abuse, it is very likely that presence of male interviewers and nonstandardized questions precluded many survivors from revealing their experiences.

Finkelhor (1979) surveyed college students about child sexual abuse. Although the sample was not a random one, it was a nonclinical one. Finkelhor defined incest as sexual experiences between family members including contact (fondling, masturbation, oral sex, intercourse) and noncontact (propositions, exhibitionism) events. Family members included step-relations as well as cousins and in-laws. Age criteria included sexual experiences between an adult and a child 12 years old and under, as well as between an adolescent 13 to 16 years old with an adult at least 10 years older. Of the

530 women students in social science classes at six New England colleges/ universities who completed self-administered questionnaires, nearly 10% were sexually abused by a relative. In a more recent random sample of 521 parents in Boston, Finkelhor (1984) reports that approximately 5% were sexually abused by a relative.

Russell (1986) suggests that Finkelhor's findings for incestuous abuse may be an underestimate of the problem because they were obtained from questions included in a study designed to obtain data on a variety of issues. Also, Finkelhor confined his interviews to parents with children aged 6 to 14 years. This excluded childless, elderly, and young women. Because the Russell (1986) data suggest that incest survivors are less likely to marry, the Finkelhor data are probably also an underestimate of the prevalence of incest.

Kercher and McShane (1984) describe an unpublished study by Riede, Capron, Ivey, Lawrence, and Somalo. The latter individuals sent a questionnaire on pornography and child sexual abuse to a random sample of 2000 Texas drivers' license holders. With a 55% return rate, the group found that 4.3% of the responders reported a sexual experience with someone in their family. Kercher and McShane suggest that one of the problems inherent in this study is that the researchers asked about sexual experiences rather than sexual abuse.

Kilpatrick and Amick (1984) utilizing the services of Louis Harris and Associates, conducted telephone interviews with a random household sample of 2004 adult women in Charleston County, South Carolina. This study focused on all experiences of completed or attempted sexual assault. Kilpatrick and Amick report that 1% (26 cases) of the women questioned had experienced incestuous abuse. Both the authors and Russell (1986) concluded that this study suffered from methodological flaws and that the prevalence obtained did not represent the actual prevalence of incest.

By contrast, Gail Wyatt conducted lengthy interviews with a sample of 248 Afro-American and white women aged 18 to 36 years in Los Angeles County. The respondents were contacted via random-digit dialing and comparable samples of Afro-American (N = 126) and white (N = 122) women were obtained. Wyatt's (1985) definition of child sexual abuse included contact of a sexual nature ranging from those involving nonbody contact to those involving body contact that occurred before age 18 with a perpetrator who was at least 5 years older than the victim. When Wyatt distinguished between contact and noncontact abuse it was found that 21% of the participants reported at least one experience of some type of incestuous abuse.

More recently, Siegel, Sorenson, Goldring, Burnam, and Stein (1987) conducted a study to determine the prevalence of childhood sexual assault in a Hispanic and non-Hispanic white community in the Los Angeles area (N = 3132). They obtained an overall prevalence of child sexual assault of 5%. However, prevalence of child sexual abuse, weighted for sampling design, and within the sample of Hispanic women (excluding men), was 7.4%. For non-Hispanic white women that value was 23.2%. With respect to incestuous abuse, 23% of all the women reporting childhood sexual assault were abused by a parent or other relative.

Perhaps the landmark epidemiological study on incest was conducted by Diana Russell (1986). The Russell survey was conducted in San Francisco and consisted of in-person interviews with 930 randomly selected adult female residents. The definition of incestuous abuse used in this survey was any kind of exploitative sexual contact or attempted contact that occurred between relatives, no matter how distant the relationship, before the victim turned 18 years old. Russell (1986) found that 16% of the women in her study were survivors of incest. Extrapolation of this figure suggested that there were at least 160,000 survivors of incestuous abuse per million female children and adolescents. When Russell considered women aged 18 to 36 years old, the prevalence of incestuous abuse increased to 19% (190,000 survivors per 3 million women). It is this latter value that provides the more appropriate basis for estimating prevalence of incest experienced by young women today, according to Russell (1986). However, she suggests that the actual value is probably higher and that the value she obtained does not include cases of repression, intentional nondisclosures, or reports from women in mental hospitals, prisons, halfway houses, and so on. Because of the sequelae associated with incest, it is highly probable that had women in these institutions been questioned, the obtained prevalence rate would have been higher.

Of all the cases reported only 2% were described as positive or neutral. Where positive or ambivalent feelings were present, the trauma experienced was often greater than when the experience was totally negative (Russell, 1986). With respect to perpetrators, stepfather–daughter incest occurred seven times more frequently relative to the numbers of respondents reared by stepfathers and compared to the numbers reared by biological fathers. In general, incestuous abuse by nonblood relatives was found to be just as traumatic as sexual abuse by blood relatives. However, incestuous abuse by biological fathers was found to be the most traumatic form of abuse. In terms of the frequencies of sexual abuse by relatives, 25% of the perpetrators were uncles, 24% were fathers (including biological, foster, and step-), 16% were first cousins, 13% were brothers, 8% were other male relatives, 6% were grandfathers, 4% were brothers-in-law, 2% were female first cousins, 2% were other female relatives, and 1% were biological mothers. In all, there were only 10 female perpetrators of incestuous abuse in the survey. This number represented 5% of all incest perpetrators. However, had male survivors been interviewed, this number probably would have been higher. Nevertheless, the literature consistently suggests that the majority of perpetrators of child sexual abuse are male (Finkelhor, 1986).

As stated earlier, father–daughter incest was found by Russell (1986) to be the most traumatic form of incest. Fathers were more likely than other perpetrators to have imposed vaginal intercourse on their daughters. Fathers also abused their daughters more frequently than other perpetrators, were more likely to use force or violence, and were at least 20 years older than their daughters at the time of abuse. The average age at which fathers committed incest was 39.6 years.

With respect to demographics, middle-class women reported as much sexual abuse as lower-class women. Indeed, upper middle-class women were overrepresented among incest victims. White women had been victims of incest as often as Afro-American and Hispanic women. Asian women, however, were less frequently abused than other groups in the San Francisco sample. Women with a Jewish religious upbringing also were less likely to be incestuously abused.

Additionally, a significant relationship was found between ethnicity and severity of sexual abuse. Of the Hispanic survivors, 83% reported extreme or considerable experience of trauma. This contrasted with 79% of Afro-American women, 50% of Asian women, 49% of white women, and 71% of women from other ethnic groups.

Russell (1986) also identified some long-term consequences of incest that were mentioned by incest survivors. They included:

1. Increased negative feelings, attitudes, or beliefs about men in general (38%)
2. Increased negative feelings, attitudes, or beliefs regarding the perpetrator (20%)
3. Increased negative feelings about herself, including low self-esteem, self-blame, self-hatred, shame, guilt, and negative body image (20%)
4. Increased negative feelings such as fear, anxiety, depression, mistrust (17%)
5. Negative impact upon sexuality (14%)
6. Increased worry regarding the safety of others (12%)
7. Negative impact on relationships with others (12%)
8. A change in behavior associated with the abuse (for example, a cessation of showing physical affection, or avoidance of particular relatives) (11%)
9. Increased likelihood of being separated or divorced at the time of the interview

To summarize, the results of epidemiological studies suggest that the prevalence of incest lies somewhere between 4.3% and 21%. The data obtained by Russell and Wyatt are undoubtedly the strongest, from a methodological point of view. Given this consideration, the data suggest that probably at least 20% of the women in this country are incest survivors. Ethnicity does not appear to be a significant risk factor for incestuous abuse, although there is some suggestion that Hispanic women may be at slightly greater risk. Being poor also does not necessarily put one at greater risk for incestuous abuse because middle-class women were just as likely to be incest survivors.

As stated earlier, upper middle-class women were somewhat overrepresented in the Russell survey. Finally, fathers, including biological, step- and foster fathers, were the most likely perpetrators, and they tended to commit the most severe forms of abuse.

CONSEQUENCES

The impact of incest and physical abuse on my life has been pervasive and intense. It has created many fears, painful feelings, and negative effects. In fact, there is not an area of my life which remains unaffected by the fallout from the abuse. These areas range from a fear of eating a family dinner indoors with my husband and three children to shaking like an aspen leaf in a heavy wind, when it's time for sex.

Because the events were so traumatic to the child who experienced them, beginning around age 4 and continuing well into adolescence, they were completely repressed until a year ago. That has made the current effects on my life even more intense.

Alcohol consumption was present in both types of abuse which I experienced. It was used by my father before he sexually abused me and by my mother when she physically abused me. Mother used to scream that it was my punishment for being unable to stop the sexual abuse. Therefore, my fear of alcohol and of my husband when he's drinking, has been almost phobic. Combine that with sex and I'm convinced I will die.

There are times when I cannot separate my husband from my abusers. So, with him, I'm often here physically, but a universe away emotionally.

Other fears, while not debilitating, are nonetheless difficult to handle. They include fears of intimacy, of conflict, of being angry, of receiving anything from gifts to affection, of not being totally in control, of going to bed alone at night, of going crazy, and of being abusive to my children. In fact, generalized fear and anxiety pervade my whole life, transfusing each waking moment with a barrage of the "cold pricklies," which at times can give way to real panic attacks.

While emotional pain is also a constant companion, it is especially intense during holiday periods when I realize that I do not have, and never did have, a family which cared about me. I feel alone and totally isolated not only from my family, but also from all mankind—like being shoved off the continent on a tiny life raft. Hopelessness has at times given way to thoughts of suicide, an option I refuse to relinquish as the ultimate alternative.

In addition to fears and pain, my life has been pervaded by many negative effects. These include perfectionism, inflexibility, compulsion which at times borders on obsession and a strong drive to achieve honors and recognition. All of these are necessary to survive and to prove that I am worthy to be alive—that I'm not the invisible person I feel that I am.

As a consequence, I push myself too far—far beyond normal physical, mental, and emotional limits without even realizing I have limits. It's almost like I'm on a self-destructive path. As a result, I usually end up physically drained and feeling used and abused once again. Boundaries haven't even been a part of my concept of life. I have been convinced that anything which is wrong is all my fault and that it's up to me to fix it. I'm totally out of touch with my feelings, can't identify them, and hence don't trust my own sense of reality.

I seem to radiate messages to family and friends . . . "Abuse me . . . I don't mind." I have been incapable of being assertive to protect myself. Instead, I withdraw when I'm uncomfortable, seeking isolation.

Other coping mechanisms have included numbing, splitting, and refusal to really trust anyone (including myself). Positive feelings are scary because I know that the ax falls next. So, having fun is frightening. In a play situation, I'm often wondering, "Are we having fun yet?" Even in a fun situation, my total lack of self-esteem is so powerful I have a hard time overcoming the flashbacks, the fears, the pain, and the myriad of negative effects in order to think I'll survive this process of working back through the abuse. However, in quiet moments with my Higher Power I KNOW that I will survive. I know that life, in the midst of facing the pain and overcoming it, is full of moments of real joy, peace, and strength which were unavailable to me as long as the memories were repressed.

The preceding essay was written by a 41-year-old incest survivor who is currently a participant in our ongoing study to determine the effectiveness of an incest survivor treatment program. It was used with the permission of the author because it so eloquently describes the pervasive impact of incestuous abuse on her adult life. This piece also illustrates an array of possible consequences that result from incestuous abuse.

Browne and Finkelhor (1986) have reviewed the literature regarding the initial and long-term effects of child sexual abuse. Some of the research considered only incest survivors and some dealt with the victims of intra- and extrafamilial abuse. The results of both types of studies will be considered in this chapter. Browne and Finkelhor (1986) categorized the long-term effects of sexual abuse as emotional reactions and self-perception issues, somatic disturbances and dissociation, effects on self-esteem, effects on interpersonal relating, effects on sexuality, and effects on social functioning.

Emotional Reactions

The symptom most commonly reported in adults who were molested as children, both in the clinical and nonclinical literature, is depression. Bagley and Ramsay (1985) found that community mental health clients with a history of childhood sexual abuse scored higher than nonabused controls on two measures of depression. Similarly, Peters (1984) reports that, in a Los Angeles community survey, sexual abuse involving physical contact was associated with a higher incidence of victim depression, a greater number of depressive episodes over time, and an increased likelihood of being hospitalized for depression. Studies of college students suggest that those who experienced sexual abuse reported more symptoms of depression and also were more likely to have been hospitalized for depression (Briere & Runtz, 1985; Sedney & Brooks, 1984). A high incidence of suicide attempts among victims of child sexual abuse has been reported (Herman, 1981), as has suicidal ideation or thoughts of self-harm (Herman; Sedney & Brooks). In the experience of Lundberg-Love, Crawford, and Geffner (1987), 88% of the incest survivors who have been studied report depression, 56% have experienced suicidal ideation, 28% have made suicide attempts, and 19% have engaged in some form of self-mutilative behavior (see Table 9.1).

TABLE 9.1.   The "3Rs" Recovery Strategy for Incest Survivors: Recount, Repair, Resolve

1. *Raising the Issue*
   Client answers affirmatively and has recall of the events (proceed to Step 2, then 4).
   Client suspects incest may have occurred but has no recall of the events (proceed to Step 2, then 3).

2. *Relaxation Training*
   a. Progressive muscle
   b. Autogenic (tape assisted)
   c. Imagery
   d. Meditative

3. *Memory Retrieval*
   a. Guided relaxation
   b. Age regression
   c. Dream diaries
   d. Family interviews
   e. "Site" visits
   f. Bibliotherapy—1st-person accounts by varied authors
   g. Educational video exposure

4. *Recounting the Incident(s)*
   This step occurs after achievement of memory retrieval. If some degree of memory retrieval does not occur within a reasonable time period, proceed to Step 10.
   a. "A Page in My Journal" (Mayer, 1983)
   b. Victim Sentence Blank (Mayer, 1983)
   c. Questionnaire on Molesting (Mayer, 1983)

5. *Identification of Feelings*
   Typical feelings include depression, anger, fear, guilt, sadness, betrayal, powerlessness, traumatization
   a. Detection of feelings
   b. Labeling of feelings
   c. Word list containing numerous adjectives

6. *Identification of Salient Issues*
   a. *Checklist* (Lundberg-Love, Crawford & Geffner, 1987)
   b. Bibliotherapy
      Outgrowing the Pain (Gil, 1983)
      The Broken Taboo (Justice and Justice, 1979)
      The Secret Trauma (Russell, 1986)
   c. Video exposure

TABLE 9.1. Continued

7. *Ventilation*

   a. Empty chair role-play
   b. Letter to perpetrator
   c. Letter to nonprotector
   d. Feelings diary or journal
   e. Autobiography

   f. Symbolic activities
      Bubble baths to eliminate "dirty" feelings
      Anger exercises
      Physical exercise
      Safety-enhancing maneuvers (security check of residence, sleeping with light on, transparent shower curtains, self-protection classes, etc.)
   g. Artistic techniques (music, poetry, etc.)

8. *Assimilation*

   a. Perpetrator's imagined response letter to survivor
   b. Nonprotector's imagined response letter to survivor
   c. Survivor's rebuttal letters to Steps 8a and 8b

   d. Guided imagery for resolution of traumatic memories
   e. Artistic techniques

9. *Confrontation of Perpetrator and Nonprotector*
   This step occurs only if and when desired by both survivor and nonprotector and is preceded by role-plays and extensive preparation.

10. *Resolution of Residual Behavioral Issues*

    a. Sexual dysfunction
       Sexual education "lecture"
       Sexual education film
       Sensate focus
       Learning to inhibit dissociation during sexual interaction
       Bibliotherapy—*For Each Other* (Barbach, 1984)

    b. Fears, phobias
       Systematic desensitization
    c. Substance abuse
       Drug education
       Alcoholics Anonymous, Alanon, Adult Children of Alcoholics, Narcotics Anonymous, Naranon
    d. Depression
       Cognitive behavior modification
       Referral for medication
       Physical exercise
       Bibliotherapy—*Feeling Good* (Burns, 1980)

    e. Eating disorders
       Cognitive behavior modification
       Dietary prescription—modification of program outlined in *Taking Charge of Your Weight and Well-Being* (Nash and Ormiston, 1980)
       Nutritional education
       Bibliotherapy—*The Deadly Diet* (Sandbek, 1984)
    f. Assertiveness training
       Education and exercises—program outlined in *How to Be an Assertive, Not Aggressive Woman* (Baer, 1979)

    g. Improvement of social skills
    h. Dealing with family of origin
    i. Prevention of further victimization
       Safety tips
       Self-defense training
       "Ropes" therapy

Note. From Lundberg-Love & Geffner, 1988.

Somatic Disturbances and Dissociation

Briere (1984) described a number of somatic disturbances that they observed in adults who were sexually victimized. They include anxiety attacks (54%), nightmares (54%), difficulty sleeping (72%), insomnia (43%), dissociation or "spacing out" (41%), dizziness (21%), fainting (7.5%), derealization (33%), out-of-body experiences (21%), and chronic muscle tension (66%). Similarly, Sedney and Brooks (1984) have identified nervousness and anxiety (59%), extreme tension (41%), and sleeping problems (51%) in their college sample. The incest survivors studied by Lundberg-Love et al. (1987) exhibited somatic complaints of various types including gastrointestinal problems, pains, and headaches (50%), eating disorders (53%), and dissociative symptoms (61%).

Self-Esteem Effects

Sexual abuse victims, in general, and incest victims, in particular, tend to feel stigmatized as adults and exhibit poor self-esteem. In Briere's (1984) study, 64% reported feelings of isolation as compared to 49% of the controls. In Herman's (1981) study of incest survivors virtually *all* of the women who had been victimized by their fathers had a sense of being branded, marked, or stigmatized by their victimization. Courtois (1979) found that 73% of her community sample of incest victims reported moderate to severe feelings of isolation and alienation. Like Herman, Lundberg-Love et al. (1987) found that 100% of incest survivors reported feeling like "damaged goods" or feeling irreparably altered as a result of their incestuous abuse.

Although poor self-esteem or a negative self-concept was not evident as an initial effect of child sexual abuse (Browne & Finkelhor, 1986), it was clearly a long-term effect of sexual abuse. Bagley and Ramsay (1985) found that 19% of child sexual abuse victims versus 5% of controls scored in the "very poor" range on the Coopersmith Self-Esteem Inventory. Only 9% of the victims scored in the "very good" category as opposed to 20% of non-victims. In general, women with poor self-esteem were nearly four times as likely to report a history of child sexual abuse as compared with nonvictims. As in the case of stigmatization, incest survivors appear to exhibit greater self-esteem problems. In Courtois's (1979) community sample, 87% reported that their "sense of self" had been moderately to severely damaged. Herman (1981) also found that 60% of the incest survivors in her study believed that they had a predominantly negative self-image as compared with 10% of women with seductive, but not incestuous, fathers. Finally, Lundberg-Love et al. (1987) found that 97% of their sample exhibited evidence of poor self-esteem, 81% felt unattractive, and 78% felt "contaminated" by their abuse. Hence, the widespread clinical impression that incest survivors possess feelings of poor self-esteem appears supported by the empirical literature.

Effects on Interpersonal Relations

Women who have been sexually victimized as children report a variety of problems within the interpersonal domain. These range from difficulty relating to both men and women, conflict with parents, and discomfort in relating to their children. DeYoung (1982) studied incest survivors and found that 79% of them had predominantly hostile feelings toward their mothers, and 52% felt hostility toward the perpetrator. Similarly, Meiselman (1978) reports that 60% of the incest survivors in her therapy sample disliked their mothers and 40% experienced strong negative feelings toward their fathers. Herman's (1981) data supported this notion. Not only did the incest survivors often direct their rage toward the mother, they also appeared to hold all women, including themselves, in contempt. The data of Lundberg-Love et al. (1987) also validate this assertion, although 89% of their sample felt anger/hostility toward their perpetrator, 75% felt hostility toward their mother, and 69% also directed their anger/hostility inward on themselves.

Incest survivors typically report problems trusting others, exhibit fear reactions, and feel a strong sense of betrayal. Briere (1984) noted fear of men in 48% of his clinical subjects versus 15% of nonvictims, and fear of women in 12% of victims versus 4% of nonvictims. Close relationships also tend to be difficult for incest survivors. In Meiselman's (1978) study, 64% of survivors as compared to 40% of the controls, reported fear of, or conflict with, husbands or sex partners. Indeed 39% of the survivors had never married. The data of Courtois (1979) support this finding; 79% of incest survivors experienced moderate or severe problems relating to men, and 40% never married. Also, recall Russell's (1986) data where 28% of incest survivors were divorced or separated and 30% never married. In the non-incest control group these values were 16% and 31%, respectively. The Lundberg-Love et al. (1987) data indicated that 89% of the incest survivors studied reported an inability to trust people, 44% had a general fear of men, 86% had difficulties with close relationships, and 39% had been married more than once or had lived with more than one significant other. At the outset of the study, 44% of the incest survivors were married, 28% were divorced, and 19% were single.

Perhaps one of the most serious interpersonal long-term effects associated with incestuous abuse is the tendency for incest survivors to be sexually revictimized during their lives. The Russell (1986) data were quite definite regarding this issue. Eighty-two percent of the survivors were victims of serious nonincestuous sexual assault at some time in their lives, and 68% of the incest survivors were victims of rape or attempted rape (nonincestuous). In a study by Fromuth (1983), who surveyed 482 female college students, women who were sexually abused before age 13 were more likely to become victims of nonconsensual sexual experiences. Additional evidence derives from a study conducted at the University of New Mexico School of

Medicine involving 341 sexual assault admittances. When comparing first-time rape victims to revictimized women, 18% of the repeat victims had incest histories as compared to only 4% of first-time victims (Miller et al., 1978). The Lundberg-Love et al. (1987) data also confirm that incest survivors are at greater risk for sexual revictimization, with 50% of them having been sexually revictimized.

Effects on Sexuality

Nearly all clinically based studies suggest that childhood sexual abuse survivors tend to have later sexual problems. This is particularly true for incest survivors. Meiselman (1978) reports that 87% of her sample of incest survivors experienced a serious problem with sexual adjustment at some point subsequent to their molestation, as compared with 20% of a sample of women who had not been sexually victimized as children. In Herman's (1981) study, 55% of incestuously victimized women reported later sexual problems. This was not significantly different, however, from the problems found in women with seductive fathers. Briere's (1984) results not only found that 45% of women sexually abused as children reported difficult sexual adjustment as adults, 42% of them also experienced an attenuated sex drive. These values compared to 15% and 29% of nonvictims, respectively.

Two studies that utilized nonclinical samples suggest that sexual problems are a legacy of incest and child sexual abuse. Courtois (1979) notes that 80% of incest survivors reported an inability to relax and enjoy sexual activity, an avoidance of or abstention from sex, or conversely a compulsive desire for sex. Finkelhor's (1979) study of college students found that child sexual abuse victims scored significantly lower on a measure of sexual self-esteem than did their nonabused classmates.

In the incest survivors studied by Lundberg-Love et al. (1987) problems with sexuality were quite common. For example, 56% reported unsatisfactory sexual relationships, 67% experienced an aversion to sexual activity, 36% complained of problems in becoming sexually aroused, and 42% experienced problems with control issues as they related to sexual interaction.

Some incest survivors report a problem that is the converse of sexual difficulty. That is, they exhibit sexual acting-out behavior, which is commonly referred to as "promiscuity" in the literature. Herman (1981) notes that 35% of incest survivors reported promiscuity and appeared to have a "repertoire of sexually stylized behavior" (p. 40). Herman suggests that such behavior was used as a mechanism for obtaining affection and/or attention. DeYoung (1982) found that 28% of her sample engaged in activities that could be termed promiscuous. Meiselman (1978) reports a frequency of 25% who exhibited this type of behavior. The data of Lundberg-Love et al. (1987) are dissimilar in this respect. Nearly 58% of the incest survivors in that study engaged in sexual acting-out behavior at some point in their lives. It is likely that the value is higher than other reports because Lundberg et al. have studied most of these women for longer than a 2-year-period, thus facilitating greater possibilities for observation and disclosure. Also, it appears that the behavior of incest survivors tends to vacillate between bipolarities across the life span (Lundberg-Love & Geffner, 1988). At times survivors may exhibit attenuated sexual behavior, and at other times they may report enhanced sexual drive. Lees (1981) also has observed what she terms bipolar patterns of affect, behavior, and cognition. In accord with the observations of Lundberg-Love and Geffner, she suggests that some survivors rigidly maintain one extreme of behavior, others the polar opposite, and some survivors alternate between the two. Nevertheless, most data describing the long-term effects of incest clearly indicate that disrupted adult sexual behavior is a sequel to childhood sexual abuse in general, and incestuous abuse in particular. Indeed, therapists at the FVRTP routinely inquire regarding the possibility of childhood sexual abuse whenever they see a female client who reports sexual problems.

Effects on Social Functioning

Within this realm of behavior, Browne and Finkelhor (1986) considered several studies of special populations. Studies of prostitutes (James & Meyerding, 1977; Silbert & Pines, 1981) suggest childhood sexual abuse is a common finding in this population. Also, incest survivors appear to be at risk for substance abuse. James and Meyerding interviewed 136 prostitutes and found that 55% were sexually abused as children by someone at least 10 years older than they were. Such abuse, of course, had occurred prior to their first experience of sexual intercourse. Similarly, Silbert and Pines found that 60% of the prostitutes they interviewed were sexually abused by an average of 2 people for a mean duration of 20 months, *before* they were 16 years old. Data reported by Fields (1981), however, failed to detect any difference among the prevalence of prostitutes who had been sexually abused as children (45%), as compared to an age-, race-, and education-matched group of nonprostitutes who were sexually abused during childhood (37%). She did report, however, that the prostitutes were sexually abused at a younger age (14.5 vs. 16.5 years) and were more likely to have experienced physical force.

With respect to substance abuse, Peters (1984) found that 17% of the sexually victimized women in her community study had symptoms of alcohol abuse as compared to 4% of nonvictimized women. Also, 27% abused at least one type of drug as compared to only 12% of nonvictimized women. Of the incest survivors studied by Herman (1981), 35% abused drugs and alcohol. This contrasted with 5% of substance-abusing women who had seductive fathers. Similarly, Briere (1984) found that 27% of adult women molested as children had a history of alcoholism and 21% a history of drug addiction as compared to 11% and 2% of nonvictims, respectively. The clinical sample studied by Lundberg-Love et al. (1987) reported a somewhat higher prevalence of substance abuse (42%) and tended to use/abuse more than one type of substance. Frequencies included alcohol 33%, amphetamine 17%, cocaine 8%, marijuana 22%, opiates 25%, sedative/hypnotics 22%, and hallucinogens 8%. In general the women in the study tended to prefer depressant drugs over stimulants because they reduced their perceptions of anxiety. However, some individuals utilized stimulants and depressants concurrently.

In summary, many of the long-term effects of child sexual abuse mentioned in the clinical literature are supported by the empirical literature. These consequences include depression, self-destructive behavior, anxiety, feelings of stigmatization and poor self-esteem, a tendency toward sexual revictimization, and substance abuse. Problems trusting others and sexual difficulties, including sexual dysfunction, impaired sexual self-esteem, sexual avoidance or abstention, and sexual dysphoria have been reported by empirical researchers, although there is less consistent agreement regarding the variables for sexual functioning (Browne & Finkelhor, 1986).

TREATMENT

Imagine that at the age of 4 you left the human race—split off into an isolated world of your own in order to survive life with parents who used you to meet their own needs.

Because of your traumatic existence, you were figuratively thrown into a life raft without food, water, or oars, towed out into the ocean, far from land . . . and then left. No one checked to see why you were missing; no one looked for you; no one even noticed you were gone. You were given no equipment or instructions on how to survive on your raft. However, you did learn survival by trial and error—how to drink the rainwater that fell in your raft and how to eat sea animals that you could catch by hand and let dry in the sun. You learned to enjoy your little life raft—isolated from mankind—because at least there you were safe. You even built a bubble around the raft to protect you further.

However, that didn't stop the assaults of your "friend" the octopus, who sometimes would sneak through a hole in the bubble, wrap its tentacles around you ("in love," he said) and almost strangle you to death. At other times the octopus would burst through the bubble, slither into the raft, hold you down and force one of his tentacles into your mouth, almost strangling you again.

After the octopus left, as you were regaining your ability to breathe, you would be assaulted by a wild and vicious hurricane which pounded you with basketball-sized hail, with ferocious winds that almost capsized your raft, and with bolts of lightning which almost destroyed you . . . all because you couldn't keep the octopus out.

The protective bubble was totally ineffective against them.

Every now and then a beautiful ocean liner would pass by; you would wave for help, but the people would just stare at you with unseeing eyes or would smilingly wave and yell, "Keep up the good work."

You lived your life on that raft—far out to sea, still surrounded by your bubble, coming close to land only occasionally to watch the rest of mankind living life.

Once the octopus died and the hurricane lost its physical fury, you still had to stay prepared for the hurricane's emotional fury—blasts of icy wind which threatened to freeze your very soul.

There are now other sea animals which circle your raft, sensing the weakness of the raft and its occupant. They attack, but you survive because, through the grace of your Higher Power you have become a SURVIVOR.

The time has come, however, to remove your protective bubble and to let your raft be led to shore. You are terrified that you might not survive. Someone might kill you or you might become so terrified and overwhelmed that you might kill yourself.

This essay was authored by the same survivor who wrote the piece included in the Consequences section of this chapter. The essay describes metaphorically what life felt like living in the shadows of incestuous abuse. It also captures the terror that is inherent in the decision to embrace therapy.

Indeed, a critical aspect of therapy for the incest survivor involves the careful dismantling of the cocoon of defenses that evolved in response to the incestuous abuse and a patient restructuring of the behavioral repertoire. As documented in the preceding section, incestuous abuse has an insidiously pervasive impact upon many aspects of behavior. Hence, it is not surprising that the effective treatment of the incest survivor may require an eclectic, multimodal approach. In this section some general treatment issues will be briefly discussed. Then, some of the general treatment strategies reviewed by Courtois (1988) will be summarized. The final part of this section will outline the treatment strategy currently being researched within the Family Violence Research and Treatment Program (FVRTP) at the University of Texas at Tyler.

General Treatment Issues

Treatment of adult survivors of incest has only recently been recognized as a discrete clinical issue, an area requiring techniques different from those utilized for child victims. Although the development of treatment programs for adult victims/survivors began in the latter 1970s with the groundbreaking work of Butler (1978), Giaretto (1976), Forward and Buck (1978), Herman and Hirschman (1977), and Meiselman (1978), the treatment literature remains descriptive and anecdotal rather than empirically based. Hence, many practitioners have had to develop their own approaches in a somewhat trial-and-error fashion. For the most part, few of these approaches have been systematically evaluated to assess their effectiveness. Nevertheless, many of the techniques possess good face validity, derive from particular theoretical perspectives, and appear to afford some relief and some degree of recovery to adult incest survivors. One axiom does seem apparent: Regardless of the therapist's theoretical perspective, treatment must be tailored to meet the unique issues of each survivor. So many combinations and permutations of variables (e.g., age of onset and termination, duration, identity of perpetrator, family organization, social supports) mediate the consequences of incestuous abuse that an inflexible, stereotyped approach to treatment is counterproductive. Indeed, Giaretto (1976) set the tone for incest survivor therapy when he said, "A variety of techniques is employed in implementing the therapeutic model. None is used for its own sake; instead I try to tune into the client and the situation and . . . apply a fitting technique" (p. 154). According to Courtois (1988), treatment should be guided by the needs of the client, her personality characteristics, the phase and intensity of her stress response, and her most salient traumagenic issues. Lundberg-Love and Geffner (1988) would also add that a therapist must consider all of the aforementioned suggestions within the context of the survivor's stage of recovery. Generally, the longer a survivor continues in therapy, the more opportunity she has had to modify existing skills and to develop new coping skills. Often the greater the array of coping skills available to the survivor, the greater the therapeutic possibilities.

Typically, treatment is conducted within an individual and/or group treatment framework. Sometimes couples/marital and family approaches are utilized, particularly when the survivor lives within the parental home. Family therapy is *not* recommended as the sole treatment modality. Rather, it should be secondary to treatment of each family member in individual, dyadic, and group formats (Giaretto, 1982). Traditional family therapy is not optimal because it tends to rebalance the family in the traditional roles (Brickman, 1984) and often treats interpersonal effects without adequate attention to the intrapsychic components that support incest transmission (Calof, 1987).

With respect to the duration of treatment, incest therapy can be strategic and time limited or time unlimited. However, Courtois (1988) emphasizes the need to be "up front" with the client in explaining that incest therapy is usually lengthy because of the complexity of the issues and the time requirements inherent in recovery. Therapeutic experience at the FVRTP also supports that recommendation. Typically, clients in this program require at least 2 years to recount, repair, and resolve the legacy of incest. This does not mean that an issue-oriented approach cannot be successful in the short run. It can. However, professionals working with the FVRTP have observed that as one "issue" resolves, another emerges. Usually, survivors need to address the trauma of their victimization directly and grieve, mourn their lost childhood, ventilate feelings, develop support networks, become educated about incest, and generally restructure their lives in order to begin recovery. Recovery appears to be a lengthy process, and some survivors would submit that the legacy of incestuous abuse is never totally resolved. However, therapy can certainly attenuate the pain, provide new alternatives to old dysfunctional patterns, promote empowerment instead of helplessness, and transform shame and guilt into self-acceptance and self-nurturance. When time-limited therapy is attempted, it must be focal, reinforce the client's strength, and preclude the developing of strong attachment to/and dependency on the therapist. These restrictions also apply to the case of time-limited group therapy (Courtois, 1988).

Treatment Strategies

Techniques utilized in the treatment of incest survivors generally derive from four basic types of categories. They include stress management/coping techniques, experiential/expressive cathartic techniques, exploratory/psychodynamic techniques, and cognitive/behavioral techniques (Courtois, 1988).

Stress Management/Coping Techniques

These techniques enable survivors to cope with the overwhelming stress inherent in dealing with the trauma of incest. Typically, the therapist, at the outset of therapy, informs the client that she probably will feel worse before she feels better, hence the need for a variety of stress management/coping skills. As outlined by Horowitz (1986), these skills range from basic relaxation techniques used with or without imagery to specific treatments for stress response syndromes. Horowitz has differentiated between two phases of stress response syndromes (the denial-numbing phase and the intrusive-repetitive phase), and he describes therapeutic strategies for each phase. For example, in the denial-numbing phase, old defenses need to be examined and interpreted. Recollection and abreaction need to be encouraged. Descriptive processes surrounding reconstruction of the survivor's memories and feelings need to be encouraged and reinforced as does the process of catharsis. The emotional aspects of relationships and experiences of the self need to be explored. The therapist also needs to encourage relationships and support to counteract the numbness (Horowitz). The techniques available to the therapist during the intrusive-repetitive phases of therapy include:

1. Supplying structure externally
2. Reducing external demands and encouraging the client to "rest"
3. Providing identification models through group membership and good leadership
4. Permitting temporary idealization
5. Providing educative and interpretive information
6. Differentiating reality from fantasy, past from current schemata, and self-attributes from object attributes

7. Interpreting the meaning and effects of environmental triggers
8. Teaching clients how to "dose" their exposure to therapeutic issues
9. Teaching desensitization and relaxation procedures

Horowitz's (1986) book, entitled *Stress Response Syndromes,* provides additional explanation for implementation of these techniques.

Experiential/Expressive Cathartic Techniques

According to Courtois (1988), techniques from Gestalt therapy, from psychodrama, and from art, music, movement, and writing therapies are useful for breaking through denial and promoting ventilation, catharsis, and abreaction of the trauma. However, a therapist must introduce and utilize such techniques cautiously. Because cathartic techniques can be very effective in dismantling various defenses and can arouse intense emotions, they must be utilized slowly and in measured doses. Otherwise, a survivor can once again feel helpless and overwhelmed. Such a reaction can disrupt client/therapist trust and endanger the therapeutic alliance.

It is not uncommon for clients to discover expressive techniques on their own, often utilizing them as another means of communicating affects and experiences to the therapist. Indeed, the majority of our clients keep personal journals, produce various works of art, write poetry or essays, and voraciously read and review books on incest and child sexual abuse. Again, the therapist needs to help the client avoid overstimulation. Most incest survivors are conscientious clients who tend to immerse themselves in treatment issues. If the therapist fails to provide guidance regarding the structuring of work and play and the importance of moderation, survivors may exhaust themselves and thereby aggravate depressive conditions.

Specific exercises that are typically used include the Gestalt empty chair technique, role-plays and role reversals, the writing of letters that may or may not be sent, mock trials of perpetrators, and role-played confrontations. Various artistic expressive techniques not only facilitate catharsis, but often promote insight by circumventing some of the defense mechanisms associated with verbalization. Mayer (1983) utilizes sentence stems, poetry, genograms, and checklists. She also suggests that art techniques are effective for recovering repressed material and uses the Kinetic Draw-A-Person Test as well as Draw-the-Assault and Draw-the-Abuser Tests. Expressive techniques can also promote mastery and empowerment. For example, writing the essays included in this chapter enabled one incest survivor to banish the last vestiges of denial of her abuse. Writing about her abuse made it real and proved she was not "crazy." Many incest survivors are plagued by feelings of "craziness" as they recover repressed memories. Even though they can acknowledge intellectually that their memories are indeed accurate, it takes time and often utilization of expressive techniques to come to grips emotionally with the reality of their abuse.

Bibliotherapy and audiovisual materials can be both educational and emotionally validating. Again, the same caveats regarding the possibility of client overstimulation are in order. Survivors should always be prepared in advance of bibliotherapy or audiovisual exposure. They should be reminded that they are in control of their exposure to the materials and encouraged to stop if they feel overwhelmed. The following list includes some of the specific books that the FVRTP has utilized (See also Table 9.1).

Bibliotherapy Sources

Kiss Daddy Goodnight (Armstrong, 1978)	*I Never Told Anyone* (Bass & Thornton, 1983)
Daddy's Girl (Allen, 1982)	*Incest Years After* (Donaldson, 1983)
Father's Days (Brady, 1979)	*Betrayal of Innocence* (Forward & Buck, 1978)
The Courage to Heal (Bass & Davis, 1987)	*The Best Kept Secret* (Rush, 1980)
Incest and Sexuality (Maltz & Holman, 1987)	*Father–Daughter Rape* (Ward, 1985)
Conspiracy of Silence (Butler, 1978)	

Finally, within the realm of expressive techniques is what Courtois (1988) terms "going public" and what FVRTP calls "making a contribution." Some incest survivors in the FVRTP feel strongly motivated to give meaning to their abuse by making a contribution to others through education, organization of self-help groups, volunteering for hotlines, peer counseling, conducting research, appearing on media programs, or producing artwork. The list is endless. Basically this behavior often stems from a desire for survivors to use their creativity to transform their pain into something they perceive as a positive response. Blank (1985) calls this the "survivor mission." Butler (1985) suggests that some survivors need to become "warriors" in order to work through their trauma. Blank also states that although such activity may not be seen as the typical response, it is within the normal range and may be crucial for some survivors' recovery. Nevertheless, therapists need to be honest with their clients regarding the possible outcomes of such endeavors and the client's psychological readiness to undertake such tasks (Courtois, 1988; Lundberg-Love & Geffner, 1988). Therapists need to help incest survivors to weigh the benefits and liabilities of engaging in such activities.

Exploratory/Psychodynamic Techniques

These techniques are derived primarily from a psychodynamic tradition and have some similarities with cathartic techniques. The psychodynamic approach attempts to explore unconscious as well as conscious material. Miller (1981, 1984) has been a leading proponent of this approach and has challenged classic analytic theory for concealing the reality of incest, thereby causing victims to deny their trauma and blame themselves. Miller suggests a return to Freud's original position regarding the role of childhood trauma in the etiology of symptom formation. Although Miller advocates the classic position of a neutral therapist, she recommends that the therapist be the advocate of the child and believe in her experience. Free association, dream analysis, and transference/countertransference analysis are techniques used in this therapeutic approach. By the analysis of defense mechanisms and through reenactments and repetitions of compulsions, childhood experiences are revealed. Brickman (1985), Greer (1986), and Pasternak (1987) also have discussed the use of a modified psychoanalytic approach to the treatment of incest survivors.

This therapeutic approach often utilizes hypnosis in the recapturing of lost memories, in the abreaction of trauma, in the identification of and reconnection with disowned parts of the self, in pain management and substance control, and as a means of relaxation via autohypnosis (Courtois, 1988).

Cognitive/Behavioral Techniques

A broad range of therapeutic techniques can be classified as cognitive/behavioral, including developmental skill-building and social learning approaches as well as traditional behavior modification protocols. Cognitive and behavioral techniques are particularly effective for remediating developmental deficits and altering conditioned responses that result from the abuse itself or from living in a dysfunctional family environment. They are also valuable for modifying the types of distorted cognitions that evolve in response to incestuous abuse and often serve as defense mechanisms. Courtois (1988) suggests that there are three categories of cognitive/behavioral techniques: developmental, cognitive, and behavioral.

The developmental techniques promote individual growth and differentiation through self-assessment and the development of new skills. Developmental deficits appear to be part of the sequel of incestuous abuse. Hence, developmental techniques typically provide opportunities and exercises for their amelioration. Helfer (1978) has a course that uses a series of graduated exercises specifically for clients who "missed" their childhoods. Part of this program encourages clients to get in touch with their senses, to differentiate between good and bad touch, and to develop a positive sense of self.

Some aspects of the treatment of incest survivors are similar to reparenting. However, it is important that a therapist maintain appropriate boundaries in this respect. Although the therapist can serve as a parental model, he or she can never restore the parenting the survivor missed, make up for the abuse, or be available as a parent. But the therapist can serve as a coach or trainer or as a guide to enable the survivor to reparent herself and seek additional parenting from appropriate surrogate parents.

Self-nurturance exercises are important for the incest survivor's development. Courtois (1988) suggests that many survivors are unaware of how hard they are on themselves and must learn how to attend to their own needs. Self-caretaking behavior is promoted by encouraging clients to engage in relaxation as well as pleasurable and positive activities. Incest survivors also should be encouraged to create a safe, aesthetically pleasing home environment for themselves to serve as a respite from the world and the pain of recovery.

In addition, self-help programs, particularly 12-step programs, can serve as developmental approaches for survivors who face compulsive or addictive behavioral problems. The development of some type of spirituality can be a source of strength and serenity during stressful times.

Finally, the use of self-affirmations and the development of more personalized and meaningful relationships with others can be growth enhancing. The survivor should be coached in the gradual development of friendships and a support network, as trust is a difficult issue and dysfunctional "rules" regarding relationships must be unlearned.

Cognitive techniques are used to correct or restructure the incest survivor's belief system about herself and her abuse. Jehu, Klassen, and Gazan (1985) have tested the efficacy of cognitive restructuring techniques in treating the distorted beliefs of 11 victims of childhood sexual abuse. Both clinically and statistically significant improvements in both beliefs and moods were obtained. The authors note the following types of distortions: all-or-nothing dichotomous thinking, overgeneralization, mislabeling, selective abstraction, disqualifying the positive, magnification and minimization, emotional reasoning, "should" statements, personalization, and jumping to conclusions. Jehu et al. provided alternatives to the distortions via provision of information, logical analysis, decatastrophizing, distancing, reattribution, and assigned activities. Cognitive techniques show promise in providing incest survivors with the possibility of altering the distorted beliefs that developed in response to the abuse.

Guided imagery and metaphor can be used alone or in conjunction with relaxation or hypnosis to promote anxiety reduction, to break through defenses, to allow memories to emerge, to enable the client to regain control, and to imagine alternative responses. For example, Groves (1987) has developed a technique for the resolution of traumatic memories using the client's expression of trauma through metaphor. Metaphors are also useful for visualizing success in therapy.

Behavioral techniques include stress inoculation training, stress management training, systematic desensitization, assertiveness training, anger management training, problem solving, goal setting, decision making, and sex therapy. These techniques usually incorporate cognitive and behavioral components. The therapist's orientation typically determines whether interventions will be first addressed cognitively or behaviorally or whether they will be addressed simultaneously. The survivor's change in behavior then affects the way she thinks or feels. Other techniques that can be considered behavioral include wilderness therapy (a variation of the Outward Bound experience) and self-defense training. Both of these approaches may be useful for replacing helplessness with empowerment. Also, self-defense techniques and assertiveness training can be helpful for preventing sexual revictimization.

Finally, a behavioral intervention that deserves mention and requires careful consideration is that of physical contact between client and therapist or between group members and their therapist(s). Courtois (1988) suggests that appropriate touching can express empathy, caring, and comforting. It can also demonstrate the difference between positive and exploitative touch. However, touch between client and therapist can be misinterpreted. Indeed, physical contact can be threatening to survivors and should never be initiated by a therapist without the client's permission and without an examination of how it will be interpreted. Forensic psychologists suggest that even appropriate, well-bounded touch can often provoke malpractice action. Courtois (1988) states that she does not maintain a hard-and-fast rule regarding touching. She always seeks permission before touching but relies on her intuition. Any physical contact is limited and serves to offer support or reassurance during times of stress or intense emotion. Courtois (1988) believes that limits and boundaries that are consistent and neither too rigid nor too permeable can be established behaviorally and cognitively.

Although the guidelines at the FVRTP are not rigid and do not forbid touch, therapists are encouraged not to touch clients unless the benefits and liabilities have been carefully weighed. Regardless of what the client says and whether the therapist uses intuition, even the most appropriate touch may somehow be reminiscent of the touch of the abuser, particularly when there is the possibility of still-repressed memories. When this occurs, trust and the therapeutic alliance can be significantly damaged. Also, therapists at the FVRTP have encountered some clients who, having experienced tactile-oriented therapists, developed the belief that the therapeutic aspect of therapy was the touching. This belief became counterproductive and often hindered the survivors' continued development. It also appeared to compromise the survivors' inclination and ability to comfort themselves, a skill all survivors need to learn. Although there is a case to be made for the therapist's modeling appropriate touch, there are also many risks inherent in this approach. However, one axiom can be stated. It is *never* appropriate for a therapist to engage in sexualized behavior with an incest survivor client.

The "3Rs" of Recovery: Recount, Repair, and Resolve

The FVRTP has developed a novel, eclectic approach to the treatment of adult incest survivors. The program has evolved in response to the variety of therapeutic problems and challenges presented by incest survivor clients. The 3Rs Recovery Program teaches stress and coping techniques, and it utilizes a multimodal, integrated approach to treatment by incorporating expressive/cathartic, cognitive/behavioral, and some psychodynamic techniques within one program. The following discussion describes the general procedure for implementation of the program, and Table 9.1 contains a detailed outline. It is also important to note that the FVRTP is currently conducting research, funded by the Hogg Foundation for Mental Health and the University of Texas at Tyler, to determine the effectiveness of its program.

For the past 3 years, the FVRTP has been responsible for the individual and group treatment of adult incest survivors. To date nearly 100 women have been treated using the strategy described in this chapter. Although some of the specific exercises have been adapted from Giaretto (1982) and Mayer (1983), this treatment strategy is an original one that has evolved in response to the challenges and problems presented by the incest survivor. The strategy for individual treatment consists of progression through five different phases:

1. Raising the issue
2. Relaxation training
3. Recounting the trauma
4. Repairing the "damage" done by the incestuous abuse
5. Resolving the residual behavior deficits of the individual

The initial stage of raising the issue is necessary because frequently incest survivors come to therapy ostensibly for reasons other than dealing with past incest. These "other reasons" often include depression, eating disorders, weight control, substance abuse, sexual dysfunction, and panic attacks. Often, unbeknown to the client, the presenting clinical issue is a sequel to early incestuous experience. Therefore, if the therapist does not inquire about the possibility of incestuous abuse, the client may never raise the issue, and therapeutic progress associated with the presenting complaint may be stymied. Thus, FVRTP therapists routinely raise the issue of sexual abuse with all female clients. They do this initially in a manner that does not require the individual necessarily to label her experience as abuse.

The second phase of treatment involves teaching the client techniques of relaxation. It is important for the therapist to teach the client a variety of approaches to relaxation because different clients respond differentially to various relaxation techniques. Hence, autogenic relaxation training, tape-assisted imagery techniques, meditative techniques, and progressive muscle relaxation are used. The majority of women prefer the psychological relaxation techniques to progressive muscle relaxation. Nevertheless, it is critical that an incest survivor be capable of performing at least one relaxation technique, so that she will have a means of calming herself when psychological discomfort occurs.

After the client has demonstrated her ability (via the use of biofeedback) to perform the relaxation techniques effectively, the client may proceed to the third phase of treatment (recounting the trauma). This phase consists of three components: recounting the incident(s), identification and labeling of feelings associated with the incident(s), and identification of salient issues surrounding the incident(s). In order to aid incest survivors in describing the abuse they experienced, the 3Rs Recovery Program utilizes some structured exercises proposed by Mayer (1983). In order to help survivors to identify their feelings and salient issues, bibliotherapy is employed. Some clients, as a result of repression, have great difficulty recalling their past abuse. With these clients an attempt is made to stimulate memory retrieval in a variety of ways, including (a) guided relaxation coupled with suggested age regression and guided imagery, (b) dream diaries, (c) bibliotherapy, (d) educational video exposure, (e) family interviews, and (f) "site" visits. Upon memory retrieval, these women then proceed to the phase of recounting the trauma. Should memory retrieval be blocked, strategic issues can be addressed until the client is safe enough or strong enough for memories to be retrievable.

After details of the abuse are known and discussed, treatment for repairing the psychological damage can ensue. This phase has two major components: ventilation and assimilation. During ventilation a variety of exercises are utilized to help the survivor "express" and "divest" herself of her emotional trauma. These include (a) empty chair role-play; (b) undelivered letter to perpetrator, including writing, reading aloud in therapy, audio taping, and replay; (c) undelivered letter to nonprotector; (d) "feelings" diary; (e) autobiography; and (f) "symbolic" activities to deal with problematic issues.

During assimilation the survivor composes the perpetrator's "imagined response" letter to her original letter. She also composes a similar "imagined response" letter from the nonprotector. Then the survivor composes two more rebuttal letters to the perpetrator and nonprotector, respectively. These letters typically are never mailed. Much symbolic work surrounding anger occurs during this phase. Therapists also use guided imagery for resolution of traumatic memories.

During the resolution phase of treatment phase the therapist works with the client in individual treatment to resolve remaining problematic behavioral issues. Such issues often include:

1. Treatment of sexual dysfunction
2. Treatment of phobias
3. Help with substance abuse
4. Cognitive behavioral modification for depression
5. Treatment of eating disorders

6. Assertiveness training
7. Prevention of further victimization

After the client has exhibited some resolution of her depressive feelings as well as her feelings of guilt and shame (as a consequence of ventilation and assimilation), she is introduced to group therapy. Typically, therapists recommend group therapy for most survivors, most often after completion of Step 7. Individual and group therapy continue concurrently until all behavioral issues are resolved. Survivors are then permitted to remain affiliated with their group until they desire separation. Although a programmatic approach has been depicted, there is often overlap of the assimilation and resolution phases of treatment.

This treatment strategy has benefited incest survivor clients tremendously. Not only are acute symptoms improved, but successful resolution of even long-standing behavioral problems appears possible. It seems likely that this treatment program has the potential to benefit most adult incest survivors.

Many treatment techniques are beneficial for the amelioration of the aftermath of incest. This chapter describes stress/coping, expressive/cathartic, psychodynamic, and cognitive/behavioral techniques for the treatment of incest survivors. Techniques need to be selected according to the therapist's orientation, the needs of the survivor, and the phase of the client's traumatic stress response or recovery status.

SUMMARY AND FUTURE DIRECTIONS

The data presented in this chapter suggest that at least 10% to 20% of the women in this country may be adult survivors of incest. The bulk of incest perpetrators are male, and their victims are female. The person most likely to commit incest is the stepfather or biological father. Because of the betrayal inherent in this type of abuse, the crime of incest can severely disrupt the development of the victim. As society becomes better educated regarding the relationship between incestuous abuse and its myriad consequences, it can be anticipated that more incest survivors will seek treatment. Hence, it is important for the practitioner to develop an awareness of the unique therapeutic needs of this special population.

Some of the long-term consequences of incestuous abuse can include depression, substance abuse, prostitution, anxiety disorders, dissociative disorders including multiple personality, and sexual dysfunction. Difficulty in trusting others, a sense of isolation, stigma, poor self-esteem, and an increased likelihood of revictimization are commonly observed in many survivors. Clients can experience many of these consequences, or few of them. Hence, treatment of adult incest survivors must be tailored to the individual's particular therapeutic requirements. Often, a therapist will need to encourage the survivor to place her therapeutic issues on a hierarchy.

Therapy can be time limited or time unlimited. The former approach, although useful, particularly in crisis intervention situations, typically is insufficient for recovery. Recovery from incestuous abuse often requires time-unlimited therapy. Because multiple treatment priorities tend to exist, a variety of therapeutic techniques are often utilized in the treatment of adult incest survivors. Courtois (1988) has reviewed some of these techniques and groups them into four categories. These include stress/coping techniques, experiential/expressive cathartic techniques, exploratory/psychodynamic techniques, and cognitive/behavioral techniques.

Strategies vary for combining and organizing the implementation of these techniques. Most therapists would agree that in some manner the incestuous abuse must be disclosed and recounted. Often, memories need to be retrieved, and feelings need to be recognized, labeled, and expressed. Cognitive distortions need to be identified and restructured. Typically, grieving and mourning of the lost childhood occurs. Developmental delays and/or discontinuities need to be addressed so that differentiation and individuation can continue. Stigmatization must be modified. Finally, education and skill building are critical. The judicious use of assessment instruments during the course of therapy is essential for evaluating treatment and for validating the survivor's progress. Group treatment appears to be important for improvement of self-esteem and survivor "networking." Potential therapists for adult incest survivors could benefit by remembering these words from Miller (1984):

> Theoretical understanding alone is still not enough. Only therapists who have had the opportunity to experience and work through their own traumatic past will be able to accompany patients on the path to truth about themselves and not hinder them on their way. Such therapists will not confuse their patients, make them anxious, or . . . misuse, or seduce them, for they no longer have to fear the eruption in themselves of feelings that were stifled long ago, and they know from experience the healing power of these feelings. (p. 314)

Even though the present treatment strategies for adult incest survivors have certain face validity, rest on theoretical bases, and afford symptomatic relief, they require systematic evaluation. Empirical studies are required to determine the effectiveness of particular techniques and various treatment packages. In order to achieve this.goal, reliable and valid assessment instruments need to be identified or created. John Briere (1984) has done groundbreaking work in this area. His efforts need to be augmented and extended by other researchers and practitioners. The FVRTP at the University of Texas at Tyler is currently conducting research with a number of instruments to evaluate its treatment program for adult incest survivors.

Programs specifically designed for male incest survivors need to be developed and evaluated. Indeed, there is a need for research studies on male incest survivors in general and a comparison study of male and female incest survivors in particular. Many therapeutic issues for the male and female incest survivors are similar, but the cognitive distortions can be different. There also may be a greater propensity for the male survivor to model the behavior of the abuser. This raises the issue of whether some techniques are more effective for male survivors than for female survivors.

Another area that requires empirical investigation is a study to evaluate the effectiveness of different techniques for memory retrieval. Practitioners also need studies to investigate the variables that mediate memory retrieval. Therapists at the FVRTP have observed differences among individuals with respect to the ease of memory retrieval. Often when memory retrieval is stymied, the issues of safety and/or control are present. The prominence of the family of origin within the survivor's present life may also be a critical variable.

Long-term follow-up information on survivors who completed time-limited treatment as compared to those who completed time-unlimited treatment is required. It appears that long-term treatment is warranted and even necessary for recovery, but it would be validating to have those data. Such information also could prove helpful to survivors, when they hit difficult times during treatment.

The brief agenda outlined here is by no means exhaustive. Rather, it highlights some obvious deficiencies in the empirical data base concerning incest survivors and, it is hoped, will stimulate the collective creativity of professionals. Clearly, much research remains to be conducted before practitioners can provide data-based answers to incest survivors regarding the most appropriate treatment strategies.

REFERENCES

Allen, V. (1982). *Daddy's girl*. New York: Berkeley.

Armstrong, L. (1978). *Kiss daddy good-night: A speak-out on incest*. New York: Hawthorne.

Armstrong, L. (1982). The cradle of sexual politics. In M. Kilpatrick (Ed.), *Women's sexual experience: Exploration of the dark continent* (pp. 109–125). New York: Plenum.

Baer, J. (1976). *How to be an assertive, not aggressive woman*. New York: Signet.

Bagley, C., & Ramsay, R. (1985). *Disrupted childhood and vulnerability to sexual assault: Long-term sequels with implications for counselling*. Paper presented at the Conference on Counselling the Sexual Abuse Survivor, Winnipeg, Manitoba.

Barbach, L. (1984). *For each other: Sharing sexual intimacy*. New York: Signet.

Bass, E., & Davis, L. (1988). *The courage to heal: Women healing from child sexual abuse*. New York: Harper & Row.

Bass, E., & Thornton, L. (Eds.). (1983). *I never told anyone: Writing by women survivors of child sexual abuse*. New York: Harper & Row.

Blank, A. (1985, March). *Lessons learned from the treatment of combat veterans relevant for crime victims.* Paper presented at the colloquium, The Aftermath of Crime: a mental Health Crisis. National Institute of Mental Health and National Organization of Victim Assistance, Washington, DC.

Brady, K. (1979). *Father's days.* New York: Dell.

Briere, J. (1984, April). *The effects of childhood sexual abuse on later psychological functioning: Defining a post-sexual abuse syndrome.* Paper presented at the Third National Conference on the Sexual Victimization of Children, Children's Hospital National Medical Center, Washington, DC.

Briere, J., & Runtz, M. (1985). *Symptomatology associated with prior sexual abuse in a non-clinical sample.* Paper presented at the annual meeting of the American Psychological Association, Los Angeles.

Brickman, J. (1984). Feminist, nonsexist, and traditional models of therapy: Implications for working with incest. *Women and Therapy, 3,* 49–67.

Brickman, J. (1985, February). *Counselling issues and techniques for working with sexual abuse survivors.* Workshop presented at the conference on Counselling the Sexual Abuse Survivor, Klinic Community Health Centre, Winnipeg, Manitoba.

Browne, A., & Finkelhor, D. (1986). Impact of child sexual abuse: A review of the literature. *Psychological Bulletin, 99,* 66–77.

Burns, D. D. (1980). *Feeling good: The new mood therapy.* New York: Signet.

Butler, S. (1978). *Conspiracy of silence: The trauma of incest.* San Francisco: Volcano.

Butler, S. (1985, February). *Treatment perspectives: A feminist view.* Presentation at the Conference on Counselling the Sexual Abuse Survior, Klinic Community Health Centre, Winnipeg, Manitoba.

Calof, D. (1987). *Treating adult survivors of incest and child abuse.* Workshop presented at The Family Network Symposium, Washington, DC.

Courtois, C. A. (1979). Characteristics of a volunteer sample of adult women who experienced incest in childhood and adolescence. *Dissertation Abstracts International, 40,* 3194A–3195A.

Courtois, C. A. (1988). *Healing the incest wound: Adult survivors in therapy.* New York: Norton.

De Young, M. (1982). *The sexual victimization of children.* Jefferson, NC: Mc-Farland.

Donaldson, M. (1983). *Incest years after: Putting the pain to rest.* Fargo, ND: Village Family Service Center.

Fields, P. J. (1981). Parent-child relationships, childhood sexual abuse, and adult interpersonal behavior in female prostitutes. *Dissertation Abstracts International, 42,* 2053B.

Finkelhor, D. (1979). *Sexually victimized children.* New York: Free Press.

Finkelhor, D. (1984). *Child sexual abuse: New theory and research.* New York: Free Press.

Finkelhor, D. (1986). *A sourcebook on child sexual abuse.* Beverly Hills: Sage.

Forward, S., & Buck, C. (1978). *Betrayal of innocence: Incest and its devastation.* Los Angeles: J. P. Tarcher.

Freud, S. (1953). Three essays on the theory of sexuality. In J. Strachey (Ed. and Trans.), *Standard edition of the complete psychological works of Sigmund Freud* (Vol. 7). London: Hogarth Press.

Fromuth, M. F. (1983). *The long term psychological impact of childhood sexual abuse*. Unpublished doctoral dissertation, Auburn University.

Giaretto, H. (1976). The treatment of father-daughter incest: A psycho-social approach. *Children Today, 34*, 2–5.

Giaretto, H. (1982). *Integrated treatment of child sexual abuse*. Palo Alto: Science and Behavior Books.

Gil, E. (1983). *Outgrowing the pain*. Walnut Creek, CA: Launch Press.

Greer, J. G. (1986). *Psychoanalytic treatment of adult incest survivors*. Paper presented at the Fourth National Medical Center, New Orleans.

Groves, D. (1987). *Resolving traumatic memories: Competency based training for mental health professionals*. Munster, IN: David Groves Seminars.

Helfer, R. E. (1978). *Childhood comes first: A crash course in childhood for adults*. East Lansing, MI: Author.

Herman, J. (1981). *Father-daughter incest*. Cambridge, MA: Harvard University Press.

Herman, J., & Hirschman, L. (1977). Father-daughter incest. *Signs, 2*, 1–22.

Horowitz, M. J. (1986). *Stress response syndromes* (2nd ed.). Northvale, NJ: Jason Aronson.

James, J., & Meyerding, J. (1977). Early sexual experiences as a factor in prostitution. *Archives of Sexual Behavior, 7*, 31–42.

Jehu, D., Klassen, C., & Gazan, M. (1985). Cognitive restructuring of distorted beliefs associated with childhood sexual abuse. *Journal of Social Work and Human Sexuality, 4*, 49–69.

Justice, B., & Justice, R. (1979). *The broken taboo: Sex in the family*. New York: Human Sciences Press.

Kercher, G., & McShane, M. (1984). The prevalence of child sexual abuse victimization in an adult sample of Texas residents. *Child Abuse and Neglect, 8*, 495–501.

Kilpatrick, D. G., & Amick, A. E. (1984, August). *Intrafamilial and extrafamilial sexual assault: Results of a random community survey*. Paper presented at the Second National Conference for Family Violence Researchers, Durham, NH.

Kinsey, A., Pomeroy, W., Martin, C., & Gebhard, P. (1953). *Sexual behavior in the human female*. Philadelphia: Saunders.

Koss, M. P. (1985). The hidden rape victim: Personality, attitudinal and situational characteristics. *Psychology of Women Quarterly, 9*, 193–212.

Lees, S. W. (1981). *Guidelines for helping female victims and survivors of incest*. Cambridge, MA: Incest Resources.

Lundberg-Love, P. K., Crawford, C. M., & Geffner, R. A. (1987, October). *Characteristics and treatment of adult incest survivors*. Paper presented at the annual meeting of the Southwestern Psychological Association, New Orleans.

Lundberg-Love, P. K., & Geffner, R. A. (1988, April). Treatment of adult incest survivors: Recount, repair, resolve. In R. A. Geffner (Chair), *Identification, treat-*

ment and prevention of sexual abuse in the family. Symposium presented at the annual meeting of the Western Psychological Association, San Francisco.

Maltz, W., & Holman, B. (1987). *Incest and sexuality.* Lexington, MA: D. C. Heath.

Mayer, A. (1983). *Incest: A treatment manual for therapy with victims, spouses and offenders.* Holmes Beach, FL: Learning Publications.

Meiselman, K. (1978). *Incest: A psychological study of causes and effects with treatment recommendations.* San Francisco: Jossey-Bass.

Miller, A. (1981). *Prisoners of childhood: The drama of the gifted child and the search for the true self.* New York: Basic Books.

Miller, A. (1984). *Thou shalt not be aware: Society's betrayal of the child.* New York: Farrar, Straus, & Giroux.

Miller, J., Moeller, D., Kaufman, A., Divasto, P., Pathak, D., & Christy, J. (1978). Recidivism among sex assault victims. *American Journal of Psychiatry, 135,* 1103–1104.

Nash, M., & Ormiston, K. (1980). *Taking charge of your weight and well-being.* Palo Alto, CA: Bull Press.

Pasternak, S. (1987, December). *The effects of childhood sexual abuse on later adult functioning and the complexities of its treatment.* Paper presented at the conference of Adult Child Therapy—Treating the Adult Survivor of Child Abuse, The Psychiatric Institute Foundation, Washington, DC.

Peters, S. D. (1984). *The relationship between childhood sexual victimization and adult depression among Afro-American and white women.* Unpublished doctoral dissertation, University of California, Los Angeles.

Rush, F. (1980). *The best kept secret: Sexual abuse of children.* Englewood Cliff, NJ: Prentice-Hall.

Russell, D. (1984). *Sexual exploitation: Rape, child sexual abuse, and sexual harassment.* Beverly Hills: Sage.

Russell, D. (1986). *The secret trauma: Incest in the lives of girls and women.* New York: Basic Books.

Sandbek, T. (1984). *The deadly diet.* Oakland, CA: New Harbinger Publications.

Sedney, M. A., & Brooks, B. (1984). Factors associated with history of childhood sexual experience in a nonclinical female population. *American Journal of Child Psychiatry, 23,* 215–218.

Siegel, J. M., Sorenson, S. B., Goldring, J. M., Burnam, M. A., & Stein, J. A. (1987). The prevalence of childhood sexual assault: The Los Angeles Epidemiologic Catchment Area project. *American Journal of Epidemiology, 126,* 1141–1153.

Silbert, M., & Pines, A. (1981). Sexual child abuse as an antecedent to prostitution. *Child Abuse and Neglect, 5,* 407–411.

Ward, E. (1985). *Father–daughter rape.* New York: Grove Press.

Wyatt, G. (1985). The sexual abuse of Afro-American and white women in childhood. *Child Abuse and Neglect, 9,* 507–519.

PART THREE

Perpetrators of Maltreatment

CHAPTER 10

Perpetrators of Child Physical Abuse

ROBERT F. SCHILLING

INTRODUCTION

It is fair to state that the public has some collective image of an abused child. That image has been shaped by literature and films, and by news stories and public service advertising in the print and electronic media. The now anachronistic term "battered child syndrome," often associated with Kempe's landmark paper (Kempe, Silverman, Steele, Droegemueller, & Silver, 1962), still evokes a powerful image of a child bruised and broken. The public's conception of the child abuser is likely less clear, inasmuch as efforts to inform the public and solicit donations typically depict victims rather than perpetrators. Many child advocates assert that child abuse is a universal phenomenon and is somehow equally distributed across all sectors of society. Evidence that conflicts with this notion is branded as a reporting artifact, attributable to factors that protect middle-class families from official detection.

In examining both the characteristics of the perpetrators of child abuse and the range of interventions to treat such persons, this chapter considers the extent to which child abuse is equally distributed across all social classes. Based on the finding that socioeconomic status is a salient correlate of abuse, the argument of this presentation is that treatment models to prevent the recurrence of child abuse cannot be divorced from the child protection system or separated from larger social policies.

CHARACTERISTICS OF PERPETRATORS

Overview

The introductory chapter of this volume underscores the complexity and interrelatedness of all forms of family violence (see Chapter 1). A review of the characteristics of the perpetrators of physical abuse shows that the same descriptors often apply to persons responsible for emotional abuse and sexual abuse, as well as to persons responsible for forms of maltreatment beyond the scope of this collection on violence. In fact, perpetrators of one form of maltreatment are often responsible for other acts of harm toward children and other family members (Becker, Kaplan, Cunningham-Rathner, & Kavoussi, 1986; Bolton & Bolton, 1987; Stark & Flitcraft, 1988).

It is tempting to look for explanatory variables that would simplify understanding the causes of child abuse and have immediate implications for treatment. Although early studies attempted to demonstrate that single factors explained abuse, it soon became clear that predicting abuse was a complex task (Starr, 1982). To comprehensively and critically analyze this substantial body of knowledge is beyond the limits of this chapter, but it is useful to review briefly some of the correlates of child abuse.

Demographic and Historical Variables

Family position and race-ethnicity are not readily alterable. Childhood experiences can be reinterpreted, but not changed after the fact. Except for socioeconomic status, which may change over time, these background variables are not subject to modification. By themselves, these variables do not suggest ways of intervening in the same way that, say, social interaction variables might. Nevertheless, such readily obtained markers often have import for program planning (Dumas & Wahler, 1983; Schilling, Schinke, & Kirkham, 1985).

Gender

Whether men or women are more often perpetrators of abuse has been a focus of some debate. Feminists, some claiming that they "have a better understanding than child welfare professionals of the causes and consequences of violence in families" (Washburne, 1983, p. 290), have criticized reporting systems that find women disproportionately represented in child abuse statistics (Martin, 1984). Single parenthood has been identified as a risk factor for abuse, and the bulk of such families are headed by women (Caplan, Watters, White, Perry, & Bates, 1984; Starr, 1988).

Mothers spend far more time with their children than fathers do, yet numerous studies find the percentage of male perpetrators equals or exceeds that of their female counterparts (Gil, 1970; Sack, Mason, & Higgins, 1985). Men are likely to be the perpetrator in incidents in which men are present (Gil, 1973; Stark & Flitcraft, 1988). An increase in recent years in the percentage of serious cases attributed to male abusers probably reflects better reporting systems and a willingness on the part of women to report serious abuse by men (Bergman, Larsen, & Mueller, 1986). Given these findings and the relationship between other forms of family violence that implicate men, it seems beyond doubt that male parent figures are more likely to inflict harm on children than are female primary caregivers. However, because they head so many single households, women will continue to be represented in perhaps half of child abuse cases. Moreover, men often are overlooked because child protection agencies have fewer opportunities to contact and investigate male parent figures.

Siblings

Violence between siblings may be more prevalent than any other form of family violence (Gelles & Cornell, 1985; Roscoe, Goodwin, & Kennedy, 1987). A study of 244 seventh-grade students found that among females, 94% and 96% reported themselves as victims and perpetrators, respectively. Among males, corresponding figures were 88% and 85% (Roscoe et al., 1987). Oddly, sibling abuse has received little attention by child abuse investigators. Society tends to view rivalry and aggression among siblings as normal, and many parents believe in intervening as little as possible. Child protection bureaus often hold parents responsible for sibling abuse, perceiving the circumstances as at least partially attributable to caregiver neglect. Because violence is, in part, learned, it is not surprising that brothers and sisters sometimes abuse each other in families that exhibit other forms of violence. Studies have repeatedly found that boys are more violent than girls and that physical aggression is common between same-sex children and closely spaced siblings. Although some progress has been made in describing normative aggression between siblings (e.g., Minnett, Vandell, & Santrock, 1983), the prevalence of child abuse by siblings has not been carefully examined.

Race–Ethnicity

It is plausible to ask whether social disadvantage and prejudice are apt to add to stress that may culminate in abuse. Problems of urban living cannot be divorced from race-ethnicity. Certainly it is possible that the experiencing of cumulative and recurrent bias and prejudice interacts with socioeconomic stress associated with poverty, resulting in increased abuse of children. Although these themes have been explored in literature and drama, they have not been contextually examined by child abuse researchers.

Viewed in a context that incorporates the historical experience of some members of racial-ethnic minority groups, differences in child-rearing patterns can be illuminating (Garbarino & Ebata, 1983). However, discussions of race must be approached carefully. Statistically significant differences in abuse rates across racial-ethnic groups are readily obtainable when large sample sizes and multiple comparisons are employed. It is often tempting to make too much of small differences, and in so doing brand a given racial-ethnic group as abusive. Factors that must be weighed in determining abuse rates across such groups include biased reporting and investigation, economic and educational variables, neighborhood and crowding indicators, family size, marital status, parental age, and child-related stressors. Observed differences in child abuse usually disappear when socioeconomic status is controlled (e.g., Department of Health and Human Services, 1988).

Socioeconomic Status

Although not the first to observe the relationship between social class and child maltreatment, Pelton (1978) was perhaps the most ardent critic of what he termed the "myth of classlessness." Along with others (American Humane Association, 1985; Garbarino & Crouter, 1978; Straus, Gelles, & Steinmetz, 1980), Pelton effectively discredited the folklore that child abuse was evenly distributed across all socioeconomic levels. However well intended, the pervasive myth of classlessness ignored a range of factors that are now recognized as salient contributors to abuse. One way to conceive socioeconomic status (SES) is as an overarching variable that correlates with a host of other risk factors. For example, unemployment, single parenthood, social isolation, stress, and personality disorders are descriptors that correlate with low income *and* with child abuse.

Child abuse is inversely related to income, but the relationship between low SES and neglect is considerably stronger (Department of Health and Human Servicesj, 1988; Larson, Doris, & Alvarez, 1987). Because abuse and neglect often are reported together as maltreatment, the strength of the relationship between abuse and SES is overstated (Wolfe, 1987). It is important to emphasize that most persons of lower socioeconomic status do not abuse their children, underscoring the notion that low income by itself is not a useful departure for intervention design.

Childhood History

Perhaps the most popular theory among both professionals and the public to explain child abuse is intergenerational violence. According to this theory, children who are abused are likely to harm their own children later in life. Abusing parents often recall that they were abused as children (Egeland, Jacobvitz, & Sroufe, 1988; Kempe & Helfer, 1972; Spinetta & Rigler, 1972; Webster-Stratton, 1985). Straus's (1983) study of 2143 parents reported mixed findings subject to multiple interpretations. Reviews by Burgess & Youngblade (1988), Jayaratne (1977), and Pagelow (1984) found little evidence to support the intergenerational hypothesis. Unquestionably, most abused children do not grow up to become abusing parents (Hunter & Kilstrom, 1979; Straus et al., 1980). Social learning theory (Bandura, 1973) posits that direct experience may contribute to future abusive patterns, and this direct pathway assumedly accounts for some abuse. But the most plausible explanation of the intergenerational hypothesis must incorporate a complex of underlying variables, all linked to social class, familial lifestyles, psychological climate, and, to some extent, genetics (Burgess & Youngblade, 1988).

Psychological Determinants

Clinicians and researchers have attempted to develop typologies describing the psychological constitution of child abusers (e.g., Merrill, 1962; Sloan &

Meier, 1983; Zalba, 1967). Berger (1980) critiqued these sorts of schema and found them to be simplistic, dependent on assessments of professionals who already know the parents' presumed involvement in abuse, and awaiting validation. Reviewing the literature on the psychological characteristics of abusing parents, Wolfe (1985) concluded, "Studies using measures of underlying personality attributes or traits have been unable to detect any patterns associated with child abuse beyond general descriptions of displeasure in the parenting role and stress-related complaints" (p. 465).

It is instructive to compare an early review of the literature on the characteristics with another review a decade later. The first paper (Spinetta & Rigler, 1972) examined a collection of mostly clinical observations. Virtually all of these articles could be characterized by a lack of methodological rigor— a common criticism of research in emerging fields. Faulting the focus on environmental factors brought to light in Gil's (1970) national survey, the authors emphasized psychological explanations of abuse. According to this view, factors within the parents themselves are of "prime importance," and indicate a "defect in character leading to a lack of inhibition in expressing frustration and other impulsive behavior" (Spinetta & Rigler, 1972, p. 302). Friedrich and Wheeler (1982) report that the evidence gathered over the next decade supported the existence of some personality variables (e.g., self-esteem, impulsivity) that discriminate abusive from nonabusive parents. However, their interpretation of the most comprehensive study reviewed (Gaines, Sandgrund, Green, & Power, 1978) found that stress overshadowed personality variables. Although they allowed that stress interacted with personality, Friedrich and Wheeler called for intervention at the societal level.

Almost all observers agree that overt psychopathology is present in no more than 20% of abusing parents. Studies examining less serious psychological deficits tend to uncover a few variables with small but statistically significant correlations that have little correspondence to similar studies. Even those few psychological descriptors that appear across multiple studies often have few immediate implications for intervention. The failure to identify a circumscribed set of personality traits has not inhibited what one critic referred to as "the endless discussion of the nonexistent abusive profile" (Bolton & Bolton, 1987, p. 56). Nevertheless, the focus of child abuse investigators has to a considerable extent shifted away from static psychological characteristics (Starr, 1988; Wolfe, 1987).

Child-Rearing Variables

Investigators have identified child-rearing patterns and attitudes toward children that indicate parents are at risk for child abuse.

Child-Rearing Patterns

It is perhaps obvious that parents who abuse their children have difficulties in disciplining family members. When compared with their nonabusing counterparts, abusing parents are often inconsistent, tend to have few defined responsibilities for their children, express unrealistic expectations of themselves as parents, and lack interpersonal competence in parental and other roles (Bauer & Twentyman, 1985; Berger, 1980; Burgess, 1985; Wolfe, 1987). Observational studies, comparing abusing and nonabusing parents, find that the former exhibit fewer positive behaviors and more negative behaviors toward their children (Lahey, Conger, Atkeson, & Treiber, 1984), are more directive (Mash, Johnston, & Kovitz, 1983), and use nagging and physical punishment at high rates (Patterson, 1982; Trickett & Kuczynski, 1986). Most observational studies find that abusing families have overall low rates of social interaction and low rates of positive interaction (e.g., Schindler & Arkowitz, 1986). Some, but not all, studies show that abusing caregivers have high rates of criticism, disobedience, and aversive exchanges (Wolfe, 1985; 1987).

Child-Rearing Attitudes

Do beliefs and attitudes of abusing parents differ from those of nonabusing parents? When compared with controls, abusing parents tend to be more protective, enjoy parenting less, perceive their children as more difficult and disobedient, discourage independence and new experience, and worry more about their children (Susman, Trickett, Iannotti, Hollenbeck, & Zahn-Waxler, 1985; Wood-Shuman & Cone, 1986). Investigators have generally failed to demonstrate that abusing parents are less apt than nonabusing parents to have an accurate understanding of children's development (Kravitz & Driscoll, 1983; Starr, 1988; Wolfe, 1985). Although the results of several investigations (e.g., Bauer & Twentyman, 1985; Reid, Kavanaugh, & Baldwin, 1987) suggest that abusing parents tend to have unfavorable and inaccurate perceptions of their children's behavior, multiple interpretations of these findings are possible. Plausibly, an abusive parent may come to view the child in an unfavorable light as a result of negative experiences in child rearing (Wolfe, 1985).

Other Social Variables

Stress

Although stress in the context of child abuse may be viewed from several perspectives, the present discussion considers it as a social phenomenon (Barth & Blythe, 1983; Farrington, 1986; Gaudin & Pollane, 1983; Straus & Kantor, 1987). According to this view, stress that contributes to child abuse may be traced to the interaction of economic and sociocultural variables, and adverse life events. Thus, social reinforcement of violence, the struggle to meet family expenses, and the difficult daily circumstances of low-income environments may interact synergistically, resulting in child abuse. Studies suggest that stress-related factors including family disharmony, divorce and single parenthood, large family size, unemployment, and neighborhood instability, are associated with child abuse (Dumas & Wahler, 1983; Kirkham, Schinke, Schilling, Meltzer, & Norelius, 1986; Young & Gately, 1988).

Social Isolation

It may seem paradoxical that abusing parents could be both isolated and living in crowded conditions characterized by high rates of interpersonal conflict. However, social connectedness is quite different from physical proximity (Schilling, 1987). Researchers have theorized that isolated families go undetected for considerable periods before neighbors, relatives, or child protection officials become aware of abusive patterns. Isolated families are unaffected by community norms, do not benefit from social support that buffers daily stress, and cannot observe effective child rearing from other parents (Garbarino & Gilliam, 1980; Gaudin & Pollane, 1983; Schilling & Schinke, 1984b; Starr, 1982).

Supporting social isolation theories are findings that abusing parents often lack social supports, social skill, and positive contacts with persons outside the family (Kirkham et al., 1986; Salzinger, Kaplan, & Artemyeff, 1983). In sum, it is clear that abusing parents often lack meaningful ties with persons outside the immediate family and may exhibit limited skills in establishing and maintaining relationships with outsiders. Thus, abusing parents are unable to draw upon others who could provide emotional and instrumental support, offer suggestions, and serve as role models to guide caregivers through difficult circumstances. Social isolation may also be conceptualized as social incompetence. According to this view, abusing families are composed of members who have minimal interpersonal skills, and this limitation impairs relationships both within and outside the family (Burgess & Youngblade, 1988).

Other Perpetrator Factors

Less important contributing factors that may account for some abuse of children include substance abuse (Famularo, Stone, Barnum, & Wharton, 1986; Leonard & Jacob, 1988), bonding failure (Ainsworth, 1980; Crittenden, 1983; Lamb, Gaensbauer, Malkin, & Schultz, 1985), intellectual limitations (Schilling, Schinke, Blythe, & Barth, 1982), and even posttraumatic stress disorder (Bolton & Bolton, 1987). Although each of these areas is of interest, findings to date are either very limited or suggest that the independent contribution of each of these variables is small.

Comment

Any discussion of perpetrator characteristics must consider the interaction between parent, child, socioeconomic, and community factors (Garbarino, Brookhouser, & Authier, 1987; Schilling & Schinke, 1984a; Schinke, Blythe,

Schilling, & Barth, 1981). Variables related to children have been covered elsewhere in this volume (Chapters 2 and 4). Here, it should be stated that the same social forces that adversely affect a parent's ability to provide a safe and nurturing environment for children also have a direct impact on a child's behavior and development. Thus, parents with the fewest caregiving assets must often care for the most difficult children.

Even without considering how special characteristics of children enter into the abuse equation, it is clear that the correlates of physical abuse are multiple, difficult to measure, and rarely observed in isolation. Social-situational or ecological theories of abuse incorporate both sociological factors, such as community norms, and situational stressors, which may include difficult child behavior or stressful events. Studies that focus on single or discrete predictors have given way to multivariate approaches to understanding the phenomenon of physical abuse. Increasingly, researchers attempt to make sense of the complex web of overlapping variables that predict child abuse. These lines of inquiry have, as yet, failed to yield models that would make it possible to predict child abusers with a high degree of confidence. Even nearly perfect predictive instruments will in any case always be viewed with suspicion by a society that values personal liberty. Nevertheless, practitioners who have an understanding of the connections between the many contributing variables, far more than those who would attribute child abuse to simple causes, will be able to weigh risks systematically and offer treatment that addresses the needs of abusing families. The next section examines some of the strategies for helping families with abused children.

TREATMENT

The first steps in the process of helping abusive families are reporting, investigation, determination, and disposition. In North America, these child protection functions are carried out by government agencies or by voluntary agencies acting as a proxy for the state. Although ongoing treatment is most often divorced from the official activities of child protection bureaus, the intervention process encompasses a spectrum of services from reporting to follow-up (Carroll & Haase, 1987; Daro, 1988; Krugman, 1987; Stein & Rzepnicki, 1983). A portion of a single chapter cannot fairly critique the child protection system now in place, nor adequately describe the multifaceted connection between child protection bureaus and community practitioners who treat perpetrators of child maltreatment (Kahn & Kamerman, 1980; Magazino, 1983). But a few comments on the child protection system will give perspective to the discussion on treatment that follows.

Inherent Limitations of Child Protection

Child protection will always be controversial and subject to the changing tides of public opinion. The state must continually balance children's rights to be protected from physical harm against families' rights to live according to their own values without government interference. Society demands that the child protection system intervene only when there is reason to believe children are being physically harmed; the system must also respect parents' rights of due process. Child protection laws recognize the special vulnerability of children and broadly empower child protection bureaus. Unlike persons accused of crimes, parents suspected of abusing their children are not always apprised of their protection from self-incrimination and may be persuaded to participate in assessment or treatment without benefit of counsel.

Despite being entrusted with this seemingly intrusive power, child protection bureaus have shown that their reach is limited. Social workers and other interested observers assert that the child protection system is charged with tasks that extend far beyond its public acceptance, lie outside the state of current knowledge, and are unrealistic given modest resources (Schilling, 1981; Stein, 1984). Casework services typically claim reabuse rates of around 50%, a troubling figure that reflects limited resources as much as ineffective intervention strategy (Cohn & Daro, 1987; Garbarino, 1983; Rivara, 1985). Still, it is probable that baseline rates for improvement would be considerably lower for untreated families (Starr, 1988).

In scarce supply are well-funded programs based on empirically derived interventions. Families usually require multiple services that may range from specialized preschools to job training, but long-term case management is a luxury not built into the system. Child protection officials have no instruments that predict rates of abuse or reabuse with precision (Altemeier, O'Connor, Vietze, Sandler, & Sherrod, 1984; Starr, 1982). Yet, caseload pressures demand that workers make risk determinations, close cases prematurely, and attend to the most recent and serious incidents of abuse (Faller, 1985; Vitulano, Lewis, Doran, Nordhaus, & Adnopoz, 1986). Follow-up often is minimal. Inevitably, some decisions will result in serious reabuse of some children in the months and years after their families were initially investigated. The many inadequacies of the child protection system should be kept in mind during the following discussion of approaches to treating abusive parents. Even the best treatment efforts are compromised by the present stresses within the child protection system.

Empirically Based Approaches

The approaches selected and the examples of effective treatment highlighted in this chapter emphasize empirically derived strategies and controlled evaluated programs. Other approaches not discussed here may well have merit, but they have not yet been subjected to scientific scrutiny (e.g., Salter, Richardson, & Martin, 1985; Timmons-Mitchell, 1986).

A review of the empirical literature on child abuse treatment uncovers two kinds of studies, each with its own limitations. Large-scale studies that measure global outcomes, such as rates of reabuse, give incomplete answers to the question "Is child abuse treatment effective?" These kinds of studies give still less satisfactory answers to the questions "What works?" or "What works with which families under what circumstances?" Although useful in incorporating treatment trends into current practice guidelines, assessing the overall effectiveness of intervention in general, and determining the need for treatment funding, such studies do not provide the degree of specificity needed by practitioners searching for practice models.

Small, carefully controlled studies typically provide practitioners and program developers with at least a brief outline to guide the design of intervention strategies for use with abusing families (Schilling, Schinke, & Gilchrist, 1985). Rarely, however, are such experiments carried out under the same conditions operable in social service settings. And intervention studies, with a few exceptions, either assess outcome immediately after treatment, or after a brief follow-up period. It would be difficult to point to more than a few studies that carefully describe the sample, community, and program setting; delineate intervention protocols; detail actual costs and disadvantages of the program; and monitor outcomes over several years.

Social workers, psychologists, other human service workers who treat abusing families, and child protection workers who monitor client progress and assess future risk of abuse cannot rely on definitive studies to guide their practice. In shaping their own definitions of "current best practice," human service workers must examine the merits of various approaches, weigh the evidence supporting each, and determine which will best serve their clients and communities. Abusing parents may be helped at the individual, interpersonal, or community level. Individual approaches focus on deficits with the individual parent that may result in physical harm to children. Other interventions assume that the interpersonal nature of child abuse should be attacked at the level of social interaction. Still other approaches focus on multiple domains and may incorporate intrapersonal and intrafamilial interventions, as well as strategies to enhance linkages with various social structures that lie beyond the boundaries of the family unit.

Not included in this treatment typology are prevention strategies that attempt to restructure neighborhoods, community agencies, and social service systems for the benefit of large numbers of families at risk for child abuse. For the most part, treatment must be concerned with a smaller scope that excludes intervention at the population level. Although potentially far more influential than any strategies or programs described in the present chapter, primary prevention strategies must be described in other discussions of proactive policies and practices.

Individual Level Treatment

Anger Management

Because child abuse often occurs in the context of parental anger, it is reasonable to consider ways of curbing this emotion that accompanies violent behavior (Deffenbacher, Story, Stark, Hogg, & Brandon, 1987). Building on Novaco's (1975) work with adult offender populations, numerous researchers have demonstrated the efficacy of anger management with parents of abused children (Nomellini & Katz, 1983). One small study (Barth, Blythe, Schinke, & Schilling, 1983) included anger control components with a group of 10 parents referred by child protection authorities. Parents met twice weekly for eight sessions led by two graduate students. Parents learned to recognize early cues of provocative situations, identify signs of angry responses, pause and take deep breaths, engage in alternative actions or thoughts, and praise themselves for their coping efforts. Written and videotape measures showed that parents made pretest-to-posttest gains in controlling their anger in stressful situations and compared favorably with a matched group of comparison controls.

A more extensive and sophisticated anger management intervention trial focused on (a) the impact of a structured intervention on parental anger toward the child, (b) intervention effects on parental child-rearing attitudes and behavior, and (c) the relationship between anger and child-rearing attitudes and behavior (Whiteman, Fanshel & Grundy, 1987). The authors compared a control condition with cognitive restructuring, relaxation, problem-solving, and composite conditions, the latter four each consisting of six sessions delivered in parents' homes. Analyses revealed that the problem-solving and composite conditions, but not the cognitive restructuring, relaxation, or control conditions, correlated with lower scores on scales measuring child and adult anger. The finding that the strongest degree of anger reduction occurred in the composite condition suggests that anger may best be controlled when persons have a repertoire of coping responses.

The focus of anger management, narrowly defined, is self-control under conditions that arouse intense emotional reactions characterized by attack responses. The obvious logic of anger management interventions may also suggest the limitations of this kind of direct and somewhat simplistic approach to treating child abuse. It appears that the most effective, or at least most convincing, anger management protocols are not entirely distinct from other cognitive-behavioral methods that provide parents with alternatives in stressful situations. Although anger management protocols have rarely been evaluated by themselves, it is difficult to fault such methods if they are employed along with strategies that deal with a broader array of human problems.

Respondent Conditioning

Intervention may also be guided by classical conditioning paradigms. Investigators have demonstrated that some abusive parents have strong physiological reactions to crying or other aversive child behavior (Starr, 1988). Although biological or learning interpretations could be applied to such findings, interventions based on respondent conditioning are responsive to either model. In classical learning terms, child abuse may occur when parents learn to associate unpleasant and angry feelings with noxious child behavior. In one study, a therapist successfully altered an abusing father's aggressive response to his daughter's crying (Sanford & Tustin, 1973).

Although theoretically elegant, respondent approaches to treating child abuse have not generated much attention from either practitioners or researchers. Respondent paradigms require that the therapist understand and have some control over conditions that can weaken the connection between the conditioned and unconditioned stimuli. In practice, it has been difficult to integrate such strategies across life domains in ways that have meaning to clients.

Personal Coping Approaches

Closely related to anger management approaches are a variety of strategies that attempt to enhance parents' coping abilities. Often referred to as stress management interventions, these approaches help parents identify sources of stress and take action either to escape from or to enervate the stressor. Methods include problem solving, self-instruction, self-reinforcement, and even deep muscle relaxation (Nomellini & Katz, 1983; Schilling, Gilchrist & Schinke, 1984; Schinke, Schilling, Barth, Gilchrist, & Maxwell, 1986). In one study (Egan, 1983), abusing parents were randomly assigned to one of four conditions: stress management, child management, combination stress and child management, and "treatment-as-usual." Interestingly, stress management and child management training had very different effects, as measured by self-report, role-play, and observational measures. Stress management participants improved on several measures related to a decrease in negative feelings or an increase in positive feelings. Members of child management groups, by contrast, improved in areas related to managing child behavior.

Interpersonal Level Treatment

Parent Training

Because child management is an obvious problem in most abusing families, psychologists, social workers, and other helping agents have developed training protocols to increase identified parents' child-rearing skills. Building on the extensive parent-training research, conducted most often with parents of developmentally disabled or conduct-disordered children (Helm & Kozlov, 1986; Kashima, Baker, & Landen, 1988; Schilling, 1988), investigators have developed and tested a rich variety of interventions to enhance child-rearing competence. In step-by-step fashion, often in group contexts, parents learn to assess behavior or developmental skills, apply behavioral teaching management techniques, and monitor progress. Strategies may include behavioral rehearsal, prompting, modeling, social reinforcement, extinction, discrimination training, and shaping. Programs may be directed to parents, abused children, or families, and may be carried out individually, in groups, or in family sessions (Egan, 1983; Shorkey, 1979; Timmons-Mitchell, 1986).

Social Skills Training

Abusing parents tend to have limited social skills, affecting their relationships both within and outside the family. In part, parent training addresses interpersonal competence in the family, especially in the area of child management. Social skills training focuses on interpersonal competence in a broader context. Parents who become proficient in interacting with others are better able to obtain social and instrumental support and may gain a sense of control and competence (Wolfe, 1987). Schilling and Kirkham (1985) employed social skills training in groups designed for parents of developmentally disabled children at risk for abuse. Parents perfected their interpersonal competence in groups, practiced newly learned social skills at home and in the community, and used these skills in advocating for their children and carrying out projects to improve conditions for handicapped children. Social skills training holds considerable promise if carried out in combination with strategies that address other deficits of abusive parents.

Social Support Development

Social support may be developed through various avenues. Tracy and Whittaker (1987) have identified several kinds of programs that seek to enhance the social supports of families. These include family support programs, which may provide respite care, home visitation, parent education, and pediatric care; network facilitation, which mobilizes informal family and community networks to either replace or supplement formal services; support groups, to activate supportive relationships among parents with similar concerns; and skills training, to teach parents how to establish and maintain supportive relationships.

Of interest is an evaluation of a 26-week group intervention to enhance the social networks of abusing mothers (Lovell & Hawkins, 1988). Program staff first assessed the mothers' social networks using data gathered from the literature, the participants, and program staff. The resulting curriculum included elements of stress management, anger management, self-reinforcement, problem solving, assertiveness, and child management. Although the intervention was specifically designed to increase social support, the expected outcomes apparently were to be achieved as by-products of the aforementioned elements that focused on other internal and child-related variables. Pretest-posttest comparisons of data on the 10 participants showed that group attendance was associated with changes in personal social networks. Overall, network changes were modest, particularly in participants' relationships with persons other than professionals. Findings point up the difficulties of trying to alter social supports of persons with long-standing deficits in their informal networks.

Integrated Approaches to Intervention

Considerations of experimental control (e.g., specification of the independent variable and measurement of outcomes), tend to narrow researchers' intervention foci. Even relatively comprehensive models that deal with anger, stress, or child management seem to ignore salient aspects of family life in other domains. Demonstration efforts often are more comprehensive than empirical studies but tend to be weak in terms of evaluation design. Typically, evaluations of innovative programs leave many questions concerning the degree to which intervention components were delivered and whether program participants improved because of the intervention or as a result of other factors. A few projects have attempted to overcome these barriers, developing and evaluating multiple component interventions that address child abuse as a complex phenomenon. Several of the studies already mentioned (Barth et al., 1983; Egan, 1983; Lovell & Hawkins, 1988) developed and tested multiple strategies, although none could be described as comprehensive in scope or length of involvement.

Three programs have successfully combined evaluation rigor and breadth of intervention scope. The Child Management Program (Wolfe, Edwards, Manion, & Koverola, 1988; Wolfe, Kaufman, Aragona, & Sandler, 1981) seeks to establish an effective and positive child-rearing experience for the parent while enhancing the adaptive abilities of the child, in conjunction with other agency-based services. Program elements include individual therapy, group instruction, and family assessment—a mixture unlikely to be funded in many settings. Program participants, when compared with controls receiving agency supervision, reported fewer behavior problems, improved parenting skills, and developmental gains.

Another comprehensive model of child abuse intervention is based on Goldstein's extensive work in the area of structured learning (Goldstein, Keller, & Erne, 1985). Working closely with a community agency, the authors developed a series of skills-building groups to teach abusing parents. Over five sessions, trained group leaders covered self-control, parenting skills, marital relationship enhancement, and interpersonal skills. A sixth session dealt with supplementary skills such as listening, giving and responding to praise, dealing with accusations, and handling group pressure. A series of studies found that participants in the structured learning groups did learn skills; were more likely to maintain gains if they viewed themselves as responsible for their own improvement; and failed to demonstrate consistent transfer of skills from group to home, except when transfer-enhancement techniques were added to the basic structured learning approach. Although this strategy attempts to cover a rather ambitious array of topics in six sessions, the clarity of the training methods outlined in the text could serve as a model for other dissemination efforts.

Probably the most expansive and extensively researched program is Project 12-Ways (Lutzker & Rice, 1987). Designed for abusing and neglecting parents, the program considers parents, children, and the family ecosystem in developing interventions. As indicated, Project 12-Ways offers stress reduction, self-control training, job finding, leisure-time counseling, social support, money management, parent training, child basic skills training, prenatal and postnatal training for single parents, home safety, home cleanliness, and alcoholism referral. Over a period of 10 years, more than 1000 families have been involved in Project 12-Ways. Recidivism data indicate that participants are substantially less likely than matched comparison families to again become involved in abuse and neglect, although differences between groups shrink over time. The most laudable aspects of Project 12-Ways are its comprehensiveness, flexibility, and obvious grounding in a non-laboratory setting. These attributes also confound efforts to determine the effects of the program as a whole and isolate the salient components of the project in reducing child maltreatment. Still, few detractors could approach the combination of pragmatics, ecological focus, and empirical soundness found in Project 12-Ways.

The paucity of studies that attempt to examine longitudinally the efficacy of comprehensive, community-based programs to treat child abuse is testimony to the many challenges that confront even the most determined investigator. The modest studies that test specific strategies over short periods offer a different sort of knowledge but collectively suggest that many kinds of interventions can have some benefit.

SUMMARY AND FUTURE DIRECTIONS

This overview of the perpetrators of child physical abuse underscores the difficulty of describing, let alone predicting or fully understanding, parents who inflict physical harm on children. More than two decades of research and public attention have yielded certain advances that bear mention. If perpetrators of child abuse defy simple description, most share one or more of the following characteristics:

They are not overtly pathological and therefore cannot be labeled as deviants who are outside the realm of "normal."

They tend to have low incomes and bear witness to many of the stressors faced by the poor.

Their ill treatment of family members is not limited to physical harm of children and may extend to spouse abuse, physical neglect, emotional abuse, and sexual abuse.

They feel, with some justification, incompetent in child rearing and in social intercourse within and beyond the family.

Their children often are difficult to manage, and they ascribe to their progeny unfavorable motivations that are perceived as a reflection of themselves.

Their own experience in growing up was less than optimal and may have both direct and indirect effects on their lack of success in parenting.

A gradual understanding of the complexity of the causes of child abuse has to some extent broadened the array of interventions for abusing parents and families. Ecologically minded practitioners, working at the individual, family, and group level, have developed multicomponent programs concerned with intrapsychic, interpersonal, and community attachments. The child protection arena has by necessity become open-minded about what constitutes effective treatment, possibly because of the dismal rates of recidivism and the long-standing interdisciplinary tradition of the field. Clinical observations, program evaluations, and tightly controlled intervention studies lend support, at least over short periods, to a variety of approaches. Behavioral and cognitive interventions have been favorably received because of their face validity and because they can be subjected to empirical scrutiny. Unfortunately, even the most optimistic overview of the outcomes of any kind of intervention suggests that many parents who abuse their children are difficult to change.

Most informed observers agree that the child protection system is overburdened. Ideally, treatment providers work closely with officials who make referrals and monitor client progress and compliance. But present conditions and funding provide for neither adequate monitoring nor support of comprehensive programs. The task for child abuse researchers is not a small one. Applied investigators should direct their energies in the following areas:

Prediction and Decision Making. The inadequacies of the underfunded child protection system are not likely to improve in the near future, but systematic efforts could result in more rational management of risk. Although screening instruments are far from perfect, prediction is now better than in the past. Investigators should continue to develop and perfect ways of predicting risk of reabuse and training workers in efficient use of available information to guide data gathering and decision making.

Determining Who Can Be Helped. The high rates of reabuse suggest that many parents cannot be helped by present methods. Without discounting the necessity of offering abusing parents multiple treatment opportunities, scarce treatment resources must be spent on families who can best use them. Researchers should gather longitudinal data on large numbers of abusing parents. Such data would shed light on how best to allocate intervention resources and integrate monitoring and intervention elements of child protection. By bringing into focus those persons who do not seem to benefit from treatment, studies would suggest systemic solutions that lie beyond present conceptualizations of service delivery.

Design and Development. The modest success of most existing intervention models and the relative paucity of carefully tested interventions indicate that creative approaches are both needed and not likely to be substantially riskier than existing treatment strategies. Methods should include focus groups, incremental pilot efforts, process evaluation, consumer satisfaction, and measurement of many immediate outcomes.

Better Intervention Research. Investigators should move beyond studies that test simple intervention strategies over short periods, unless the experimental treatment is particularly novel. Studies can serve both ethical and methodological requirements if comparison designs are employed. Outcome determinations should include immediate gains, rates of attrition and reabuse, parent satisfaction with and actual use of various program elements, and longitudinal follow-up. Intervention components should be carefully delineated, along with details about the training of intervention personnel. Intervention researchers should collaborate with program evaluators in conducting outcome studies that consider treatment in the context of the entire process of reporting, investigation, disposition, referral, and follow-up. Studies of dissemination and utilization could emerge if treatment experts come to agree on what constitutes optimal treatment.

Child abuse treatment remains at the levels of art and opinion, rather than science and understanding. The best treatment studies leave much to be desired, largely because the problems of abusing families are difficult and child protection regulations do not easily accommodate research designs. The poor outcomes of present efforts to protect children from repeated physical harm are a challenge to treatment researchers and program developers. Nothing less than bold and creative efforts are required.

REFERENCES

Ainsworth, M. D. (1980). Attachment and child abuse. In G. Gerber, C. J. Ross, and E. Zigler (Eds.), *Child abuse: An agenda for action* (pp. 35–47). New York: Oxford University Press.

Altemeier, W. A., O'Connor, S., Vietze, P., Sandler, H., & Sherrod, K. (1984). Prediction of child abuse: A prospective study of feasibility. *Child Abuse and Neglect, 8,* 393–400.

American Humane Association. (1985). *Highlights of official child neglect and abuse reporting 1983.* Denver, CO: Author.

Bandura, A. (1973). *Aggression: A social learning analysis.* Englewood Cliffs, NJ: Prentice-Hall.

Barth, R. P., & Blythe, B. J. (1983). The contribution of stress to child abuse. *Social Service Review, 57,* 477–489.

Barth, R. P., Blythe, B. J., Schinke, S. P., & Schilling, R. F. (1983). Self-control training with maltreating parents. *Child Welfare, 62,* 313–324.

Bauer, W. T., & Twentyman, C. T. (1985). Abusing, neglectful, and comparsion mothers' responses to child-related and non-child related stressors. *Journal of Consulting and Clinical Psychology, 53,* 335–343.

Becker, J. V., Kaplan, M. S., Cunningham-Rathner, J., & Kavoussi, R. (1986). Characteristics of adolescent incest sexual perpetrators: Preliminary findings. *Journal of Family Violence, 1*, 85–97.

Berger, A. M. (1980). The child abusing family: II. Child and child-rearing variables, environmental factors, and typologies of abusing families. *American Journal of Family Therapy, 8*, 52–68.

Bergman, A., Larsen, R. M., & Mueller, B. (1986). Changing spectrum of serious child abuse. *Pediatrics, 77*, 113–116.

Bolton, F. G., & Bolton, S. R. (1987). *Working with violent families*. Newbury Park, CA: Sage.

Burgess, R. L. (1985). Social incompetence as a precipitant to and consequence of child maltreatment. *Victimology: An International Journal, 10*, 72–86.

Burgess, R. L., & Youngblade, L. M. (1988). Social incompetence and the intergenerational transmission of abusive parental practices. In G. T. Hotaling, D. Finkelhor, J. T. Kirkpatrick, & M. A. Straus (Eds.), *Family abuse and its consequences* (pp. 38–60). Newbury Park, CA: Sage.

Caplan, D. J., Watters, J., White, G., Perry, R., & Bates, R. (1984). Toronto Multiagency Child Abuse Research Project: The abused and the abuser. *Child Abuse and Neglect, 8*, 343–351.

Carroll, C. A., & Haase, C. C. (1987). The function of protective services in child abuse and neglect. In R. E. Helfer & R. S. Kempe (Eds.), *The battered child* (4th ed., pp. 137–151). Chicago: University of Chicago Press.

Cohn, A. H., & Daro, D. (1987). Is treatment too late: What ten years of evaluative research tell us. *Child Abuse and Neglect, 11*, 433–442.

Crittenden, P. M. (1983). The effect of mandatory protective daycare on mutual attachment in maltreating mother–infant dyads. *Child Abuse and Neglect, 7*, 297–300.

Daro, D. (1988). *Confronting child abuse: Research for effective program design*. New York: Free Press.

Deffenbacher, J. L., Story, D. A., Stark, R. S., Hogg, J. A., & Brandon, A. D. (1987). Cognitive-relaxation and social skills interventions in the treatment of general anger. *Journal of Counseling Psychology, 34*, 171–176.

Department of Health and Human Services. (1988). *Study of national incidence and prevalence of child abuse and neglect*. Washington, DC: Office of Human Development Services.

Dumas, J. E., & Wahler, R. G. (1983). Predictors of treatment outcome in parent training: Mother insularity and socioeconomic disadvantage. *Behavioral Assessment, 5*, 301–313.

Egan, K. J. (1983). Stress management and child management with abusive parents. *Journal of Clinical Child Psychology, 12*, 292–299.

Egeland, B., Jacobvitz, D., & Sroufe, L. A. (1988). Breaking the cycle of abuse. *Child Development, 59*, 1080–1088.

Faller, K. C. (1985). Unanticipated problems in the United States child protection system. *Child Abuse and Neglect, 9*, 63–69.

Famularo, R., Stone, K., Barnum, R., & Wharton, R. (1986). Alcoholism and severe child maltreatment. *American Journal of Orthopsychiatry, 56*, 481–485.

Farrington, K. (1986). The application of stress theory to the study of family violence: Principles, problems, and prospects. *Journal of Family Violence, 1,* 131–147.

Friedrich, W. N., & Einbender, A. J. (1983). The abused child: A psychological review. *Journal of Clinical Child Psychology, 12,* 244–256.

Friedrich, W. N., & Wheeler, K. K. (1982). The abusing parent revisited: A decade of psychological research. *Journal of Nervous and Mental Disease, 170,* 577–587.

Gaines, R., Sandgrund, A., Green, A. H., & Power, E. (1978). Etiological factors in child maltreatment: A multivariate study of abusing, neglecting, and normal mothers. *Journal of the American Academy of Child Psychiatry, 18,* 236–250.

Garbarino, J. (1983). What we know about child maltreatment. *Children and Youth Services Review, 5,* 3–6.

Garbarino, J., Brookhouser, P. E., & Authier, K. J. (1987). *Special children—special risks: The maltreatment of children with disabilities.* New York: Aldine de Gruyter.

Garbarino, J., & Crouter, A. (1978). A note on the problem of construct validity in assessing the usefulness of child maltreatment report data. *American Journal of Public Health, 68,* 598–600.

Garbarino, J., & Ebata, A. (1983). The significance of ethnic and cultural differences in child maltreatment. *Journal of Marriage and the Family, 45,* 773–783.

Garbarino, J., & Gilliam, G. (1980). *Understanding abusive families.* Lexington, MA: Lexington Books.

Gaudin, J. M., & Pollane, L. (1983). Social networks, stress, and child abuse. *Children and Youth Services Review, 5,* 91–102.

Gelles, R. J., & Cornell, C. P. (1985). *Intimative violence in families.* Beverly Hills, CA: Sage.

Gil, D. G. (1970). *Violence against children.* Cambridge, MA: Harvard University Press.

Gil, D. G. (1973). *Violence against children: Physical child abuse in the United States.* Cambridge, MA: Harvard University Press.

Goldstein, A. P., Keller, H., & Erne, D. (1985). *Changing the abusive parent.* Champaign, IL: Research Press.

Helm, D. T., & Kozlov, M. A. (1986). Research on parent training: Shortcomings and remedies. *Journal of Autism and Developmental Disorders, 16,* 1–21.

Hunter, R. S., & Kilstrom, N. (1979). Breaking the cycle in abusive families. *American Journal of Psychiatry, 136,* 1320–1322.

Jayaratne, S. (1977). Child abusers as parents and children: A review. *Social Work, 22,* 5–9.

Kahn, A. J., & Kamerman, S. B. (1980). Child abuse: A comparative perspective. In G. Gerbner, C. J. Ross, & E. Zigler (Eds.), *Child abuse: An agenda for action* (pp. 118–132). New York: Oxford University Press.

Kashima, K., Baker, B. L., & Landen, S. J. (1988). Media-based versus professionally led training for parents of mentally retarded children. *American Journal on Mental Retardation, 93,* 209–217.

Kempe, C. H., & Helfer, R. E. (1972). *Helping the battered child and his family.* Philadelphia: Lippincott.

Kempe, C. H., Silverman, F. N., Steele, B. F., Droegemueller, W., & Silver, H. K. (1962). The battered child syndrome. *Journal of the American Medical Association, 181,* 17–24.

Kirkham, M. A., Schinke, S. P., Schilling, R. F., Meltzer, N. J., & Norelius, K. L. (1986). Cognitive-behavioral skills, social supports, and child abuse potential among mothers of handicapped children. *Journal of Family Violence, 1,* 235–245.

Kravitz, R. I., & Driscoll, J. M. (1983). Expectations for childhood development among child-abusing and non-abusing parents. *American Journal of Orthopsychiatry, 53,* 336–344.

Krugman, R. (1987). The assessment process of a child protection team. In R. E. Helfer & R. S. Kempe (Eds.), *The battered child* (4th ed., pp. 127–136). Chicago: University of Chicago Press.

Lahey, B. B., Conger, R. D., Atkeson, B. M., & Treiber, F. A. (1984). Parenting behavior and emotional status of physically abusive mothers. *Journal of Counseling and Clinical Psychology, 52,* 1062–1071.

Lamb, M. E., Gaensbauer, T. J., Malkin, C. M., & Schultz, L. (1985). The effects of child abuse and neglect on security of infant–adult attachment. *Infant Behavior and Development, 8,* 1–14.

Larson, O. W., Doris, J., & Alvarez, W. F. (1987). Child maltreatment among U.S. East Coast migrant farm workers. *Child Abuse and Neglect, 11,* 281–291.

Leonard, K. K., & Jacob, T. (1988). Alcohol, alcoholism, and family violence. In V. B. Van Hasselt, R. L. Morrison, A. S. Bellack, & M. Hersen (Eds.), *Handbook of Family Violence* (pp. 383–406). New York: Plenum.

Lovell, M. L., & Hawkins, J. D. (1988). An evaluation of a group intervention to increase the personal social networks of abusive mothers. *Children and Youth Services Review, 10,* 175–188.

Lutzker, J. R., & Rice, J. M. (1987). Using recidivism data to evaluate Project 12-Ways: An ecobehavioral approach to the treatment and prevention of child abuse and neglect. *Journal of Family Violence, 2,* 283–290.

Magazino, C. J. (1983). Services to children and families at risk of separation. In Brenda G. McGowan & William Meezan (Eds.), *Child welfare: Current dilemmas, future directions* (pp. 211–254). Itasca, IL: F. E. Peacock.

Martin, J. A. (1984). Neglected fathers: Limitations in diagnostic and treatment resources for violent men. *Child Abuse and Neglect, 8,* 387–392.

Mash, E. J., Johnston, C., & Kovitz, K. (1983). A comparison of the mother–child interactions of physically abused and non-abused children during play and task situations. *Journal of Clinical Child Psychology, 12,* 337–346.

Merrill, E. J. (1962). Physical abuse of children: An agency study. In V. DeFrancis (Ed.), *Protecting the battered child* (pp. 1–15). Denver, CO: American Humane Association.

Minnett, A. M., Vandell, D. L., & Santrock, J. W. (1983). The effects of sibling status on sibling interaction: Influence of sex of child, birth order, and age spacing. *Child Development, 54,* 1064–1072.

Nomellini, S., & Katz, R. C. (1983). Effects of anger control training on abusive parents. *Cognitive Therapy and Research, 7,* 57–68.

Novaco, R. W. (1975). *Anger control: The development and evaluation of an experimental treatment*. Lexington, MA: Lexington Books.

Pagelow, M. D. (1984). *Family violence*. New York: Praeger.

Patterson, G. R. (1982). *Coercive family process*. Eugene, OR: Castalia.

Pelton, L. H. (1978). Child abuse and neglect: The myth of classlessness. *American Journal of Orthopsychiatry, 48,* 608–617.

Reid, J. B., Kavanaugh, K., & Baldwin, D. V. (1987). Abusive parents' perceptions of child problem behaviors: An example of parental bias. *Journal of Abnormal Child Psychology, 15,* 457–466.

Rivara, F. P. (1985). Physical abuse of children under two: A study of therapeutic outcomes. *Child Abuse and Neglect, 9,* 81–87.

Roscoe, B., Goodwin, M. P., & Kennedy, D. (1987). Sibling violence and agnostic interactions experienced by early adolescents. *Journal of Family Violence, 2,* 121–137.

Sack, W. H., Mason, R., & Higgins, J. E. (1985). The single-parent family and abusive child punishment. *American Journal of Orthopsychiatry, 55,* 252–259.

Salter, A. C., Richardson, C. M., & Martin, P. A. (1985). Treating abusive parents. *Child Welfare, 64,* 327–341.

Salzinger, S., Kaplan, S., & Artemyeff, C. (1983). Mothers' personal social networks and child maltreatment. *Journal of Abnormal Psychology, 92,* 68–76.

Sanford, D. A., & Tustin, R. D. (1973). Behavioral treatment of parental assault on a child. *New Zealand Psychologist, 2,* 76–82.

Schilling, R. F. (1981). Treatment of child abuse. In S. P. Schinke (Ed.), *Behavioral methods in social welfare* (pp. 107–129). New York: Aldine.

Schilling, R. F. (1987). Limitations of social support. *Social Service Review, 61,* 19–31.

Schilling, R. F. (1988). Helping families with developmentally disabled members. In C. Chilman, F. Cox, & E. Nunnally (Eds.), *Troubled families: Vol. 2. Families with disabled members* (pp. 171–92). Beverly Hills, CA: Sage.

Schilling, R. F., Gilchrist, L. D., & Schinke, S. P. (1984). Coping and social support in families of developmentally disabled children. *Family Relations, 33,* 47–54.

Schilling, R. F., & Kirkham, M. A. (1985). Preventing maltreatment of handicapped children. In L. D. Gilchrist & S. P. Schinke (Eds.), *Preventing social and health problems through life skills training* (pp. 29–42). Monograph No. 3, University of Washington, Seattle.

Schilling, R. F., & Schinke, S. P. (1984a). Maltreatment and mental retardation. In J. M. Berg (Ed.), *Perspectives and progress in mental retardation* (Vol. I, pp. 11–22). Baltimore: University Park Press.

Schilling, R. F., & Schinke, S. P. (1984b). Personal coping and social support for parents of handicapped children. *Children and Youth Services Review, 6,* 195–206.

Schilling, R. F., Schinke, S. P., Blythe, B. J., & Barth, R. P. (1982). Child maltreatment and mentally retarded parents: Is there a relationship? *Mental Retardation, 20,* 201–209.

Schilling, R. F., Schinke, S. P., & Gilchrist, L. D. (1985). Utilization of social work research: Reaching the practitioner. *Social Work, 30,* 527–529.

Schilling, R. F., Schinke, S. P., & Kirkham, M. A. (1985). Coping with a handicapped child: Differences between mothers and fathers. *Social Science and Medicine, 8,* 857–863.

Schindler, F., & Arkowitz, H. (1986). The assessment of mother–child interactions in physically abusive and nonabusive families. *Journal of Family Violence, 1,* 247–257.

Schinke, S. P., Blythe, B. J., Schilling, R. F., & Barth, R. P. (1981). Neglect of mentally retarded persons. *Education and Training of the Mentally Retarded, 16,* 299–303.

Schinke, S. P., Schilling, R. F., Barth, R. P., Gilchrist, L. D., & Maxwell, J. S. (1986). Stress-management intervention to prevent family violence. *Journal of Family Violence, 1,* 13–26.

Shorkey, C. T. (1979). A review of methods used in the treatment of child abuse. *Social Casework, 60,* 360–366.

Sloan, M. P., & Meier, J. H. (1983). Typology for parents of abused children. *Child Abuse and Neglect, 7,* 443–450.

Spinetta, J., & Rigler, D. (1972). The child abusing parent: A psychological review. *Psychological Bulletin, 77,* 296–304.

Stark, E., & Flitcraft, A. H. (1988). Women and children at risk: A feminist perspective on child abuse. *International Journal of Health Services, 18,* 97–118.

Starr, R. H., Jr. (1982). A research-based approach to the prediction of child abuse. In R. H. Starr, Jr. (Ed.), *Child abuse prediction: Policy implications* (pp. 105–134). Cambridge, MA: Ballinger.

Starr, R. H., Jr. (1988). Physical abuse of children. In V. B. Van Hasselt, R. L. Morrison, A. S. Bellack, & M. Hersen (Eds.), *Handbook of family violence* (pp. 119–155). New York: Plenum.

Stein, T. J. (1984). The child abuse prevention and treatment act. *Social Service Review, 58,* 302–314.

Stein, T. J., & Rzepnicki, T. L. (1983). *Decision making at child welfare intake.* New York: Child Welfare League of America.

Straus, M. A. (1983). Ordinary violence, child abuse, and wife-beating: What they have in common. In D. Finkelhor, R. J. Gelles, G. T. Hotaling, & M. A. Straus (Eds.), *The Dark Side of Families* (pp. 213–234). Beverly Hills: Sage.

Straus, M. A., Gelles, R. J., & Steinmetz, S. K. (1980). *Behind closed doors: Violence in the American family.* Garden City, NY: Anchor Books.

Straus, M. A., & Kantor, G. K. (1987). Stress and child abuse. In R. E. Helfer & R. S. Kempe (Eds.), *The battered child* (4th ed., pp. 42–59). Chicago: University of Chicago Press.

Susman, E. J., Trickett, P. K., Iannotti, R. J., Hollenbeck, B. E., & Zahn-Waxler, C. (1985). Child-rearing patterns in depressed, abusive, and normal mothers. *American Journal of Orthopsychiatry, 55,* 237–251.

Timmons-Mitchell, J. (1986). Containing aggressive acting out in abused children. *Child Welfare, 65,* 459–468.

Tracy, E. M., & Whittaker, J. K. (1987). The evidence base for social support interventions in child and family practice: Emerging issues for research and practice. *Children and Youth Services Review, 9,* 249–270.

Trickett, P. K., & Kuczynski, L. (1986). Children's misbehaviors and parental discipline strategies in abusive and nonabusive families. *Developmental Psychology, 22*, 115–123.

Vitulano, L. A., Lewis, M., Doran, L. D., Nordhaus, B., & Adnopoz, J. (1986). Treatment recommendation, implementation, and follow-up in child abuse. *American Journal of Orthopsychiatry, 56*, 478–480.

Washburne, C. K. (1983). A feminist analysis of child abuse and neglect. In D. Finkelhor, R. J. Gelles, G. T. Hotaling, & M. A. Straus (Eds.), *The Dark Side of Families* (pp. 289–292). Beverly Hills: Sage.

Webster-Stratton, C. (1985). Comparison of abusive and non-abusive families with conduct-disordered children. *American Journal of Orthopsychiatry, 55*, 59–69.

Whiteman, M., Fanshel, D., & Grundy, J. F. (1987). Cognitive-behavioral interventions aimed at anger of parents at risk of child abuse. *Social Work, 32*, 469–474.

Wolfe, D. A. (1985). Child-abusive parents: An empirical review and analysis. *Psychological Bulletin, 97*, 462–482.

Wolfe, D. A. (1987). *Child abuse: Implications for child development and psychopathology.* Newbury Park, CA: Sage.

Wolfe, D. A., Edwards, B., Manion, I., & Koverola, C. (1988). Early intervention for parents at risk of child abuse and neglect: A preliminary investigation. *Journal of Consulting and Clinical Psychology, 56*, 40–47.

Wolfe, D. A., Kaufman, K., Aragona, J., & Sandler, J. (1981). *The child management program for abusive parents.* Winter Park, FL: Anna.

Wood-Shuman, S., & Cone, J. D. (1986). Differences in abusive, at-risk for abuse, and control mothers' descriptions of normal child behavior. *Child Abuse and Neglect, 10*, 397–405.

Young, G., & Gately, T. (1988). Neighborhood impoverishment and child maltreatment. *Journal of Family Issues, 9*, 240–254.

Zalba, S. R. (1967). The abused child: II. A typology for classification and treatment. *Social Work, 12*, 70–79.

CHAPTER 11

Perpetrators of Child Sexual Abuse

JUDITH V. BECKER AND MEG S. KAPLAN

INTRODUCTION

Child sexual abuse within the family is a serious problem and more common than generally recognized. Although the exact occurrence is unknown, incidence rates suggest that each year approximately 50,000 to 60,000 children are victims of intrafamily sexual abuse (Giarretto, 1976; NCCAN, 1981). Previous early studies consisted largely of reported cases to courts and social service agencies. However, more recent studies have demonstrated that intrafamily sexual abuse is more prevalent than reported, because families tend to conceal the occurrence. For example, Herman and Hirschman (1981) found that in a sample of 40 women in psychotherapy for father–daughter incest, over 90% of the cases were unknown to mental health facilities or social service agencies.

In studies that have been conducted to date many of the reported rates vary considerably. These studies estimate prevalence or percentage of sexual abuse in a specific population.

Finkelhor (1979) surveyed 530 female and 266 male college students. Twenty-eight percent of the females and 23% of the males reported a sexual experience with a relative. The definition included all types of contact and non-contact abuse.

In another recent study, Russell (1983) interviewed 930 adult women; 16% reported at least one experience of intrafamilial sexual contact before the age of 18 years; 12% had been sexually abused by a relative before the age of 14. The definition used was "any kind of exploitive sexual contact that occurred between relatives, no matter how distant the relationship" (p. 116), including noncontact abuse such as exhibitionism or solicitation.

Husain and Chapel (1983) studied 437 hospitalized female psychiatric inpatients, aged 18 and younger; 61 (13.9%) admitted to having been involved in an incestuous relationship.

CHARACTERISTICS OF PERPETRATORS

The terms *intrafamily child sexual abuse* and *incest* have been defined in various ways. The sexual acts may range from such behavior as exhibitionism and fondling, to forcible penetration between a child and a family member (biologically related or living as a family member, such as parent figure, guardian, or person in a role of authority in the home).

The revised *Diagnostic and Statistical Manual of Mental Disorders* (DSM-III-R; American Psychiatric Association, 1987) describes the diagnostic class of sexual disorders that include paraphilias or sexual deviations. These are characterized by repetitive sexual acts that involve nonconsenting partners or preference for use of a nonhuman object for sexual arousal. Pedophilia describes adults whose preferred or exclusive method of achieving sexual excitement is in the act or fantasy of engaging in sexual activity with pre-pubescent children (generally aged 13 years or younger). The minimum difference in age between the adult (who must be at least 16 years of age) and the prepubescent child is 5 years. For late adolescents with this disorder, no precise age difference is specified (American Psychiatric Association, 1987, p. 284). The diagnosis of pedophilia can include or be limited to incest. However, incest is not always characterized as a paraphilia. Isolated acts can be precipitated by marital problems, illness, or loneliness.

One of the difficulties in diagnosis is that the traditional psychiatric literature suggests that paraphiliacs offend only within their families, or only against nonfamily members, but rarely against both.

A recent study by Abel, Becker, Cunningham-Rathner, Mittelman, and Rouleau (1987) found that, of 561 voluntary adult male pedophiles, 131 (23%) had offended against both family and nonfamily targets; the average number of paraphilias by diagnosis was 3 to 5 paraphilias per diagnostic category.

Frequency of Different Forms of Intrafamilial Sexual Abuse

Most studies have focused primarily on father–daughter incest (Becker and Coleman, 1988; Cavallin, 1966; Weinberg, 1955). However, research also has concentrated on persons in the same age group, such as siblings and cousins. Recently, researchers have focused attention on the adolescent incest perpetrator. These studies have found the onset of deviant sexual interest patterns to be prior to the age of 19 years (Abel, Mittelman, & Becker, 1985; Brecher, 1978; Groth & Birnbaum, 1979).

Finkelhor (1979) conducted a survey of 796 female college students and found that one third of the women reporting victimization indicated that the molester was a male youth, aged 10 to 19, who was likely to have been a family or extended family member. Further, Finkelhor (1980) reported that 15% of the females and 10% of the males reported a sexual experience with a sibling. However, identification of adolescent incest perpetrators is difficult because most cases go unreported. It is believed that families often deny that their child has engaged in sibling incest for fear of opening the family to professional scrutiny (Deisher, Wenet, Paperny, Clark, & Fehrenbach, 1982).

In one recent study, Becker, Kaplan, Cunningham-Rathner, and Kavoussi (1986) interviewed 22 adolescent males who had been charged with or convicted of a sexual crime against a family member. Their results indicated that 59% of the subjects (mean age 14 years) reported a prior nondeviant genital experience (mean age 12.3 years) whereas the majority of adolescents reported engaging in deviant sexual behavior after 14 years of age. The finding that the mean age of onset of nondeviant genital behavior predated the onset of deviant sexual behavior is consistent with Groth's (1977) data showing that the sexual assault is not the first interpersonal experience in the perpetrator's life. He challenges the assumption that sex crimes of adolescents are merely attempts to learn about sex and can therefore be viewed as sexual exploratory behavior.

Previous work had suggested that adolescents rarely repeat their offenses. Of the 22 incest cases in the sample, there was a total of 13 attempted sexual crimes and 415 completed sexual crimes (however, 1 adolescent accounted for 229 of those offenses). This indicates that a number of adolescents do continue to engage in deviant sexual behavior.

INCEST OFFENDERS: PEDOPHILES

An important issue concerning men who involve themselves sexually with children in the family relates to whether these men are etiologically different from pedophiles. Researchers have attempted to determine if incest offenders have specific sexual preference for children in general or only for family members.

Quinsey (1977) compared recidivism rates of heterosexual pedophiles to heterosexual incest cases and found the rates of incest cases to be lower. He hypothesized that etiologies may be different for these two groups.

Abel, Becker, Murphy, and Flanagan (1979) used a psychophysiologic assessment to compare incest offenders to pedophiles in order to determine if the arousal patterns of these two groups differed. They found "The cases of heterosexual incest are not different in their preferences from heterosexual pedophiles, since both groups are highly aroused by young children other than their female relatives" (p. 25).

In a more recent study, Abel and his colleagues (1987) assessed 159 incest offender subjects. Of those who reported involvement with female incest pedophilia, 49% had histories of also having been involved in nonincest pedophilia, 12% in male nonincest pedophilia, and 12% in male incest pedophilia. Of the 44 subjects who reported involvement with male incest pedophilia, 61% had histories of also having been involved with female nonincest pedophilia, 68% with male nonincest pedophilia, and 43% with female incest pedophilia. From these data, it becomes apparent that child molesters have a very high incidence of deviant behavior with both family and nonfamily targets. Furthermore, these data also suggest that, contrary to traditional belief, a significant number of incestuous child molesters have been involved with children outside the home.

Thus, the preceding studies indicate that some incest offenders have an arousal preference for children that is not limited to their own children.

Various theories have been proposed to explain the development of a paraphilia, but to date none has been empirically tested. There are those theorists who posit that sexually abusive behavior is the result of intrapsychic conflict, others who believe it is caused by biological excesses or deficiencies, and those who argue that the behavior is learned. Psychoanalytic theory views paraphilia, or perversion, as an expression of unresolved problems in childhood development. Freud (1938) first theorized that the choice of an immature sexual object is a result of either a fixation at an infantile level or an unresolved Oedipus complex. He hypothesized that excessive gratification could stop at one level of childhood development and never allow the advance of adult sexual development. For example, the sexual deviant, unable to deal with adult heterosexuality because of castration fears, resorts to safer, more developmentally primitive forms of sexual expression. Freud later emphasized the notion that perversion may be a regression to perverse sexuality, an early state of sensual gratification (Cook & Howells, 1981; Mohr & Jerry, 1964; Stoller, 1979). These psychoanalytic writers share the belief that the perversion is a product of unresolved problems in libidinal and family development.

Oedipal theory posits the existence of incestuous fantasies among children for their opposite sex parents. Freud hypothesized that neuroses were the result of the incest taboo not preventing unconscious sexual desires.

Those who adhere to a biological model treat the paraphilias with drugs to decrease androgen levels. Antipsychotic medications have also been used with psychotic offenders. Unfortunately, to date, no theory has been empirically tested.

According to social learning theory, individuals are not born with complex repertories of behaviors but learn them (Bandura, 1973). "The theoretical basis for behavior therapy is that the symptom or behavior to be treated has been learned at some time in the past and can be changed by the learning of a new pattern of behavior" (McQuire, Carlyle & Young, 1965, p. 185). Numerous researchers describe the importance of learning theory.

Ford and Beach (1955) state:

Human sexuality is affected by experience in two ways. First, the kinds of situations that become capable of evoking sexual excitement are determined in a large measure by learning. Second, the overt behavior through which this excitement is expressed depends largely upon the individual's previous experience. (p. 262)

Kinsey, Pomeroy, Martin, and Gebhard (1953) also concluded:

The sexual capacities which an individual inherits at birth appear to be nothing more than the necessary anatomy and the physiologic capacity to respond to a sufficient physical or psychological stimulus . . . but apart from these few inherent capacities, most other aspects of human sexual behavior appear to be the product of learning and conditioning. (p. 644)

McQuire et al. (1965) have postulated that learning is established by the process of fantasizing the initial deviant experience. It is postulated that the deviant frequently recalls his first sexual experience. The repeated pairing of these fantasies with orgasm results in their acquiring sexually arousing properties, which are reinforced.

In summary, social learning theory views sex offenses as conditioned behavior learned as a result of inappropriate fantasies that can be changed by learning new patterns of behavior.

Becker and Kaplan (1988a) have proposed a model to explain the acquisition and maintenance of deviant sexual arousal. They propose that the deviant behavior is learned in any number of different ways (e.g., observation of the behavior; being the victim of physical or sexual aggression, which predisposes an individual to model that behavior). They theorize that other events must occur for the development of a deviant sexual interest pattern. This relates to the recall of the initial deviant sex act during masturbation-orgasm activities.

Risk Factors In Intrafamilial Sexual Abuse

Research and therapy regarding incestuous behavior have been approached from the point of view of family dysfunction, as shown in the contributory characteristics of the fathers, mothers, and children. Several of the major theories and studies will be reviewed here. Because intrafamilial sexual abuse occurs in the presence of multiple problems, there is no known direct cause and effect.

Justice and Justice (1979) state that some of the factors involved include (a) the personalities of the individuals involved; (b) their situations, setting, and circumstances; (c) the change or crises that have recently occurred in their lives.

According to Kempe and Kempe (1984) research is needed to clarify the contributing factors of various types of incest.

Mrazek (1981) cites the most predictive factors of incest in general as the absence of a strong satisfying marital bond and prior incestuous behavior somewhere in the family. Researchers stress that the interacting system of individual and family must be evaluated in a contextual view to assess the correct intervention.

In the family dynamics model of incest, the marital relationship is dysfunctional, the mother is emotionally alienated, and the father turns to his daughter as a substitute for gratification (Gebhard, Gagnon, Pomeroy, & Christenson, 1965). Within their subject population, Gebhard and his colleagues also found that incest always occurred during periods of marital stress. Mayer (1983) has also stated that father–daughter incest most often occurs in dysfunctional isolated families, and cites the following typical patterns:

1. Marital discord and a poor sexual relationship between the parents
2. Unwillingness of the father to seek sexual relationships outside of the family
3. Role reversal between mother and daughter
4. The mother's condoning (consciously or unconsciously) the relationship between father and daughter (p. 25)

Thorman (1983) has cited the following as deficient areas in the family.

1. Lack of strong correlation between the parents
2. Mothers who are physically or psychologically absent
3. Reversed mother–daughter roles
4. Unequally distributed power between husband and wife
5. Conflict resolved through scapegoating
6. Family affect not supportive to family members
7. Lack of autonomy among family members
8. Confused communication
9. Socially isolated family members who are unable to cope with stress (pp. 77–78)

Herman and Hirschman (1981) found that families that were at particular risk for incest were those in which there was a violent father, a powerless or disabled mother, or an acting-out adolescent girl.

Paveza (1988) recently reported on a study of 34 families in which incest had occurred and a control group of 68 nonincest families. Subjects responded to a self-administered questionnaire. Four variables were identified as having a relationship in terms of presenting a risk factor for sexual abuse. The variables were income (lower income, greater risk), closeness of mother–daughter relationship, marital satisfaction, and violence between abuser and spouse.

According to the feminist model of incest, the excesses of patriarchal authority account for lowered inhibitions; men, viewing their wives and children as property, have the socially approved authority to treat them as they wish (Becker & Coleman, 1988; Rush, 1980).

Specific Characteristics

According to Finkelhor (1986):

> A serious problem in the field of research on child molesters has been the tendency to try to explain all child molesting with single-factor theories—for example, the theory that child molesters are all immature, or that child molesters all have some kind of hormonal problem. So far the research has shown that no single factor can begin to explain fully all sexual abuse. (p. 119)

However, various individual characteristics are cited in the literature. Weinberg (1955) divided incest offenders into three groups:

1. Indiscriminate promiscuity where incest is part of a pattern of sexual psychopathology;
2. Pedophilia in which incestuous behavior is also included
3. Intrafamilial incest, confined only to family members

Weinberg has suggested that some men may seek out their own children rather than other adult women because of taboos against extramarital affairs.

Several researchers have theorized that adults who involve themselves sexually with children have themselves been sexually or physically abused as children. A number of studies have found various rates of prior victimization in samples of sex offenders (Abel et al., 1984; Gebhard et al., 1965; Groth & Birnbaum, 1979).

A large body of research suggests that sex offenders have difficulties in social skills with adult females. Gebhard et al. (1965) found problems in social relationships for incest offenders as well as other offender groups. Other researchers have reached similar conclusions (Bell & Hall, 1976; Howells, 1981; Langevin, 1983).

Alcohol abuse has also been cited as a possible risk factor in the commission of sex offenses. Aarens et al. (1978) reviewed several studies and concluded that incestuous sex offenders had a higher degree of alcoholism and alcohol use at the time of the offense than nonincestuous child molesters.

According to researchers, presence of a stepfather increases the risk for sexual molestation (Finkelhor, 1979). Russell (1984) in an analysis of interviews obtained from a random sample of 930 women, found that among those who had a stepfather as a principal figure in their childhood years, 17% were sexually abused by him. The comparable figures for biological fathers was 2%. One explanation for this is that because a stepfather has not lived with the child since her birth, lack of early parental contact as a caretaker may result in less concern and lowered inhibitions. Husain and Chapel (1983) theorize that stepfathers may not develop incest taboos because they come into the family as strangers and are as aroused sexually by the child as by her mother.

Assessing Incest Offenders

Frequently clinicians are called upon to evaluate an alleged offender when incest has been disclosed. It is common for the alleged offender to deny or minimize the behavior because of fear of consequences.

Short of the person admitting that he or she committed the sexual offense, no definitive assessment instrument can speak to guilt or innocence.

The clinician's task is difficult because no test or combination of tests can determine "definitively" whether a person has committed a sexual crime. Unfortunately, there is no empirically derived profile of an incest offender with which to compare the alleged offender.

Several studies have evaluated offender samples. Becker and Kaplan (1988b) discuss in detail assessment techniques with adult sex offenders.

In general, assessments usually consist of a clinical interview, with particular emphasis placed on obtaining a sex history of paraphilic and non-paraphilic behavior as well as a history of physical, sexual, and/or substance abuse. A psychiatric assessment is conducted to determine whether the behavior may have been associated with impaired cognitive abilities or psychosis. Behaviorists have utilized the penile plethysmograph as part of a comprehensive evaluation to assess sexual response patterns. This assessment involves the direct measurement of changes in penile response to paraphilic and nonparaphilic stimuli. Penile response is, however, subject to some voluntary control or faking. Consequently, the validity is questionable when assessing alleged offenders (see Murphy & Barbaree, 1988, for an extensive review of the use of erection measures with offenders).

Other psychometric instruments that have been utilized in assessing incest offenders include a Sexual Interest Cardsort and a Cognitions Scale (Abel, Becker, Rathner, Kaplan, & Reich, 1984).

A number of studies have reported on the use of the MMPI (Minnesota Multiphasic Personality Inventory) in the assessment of offenders. Levin and Stava (1987), in a review of MMPI studies with sex offender populations, note that studies are marked by methodological problems: "In general, negative or inconsistent findings outweigh those of a positive nature" (p. 69).

In summary, although psychological tests are useful in delineating treatment needs of those offenders who acknowledge their deviant behavior and are seeking treatment, they cannot speak to guilt or innocence.

TREATMENT

Because a variety of theoretical orientations have been proposed to explain incestuous behavior, treatment strategies have been implemented based on those theories. Traditionally, psychoanalysis has been the treatment for the paraphilias; it seeks to undo the repression that is believed to be the cause. Treatment is usually reconstructive psychotherapy. Unfortunately, evaluating results is extremely complicated because there are no common standards of measurement. Moreover, several investigators have reported disappointment with the results of psychoanalysis or psychotherapy as the sole form of treatment in cases of deviant sexual behavior (e.g., Cook & Howells, 1981).

Family Therapy

Giarretto, Giarretto, and Sgroi (1978) describe a treatment program for families in which incest has occurred. The primary emphasis of the program is to maintain family integrity, and it combines individual therapy, group therapy, and self-help groups. Therapy begins with counseling of the daughter, then individual counseling of the mother, and joint mother–daughter counseling. If there are other siblings, they then join in the counseling with the mother and victim. The perpetrator receives marital counseling. The father is finally placed in the family counseling. Such counseling is supplemented with participation in the self-help groups known as Daughters and Parents United.

Behavioral Treatment

Because sexual disorders can occur in individuals who have no other psychological symptoms, behavior therapy, based on social learning theory, has been implemented (Bandura, 1973). Sex offenders have arousal to deviant behavior so the focus is on teaching them self-control over sexual interests as well as altering other behavioral excesses or deficits (such as social skills training to improve their ability to communicate with adult partners). A number of researchers have used specific behavioral treatment techniques to teach control over deviant sexual interest patterns (Abel, Barlow, Blanchard, & Guild, 1977; Abel, Blanchard, Barlow, & Mavissakalian, 1975; Abel, Blanchard, Becker, & Djenderedijian, 1978; Barlow & Abel, 1976).

Abel and his colleagues (1984) describe a multicomponent treatment program for child molesters.

1. *Satiation.* The individual learns how to use his deviant fantasies postorgasm in a repetitive manner to the point of satiating himself with the very stimuli that used to arouse him. The client is given precise instructions for carrying out the procedure at home. The treatment consists of having the client masturbate to adult consensual imagery to orgasm for a short period of time and then to deviant imagery for a prolonged period of time. The client taperecords the fantasies and brings them to the sessions. Self-administered satiation is particularly useful because it can be employed by the client any time reduction of deviant arousal is necessary.

2. *Covert Sensitization.* This technique decreases deviant arousal and disrupts the behaviors that are antecedent to the client's actually coming in

contact with his victim. Covert sensitization involves the client's imagining the various feelings or experiences that begin to lead him toward committing a deviant sexual act; he then immediately brings to mind very aversive images that reflect the negative consequences of proceeding in that direction. Covert sensitization appears to sensitize the client to those behaviors early in the chain of events that leads to his paraphiliac act. Some clients may never be completely successful in eliminating their arousal to deviant acts. Consequently, they always will need to be able to disrupt the very behaviors that lead them toward commission of the act. As with satiation, covert sensitization is self-administered at home. The client records the session and the therapist checks the tapes to ensure compliance and to refine antecedents and consequences.

Both satiation and covert sensitization are self-control procedures that clients are instructed to use in the future when they experience deviant fantasies or urges.

3. *Assertiveness and Social Skills Training.* Without appropriate social skills, the client might continue to be involved with children or family members with whom appropriate social skills are less necessary. Social skills training involves a role rehearsal procedure that allows the client to model appropriate social skills, practice those skills in his real life, get feedback from the therapist about his performance, and then learn more complicated skills through a similar process.

4. *Cognitive Restructuring.* The majority of pedophiles know that their deviant behavior is contrary to the morals and ethics of our society, yet they give themselves permission to engage in such behavior. These "permission-giving statements" are cognitive distortions used to justify behaviors.

Treatment requires teaching the client how cognitive distortions develop and why it is essential for him to recognize that his own distortions have allowed him to accept his deviant behavior.

5. *Sex Education and Values Clarification.* The client is taught about sexual myths, sexual dysfunction, and appropriate sexual behavior.

Abel et al. (1984) entered 192 adult pedophiles into their treatment program. Therapy was conducted in a group format. Sessions were held weekly.

Of the 192 offenders who entered the program, 65% completed treatment. Of the 98 offenders who presented for a 1-year follow-up, 12 had reoffended. Factors associated with recidivism included (a) marital status (single and divorced offenders were more likely to reoffend); (b) program endorsement (those who reoffended were less likely to have endorsed the goals of the treatment program); (c) type of sexual crime (reoffenders were more likely to have committed sexual crimes against both males and females and children and adolescents).

For a detailed review of treatment strategies, readers are referred to Dixen and Jenkins (1981) and Kelly (1982).

SUMMARY AND FUTURE DIRECTIONS

Although a body of literature has been adduced on incest perpetrators, much research needs to be done. The field lacks an empirically derived and tested theory to explain why some people engage in sexual behavior with child relatives. Some reports indicate that dysfunctional families may play an etiological role, but this hypothesis has not been formally evaluated. When family members are evaluated after disclosure of abuse, the family indeed looks dysfunctional. But is this the case as a result of the stress and strain of the disclosure and subsequent investigations, or was the family originally dysfunctional? There is no doubt that many families are marked by dysfunction and marital problems, yet in the majority of these families parents do not turn to their children or stepchildren for sexual gratification.

Because the development of sexual interest and arousal is a complex process, a multifactor theory that incorporates biological, intrapsychic, environmental, and familial factors is needed. Research should focus on why some people engage in extrafamilial as well as intrafamilial sexual abuse, whereas others only in the intrafamilial mode.

Future research needs to focus on the development of a typology of incest offenders. Various treatment strategies need evaluation. The public and the criminal justice system need to be informed of the availability and success of various treatment strategies. As noted by Faller (1988), recommendations made regarding perpetrators are often contradictory. Some treatment programs require an admission to the deviant behavior as a prerequisite of therapy; others see it as a goal of therapy.

Another controversial issue needing investigation is whether the goal of therapy should be to reunite the family. Although in some cases this might be advisable, in other cases it might prove detrimental. Research should focus on the development of criteria to assist clinicians in helping families establish therapeutic goals.

A third issue concerns what form or combination of forms of therapy works best with which perpetrator and family. Whereas treatment that specifically addresses inappropriate sexual arousal has been demonstrated to be effective, research evaluating the effectiveness of other forms of therapy needs to be conducted. Long-term follow-ups of treated offenders must be conducted to assess what factors are associated with maintenance of treatment effects and which contribute to relapse.

Finally, victims of child sexual abuse must receive evaluations and treatment when warranted. Providing treatment to these victims may prevent future abuse.

REFERENCES

Aarens, M., Cameron, T., Roizen, J., Room, R., Schneberk, D., & Wingard, D. (1978). *Alcohol, casualties and crime.* Berkeley, CA: Social Research Group.

Abel, G., Barlow, D., Blanchard, E., & Guild, D. (1977). The components of rapists' sexual arousal. *Archives of General Psychiatry, 34,* 895–903.

Abel, G., Becker, J., Cunningham-Rathner, J., Mittelman, M., & Rouleau, J. (1987). Multiple paraphilic diagnoses among sex offenders. *American Academy of Psychiatry and the Law, 16,* 153–168.

Abel, G., Becker, J., Murphy, W., & Flanagan, B. (1979, March). *Identifying dangerous child molesters.* 11th Banff International Conference on Behavior Modification, Banff, Canada.

Abel, G., Becker, J., Rathner, J., Kaplan, M., & Reich, J. *Treatment manual for child molesters* (1984). Unpublished manual, available from the Sexual Behavior Clinic, NYS Psychiatric Institute, N.Y.

Abel, G., Blanchard, E., Barlow, D., & Mavissakalian, M. (1975). Identifying specific erotic cues in sexual deviation by audio-taped descriptions. *Journal of Applied Behavior Analysis, 8,* 247–260.

Abel, G., Blanchard, E., Becker, J., & Djenderediian, A. (1978). Differentiating sexual aggressives with penile measures. *Criminal Justice and Behavior, 5,* 315–332.

Abel, G. G., Mittelman, M. S., & Becker, J. V. (1985). Sexual offenders: Results of assessment and recommendations for treatment. In M. H. Ben-Aron, S. J. Hucker, & C. D. Webster (Eds.), *Clinical criminology: Current concepts.* Toronto: M & M Graphics.

American Psychiatric Association (1987). *Diagnostic and statistical manual of mental disorders* (DSM-III-R; 3rd ed.-rev.). Washington, DC: Author.

Bandura, A. (1973). *Aggression: A social learning analysis.* New Jersey: Prentice-Hall.

Barlow, D. H., & Abel, G. G. (1976). Sexual Deviation. In W. Craighead, A. Kazdin, & M. Mahoney (Eds.), *Behavior modification: Principles, issues, and applications.* (pp. 341–360). Atlanta, GA: Houghton Mifflin.

Becker, J., & Coleman, E. (1988). Incest. In V. B. Van Hasselt, R. L. Morrison, A. S. Bellack, & M. Hersen (Eds.), *Handbook of family violence* (pp. 187–205). New York: Plenum.

Becker, J., & Kaplan, M. (1988a). Assessment of adolescent sexual offenders. In R. Prinz (Ed.), *Advances in behavioral assessment of children and families: Vol. 4.,* Greenwich, CT: JAI Press.

Becker, J., & Kaplan, M. (1988b). Assessment and treatment of the male sex offender. In A. Green & D. Schetky (Eds.), *Child sexual abuse: Intervention, treatment and prevention* (pp. 136–149). New York: Bruner/Mazel.

Becker, J. V., Kaplan, M. S., Cunningham-Rathner, J., & Kavoussi, R. J. (1986). Characteristics of adolescent incest sexual perpetrators: Preliminary findings. *Journal of Family Violence, 1,* 85–97.

Bell, A., & Hall, C. (1976). The personality of a child molester. In M. S. Weinberg (Ed.), *Sex research: Studies from the Kinsey Institute* (pp. 184–202). New York: Oxford University Press.

Brecher, E. (1978). *Treatment programs for sex offenders.* Washington, DC: U.S. Department of Justice.

Cavallin, H. (1966). Incestuous fathers: A clinical report. *American Journal of Psychiatry, 122,* 1132–1138.

Cook, M., & Howells, K. (Eds.). (1981). *Adult sexual interest in children*. New York: Academic Press.

Deisher, R., Wenet, G., Paperny, D., Clark, T., & Fehrenbach, P. (1982). Adolescent sexual offense behavior: The role of the physician. *Journal of Adolescent Health Care, 2,* 279–286.

Dixen, J., & Jenkins, J. (1981). Incestuous child sexual abuse: A review of treatment strategies. *Clinical Psychology Review, 1,* 211–222.

Faller, K. (1988). Decision making in cases of intrafamilial child sexual abuse. *American Journal of Orthopsychiatry, 58,* 121–128.

Finkelhor, D. (1979). *Sexually victimized children*. New York: Free Press.

Finkelhor, D. (1980). Risk factors in the sexual victimization of children. *Child Abuse and Neglect, 4,* 265–273.

Finkelhor, D. (1986). *A sourcebook on child sexual abuse*. Los Angeles: Sage.

Ford, C., & Beach, F. (1955). *Patterns of sexual behavior*. New York: Harper & Row.

Freud, S. (1938). Three contributions to the theory of sex. In A. A. Brill (Ed.), *The basic writings of Sigmund Freud* (pp. 555–629). New York: Random House.

Gebhard, P., Gagnon, J., Pomeroy, W., & Christenson, C. (1965). *Sex offenders: An analysis of types*. New York: Harper & Row.

Giarretto, H. (1976). Humanistic treatment of father–daughter incest. In R. E. Helfer & C. H. Kemp (Eds.), *Child abuse and neglect: The family and the community*. Cambridge, MA: Ballinger.

Giarretto, H., Giarretto, A., & Sgroi, S. (1978). Coordinated community treatment of incest. In A. Burgess, A. N. Groth, L. L. Holmstrom, & S. M. Sgroi (Eds.), *Sexual assault of children and adolescents* (pp. 231–240). Lexington, MA: Lexington Books.

Groth, A. (1977). The adolescent sex offender and his prey. *International Journal of Offender Therapy: Comparative Criminology, 21,* 249–254.

Groth, A., & Birnbaum, H. (1979). *Men who rape: The psychology of the offender*. New York: Plenum.

Herman, J., & Hirschman, L. (1981). Families at risk for father–daughter incest. *American Journal of Psychiatry, 138,* 967–970.

Howells, K. (1981). Adult sexual interest in children: Considerations relevant to theories of aetiology. In M. Cook & K. Howells (Eds.), *Adult sexual interest in children* (pp. ??). New York: Academic Press.

Husain, A., & Chapel, J. (1983). History of incest in girls admitted to a psychiatric hospital. *American Journal of Psychiatry, 140,* 591–593.

Justice, B., & Justice, R. (1979). *The broken taboo: Sex in the family*. New York: Human Sciences Press.

Kelly, R. (1982). Behavioral reorientation of pedophiliacs: Can it be done? *Clinical Psychology Review, 2,* 387–408.

Kempe, R. S., & Kempe, C. H. (1984). *The common secret of sexual abuse of children and adolescents*. New York: W. H. Freeman.

Kinsey, A., Pomeroy, W., Martin, C., & Gebhard, P. (1953). *Sexual behavior in the human female*. Philadelphia, PA: W. B. Saunders.

Langevin, R. (1983). *Sexual strands: Understanding and treating sexual anomalies in men*. Hillside, NJ: Erlbaum.

Levin, S. M., & Stava, L. (1987). Personality characteristics of sex offenders: A review. *Archives of Sexual Behavior, 16*, 1.

Mayer, A. (1983). *Incest: A treatment manual for therapy with victims, spouses and offenders*. Holmes Beach, FL: Learning Publications.

McQuire, R., Carlyle, J., & Young, B. (1965). Sexual deviations as conditioned behavior: A hypothesis. *Behaviour Research and Therapy, 2*, 185–190.

Meiselman, K. (1978). *Incest: A psychological study of causes and effects with treatment recommendations*. San Francisco: Jossey-Bass.

Mohr, R., Turner, R., & Jerry, J. (1964). *Pedophilia and exhibitionism*. Toronto: University of Toronto Press.

Mrazek, P. (1981). The nature of incest: A review of contributing factors. In P. Mrazek & H. Kempe (Eds.), *Sexually abused children and their families*. New York: Pergamon.

Murphy, W., & Barbaree, H. (1988). *Assessments of sexual offenders by measures of erectile response. Psychometric properties and decision making*. Unpublished manuscript prepared under contract with the National Institute of Mental Health (Order No. 86 M0506500501D).

National Center for Child Abuse and Neglect (NCCAN) (1981). *Study findings: National study of incidence and severity of child abuse and neglect*. Washington, DC: Department of Health, Education, and Welfare.

Paveza, G. (1988). Risk factors in father–daughter child sexual abuse. *Journal of Interpersonal Violence, 3*, 290–306.

Quinsey, V. (1977). The assessment and treatment of child molesters: A review. *Canadian Psychological Review, 18*, 204–220.

Rush, F. (1980). *The best kept secret: Sexual abuse of children*. Englewood Cliffs, NJ: Prentice-Hall.

Russell, D. (1983). The incidence and prevalence of intrafamilial and extrafamilial sexual abuse of female children. *Child Abuse and Neglect, 7*, 133–146.

Russell, D. (1984). The prevalence and seriousness of incestuous abuse: Stepfathers vs. biological fathers. *Child Abuse and Neglect, 8*, 15–22.

Stoller, R. (1979). *Sexual excitement*. New York: Pantheon Books.

Thorman, G. (1983). *Incestuous families*. Springfield, IL: Charles C Thomas.

Weinberg, S. K. (1955). *Incest behavior*. New York: Citadel Press.

CHAPTER 12

Perpetrators of Spouse Abuse

ALAN ROSENBAUM AND ROLAND D. MAIURO

Perhaps when more is known about batterers, we will need to view them also as victims.
Certainly those I have known did not commit their crimes without severe psychological distress.

L. E. A. WALKER (1979, p. xvii)

INTRODUCTION

In the past 15 years interest in all forms of domestic aggression has increased dramatically. Public awareness of the magnitude of spousal violence has provoked important changes in the social and legal responses to this problem. Shelters for abused women, often providing legal services, advocacy, social services, and therapy, can be found in almost every major population center. Services for batterers are less common, less well organized, and inadequately supported. This is not surprising given the stiff competition for the limited financial resources allotted to this population. Money spent treating batterers may be seen as money that will not be available to help victims. This is surprising, however, given the prevailing belief that the male batterer is largely, if not solely, responsible for spousal aggression. If this latter view is accepted, it follows that treatment of the batterer is essential to the reduction and elimination of this problem. It might be argued that treatment of batterers promotes the (some would say fallacious) belief that abusive marriages can and should be preserved. However, regardless of what one believes and despite the best advice from professionals, innumerable abusive relationships do continue; and further, even if they do not continue, it is likely that an untreated batterer will continue his aggressive behavior with subsequent partners. From this perspective, the plight of battered women can only be improved by treating batterers.

This chapter begins with a discussion of the characteristics that have been associated with batterers and some models for understanding aggression in intimate relationships. Many of these factors are already addressed by existing treatment programs. The remainder of the chapter will deal with the treatment of batterers, focusing on assessment, structure (group vs. individual vs. couples), issues addressed, techniques for aggression control, ethical issues, and outcome. It ends with suggestions of some relevant foci for future research and treatment.

The lack of carefully performed descriptive research on the abusive husband in early studies of domestic violence has given rise to stereotypic thinking regarding his traits and motives. Often portrayed as a sadistic tyrant who terrorizes and brutalizes his loved ones, causing pain and sometimes disfigurement, physical injury, or even death, he elicits little sympathy and much animosity. The sadistic tyrant exists, but is the typical abusive husband a sadistic tyrant? The sensationalistic examples, sufficiently violent to be newsworthy, are indeed nonfiction. To what degree, however, are they representative?

Early inquiries regarding the dynamics of marital violence* often focused on the "wife/victim" rather than on the "husband/perpetrator." The abused wife, having sought agency services or police assistance, often was a cooperative informant regarding the violent marriage. The abusive husband was rarely accessible. With the growth of programs for batterers, however, firsthand information about the characteristics of partner-abusive men has become available.

A danger in describing the typical batterer is that it conveys the message that batterers are a homogeneous group. It has become increasingly clear that they are not. Describing the characteristics that are associated with substantial percentages of batterers is more concordant with the belief that relationship aggression is multidetermined. Our knowledge of the characteristics of batterers is derived from the current research literature, consequently a preliminary caveat seems in order. The research literature on marital aggression, including that on male batterers, is inconsistent in methodology, sampling, and, not surprisingly, findings. Information obtained from samples of court-mandated men may not be consistent with that from self-referred samples. Dutton (1988) refers to this as "variation as a function of available sample." Similarly, information collected via self-report might conflict with that derived from observation, quantitative measures, or partner informants. Because a review of methodological considerations is beyond the scope of this chapter, the reader is referred to reviews by Rosenbaum (1988) and Hotaling and Sugarman (1986) for further elaboration of these issues. Further, we will not attempt to reconcile the inconsistencies in the literature other than to suggest that methodological and sampling differences probably account for much of the variance. These concerns notwithstanding, we will attempt to review some of the common features reported for domestically violent men.

*Throughout this chapter, the terms *marital violence, marital aggression, relationship aggression, spousal violence, wife abuse,* and numerous other combinations will be used interchangeably, as they generally are in the literature. Similarly, referring to the male as *husband* does not necessarily connote a married couple, because many batterers are not married. Variety in the choice of terminology has been employed to enhance readability.

CHARACTERISTICS OF PERPETRATORS

Exposure to Violence in Family of Origin

Exposure to violence in the batterer's family of origin is consistently associated with relationship aggression (Caesar, 1988; Hotaling & Sugarman, 1986; Rosenbaum & O'Leary, 1981). Batterers are often subjected to corporal punishment as children, by either or both parents (Kalmuss, 1984; Rosenbaum & O'Leary, 1981), and sometimes the label "child abuse" is retrospectively applied. Witnessing interparental aggression, however, appears to be more strongly correlated with subsequent marital aggression (Caesar, 1988; Hotaling & Sugarman, 1986; Kalmuss, 1984). These findings are consistent with a social learning approach that posits that aggression is learned from familial role models. There is, however, a question of "what" is being modeled, because as Kalmuss reported, violent husbands were as likely to have witnessed their mothers hitting their fathers as vice versa. It should also be emphasized that Caesar (1988) found that 38% of her sample had neither witnessed interparental aggression nor experienced physical abuse as children. Although strongly related, exposure to family violence does not appear to be a prerequisite for the perpetration of relationship aggression.

Sex Role and Self-Image

Rosenbaum (1986b) examined the sex-role identities of abusive males. It was hypothesized that abusers, lacking a stable sex-role identity, would display the media caricature of the "macho man," which often includes aggression. Instead, it was observed that abusers were more likely to have undifferentiated sex-role identities (i.e., scoring low in measures of both masculinity and femininity), a finding replicated by LaViolette, Barnett, and Miller (1984). Such findings suggest that inadequately or poorly developed identity, more than hypermasculine identity, may be associated with husband-to-wife violence.

Several studies have confirmed that abusers generally have defective self-images (Goldstein & Rosenbaum, 1985; Neidig, Friedman, & Collins, 1986). The "approval seeker," one of the four subgroups of batterers described by Elbow (1977), is purportedly motivated to his abusive behavior by defective self-esteem. Hotaling and Sugarman (1986) identified self-esteem as an inconsistent risk marker for husband-to-wife violence. However, in three of the five studies reviewed, the investigators reported a significant and negative relationship between the batterers' self-esteem and aggression. Furthermore, if Goldstein and Rosenbaum (1985) and Neidig et al. (1986) are added to the five studies included in the Hotaling and Sugarman (1986) review, the finding is supported in five of the seven studies. Interestingly, Goldstein and Rosenbaum (1985) also reported that abusers were significantly more likely than their nonaggressive counterparts to interpret their spouses' behavior as damaging to their self-esteem. This latter finding suggests that a cognitive mediational component specifically related to a vulnerable sense of self-esteem may be at work in the dynamics of marital aggression.

Verbal Skill Deficits

Several observers have suggested that the verbal skills of batterers are inferior to those of their wives (Ganley, 1981; Rounsaville, 1978) and that batterers may resort to aggression to compensate instrumentally for this deficit or as an affective response to frustration. Although general verbal skill deficits have yet to be demonstrated, several studies have shown abusers to have deficits in spouse-specific, verbal assertiveness (Dutton & Strachan, 1987; Maiuro, Cahn, & Vitaliano, 1986; Rosenbaum & O'Leary, 1981b). Moreover, these deficits have been demonstrated to be significantly related to aggressive tendencies (Maiuro, Cahn, & Vitaliano, 1986). Using a discriminant analysis, Dutton and Strachan (1987) report that high power needs (as assessed with the Thematic Apperception Test) in combination with low spouse-specific assertiveness correctly classified abusers and maritally conflicted males into their respective groups 90% of the time.

Psychopathology

The association of battering with known patterns of psychological disorder or psychopathology has a checkered history. In the forward to Gelles's (1972) early volume on the subject, Straus opined, "Individual (psycho) pathology is but a minor element," and "Few, if any, of the people he [Gelles] studied can be considered as suffering from any gross abnormality" (p. 16). However, in a comprehensive review of research conducted in the interim, Hotaling and Sugarman (1986) concluded that the data pointed toward serious and enduring patterns of maladjustment in batterers, with many cases appearing to evidence some form of personality disorder.

Hamberger and Hastings (1986) assessed a sample of batterers with a standardized measure of dysfunctional personality patterns, the Millon Clinical Multiaxial Inventory (MCMI) (Millon, 1983). The investigators identified three personality factors (schizoidal/borderline, narcissistic/antisocial, and dependent/compulsive), which they combined to yield "eight distinct and reliable subgroupings" of batterers (Hastings & Hamberger 1988, p. 32). Furthermore they report "discernible pathology" existed in all but 15% of their sample.

Hastings and Hamberger (1988) extended their study of personality disorder in batterers by including comparison groups of maritally satisfied and maritally discordant but nonviolent men. They reported that batterers scored significantly higher than nonbatterers in the areas of borderline personality disorder symptomatology and in negativistic, passive-aggressive tendencies.

Dysphoric symptoms were also significantly elevated in the batterer group. As previously reported by Caesar (1986), using the Minnesota Multiphasic Personality Inventory (MMPI), the authors were unable to discriminate batterers from a clinical sample of nonbatterers who were maritally discordant or in treatment for problems other than violence. Despite the presence of multiple elevations, Hastings and Hamberger also observed quite a bit of variance and heterogeneity within the batterer sample, as none of the mean MCMI scale scores exceeded the usual cutoff for clinical pathology.

In evaluating well over 1000 cases of domestic violence, Maiuro and his colleagues at the Harborview Anger Management Program report a broad spectrum of diagnosable profiles in batterers (Helping Angry and Violent People, 1987). In accord with the findings of previous investigators, they have found many cases meeting criteria for personality disorders. They have also observed various types of depression (Maiuro, Cahn, Vitaliano, Wagner, & Zegree, 1988), impulse control disorder, unresolved learning disabilities or attention deficit disorders, alcohol abuse (Maiuro, Vitaliano, Cahn, & Hall, 1987), cyclic mood or arousal disorders, adjustment reactions, organic personality syndromes, and, to a lesser extent, formal thought disorder. Despite the observed prevalence of such conditions, Maiuro has argued that domestically violent behavior is multiply determined and that psychopathology variables should be viewed as vulnerability factors rather than causal entities (Rosenbaum & Maiuro, 1989).

When taken together, current studies suggest that batterers as a group may demonstrate more psychopathology, particularly features of personality disorder, than the general population. However, given the multitude of problems described, there may not be a single, distinct, and replicable batterer profile. The retrospective nature of the research designs employed in these studies also raises questions regarding the directionality of some of the pathology relationships observed. In this regard, some aspects of batterers' clinical presentation may occur in response to the consequences of their behavior, or as a function of their course through the criminal-justice system. Other features, however, may be more long-standing and enduring, as well as indicative of more dysfunction in some cases than suggested by earlier reports.

Alcohol Abuse

As in other types of violence, alcohol abuse has been identified as a common feature of domestic violence cases. Although incidence rates vary widely depending on the sampling procedures employed, more common estimates range from about 40% to 50% (Byles, 1978; Fagan, Stewart, & Hansen, 1983; Gelles, 1972). Most clinicians believe that alcohol plays an important role in violent behavior, but the exact mechanisms remain unclear.

In a study of 393 couples planning to marry, O'Leary, Arias, Rosenbaum, and Barling (1985) found that alcohol abuse, measured by the Short Michigan Alcohol Screening Test, was significantly associated with physical aggression in both men and women. They further found that heavy drinkers endorsed more severe forms of physical assault than did light drinkers.

Kantor and Straus (1986) reviewed 15 studies reporting on the alcohol–wife abuse link. They generated incidence figures ranging from a low of 6% (Bard & Zacker, 1974) to a high of 85% (Roy, 1977). Only 6 studies provided statistical comparisons with a nonabusive sample and all 6 reported significantly more alcohol use among spouse abusers. However, Kantor and Straus (1986) examined drinking behavior at the time of violent incidents and found that in almost 74% of the incidents neither party had been drinking. In dividing their sample (the 1985 national probability sample of 4032 households) by level of alcohol use, they found rates of wife abuse by high and binge drinkers were 2.3 to 3 times higher than the rates for moderate drinkers. They also reported that 80% of the men in the high- and binge-drinking groups had not hit their wives at all during the year being examined.

Clearly, there is much alcohol abuse among spouse abusers and much wife abuse among alcohol abusers. However, it is also true that the large majority of spouse abusers do not drink prior to their violent episodes and that a large percentage of alcoholics are not violent toward their wives. Kantor and Straus (1986) concluded: "Alcohol use is associated with an increased probability of wife abuse, even though the linkage is neither necessary nor sufficient" (p. 13). In this regard, a recent study by Maiuro, Vitaliano, Cahn, and Hall (1987) compared domestically violent men who abused alcohol at the time of their offense to a demographically matched comparison group who did not abuse alcohol. Although some differences were found in the strength of the relationship between anger indices and aggressive behavior in these groups, both groups evidenced significant problems with anger, hostility, depression, and coping deficits in comparison to a nonviolent control group.

There are several ways to view the mechanism by which alcohol influences the occurrence of marital aggression. Chritchlow (1986) has suggested that the effect of alcohol ingestion on violence may be more psychologically and socioculturally bound than physiologically dictated. Alcohol is a known disinhibitor or releaser of all forms of constrained behavior, both appropriate (e.g., asking for a dance or a date) and inappropriate (e.g., violent attack). Alcohol intoxication may also function as a rationalization for socially undesirable behavior. Indeed, men in treatment groups often invoke alcohol use to disavow responsibility for their aggressiveness (Rosenbaum & Maiuro, 1989). This clinical observation is consonant with Gelles's (1972) early suggestion that substance abuse serves to excuse the violence. Alternatively, excessive alcohol use may trigger arguments regarding irresponsibility that eventuate in aggression and may interact with concurrent stressors (e.g., money spent on drink exacerbating financial problems or undermining employment).

Current Typologies

The growing base of both empirical data and clinical reports regarding the diversity of batterers has stimulated attempts to identify clinically meaning-ful, replicable subgroups of batterers. In an early attempt to develop a ty-pology, Elbow (1977) identified four subtypes—the controller, the defender, the approval seeker, and the incorporator. These subtypes were based on observation and have not been validated. Caesar (1986) also offered four subtypes: the exposed rescuer, the nonexposed altruist, the psychotic, and the tyrant. Caesar, however, employed a small sample ($N = 26$) and was unable to differentiate her subgroups on the basis of MMPI scores, relying instead on a content analysis of interview material (Dutton, 1988).

Gondolf (1988) advocates a behaviorally based, as opposed to personality based, typology of the batterer. Drawing on data collected at shelters for battered women, Gondolf employed a cluster analysis to classify three abuse variables (physical abuse, verbal abuse, and blame after abuse) and three antisocial variables (substance abuse, general violence, previous arrests). This resulted in a three-cluster solution, "two clusters (I and II) of severely abusive and extremely antisocial men (comprising 48% of the sample) and one cluster (III) of less severely abusive and minimally antisocial batterers (52%)" (p. 193). In addition to engaging in severe physical and verbal abuse of their wives, batterers in Groups I and II were characterized by general violence directed at a wide range of targets, including their children, and were significantly more likely than Group III batterers to have been arrested.

These findings are somewhat inconsistent with those of Hershorn (1986) who differentiated two groups of batterers, over- and undercontrolled (OH and UH, respectively), using the Megargee (1967) scale derived from the MMPI. He reported that OH batterers were more severely, but less fre-quently, violent than UH batterers. OH batterers were also less likely to fight with people other than their wives. UH batterers were generally more hostile, as assessed by the Buss-Durkee Hostility Inventory and were more likely to have witnessed interparental aggression in the family of origin. It should be noted that Hershorn assessed his constructs via standardized instruments completed by a sample of batterers attending a treatment pro-gram for marital aggression, whereas Gondolf based his study on data pro-vided about the batterers by their female victims.

The trend toward identifying subgroups of batterers based on a variety of personality, behavioral, biological, and background variables is promising. Profiles based on victim reports have suggested a power-oriented, tyrannical offender. Direct clinical assessments of domestically violent men have re-vealed at least three different profiles, only one of which is consistent with this portrayal (Dutton, 1988). Other features that appear to have growing empirical support include passive-aggressive and unassertive (Dutton & Stra-chan, 1987) and angry, hostile-dependent (Maiuro, Cahn, Vitaliano, Wagner, & Zegree, 1988). At the present time, the development of typologies is very much in progress. As investigators include different variables, access different samples, and utilize different analyses, understanding of these men will evolve considerably.

Dynamic Models

Batterers frequently attribute their behavior to provocation by their partner (Dutton, 1986b). This may take the form of physical aggression ("She hit me first"); verbal abuse, such as criticism, name calling, and nagging; offensive behavior, as in the wife's going out and drinking with a friend, inadequate mothering, or poor housekeeping; or disobedience, exemplified by refusal to have sex or failure to have dinner ready when requested. Remembering that provocation does not justify aggression, it may still be useful to examine the role of provocation. There is also mounting evidence that a significant proportion of the interspousal aggression is female-to-male. Makepeace (1981) reports equivalent rates for male-to-female and female-to-male aggression in dating populations. Several studies similarly report no differences in married populations (Straus, Gelles, & Steinmetz, 1980; Straus & Gelles, 1986). Recently, O'Leary et al. (1989) reported higher rates for female-to-male aggression than for the reverse in beginning marriages. Such findings are usually accompanied by legitimate disclaimers asserting that male-to-female aggression is more damaging (O'Leary, 1988) and that much of the female-to-male aggression is probably retaliatory. However, if the goal is to understand the dynamics of marital aggression, rather than to assign blame, then such findings should not be dismissed or discounted.

The importance of provocation in the dynamics of wife battering can be better appreciated by examining a more general theory of aggression. Bandura (1983) proposes that people have a neurophysiological capacity to behave aggressively, but do not do so without appropriate stimulation. Further, he asserts that this process is subject to cognitive control. Individuals can either exacerbate or mitigate anger by cognitive means. According to Dutton (1988), "Aggression is increased when we perceive the actions of others as intended to hurt us, as threatening to our self-esteem or as causing our own aversive arousal" (p. 15). Abusers may be particularly prone to view their partner's behavior as a threat to an already defective sense of self-worth. Bandura (1983) also suggests that individuals can prolong anger arousal or regenerate anger that may have already subsided through rumination on anger-provoking thoughts. This is consistent with the reports of batterers who say that they have difficulty "letting go" of a perceived insult from their partners.

Zillman (1983) describes a linear relationship between provocation and aggression in which stronger provocations are more highly arousing and produce more intense aggressive behavior. He proposes that, at very high levels, hostile and aggressive behaviors become impulsive in that they "become behaviors composed of learned reactions associated with great habit strength" (p. 94). At very high levels of arousal cognitive control of behavior becomes impaired. Possibly, this is what abusers are referring to when they describe themselves as "losing control" during a violent incident. This also is consistent with their claim to be "out of control," even though their behavior seems not to be, as evidenced by there typically being clear limits and constraints on the behavior (e.g., they usually do not seriously hurt or kill their wives, typically do not engage in abusive behaviors in the presence of others, and can sometimes delay the aggression). Bandura (1983) argues that the form of the aggressive behavior is acquired through learning. Thus, abusers, who have learned spousal aggression in their families of origin (behaviors that may have acquired substantial habit strength), might resort to this type of behavior when highly aroused.

Consistent with this model, factors that reduce impulse control (e.g., alcohol) would increase the probability of aggression by lowering the level of arousal necessary to shift control to "automatic pilot." Neurological factors might represent another relevant factor. Dorothy Lewis and her colleagues (Lewis et al., 1986, 1988) have reported a strong relationship between head injury and generalized aggression in both juvenile and adult violent offenders. Rosenbaum and Hoge (1989) assessed the occurrence of severe head injury in the medical histories of 31 wife batterers, and found that 19 (61.3%) reported having experienced a head injury severe enough to have produced a loss of consciousness or to have been diagnosed as a concussion.

Other dynamic models that appear to have merit include the cognitive-behavioral formulations of Bandura (1983) and Zillman (1983). An adaptation of these formulations to the case of the batterer might include the following dynamics: The batterer is subjectively provoked (perceives or interprets some aspect of his partner's behavior as somehow threatening to himself or his self-esteem). He engages in self-talk that engenders a sense of injustice and anger (e.g., "She's not home yet," "She knows damn well when I get home and just doesn't care"). He responds to the instigating events by cognitively exacerbating his anger through self-talk that further fans the flames of his emotional reactivity ("She's probably spending time with somebody else, probably some other guy"). Spouse-specific assertion deficits reduce the probability that he will confront his wife with his feelings of insecurity, jealousy, and upset. This skill deficit, in turn, deprives his partner of the opportunity to clarify the facts or reassure him ("Sorry I'm late but the car broke down"). Narcissistic, borderline, or hostile-dependent personality traits further magnify the reaction to the perceived injury to irrational proportions. Arousal increases to the point where behavior becomes difficult to control, and the batterer impulsively resorts to aggression. The specific abusive behavior may have been learned in the family of origin. It may be further reinforced by past experiences wherein the aggression had the desired effects of punishing the perceived wrongdoer and forcibly demanding a preferred behavior.

Although this formulation still requires much in the way of empirical validation and may only be applicable to a subsample of the total population of batterers, the foci and strategies for intervention suggested are remarkably similar to those that characterize many existing treatment programs.

ASSESSMENT AND TREATMENT

Although differing profiles may result in part from differences in the ideology, methodology, and the sampling procedures used by investigators, they also reflect the complex etiology and multifaceted nature of this type of assault (Rosenbaum & Maiuro, 1989). Whatever the theoretical and classification schemes used for describing and explaining the phenomena, the professional must eventually assume a problem-oriented approach in treating marital violence. The following sections discuss some of the basic issues involved in assessing and treating domestically violent men.

The Clinical Interview

Effective management of the domestic violence case requires in-depth knowledge of the circumstances surrounding the request for treatment, the current relationship of the abuser to recent or potential victims, a comprehensive history of the client's experience with abuse and violence, an assessment of vulnerability factors that increase the likelihood of further violent behavior, and current sources of social support. Whether an individual seeks treatment on a voluntary basis or is among the increasing number of cases that are court referred for domestic assault (Finn, 1987), it is not uncommon for individuals to feel distressed and ambivalent about their need for help. Sufficient time must be allowed for the offender to overcome the discomfort associated with sharing socially undesirable acts and attitudes. It may take a number of visits before sufficient trust is established between the intake worker and the client, and a multiple-stage assessment process should be considered.

It is important for the clinician to know about the client's source of motivation for seeking help (e.g., court, family, personal dissatisfaction), potential stressors or impending losses, and the consequences associated with the violent and abusive behavior (e.g., divorce, separation, reconciliation, access to children, fines, legal proceedings, conditions of probation). Although some therapists may use such information to help determine amenability to their particular approach or program, there is currently little data to suggest that these variables have predictive power regarding outcome in the individual case. They do, however, appear to be useful in alerting the clinician to areas that may require further assessment, case management, clarification regarding client expectations, and strategies to overcome treatment resistance and compliance problems.

Whether the wife is to be actively involved in the treatment process, it is important to involve her in the assessment stage. As pointed out by Jouriles and O'Leary (1985), descriptions of problems, and estimates of their frequency and severity, will often vary between husband and wife. Depending on the informant and the nature of the relationship (e.g., husband-to-wife assault only versus mutual violence), the wife may be a more reliable source for describing the violence because she is on the receiving end of the punches, pushes, and blows. Some clinicians believe that the memory of perpetrators may be impaired or limited during periods of extreme rage and that this adds to the risk of underreporting already created by psychological defensiveness and social undesirability (Elliot, 1976). In addition, it is essential to establish contact with the spouse for purposes of assessing and monitoring dangerousness. It should be noted that many cases of spousal abuse also involve child abuse (Rosenbaum & O'Leary, 1981a), making knowledge of parenting practices as well as the ages, number of, and accessibility to children important for the clinician.

A thorough history of violent behavior is perhaps the most essential component of the intake process. This assessment should include developmental history related to violence and abuse in the client's family of origin, including an account of the batterer's own victimization experiences. A personal history of physical abuse, sexual abuse, psychological abuse, and observation of abuse between parents have all been linked to spousal assault in later life (Caesar, 1988).

Men who batter commonly have histories of other aggressive and criminal acts that may or may not have been adjudicated and documented by law enforcement officials. For this reason, it is also important to ask a full range of questions pertaining to the assault of nonintimates outside the family, motor vehicle violations, as well as drug- and alcohol-related incidents such as driving while intoxicated. Such information can be useful in determining how generalized and ingrained the impulse control problems are in a given case.

In recent years increased attention has been given to the role of individual vulnerability factors as contributing elements to domestic violence episodes. The preceding review of the various types of psychopathology sometimes observed with these cases should alert the clinician to the complexity of this problem and the value of going beyond a simple behavioral approach. Such data suggest the need for broad-based assessment and a multidisciplinary approach to intervention in many cases of domestic violence.

Assessment of Dangerousness

During the past decade various court decisions have underscored and broadened the therapist's duty to protect potential victims from violence-prone clients (Gross, Southard, Lamb, & Weinberger, 1987; Sonkin & Ellison, 1986). *Tarasoff v. Regents of the University of California* (1976) established the need to act in cases in which a specific threat is made toward an identifiable victim. *Jablonski by Pahls v. United States* (1983) extended this duty to include situations in which the client behaves or is judged to be potentially dangerous regardless of a specific threat toward another. The need to protect was further expanded to include unintended victims who might be situationally at risk by virtue of proximity to a potential victim such as children, other family members, and friends (*Hedlund v. Superior Court of Orange County*, 1983). Although these court rulings have stimulated considerable debate among professionals regarding the practical limitations and therapeutic complications associated with such decisions, they have been generally supported by a variety of legal (e.g., Parker's Evidence Code of California, 1986) and ethical statutes (American Psychological Association Committee on Legal Issues, 1985). These statutes explicitly limit the privilege of confidentiality in such matters and, in some cases, obligate the clinician to take a variety of specific actions to help safeguard victims.

There is a consensus among mental health professionals that it is beyond the expertise and capability of any therapist to absolutely predict violence in the individual case (American Psychological Association Committee on Legal Issues, 1985). However, it is important for all clinicians dealing with marital violence to be familiar with the factors that increase or decrease the likelihood of such acts. Knowledge of such factors can permit the therapist to take prudent action to help protect potential victims, the client, and the community.

Studies of homicide have indicated that a history of previous physical abuse precedes lethal acts of violence in most cases (Bourdouris, 1971). In a review of current clinical knowledge related to assessments of dangerousness, Monahan (1982) stressed the importance of considering historical and demographic variables as well as current mental status and situational variables.

By definition, all marital violence cases have some history of violent behavior as the core of their presenting problem. Therefore, clinical protocols are typically directed at identifying risk factors for serious forms of injury. It is important to ask questions focused on frequency, severity, and nature of injuries associated with previous violent episodes, specific intent to harm, and the availability of weapons. A number of investigators have also found similarities in the emotional state of suicidal and homicidal men (Maiuro, O'Sullivan, Michael, & Vitaliano, 1989), indicating the need to ask about the history of suicide in the family, personal attempts, threats, and ideation. Walker (1979) found domestically violent men to be at particularly high risk for suicide after battering incidents in which the woman exits the relationship. Alcohol or substance abuse has been associated with violent episodes of longer duration on the part of offenders and greater vulnerability in victims (Virkkunen, 1974). In comparing cases in which marital homicide had occurred (female to male) in comparison to abuse only cases, Browne (1984) found all of the preceding factors to be useful in distinguishing the two groups. Browne also found that actual or threatened instances of forced sexual activity to be associated with increased likelihood of lethal outcomes.

There is, as yet, no scientific formula for determining when a client has crossed the threshold into the realm of dangerousness. It remains a matter of clinical judgment guided by experience and knowledge of the research literature on interpersonal violence. Recent escalation of any of the preceding variables should lead a clinician to consider a case to be in the high-risk category for future violence. All instances in which a previous or potential victim expresses acute concern about her safety should be taken seriously. In fact, studies indicate that given the stakes in such matters, most clinicians err on the side of taking precautions (Wise, 1978).

As in other matters related to treatment, client accountability is critical to the assessment of dangerousness. Open discussion of the matter with the client is encouraged to ascertain whether the client feels in enough control to assure the therapist that he will not be violent. Some clinicians formalize this process by having the client enter into a "nonviolence contract" as is commonly done in cases of suicidal ideation. Special concern is warranted in cases where clients demonstrate that they are grossly unreliable in their reporting, acutely depressed, or fixated or obsessed with controlling or getting even with their spouse in a "no way out" or "exit blocking" fashion. To enhance personal support and ensure a thorough review of pertinent issues, many professionals and agencies recommend that therapists develop a policy of consulting with colleagues or supervisors when questions of dangerousness arise. Careful record keeping with respect to data base and contacts made is essential to document that the duty to protect has been handled responsibly and within the scope of professional standards.

Treatment Considerations

Over the years a variety of community-based and institution-based intervention programs have appeared for men who batter (see Eddy & Myers, 1984; Jennings, 1987). Although developed, to some extent, with different ideologies, many of the programs share some common goals and components. Specialized treatment programs for men who batter all have the primary goal and focus of eliminating violent behavior and abusive interchanges. Through one method or another they attempt to (a) increase the clients' awareness, appreciation, and accountability for their acts; (b) enhance the clients' ability to identify and manage the attitudes and emotions that are associated with violent behavior; (c) decrease social isolation and provide a supportive milieu for change; (d) decrease unhealthy, hostile-dependent relationships; and (e) develop nonviolent and constructive conflict resolution skills.

Group Treatment

Most specialized programs for maritally violent men utilize group therapy approaches. Although there have been no comparative studies of efficacy across treatment modality, a number of advantages can be identified for group methods. Social isolation has been cited as a risk factor for domestic violence (Hotaling & Sugarman, 1986; Straus, 1980). Treatment groups can provide a structured form of peer support and a safe place for violence-prone men to ventilate acute concerns (Lion, Christopher, & Madden, 1977). Many therapists have also recognized the confrontive value of groups for male offenders of various types (Bernard & Bernard, 1984). When support-ively guided by a trained therapist, such confrontation can be useful in identifying and modifying interpersonal insensitivity, cognitive distortions, and the type of minimization and denial often evidenced by maritally violent men. Group modalities also allow for a variety of vicarious learning expe-riences. Being a resistant population, some members will be slow to engage in treatment and can benefit from the desensitization and multiple exposures to group exercises provided by other men.

Because a group comprises peers with similar problems, the group format also provides exposure to "coping" models in addition to therapist "mas-tery" models (Meichenbaum, 1971). Coping models, who begin with a variety of fears and failings and then progressively gain skills and positive social judgments, can surpass mastery models in social influence (Kazdin, 1973; Meichenbaum, 1971). The use of coping models may be particularly relevant in the case of batterers, as some may have generalized conflicts with au-thority figures (Fagan, Stewart, & Hansen, 1983). Moreover, those men who present with a "macho" identity may require the social support of other aggressive males in order to let go of their defenses and consider alternatives to their psychological and behavioral weaponry.

Another attribute of group interventions relates to economy and efficiency of service delivery. Although domestic violence occurs across all socioeco-nomic levels, a large proportion of cases come from low socioeconomic strata (Hotaling & Sugarman, 1986; Straus, Gelles, & Steinmetz, 1980). By offering relatively less expensive group services, the therapist can decrease financial barriers to treatment for clients who lack comprehensive health insurance, have modest incomes, or partial employment. A related issue deals with the sheer magnitude of marital violence as a problem. Survey statistics suggest that at least 12% of American wives experience some form of violence from their mates in any given year, with approximately 4% reporting *serious* forms of assault, such as being punched, kicked, beaten with an object, or assaulted with a weapon (Straus et al., 1980). Even though individualized services may be indicated in some cases, such prevalence rates demand efficient service delivery methods to accommodate the needs of the community.

Group Treatment Parameters

Little program evaluation research exists to indicate the effect of various group treatment parameters on outcome (Ptacek, 1984). There is consider-able variability in the structure of men's groups (Rosenbaum, 1986a), with some being open-ended and some closed-ended, and the number of sessions ranging from as few as 5 or 6 to as many as 50 or more. Recognizing the resistant and ingrained nature of many batterers' problems, a variety of programs set a minimum length of treatment at approximately 6 months (Sonkin, 1988) but allow for more extended treatment as indicated. Many clinicians believe that time-limited treatment enhances compliance in that it is more predictable and less vague than open-ended models.

Psychoeducational approaches are commonly employed by treatment programs for batterers. Such programming is congruent with the current popularity of cognitive-behavioral strategies (Novaco, 1975) and the application of social learning principles to violent behavior during recent years (Bandura, 1973). It tends to be highly structured and directive in nature and well suited for clients with impulse control problems. Some practitioners also feel that psychoeducational programming is less threatening to clients than traditional process-oriented therapy. It is generally couched in the idiom of competence and self-fulfillment (educational classes, personal growth workshops) rather than illness or pathology and, thus, may facilitate the entry of clients who might otherwise be reluctant to seek services (Gondolf, 1985a; Womack, Maiuro, Russo, & Vitaliano, 1983). Depending on the treatment setting and availability of specialized staff, psychoeducational programming may be offered alone or in conjunction with a comprehensive array of other psychological, medical, and psychiatric services (Rosenbaum & Maiuro, 1989).

Some clinicians have advocated the use of a male-female coleader team for group treatment of batterers (Helping Angry and Violent People, 1987; Rosenbaum & Maiuro, 1989). This leadership structure serves several purposes. Because the primary referral problem involves violence toward women, it is important to draw out and observe the men's reactions to female figures. The presence of both a male and female leader can sometimes reveal a pattern of differential responding in the participants that can be used for diagnostic and therapeutic purposes.

From a process perspective, the coleaders can also provide a model of a couple in which power is shared and negotiated. Care must be taken to ensure that the coleaders model an egalitarian relationship, taking turns starting and ending sessions, sharing duties within the group, and participating equally. The use of a female coleader also provides a model of a woman in a professional role. This role stands in contrast to the narrow or negative opinion that some batterers have of women and helps them to confront these destructive attitudes. Additionally, the presence of a female coleader can short-circuit the development of an "all male" camaraderie that sometimes reinforces sex role rigidity and "macho" attitudes toward violence and victimization.

Specific Treatment Techniques

Dealing with Anger

Recent studies suggest that maritally violent men have major difficulties identifying and regulating angry affect (Maiuro et al., 1988). As a result, most specialized programs include some form of anger management training as a core component of the treatment process (Feazell, Mayers, & Deschner, 1984). This programming may use standard cognitive-behavioral strategies advocated by Novaco (1975), multimodal interventions that utilize psychological assessment (Maiuro, Vitaliano, & Cahn, 1987), and videotape technology (Maiuro, Eberle, Muscatel, & Donovan, 1981) to enhance the client's self-awareness and appreciation of these issues (Helping Angry and Violent People, 1987).

The basic aim of anger management techniques is to help clients recognize and short-circuit an aggressive response in the early stages of arousal. Clients are typically taught a variety of cognitive, behavioral, and physiological signals related to anger and impending loss of control. Discrimination training helps clients differentiate their emotional response (anger, frustration, threat) from their behavioral response or expression (verbal abuse, violent tirade).

Effective intervention with anger problems in maritally violent men is often a difficult and time-consuming process. Angry affect may be covered and distorted by a variety of defense mechanisms including denial, minimization, suppression, repression, and isolation. Once identified and acknowledged, expressions of anger, even abusive forms, are often justified through processes of externalization ("She made me do it"), projection ("She's the one with the problem"), and/or lack of alternative skills ("What else could I do?").

Anger reactions in many batterers appear to be deeply ingrained traits (Maiuro et al., 1988) that are experienced as "automatic" or reflexive reactions. Cognitive restructuring techniques such as Ellis's ABC model of emotional response can be useful in pinpointing the self-generated components of an anger response (Ellis, 1977). Having the client repeatedly record and examine the antecedent events and the mediating appraisals or beliefs that are associated with his emotional response can help foster the development of self-control strategies.

Early workers in the field emphasized the power and control that can be derived from angry, threatening, and violent acts (Dutton & Strachan, 1987; Gondolf, 1985b). In this manner, angry and violent behavior can be inadvertently reinforced by fear-induced deference and compliance on the part of the spouse, becoming habitual and recurrent in nature. From a client-centered perspective, it is often useful to acknowledge rather than condemn the apparent short-term "benefits" of anger and aggressive posturing. This understanding can then be used to provide a framework for comprehending the negative and damaging consequences of such behavior for themselves (e.g., dislike, alienation, criminal record, possible abandonment) as well as loved ones (e.g., physical and emotional injury, pathological modeling for children).

Clinicians working with domestically violent males have long recognized the tendency to immediately transform feelings of hurt, insecurity, and fear into anger and violence (Ganley, 1981; Sonkin & Durphy, 1982). In this way anger may be used to mask a variety of other feelings related to threat and vulnerability. Moreover, the powerful surge of adrenaline experienced during an angry and violent tirade can dissipate feelings of hurt and helplessness and result in a vicious and addictive cycle of dyscontrol. Some programs (Helping Angry and Violent People, 1987; Sonkin & Durphy, 1982) employ a variety of structured exercises (feeling journals, videotaped scenarios and discussion) to help spouse abusers recognize and label a more flexible range of emotions and feelings. These exercises are designed to help the men develop alternatives to anger and to desensitize them to emotions that may have been socially or developmentally counterconditioned (e.g., hurt, sadness) or anxiety provoking (e.g., fear, jealousy, insecurity).

Relaxation and Arousal Reduction Techniques

Intense arousal can interfere with higher cortical functioning (Mandler, 1984) and interpersonal problem solving during stressful encounters (Janis, 1974). Clients can be taught a variety of arousal reduction strategies such as progressive muscle relaxation, imagery, and deep breathing exercises. Other clients may employ more naturalistic techniques such as going for a walk or listening to soothing music. Such "self-control" techniques can help increase the probability that the client will be in a state of body and mind that is conducive to good communication and rational problem solving.

There are also a number of strategies that clients can use in vivo during conflict situations. Rosenbaum (1986a) suggests employing techniques that decrease nonverbal aspects of aggressive posturing in spouses. Behaviors incompatible with physical violence are encouraged, such as sitting down rather than standing up during an argument, leaning back rather than looming forward, using the telephone rather than "in person" encounters during times of intense conflict, and speaking softly rather than yelling when disagreement develops. Although these strategies may initially appear as gimmicks or quick fixes to deeper problems, they can be useful adjuncts when establishing interpersonal contracts or conflict protocols to limit the likelihood of recurring violence early in treatment.

"Time-Out" Training

Studies of interpersonal problem solving between abusers and their mates indicate that a form of "negative reciprocity" often occurs that personalizes and escalates the conflict rather than resolves it (Deschner, 1984; Margolin, John, & Gleberman, 1988). In those cases where the spouse is available and willing to participate in the abuser's treatment (and such involvement is not contraindicated by basic safety concerns), training both partners in the appropriate use of "time-out" techniques can be useful. Utilizing such techniques is particularly important during those phases of treatment when other self-control skills are not well developed, or in the inevitable situation when conflict resolution skills may be tested and overwhelmed. Careful attention must be given to avoid the possibility that the technique will be used in a passive-aggressive fashion to cut off or ignore the partner's concerns. This strategy provides a behavioral safety valve to decrease the likelihood of continued abuse and an opportunity for dearousal to promote rational problem solving.

Sonkin and Durphy (1982) have summarized the time-out procedure as the systematic application of the following steps:

1. The abuser recognizes cues that signal the presence of intense anger.
2. He assertively states that he needs to take a time-out or simply makes a "T" sign with his hands without speaking.
3. He leaves the house for a specified period of time (up to 1 hour) to "cool off" and collect his thoughts. (Some practitioners suggest seeking the social support of a friend or group member, although drinking, driving, or going to a bar or tavern are all discouraged.)
4. He returns home at the specified time, to reestablish contact, rebuild trust, and discourage avoidance as a coping strategy.
5. He "checks in" and calmly states and discusses the issue related to his anger.

Changing Cognitions and Attitudes

Spouse abusers often experience distorted views and attitudes toward their partners and the act of violence that precipitated their entry into treatment. Dehumanizing attitudes and labels for victims (e.g., "bitch," "the little woman," "dumb broad," "a woman's place is . . .") that result from sex role stereotypes and objectification, or "thinging," must be confronted. The abuser needs to be educated regarding the hostile dynamics and violence-facilitating properties of such attitudes and behavior.

A variety of strategies can be employed to deal with sexist and dehumanizing attitudes and cognitions. At the most basic level, one can focus on the client's language structure or attributions. Language targeting the person or negatively labeling the woman's personality as the problem must be identified as an ineffective and conflict-escalating pattern of behavior. The clinician must help the client break the habit of "name calling" in favor of focusing on specific problem behaviors.

The therapist can also confront these issues through evocative techniques. Some practitioners use educational films and female speakers from shelters and victim agencies, or have abused women participate in the group to help discuss and confront these issues (Gondolf, 1985a). The women's firsthand, personal accounts of abusive and harassing experiences can have a dramatic effect on the mindset of a group of abusing men. The therapeutic group provides a unique and safe setting in which women can relate the pain and degradation of being on the receiving end of such attitudes and helps engender a sense of empathy for the victim.

Many maritally violent men not only need to examine their attitudes toward women but also toward themselves. Abusers are frequently saddled with traditional, patriarchal notions that men should be dominant, omniscient, omnipotent, and infallible. Such distorted views of the husband's role in a marital relationship sometimes compel the batterer to fulfill unrealistic expectations. Batterers typically are unable to ask their wives for help with tasks that they feel are "the man's job." They may believe that it is a sign of weakness or failure to be wrong in front of one's family, and even worse to admit being wrong in an argument with one's spouse. As in the case of other self-defeating cognitive beliefs, a rational-emotive approach (Ellis, 1977) may be helpful in uncovering these thought patterns. The clinician may also lead the man to examine the socially destructive, growth-limiting aspects of a stereotypic male role (Gondolf, 1985a), as well as the increased health risks associated with male-dominant behavior patterns (Goldberg, 1976).

Communications and Assertion Training

A number of clinicians have identified a lack of assertive skills as an area of dysfunction in domestically violent men (Ganley, 1981; Saunders, 1984; Sonkin, Martin, & Walker, 1985; Steinmetz, 1977). In an empirical study, Rosenbaum and O'Leary (1981b) reported that abusive husbands were less able to assert themselves to their wives than nonviolent husbands in maritally conflicted or maritally satisfied relationships. Maiuro, Cahn, and Vitaliano (1986) similarly found maritally aggressive men to have assertiveness deficits. Their research indicated that skill deficits were particularly notable in the area of request behavior including the expression of needs and wants in a positive and growth-oriented fashion. They also demonstrated that assertiveness deficits were significantly and inversely related to the amount of anger and aggression that the men expressed.

A wealth of resource materials exists for helping spouse abusers develop better assertiveness skills (Alberti & Emmons, 1982; Lange & Jakubowski, 1976). In our experience, the assertiveness deficits fall into two general domains: skill deficits and discrimination problems in which the individual confuses assertiveness with aggressiveness. Skill deficits can stem from a lack of cognitive skills for implementing the behavior or from performance anxiety resulting in an inhibition or avoidance of the behavior. These deficits can be addressed with a variety of techniques including bibliotherapy (providing reading assignments defining, describing, and legitimatizing assertive behavior, as in Mantooth, Geffner, Franks, & Patrick, 1987), therapist modeling, role-play methods, and videotaped feedback focused on discrimination training in noncoercive and nonabusive communication styles.

Adjunctive Treatment Strategies

Individual Treatment

Although group therapy formats are preferred by many clinicians, there are circumstances in which individual intervention modalities may be appropriate. As described earlier, many assessment issues involve the collection of detailed information in an individualized fashion. Acute concerns regarding dangerousness to self or others usually require more intensive intervention on a one-to-one basis. The clinician should also be prepared to deal with issues of trust, defensiveness, and resistance in a maximally supportive fashion. This may require individualized services to avoid premature termination or dropout, especially in cases where the client is voluntarily seeking services, is well known in the community, and is concerned about further damage to his reputation and family.

However, the choice of individual versus group methods need not be an either-or decision for the clinician. A number of investigators have found that offering individualized "pregroup" sessions can enhance the efficacy and impact of group programming (Helping Angry and Violent People, 1987; Yalom, Houts, Newell, & Rand, 1967). It can be useful for clarifying client expectations, allaying fears regarding faulty perceptions and myths surrounding group therapy, and for presenting models of expected client behavior. In an empirical study, Yalom, Peters, Sheldon, and Rand (1967) found that group therapy participants who had received such attention often engaged in the group process more quickly and were less likely to drop out of treatment prematurely.

Conjoint Couples Counseling

There are a number of issues to consider before selecting conjoint therapy as a treatment modality in marital violence. The considerations differ significantly from routine marital therapy in that the subject matter goes far beyond simple enhancement of a relationship. Marital violence involves criminal assault and life-threatening acts, and it requires careful assessment and screening, specialized treatment strategies, and constant monitoring by the clinician. Prior to accepting a case for couples treatment, Rosenbaum and O'Leary (1986) have suggested that a formal evaluation be conducted to determine whether (a) the wife is safe, (b) the wife is aware and informed of alternative interventions, and (c) rehabilitation of the marriage is viable given the dynamics of the relationship and the tools available to the clinician.

Because of the damaging effects of battering, not all clients will have a spouse available or willing to enter therapy. Even in cases where the spouse is willing and available, couples therapy is not always recommended or indicated. Care must be taken to avoid mislabeling the man's violence as a couple's problem, thus blaming the victim for her own abuse. Although marital discord is a couple's problem, the husband must assume responsibility for serious forms of physical violence in the majority of cases. Even in those cases where violence is reciprocal, care must be taken to recognize that many women may react in self-defense (Pleck, Pleck, Grossman, & Bart, 1978). On the other hand, some researchers have suggested that mutually occurring violence is more common than previously indicated in the literature (O'Leary & Arias, in press; Steinmetz & Lucca, 1987) and that certain aspects of treatment for the husband (e.g., time-out techniques) can be more effective if the spouse is involved (Rosenbaum & Maiuro, 1989).

Some practitioners advocate treating the batterer's aggression prior to considering couples counseling (Rosenbaum & Maiuro, 1989). This clearly sends the message that the aggression is the man's problem and that he must deal with it before any marital reconciliation can be attempted. It also allows time for the wife to make decisions about whether she wishes to remain in the relationship. If she decides to remain, the additional time also provides a margin of safety because it gives the therapist(s) an opportunity to assess whether the aggression is controlled sufficiently to permit conjoint therapy.

Informed consent for couples treatment also necessitates a frank discussion of the potential benefits and drawbacks of such an intervention, along with the alternatives available to the wife (e.g., women's shelter programs, divorce mediation, legal advocacy). The clinician is advised to assume a public health role in such cases and to become acquainted with existing shelter and advocacy programs for victims of domestic violence. This role should include being prepared to encourage the wife to have her husband arrested if further abuse occurs. Many specialists feel that the best outcomes are obtained through a combination of criminal-justice and rehabilitative interventions (Ganley, 1981; Rosenbaum & Maiuro, 1989). In a controlled test of the effects of arrest on spousal abuse, Sherman and Berk (1984) concluded that arrest was a more effective deterrent than brief separation or counseling of the couple.

A number of treatment models have been proposed for conjoint therapy (Deschner, 1984; Harbin, 1977; Margolin, 1979; Neidig & Friedman, 1984). As in the case of treatments primarily focused on the male batterer, the primary objective is to stop the abuse. The specific strategies are similar to those employed in treating the batterer alone and include having the violent spouse assume responsibility for his aggressive acts, having both parties agree that physical aggression is not a legitimate response to conflict and that it will not be tolerated, and developing nonviolent and less destructive behaviors such as problem-solving skills for resolving conflict. The dyadic and interactional nature of marital approaches also permits direct observation and intervention with communication patterns that are associated with emotional escalation and violent episodes.

The unique aspect of a couples approach lies in the opportunity to identify spouse-specific interactional cycles associated with rising tempers and abuse. Both partners can help identify cues in themselves and each other that violence on the part of the man may be imminent. The negative aspects of the relationship can be countered with positive strategies directed at enhancing sharing feelings and responsibilities, increasing intimacy, and strengthening mutual support systems (Bedrosian, 1982).

Alcohol Abuse Rehabilitation

The available evidence suggests that alcohol abuse is neither a necessary or sufficient condition for violent behavior. When carefully questioned, the majority of alcohol-abusing men acknowledge that they also have been violent while not under the influence of alcohol (Sonkin, Martin, & Walker, 1985). Nonetheless, in those cases in which it is presented, it appears to exacerbate preexisting impulse control and emotional problems, increase the likelihood of more serious injury (Coleman, 1980), and cloud responsibility and accountability for behavior.

If a domestically violent man is indeed an alcohol or drug abuser, he needs specialized treatment for *both* spousal abuse and substance abuse. Uncontrolled or abusive drinking can severely disrupt the therapy process, and attention to this problem prior or concomitant to treatment for battering should be considered. In either case, it is a good idea to establish ground rules prohibiting attendance at sessions (group, couple, or individual) while under the influence. As in the case of the primary presenting problem of violent behavior, alcohol abuse patterns may be ingrained and habitual. Indeed, many batterers report that their fathers were alcoholic. In such cases, long-term support programs (e.g., Alcoholics Anonymous, groups for adult children of alcoholics), may be helpful in sustaining gains made in the course of treatment.

Treatment Outcome

Treating batterers can be a frustrating endeavor, but it can also be extremely rewarding. Dropout rates are high. In her literature review, Russell (1988) reported dropout rates ranging from one third to two thirds for nonmandated populations. Despite the presence of court intervention and probationary monitoring, many court-mandated cases will also discontinue treatment. Long-term prospects for continued nonviolence are uncertain. Although reported success rates at follow-up are frequently in the range of 70% to 84% (Dutton, 1986a; Edleson & Grusznski, 1988; Rosenbaum & Maiuro, 1989), there is great variability in the length of the follow-up interval, outcome criteria, and the source of the data employed in such studies.

Should reductions in aggression be considered a successful outcome? Citing problems in the scaling of severity, the equating of severity and frequency, and a lack of evidence that certain quantitative differences result in substantive behavioral change, Rosenbaum (1986a) has argued that elimination of aggression be the standard. Mantooth et al. (1987), on the other hand, feel that violence and abuse reduction may be a more realistic outcome than total elimination of such behavior. Such an argument may have merit in view of the developing nature of the therapeutic technology in this area.

The length of the follow-up interval is also relevant to definitions of success. Purdy and Nickle (1981) employed a 6-month follow-up, Edleson et al. (1985) reported outcome after 4 months, and Maiuro, Cahn, Vitaliano, and Zegree (1987) presented follow-up data 1 year after termination of treatment. Rosenbaum and O'Leary (1986) recommended a minimum 6-month interval to compensate for the "honeymoon" period that often accompanies participation in treatment and for the violence-free periods of several months that are common, even in untreated populations. These issues and other methodological concerns are discussed more fully by Geffner, Rosenbaum, and Hughes (1988) and Rosenbaum (1988).

SUMMARY AND FUTURE DIRECTIONS

Numerous issues and questions remain that suggest future research directions. Further descriptive work is needed in defining the broad range of violent men currently described as spouse abusers. The batterers that many clinicians see in treatment may not be the same men that are being described by battered women in shelters. It is likely that some subtypes are untreatable by existing technologies and are best handled by the criminal-justice system, without the expenditure of mental health resources. However, the available data suggest that a major proportion of spouse abusers are not callous, sadistic thugs who enjoy beating women. They are often unhappy men, dissatisfied and ashamed of their behavior, who wish they could undo the damage they have inflicted on their families and themselves. They are frequently victims of abusive, alcoholic fathers, and abused, ineffectual mothers, who are trapped in a repetitive cycle in which violence is transmitted and passed on to those with whom they have the most intimate contact. As relative newcomers to evaluation and treatment, they constitute an important national health priority and are worthy of our attention.

Preliminary outcome studies are encouraging, and treatment of batterers and aggressive couples continues, as it should. However, studies comparing the various treatment configurations have not been performed. What is the best treatment? Under what conditions is treatment of couples desirable, effective, safe, or unsafe? What are the key ingredients or components? Can various subtypes of batterers and relationships be effectively matched to different treatments?

Much work also remains in defining and delineating the mechanisms involved in spouse abuse. Although a host of cognitive and attitudinal processes have been implicated in wife battering, there have been few direct assessments of the cognitions of abusive males as compared to appropriate comparison groups (O'Leary, 1988). It has also been observed that batterers are less articulate than their nonbattering peers, yet the only information available in this regard comprises clinical impressions and several studies examining spouse-specific assertiveness. Psychological theory and developmental research have taught professionals much about the complexity of verbal behavior, and there is a need for more basic experimental research with domestically violent samples, particularly in relation to the articulation of conflicts and feelings. Existing evidence for the transgenerational transmission of interpersonal violence suggests that interventions can be developed to prevent its occurrence. Longitudinal studies of intervention with high-risk families are greatly needed and would be a worthy investment for investigators and funding agencies.

Although there is a growing trend toward multidisciplinary perspectives and biopsychosocial models of human behavior (Maiuro & Eberle, 1989), the potential role of physiological factors in marital aggression is virtually unexplored. Roy (1977) stated, "Physical disorders of the brain are sometimes responsible for wife battery, though, as yet, there is [sic] no data on what proportion of wife batterers are so affected" (p. 98). At the time of this writing, some 12 years later, there are still no data addressing this question. The potential contribution of such factors in select cases does not conflict with an appreciation of the broader psychological, social, and cultural influences already postulated and advanced. It is clear that spouse abuse is a large, unsolved problem that requires broad thinking and a willingness to ask many more questions with more sophisticated models and experimental designs.

REFERENCES

Alberti, R. E., & Emmons, M. L. (1982). *Your perfect right: A guide to assertive living* (4th ed.). San Luis Obispo, CA: Impact.

American Psychological Association Committee on Legal Issues. (1985). *White paper on duty to warn*. Englewood Cliffs, NJ: Prentice-Hall.

Bandura, A. (1973). *Aggression: A social learning analysis*. Englewood Cliffs, NJ: Prentice-Hall. pp. 1–40

Bandura, A. (1983). Psychological mechanisms of aggression. In R. G. Geen & E. I. Donnerstein (Eds.), *Aggression: Theoretical and empirical reviews* (Vol. 1, p.). New York: Academic Press.

Bard, M., & Zacker, J. (1974). Assaultiveness and alcohol use in family disputes. *Criminology, 12*, 283–292.

Bedrosian, R. C. (1982). Using cognitive and systems intervention in the treatment of marital violence. In L. R. Barnhill (Ed.), *Clinical approaches to family violence* (pp. 117–138). Rockville, MD: Aspen.

Bernard, J., & Bernard, M. (1984). The abusive male seeking treatment: Jekyll and Hyde. *Family Relations, 33*, 545–547.

Bourdouris, J. (1971). Homicide in the family. *Journal of Marriage and the Family, 33*, 667–676.

Browne, A. (1984). Assault and homicide at home: When battered women kill. In M. J. Saks & L. Saks (Eds.), *Advances in applied social psychology* (Vol. 3). Hillsdale, NJ: Erlbaum.

Byles, J. A. (1978). Violence, alcohol problems and other problems in disintegrating families. *Journal of Studies on Alcohol, 39*, 551–553.

Caesar, P. L. (1986, August). *Men who batter: A heterogeneous group*. Paper presented at the annual meeting of the American Psychological Association, Washington, DC.

Caesar, P. L. (1988). Exposure to violence in the families-of-origin among wife abusers and maritally nonviolent men. *Violence and Victims, 3,* 49–63.

Chritchlow, B. (1986). The powers of John Barleycorn: Beliefs about the effects of alcohol on social behavior. *American Psychologist, 41,* 751–764.

Coleman, K. H. (1980). Conjugal violence: What 33 men report. *Journal of Marriage and the Family, 6,* 207–313.

Deschner, J. (1984). *The hitting habit: Anger control for battering couples.* New York: Free Press.

Dutton, D. G. (1986a). The outcome of court-mandated treatment for wife assault: A quasi-experimental evaluation. *Violence and Victims, 1,* 163–175.

Dutton, D. G. (1986b). Wife assaulters' explanations for assault: The neutralization of self punishment. *Canadian Journal of Behavioral Sciences, 18,* 381–390.

Dutton, D. G. (1988). Profiling of wife assaulters: Preliminary evidence for a trimodal analysis. *Violence and Victims, 3,* 5–29.

Dutton, D. G., & Strachan, C. E. (1987). Motivational needs for power and spouse-specific assertiveness in assaultive and nonassaultive men. *Violence and Victims, 3,* 145–156.

Eddy, M. J., & Myers, T. (1984). *Helping men who batter: A profile of programs in the U.S.* Arlington, TX: Texas Council on Family Violence.

Edleson, J. L., Eiskovits, Z., & Guttman, E. (1985). Men who batter women: A critical review of the evidence. *Journal of Family Issues, 6,* 229–247.

Edleson, J. L., & Grusznski, R. J. (1988). Treating men who batter: Four years of outcome data from the domestic abuse project. *Journal of Social Service Research, 12,* 3–22.

Elbow, M. (1977). Theoretical considerations of violent marriages. *Social Casework, 58,* 515–526.

Elliot, F. A. (1976). The neurology of explosive rage: The dyscontrol syndrome. *The Practitioner, 217,* 51–60.

Ellis, A. (1977). *Anger: How to live with and without it.* Secaucus, NJ: Citadel Press.

Fagan, J. A., Stewart, D. K., & Hansen, D. K. (1983). Violent men or violent husbands? Background factors and situational correlates. In D. Finkelhor, R. J. Gelles, G. T. Hotaling, & M. A. Straus (Eds.), *The dark side of families: Current family violence research* (pp. 49–67). Beverly Hills, CA: Sage.

Feazell, C., Mayers, R., & Deschner, J. (1984). Services for men who batter: Implications for programs and policies. *Family Relations, 33,* 217–223.

Finn, J. (1987). Men's domestic violence treatment: The court referral component. *Journal of Interpersonal Violence, 2,* 154–165.

Ganley, A. L. (1981). *Court-mandated counseling for men who batter: A three-day workshop for mental health professionals.* Washington, DC: Center for Women's Policy Studies.

Geffner, R., Rosenbaum, A., & Hughes, H. (1988). Research issues concerning family violence. In V. B. Van Hasselt, R. L. Morrison, A. S. Bellack, & M. Hersen (Eds.), *Handbook of Family Violence* (pp. 457–482). New York: Plenum.

Gelles, R. J. (1972). *The violent home: A study of physical aggression between husbands and wives.* Beverly Hills, CA: Sage.

Goldstein, D., & Rosenbaum, A. (1985). An evaluation of the self-esteem of maritally violent men. *Family Relations, 34,* 425–428.

Gondolf, E. W. (1985a). Anger and oppression in men who batter: Empiricist and feminist perspectives and their implications for research. *Victimology: An International Journal, 10,* 311–324.

Gondolf, E. W. (1985b). *Men who batter: An integrated approach for stopping wife abuse.* Holmes Beach, FL: Learning Publications.

Gondolf, E. W. (1988). Who are these guys? Toward a behavioral typology of batterers. *Violence and Victims, 3,* 187–203.

Goldberg, H. (1976). *The hazards of being male.* New York: Nash.

Gross, B. H., Southard, M. J., Lamb, H. R., & Weinberger, L. E. (1987). Assessing dangerousness and responding appropriately: *Hedlund* expands the clinician's liability established by *Tarasoff. Journal of Clinical Psychiatry, 48,* 9–12.

Hamberger, L. K., & Hastings, J. E. (1986). Personality correlates of men who abuse their partners: A cross-validation study. *Journal of Family Violence, 1,* 323–341.

Harbin, H. (1977). Episodic dyscontrol and family dynamics. *American Journal of Psychiatry, 134,* 1113–1116.

Hastings, J. E., & Hamberger, L. K. (1988). Personality characteristics of spouse abusers: A controlled comparison. *Violence and Victims, 3,* 31–48.

Hedlund v. Superior Court, 34 Cal. 3d 695, 194 Cal. Rptr. 805 (1983).

Helping Angry and Violent People Manage Their Emotions and Behavior: Harborview Anger Management Program. (1987, November). *Hospital and Community Psychiatry, 38,* 1207–1210.

Hershorn, M. (1986). *Over- vs. undercontrolled hostility: Construct validation of the concept as applied to maritally violent men.* Unpublished doctoral dissertation, Syracuse University, Syracuse, NY.

Hotaling, G. T., & Sugarman, D. B. (1986). An analysis of risk markers in husband to wife violence: The current state of knowledge. *Violence and Victims, 1,* 101–124.

Jablonski by Pahls v. United States, 712 F.2d 391 (1983).

Janis, I. L. (1974). Vigilance and decision-making in personal crisis. In G. V. Coehlo, D. A. Hamburg & J. E. Adams (Eds.), *Coping and adaptation.* New York: Basic Books.

Jennings, J. L. (1987). History and issues in the treatment of battering men: A case for unstructured group therapy. *Journal of Family Violence, 2,* 193–213.

Jouriles, E. N., & O'Leary, K. D. (1985). Interspousal reliability of reports of marital violence. *Journal of Consulting and Clinical Psychology, 53,* 419–421.

Kalmuss, D. (1984). The intergenerational transmission of marital aggression. *Journal of Marriage and the Family, 46,* 11–19.

Kantor, G. K., & Straus, M. A. (1986, April). *The drunken bum theory of wife beating.* Paper presented at the National Alcoholism Forum Conference of Alcohol and the Family, San Francisco.

Kazdin, A. E. (1973). Covert modeling and the reduction of avoidance behavior. *Journal of Abnormal Psychology, 81,* 87–95.

Kazdin, A. E. (1974). Covert modeling, model similarity, and reduction of avoidance behavior. *Behavior Therapy, 5,* 325–340.

Laird, J. D. (1974). Self attribution of emotion: The effects of expressive behavior on the quality of emotional experience. *Journal of Personality and Social Psychology, 29*, 475–486.

Lange, A. & Jakubowski, P. (1976). *Responsible assertive behavior*. Champaign, IL: Research Press.

LaViolette, A. D., Barnett, O. W., & Miller, C. L. (1984, August). *A classification of wife abusers on the Bem Sex Role Inventory*. Paper presented at the Second National Conference of Research on Domestic Violence, Durham, NH.

Lewis, D. O., Pincus, J. H., Bard, B., Richardson, E., Prichep, L. S., Feldman, M., & Yeager, (1988). Neuropsychiatric, psychoeducational, and family characteristics of 14 juveniles condemned to death in the United States. *American Journal of Psychiatry, 145*, 584–589.

Lewis, D. O., Pincus, J. H., Feldman, M., Jackson, L., & Bard, B. (1986). Psychiatric, neurological, and psychoeducational characteristics of 15 death row inmates in the United States. *American Journal of Psychiatry, 143*, 838–845.

Lion, J. R., Christopher, R. L., & Madden, D. J. (1977). A group approach with violent outpatients. *International Journal of Group Psychotherapy, 27*, 67–74.

Maiuro, R. D., Cahn, T. S., & Vitaliano, P. P. (1986). Assertiveness and hostility in domestically violent men. *Violence and Victims, 1*, 279–289.

Maiuro, R. D., Cahn, T. S., Vitaliano, P. P., Wagner, B. C., & Zegree, J. B. (1988). Anger, hostility, and depression in domestically violent versus generally assaultive men and nonviolent control subjects. *Journal of Consulting and Clinical Psychology, 56*, 17–23.

Maiuro, R. D., Cahn, T. S., Vitaliano, P. P., & Zegree, J. B. (1987, August). *Treatment for domestically violent men: Outcome and follow-up data*. Paper presented at the annual meeting of the American Psychological Association, New York.

Maiuro, R. D., & Eberle, J. A. (1989). New developments in research on aggression: An international report. *Violence and Victims, 4*, 3–15.

Maiuro, R. D., Eberle, J., Muscatel, K., & Donovan, D. (1981). *Anger management*. Videotape Production: Instructional Media Services, University of Washington, Seattle.

Maiuro, R. D., O'Sullivan, M. J., Michael, M. C., & Vitaliano, P. P. (1989). Anger, hostility, and depression in assaultive versus suicide attempting males. *Journal of Clinical Psychology, 45*, 531–541.

Maiuro, R. D., Vitaliano, P. P., & Cahn, T. C. (1987). A brief measure for the assessment of anger and aggression. *Journal of Interpersonal Violence, 2*, 166–178.

Maiuro, R. D., Vitaliano, P. P., Cahn, T. S., & Hall, G. C. (1987, July). *Anger, depression, and coping in alcohol abusing versus non-alcohol abusing domestically violent men*. Paper presented at the Third National Family Violence Research Conference, Durham, NH.

Makepeace, J. M. (1981). Violence among college students. *Family Relations, 30*, 97–102.

Mandler, G. (1984). *Mind and body: The psychology of emotion and stress*. New York: W. W. Norton.

Mantooth, C. M., Geffner, R., Franks, D., & Patrick, J. (1987). *Family preservation: A treatment manual for reducing couple violence.* Tyler, TX: East Texas Crisis Center.

Margolin, G. (1979). Conjoint marital therapy to enhance anger management and reduce spouse abuse. *American Journal of Family Therapy, 7,* 13–23.

Margolin, G., John, R. S., & Gleberman, L. (1988). Affective responses to conflictual discussions in violent and nonviolent couples. *Journal of Consulting and Clinical Psychology, 56,* 24–33.

Megargee, E. I. (1967). Development and validation of an MMPI scale. *Journal of Abnormal Psychology, 72,* 519–528.

Meichenbaum, D. (1971). Examination of model characteristics in reducing avoidance behavior. *Journal of Personality and Social Psychology, 17,* 298–307.

Millon, T. (1983). *Millon Clinical Multiaxial Inventory manual.* Minneapolis: Interpretive Scoring Systems.

Monahan, J. (1982). *Predicting violent behavior: An assessment of clinical techniques.* Beverly Hills, CA: Sage.

Neidig, P. H. & Friedman, D. H. (1984). *Spouse abuse: A treatment program for couples.* Champaign, IL: Research Press.

Neidig, P. H., Friedman, D. H., & Collins, B. S. (1986). Attitudinal characteristics of males who have engaged in spouse abuse. *Journal of Family Violence, 1,* 223–233.

Novaco, R. W. (1975). *Anger control: The development and evaluation of an experimental treatment.* Lexington, MA: Lexington Books.

O'Leary, K. D. (1988). Physical aggression between spouses. In V. B. Van Hasselt, R. L. Morrison, A. S. Bellack, & M. Hersen (Eds.), *Handbook of family violence* (pp. 31–56). New York: Plenum.

O'Leary, K. D., & Arias, I. (in press). Prevalence, correlates, and development of spouse abuse. In R. DeV. Peters & R. J. McMahon (Eds.), *Marriage and families: Behavioral treatments and processes.* New York: Brunner/Mazel.

O'Leary, K. D., Arias, I., Rosenbaum, A., & Barling, J. (1985). *Premarital physical aggression.* Unpublished manuscript. State University of New York, Stony Brook.

O'Leary, K. D., Barling, J., Arias, I., Rosenbaum, A., Malone, J., & Tyree, A. (1989). Prevalence and stability of spousal aggression. *Journal of Consulting and Clinical Psychology, 57, 2,* 263–268.

Parker's Evidence Code of California (1986). Los Angeles: Parker & Sons.

Pleck, E., Pleck, J., Grossman, M., & Bart, P. (1978). The battered data syndrome: A reply to Steinmetz. *Victimology, 2,* 680–683.

Ptacek, J. (1984, August). *The clinical literature on men who batter: A review and critique.* Paper presented at the Second National Conference for Family Violence Researchers, Durham, NH.

Purdy, F., & Nickle, N. (1981). Practice principles for working with groups of men who batter. *Social Work Groups, 4,* 111–122.

Rosenbaum, A. (1986a, August). *Group treatment of wife abusers: Process and outcome.* Paper presented at the annual meeting of the American Psychological Association, Washington, DC.

Rosenbaum, A. (1986b). Of men, macho, and marital violence. *Journal of Family Violence, 1,* 121–129.

Rosenbaum, A. (1988). Methodological issues in marital violence research. *Journal of Family Violence, 3,* 91–104.

Rosenbaum, A., & Hoge, S. K. (1989). *Head injury and marital aggression.* Unpublished manuscript, University of Massachussetts Medical School, Worcester.

Rosenbaum, A., & Maiuro, R. D. (1989). In P. L. Caesar & L. K. Hamberger (Eds.), Eclectic approaches in working with men who batter. *Therapeutic interventions with batterers: Theory, practice, and programs* (pp. 165–195). New York: Springer.

Rosenbaum, A., & O'Leary, D. K. (1981a). Children: The unintended victims of marital violence. *American Journal of Orthopsychiatry, 51,* 692–699.

Rosenbaum, A., & O'Leary, D. K. (1981b). Marital violence: Characteristics of abusive couples. *Journal of Consulting and Clinical Psychology, 49,* 63–71.

Rosenbaum, A., & O'Leary, K. D. (1986). Treatment of marital violence. In N. Jacobson & A. Gurman (Eds.), *Clinical handbook of marital therapy* (pp. 385–405). New York: Guilford.

Rounsaville, B. (1978). Theories in marital violence: Evidence from a study of battered women. *Victimology: An International Journal, 3,* 11–31.

Roy, M. (1977). *Battered women.* New York: Van Nostrand Reinhold.

Russell, M. (1988). Wife assault theory, research, and treatment: A literature review. *Journal of Family Violence, 3,* 193–208.

Saunders, D. (1984). Helping husbands who batter. *Social Casework, 65,* 347–353.

Sherman, L., & Berk, R. A. (1984, April). The Minneapolis domestic violence experiment. *Police Foundation Reports,* 1–8.

Sonkin, D. J. (1988). The male batterer: Clinical and research issues. *Violence and Victims, 3,* 65–79.

Sonkin, D. J. & Durphy, M. (1982). *Learning to live without violence: A handbook for men.* San Francisco: Volcano Press.

Sonkin, D. J., & Ellison, J. (1986). The therapist's duty to protect victims of domestic violence: Where we have been and where we are going. *Violence and Victims, 1,* 205–214.

Sonkin, D., Martin, D., & Walker, L. (1985). *The male batterer: A treatment approach.* New York: Springer.

Steinmetz, S. K. (1977). *The cycle of violence.* New York: Praeger.

Steinmetz, S. K., & Lucca, J. (1987). Husband battering. In V. B. Van Hasselt, R. L. Morrison, A. S. Bellack, & M. Hersen (Eds.), *Handbook of family violence* (pp. 223–246). New York: Plenum.

Straus, M. A. (1980). Social stress and marital violence in a national sample of American families. In F. Wright, C. Bahn, & R. W. Rieber (Eds.), *Forensic psychology and psychiatry: Annals of the New York Academy of Sciences* (Vol. 347, pp. 229–250) Durham, NH: University of New Hampshire.

Straus, M. A., & Gelles, R. J. (1986). Societal change and change in family violence from 1975 to 1985 as revealed by two national surveys. *Journal of Marriage and the Family, 48,* 465–479.

Straus, M. A., Gelles, R. J., & Steinmetz, S. (1980). *Behind closed doors: Violence in the American family.* New York: Doubleday/Anchor.

Tarasoff v. Regents of the University of California, 17 Cal. 3d 425, 551 P.2d 334 (1976).

Virkkunen, M. (1974). Alcohol as a factor precipitating aggression and conflict behaviour leading to homicide. *British Journal of Addiction, 69,* 149–154.

Walker, L. E. A. (1979). *The battered woman.* New York: Harper & Row.

Wise, T. (1978). Where the public peril begins: A survey of psychotherapists to determine the effects of *Tarasoff. Stanford Law Review, 31,* 165–190.

Womack, W. M., Maiuro, R. D., Russo, J., & Vitaliano, P. P. (1983). Psychoeducational courses for a nonpatient clientele at a mental health center. *Hospital and Community Psychiatry, 34,* 1158–1160.

Yalom, I. D., Houts, P. S., Newell, G. & Rand, K. H. (1967). Preparation of patients for group therapy. *Archives of General Psychiatry, 17,* 416–427.

Yalom, I. D., Peters, H. S. Sheldon, M. Z., & Rand, K. H. (1967). Prediction of success in group therapy. *Archives of General Psychiatry, 17,* 159–168.

Zillman, D. (1983). Arousal and aggression. In R. G. Geen & E. I. Donnerstein (Eds.), *Aggression: Theoretical and empirical reviews* (Vol 1, pp. 75–101). New York: Academic Press.

CHAPTER 13

Perpetrators of Elder Abuse

ROSALIE S. WOLF

INTRODUCTION

Only now, more than 10 years after the first public disclosure of elder abuse, is the picture of the perpetrator and the circumstances surrounding abuse and neglect of older persons coming into sharper focus. The intent of this chapter is to examine what has been learned about perpetrators in the past decade and how this information can be helpful in designing intervention strategies that will reduce or eliminate the maltreatment of elderly individuals.

The definition of elder mistreatment suggested by Margaret Hudson (1988) provides a framework in which to discuss the topic:

> Elder mistreatment is destructive behavior which is directed toward an older adult, occurs within the context of a relationship connoting trust, and is of sufficient intensity and/or frequency to produce harmful physical, psychological, social and/or financial effects of unnecessary suffering, injury, pain, loss and/or violation of human rights and decreased quality of life for the older adult. (p. 162)

It includes acts of commission (abuse) and omission (neglect), intentional and unintentional. Although such deeds can take place in any setting or at the hands of anyone, for the purpose here, they will be limited to conflict in the home by family members or persons who have a significant relationship with the older person. Thus, perpetrators are individuals whose behavior toward older adults with whom they have a personal or social relationship results in unnecessary suffering for those older adults. The behavior can be described as physical abuse, psychological abuse, and material abuse (financial exploitation), or neglect in any of these areas.

CHARACTERISTICS OF PERPETRATORS

Early Findings

Although the early attempts (Block & Sinnott, 1979; Chen et al., 1981; Lau & Kosberg, 1979; O'Malley et al., 1979; Sengstock & Liang, 1982; U.S. House Select Committee on Aging, 1981) to examine systematically the issue of elder abuse and neglect failed to provide a clear statement about perpetrators, certain themes did emerge. On the average, adult children were identified as perpetrators in almost half of the cases reported in the preceding studies. Spouses were implicated in one eighth to one fourth of the cases; and other relatives and nonrelatives, in still smaller proportions. Generally, perpetrators were male. Stress appeared to be a common element in their lives. Not only was the victim viewed as a source of this stress, but the perpetrators were experiencing alcohol, drug, financial, and marital problems. In these same reports, the victim was depicted as female, very old, with physical and mental impairments, and dependent on the perpetrator.

Although these early studies were useful in documenting the existence of abuse and neglect and suggesting possible explanations of elder mistreatment, at best they could be considered only exploratory. The small and unrepresentative samples, absence of control groups, and reliance on case records raised serious questions about their substantiality and replicability. Yet, the portrait of elder abuse that they represented was adopted by the media, the public, and policymakers. From the first public disclosure of elder abuse, the problem tended to be framed as one of the overburdened caregiver, usually a daughter, taking care of an infirm elderly parent (Wolf & Pillemer, 1989).

The next series of studies attempted to overcome some of these limitations, and in the process a more valid characterization of the perpetrator began to appear. In a comparison of abuse and neglect cases analyzed for statistical differences, Crouse, Kobb, Harris, Kopecky, and Poertner (1981) reported that neglect was far more likely to be associated with a victim who had a physical disability (and somewhat likely in the case of a mental disability), but that abuse was more apt to be related to the characteristics of the abuser.

Giordano and Giordano (1983) also did a comparative analysis but utilized cases of abused (600) and nonabused elders (150) obtained from the files of the Aging and Adult Services units in 5 Florida counties. They were interested in learning how various individual and familial circumstances related to four types of abuse: physical (bodily harm), neglect (breach of duty, violation of rights), psychological (fear, anxiety, or isolation), and financial exploitation (theft or conversion of money or material possessions). Using multivariate analysis, they showed, as did the Crouse survey, that specific characteristics were related to different types of abuse. The physically abused person was apt to be physically ill, sustain a number of abuses, and live with the perpetrator, whereas the neglected elder was likely to be intellectually and physically impaired. The number of abuses and the adult child–parent conflict were factors associated with psychological abuse and financial problems; income, age, and living with the abuser were identified with financial exploitation. Their most important finding, according to the authors, was the emergence of spouse abuse as a dominant variable in physical, psychological, and multiple abuse cases. Not only did this report present a more complex image of elder abuse than the first studies had suggested, but it also challenged the belief that the adult child was the primary perpetrator in certain categories of abuse.

Later Studies

Using data from 39 cases of appropriate care and 29 cases of abusive situations (reported by homemakers and media-initiated community reports), Bristowe and Collins (1989) sought to identify risk factors that could be used in planning precrisis interventions. Their principal findings were (a) alcohol use by the caregivers, but not the care recipients; (b) abuse by male caregivers (usually their husbands) of frail elderly women; (c) caregivers who suffered from confusion and depression; and (d) recipients in the abusive situations who suffered more depression than their counterparts in appropriate care settings. Bristowe and Collins concluded that in their sample the caregiver characteristics were more predictive of potential abuse than were the frailties of the victim.

Unlike the studies referred to earlier, Pillemer (1986) chose to restrict his investigation to cases of physical/verbal abuse, to interview victim and perpetrator directly, and to use a matched nonabused control group. Five potential causes of abuse were examined: intraindividual dynamics, dependency, external stress, social isolation, and intergenerational transmission of violence. When the cases were compared with the controls on the psychological factors, the abusers were much more likely to have mental or emotional problems, to abuse alcohol, and to have been hospitalized for psychiatric reasons. The results on the dependence criteria indicated that abused elders were not in poor health and were, in fact, less disabled in a number of areas than the control group. The victims were not more dependent on their kin for assistance with activities of daily living, but the perpetrators were more likely to be financially dependent on their elderly victims than were the control relatives.

In regard to the external stress items, Pillemer found that the three that differentiated the abused and nonabused families (someone moving in, someone leaving, and someone getting arrested) could be attributed to the perpetrator rather than external events. Of the five social resources scales used to measure socialization, the abuse cases scored more poorly on three of them; they had fewer overall contacts, were less satisfied with them, and rated lower on a composite extent-of-satisfaction index. Findings on intergenerational transmission of abuse were not significant. Abused elders did not report more physical punishment of children nor did they indicate that the perpetrator had been a victim of child abuse. Although Pillemer's intention was to interview the perpetrators, he was forced to drop this subsample from the investigation because more than half of the group was unavailable; some were incarcerated, institutionalized, living in unknown locations, unwilling to be interviewed, or too impaired to respond.

On the other hand, Anetzberger (1987) deliberately chose perpetrators as the sample for her study of the etiology of elder abuse, but she too had difficulty in reaching the numbers that she had proposed. Participating hospitals and human service agencies identified 40 as qualified for inclusion in the study; only 15 were willing to be interviewed, although background information was obtained from the referral source caseworkers on the total group. Also, like Pillemer (1986), she limited her study to physical abuse situations, but she restricted it to those involving adult children and their aged parents. Her conceptual framework included a combination of existing theoretical approaches: primarily, social learning and, secondarily, stress and pathology. Based on her findings, she revised the conceptual framework, deemphasizing the role of history of family violence and external stresses. She suggested that the etiology of physical abuse of elderly parents by their adult offspring could be traced to certain pathological personality characteristics of the adult children, the acute stress in their lives, and their social isolation. Also, vulnerability of the elder parents and "prolonged and profound" (p. 97) intimacy between the adult offspring and the elder parent were major factors. The typical abusing adult offspring was found to have some characteristic pathology, usually emotional distress, mental illness, or alcoholism, but was not under stress from recent life crisis events. He/she was burdened by close contact with the elder parent, the parent's disturbing behaviors, lack of time for personal pursuits, and absence of support from other family members.

Anetzberger then categorized the sample of perpetrators into three types. The first group was labeled "hostiles." They were aggressive, hated authority, were outspoken, and angry at everyone. For them, contact with the elder parent was a very negative experience. They were also the most abusive of the three types.

The "authoritarians" in the sample were the least likely to have any psychopathology. However, they were rigid in their expectations regarding the elder parent, critical, impatient, and generally unsympathetic to the elder's situation. The third group was composed of the "dependents," who were mainly distinguished from the others by their financial dependence on the elder parent. Anetzberger writes:

The dependents had never achieved the social, economic or emotional status expected of American adults. Rather, they seemed to remain attached to the elder parent in a childlike dependency, impassive in their desire to alter the present situation. (p. 90)

Perpetrator Profiles

The increasing importance of perpetrator characteristics as causal factors in elder abuse and neglect was very apparent in results of the model project evaluation (Wolf, Godkin, & Pillemer, 1984, 1986), of which the Pillemer (1986) study was a part. A comparative analysis of types of abuse and neglect (physical, psychological, and material abuse, active and passive neglect) was carried out using the data from comprehensive assessments of 328 cases seen by the model projects over a 2-year period. Four of the five risk factors identified by Pillemer (intergenerational transmission of violence was dropped because of lack of data) formed the basis of the comparison. Because more than one form of abuse or neglect usually was present in a single case, it was not possible to work with mutually exclusive categories. Therefore, the analysis was set up to examine, for instance, all cases in which physical abuse was present compared to cases in which it was absent. This process was repeated for the five different forms of maltreatment.

The cases of physical abuse were more likely to involve victims and perpetrators in poorer emotional health than those cases without physical violence. Surprisingly, the victims, in spite of emotional problems, were generally independent in most activities of daily living. On the other hand, the perpetrators were apt to abuse alcohol, to have had a history of mental illness, and to have undergone a recent decline in both mental and physical health status. In this type of mistreatment, it was the perpetrator who had experienced an increase in dependency.

Psychological abuse also appeared to be related to the mental health of the parties involved. The victims were relatively unimpaired, cognitively and functionally, and were independent in meeting their daily needs, but were more likely to be in poor emotional health. The abusers were apt to have had a history of mental illness, a recent decline in mental health, and both recent and long-term medical problems.

A somewhat different profile was presented by the financial exploitation cases. This form of abuse appeared to be motivated by the financial needs of the perpetrators, who were more likely to have long-term and recent financial problems and/or to have undergone a change in their financial or job status. Alcohol abuse was also a significant factor in this group. The relative isolation of the victims may have played a role, because the data showed that they were more apt to be widowed and to have suffered losses in their social network. The perpetrators were generally distant relatives or nonrelatives, who were not so emotionally connected to their victims as in the other forms of mistreatment.

In marked contrast to the physical or psychological abuse cases, those involving neglect appeared to be very much related to the dependency needs of the victims. The neglected older persons had significant problems with cognitive and physical functioning that forced them to depend on their caretakers, generally female, for assistance with many activities of daily living. Because of their infirmities and advanced age, they were more likely to be a source of stress to their relatives. The perpetrators were not as financially dependent on their victims or beset with mental problems as were the perpetrators of physical or material abuse. Social isolation was a contributing factor, being evidenced by a loss of social supports in cases of passive neglect and a lack of emergency contacts for victims of active neglect.

The model project evaluation provided still another analysis of interest—a comparison of cases in which spouses and adult children were the perpetrators (Wolf & Pillemer, 1989). Elders mistreated by spouses were more often victims of physical abuse than other forms of maltreatment, were in poorer emotional health, and were dependent on their abusers for companionship. Adult children were more likely to commit acts of psychological abuse and neglect with more severe ramifications than those perpetrated by spouses. These children were more likely to have money problems, to be financially dependent on their elderly parents, and to have a history of mental illness and alcoholism. On the other hand, the spousal perpetrators were more apt to have had both recent and long-term medical complaints and to have experienced a recent decline in physical health.

When the cases of parent abuse were analyzed for gender differences, very few of the sociodemographic, physical, psychological, functional, and social variables proved to be significant. Among cases in which daughters were the perpetrators, there was a larger proportion of victims whose health had been declining and who needed assistance with financial management than those involving sons. However, sons were more apt to abuse alcohol.

In looking for correlates of abuse and neglect in a case-control study of elders living in the community who reported physical abuse, verbal aggression, and neglect by adult children, Finkelhor and Pillemer (1989) also found that abuser deviance and dependency and, to a lesser degree, abuser stress, were the strongest predictors, with victim dependency and disability of much less significance. When cases of spousal abuse were analyzed, abuser deviance was again the most important factor predicting abuse. These families also exhibited a high level of spousal conflict.

Although research into the nature of elder abuse is still in its early stages, there is now evidence that the phenomenon is much more complex than first portrayed. These studies also suggest that the perpetrator may be a more useful frame of reference than the victim in the search for causes and treatment.

TREATMENT

Theoretical and Practical Models

In addition to determining the characteristics of victims, perpetrators, and abuse situations, the early investigators also described some of the interventions that were in use at that time and suggested other forms of treatment based on their findings. Thus, Lau and Kosberg (1979) in one of the first reports on the subject recommended counseling, homemakers, nursing, and medical care as strategies for reducing caregiver stress, which they saw as a strong causal factor in elder abuse. In surveys of the Baltimore–Washington area, Block and Sinnott (1979) found that social services, civil sanctions, and criminal proceedings were utilized in treating these cases, but often removal of the victim from the home situation was thought to be the only remedy. This view was also expressed by O'Malley, Segars, Perez, Mitchell, and Knuepfel (1979), after their survey of professionals and paraprofessionals in Massachusetts, which found that relocation of the victim, either placement in another setting or hospitalization, was the most frequently cited action by the respondents. Gioglio and Blakemore (1983), at the conclusion of their prevalence survey of elder abuse in New Jersey, wrote that more legal options and resources should be available for the protective services departments handling abuse cases.

The more recent contributions to the literature have gone beyond recommendations regarding treatment and preventive services to the formulation of theoretical models for intervention. The strong association between the dependency of the abuser and mistreatment led Pillemer (1986) to suggest a model of intervention based on the "social exchange theory," in which the rewards of reducing dependency on the elder and/or the costs of abusing the elder are increased. Phillips (1986) advanced "symbolic interactionism" as a more accurate account of the social interaction between victim and perpetrator, because it takes into account the individual's impressions of past experiences. Although this view may be promising for explaining the dynamic nature of the situation, it cannot be readily translated into a set of intervention strategies. On the other hand, the "environmental press model" described by Ansello, King, and Taler (1986) does have practical implications. According to this paradigm, if an individual's level of competence and the environment's demand (or "press") are not in synchrony, maladaption occurs. Thus, the goal of intervention is to reduce the environmental press on caregivers by increasing their level of competence and at the same time to increase environmental demand on the frail elder through greater stimulation and socialization.

Actually, because of the paucity of research on elder mistreatment, practitioners have been left to rely on field experience and professional training in designing treatment modalities. One of the first efforts and the most complete is the Elder Abuse Diagnosis and Intervention Model, developed by

Quinn and Tomita (1986). In their book they lay out the principles and methods for diagnosis, based on traditional psychosocial casework, and for an intervention phase that incorporates crisis, short-term, and long-term intervention methodology. Counseling is at the heart of their model, but they also include an array of elder services that can be utilized in the development of individual care plans.

Fulmer and O'Malley (1987) approach intervention from an entirely different perspective. Using "inadequate care" as the paradigm, they have designed decision trees for various categories of cases based on (a) the needs of the client, and (b) the significance of the caretaking role of the individual believed to be responsible for the inadequate care. The model is most appropriate for health care professionals and, in particular, hospital emergency room personnel, although it too recognizes the need to have access to a wide variety of social, psychological, environmental, and legal services following the hospital encounter.

It is the multiplicity of problems requiring the attention of many different providers that distinguishes abuse and neglect cases from nonabuse cases. In an analysis of state legislation related to elder abuse, the American Public Welfare Association and the National Association of State Units on Aging (1986) established 27 different categories to encompass all those services listed in the laws. Medical care, mental health services, counseling, transportation, day care, food, clothing, in-home services, emergency shelter, and legal services are some of them. The treatment process has also been addressed in the legislation, with 26 of the 50 states specifying identification, assessment, evaluation, service plan development, and coordination of services as required activities for their protective services agencies.

Intervention Models

The manner in which the service system is organized may also affect the nature of the treatment. A useful characterization is the one that was described in a study commissioned by the Illinois Department on Aging (Crouse et al., 1981) and that, in fact, became the basis of a demonstration project carried out by the Department (Illinois Department on Aging, 1987). There are three variations:

1. *The Child Abuse or Mandatory Reporting Model.* This model is adapted from the service system used for abused and neglected children and is probably the most common approach of the states. Certain designated professionals who work with older persons are required to report suspected cases of elder abuse to specified agencies.

2. *The Legal Intervention Model.* In this version, the legal system is considered a primary source of assistance for case resolution through such

means as restraining orders, complaints to the police and the courts, and collection of accurate case data for use in possible prosecution.

3. *The Advocacy Model.* The assumption in this model is that the lowest level of intervention would be used in assisting the victims. The service provider is not to intrude unnecessarily in the life of the elder, but to use a broad range of formal and informal services to assist the older person in attaining his/her goals.

Because the immediate concern in handling any elder abuse and neglect case is the safety of the elderly person, the intake and assessment forms used in most agencies have centered on the victim. There is a trend, however, among protective service departments and other agencies to update their assessment forms to conform more closely to the current state of knowledge. Questions pertaining to abusers now appear on assessment forms, but more often as criteria for determination of risk level for the victim than for the design of care plans for the perpetrator. The contention of this chapter is that the needs of the perpetrator must be part of the solution to the problem of elder abuse.

Perpetrator Types and Intervention

From the results of the more recent elder abuse studies and the experience of elder abuse workers it is possible to identify four perpetrator types—the "stressed-out" daughter, the dependent son, the impaired spouse, and the avaricious friend. Obviously, these categories are not intended to represent all cases, but this typology does provide a useful framework for discussing elder abuse treatment from the perspective of the perpetrator.

The Stressed-Out Daughter

The stressed-out daughter is the most familiar abuser type and has received the most attention in the literature and media. Because these perpetrators are more apt to be involved in neglect cases, the immediate response, once a reported case has been substantiated and an assessment is underway, is to provide needed care to the victim and to relieve the burden and strain on the caregiver. If the situation is of an emergency nature, the elderly person may be hospitalized. Most often, however, treatment consists of bringing help to the family in the form of skilled nursing care, homemaker assistance, personal care, meals-on-wheels, chore services, respite care, or adult day care.

The concept of relief for the perpetrator has been accepted as the primary strategy in these cases. From the viewpoint of the perpetrators, the goal of intervention should be to enhance their ability to cope with their situation. Counseling, training, and skills building are activities that can be carried out in the home or in a group setting for this purpose.

The Dependent Son

The second perpetrator type, the dependent son, is most closely associated with incidents of physical abuse, rather than neglect. This abuser has mental, social, and financial problems, with resulting dependency on his elderly parent(s). Unable to cope with the demands of everyday living, he responds to feelings of inadequacy and powerlessness with anger, hostility, and violence. Here, too, the immediate concern is the safety of the victim, but obviously, the treatment plan must focus on the perpetrator. Mental health and alcohol treatment programs systems are important partners with adult protective services in this endeavor. Vocational counseling, job placement, housing assistance, and financial support may all be necessary to enable this adult child to achieve independence, or at least independence within a structured environment. Simultaneously, the victim needs help in overcoming the sense of shame, guilt, and fear, as well as the emotional dependency that has characterized the relationship with the son. Because battering is a felony or criminal offense, legal steps can be taken to end the mistreatment. A court order limiting or stopping the perpetrator from contacting the victim may be necessary. Increasing awareness, interest, and activity by the criminal justice system in elder abuse may encourage more extensive use of legal sanctions.

The Impaired Spouse

For some couples, the stresses of later life, particularly physical illness, can exacerbate an already tension-filled and unhappy marriage. The impaired spouse, the third perpetrator type, is often locked into such a relationship, unable to manage the growing demands that aging and illness bring, especially when he or she may be in failing health, too. Restoring equilibrium in the marital partnership will require treating the social, psychological, and physical needs of both spouses. As with other forms of maltreatment, life-threatening situations must be addressed first. Hospitalization of one or both spouses may be necessary. This separation may also allow for a "cooling off" period. Home care services to reduce burden and strain on the caregiver spouse, coupled with professional help for alcohol and emotional problems that are often present, are important steps in reducing dependency and violence. Finally, marital counseling can offer an opportunity for older couples to explore the resentments and anger they harbor against each other and to work toward a more harmonious relationship.

The Avaricious Friend

Although financial exploitation is a punishable offense under law, dealing with the avaricious friend may not be as simple as it first appears. The nature of the association between the victim and perpetrator may make it difficult to prove fraud or to obtain agreement from the victim to press charges. Financial institutions, legal services, law enforcement, and the judicial system are potential allies in successful intervention.

Barriers to Treatment of Perpetrators

It is clear that, within the classification of perpetrators of elder abuse, the circumstances surrounding the incidents, the dynamics within the family setting, and the factors giving rise to violent behavior are diverse, and consequently the treatment modalities must be different. The need to include the perpetrator as a major participant in the treatment plan is obvious. However, a number of obstacles make this goal often unattainable. The first barrier is inherent in adult protection statutes. Because the objective of such laws is to protect the victim, the content deals primarily with the victims. The services mandated under the laws, although sometimes very broad in scope, are intended to respond to the needs of the abused or neglected elderly person. The following are just a few examples from various state statutes (APWA/NASUA, 1986): "Protective services may be arranged when an adult is in need of care and protection because of danger to his health or safety" (Alabama) (p. 167); "Protective services are those needed to protect the endangered adult from himself and others" (Arkansas) (p. 177); "Protective services are defined as the services necessary to protect the disabled adult from abuse, neglect, or exploitation, consisting of the evaluation of the need for service and the mobilization of essential services on behalf of the disabled adults" (North Carolina) (p. 288); and Services to be provided under the law are those services with the objective to protect an aged or disabled person" (Florida) (p. 197).

References in the legislation to the perpetrator, when included, are generally limited to penalties: "Guilty of Class D felony [neglect] . . . Class B misdemeanor [abuse]" (Arkansas) (p. 175–176); "[In the case of] an indication of abuse or exploitation which appears to be criminal, the director . . . shall forward the information to the appropriate law enforcement officials" (Maryland) (p. 238). It is interesting that the most extensive coverage given to perpetrators appears in the Illinois law, which is actually a domestic violence statute, but was, until the passage of the new elder abuse legislation in 1988, the only statewide legislation that covered elders who were mistreated. Regarding penalties for the perpetrator, this law specifies a list of eight "remedies," among which is "requiring or recommending the respondent to undergo counseling for a specified duration." (p. 211) In addition to not including the perpetrator as a recipient of services, except in terms of sanctions, the states on the whole provide very little additional funds for protective services of older persons so that priority is given to the victims. Other community agencies are supposed to work with the perpetrators.

A second barrier is the refusal of the perpetrator to accept services. The model project study reported by Wolf and Pillemer (1989) examined the effect of certain barriers on the delivery of appropriate services to the elder abuse cases. Of 11 potential barriers (unavailability of services, bureaucratic redtape, fragmentation of services, uncoordinated agencies, legal implications of interventions, number of agencies involved, lack of protective services, lack of respite care, lack of support groups for caregivers, reluctance of the victim to receive help, and reluctance of the perpetrator to receive help), the caseworkers in the three sites all agreed that the greatest hindrance was the reluctance of the perpetrator to receive help (which occurred in five of six cases). To be sure, victims were also reluctant to accept assistance, but in somewhat smaller proportions. A related problem is that about one third of the perpetrators were not available for assessment or treatment.

The question of the abuser's willingness to undergo treatment was addressed in Iris's (1987) evaluation of the North Suburban Cook County Elder Abuse Project, one of the four Illinois demonstration projects. Data were available to the workers on only 161 perpetrators out of a total of 219 cases. Of the 161, 55% were thought to be unwilling to make a change in their situations. When the caseworkers were asked to assess the abusers' willingness to effect change in themselves, such a change was viewed as not very difficult to achieve for only 10% of the abusers, somewhat difficult for 42% and very difficult for 49%.

Still another barrier to treatment for the perpetrator is the lack of knowledge among workers about the various risk factors leading to elder abuse and neglect and the role of the perpetrator. Those services that might be especially appropriate for perpetrators have generally not been viewed as particularly useful or necessary by most service providers. When respondents in a national survey of agencies serving abused and neglect elders were asked to rank 36 components that might make up an ideal, comprehensive, local service system for elder abuse and neglect, those that specifically referred to the perpetrator, exclusive of the stressed-out daughter type, received low ratings. Employment assistance ranked 36; civil commitment procedures, 33, alcohol counseling, 29, and caregiver training/counseling, 19 (Wolf & McMurray Anderson, in press). Sengstock, Hwalek, and Petrone (1987) found similar results in their analysis of the services used in the four Illinois Department on Aging demonstration sites. They noted that legal services tended to be the least used, and job assistance was only provided in a few cases. Of particular interest is that in five out of six cases, only the victim received services. In their analysis, the cases of physical abuse involved the highest number of abusers in treatment; only very few perpetrators of neglect or financial abuse were part of the service plan. Yet, they add, one would expect that respite care or caregiver training would be appropriate for neglect cases, and job training, aid in finding employment, or welfare assistance would make the abuser less dependent in financial exploitation cases.

Treatment Outcome

With so little attention given to treatment of perpetrators in the law and in practice, there have been virtually no empirical data to indicate what intervention strategies are the most effective. One exception is the treatment outcome study conducted by the University of Alabama (Beall et al., 1988) to determine the effectiveness of a training program that would provide caregivers of frail or impaired older adults with information and skills to assist them in performing caregiving tasks and in coping with demands of the caregiving role. Although the initial intent was to obtain referrals of abusers who would be required by local district attorneys to attend the 8-week training session as an alternative to criminal prosecution, these referrals did not materialize because, as the authors explain, few cases of abuse were prosecuted, the victims were reluctant to sign a complaint or warrant, and Alabama law failed to redress for neglect. Therefore, the participation was broadened to include caregivers who were identified by mental health workers as being "at risk." Using two community control groups, the authors conducted eight 2-hour sessions on aging, community resource information, problem-solving and management skills, and stress and anger management techniques. The results indicated that the program was most effective in reducing symptoms of psychiatric distress. Its efficacy may be as a primary preventive measure, rather than as a treatment because none of the participants were known abusers.

SUMMARY AND FUTURE DIRECTIONS

From the depiction of elder abuse as involving a very dependent and impaired elderly woman who is mistreated by a well-meaning, but overburdened adult child caregiver, the concept has evolved into a much more complex set of players and relationships. Rather than placing the blame on the victim, professionals now recognize the perpetrator as an equal partner, if not a major cause, of the mistreatment. The work of Crouse et al. (1981) and Bristowe and Collins (1989) has alerted researchers that the characteristics of the caregiver may be more predictive of abuse than the frailties of the victim. Indeed, Anetzberger (1987) and Pillemer (1986) have provided some of the distinctive risk factors. The value of differentiating forms of abuse, reported first by Giordano and Giordano (1983), was also apparent in the series of analyses of the model project data identifying three diverse profiles of victims and perpetrators associated with the specific forms of abuse and neglect.

Physical and psychological abuse represented one profile, in which the victim suffered from emotional problems but was relatively independent in the activities of daily living. The perpetrator in these cases had a history of psychopathology and was dependent on the victim for financial resources.

The second profile, characteristic of neglect, was of an older, widowed victim who had cognitive and functional problems and little social support. These perpetrators neither had psychological problems nor were they financially dependent on the victim. For them, the victim was a source of stress. The third profile was that of material abuse. Here the motivation was, simply put, greed. The victims were generally unmarried with few social supports. The perpetrators had financial problems, sometimes traceable to a history of substance abuse. For them, the single, lonely elder was an easy target for exploitation.

In searching for explanations of elder mistreatment, researchers have proposed the social exchange theory, symbolic interactionism, and the environmental press model among others. Some clinicians have suggested a diagnosis and intervention model, based on psychosocial casework and an inadequate care paradigm, related to the needs of the client and caretaker as examples of treatment modalities. Lacking empirical data, service providers have patterned their response after other forms of family violence or aging programs, sometimes referred to as the child abuse model, the legal intervention model, and the advocacy model. The emphasis, and rightly so, has been on protecting the victim, with peripheral attention to the perpetrator.

However, the results of the more recent elder abuse studies indicate that working with the perpetrators may be a more successful way of reducing the incidence and prevalence of elder abuse. The existence of a range of perpetrator types suggests that diverse interventions should be considered, such as home services, respite care, crisis intervention, temporary separation, skill development, anger management, job placement, alcohol counseling, mental health care, legal restraints, and incarceration. Unfortunately, a number of barriers make it difficult to work with perpetrators, including the present organization and delivery of elder abuse services that focus primarily on the victim, the absence of the perpetrator from the case or his/her refusal to accept help, the inadequacy or unavailability of services, and the lack of knowledge of practitioners concerning the risk factors for abuse and neglect. Despite these limitations, this strategy holds the most promise in reducing the potential for elder mistreatment.

Finkelhor and Pillemer (1984) argue that it may be useful to start examining elder abuse for parallels with spouse abuse situations rather than child abuse, because the individuals involved are legally independent adults and because the model allows for consideration of the dependency of the abuser on the abused. Furthermore, spouse abuse represents a considerable proportion of the cases that are reported and a majority of those that exist in the community. From this perspective, elder abuse is no longer just an aging issue but a more broadly conceived family problem, exacerbated by alcoholism, mental illness, social isolation, and stress (Pillemer & Finkelhor, 1988). Considered in these terms, elder abuse may be more amenable to family-oriented intervention, which works toward strengthening the family's functioning, than treatment that concentrates on the older person's state (Edinburg, 1986). A family systems approach may be particularly appropriate in those instances in which victim and perpetrator are entangled in a "web of mutual dependency" (p. 69, Wolf, Strugnell, & Godkin, 1983).

The reconceptualization of elder abuse from a child abuse model to domestic violence offers new possibilities for treatment and prevention. Criticism of both the police and prosecutors for failing to respond to family violence, especially wife battering, has given rise to significant reforms and experiments that focus more on sanction and control of offenders than on victim protection (Fagen, 1988). One answer to the accumulated evidence of the ineffectiveness of the informal police dispositions of family violence calls has been mandatory arrest policies. Support for this practice has come from the Minneapolis Domestic Violence Study (Sherman & Berk, 1984), which found that of three randomly applied interventions—arrest, removing the husband from the home, and advice/mediation—arrest resulted in fewer calls for help and less repeated violence. Although there has been some question about the effectiveness of arrest procedures for those who commit repeated acts of violence and/or are at high risk of formal punishment, the study has helped to shape police policy and legislation nationwide. In fact, one of the recommendations of the Attorney General's Task Force on Family Violence (U.S. Department of Justice, 1984) was the establishment of arrest by law enforcement agencies as the preferred response in cases of family violence.

Similarly, prosecutors have been criticized for failing to file charges or pursue convictions and sanctions against offenders. Changes in adjudication processes, victim-witness programs, legal advocacy efforts, and special prosecution units in some jurisdictions have led to an increase in the percentage of cases formally prosecuted, but such activities are still not commonplace (Fagen, 1988).

Although only a minority of the nation's police agencies have special programs dealing with elder abuse, there is a growing awareness of the problem and its seriousness. A subset of 28 agencies responding to a survey of 175 police departments (from a stratified sample of 4733 police departments) conducted by the Police Executive Research Foundation (Plotkin, 1988), placed "defining elder abuse as a crime" among the highest ranked initiatives police would like policymakers to consider in setting legislative priorities.

The criminalization of elder abuse is evident in the increased interest in the topic by the criminal justice system. One district attorney (Harshbarger, 1988) addressing a conference for adult protective services workers articulated this position:

> Prosecution of these serious, complex cases is not the only solution but it does treat these acts of abuse and neglect for what they are—crimes—and forces professional and public awareness, responses and accountability. More posi-

tively, prosecution aids in therapy; the leverage is crucial to get offenders into treatment and to acknowledge wrongdoing. Prosecution also validates the victim and removes the stigma of inferiority, helplessness and sense of guilt—it helps to demonstrate that the victim is not at fault. (p. 6)

Certainly, not all acts of elder mistreatment would require this type of response. Physical abuse and financial exploitation may fit more comfortably within the structure and philosophy of the criminal justice system whereas acts of psychological abuse and neglect may not be appropriate. Although there is still a debate about the effectiveness of tougher criminal sanctions in reducing family violence (Hampton, 1988), for certain cases of elder abuse it is an approach that may be worth a trial.

Involving police and prosecutors, along with adult protective service workers, mental health professionals, lawyers, physicians, nurses, social workers, alcohol counselors, employment personnel, and aging advocates in communitywide problem solving of elder abuse cases may be the most successful strategy in the end. Across the country, representatives of such groups have joined together in local multidisciplinary teams, agency coalitions, or organization consortia to deal with the complex issues presented in cases of elder abuse and neglect. Within this context, the needs of the perpetrator as well as the victim and other members of the family can be addressed. Such ventures hold great promise not only in sensitizing the various sectors of society about abuse and neglect in the aging population, but in bringing about new solutions to some old societal problems.

REFERENCES

American Public Welfare Association & National Association of State Units on Aging (APWA/NASUA). (1986). *A comprehensive analysis of state policy and practice related to elder abuse*. Washington, DC: American Public Welfare Association and National Association of State Units on Aging.

Anetzberger, G. (1987). *The etiology of elder abuse by adult offspring*. Springfield, IL: Charles C Thomas.

Ansello, E. F., King, N. R., & Taler, G. (1986). The environmental press model: A theoretical framework for intervention in elder abuse. In K. A. Pillemer & R. S. Wolf (Eds.), *Elder abuse: Conflict in the family* (pp. 314–330). Dover, MA: Auburn House.

Beall, S. C., Baumhover, L. A., Bolland, J. M., Grote, N. P., Pieroni, R. E., & Scrogin, F. (1988, November). *Elder abuse intervention: A statewide program*. A paper presented at the Annual Scientific Meeting of the Gerontological Society of America, San Francisco.

Block, M. R., & Sinnott, J. D. (1979). *The battered elder syndrome: An exploratory study*. College Park: University of Maryland, Center on Aging.

Bristowe, E., & Collins, J. B. (1989). Family mediated abuse of noninstitutionalized frail elderly men and women living in British Columbia. *Journal of Elder Abuse & Neglect, 1,* 45–64.

Chen, P. N., Bell, S. S., Dolinsky, D. L., Doyle, J. & Dunn, M. (1981). Elderly abuse in domestic settings: A pilot study. *Journal of Gerontological Social Work, 4*(1), 3–17.

Crouse, J. S., Kobb, D. C., Harris, B. B., Kopecky, F. J., & Poertner, J. (1981). *Abuse and neglect of the elderly in Illinois.* Springfield: Illinois Department on Aging.

Edinburg, M. A. (1986). Developing and integrating family-oriented approaches in care of the elderly. In K. A. Pillemer & R. S. Wolf (Eds.), *Elder abuse: Conflict in the family* (pp. 267–282). Dover, MA: Auburn House.

Fagen, J. (1988). Contributions of family violence research to criminal justice policy on wife assault: Paradigms of science and social control. *Violence and Victims, 3*(3), 159–186.

Finkelhor, D., & Pillemer, K. A. (1984, August). *Elder abuse: Its relationship to other forms of domestic violence.* Paper presented at the Second National Conference for Family Violence Researchers, Durham, NH.

Fulmer, T. T., & O'Malley, T. A. (1987). *Inadequate care of the elderly: A health care perspective on abuse and neglect.* New York: Springer.

Gioglio, G. R., & Blakemore, P. (1983). *Elder abuse in New Jersey: The knowledge and experience of abuse among older New Jerseyans.* Trenton: New Jersey Department of Human Services.

Giordano, N. H., & Giordano, J. A. (1983, November). *Individual and family correlates of elder abuse.* Paper presented at the Annual Scientific Meeting of the Gerontological Society of America, San Francisco.

Hampton, R. L. (1988). Physical victimization across the life span. In M. B. Straus (Ed.), *Abuse and victimization across the life span* (pp. 203–222). Baltimore: Johns Hopkins University Press.

Harshbarger, S. (1988, November). *A prosecutor's perspective on protecting Older Americans.* Presentation at the 5th Annual Adult Protective Services Conference, San Antonio.

Hudson, M. F. (1988). A delphi study of elder mistreatment: Theoretical definitions, empirical referents, and taxonomy. Unpublished doctoral dissertation, University of Texas, Austin.

Illinois Department on Aging (1987). *Elder abuse demonstration project. Third interim report of the Illinois General Assembly on Public Acts 83-129 and 83-1432.* Springfield, IL: Author.

Iris, M. (1987). *North Suburban Cook County elder abuse project: Final Report.* Chicago: The Metropolitan Chicago Coalition on Aging.

Lau, E., & Kosberg, J. (1979). Abuse of the elderly by informal care providers. *Aging* 10–15.

O'Malley, H., Segars, H., Perez, R., Mitchell, V., & Knuepfel, G. M. (1979). *Elder abuse in Massachusetts: A survey of professionals and paraprofessionals.* Boston: Legal Research and Services for the Elderly.

Phillips, L. R. (1986). Theoretical explanations of elder abuse: Competing hypotheses and unresolved issues. In K. A. Pillemer & R. S. Wolf (Eds.), *Elder abuse: Conflict in the family* (pp. 197–217). Dover, MA: Auburn House.

Pillemer, K. A. (1986). Risk factors in elder abuse: Results from a case-control study. In K. A. Pillemer & R. S. Wolf (Eds.), *Elder abuse: Conflict in the family* (pp. 239–263). Dover, MA: Auburn House.

Pillemer, K. A., & Finkelhor, D. (1988). The prevalence of elder abuse: A random sample survey. *Gerontologist 28*(1), 51–57.

Pillemer, K. A. & Finkelhor, D. (1989). Causes of elder abuse: Caregiver stress vs. problem relatives. *American Journal of Orthopsychiatry, 51*(2), 179–187.

Plotkin, M. R. (1988). *A time for dignity: Police and domestic abuse of the elderly.* Washington, DC: Police Executive Research Forum and American Association of Retired Persons.

Quinn, J. J., & Tomita, S. K. (1986). *Elder abuse and neglect: Causes, diagnosis, and intervention strategies.* New York: Springer.

Sengstock, M. C., Hwalek, M., & Petrone, S. (1987, November). *Services for elderly victims of abuse: An analysis of four model programs.* Paper presented at the Annual Scientific Meeting of the Gerontological Society of America, Washington, DC.

Sengstock, M. C., & Liang, J. (1982). *Identifying and characterizing elder abuse.* Detroit: Wayne State University, Institute of Gerontology.

Sherman, L. W., & Berk, R. A. (1984). The Minneapolis domestic violence experiment. *Police Foundation Reports, 1,* 1.

U.S. Department of Justice (1984). *Report of the Attorney General's task force on family violence.* Washington, DC: U.S. Government Printing Office.

U.S. House of Representatives, Select Committee on Aging (1981). *Elder abuse: An examination of a hidden problem.* Washington, DC.: U.S. Government Printing Office.

Wolf, R. S., Godkin, M. A., & Pillemer, K. A. (1984). *Elder abuse and neglect: Report from three model projects.* Worcester: University of Massachusetts Medical Center, University Center on Aging.

Wolf, R. S., Godkin, M. A., & Pillemer, K. A. (1986). Maltreatment of the elderly: A comparative analysis. *Pride Institute Journal of Long Term Home Health Care 5,* 10–14.

Wolf, R. S., & McMurray Anderson, S. (in press). Elder abuse services in the local area: Adequacy and need. *Journal of Health and Human Services Administration.*

Wolf, R. S. & Pillemer, K. A. (1989). *Helping elderly victims: The reality of elder abuse.* New York: Columbia University Press.

Wolf, R. S., Strugnell, C. P., & Godkin, M. A. (1982). *Preliminary findings from three model projects on elderly abuse.* Worcester: University of Massachusetts Medical Center, University Center on Aging.

PART FOUR

Prevention of Family Violence

CHAPTER 14

Prevention of Child Physical Abuse

DEBORAH DARO

INTRODUCTION

In November 1987 the nation was outraged at the story of Lisa Steinberg, a 6-year-old New York City schoolchild who died allegedly as a result of beatings by her adoptive father. Across the country, the public asked how such violence toward a child could have been perpetrated by her so-called caretaker and, more importantly, how her death could have been prevented. Lisa's unhappy childhood and the injuries she had suffered from previous abuse were well documented. She had been reported as a suspected abuse victim on prior occasions, and the majority of her neighbors had noted disturbing patterns in her behaviors and those of her parents. Was her death the result of her parents' emotional problems? Was Lisa the victim of an image that suggests that only poorly educated, welfare recipients physically mistreat their children? Was Lisa the victim of an overworked and under-funded child protective service system unable to follow up thoroughly on all of the abuse reports it receives? Did Lisa die because professionals and community residents were reluctant to intrude on a family's right to privacy?

Tragically, her death was the cumulative result of all of these factors. Although physical abuse is the most widely recognized and "classic" form of child maltreatment, professional and public concern with this issue often begins only after a child has suffered physical battering and injury. Severe physical mistreatment by a parent or caretaker is generally considered child abuse and, in extreme cases, it justifies quick and extensive public intervention into the private family (Giovannoni & Becerra, 1979; Magura & Moses, 1986). Public concern and intervention before serious injury occurs, however, has not been the norm.

Reluctance to get involved before physical mistreatment results in observable injuries is supported by several misperceptions regarding the physical abuse process and parental responsibilities. Because child protective service caseworkers respond to over 2 million maltreatment reports annually, many believe intervention should be limited to the most extreme cases of abuse (Besharov, 1986). They consider physical abuse, as opposed to physical punishment, to be a relatively rare and predictable event, found only in families with visible and easily documented emotional and economic difficulties. When such indicators are absent or if the reported offense has not seriously injured the child, parents are given the right in our society to rear their children in the manner they see fit, including the use of physical punishment.

Does such a policy offer children the maximum protection possible? Unfortunately, intervening only after a child has suffered is too late for the child, for the family, and for a society that values its future. In many respects, child abuse follows a developmental pattern not unlike that of a disease— left untreated minor symptoms and discomforts can mushroom into serious, even fatal, disorders. Preventing physical abuse requires that action be taken against those individual and cultural factors that condone or nurture this more general abuse process.

The need for a comprehensive prevention strategy for physical abuse is justified for at least three reasons: The vast majority of treatment programs leave a sizable number of children at risk for future maltreatment; child maltreatment has serious and often fatal consequences for children, consequences from which they should be protected; and providing services only after a child is abused represents an enormous waste of scarce public resources.

Evaluations of child abuse treatment programs over the past 10 years have consistently underscored the limitations of these efforts (Cohn & Daro, 1988; Daro, 1988). Frankly, treatment programs have not been terribly successful in protecting children from continued abuse. Among protective service caseloads, reincidence rates of 30% to 40% are common (Herrenkohl, Herrenkohl, Egolf, & Seech, 1979; Laughlin & Weiss, 1981). Federal and state-funded evaluations of sophisticated clinical demonstration projects, often consisting of weekly contact for 12 to 18 months, report reincidence among one third to one half of all clients (Cohn & Daro, 1988). Further, at termination, more than half of the clients served by these programs remain at risk of abusing their children in the future.

Prevention services also are necessary to protect children from the extensive emotional and physical damage they suffer as the result of abuse. The documented consequences of abuse include chronic health problems; cognitive and language disorders as reflected in poor performances on virtually every standard measure available; socioemotional problems such as low self-esteem, lack of trust, low frustration tolerance, and poor relationships with adults and peers; difficulties in school including poor attendance, misconduct, and learning disorders serious enough to warrant special education classes; and self-mutilative or other self-destructive behaviors. One evaluation of abused children who received therapeutic services from federally funded treatment programs reported that 14% of the victims under 12 years of age and 40% of the adolescent victims had attempted suicide or self-injury (Daro, 1988).

Of course, the ultimate damage from abuse is death. Annual telephone surveys of all 50 states conducted by the National Committee for Prevention of Child Abuse (NCPCA) found that in 1986 and 1987 an average of three children a day were reported as fatal victims of maltreatment. Perhaps more alarming is that between 25% and 50% of these children were currently on child protective service caseloads or known to local protective service workers at the time of death (Daro & Mitchel, 1988).

Developing prevention services is not only good program planning, it is good economic planning. Quite simply, the costs associated with remediating the consequences of maltreatment are staggering, as reported in a detailed benefit–cost analysis developed by Daro (1988). Initially, serious physical abuse cases, a category that represents only 3% of all reports, cost society annually at least $20 million in hospitalization and $7 million in rehabilitation to address the victim's immediate physical injuries and developmental problems. Further, in 1983, reported cases of child abuse cost society a minimum of $460 million in administrative and foster care placement costs. Intensive treatment services for this population can run between $2,860 per family per year for lay therapy and supportive services to over $28,000 per family per year for comprehensive therapeutic services, including remedial services for children. If only the severely abused children reported in 1983 received these intensive therapeutic services for one year, the costs would have exceeded $662 million.

In addition to these initial costs, those of maltreatment extend over time. Again, using Daro's conservative estimates, the long-term costs of abuse include $14.8 million for juvenile court and detention and $664 million in long-term foster care. Most disturbing, are the limitations serious physical abuse place on our nation's ability to be economically competitive. The 1,200 child abuse fatalities reported in 1986 cost society $645 million in potential future earnings. In 1987, another $608 million in potential earnings were eliminated from our economic future as a result of fatal child maltreatment. Can a society that hopes to compete in the world economy afford to suffer this continuous drain on its future labor pool? Further, the domestic need for a more productive labor force also is growing. Whereas today each 100 workers support 19 elderly persons, these same 100 workers will have to support 38 elders by the end of this century (Ozawa, 1985). Every case of child abuse undercuts our nation's ability to achieve these productivity levels.

The efficient and effective use of public monies to prevent physical abuse is a worthwhile goal. However, generating support for intervention into the private family prior to an overt failure on the part of parents to adequately care for or discipline their children is a complex issue. To date, the majority of prevention programs have targeted at risk populations as defined by various causal theories of maltreatment. As discussed later in this chapter, a wide range of educational and support services have been developed for new parents, teen parents, low-income families, families with special needs children, and parents exhibiting various behavioral or emotional problems. Future prevention efforts, however, need to move beyond these types of targeted efforts and incorporate strategies that alter the normative standards of discipline and enhance a sense of communitywide responsibility for a child's well-being.

With such an objective in mind, this chapter begins with an overview of the issues facing prevention planners, paying particular attention to the contributions various causal theories of abuse make to the creation of a prevention service continuum. Attention is then focused on the empirical evidence generated by program evaluations, highlighting those specific prevention programs which offer the most promising avenues for success. The discussion concludes with a suggested prevention continuum and strategies for establishing this array of services in all communities across the country.

ISSUES IN PREVENTION

Enhancing future prevention efforts requires attention to two broad sets of issues—those individual and societal factors that contribute to an elevated risk of maltreatment and those factors that limit the capacity of prevention efforts to reach beyond their current, narrowly defined target populations. Identification of the first set of factors is facilitated by a careful review of prevailing causal theories of maltreatment. Reviewing the process through which prevention services are generally made available to individual families contributes to a keener understanding of the second set of issues.

Causal Theories of Abuse and Their Implications for Prevention

Broad causal theories have been used to explain the general relationship between specific individual or environmental conditions and child abuse. Theoretical accounts most commonly found in the literature range from interpersonal functioning theories, such as psychodynamic and learning theories, to systemic and social explanations for maltreatment, as suggested by theories of stress and poverty (Newberger & Newberger, 1982). For purposes of developing useful prevention strategies, most of these theories can be classified into four general groups according to their suggested approach:

Psychodynamic Theories. Parents would be less abusive if they better understood themselves and their role as parents.

Learning Theories. Parents would be less abusive if they knew, more specifically, how best to care for their children.

Environmental Theories. Parents would be less abusive if they had greater resources available to them in terms of material support or social support for a given set of actions.

Ecological Theories. Parents would be less abusive if a network of services or supports existed to compensate for individual, situational, and environmental shortcomings.

Each of these theoretical frameworks is intuitively appealing in its capacity to explain the phenomenon of physical abuse and to offer creative ways to prevent its occurrence.

Psychodynamic theories place a heavy emphasis on the parent's level of functioning in explaining abusive behavior (Bolton & Bolton, 1987). Individuals with diminished capacity because of developmental disabilities or substance dependency or abuse are less able to care for their children adequately than individuals without these functional limitations. Individuals who have difficulty managing their personal choices and emotions often find it difficult, if not impossible, to manage and care for children, particularly if the children are unusually demanding or needy. Although these individuals may have an adequate understanding of appropriate parenting skills, they lack the personal capacity to implement these skills in a consistent and effective manner. Similarly, individuals suffering from severe or even relatively moderate psychological disorders may be less able to cope with the unpredictable nature of children or the routine demands of child care.

Parents who are unable to establish emotional attachments to their children or who exhibit serious psychological problems are generally very poor candidates for prevention services. Fortunately, a small percentage, roughly 10% to 20% of all abusive parents, present overt psychopathology (Kempe & Kempe, 1978, 1984). The vast majority of parents presenting such problems as distorted dependencies, immaturity, feelings of helplessness or isolation, low self-esteem, or an inability to manage anger are amenable to interventions, either prior to or after becoming parents. Formal therapeutic services, such as individual, family, or group therapy, or more informal self-help groups, offer opportunities for individuals to address the underlying causes of these difficulties. Such efforts play an important role in the prevention continuum by reducing those personal barriers that can limit a well-intentioned parent's capacity to care for his or her child.

Although it still focuses on the parent, learning theory emphasizes the lack of skills and knowledge rather than poor psychological functioning. Under this model, abuse occurs because parents simply do not know how to care for their children, have a limited repertoire of discipline, or use child care techniques that are either harmful or ineffective. These adults also may have a history of maltreatment and poor parenting, or they may be too young or too inexperienced to comprehend what is expected of them as parents. The intuitive appeal of this model is that if parents can be trained or taught how to parent effectively, the cycle of abuse could be broken through consistent intervention with all first-time parents. Parenting education programs are well suited to filling this type of informational gap either through written material, group presentations, or individual home instruction. In many respects, conveying this type of basic knowledge to parents may be the easiest task in improving parenting potential.

Beyond providing parents with general information, however, lies the more difficult task of helping parents translate knowledge into behavior. For some parents, this transition will be a natural extension of having received the information or of having observed appropriate caregiving. For other parents, the transition will be significantly more difficult. Parents who experienced healthy care as children (or who observed or perhaps assisted their parents in the care of younger siblings) will have less difficulty making use of the knowledge offered by parenting education resources than will parents who lack concrete, positive experiences. For the latter group of parents, identifying and addressing the barriers they face in meeting their child's needs can be a complex and time-consuming task for practitioners. Service providers may need to spend several sessions simply modeling the implementation of basic parenting information or assisting parents in securing necessary support services, such as medical care or day care.

The third theoretical approach moves the discussion away from a focus on individual characteristics and toward the broader structural and cultural environment. Rather than viewing maltreatment as emanating from a lack of motivation or skill on the parent's part, this causal theory focuses on the potentially dominant role of certain societal conditions and values. Poverty with its corresponding limits on personal choice and societal values that condone violence, racism, and sexism are forces that often overwhelm the limited resistance of families who find themselves trapped in a cycle of distress (Pelton, 1981). Depending on the type of abuse in question, the social features that contribute to the problem differ but the direction and intensity of the impacts remain. Attitudes that condone, even promote, corporal punishment, and the importance placed on individualism, competition, and the family privacy contribute to a generally violent environment (Garbarino, 1987; Gelles & Straus, 1988).

As one might expect, the prevention services generated by this theory seek changes within communities and value systems. Attacking the underlying causes of abuse under this theoretical assumption requires changes in social attitudes and practices. In addition to broad-scale public awareness campaigns to clarify the relationship between certain societal norms and potential maltreatment, proponents of this approach support policy changes to reduce the level of stress families face because of poverty or the shortage of necessary support services. Improvements in housing, health care systems, and educational services, as well as increased access to job training and employment opportunities are among the strategies frequently promoted within the context of an environmental explanation for maltreatment (Wolock & Horowitz, 1979).

Each of these three theoretical approaches is partially correct in its explanation of maltreatment; none, however, can adequately explain on its own the entire riddle of abuse. The final theoretical framework cited earlier, the ecological model, integrates the interpersonal characteristics of a family with its surrounding environmental and cultural realities (Belsky, 1980; Brofenbrenner 1979; Garbarino 1977). This theory focuses not merely on the functioning of individuals and the functioning of the various spheres in which they operate (e.g., the family, the community, and the broader social/political environment), but rather on the interaction of these spheres. Some have classified these interactions in terms of a hierarchical structure, differentiating between sufficient causes and necessary causes (Garbarino, 1977). Framing the interactions in a different way, Cicchetti and Rizley (1981) allocate risk factors into one of two broad categories: potentiating factors that increase the probability of the occurrence of maltreatment, and compensatory factors that decrease the risk of maltreatment. The risk factors attributed to each of these categories are further divided into transient "state" factors and more permanent "trait" factors. According to Cicchetti and Rizley, abuse occurs only in those situations where the potentiating factors exceed the compensatory or buffering conditions.

There are two implications of the ecological theory for prevention planning. First, the theory underscores the need to simultaneously address the problem from a number of levels, including changes in the individual, the manner in which that individual relates to other family members, and the manner in which the family unit interacts with its immediate community as well as with broader social and cultural norms. No single prevention approach will address the multiple causes of maltreatment nor the way these causal factors influence the actions of an individual parent. Second, the transactional risk model highlights that emphasis must be placed not only on minimizing the characteristics of individuals or communities viewed as elevating risk of maltreatment, but also on maximizing the characteristics of individuals or communities that buffer families against abuse. It is not sufficient merely to suggest that parents not use physical force in disciplining their children. An effective prevention system must also offer alternative discipline methods and address the conditions that lead a parent to consider the use of physical discipline not only appropriate but necessary.

Barriers to Effective Prevention Planning

Several fiscal, demographic, and programmatic barriers exist to expanding prevention services. First, none of the solutions being debated is inexpensive. Even the most modest programs, involving short-term informational services to first-time parents, would require significant funding. Simply supplying the 3.7 million women who give birth each year with $5 worth of printed material, with no personalized explanations, would cost $18.5 million annually. If every woman giving birth received one hour of parenting advice and information, at an average per client cost of $14, the annual costs would exceed $52 million (Daro, 1988). Although the costs of new parent services can be minimized through integration with existing service systems and through the use of paraprofessional staff and volunteers, significant expenditures are inevitable.

In the long run, however, prevention is cost-effective. Initial spending on health care and day-care services around the time of birth can result in significant system savings in local welfare and special education budgets. For example, Seitz, Rosenbaum, and Apfel (1985) noted considerable long-term savings in such costs for high-risk families randomly selected to receive intensive medical and support services following the birth of their child. Compared to a similar group of families not receiving such services, they found the 15 treatment families used $40,000 less in welfare benefits and special educational services in the single year in which the 10-year follow-up study was conducted. Considering the broader prevention network, Daro (1988) estimates that even if such services were successful in reducing the level of serious physical abuse by only 20%, some $362 million would be saved each year in reduced foster care costs, hospitalization and medical costs, rehabilitative services, juvenile court costs, and lost future productivity. Unfortunately, policy is rarely made with an eye toward long-term savings. Calls for a balanced budget make legislatures uncomfortable with even moderate spending if savings cannot be realized in the same fiscal year. For at least some period of time, it is reasonable to assume that significant dollars need to be placed in both treatment and prevention. Although prevention dollars spent today eventually will lead to a reduction in the demand for treatment services, the increasing number of current victims as evidenced by higher reporting and child fatality rates suggests that this transfer point has not been reached. Being committed to prevention means being committed to devoting professional energies and fiscal resources to the planning and implementation of an intervention that may not produce aggregate, measurable cost savings for some time.

Second, the health and welfare of the nation's children is influenced by a myriad of sociological and demographic trends that in turn influence both the potential for child abuse and the capacity to prevent it. Divorce, women in the labor force, teenage pregnancy, domestic violence, school failures and dropout rates, drug use, a mismatch between the skills of the workforce and the jobs that are available, the lack of affordable housing, and an erosion of the social service safety net add stress to the parenting process and place a growing number of families at an elevated risk for maltreatment. One challenge facing those concerned with prevention is selecting from among these issues those trends they will try to reduce and those they will accept as a given. Such a selection process reflects different ideological points of view and different concepts of family structure. Policies whose success depend on an increase in two-parent households where one parent remains home to care for the child face a tough battle. As reported by the U.S. House of Representatives Select Committee on Children, Youth, and Families (1987), few families resemble this model. At any one time, almost a quarter of all families are headed by single parents and over 70% of all children will face life in a single-parent household at least some time before they turn 18. Further, by 1995, 67% of all preschoolers, and 80% of all children aged 7 to 18 years will have working mothers. Prevention efforts need to be compatible with these realities.

Finally, a chronic criticism of prevention services is that the only parents who use them are the ones who would most likely not abuse or neglect their children. Parents who recognize the need to seek out parenting services, the argument goes, are exactly the type of parents one would expect to be successful in the use of such services. To a certain extent the voluntary nature of prevention services do allow the most violent and most seriously dysfunctional families to avoid early intervention. For example, Schverman, Wulczyn, and Farber (1984) confirmed this theory with respect to the types of teen parents electing to participate in Parents Too Soon, an educational and support program in Illinois. Those youths who had ever held a job, who perceived work as better than welfare, and who saw themselves as having problems were three times more likely to enroll in the program than youth with none of these characteristics.

Such findings may indeed suggest a self-selection process, but this process may not be detrimental to the efficient use of prevention resources. Simply put, severely dysfunctional families may not be good candidates for prevention services. Wauchope and Straus (1987) noted that roughly 4% to 6% of the randomly selected households they interviewed demonstrated severe violence toward their children irrespective of the child's age. One interpretation of this finding is that physical violence in these families is not a result of a lack of child development knowledge or unrealistic expectations for children. Families in this group appear to communicate through violence and to cope with stress and disappointment by physically mistreating each other. Simply providing parenting education services and support groups to these families has little chance of breaking this very severe pattern of violence.

Protecting children who live in such violent environments may well require nonvoluntary programs and cohesive interventions. On the other hand, prevention services, almost by definition, have an inherent voluntary quality to them. The minute a program shifts from voluntary to mandatory it shifts from social support to social control. One of the major dilemmas facing the prevention field is how to reach down into those families at highest risk without altering the supportive and positive image of prevention.

PREVENTION PROGRAMS AND EVALUATION

Effectively preventing physical abuse can be accomplished only through the combined efforts of practitioners, policy makers, and researchers. Certainly, reducing levels of serious injury to young children and enhancing a child's healthy development and well-being demand the design and implementation of a diversified prevention service network. The specific components of such a system articulated by the National Committee for Prevention of Child Abuse include:

Educational and support services for all new parents around the time their children are born

Continued opportunities for parenting education to help parents adjust to the ever-changing demands of their children

Early and regular child and family screening and treatment to ensure prompt attention to any health or developmental problems

Adequate child care opportunities to furnish parents with quality regular and occasional out-of-home care for their children

Programs for abused and neglected children to remediate the immediate consequences of maltreatment and to minimize the risk of additional functioning problems as the child matures

Life skills training for children and young adults to equip them with the interpersonal skills and knowledge valuable in their future adult roles and in protecting themselves from being abused

Self-help groups and other neighborhood supports to foster a sense of community responsibility and care for the well-being of parents and children

Public awareness campaigns to educate parents and future parents that being a parent is not easy, that it is all right to reach out for help, and that prevention is everyone's responsibility

Systemic changes to address institutional and cultural barriers that foster the use of violence toward children (Cohn, 1983)

At present, these prevention efforts exist all across the country. A recent survey of service providers in 29 randomly selected counties found that over 75% of the hospitals, school districts, and community-based agencies contacted offer some form of educational or support services to parents or youth as a strategy to prevent child abuse (Daro, Abrahams, & Robson, 1988). Virtually every community offers parents a way to reach out for help in times of stress, either through crisis hotlines or respite care centers. Further, national media campaigns to promote public awareness of the problem and to urge parents to "take time out; don't take it out on your kid" have been developed and disseminated by the National Committee for Prevention of Child Abuse for longer than 10 years.

The richest body of empirical evidence regarding the effectiveness of prevention services is found among those programs that offer specific services to high-risk parents. Although the content and structure of these programs vary, critical service goals include:

Increasing the parents' knowledge of child development and the demands of parenting

Enhancing the parents' skill in coping with the stresses of infant and child care

Enhancing parent–child bonding, emotional ties, and communication

Increasing the parents' skill in coping with the stress of caring for children with special needs

Increasing the parents' knowledge about home and child management

Reducing the burden of child care

Increasing access to social and health services for all family members

Both home-based programs and center-based programs incorporating these goals have demonstrated a wide range of positive client outcomes. Specific gains have included improved mother–infant bonding and maternal capacity to respond to the child's emotional needs (Affholter, Connell, & Nauta, 1983; Dickie & Gerber 1980; Field, Widmayer, Stringer, & Ignatoff, 1980; O'Connor, Vietze, Sherrod, Sandler, & Altemeier, 1980); demonstrated ability to care for the child's physical and developmental needs (Field et al., 1980; Gabinet, 1979; Gray, 1983; Gutelius, Kirsch, MacDonald, Brooks, & McErlean, 1977; Larson, 1980; Love, Nauta, Coelen, Hewett, & Ruopp, 1976; Olds, Chamberlin, & Tatlebaum, 1986; Travers, Nauta, & Irwin, 1982); fewer subsequent pregnancies (Badger, 1981; McAnarney et al., 1978; Olds et al., 1986) more consistent use of health care services and job-training opportunities (Powell, 1986); and lower welfare use, higher school completion rates, and higher employment rates (Badger, 1981; Gutelius et al., 1977; Polit, 1987; Powell, 1986; Seitz et al., 1985). In identifying the types of parents most likely to benefit from these educational and supportive services, several have noted particular success with young, relatively poor mothers (Badger, 1981; Gabinet, 1979; Olds et al., 1986) and with mothers who felt confident in their lives prior to enrolling in the program (Powell, 1986).

At least two longitudinal studies suggest that comprehensive parenting services not only produce initial gains but that these gains are strengthened over time. Seitz and her colleagues (1985) successfully tracked, 10 years later, 15 of 17 matched sets of low-income, first-time parents, half of whom had received a coordinated set of medical and social services, including day care for their children. Each family received 13 to 17 well-baby visits; an average of 28 home visits by a social worker, psychologist, or nurse; and 2 to 28 months of day-care services over the entire treatment period. Families were enrolled from pregnancy through 20 months postpartum.

Although the sample is small and was limited to first-time mothers, repeated follow-up studies on the treatment families noted a steady improvement from termination, to 5 years later, to the current 10-year posttermination study. Average educational achievement for treatment mothers was 13.0 years, whereas the control sample had an average of only 11.7. The study team found 13 of the 15 treatment families had at least one full-time wageearner or full-time equivalent between both adult partners in the home, a situation that was found in only 8 of the 15 control families. Significant differences also were noted in the school performance of the two groups of children. Only 4 of the 15 control children were judged by their teachers to have good school adjustment, a rating given to 10 of the 16 treatment children.

Similar gains were noted by Wieder, Poisson, Lourie, and Greenspan (1988) in a 5-year follow-up of 32 multirisk families who received intensive, comprehensive services through the Clinical Infant Development Program (CIDP) of the National Institute of Mental Health. Unlike the previous study, all of the women in this sample had at least one other child prior to project enrollment. The three components of this multiyear program included organizing basic services for adequate food, housing, medical care, and educational opportunities; providing a constant emotional relationship with the family in order to establish trust; and providing specialized services to the infant and parents, geared to meet the challenges at each stage of development.

Significant gains were noted on all of the dimensions tested. Although many of the families continued to exhibit some functional problems, economic and personal improvements were significant. Over 60% of the adult mothers and almost 75% of the women initially seen as teen parents were employed at follow-up as contrasted to the 20% employment rate for adults and the 7% employment rate for teens noted at intake. Although 75% of the teen parent participants had been receiving public assistance at the time services terminated, none of the 13 adolescent clients contacted 5 years later were welfare recipients. Further, only 5% of the adult program participants were reported for child abuse during the 5-year period and none of these reports involved the child who had received services as part of this program.

The work of David Olds and his colleagues (1986) has provided some of the best empirical evidence to date that the provision of a specific service model does indeed reduce the incidence of child abuse. The 400 participants in this study, all of whom were first-time mothers, were randomly assigned to one of four conditions in which the most intensive level of services involved regular pre- and postnatal home visits by a nurse practitioner. The home visitors carried out three major activities: parent education regarding fetal and infant development; the involvement of family members and friends in child care and support of the mother; and the linkage of family members with other health and human services.

Those who received the most intensive intervention had a significantly lower incidence of reported child abuse over the 2-year postbirth study period. Whereas 19% of the comparison group at greatest risk for maltreatment (i.e., poor, unmarried teens) were reported for abuse or neglect, only 4% of their nurse-visited counterparts were reported. Of these cases, 50% involved reports of neglect only and 50% involved reports of neglect and physical abuse. Although these results were not true for older program participants, the dramatic gains realized with first-time, teen mothers suggest that this group may benefit particularly from prevention services. In addition to having a lower reported rate of child abuse, those infants whose mothers received ongoing home visits had fewer accidents and were less likely to require emergency room care. The mothers also reported less frequent need to punish or restrict their children.

The use of home visitors has been identified by others as achieving notable gains in parent–child interactions and in improving the child's developmental progress. For example, Project 12-Ways, a multifaceted home-based service program in central Illinois, provides intensive services to families who have been reported for actual maltreatment or for being at risk of maltreatment. Services are provided in the client's home by advanced graduate students and cover such topics as parenting skills, stress management, self-control, assertiveness training, health maintenance, job placement, and marital counseling. Repeated evaluations of the program by Lutzker and Rice (1984, 1987) have documented significantly fewer repeated abuse and neglect incidents among program recipients than among similar families not receiving this intervention. While enrolled in the program, only 2% of a randomly selected number of clients from Project 12-Ways were reported for maltreatment compared to 11% of the control group. In the year following termination of services, 10% of the treatment families and 21% of the nontreatment families were reported for maltreatment.

Larson (1980) noted similar gains in an assessment of the Prenatal Intervention Project in Montreal, but only in cases in which such visits began prior to the child's birth. In this case, the home visitors were women with undergraduate degrees in child psychology who had received special training in preventive child health care. The home visits were designed to provide information about general caretaking topics, such as feeding, sleep schedules, clothing, accident prevention, and the need for regular well-child care. The visitors also encouraged the mothers to talk to their infants during caregiving and to respond to their vocalizations. Child development counseling involved reviewing with the mother her child's developmental competence and suggesting types of activities she could engage in to promote the child's capabilities.

Children whose mothers began receiving services in the 7th month of pregnancy had a lower accident rate and exhibited fewer feeding problems. In addition, the mothers scored higher on assessments of maternal behavior and in providing appropriate and stimulating home environments.

The use of trained, lay volunteers as home visitors also has been found effective in reducing the risk of abuse. The C. Henry Kempe National Center for the Treatment and Prevention of Child Abuse and Neglect pioneered the use of lay home visitors with at-risk mothers. Gray, Cutler, Dean, and Kempe's (1979) evaluations of this effort found this method reduced child abuse potential and enhanced mother–infant relationships. Although it did not measure a reduction in child abuse and neglect directly, the Ford Foundation's Child Survival/Fair Start Initiative suggests that well-trained community volunteers offer a unique opportunity to successfully engage at-risk mothers, particularly those who lack the ability to trust anyone outside of their immediate family. Larner and Halpren (1987) report that for many of the families, the home visits were sufficient to resolve the majority of their situational and personal difficulties. Many multiproblem families, however, required additional, more directed professional assistance in the areas of health care, child care, and mental health services.

Recently, positive findings have been noted among programs providing services for a relatively short period of time. For example, Taylor and Beauchamp (1988) report notable differences in parenting knowledge, skills, and attitudes among participants receiving four visits by a student nurse volunteer compared to a no service control group. Program participants received one visit while in the hospital and three subsequent home visits, 1, 2, and 3 months postpartum. Those who received the visits scored significantly higher on tests of child development, expressed more democratic ideas regarding child rearing, demonstrated more positive parent–infant interactions, and evinced greater problem-solving abilities.

A number of parenting enhancement models utilizing a center-based service delivery method also have produced positive gains in overall parenting skills and in the use of community resources (Levine, 1988). Many of these programs are school-based initiatives. For example, the New Futures School, in Albuquerque, New Mexico, reports a very positive response of teen mothers to their school-based educational and support program. A 1981 follow-up study on youth who were served by the program between 1974 and 1980 found that over 80% of the teens had completed high school and, as a group, they had a repeat pregnancy rate that was one third the national average.

Integrating parent support programs into a community's broader self-help system also has produced notable gains. For example, Avancé Educational Programs for Parents and Teens serves a predominantly low-income Mexican-American community in San Antonio, Texas, through the provision of comprehensive parenting education. The 9-month service period includes center-based weekly bilingual discussions on child growth and development, toy-making classes, day-care practicum, field trips, library use, transportation, information and referral, and communal holiday celebrations. Evaluations of these efforts have found participants to be more hopeful about the future, and more willing to assume the role of educator with their children, to hold less severe conceptions of punishment, and to be more willing to utilize social supports to gain help (Rodriguez & Cortez, 1983).

One of the most widely disseminated group-based models is the Minnesota Early Learning Demonstration (MELD), an intensive 2-year parenting education and support program. MELD's mission is to get families off to a good start and to eliminate the potential for maltreatment by preventing the development of abusive or neglectful patterns. The MELD staff believe that there is no one right way to parent, and participants are encouraged to make the child-rearing choices that are appropriate for them and their children. The program demonstrates that if participants are supported in their efforts to be good parents, if they are exposed to good information and alternative ways of addressing child-rearing issues, they will be able to make the choices that enhance their children's well-being as well as their own.

Although the program has never been evaluated in terms of child abuse prevention, the immediate outcomes demonstrated by program participants are encouraging (Ellwood, 1988; Miller, 1988). A recent evaluation of the MELD Young Moms program conducted by the Child Welfare League of America noted that 80% of the participants had finished or were completing high school compared to an overall school completion rate of only 20% for the general adolescent parent population. Also, whereas 25% of all teenage mothers experience a repeat pregnancy within a year of their first birth, MELD Young Mom participants have a repeat pregnancy rate of only 10% to 15%. Changes also were noted in the parents' use of discipline, in that the percentage of parents who spanked their children decreased from 56% at the start of the program to only 12% at the conclusion of services.

The collective results outlined here underscore the difficulty in addressing the myriad of issues associated with an increased risk for maltreatment under the rubric of a single service framework. Reaching the full spectrum of the at-risk population requires some combination of both home-based and center-based programs. Center-based services, particularly if they are associated with local junior high and senior high school programs for adolescent parents, offer excellent opportunities for a highly motivated teenage mother not only to improve her parenting skills but also to continue her education and to establish a stable life for herself and her infant. Home-based programs, with their more individualized and flexible service delivery system, will be particularly useful with a more isolated population and with those mothers lacking the interest or motivation to participate in a group program. Crisis intervention should augment both of these strategies, and respite services also are needed as a safety valve for new parents.

SUMMARY AND FUTURE DIRECTIONS

The prevention of physical abuse has focused primarily on altering parental behavior or on providing parents under stress an opportunity to seek help before they strike out at their child. The most common and best evaluated of these strategies include home visitor programs, parenting education classes, and support groups. Such efforts serve both to strengthen the abilities of parents to care for their children and to remediate or correct the psychological, knowledge, and skill barriers that impede positive parenting. To be most effective, however, these efforts must reach a greater percentage of the population and be augmented by strategies that attack the underlying cultural and environmental factors contributing to elevated risk of maltreatment.

How should efforts to prevent physical abuse be expanded? At a minimum, energies need to focus on four fronts:

Expanding the availability of educational and support services for all parents

Providing quality therapeutic and remedial services to all victims of abuse

Encouraging all individuals to serve as a resource for parents under stress

Eliminating cultural norms and values that promote the use of violence toward children

Expansion of Services and Supports for Parents

Beginning where the field is at, it remains important for all parents to receive quality assistance throughout the child-rearing years. To accomplish this task, prevention services need to be more fully integrated into those institutions that interact with parents. For example, all local hospitals with maternity wards need to develop education and supportive services for all women delivering at their facilities. Initially these services might be limited to first-time parents, gradually expanding to include all births. Further, all local junior and senior high school administrators need to integrate parenting and family life education into the standard curriculum. In addition, all high school districts should develop and implement a comprehensive educational and support program for pregnant and parenting teens. Key services to include in such a program would be day care, vocational training, support groups, and financial planning.

The provision of parenting classes through local school districts is already under way in Missouri and Minnesota, although in both cases funding for these programs is woefully inadequate. The Early Childhood Family Education Program in Minnesota establishes weekly in-class discussions for all adults who are pregnant or who have children under the age of 5 years. Each session includes a 15- to 45-minute parent–child interaction period. Although available for all parents, only 6% of the target population was served in 1987. Similarly, the Missouri Parents as Teachers program provides funding for only 30% of the parents of children under the age of 3 years, although all parents are technically eligible.

Finally, prevention advocates need to integrate parent enhancement services into the broad range of organizations with which parents interact. Both home visitor programs as well as center-based education and support groups need to be established, thereby providing a network of services for parents with different personal skills and needs. Local churches, recreational centers, housing associations, day-care collectives, and civic organizations all must be engaged in supporting parents in their local community, either directly through the development and implementation of a new parent program, or indirectly through contributing volunteers or funding to existing efforts.

Central to expanding service levels is to generate additional revenues. Among the most innovative and widely disseminated sources for child abuse prevention funding are the Children's Trust and Prevention Funds, based on a concept conceived in the late 1970s by Dr. Ray Helfer of Michigan State University, School of Medicine. A pioneer in the area of child abuse identification and treatment, Dr. Helfer designed the funds as a way of securing permanent support for prevention. Currently operating in 49 states, these trust and prevention funds raise money by building in surcharges on marriage licenses, birth certificates, or divorce decrees, or through specially designed tax refunds. More recently, a number of the funds have generated revenues through direct appropriations and private donations. In 1987, these funds collectively distributed over $21 million to support 1250 prevention programs nationwide.

Individual counties also are drafting local taxing schemes to increase the resources available for children's programs. In Florida, for example, over a dozen counties have passed or initiated referendums to assess homeowners an additional $25 per year to support a Juvenile Welfare Board. These boards assess the service needs for local children, coordinate efforts presently underway to meet these needs, and support new service initiatives when present efforts prove inadequate (Volsky, 1988). These and similar strategies attest to the possibilities of expanding child abuse prevention resources even within the context of limited public budgets.

Expansion of Therapeutic Services for Abuse Victims

Many of the theoretical explanations for child abuse underscore an association between being abused as a child and becoming an abusive parent. Certainly, this association is not perfect. Kaufman and Zigler (1989) found that only one third of abuse victims become abusive parents. However, looking at this statistic in terms of increased probability, parents who were abused children are six times more likely to mistreat their own children than are parents who were nonabused. Given such increased propensity toward maltreatment, it seems that the provision of therapeutic services to remediate the psychological and physical damage from violence experienced as a child would be a critical component in any plan to break the cycle of abuse.

Unfortunately, the victims of maltreatment are not presently receiving this benefit. Local child protective service administrators report that they are able to provide remedial or therapeutic services to less than one third of the victims they identify (Daro & Mitchel, 1988). Increasing the percentage of abuse victims receiving services is essential to reducing abuse rates in the next generation. Research on both children and adolescent victims of maltreatment suggests that therapeutic and support services do indeed remediate the consequences of maltreatment. Recipients of such services as therapeutic preschool, play therapy, group, and individual counseling demonstrate improved self-esteem, physical and emotional development, interactions with peers, and parental and sibling relationships (Daro, 1988; Delson & Clark, 1981; MacFarlane et al., 1986; Porter, Blick, & Sgroi, 1982). Failure to provide therapeutic services to abuse victims represents a lost opportunity society can ill afford.

Encouraging Individuals to Become Involved

Preventing child abuse requires not only an expansion of formal service systems but also an increased capacity among informal sources of support. Simply put, individuals need to become more directly concerned and involved in the prevention process throughout all aspects of their lives. Public opinion polls conducted for NCPCA over the past 2 years have noted that two thirds of the American public feel that they can do much to prevent child abuse and one fourth report actually having taken steps to prevent child abuse in the past year. Among the personal activities respondents listed were reporting someone for abuse (21%); not abusing or hitting their own children (16%); working as a volunteer or counselor (17%); speaking to a friend or relative about abuse (13%); educating adults on how not to be abusive of children or how not to be victimized (12%); stopping someone from hitting a child (5%); and serving as foster parents (3%).

Many individuals find it the most difficult to interfere in the rearing of children and are reluctant to talk with close friends or relatives about their parenting (not to mention approaching a stranger). However, until individuals demonstrate such concern, family violence will continue to be sanctioned. In order to assist individuals in overcoming their fears of reaching out and offering assistance to parents in stress, the Franklin County Children's Task Force in Farmington, Maine, published the following supportive statements to make to parents and children in abusive or near-abusive situations:

"She seems to be trying your patience."

"It looks like it's been a long day for both of you."

"He has beautiful [eyes]," to get the parent in a more positive mood.

"My child used to get upset like that."

"Children can wear you out, can't they? Is there anything I can do to help?"

Strike up a conversation with the adult. See if you can redirect his/her attention away from the child.

Sympathize with the parent, even if it's just a knowing glance or smile.

Divert the child's attention (if he/she is misbehaving), by talking to or engaging him/her in conversation.

Praise the child and/or parent at the first opportunity.

If the child is in danger, offer assistance. For example, if the child was left unattended in a grocery cart, go stand by the child until the parent returns.

Offering such assistance to parents under stress might be viewed as an intrusion into their privacy. However, when such support is offered in a nonjudgmental manner, it not only provides a break in a potentially escalating cycle of violence but also conveys the message that parents are not alone in rearing their children. To the extent society wants to reap the benefits of a productive next generation, each member of that society has the responsibility to protect children from behaviors that might limit their potential to achieve these objectives.

Ending Violence toward Children

Preventing physical abuse requires the elimination of all forms of violence toward children. Gelles and Straus (1988) have called for the development of a cultural ethic that views hitting children as inappropriate, citing the ban on corporal punishment passed by Swedish legislators in 1979. Gelles and Straus write:

> After nearly two decades of research on the causes and consequences of family violence, we are convinced that our society must abandon its reliance on spanking children if we are to prevent intimate violence. If we are ever to accomplish this goal, we must reject the belief that spanking is an effective discipline tool and we must abolish corporal punishment for all time. (p. 197)

The widespread acceptance of physical punishment, as evidenced by Gelles and Straus's own work, bode against achieving any type of legislative ban on spanking in the near future. However, several interim steps toward this long-term objective can be implemented. First, every state can ban the use of corporal punishment in their schools. As of 1988, 11 states and several local municipalities have passed such legislation, suggesting that political resources and public support can be successfully marshaled with respect to this issue (Scott & Moelis, 1988). Second, organizations and parent groups that are reluctant to support an outright ban on corporal punishment should find greater agreement among their membership regarding a ban on the use of corporal punishment with infants. Although over 90% of parents with 3- or 4-year-olds report using physical punishment, only 21% of parents with infants report using this method of discipline (Wauchope & Straus, 1987). Certainly, members of any group concerned with the welfare of children would agree that the most vulnerable members of society, those children less than 1 year of age, should be afforded maximum protection from physical mistreatment regardless of the label used. Finally, parenting education and support services need to offer parents clear and workable alternatives to physical punishment. Haeuser (1988) suggests that unlike Swedish society, which for a variety of reasons can accept a law prohibiting all physical punishment, our society must depend on establishing a child-rearing norm that is highly visible and that parents can voluntarily adopt. Greater care must be taken in documenting not only the negative consequences of repeated and often excessive physical punishment but also the positive results of alternative discipline methods. Behavioral modification techniques that rely on consistency, fairness, and negotiations move children away from negative behaviors, while also instilling the positive values and skills necessary for healthy personal development and social integration. To the extent parents learn that they and their children have much to gain by not managing their relationship with corporal punishment, the more likely they are to voluntarily withdraw from this most damaging practice.

Some argue that prevention is extremely problematic within any reasonable scope of fiscal effort and within the values of a free society that gives people the right to be left alone. Also, to promote new discipline standards that do not rely on the use of corporal punishment is to advocate behavior contrary to the parenting realities found in the majority of American homes. Despite these difficulties, responding only after the fact ensures the continuous need for society to deal with the victims that dysfunctional families, individuals, and social policies will inevitably produce. Just as the hallmark of good leaders is the ability of their followers to operate efficiently without them, one might argue that the best child welfare system will be one that eventually is able to reduce its overall size and scope, not by definition (i.e., not by ignoring the precursors of specific social ills), but rather by reducing the number of physically abused children through thoughtful and coordinated early intervention.

REFERENCES

Affholter, D., Connell, D., & Nauta, M. (1983). Evaluation of the child and family resource program: Early evidence of parent-child interaction effects. *Evaluation Review, 7,* 65–79.

Badger, E. (1981). Effects of a parent education program on teenage mothers and their offspring, in K. G. Scott, T. Field, & E. Robertson (Eds.), *Teenage parents and their offspring,* (pp. 283–309) New York: Grune & Stratton.

Belsky, J. (1980). Child maltreatment: An ecological integration. *American Psychologist, 35,* 320–335.

Bersharov, D. (1986). Unfounded allegations—A new child abuse problem. *The Public Interest, 83,* 18–33.

Bolton, F., & Bolton, S. (1987). *Working with violent families: A guide for clinical and legal practitioners.* Newbury Park, CA: Sage.

Brofenbrenner, U. (1979). *The ecology of human development*. Cambridge, MA: Harvard University Press.

Cicchetti, D., & Rizley, R. (1981). Developmental perspectives on the etiology, intergenerational transmission, and sequence of child maltreatment. *New Directions for Child Development, 11,* 31–55.

Cohn, A. (1983). Effective treatment of child abuse and neglect. *Social Work, 24,* 513–519.

Cohn, A., & Daro, D. (1988). Is treatment too late: What teen years of evaluative research tell us. *Child Abuse and Neglect, 11,* 433–442.

Daro, D. (1988). *Confronting child abuse*. New York: Free Press.

Daro, D., Abrahams, N., & Robson, K. (1988). *Reducing child abuse 20% by 1990: 1985–1986 baseline data*. Chicago, IL: National Committee for Prevention of Child Abuse.

Daro, D., & Mitchel, L. (1988). *Child abuse fatalities remain high: The results of the Annual Fifty State Survey*. Chicago, IL: National Committee for Prevention of Child Abuse.

Delson, N., & Clark, M. (1981). Group therapy with sexually molested children. *Child Welfare, 60,* 175–182.

Dickie, J., & Gerber, S. (1980). Training in social competence: the effects on mothers, fathers and infants. *Child Development, 51,* 1248–1251.

Ellwood, A. (1988). Prove to me that MELD makes a difference. In H. Weiss, & F. Jacobs (Eds.), *Evaluating family programs* (pp. 303–314) New York: Aldine.

Field, T., Widmayer, S., Stringer, S. & Ignatoff, E. (1980). Teenage, lower-class, black mothers and their preterm infants: An intervention and developmental follow-up. *Child Development, 5,* 426–436.

Gabinet, L. (1979). Prevention of child abuse and neglect in an inner-city population. II: The program and the results. *Child Abuse and Neglect, 3,* 809–817.

Garbarino, J. (1977). The human ecology of child maltreatment: A conceptual model for research. *Journal of Marriage and the Family, 39,* 721–735.

Garbarino, J. (1987). Family support and the prevention of child maltreatment. In S. Kagan, D. Powell, D., Weissbourd, & E. Zigler (Eds.), *America's family support programs* (pp. 99–114) New Haven, CT: Yale University Press.

Gelles, R., & Straus, M. (1988). *Intimate violence: The causes and consequences of abuse in the American family*. New York: Simon & Schuster.

Giovannoni, J. M., & Becerra, R. (1979). *Defining child abuse*. New York: Free Press.

Gray, E. (1983). What have we learned about preventing child abuse: An overview of the "Community and Minority Group Action" program. Chicago: National Committee for Prevention of Child Abuse.

Gray, J., Cutler, C. A., Dean, J. G., & Kempe, C. H. (1979). Prediction and prevention of child abuse and neglect. *Journal of Social Issues, 35,* 127–139.

Gutelius, M., Kirsch, A., MacDonald, S., Brooks, M., & McErlean, T. (1977). Controlled study of child health supervision: Behavior results. *Pediatrics, 60,* 294–304.

Haeuser, A. (1988, April). *The physical punishment neurosis: Can it be cured?* Paper presented at the National Symposium on Child Victimization, Anaheim, CA.

Herrenkohl, R., Herrenkohl, E., Egolf, B., & Seech, M. (1979). The repetition of child abuse: How often does it occur? *Child Abuse and Neglect, 3,* 67–72.

Kaufman, J., & Zigler, E. (1989). The intergenerational transmission of child abuse. In D. Cicchetti & V. Carlson (Eds.), *Child maltreatment: Theory and research on the causes and consequences of child abuse & neglect* (pp. 129–150) Cambridge: Cambridge University Press.

Kempe, R., & Kempe, C. H. (1978). *Child abuse.* Cambridge, MA: Harvard University Press.

Kempe, R., & Kempe, C. H. (1984). *The common secret: Sexual abuse of children and adolescents.* New York: W. H. Freeman.

Larner, M., & Halpren, R. (1987). Lay home visiting programs: strengths, tensions, and challenges. *Zero to Three, 8,* 1–7.

Larson, C. (1980). Efficacy of prenatal and postpartum home visits on child health and development. *Pediatrics, 66,* 191–197.

Laughlin, J., & Weiss, M. (1981). An outpatient milieu therapy approach to treatment of child abuse and neglect problems. *Social Casework, 62,* 106–109.

Levine, C. (Ed.). (1988). *Programs to strengthen families.* Chicago, IL: Family Resource Coalition.

Love, J., Nauta, M., Coelen, C., Hewett, K., & Ruopp, R. (1976). *National home start evaluation: Final report, findings and implications.* Ypsilanti, MI: High scope Educational Research Foundation.

Lutzker, J., & Rice, J. (1984). Project 12-Ways: Measuring outcome of a large in-home service for treatment and prevention of child abuse and neglect. *Child Abuse and Neglect, 8,* 519–524.

Lutzker, J., & Rice, J. (1987). Using recidivism data to evaluate Project 12-Ways: An ecobehavioral approach to the treatment and prevention of child abuse and neglect. *Journal of Family Violence, 2,* 283–290.

MacFarlane, K., Waterman, J., Conerly, S., Damon, L., Durfee, M., & Long, S. (1986). *Sexual abuse of young children.* New York: Guilford.

Magura, S., & Moses, B. (1986). Are services to prevent foster care effective? *Children and Youth Services Review, 3,* 193–212.

McAnarney, E., Roghmann, K., Adams, B., Tatlebaum, R., Kash, C., Coulter, M., Plume, M., & Charney, E. (1978). Obstetric, neonatal, and psychosocial outcome of pregnant adolescents. *Pediatrics, 61,* 191–205.

Miller, S. (1988). The Child Welfare League of America's adolescent parents projects. in H. Weiss, & F. Jacobs, (Eds.), *Evaluating Family Programs.* (pp. 371–388) New York: Aldine.

Newberger, C., & Newberger, E. (1982). Prevention of child abuse: Theory, myth, and practice. *Journal of Prevention Psychiatry, 1,* 443–451.

O'Connor, S., Vietze, P., Sherrod, K., Sandler, H., & Altemeier, W. (1980). Reduced incidence of parenting inadequacy following rooming-in. *Pediatrics, 66,* 176–182.

Olds, D., Chamberlin, R., & Tatlebaum, R. (1986). Preventing child abuse and neglect: A randomized trial of nurse home visitation. *Pediatrics, 78,* 65–78.

Ozawa, M. (1985, April). *Public interest in children*. Paper presented at the Seabury Lecture, School of Social Welfare, University of California, Berkeley.

Pelton, L. (1981). *Social context of child abuse and neglect*. New York: Human Services Press.

Polit, D. (1987, Jan.–Feb.). Routes to self-sufficiency: Teenage mothers and employment. *Children Today*, pp. 6–11.

Porter, F., Blick, L., & Sgroi, S. (1982). Treatment of the sexually abused child. In S. M. Sgroi (Ed.), *Handbook of clinical intervention in child sexual abuse* (pp. 109–145). Lexington, MA: Lexington Books.

Powell, D. (1986, March). Parent education and support programs. *Young Children*, pp. 47–53.

Rodriguez, G., & Cortez, C. (1988). The evaluation experience of the Avance Parent-Child Education Program. In H. Weiss & F. Jacobs (Eds.), *Evaluating family programs* (pp. 287–302). New York: Aldine.

Schverman, J., Wulczyn, F., & Farber, N. (1984, November). *Evaluation of the Illinois Department of Public Aid Young Parent program*.

Scott, J., & Moelis, C. (1988). *Abolishing corporal punishment in the schools: A call for action*. Chicago, IL: National Committee for Prevention of Child Abuse.

Seitz, V., Rosenbaum, L., & Apfel, N. (1985). Effects of family support intervention: A ten-year follow-up. *Child Development, 56,* 376–391.

U.S. House of Representatives, Select Committee on Children, Youth, and Families. (1987). *Abused children in America: Victims of official neglect*. Washington, DC: U.S. Government Printing Office.

Taylor, D., & Beauchamp, C. (1988). Hospital-based primary prevention strategy in child abuse: A multi-level needs assessment. *Child Abuse and Neglect, 12,* 343–354.

Travers, J., Nauta, M. & Irwin, N. (1982). *The effects of a social program: Final report of the Child and Family Resource Program's infant and toddler component*. Cambridge, MA: ABT Associates.

Volsky, G. (1988, September 4). Florida county will vote on child welfare plan. *New York Times*, p. 15.

Wauchope, B., & Straus, M. (1987, July). *Age, class, and gender difference in physical punishment and physical abuse of American children*. Paper presented at the Third National Conference on Family Violence Research, Durham, NH.

Wieder, S., Poisson, S., Lourie, R., & Greenspan, S. (1988). Enduring gains: A five-year follow-up report on the Clinical Infant Development Program. *Zero to Three, 8,* 6–11.

Wolock, I., & Horowitz, B. (1979). Child maltreatment and material deprivation among AFDC-recipient families. *Social Service Review, 53,* 175–194.

CHAPTER 15

Prevention of Child Sexual Abuse

ANN P. HAZZARD

INTRODUCTION

Over the past decade, sexual abuse prevention programs have been implemented on a widespread basis as professional and public awareness about child sexual abuse has grown. In part, recognition of the high incidence of sexual abuse and its negative psychological consequences has spawned preventive efforts. Furthermore, the secrecy that is an integral aspect of sexual abuse suggests the need for a proactive, rather than only reactive, response to the problem. Finally, there are limited treatment resources available, even for those victims who do disclose sexual abuse. For all of these reasons, a variety of preventive approaches to child sexual abuse have evolved.

Finkelhor's (1984) four-factor model of child sexual abuse is helpful in conceptualizing the array of preventive approaches to child sexual abuse. He asserts that sexual abuse occurs when a potential offender has an internal predisposition to abuse, overcomes his own internal inhibitions against abuse, overcomes external impediments to abuse, and overcomes a child's resistance. Some preventive efforts, such as attempts to reduce the availability of child pornography, are targeted at decreasing offenders' motivation or raising offenders' inhibitions against child sexual abuse. Efforts to educate parents or other child caretakers about sexual abuse aim to increase external impediments to abuse by enhancing adults' ability to protect children. However, most preventive efforts have focused on improving the child's ability to resist sexual abuse attempts, primarily through school-based education.

In fact, in 1984 the California General Assembly mandated and funded child abuse prevention training for public school children five times in their school careers. A national survey completed by the National Committee for the Prevention of Child Abuse found that over 25% of all public schools provide this type of instruction to at least one grade level (Daro, Duerr, & LeProhn, 1986). Despite the proliferation of school-based prevention programs, many questions remain unanswered about how best to protect children from sexual abuse.

The questions that children themselves ask about the topic reflect the many dilemmas encountered by prevention educators. Over the past 3 years, my colleagues and I have conducted research on sexual abuse prevention using the *Feeling Yes, Feeling No* curriculum (Hazzard, Webb, & Kleemeier, 1988). In our prevention program, like many others, a "Question Box" is placed in the classroom, so that children can write down anonymous questions to be answered later by the trainer.

Often questions reveal children's sense of vulnerability and helplessness in the face of what they perceive as a violent and dangerous world:

"Can a stranger kill you?"

"What if someone holds a gun to your head and takes off all your clothes?"

"What if someone sneaks up from behind you and knocks you out and then ties you up and while you are asleep sexually abuses you for a long time and then when you wake up, they threaten you?"

These types of questions sensitize one to the important issue of how much responsibility for preventing sexual abuse children should be encouraged to assume. Furthermore, can children be given helpful prevention information without increasing their anxiety or engendering other negative side effects?

Other questions reveal children's uncertainty about sexuality in general and their difficulty in distinguishing between healthy, positive sexuality and sexual abuse:

"Can you sexually abuse yourself?"

"Why are gay people gay?"

"What if your boyfriend touches you and the no feeling doesn't come out and you keep saying yes, yes, yes, what do you do?"

In these questions we see reflections of our society's ambivalence and confusion about sexuality, which on a cultural level, may set the stage for the high incidence of sexual abuse. One becomes aware of the importance of designing prevention programs that do not leave children feeling that all sexual touches are negative.

And finally, the question asked repeatedly in virtually all of the classrooms in which we have conducted prevention training:

"Why do people have to sexually assault kids?"

In the struggle to give an answer, my colleagues and I have become painfully aware of how little we as professionals truly understand about the etiology of child sexual abuse. As the rush of initial enthusiasm and optimism about sexual abuse prevention programs for children has abated, there is growing recognition that these programs can at best be one small part of the solution to a complex social problem.

ISSUES IN PREVENTION

The majority of professional attention has been directed toward child-focused, school-based sexual abuse prevention programs. Professionals designing and conducting these programs have had to address two types of programmatic issues: how to develop community support for a sexual abuse prevention program, and how to present prevention concepts to children of different ages and backgrounds.

Program Acceptance Issues

To gain community acceptance for a sexual abuse prevention program, professionals typically work with key individuals within school systems, parent organizations, protective services agencies, police departments, and/or mental health agencies. Initial goals are to raise awareness concerning the incidence and consequences of child sexual abuse and to present a rationale for a preventive approach (Illusion Theatre, 1983).

In this process, professionals often confront questions from community members about how children are likely to respond to programs. Parents or school administrators are sometimes concerned about whether prevention programs will (a) increase children's anxiety, (b) introduce children prematurely to sexual information, (c) encourage children to say no to appropriate adult requests, (d) make children uncomfortable with normal displays of affection from adults, or (e) perhaps lead to false reports of abuse.

Research data, to be discussed in the next section, are now available to allay many of these concerns about potential negative consequences of prevention programs. In general, most prevention educators carefully adopt a nonthreatening and balanced approach to the problem. For example, the Committee for Children in Seattle, which has developed many excellent prevention resources, introduces parents to their program in this way (Downer, 1984a):

> *Talking About Touching* is a safety, not sex education, curriculum. . . . A safety curriculum on touching is no more likely to produce unnecessary fears about touching than a traffic safety curriculum is likely to produce an extreme fear of trucks. . . . The unknown is usually a greater source of fear in children and adults. Practical information on personal safety . . . provides children with a sense of security based on knowledge of safe options in potentially dangerous situations. (p. 78)

Although it is important for prevention professionals to be aware of potential community concerns about program implementation, it also is important to note that, for the most part, community members have welcomed sexual abuse prevention programs. Higgs (1982) reports on the positive community responses to several sexual abuse demonstration projects funded in

1980 by the National Center on Child Abuse and Neglect. Even at that time, when prevention programs were relatively new and untested, community surveys indicated no organized opposition to prevention program development and found instead that most community leaders felt that there was a need for prevention education.

In addition to mobilizing community support for prevention programs on a systemic level, professionals also must decide how to handle questions concerning individual children's participation. Prevention programs that include a formal research component require parents to sign detailed consent forms before their children participate. However, most prevention educators simply inform parents about the program via a letter and/or a parent meeting. Some school systems allow parents to request that their children not participate but, in the absence of parental prohibition, assume parental consent.

There appear to be several benefits to informing parents about prevention programs. Informational materials often reassure parents who may have some initial concerns about the program and encourage parents to talk to their children about the topic, thereby reinforcing prevention concepts. Parents who are informed through parent meetings or written materials may become better able to recognize indicators of abuse and to respond appropriately to child disclosures. Finally, after notifying parents about the program, professionals are often contacted by parents whose children have already disclosed previous sexual abuse. These parents are appropriately concerned about whether the program is likely to be beneficial or to produce anxiety in their already-victimized children. After discussing the pros and cons with a project staff member, almost all parents decide to allow their children to participate. Being aware of a child's previous victimization enables trainers to be more sensitive to the child's reactions during the program and to respond supportively.

The major negative consequence of informing parents prior to prevention program implementation is that families in which abuse is ongoing may refuse to allow their children to participate. Therefore, in our project, we encouraged teachers to be alert for behavioral indicators of possible abuse among nonparticipating students and, when concerned, to initiate open-ended conversations with these students.

Program Content Issues

A wide variety of sexual abuse prevention materials currently are available. Several annotated bibliographies also have been published (Clark, 1985; Hallingby & Brick, 1984; National Committee for the Prevention of Child Abuse, 1984; Schroeder, Gordon, & McConnell, 1986).

Prevention information has been presented in a number of ways. Written materials include books to be read with children (Hindman, 1983; Wachter, 1982), coloring books (Stowell & Dietzel, 1982), and a Spiderman comic book on sexual abuse developed by the National Committee for the Prevention of Child Abuse and Marvel Comics (1984). Written materials for adults also have been developed, primarily aimed at parents (Adams & Fay, 1981; Spelman, 1985) and teachers (Broadhurst, 1986; Nelson & Clark, 1986).

Several organizations have traveling groups of actors and actresses who make dramatic presentations related to abuse (e.g., Citykids, New York, NY; Illusion Theatre, Minneapolis, MN; Bubblylonian Encounters, Overland, KS; Bridgework Theatre, Goshen, IN). Some of these organizations have produced videotapes of their dramatic presentations, such as "Touch," produced by Illusion Theatre Company and Media Ventures (1984). A variety of other audiovisual materials have been developed as prevention resources, such as:

1. *Better Safe Than Sorry I, II, III* (Filmfair Communications, 1978; 1983; 1985)
2. *Child Sexual Abuse: A Solution* (James Stanfield & Co., 1985)
3. *Incest: The Victim Nobody Believes* (J. Gary Mitchell Film Co., 1976)
4. *Identifying, Reporting, and Handling Disclosure of the Sexually Abused Child* (Committee for Children, 1985)
5. *Yes, You Can Say No* (Committee for Children, 1986)

Many multimedia curricula for children have been developed, some of which include videotapes. Most curricula include group discussions and role-plays between trainers, students, and/or puppets. Curricula range in length from (a) one- to two-session programs (Child Assault Prevention Project, 1983), (b) three- to five-session programs (Morgan, 1985; Plummer, 1984a), and (c) extended programs presented in 15 to 45 brief sessions (Committee for Children, 1984; National Film Board of Canada, 1985).

The content of these programs is similar although there are some important differences and areas of controversy. Three controversial issues in prevention programs that have to do with defining sexual abuse are whether touches are defined as *bad* or *good*, whether feelings or intuition are used to help define a touch as abusive, and whether anatomically correct names for body parts are used to define sexual abuse.

Although *good touch* and *bad touch* were frequently used terms in early prevention programs, currently *unsafe touch* or *secret touch* are being used more often to introduce the notion of sexual abuse. Many prevention educators have argued that good touch and bad touch are detrimental labels, because often sexual abuse begins with touches that feel good to children, such as caresses, and some sexual abuse itself may be physically pleasurable to children. Furthermore, use of these terms may encourage children to overgeneralize and conclude that healthy sexuality is bad. Finally, labeling sexual abuse as bad touch may increase the guilt of already abused children (Hindman, 1987).

A related definitional dilemma is whether children should be taught to use feelings to decide whether a touch is appropriate or inappropriate. Although this approach has been used in many programs, recently many prevention professionals have expressed concerns that trusting [one's] feelings to define sexual abuse may be an overly difficult task, particularly for preschoolers. Several preschool programs such as *Talking about Touching II* (Beland, 1986b) and Behavioral Skills Training (BST) (Wurtele, 1987) are instead defining sexual abuse in concrete, descriptive terms. For example, the BST program teaches children, "No one who is bigger or older than you should look at or touch your private parts, nor should you look at or touch their private parts" (p. 486). The exceptions to the rule are when private parts need to be looked at or touched for hygienic or health reasons (Wurtele, 1987). Research concerning this issue is presented in the section on preschool program evaluation.

A final definitional issue is whether to use anatomically correct terms to define sexual abuse. Presumably because of concerns about community acceptance, many programs have referred to sexual organs as "private parts," "private zones," or "the parts of your body covered by a bathing suit." However, many prevention educators have argued that some children do not disclose abuse because they lack the vocabulary to describe what has happened; if so, avoiding the use of anatomically correct terms may be a disservice. Furthermore, although children in prevention programs are encouraged to tell about sexual abuse, when they hear adults using euphemisms, they may conclude that it is not really permissible to discuss this issue openly.

In our prevention project (Hazzard et al., 1988), we used the terms *breasts, buttocks, penis,* and *vagina* to define sexual abuse. We encountered little resistance from parents or teachers after we explained our rationale for using anatomically correct language. When children were interviewed individually afterward and asked what they thought about learning the names of the private parts of the body, 71% stated that it was all right or a good idea and 21% stated either that they did not like it or thought it was embarrassing (Pohl & Hazzard, 1988). Further research is needed to determine if the potential benefits of using explicit language outweigh any risks of engendering embarrassment among a minority of children.

After defining sexual abuse, most prevention programs teach children that abuse can happen to boys as well as girls, and that abusers can be strangers or persons whom one knows and perhaps likes. Programs typically teach children three preventive strategies: Say no, get away if you can, and tell a trusted adult. Thus, programs teach children to avoid or resist abuse (a primary prevention goal) as well as to disclose immediately abuse that they are unable to prevent, so that chronic abuse will not occur and immediate treatment can be provided (a secondary prevention goal).

Recent discussion among prevention experts has focused on whether it is realistic to expect a child to be able to say no in many sexually abusive situations, particularly when a molester may be a trusted, powerful adult in the child's life and/or may skillfully use psychological manipulation or coercive threats to gain the child's cooperation. Some prevention professionals have suggested that a greater emphasis should be placed on encouraging the child to disclose any abusive encounter (Berliner & Conte, 1988).

Another controversial question is whether children should be taught self-defense strategies such as a self-defense yell or physical self-defense. These strategies are primarily employed by Child Assault Prevention (CAP) programs that were developed by feminist-oriented rape crisis centers (Child Assault Prevention Project, 1983). Advocates of teaching children self-defense strategies argue that children are "empowered" by knowing that they have a right to physically resist abuse. Critics are concerned that children cannot effectively physically resist an older and presumably stronger molester or that children may elicit more physical violence toward themselves by using these strategies.

There also has been some debate about how to teach prevention skills, particularly assertion skills, while respecting cultural differences in what is considered appropriate behavior. For example, it is probably not useful to teach direct eye contact as a component of assertiveness to children from cultures in which direct eye contact with adults is considered rude. Instead, some programs encourage children to say no "like you really mean it," thereby encouraging children to behave assertively within their own cultural context.

Finally, there is controversy concerning how to handle the question of personal responsibility in sexual abuse prevention programs. Most programs teach children several strategies to prevent abuse and then include the somewhat antithetical message that it is not the child's fault if abuse occurs. Trainers in such programs may find it difficult to convince some concrete-operational children that abuse is not the child's fault in situations in which the child fails to follow a safety rule or to use a preventive strategy, even in the face of manipulation by a perpetrator. In response to this difficulty, rather than teaching children rules or prevention skills they *should* use, some programs present prevention skills as responses children *can* use. Programs also may include discussions of why it is often difficult to say no or tell an adult.

Most prevention programs are based on the assumption that victim self-blame is maladaptive, given the clinical research documenting depression, lowered self-esteem, and increased rates of revictimization among victims. However, some authors argue that victim self-blame may be adaptive because it gives children a sense of control over the events in their lives. Until research has clarified the meaning of victim-blame for victims and non-victims, the stance taken by prevention programmers on this issue is likely to continue to reflect a value judgment rather than an empirically based decision.

PREVENTION PROGRAMS AND EVALUATION

Although research on sexual abuse prevention has lagged behind program development and implementation, a number of evaluation studies have been conducted, most within the past 5 years. Several recent reviews of the literature have been published (Conte, 1984; Finkelhor & Strapko, 1987; Haugaard & Reppucci, 1988; Kolko, 1988; Wurtele, 1987). In this section, I will review literature concerning programs for elementary schoolchildren, preschool children, adolescents, disabled persons, and caretaking adults such as parents and teachers.

Elementary School Program Evaluation

Most of the research in this field has focused on programs for elementary schoolchildren (Grades K through 6). Studies have examined knowledge gains, skill gains, retention of gains at follow-up, disclosures, potential negative effects, and differential program effectiveness according to subject or program variables.

Knowledge Gains

Several studies have documented statistically and clinically significant gains in knowledge for children who have participated in prevention programs as compared to control children (Conte, Rosen, Saperstein, & Shermach, 1985; Hazzard, Webb, & Kleemeier, 1988; Saslawsky & Wurtele 1986; Wurtele, Marrs, & Miller-Perrin, 1987; Wurtele, Saslawsky, Miller, Marrs, & Britcher, 1986). A number of other studies have found statistically significant pre-post or treatment-control differences in knowledge, but these studies include a number of methodological problems, such as (a) no control group (Binder & McNiel, 1987; Kenning, Gallmeier, Jackson, & Plemons, 1987; Lansing Public Schools, 1987; Plummer, 1984b); (b) no pretests (Nelson, 1985; Wolfe, MacPherson, Blount, & Wolfe, 1986); (c) questionnaires with unreported or inadequate reliability (Downer, 1984a; Gardner-Frum & Fontanella, 1985; Kolko, Moser, Litz, & Hughes, 1987; Lansing Public Schools, 1987; Nelson, 1985; Plummer, 1984b; Wolfe et al., 1986); (d) clinically insignificant gains, often because of questionnaire ceiling effects (Binder & McNiel, 1987; Gallmeier, Kenning, & Plemons, 1988; Gardner-Frum & Fontanella, 1985; Lutter & Weisman, 1985; Wolfe et al., 1986; Woods & Dean, 1986); (e) item-by-item analyses that make it difficult to gauge overall results (Kolko et al., 1987; Plummer, 1984b); and (f) other questionable statistical analyses (Gallmeier et al., 1988; Gardner-Frum & Fontanella, 1985; Lansing Public Schools, 1987; Nelson, 1985; Woods & Dean, 1986).

Skill Gains

Demonstrating increases in knowledge does not ensure that children have learned behavioral prevention skills (say no, leave, and tell an adult) or that they would use these skills if confronted with a potentially abusive situation. To assess skills, researchers have used a variety of analogue techniques, including role-plays between puppets (Downer, 1984a; Kenning et al., 1987) or between trainer and child (Miltenberger & Thiesse-Duffy, 1988), written or verbal vignettes (Miltenberger & Thiesse-Duffy, 1988; Wurtele, Miller-Perrin, Kondrick, Morris, & Bratcher, 1988), and videotaped vignettes (Hazzard, Webb, & Kleemeier, 1988; Swan, Press, & Briggs, 1985). Results have been mixed using these measures, with Miltenberger and Thiesse-Duffy (1988) and Saslawsky and Wurtele (1986) finding the clearest evidence of skill gains after prevention program participation.

To assess whether children actually use prevention skills, several researchers have employed in vivo simulations of abduction scenarios. This methodology raises some ethical concerns (Conte, 1987), although most researchers have been very sensitive to issues of informed consent and subject welfare. However, in vivo techniques are limited to abduction situations, which are relatively infrequent compared to other abusive encounters.

Fryer, Kraizer, & Miyoshi (1987a) contrasted the performance of 23 children (Grades K-2) who participated in an eight-session classroom prevention program with 21 control children. Significantly more treatment children resisted the request of a stranger to accompany him outdoors at posttesting (78.3%) than at pretesting (43.5%), whereas about half of the control children continued to agree to go with the stranger.

Results of the few studies that investigate how knowledge and skills measures relate to each other are somewhat inconsistent. Wurtele et al. (1988) reported a moderate correlation ($r = .57$) between children's scores on a knowledge measure and a verbal vignettes measure of skills. Fryer et al. (1987a) found that knowledge scores did not predict children's pretest abduction response. However, there were significant differences in pre-self-esteem and postknowledge scores between children who successfully resisted the postabduction simulation and those who did not. Fryer et al. (1987a) hypothesize that children with positive self-esteems are better able to assimilate and act on prevention knowledge. The research results of Hazzard and colleagues have been mixed. In their first study, knowledge scores and scores on videotape vignettes measure of skills were not significantly related (Hazzard et al., 1988). In the second study, they were able to replicate Fryer et al.'s (1987a) results: A multiple regression equation using pre-self-esteem scores and postknowledge scores to predict vignettes skill scores was statistically significant (Hazzard & Kleemeier, 1988). Further research obviously is needed to clarify how cognitive, affective, and behavioral dimensions of prevention skills are related.

Retention of Gains at Follow-Up

Several studies have demonstrated that children's gains in prevention knowledge are maintained at 1- to 3-month follow-up (Hazzard, et al., 1988; Saslawsky & Wurtele, 1986; Wurtele, Marrs, & Miller-Perrin, 1987; Wurtele et al., 1986), at 6-month follow-up (Gallmeier et al., 1988; Ray & Dietzel, 1984), and at 1-year follow-up (Lutter & Weisman, 1985; Pohl, Angert, & Hazzard, 1988). Other researchers conducting item-by-item follow-up analyses have found more mixed results (Kolko et al., 1987; Plummer, 1984b). For example, although Plummer (1984b) found that children maintained knowledge gains on most questions at 8-month follow-up, their responses shifted toward baseline levels on items assessing whether promises could sometimes be broken, whether abusers could be known adults, whether sexual abuse was the same as getting "beat up," and whether abuse could be the child's fault. Another less encouraging result is Lutter and Weisman's (1985) finding that treatment-control differences had diminished at 18-month follow-up, although these results should be interpreted cautiously because her treatment sample included only 14 subjects.

Several authors have reported retention of prevention skills on analogue measures over 1- to 3-month periods (Saslawsky & Wurtele, 1986; Wurtele et al., 1986; Wurtele et al., 1987), and over a 1-year follow-up period (Pohl et al., 1988). Similarly, retention of abduction avoidance skills has been demonstrated by Miltenberger and Thiesse-Duffy (1988) for 6- and 7-year-olds over a 2-month period and by Fryer, Kraizer, and Miyoshi (1987b) for 5- to 7-year-olds over a 6-month period.

Three studies have investigated whether review sessions or "booster shots" are helpful in increasing or maintaining children's knowledge or skills. Ray and Dietzel (1984) evaluated a booster shot delivered before the 1-month follow-up and Gallmeier et al. (1988) evaluated a booster shot delivered 4 months after the original program. Both investigations revealed significant effects for the booster shot, but because of problems with measurement ceiling effects and questionable statistical analyses, these conclusions are debatable. Pohl et al. (1988) evaluated a booster-shot session conducted 1 year after program implementation. The review lesson did not result in knowledge gains but did result in small but significant increases in prevention skill levels.

Prevention educators agree that it is important for prevention information to be presented several times throughout childhood. The nature of the information about sexual abuse that children need and can assimilate is obviously different at various stages of development. Further research would be helpful in determining the optimal timing and sequencing of prevention information to promote retention of developmentally appropriate knowledge and skills.

Disclosures

Several researchers have tabulated child disclosures of abuse to determine whether programs are attaining their secondary prevention goal of encouraging early disclosure and treatment of abuse. However, because of differences in the way that disclosures have been measured and other methodological problems, these data are difficult to interpret. Most researchers have tabulated verbal disclosures made to school or program personnel or reported to Protective Services agencies (Beland, 1986a; Lansing Public Schools, 1987; Hazzard & Kleemeier, 1988; Hazzard et al., 1988). Kolko et al. (1987) used a very different methodology and included questions about inappropriate touch in follow-up written questionnaires with parents and children. There are several methodological problems with Kolko's approach; nevertheless, his post and follow-up disclosure rates among treatment groups varied from 1.8% to 9.7%. These rates are generally consistent with the 5% rate of verbally reported and clinically validated disclosures found in the sample of Hazzard et al. (1988).

Only one study includes disclosure data adequate enough to draw tentative conclusions about the impact of prevention programs on disclosures. Beland (1986a) compared disclosure rates of 45 schools participating in the Talking about Touching Program to 7 control schools. In the year prior to program implementation, treatment and control schools did not vary in disclosure rates. During the year that prevention programs were implemented, treatment schools reported significantly more sexual abuse disclosures ($X = 2.04$ cases per school) than control schools ($X = .63$ cases).

The possibility that prevention programs encourage false reports of abuse has been mentioned as a concern of some community members. Data concerning this issue have not been reported by any researchers. However, Hazzard et al. (1988) were not made aware in their study that any of the disclosures were, upon subsequent investigation, believed to be false allegations.

Negative Effects

A number of researchers have assessed whether children have any negative reactions to prevention programs, focusing primarily on increased anxiety, increased disobedience, or changed reactions to appropriate physical affection. Researchers typically have used child-completed measures of general anxiety or specific fears and parent reports of child behaviors and feelings. Most studies have found no treatment-control or no pre-post differences on these measures (Binder & McNeil, 1987; Hazzard et al., 1988; Kolko et al., 1987; Miller-Perrin & Wurtele, 1986; Wurtele, 1988; Wurtele & Miller-Perrin, 1987). In fact, most global program ratings by parents have been quite positive. For example, from 95% (Hazzard et al., 1988) to 99% of parents (Wurtele, 1988) have reported that they would let their child participate again in a prevention program.

A few researchers have found indications of some child distress related to prevention program participation. For example, Garbarino (1987) evaluated the Spiderman comic book on prevention and found that from 17% to 50% of children (depending on the sex-grade combination) responded "yes" when asked if the comic book "made you feel worried." In an evaluation of the Talking about Touching Program, Beland (1986a) found that 66% of parents rated their children as "not frightened" by the program, whereas 21% rated their children as "frightened some." Swan, Press, and Briggs (1985) reported that 75% of parents surveyed after the Bubbylonian Encounters program were "positive" about their child's attendance, whereas 25% were "uncertain." Wurtele (1988) found that both treatment and control children's fear of strangers increased over time, similar to the findings of Hazzard et al., 1988. This increased fear of strangers appears to result from testing effects or other variables unrelated to the actual prevention program, because in both studies there were no treatment-control differences.

It is unclear whether these reports of anxiety among a minority of children are related to particular program approaches and/or to how the question was asked. For example, Pohl and Hazzard (in press) report that in their first study children were asked "Since you've participated in the Personal Safety Program, how do you feel?" Ninety percent of the children said they felt "more safe than before," with 10% responding "about as safe as before" or "less safe than before."

Subject Variables

A variety of studies have investigated whether prevention program impact varies according to subject variables, such as age, sex, achievement, and race. Several researchers have found the predictable result that older children score higher than younger children on prevention knowledge questionnaires (Conte, Rosen, Saperstein, & Shermach, 1985; Hazzard & Kleemeier, 1988; Hazzard et al., 1988; Saslawsky & Wurtele, 1986; Wurtele et al., 1986). Wurtele and her colleagues have found similar results on their verbal vignettes measure of prevention skills (Saslawsky & Wurtele, 1986; Wurtele et al., 1986). However, with the exception of Conte et al. (1985), these same authors have not found that older children demonstrate larger *increases* in knowledge or skills following prevention program participation.

Some researchers have found no sex differences in prevention knowledge (Conte et al., 1985; Kenning et al., 1987; Saslawsky & Wurtele, 1986; Wolfe et al., 1986). In other research, slightly higher scores were found for girls than boys on knowledge questionnaires (Hazzard & Kleemeier, 1988; Hazzard et al., 1988). However, there have been few reports of differences in knowledge or skill gains according to subject sex. Garbarino (1987) reported that boys performed somewhat better than girls on his post-only measure, but hypothesized that this sex difference might be specific to the Spiderman comic book he evaluated, which may appeal more to boys than to girls.

Hazzard et al. (1988) found no differences in prevention knowledge according to subject race or achievement level. However, Hazzard and Kleemeier (1988) found that high achievers scored better on preknowledge questionnaires but made relatively smaller gains following the prevention program, perhaps because of questionnaire ceiling effects. Black children also scored slightly lower on the knowledge measure than Caucasian children, although they made equivalent knowledge gains. This small race effect may be confounded with socioeconomic status (SES), which was not assessed. Nelson (1985) reported that low SES students had lower prevention knowledge scores than high SES students.

Program Variables

Other research has explored how program effectiveness may vary according to program format and content. Generally, results suggest that action-oriented approaches may be superior to videotape-only approaches, which in turn may be superior to didactic approaches such as lectures and written materials (Nelson, 1985; Woods & Dean, 1986; Wurtele et al., 1986; Wurtele et al., 1987).

Another programmatic issue that has been investigated is whether program effectiveness varies according to type of trainer. Typically, programs are either implemented by regular teachers who have received some special training, or by expert consultants from outside the school system, usually mental health professionals or paraprofessionals with some expertise in sexual abuse. Each approach has potential merits and drawbacks. Teachers may be more effective presenters because of their general teaching expertise and because their position within the school system allows for more longitudinal presentation of prevention concepts. On the other hand, experts may be more effective because of their greater knowledge and comfort discussing sexual assault. Also, it is unclear whether children are more likely to disclose abuse to a teacher, whom they may trust, or to a sympathetic outside expert, with whom they may feel less embarrassment.

A study was conducted in which teachers received 12 hours of training to prepare them to present sexual abuse prevention programs (Hazzard & Kleemeier, 1988). Teacher training included a 6-hour workshop, observation of an expert presenting the three-session "Feeling Yes, Feeling No" program to a classroom, and follow-up consultation. Responses of children in 23 classrooms taught by a teacher were compared with 10 classrooms taught by an expert consultant. There were no significant differences between conditions in terms of prevention knowledge gains, performance on a video vignettes measure of prevention skills, subjective response to the program, and number of disclosures. Thus, although program impact may vary according to individual trainer characteristics, there do not appear to be any overriding advantages or disadvantages to having either teachers or experts present prevention programs.

On the other hand, Miltenberger and Thiesse-Duffy (1988) found that children taught prevention skills by parents, using the *Red Flag Green Flag Prevention Book* (Rape and Abuse Crisis Center, 1986), did not reach criterion performance on measures of prevention skills, even when parents were given additional instructions on how to behaviorally rehearse and reinforce prevention responses with their children. If these results are replicated, they suggest that prevention resources utilized by relatively untrained parents may have minimal impact.

Preschool Program Evaluations

Much less research has been conducted on preschool prevention programs, probably because of the methodological difficulties inherent in assessing young children's knowledge, feelings, and behaviors. Yet, prevention programs for preschoolers (aged 3 to 5 years) have been the focus of much recent controversy. Following well-publicized sexual abuse cases in day-care centers, many parents have been eager for their preschool children to receive prevention education. Yet, some day-care providers fear that prevention programs may lead children to misinterpret their appropriate care-taking touches, such as providing assistance with toileting or changing clothes. Some child development specialists have questioned whether most preschool programs present prevention concepts in a developmentally appropriate manner, or indeed, whether this task is even possible, given preschoolers' concrete thinking styles and age-appropriate dependence on adults.

In this section, I will review evaluations of preschool prevention programs in terms of knowledge gains, skill gains, follow-up results, negative effects, and the relationship of subject and program variables to prevention knowledge. No investigations to date have examined the extent to which preschool prevention programs elicit disclosures.

With the exception of two behavioral, single-subject design studies (Miltenberger & Thiesse-Duffy, 1988; Poche, Brouwer, & Swearington, 1981) and a study by Wurtele et al. (1988), most of the evaluations have significant methodological problems. Most do not include control groups (Borkin & Frank, 1986; Gilbert, Daro, Duerr, LeProhn, & Nyman, 1988; Kearny, 1986), and the reliability and validity of the assessment instruments used are questionable. Thus, given these methodological shortcomings, only tentative conclusions can be drawn from these studies.

Knowledge Gains

Two studies have reported moderate knowledge gains for preschoolers participating in lengthy prevention programs presented in a number of sessions over several weeks. On a post-only interview measure, Lidell, Young, and Yamagishi (1986) found significant differences between two preschool treatment groups and a control group. In addition, Kearny (1986) found positive pre-post changes for preschoolers participating in a prevention program on all concept areas assessed in a content-coded interview.

Less encouraging results have been reported in two other investigations. Four to 6 weeks after a prevention puppet show, Borkin and Frank (1986) asked preschoolers: "What should you do if someone tries to touch you in a way that doesn't feel good?" Any one of the basic prevention responses (say no, leave, tell someone) was considered correct. Only one 3-year-old (4%) answered correctly, whereas 43% of the 4- and 5-year-olds answered correctly.

Gilbert et al. (1988) evaluated seven different preschool prevention programs ranging from 1 to 24 sessions, with most lasting from 1 to 3 sessions. They utilized multiple assessment instruments, using "bunnies" to represent interpersonal situations. On one measure, children were asked to respond to a picture in which "a big bunny has told the little bunny something and has told the little bunny not to tell anyone. The little bunny looks all mixed up." After the prevention program, the percentage of children who said that the little bunny should tell someone about the confusing secret increased from pretesting; still, only 56% of children said they would tell at posttesting. After program participation, preschoolers also improved in their ability to logically connect feelings to various pictured touch situations (hugging, tickling, bathing, hitting), but even at posttesting only 50% of children gave logical explanations for all four touch–feeling relationships. Most preschoolers had difficulty grasping the concept of a touch that could change so as to produce different feelings or the concept of a "confused" feeling, which was seldom chosen by the children to describe the touch situations.

Wurtele et al. (1988) also investigated how feeling labels affect children's judgments concerning the appropriateness of touches. Kindergarten children were read six verbal vignettes that varied in terms of appropriateness of touch request (appropriate, inappropriate) and feeling of the child in the vignette (good, bad, confused). After each vignette, children were asked standard questions to determine whether they thought the touch was appropriate and what they would say and do. Wurtele et al. (1988) found that when the "bad" feeling label was applied, children overgeneralized and responded as if the touch were inappropriate, even if the touch was appropriate. Conversely, when "good" or "confused" feeling labels were associated with inappropriate touch situations, children responded as if the touch were appropriate. Wurtele et al. (1988) concluded that even for kindergarteners (the oldest children in the preschool range), it may not be effective to teach children to make safety decisions according to their affective state.

It is difficult to draw conclusions from these studies because of the differences in the programs evaluated and the measures utilized. However, the work of Gilbert et al. (1988) and Wurtele et al. (1988) suggest that preschool prevention programs may be more effective if they focus on teaching concrete rules. Prevention concepts such as "touches that give you a confused feeling," "touches that change from feeling bad to good," "bad secrets versus good secrets," or "secrets versus surprises" appear to be too difficult for preoperational preschoolers to comprehend. More positive results also were reported by researchers who evaluated longer, multisession programs. It would be helpful for researchers to evaluate the impact of program length on outcome: Preschoolers may need much repetition to master even concrete prevention rules and concepts.

Skill Gains

Gilbert et al. (1988) also used a role-play measure to assess how preschool children, when taking the part of a "little bunny," would respond to various requests from a "big rabbit the little bunny does not know." Although preschoolers improved from pre- to posttesting in resisting stranger lures, only 42% did not get in the stranger bunny's car at posttesting. However, some authors have criticized this methodology, noting that children may respond differently to scenarios involving rabbit characters than to actual stranger situations (Nibert, Cooper, Fitch, & Ford, 1988; Ray-Keil, 1988).

More positive results were found by Nibert et al. (1988), who used four illustrated verbal vignettes to assess whether preschoolers' prevention skills improved after participating in a three-session Child Assault Prevention Program. In one study with no control group, the percentage of children who gave at least one correct preventive response to all four vignettes increased significantly from pre- to posttesting. At posttesting, over 80% of the children were able to give correct responses to two stranger scenarios and a scenario involving a known abuser. However, only 64% gave a correct preventive response to a bully; many children incorrectly suggested hitting the bully. In a second study, there were not clear control-treatment differences and Nibert et al. (1988) suggest that the pretest may have resulted in posttest gains for control children. These results highlight the difficulty of interpreting many of these preschool evaluations that do not include control groups, because pre-post differences in the experimental group may be due to testing effects or other variables, rather than the prevention program itself.

Two other studies have examined preschoolers' mastery of stranger avoidance skills (Poche et al., 1981; Miltenberger & Thiesse-Duffy, 1988). Both investigations reported that, after individual instruction and behavioral rehearsal, preschoolers were able to resist simulated abduction lures during in vivo assessments. These findings are encouraging, but two important questions remain. First, can preschoolers be successfully taught skills to avoid stranger abduction in group settings? And second, can preschoolers be taught to use prevention skills in the more common and more complex situations involving known abusers?

Follow-Up

No studies have been published concerning preschoolers' retention of prevention knowledge. Unfortunately, the data concerning retention of abduction avoidance skills are not encouraging. Both Miltenberger and Thiesse-Duffy (1988) and Poche et al. (1981) report only partial retention of these skills in 2- to 3-month follow-ups with preschoolers.

Negative Effects

Gilbert et al. (1988) are the only researchers who have attempted to assess potential negative effects of prevention programs for preschoolers. On one measure, children moved a bunny's arms to indicate how "scared and worried" the bunny would be about different types of touches. No pre-post differences were found, suggesting no overall increase in children's anxiety about touches.

On another measure, children's affective associations to a hugging picture remained positive. However, their affective associations to tickling, bathing, and hitting pictures became more negative from pre- to posttesting. One possible interpretation of this finding is that preschoolers may overgeneralize negative feelings to ambiguous touching situations such as tickling and bathing. Alternatively, some preschoolers may have been given permission by prevention programs to assert genuine feelings of discomfort with these situations.

Subject Variables

Several researchers have found age differences on their measures of prevention knowledge, with children performing better as their age increased from 3 to 4 to 5 (Borkin & Frank, 1986; Kearny, 1986; Lidell et al., 1986). However, Nibert et al. (1988) did not find consistent age differences, nor did they find differences according to subject sex or socioeconomic status.

Program Variables

Crisci and Kearny (1988) compared two curricula for kindergarten children that varied in terms of the degree of program structure and specificity and the amount of teacher education and support. They concluded that the more structured program with greater teacher support produced greater gains in child knowledge about feelings, touches, and assertiveness, but not about support systems. Although this study included a control group, measurement and analysis problems limit the strength of the findings.

Adolescent Programs

Both crime report and survey data suggest that a significant number of adolescents have experienced sexual assault, as either victims and/or perpetrators (Ageton, 1983; Burgess, 1985; Fehrenbach, Smith, Monastersky, & Deisher, 1986; Hall & Flannery, 1984). Adolescent sexual abuse includes molestation by adults as well as forced sexual activity with peers, including acquaintance rape.

A number of sexual abuse prevention curricula for adolescents have been developed (Anderson-Kent, 1982; Children's Self-Help Project, 1988; Downer & Beland, 1985; Fortune, 1983; Kassees & Hall, 1987; Montgomery & Anlauf, 1988; Strong, Tate, Wehman, & Wyss, 1986). Some of these curricula address both child molestation and sexual assault among peers, whereas others focus specifically on acquaintance rape prevention. The curricula also vary in terms of whether the program is intended for potential victims, potential perpetrators, or both.

In the past few years, many prevention educators have advocated an increased emphasis on perpetrator prevention, as opposed to victim-oriented approaches. This trend has been particularly evident in adolescent sexual abuse prevention programs. It is intuitively appealing to place more responsibility for preventing sexual abuse on the potential perpetrator rather than the victim. However, we do not know whether this approach is at all effective. Surprisingly, there are no published evaluations of sexual abuse prevention programs for adolescents.

In addition, most prevention programs aimed at potential adolescent perpetrators are not well-grounded in the literature. Treatment programs for juvenile sexual offenders have only recently begun in many communities so knowledge concerning the etiology of adolescent sexual abuse is limited. The literature concerning adolescent offenders who molest younger children has focused primarily on individual and family psychopathology, factors that may be difficult to address with a preventive intervention. In contrast, the literature on acquaintance rape has focused more on attitudinal precursors to sexual abuse. For example, research suggests that sexually coercive college students are more likely to endorse victim-blaming rape myths and to believe that heterosexual relationships are exploitative and that aggression is justified to attain one's goals (Briere & Malamuth, 1983; Koss, Leonard, Beezley, & Oros, 1985; Muehlenhard & Linton, 1987). Researchers also have focused on male–female misperceptions and miscommunications about sexual expectations (Abbey, 1982; Zellman, Johnson, Giarrusso, & Goodchilds, 1979).

Adolescent sexual abuse is clearly a complex, multidetermined phenomenon. Prevention educators need to use research results to develop conceptually sound curricula, which then need to be evaluated in terms of impact.

Programs for Disabled Children

Disabled children have been hypothesized to be at increased risk for sexual victimization because of their greater dependence on caretaking adults and because their communication deficits make it more difficult for them to disclose abuse. Several prevention curricula have been developed for elementary children and adolescents with various disabilities (LaBarre & Hinkley, 1986; O'Day, 1983; Seattle Rape Relief, 1979). Only one program is available for preschool disabled children (Krents & Atkins, 1985).

Prevention educators are only beginning to meet the challenge of developing prevention programs that are appropriate for students with various disabilities. Although evaluation of these programs will be methodologically difficult, it is critical to ensure program efficacy.

Caretaking Adults

Many programs have been developed to educate adults about sexual abuse prevention, often in conjunction with programs for children. This section will focus on evaluations of prevention education for parents, teachers, and other professionals.

Parents

Several studies have examined what parents tell their children about sexual abuse. Finkelhor (1984) found fewer parents (29%) talked to their children about sexual abuse than other difficult topics (e.g., death, pregnancy, homosexuality, abortion). However, three more recent studies have found greater numbers of parents, from 47% to 74%, reporting discussions of sexual abuse with their children (Hazzard et al., 1988; Porch & Petretic-Jackson, 1986; Wurtele & Miller-Perrin, 1987). This increase may reflect sample selection bias in the more recent studies or may represent a real increase in parents' attention to this topic, as public awareness about child sexual abuse has grown.

However, all of these studies have found that parents often omit important information in their discussions of sexual abuse with their children. Most parents focus primarily on rules involving strangers. Fewer parents explicitly discuss potential sexually abusive activities with their children or let their children know that they could be abused by a known adult. Although most parents encourage their children to tell them about abuse, fewer parents recommend assertive responses (e.g., say no) to abusive approaches. Also, some parents may communicate their own anxiety to children when discussing sexual abuse. For example, Garbarino (1987) found that among fourth graders in his sample, 80% of the children whose parents read the Spiderman prevention comicbook with them reported being anxious, as compared to 50% of children whose parents did not read it with them.

Most educational programs for parents emphasize secondary prevention goals. Programs aim to increase parents' awareness of the problem of sexual abuse, sensitize them to behavioral indicators of potential abuse that facilitate early identification of victims, and inform them about community resources to promote appropriate intervention after disclosure.

Several studies have examined the effectiveness of parent programs, although all of the studies have methodological shortcomings. The most encouraging results were reported by Porch and Petretic-Jackson (1986), who found significant pre-post increases in knowledge about sexual abuse for parents who participated in a prevention workshop. Without a control group, however, it is difficult to interpret the significance of these gains. On the other hand, although Gardner-Frum and Fontanella (1985) found that parents who attended a prevention workshop had more knowledge than parents who did not attend the workshop, attending parents still answered only 53% of the knowledge questions correctly at posttesting. Similarly, Gilbert et al. (1988) found that parents made few knowledge gains after a parent prevention workshop. Most parents still believed that they would know intuitively if their child were abused and a minority said they would involve a public agency after a disclosure of sexual abuse. Similarly, in a study conducted in the Lansing Public Schools (1987), 66% of parents reported that they had not learned anything new in the parent prevention workshop. Finally, many researchers note the difficulty of getting even a majority of parents to attend prevention education meetings.

Parent education programs also often encourage parents to provide primary prevention information to their children. Several researchers have reported an increase in parent–child discussions about sexual abuse following parent education programs (Binder & McNeil, 1987; Gardner-Frum & Fontanella, 1985; Porch & Petretic-Jackson, 1986). For example, Porch and Petretic-Jackson found that the percentage of parents who reported warning their children about sexual abuse by known adults increased from 41% to 84%. However, in some studies, increases in parent–child communication may have been partially related to concurrent school-based child prevention programs (Binder & McNeil, 1987; Gardner-Frum & Fontanella, 1985; Hazzard et al., 1988; Wurtele & Miller-Perrin, 1987). Furthermore, no research has examined the quality or impact of increased parent–child discussion of sexual abuse.

Teachers

Teachers, by virtue of their accessibility to the children in their classrooms and their expertise in child development, are in a unique position to intervene with sexually abused children. However, teachers have traditionally had limited training in child abuse. Hazzard and Rupp (1986) found that teachers were significantly less knowledgeable about child abuse than pediatricians or mental health professionals. Levin's (1983) survey of 285 teachers revealed that most teachers rated themselves as lacking knowledge about behavioral symptoms of child abuse, particularly sexual abuse. In Levin's survey, only 5% of teachers had ever reported a suspected sexual abuse case. However, in a more recent study, 40% of teachers had reported one or more suspected sexual abuse cases (Kleemeier, Webb, Hazzard, & Pohl, 1988). The increase may be a result of increased public awareness and enhanced teacher training in child abuse. In this sample, teachers reported an average of 3.6 hours of previous education about child abuse in general and 4.6 hours of previous education about sexual abuse.

Several studies have examined the impact of sexual abuse prevention workshops on teachers' knowledge, attitudes, and/or behaviors. Like prevention programs for parents, teacher workshops generally have a secondary prevention focus, aiming to enhance teacher skills in victim identification, support, and referral.

Teachers appear to increase in knowledge about sexual abuse following workshop participation (Beland, 1986a; Higgs, 1982; Lansing Public Schools, 1987; Swift, 1982). Higgs also found that teachers developed more accepting attitudes toward victims, offenders, and the nonoffending parent, while Lutter and Weisman (1985) found that Campfire Girl leaders rated themselves as more comfortable discussing sexual abuse issues. Swift (1982) found that school personnel (primarily nurses) in one school district who participated in a 33-hour training program on sexual abuse increased their reporting rate

500% from the year preintervention to the year postintervention. However, all of these studies are limited by their lack of control groups.

Kleemeier et al. (1988) evaluated the impact of a 6-hour prevention training workshop with teachers from 8 randomly assigned treatment and control schools. Compared to control teachers, trained teachers increased dramatically in knowledge about the scope of the problem, dynamics of child sexual abuse, behavioral indicators, reporting procedures, treatment alternatives, and prevention concepts. Furthermore, trained teachers appeared to be able to apply their knowledge to hypothetical situations that teachers might actually face. On a vignettes measure, trained teachers were better able than control teachers to identify specific indicators of sexual abuse and to respond to hypothetical sexually abused children in helpful ways.

Trained teachers also exhibited changes in their attitudes relative to control teachers, although these changes were smaller in magnitude than observed changes on the knowledge and vignettes measures. Trained teachers were more willing to acknowledge the severity of the problem of child sexual abuse, less blaming of the victim, more likely to see community agencies such as Child Protective Services as helpful, more supportive of prevention programs for children, and more confident of their own role in addressing the problem.

However, on a 6-week follow-up measure, trained teachers were not significantly different from control teachers in terms of self-reported behaviors such as conducting classroom prevention activities, discussing potential abuse with individual students, or reporting suspected abuse cases. The absence of behavioral changes may be partially due to the short follow-up period, or control teachers may have been motivated to deal with the abuse issue as a result of completing the measures. Also, in half of the teachers' classrooms, research staff presented prevention programs to the children as part of a related project; therefore, teachers probably felt less personal responsibility for discussing abuse with their classes or individual children. Nevertheless, additional research needs to focus on how to enhance the impact of teacher training on actual preventive behaviors by teachers.

Other Professionals

A variety of other professional adults often come into contact with sexually abused children and could potentially benefit from secondary prevention education. These professionals include day-care workers, clergy, pediatricians, mental health professionals, child protective services staff, and police officers. The literature on sexual abuse prevention efforts with these professionals is quite limited.

Two studies provide some normative information concerning professionals' knowledge about abuse. Hazzard and Rupp (1986) found that pediatricians were less informed than mental health professionals about child abuse in general. Attias and Goodwin (1984) found that psychiatrists and pediatricians were less knowledgeable about incest than psychologists or mental health counselors, although most professionals were fairly knowledgeable, answering over 75% of questionnaire items correctly. Differences among professional groups may actually reflect a sex difference, since female professionals were somewhat more knowledgeable than males and were disproportionately distributed among professional groups. Attias and Goodwin also noted specific knowledge deficits associated with particular professional groups. For example, as one might expect, fewer mental health professionals than pediatricians recognized the need for physical exams for sexual abuse victims. Psychiatrists appeared most likely to overestimate the likelihood of children's accusations being fantasies and least likely to refer a case to Protective Services after a retraction.

Certainly, there appear to be deficits in the knowledge of some professionals concerning child sexual abuse. However, there is no literature on sexual abuse prevention training for day-care workers, clergy, or pediatricians. Swift (1982) evaluated training workshops (4 to 33 hours) for police officers, community mental health center staff, child protection workers, and school personnel. Overall, professionals scored significantly higher on knowledge posttests than pretests. However, no control group was used in this study. There was a 15% increase in reported sexual abuse cases by participating agencies from the year pre- to the year posttraining. However, the two police agencies receiving training both showed a slight decline in reported cases, possibly because of the brevity of the intervention for police (4 hours) and the institutional practice of rotating officers, which may have removed trained officers from participation in sexual abuse investigations.

SUMMARY AND FUTURE DIRECTIONS

In the past decade, a great deal of creative energy has gone into developing sexual abuse prevention programs as well as designing studies to assess the impact of these programs. Considering the recency of sexual abuse prevention efforts, an impressive array of program materials and research results has been amassed.

School-based prevention programs for elementary children have been most widely implemented and evaluated. Elementary schoolchildren clearly appear to gain in knowledge as a result of these programs and to retain knowledge gains at 1-year follow-up. However, the issue of whether these children are using their increased knowledge to prevent sexual abuse is unresolved. Some research suggests that children do exhibit enhanced prevention skills on analogue measures, such as verbal or videotape vignettes, or during in vivo simulations of abduction scenarios. Prevention programs also appear to encourage disclosures of abuse, which is a secondary prevention outcome.

Most studies of potential negative effects suggest that children participating in elementary prevention programs do not, as a group, exhibit increased anxiety, inappropriate noncompliance, or feelings of discomfort about appropriate physical affection. A minority of children may experience some embarrassment, related to discussing sexually explicit material, or an increased fear of strangers. As with other sensitive topics, educators and parents must weigh the potential benefits of sexual abuse prevention education against its potential risks.

There is much less literature, and a great deal more controversy, about sexual abuse prevention education for other child populations: preschoolers, disabled children, and adolescents. The evidence concerning the efficacy of preschool prevention education is not strong. There seems to be a growing consensus that many of the abstract concepts in elementary programs, such as associating feelings with different touches, are too cognitively complex for preschoolers. Thus, prevention educators are increasingly focusing on teaching preschoolers concrete rules about when genital touching is or is not appropriate. It is hoped that there will soon be more methodologically sound research to determine how variables such as program length and conceptual basis affect preschool program impact.

Similar issues arise when considering prevention education for disabled children. Not only must these programs be developmentally appropriate, but they must take into account the communication difficulties experienced by children with various disabilities. These difficulties have apparently inhibited program development and program evaluation efforts thus far.

Although many prevention programs for adolescents have been recently developed, most lack a clear theoretical basis. It has been difficult for prevention educators to integrate the literature on child molestation and acquaintance rape and to conceptually distinguish perpetrator issues from victim issues. Furthermore, there is no published evaluative research on adolescent prevention programs.

Prevention educators have accomplished much in the past decade, but many opportunities for further growth and innovation remain. With respect to school-based programs, there are many unresolved conceptual issues as well as program evaluation dilemmas. Moreover, many prevention professionals have begun looking beyond school-based programs for children to consider other approaches to prevention.

Conceptually, school-based programs are developing in several new directions. First, prevention professionals are beginning to utilize the literature on children's cognitive and moral development to make prevention programs more developmentally appropriate. Second, prevention programmers are increasingly considering how to integrate prevention messages with other sociobehavioral education in the classroom. For example, should prevention programs also address other types of abuse such as physical abuse and neglect? What is the optimal relationship between sexual abuse prevention programs and sex education programs? And, should programs teaching specific sexual abuse prevention skills be integrated with programs addressing related issues such as assertion, anger management, empathy, and self-esteem? For example, the Committee for Children (1988) has developed the Second Steps elementary curriculum, which aims to reduce physical and sexual aggression by teaching potential perpetrators empathy, impulse control, anger management, and decision-making skills.

Finally, Conte, Wolf, and Smith (1988) have begun conducting research with perpetrators to find out more about the process of victimization, so that prevention programs can be revised to provide children with more accurate and potentially effective information. For example, perpetrator interviews have revealed the subtlety of the grooming and sexual desensitization processes used by molesters. Conte et al. (1988) argue that it is not realistic to teach children to recognize early warning signs of abuse, because so many grooming behaviors are normal aspects of adult–child relationships (e.g., an adult paying attention to or being physically affectionate with a child). Rather, prevention programs need to give children permission to say no to touches that have become sexual, even if they said yes or said nothing to other touches or activities during the grooming process. It would also be helpful to study victims in greater depth, perhaps investigating variables that distinguish long-term victims from children who were able to avoid or immediately disclose an abusive incident. Were avoiders more knowledgeable about the inappropriateness of the sexually abusive approach, less fearful of the consequences of disclosure, or more assertive and confident overall? In-depth studies of perpetrators and victims can help refine the content of prevention programs on an empirical basis.

As prevention programs are becoming more conceptually sophisticated, researchers are struggling to develop methodologies adequate to address the many unanswered evaluation questions. The biggest gap in the literature is the absence of any long-term, large-scale follow-up studies to determine whether children are indeed better able to protect themselves after prevention education. In addition to the ethical and pragmatic problems involved in such studies, researchers also face the dilemma of how to interpret disclosures. Because programs teach prevention skills *and* encourage reports, a high frequency of disclosures from trained children does not necessarily mean the program has failed. As Finkelhor and Strapko (1987) point out, researchers need to examine the types of disclosures from a trained versus an untrained group: the trained group should disclose more short-term molestations or molestation attempts that were disclosed immediately. Another approach to the question of ultimate program outcome is to assess impact on a community level, rather than to use a treatment-control group design. A community having extensive sexual abuse prevention programming could be contrasted with a comparable community without prevention programming, examining variables such as frequency and type of abuse reports.

In addition to evaluating long-term program effectiveness in preventing sexual abuse, researchers need to assess other dimensions of program impact. It is unclear how these programs affect children's feelings about sexuality or how these effects vary depending on how sex education is handled at home and school. For example, do prevention programs inadvertently contribute to children's guilt or confusion about nonabusive sex play with peers? How do prevention programs affect children's feelings and behaviors as they make decisions about sexuality in adolescence? Furthermore, researchers have not investigated how programs affect already victimized children or children who may be victimized in the future. For example, does prevention education increase or decrease guilt among victims?

In addition to refining current school-based programs, prevention educators are expanding the focus of their efforts. There is a trend toward placing more responsibility for prevention on adults, rather than children. There is increasing attention to developing programs that more effectively serve caretaking adults such as parents, particularly as a component of preschool prevention education. It also might be helpful to integrate prevention information into programs which serve high-risk parents such as stepparents or incest survivors. Sexual abuse prevention education needs to be integrated into the standard undergraduate or graduate curricula for child care professionals such as teachers, mental health professionals and pediatricians, instead of being presented via special workshops as is now the case. Preventive interventions targeting adult molesters are also being developed, in addition to the perpetrator prevention programs for elementary students and adolescents that have already been mentioned. For example, the Committee for Children has developed a public service announcement aimed at perpetrators and the National Committee for the Prevention of Child Abuse has published a pamphlet entitled "You Don't Have to Molest That Child" (Smith, 1987).

Finally, many prevention educators continue to discuss how sexual abuse is supported by cultural attitudes that sanction interpersonal aggression and male domination of women and children. The broader focus of these prevention advocates and their political activism highlight the fallacy of assuming that sexual abuse can be eradicated solely by teaching prevention skills to children. Child sexual abuse is a complex, multidetermined problem that must be addressed by prevention efforts aimed at individual, family, and societal levels.

REFERENCES

Abbey, A. (1982). Sex differences in attributions for friendly behavior: Do males misperceive females' friendliness? *Journal of Personality and Social Psychology, 42,* 830–838.

Adams, C., & Fay, J. (1981). *No more secrets.* Santa Cruz, California: Network Publications.

Ageton, S. (1983). *Sexual assault among adolescents.* Lexington, MA: Lexington Books.

Anderson-Kent, C. (1982). *No easy answers.* Minneapolis: Illusion Theatre.

Attias, R., & Goodwin, J. (1984, September). *Knowledge and management strategies in incest cases: A survey of physicians, psychologists, and family counselors.* Paper presented at the Fifth International Congress on Child Abuse and Neglect, Montreal.

Beland, K. (1986a). *Preventing child sexual victimization: A school-based statewide prevention model.* Seattle: Committee for Children.

Beland, K. (1986b). *Talking about touching II.* Seattle: Committee for Children.

Berliner, L., & Conte, J. (1988). *The process of victimization: The victim's perspective.* Unpublished manuscript, University of Chicago, School of Social Service Administration, Chicago.

Binder, R., & McNiel, D. (1987). Evaluation of a school-based sexual abuse prevention program: Cognitive and emotional effects. *Child Abuse and Neglect, 11,* 497–506.

Borkin, J., & Frank, L. (1986). Sexual abuse prevention for preschoolers: A pilot program. *Child Welfare, 65,* 75–82.

Briere, J., & Malamuth, N. (1983). Self-reported likelihood of sexually aggressive behavior: Attitudinal versus sexual explanations. *Journal of Research in Personality, 17,* 315–323.

Broadhurst, D. (1986). *Educators, schools, and child abuse.* Chicago: National Committee for the Prevention of Child Abuse.

Burgess, A. (1985). Sexual victimization of adolescents. In A. Burgess (Ed.), *Rape and sexual assault: A research handbook* (pp. 123–138). New York: Garland Publishing.

Child Assault Prevention Project. (1983). *Strategies for free children.* Columbus, OH: Author.

Children's Self-Help Project. (1988). *Middle school and high school sexual abuse prevention programs.* San Francisco: Author.

Clark, K. (1985). *Sexual abuse prevention education: An annotated bibliography.* Santa Cruz, CA: Network Publications.

Committee for Children. (1984). *Talking about touching.* Seattle: Author.

Committee for Children. (1985). *Identifying, reporting, and handling disclosure of the sexually abused child* (Videotape). Seattle: Author.

Committee for Children. (1986). *Yes, You Can Say No* (Videotape). Seattle: Author.

Committee for Children. (1988). *Second step: A skill training curriculum to prevent violence.* Seattle: Author.

Conte, J. (1984, August). *Research on the prevention of sexual abuse of children.* Paper presented at the Second National Conference for Family Violence Researchers, Durham, NH.

Conte, J. (1987). Ethical issues in evaluation of prevention programs. *Child Abuse and Neglect, 11,* 171–172.

Conte, J., Rosen, C., Saperstein, L., & Shermach, R. (1985). An evaluation of a program to prevent the sexual victimization of young children. *Child Abuse and Neglect, 9,* 319–328.

Conte, J., Wolf, S., & Smith, T. (1988, July). *What sexual offenders tell us about prevention findings.* Paper presented at the Third National Family Violence Conference, Durham, NH.

Crisci, G., & Kearney, D. (1988, April). *Child sexual abuse prevention: Preschool evaluation study*. Paper presented at the National Symposium on Child Victimization, Anaheim, CA.

Daro, D., Duerr, J., & LeProhn, N. (1986). *Child assault prevention instruction: What works with preschoolers*. Chicago: National Committee for the Prevention of Child Abuse.

Downer, A. (1984a). *Prevention of child sexual abuse: A trainer's manual*. Seattle: Committee for Children.

Downer, A. (1984b). *Evaluation of talking about touching*. Seattle: Committee for Children.

Downer, A., & Beland, K. (1985). *Personal safety and decision-making*. Seattle: Committee for Children.

Fehrenbach, P., Smith, W., Monastersky, C., & Deisher, R. (1986). Adolescent sexual offenders: Offender and offense characteristics. *American Journal of Orthopsychiatry, 56*, 225–233.

Filmfair Communications (1978). *Better safe than sorry I* (Videotape). Studio City, CA: Author.

Filmfair Communications (1983). *Better safe than sorry II* (Videotape). Studio City, CA: Author.

Filmfair Communications (1986). *Better safe than sorry III* (Videotape). Studio City, CA: Author.

Finkelhor, D. (1984). *Child sexual abuse: New theory and research*. New York: Free Press.

Finkelhor, D., & Strapko, N. (1987). Sexual abuse prevention education: A review of evaluation studies. In D. Willis, W. Holder, & M. Rosenberg (Eds.), *Child abuse prevention*. New York: Wiley.

Fortune, M. (1983). *Sexual abuse prevention: A study for teenagers:* New York: United Church Press.

Fryer, G. E., Kraizer, S. K., & Miyoshi, T. (1987a). Measuring actual reduction of risk to child abuse: A new approach. *Child Abuse and Neglect, 11*, 173–179.

Fryer, G. E., Kraizer, S. K., & Miyoshi, T. (1987b). Measuring children's retention of skills to resist stranger abduction: Use of the simulation technique. *Child Abuse and Neglect, 11*, 181–185.

Gallmeier, T., Kenning, M., & Plemons, S. (1988, April). *Evaluation of a school-based child sexual abuse prevention program*. Paper presented at the National Symposium on Child Victimization, Anaheim, CA.

Garbarino, J. (1987). Children's response to a sexual abuse prevention program: A study of the Spiderman Comic. *Child Abuse and Neglect, 11*, 143–148.

Gardner-Frum, M., & Fontanella, J. (1985). *Sexual abuse prevention project annual report: Year 3*. Meriden, CT: Child Guidance Clinic for Central Connecticut.

Gilbert, N., Daro, D., Duerr, J., LeProhn, N., & Nyman, N. (1988). *Child sexual abuse prevention: Evaluation of educational materials for preschool programs*. Berkeley, CA: Family Welfare Research Group.

Hall, E., & Flannery, P. (1984). Prevalence and correlates of sexual assault experiences in adolescents. *Victimology: An International Journal, 9*, 398–406.

Hallingby, L., & Brick, P. (1984). Child sexual abuse education and prevention: A selected bibliography of materials for sale. *Siecus Report, 13,* 13–16.

Haugaard, J., & Reppucci, N. D. (1988). Preventing child sexual abuse. In *The sexual abuse of young children.* San Francisco: Jossey-Bass.

Hazzard, A., & Kleemeier, C. (1988, August). *Teacher vs. expert presentations of sexual abuse prevention programs.* Paper presented at the annual meeting of the American Psychological Association, Atlanta.

Hazzard, A., & Rupp, G. (1986). A note on the knowledge and attitudes of professional groups toward child abuse. *Journal of Community Psychology, 14,* 219–223.

Hazzard, A., Webb, C., & Kleemeier, C. (1988, April). *Child sexual abuse prevention programs: Helpful or harmful?* Paper presented at the National Symposium on Child Victimization, Anaheim, CA.

Higgs, C. (1982). *Sexual abuse preventive education demonstration projects: Program evaluation final report.* Alexandria, VA: Graham Mcwhorter Research.

Hindman, J. (1983). *A very touching book.* Ontario, OR: Alexandria Assoc.

Hindman, J. (1987). *Abuses to sexual abuse prevention programs.* Ontario, OR: Alexandria Assoc.

Illusion Theatre Company. (1983). *How to take the first steps.* Minneapolis: Author.

Illusion Theatre Company & Media Ventures (Coproducers). (1984). *Touch* (Film). Deerfield, IL: MTI Teleprograms.

J. Gary Mitchell Film Company. (1976). *Incest: The victim nobody believes* (Film). Deerfield, IL: MTI Teleprograms.

James Stanfield & Company. (1985). *Child sexual abuse: A solution* (Videotape). Santa Monica, CA: Author.

Kassees, J., & Hall, R. (1987). *Adolescent sexual abuse project.* Wilmington, DE: Parents Anonymous of Delaware.

Kearny, D. (1986). *Hamden and Hampshire County preschool study of the personal safety programs combination puppet show/curriculum.* (Available from 165 Front Street, Bldg., D-5th, Chicopee, MA 01013)

Kenning, M., Gallmeier, T., Jackson, T., & Plemons, S. (1987). *Evaluation of child sexual abuse prevention programs: A summary of two studies.* Paper presented at the National Conference on Family Violence, Durham, NH.

Kleemeier, C., Webb, C., Hazzard, A., & Pohl, J. (1988). Child sexual abuse prevention: Evaluation of a teacher training model. *Child Abuse and Neglect, 12,* 555–561.

Kolko, D. (1988). Educational programs to promote awareness and prevention of child sexual victimization: A review and methodological critique. *Clinical Psychology Review, 8,* 195–209.

Kolko, D., Moser, J., Litz, J., & Hughes, J. (1987). Promoting awareness and prevention of child sexual victimization using the Red Flag/Green Flag Program: An evaluation with follow-up. *Journal of Family Violence, 2,* 11–35.

Koss, M., Leonard, K., Beezley, D., & Oros, C. (1985). Non-stranger sexual aggression: A discriminant analysis of the psychological characteristics of undetected offenders. *Sex Roles, 12,* 981–992.

Krents, E., & Atkins, D. (1985). *No-Go-Tell! A child protection curriculum for very young disabled children.* New York: Lexington Center.

LaBarre, A. & Hinkley, K. (1986). *Sexual abuse! What is it? An informational book for the hearing impaired.* St. Paul: St. Paul-Ramsey Foundation.

Lansing Public Schools Office of Research and Evaluation. (1987). *Final evaluation report of aware kids/safe kids: A comprehensive program for school based child sexual abuse prevention.* Lansing, MI: Author.

Levin, P. (1983). Teacher's perceptions, attitudes, and reporting of child abuse/neglect. *Child Welfare, 62,* 14–20.

Lidell, T., Young, B., & Yamagishi, M. (1986). *Implementation and evaluation of a preschool sexual abuse prevention resource.* Seattle: Committee for Children.

Lutter, Y., & Weisman, A. (1985). *Sexual victimization prevention project: Final report* (Federal Grant No. R18MH37549). (Available from P.O. Box 229, Greendale Station, Worcester, MA 01609)

Marvel Comics (1984). *Spiderman and Power Pack.* New York: Author.

Miller-Perrin, C., & Wurtele, S. (1986, August). *Harmful effects of school-based sexual abuse prevention programs? Reassure the parents.* Paper presented at the annual meeting of the American Psychological Association, Washington, DC.

Miltenberger, R., & Thiesse-Duffy, E. (1988). Evaluation of home-based programs for teaching personal safety skills to children. *Journal of Applied Behavior Analysis, 21,* 81–87.

Montgomery, B., & Anlauf, K. (1988). *Sexual health and responsibility program.* St. Paul: Department of Human Services.

Morgan, M. (1985). *Safe Touch.* Eugene, OR: Rape Crisis Network.

Muehlenhard, C., & Linton, M. (1987). Date rape and sexual aggression in dating situations: Incidence and risk factors. *Journal of Counseling Psychology, 34,* 186–196.

National Committee for the Prevention of Child Abuse (1984). *Child sexual abuse prevention resources.* Chicago: Author.

National Film Board of Canada. (1985). *Feeling yes, feeling no.* Evanston, IL: Perennial Education.

Nelson, D. (1985). *An evaluation of the student outcomes and instructional characteristics of the "You're in Charge" program.* (Available from Utah State Office of Education, Salt Lake City, UT 84111)

Nelson, M., & Clark, K. (1986). *The educator's guide to preventing child sexual abuse.* Santa Cruz: Network Publications.

Nibert, D., Cooper, S., Fitch, L., & Ford, J. (1988). *Prevention of abuse of young children.* Columbus, OH: National Assault Prevention Center.

O'Day, B. (1983). *Preventing sexual abuse of persons with disabilities: A curriculum for hearing impaired, physically disabled, blind and mentally retarded students.* St. Paul, MN: Program for Victims of Sexual Assault, Department of Corrections.

Plummer, C. (1984a). *Preventing sexual abuse.* Holmes Beach, FL: Learning Publications.

Plummer, C. (1984b). *Preventing sexual abuse: What in-school programs teach children.* Paper presented at the Second National Conference for Family Violence Researchers, Durham, NH.

Poche, C., Brouwer, R., & Swearington, M. (1981). Teaching self-protection to young children. *Journal of Applied Behavior Analysis, 14,* 169–176.

Pohl, J., Angert, A., & Hazzard, A. (1988, August). *Child sexual abuse prevention: One year follow-up and booster shot.* Paper presented at the annual meeting of the American Psychological Association, Atlanta.

Pohl, J., & Hazzard, A. (in press). Reactions of children, parents, and teachers to child sexual abuse prevention programs. *Education.*

Porch, T., & Petretic-Jackson, P. (1986). *Child assault prevention: Evaluating parent education workshops.* Paper presented at the American Psychological Association Convention, Washington, DC.

Rape and Abuse Crisis Center. (1986). *Red flag green flag prevention book.* Fargo, ND: Author.

Ray, J., & Dietzel, M. (1984). *Teaching child sexual abuse prevention.* Spokane: Rape Crisis Network.

Ray-Keil, A. (1988). *Prevention for preschoolers: Good, bad, or confusing.* Seattle: Committee for Children.

Saslawsky, D., & Wurtele, S. (1986). Educating children about sexual abuse: Implications for pediatric intervention and possible prevention. *Journal of Pediatric Psychology, 11,* 235–245.

Schroeder, C. S., Gordon, B. N., & McConnell, P. (1986). Books for parents and children on sexual abuse prevention. *Journal of Clinical Child Psychology, 15,* 178–185.

Seattle Rape Relief. (1979). *Sexual exploitation of handicapped students: Levels I and II.* Seattle: Author.

Smith, T. (1987). *You don't have to molest that child.* Chicago: National Committee for the Prevention of Child Abuse.

Spelman, C. (1985). *Talking about child sexual abuse.* Chicago: National Committee for the Prevention of Child Abuse.

Stowell, J., & Dietzel, M. (1982). *My very own book about me.* Spokane: Lutheran Social Services of Washington.

Strong, K., Tate, J., Wehman, B., & Wyss, A. (1986). *Project Safe: A sexual assault perpetrator prevention curriculum for junior high school students.* Cumberland, WI: Human Growth and Development Program.

Swan, H., Press, A., & Briggs, S. (1985). Child sexual abuse prevention: Does it work. *Child Welfare, 54,* 395–405.

Swift, C. (1982). *Consultation in the area of child sexual abuse: Final report* (Report No. NIMH 83-213). Rockville, Maryland: National Institute of Mental Health.

Wachter, O. (1982). *No more secrets for me.* Boston: Little-Brown.

Wolfe, D., MacPherson, T., Blount, R., & Wolfe, V. (1986). Evaluation of a brief intervention for educating school children in awareness of physical and sexual abuse. *Child Abuse and Neglect, 10,* 85–92.

Woods, S., & Dean, K. (1986). *Community-based options for maltreatment prevention: Augmenting self-sufficiency final report.* (Available from Child and Family Services, 2602 E. Fifth Avenue, Knoxville, TN 37914)

Wurtele, S. (1987). School-based sexual abuse prevention programs: A review. *Child Abuse and Neglect, 11,* 483–495.

Wurtele, S. (1988, August). *Harmful effects of sexual abuse prevention programs?*

Results and implications. Paper presented at the annual meeting of the American Psychological Association, Atlanta.

Wurtele, S., Marrs, S., & Miller-Perrin, C. (1987). Practice makes perfect? The role of participant modeling in sexual abuse prevention programs. *Journal of Consulting and Clinical Psychology, 55*, 599–602.

Wurtele, S., & Miller-Perrin, C. (1987). An evaluation of side effects associated with participation in a child sexual abuse prevention program. *Journal of School Health, 57*, 228–231.

Wurtele, S., Miller-Perrin, C., Kondrick, P., Morris, D., & Bratcher, K. (1988, August). *Development of an instrument to measure children's responses to sexual abuse prevention programs*. Paper presented at the annual meeting of the American Psychological Association, Atlanta.

Wurtele, S., Saslawsky, D., Miller, C., Marrs, S., & Britcher, J. (1986). Teaching personal safety skills for potential prevention of sexual abuse: A comparison of treatments. *Journal of Consulting and Clinical Psychology, 54*, 688–692.

Zellman, G., Johnson, P., Giarrusso, R., & Goodchilds, J. (1979, August). *Adolescent expectations for dating relationships: Consensus and conflict between the sexes*. Paper presented at the annual meeting of the American Psychological Association.

CHAPTER 16

Prevention of Wife Assault

GERALD T. HOTALING AND DAVID B. SUGARMAN

INTRODUCTION

In the past 10 years, an extensive amount of research has been produced about the individual, relational, and cultural factors that place women at risk for violence in close relationships with men. Less attention has been paid to the application of this knowledge to issues of prevention, especially primary prevention. It is ironic that one of the main stumbling blocks to this application of knowledge is the assumption that "all of the facts are in" and that there is no longer a need to search for the causes of wife assault and other forms of family violence and to continue refining theories to explain their occurrence. For example, in a recent book review, Gil (1989) states:

> We have known for a long time how to reduce the incidence of intimate violence. To start that process we need to eliminate unemployment and poverty, humanize and democratize work, develop publicly maintained systems of comprehensive, quality education and health care for all, and provide means for voluntary prevention of unintended births. While we have the resources and knowledge to carry out these measures, we have actually moved in recent years in the opposite direction, due to lack of political will. (p. 238)

Not many would dispute that these social changes would significantly reduce the suffering of many people, but would they reduce the incidence of wife assault? Some evidence would suggest the answer is "no," but the real point is simply that no one knows. Current knowledge about wife assault is not advanced enough to speak with certainty about the complex interplay of factors that promote its occurrence.

This research was supported under Contract No. 299-84-0755 from the Department of Health and Human Services through the Violence Epidemiology Branch of the Department of Health and Human Services at the Centers for Disease Control, Atlanta, GA, and by a grant from the National Institute of Mental Health (No. MH 15161-07) through the University of New Hampshire. The views and conclusions expressed in this paper are solely those of the authors and do not necessarily reflect the views of above-mentioned organizations.

The purpose of this chapter is to review current knowledge about wife assault and assess its utility for primary prevention. It first presents some facts about the extent and consequences of wife assault, followed by a discussion of the difficulties in applying a public health prevention approach to social problems.

ISSUES IN PREVENTION

The Incidence and Consequences of Wife Assault*

Wife assault is quite common in the United States. Two national studies report that between 11% and 12% of couples reported one or more acts of wife assault during a 12-month period (Straus & Gelles, 1986; Straus, Gelles, & Steinmetz, 1980). This translates to an estimated 1.6 to 2.0 million women who are targets of wife assault each year. If one attempts to estimate the number of women who will be assaulted by male partners over the entire course of their relationship, the numbers become even more staggering. These studies report that 20% to 30% of surveyed women are assaulted at some point in the marital relationship (Gentemann, 1980; Nisenoff & Bitman, 1979; Schulman, 1979; Straus & Gelles, 1986; Straus et al., 1980; Teske & Parker, 1983).

Many of these women are victims of serious assaults. The National Family Violence Resurvey (Straus & Gelles, 1986) found that 39% of the violent incidents toward wives involved punching with a fist, kicking, biting, beating, and attacks with knives and guns. Furthermore, the seriousness of these assaults is underscored by U.S. homicide statistics. Unpublished data from the Supplementary Homicide Report collected as part of the Uniform Crime Reporting Program of the Federal Bureau of Investigation indicate that of women who were age 18 or older, 12,582 were killed in one-to-one homicide events during 1980–1984. Of these women, 52% were killed by a husband, ex-husband, common-law husband, or boyfriend (Carmody & Williams, 1987).

Death is certainly the most serious but not the only consequence of wife

---

*The term *assault* is used in this chapter rather than *violence* or *abuse* because it focuses on acts instead of injuries. As Marcus (1983, p. 89) states: "Physical contact is not an element of assault," or as the Uniform Crime Reports puts it: "Attempts are included (in the tabulation of aggravated assault) because it is not necessary that an injury result" (U.S. Department of Justice, 1985, p. 21). The notion of assault resembles the definition of violence used by Gelles and Straus (1979) in their studies of family violence. Violence is defined as an act carried out with the intention of causing pain or physical injury to another person. It is similar to assault in that it includes unsuccessful attempts but different because not all violence is a common law or statutory crime. Some violent acts, in fact, are required by law, for example, capital punishment. Abuse, on the other hand, is usually gauged by the severity of the act of violence or assault and is more like the legal concept of battery. Abuse is typically measured by reference to psychological or physical harm. Because this chapter considers actual or attempted acts of illegal violence, *assault* seems the most appropriate term.

assault. Stets and Straus (in press) have documented the numerous ways in which victimization is associated with a plethora of physical and mental health problems. The effects of victimization include almost double the number of days in bed from illness, double the incidence of headaches, four times the rate of feeling depressed, and over five times the rate of suicide attempts.

The harmful consequences of wife assault are broader still when the effects on children who witness these assaults are taken into account. Prior research has documented that a key risk factor in husband-to-wife violence is the childhood witnessing of parental violence by the male (Hotaling & Sugarman, 1986). In addition, children who have witnessed parental assault are more likely to have assaulted someone outside the family and to have committed property crimes than children who have not witnessed parental violence. These findings hold regardless of the child's gender or the family's social class (Hotaling, Straus, & Lincoln, 1989).

Even though wife assault is an extreme and serious problem, discussions of primary prevention have largely been ignored. In part, this is attributable to three major issues: the lack of acceptance of the idea of primary prevention, problems in the application of a public health model of prevention to social phenomena, and the inadequate study of risk factors. Each of these issues is discussed in the following sections.

The Need for Primary Prevention of Wife Assault

The concept of primary prevention is borrowed from the fields of public health and mental health where it refers to steps that inhibit the development of a disease before it occurs. In current usage, it has a more elaborate meaning. The term has been extended now to include activities that also interrupt or inhibit the progression of disease (Mausner & Bahn, 1974). Under this schema, prevention can occur at any of three levels depending on the stage at which one applies prevention measures (Sedlak, 1988).

Primary prevention refers to any activity that stops the problem prior to disease exposure or the occurrence of the first symptoms. This form of prevention consists of measures that fall into two major categories. First, interventions can be directed at reducing the individual's exposure to environmental factors that may place the person at risk to the disease (e.g., elimination of the use of asbestos in construction to reduce the risk of lung cancer, reduction of environmental stressors to decrease the likelihood of wife assault). Second, interventions can reduce the individual's susceptibility to the disease by increasing available resources (e.g., childhood immunization programs, training courses in the management of stress).

Secondary prevention involves activities designed to eliminate the problem in its early stages after the initial signs of symptomology have appeared. The goal of secondary prevention is to end the problem or slow its progression toward more serious stages. As with primary prevention, secondary prevention can be directed at reducing exposure to the environmental factors that cause the symptoms (e.g., toxic waste cleanup) or at increasing the individual's ability to fight the disease (e.g., penicillin for the eradication of venereal disease).

Tertiary prevention focuses on interventions that are used when the problem has entered a chronic phase exhibiting a stable pattern of symptomology (e.g., mental health institutionalization). They are designed to reduce the duration and/or severity of symptoms and the likelihood of recurrence.

For a variety of reasons, this chapter considers the primary prevention of wife assault. First of all, there are at least two recent comprehensive works that chronicle and evaluate secondary and tertiary prevention measures for wife abuse (see Saunders & Azar, 1989; Sedlak, 1988). Second, there are practical limitations to secondary and tertiary prevention measures for sharply reducing the incidence of wife abuse. The most obvious limitations of treatment approaches to wife abuse stem from the sheer size of the problem and the many serious consequences that result from it (Straus & Smith, 1989). There is a vast imbalance between the available organizational resources for aid and the number of individuals who require help. Kantor and Straus (in press), for example, report that only about 7% of assaults between spouses are reported to the police and a very small proportion of those reports result in arrest. In fact, it is estimated that arrest occurs in less than one in a hundred marital assaults. Furthermore, there are only approximately 1000 shelters available to women in the United States (Gelles & Straus, 1988). The mental health system is also unlikely to provide assistance to more than a minute fraction of those in need of help. If incidence figures on wife assault are a true representation of the size of the problem, there is little possibility of providing sufficient mental health treatment to more than a few of the victims and/or offenders of wife assault.

Primary prevention has been a low priority in the field of family violence because the immediate need to assist victims has emphasized the development of information about secondary and tertiary prevention efforts. This chapter is a small step to remedy that situation. Significant reductions in the incidence of assaultive behaviors within families will only come about when those harmful factors that produce violence are identified and modified. A great deal of work has been devoted to the identification of risk markers and it is the duty of researchers to explicitly draw out prevention implications.

Problems in the Application of the Concept of Prevention to Social Phenomena

The public health model of prevention developed in response to clearly defined physical disease entities. In this arena, interventions are designed to either eliminate or reduce the intensity of noxious agent(s) or to strengthen the host and thereby reduce susceptibility to disease. This model applies awkwardly to social phenomena (Sedlak, 1988), especially when utilized in situations in which both the disease agent and host are human beings (Swift, 1988). Nontrivial conceptual, ethical, and political problems arise when this model is applied to a social problem such as wife assault. Conceptually, there is little consensus about the exact meaning of wife assault or about the exact role of causal factors in its onset. These problems must be stated as clearly as possible in order to implement a primary prevention model. A larger problem concerns the specification of the target in a primary prevention approach. This decision must be based on some idea of just who or what constitutes the disease entity. There appear to be at least three choices. The first choice is to eliminate or reduce the intensity of the noxious agent or offending entity. In the case of wife assault, this means the eradication, imprisonment, or rehabilitation of the male offender. Second, the host population can be strengthened by teaching women in intimate relationships how to resist or effectively avoid violent encounters. The ethical problem here is obvious: It places the burden of prevention on the victim and thus holds her potentially accountable for the problem (Swift, 1988).

A third alternative is to choose the relationship as the unit of concern. Here, the relationship itself is *both* the disease and the host. This perspective runs counter to the dichotomous logic of the classic prevention model but does reflect the complexity of violent intimate relationships. Prevention measures here would include radical adjustments of conduct in relationships to ensure nonassaultive interactions. From this perspective, the health problem (in this case, wife assault) is not understandable or modifiable by reference to either the characteristics of the offender or the characteristics of the victim in isolation. It is only through the interaction of offender *and* victim that the dynamics of the health problem become apparent.

Inadequate Study of Risk Markers

Whether preventive interventions should be directed at offenders, victims, or relationships is a question that can be addressed empirically through the study of risk markers of wife assault. In fact, any primary prevention effort must rely heavily on knowledge of these markers. A risk marker in the case of wife assault refers to an attribute or characteristic that is associated with an increased likelihood of such assault. Risk markers do not refer to consequences of assault, and risk factors are not necessarily causal factors although they can be (see Last, 1983). As Sedlak (1988) indicates, risk markers can be identified on the basis of whether they are related to either the occurrence of wife assault, to the level of assault severity, or to both occurrence and severity.

Much of the research work on wife assault has been inadequate for the purpose of identifying risk markers and, consequently, unhelpful in the design of primary prevention measures. Two major problems are relevant here. First, the design of many studies does not allow for a calculation of risk. Much of wife assault research can be described at best as profile analyses in which characteristics of either violent men or victimized women are examined in the absence of appropriate comparison groups. These studies often make assertions about a potential characteristic's impact on wife assault without reference to that characteristic among nonassaultive persons. For example, if 65% of men who assault their wives have witnessed violent behavior between their parents while growing up, nothing is learned about the role of witnessing parental violence as a risk marker. One still requires a measure of the extent of the childhood witnessing parental violence among a group of nonassaultive husbands. This permits an evaluation of the effect of witnessing parental violence on later violence. This argument should not be construed as viewing profile analysis research as worthless or inferior. Indeed, this type of study permits the generating of risk-marker hypotheses that can subsequently be confirmed in multiple-group studies. Also, profile analysis can be immensely valuable for the purpose of secondary or tertiary prevention where detailed knowledge of a client population is a clear asset. But it has little direct value for the determination of risk markers and, therefore, for use in primary prevention.

In order to identify individuals at risk of assaulting or being assaulted, it is necessary to use a case-comparison research design. There are an increasing number of studies that have employed this design to study wife assault (see Hotaling & Sugarman, 1986). Generally, researchers implement this design by means of either a *target sample strategy* or a *community survey strategy*. A target sample strategy employs an assault group and at least one comparison group composed of persons not experiencing assaultive acts or engaging in assaultive acts (e.g., Rosenbaum & O'Leary, 1981; Telch & Lindquist, 1984). This approach attempts to separate participants into assault or nonassault groups *prior* to data collection and analysis. For example, a group of men in marital counseling who assault their wives can be compared to a group of men in marital counseling who have not engaged in assaultive behavior. A comparison of these two groups on a number of characteristics would identify factors that increase the likelihood or risk of assaultive behavior. A community survey strategy derives comparison groups *after* data collection on the basis of responses to standard measures (e.g., the Conflict Tactics Scale, Straus, 1979) via statistical manipulation (e.g., Sugarman & Hotaling, 1986, 1987).

These two research strategies are not necessarily equivalent. Generally, the target sample strategy will have a relatively small number of participants, and attempts are made to match the assaultive/assaulted group and the nonassaultive/nonassaulted group on a range of demographic variables (e.g., age, years of education). These studies tend to focus on differences that may be attributable to psychological and interactional factors, such as self-esteem (Telch & Lindquist, 1984), assertiveness (Rosenbaum & O'Leary, 1981), power tactics usage (Frieze, 1979), and marital satisfaction (Hudson & McIntosh, 1981). Essentially, the generalizability of these studies is restricted in order to gain greater internal validity. Being based on more representative samples, community survey studies are particularly useful in evaluating the impact of demographic and societal structural factors on wife assault (Straus et al., 1980).

A second problem that affects risk marker research centers on the potential relationships among markers. A hypothetical study might reveal that assaultive husbands are more likely to be unemployed, have less formal education, and lower personal incomes than nonassaultive husbands. This would suggest that three factors are predictive of wife assault at the univariate level. However, this analysis does not account for the relationships among the factors (e.g., being unemployed will be associated with lower levels of personal income). A second analysis strategy may be to use regression techniques in order to predict group membership based on these three factors. This approach takes into account the relationships among the variables but answers a distinctly different question. That is, which factor contributes most to the observed between-group differences? In addition, an intuitive researcher would observe that these three factors seem to be a conceptual unit (e.g., all measures of socioeconomic status).

This observation should promote a third approach that focuses on viewing a number of markers as a multivariate package representing some latent variable. Consequently, factor analyzing potential risk markers prior to between-group analysis permits the identification of potential latent variables. Furthermore, the between-group analysis then allows for the evaluation of risk on a specific latent variable independent of other latent variables in the analysis. Besides offering researchers information with respect to potential risk markers, this multivariate approach can aid in clarifying the complexity of potential causal factors.

The purpose of the remainder of this chapter is to (a) assess the current knowledge base on risk markers of wife assault, (b) present the results of a statistical analysis of these risk markers that will allow for an assessment of their independent effect on wife assault, and (c) outline the implications of these findings for the primary prevention of wife assault.

A Risk Marker Analysis

Three reviews of case comparison studies have identified a number of important individual and relationship level risk factors of wife assault (Hotaling & Sugarman, 1984, 1986; Sedlak, 1988). The analyses of Hotaling and Sugarman were based on findings from case-comparison investigations that were drawn from over 400 empirical reports on husband-to-wife violence. These reports were derived from four sources:

1. A search was made of *Psychological Abstracts* and *Sociological Abstracts* for the years 1970 to 1984.
2. *Dissertation Abstracts International* for the years 1970 to 1985 were reviewed.

3. The agenda programs from two national conferences on family violence research held in 1981 and 1984 were abstracted.

4. A network of research sources was assessed, including available conference paper presentations, governmental technical reports, and manuscripts submitted for publication.

In addition to being a case-comparison design, the study had to present a statistical analysis of data in order to be considered. For those that did not, statistical tests were performed if the document presented enough data. To be classified as a consistent risk factor, the variable had to be measured in at least three independent investigations and found to be statistically related ($p < .05$) to wife assault in at least 70% of these investigations.* As shown in the following list, risk factors were classified into three categories: characteristics of the offender, the victim, and the relationship.

Characteristics of the Offender

Experiencing of parental violence as a child
Witnessing of parental violence as a child
Low occupational status
Low assertiveness
Low income
Frequent alcohol use
Low self-esteem

Characteristics of the Victim

Experiencing of parental violence as a child
Witnessing of parental violence as a child
Low self-esteem

Characteristics of the Relationship

Marital conflict
Verbal aggression
Low family income
Religious incompatibility
Nonmarried status
Educational incompatibility

---

*In her review of wife assault Sedlak (1988) used criteria in evaluating risk markers that were somewhat different from the ones used by Hotaling and Sugarman (1984, 1986). She included studies using normative data as a proxy for actual comparison groups, viewed as a significant risk marker any variable that was related to wife assault in two thirds of relevant studies, and gave preferential weight to findings from representative surveys.

Occupational incompatibility

Traditional expectations about couple division of labor

It is apparent from a glance at this list that a risk-marker–based primary prevention program directed at victims would not be very successful. Thirty-nine of 42 risk markers concerned with characteristics of women failed to discriminate victims from nonvictims of wife assault (Hotaling & Sugarman, 1984, 1986). Only three victim risk markers emerge as consistent correlates of wife assault; two of them concern her exposure to family violence as a child, and a third, self-esteem, is probably a consequence of wife assault, rather than a cause (Stark et al., 1981). There is no evidence that the status a woman occupies, the roles she performs, her demographic profile, or her personality characteristics consistently influence her chances of becoming a victim of wife assault.

An examination of offender and relationship risk markers offers a different picture. Male assaulters are exposed early in life to parental violence, are less assertive than other men, abuse alcohol, and possess fewer educational and economic resources than nonassaultive males. Relationships marked by conflict, verbal aggression, and religious incompatibility also are more likely to experience wife assault. Low family income and unmarried status were further found to be consistent risk markers.

These risk factors, however, may be highly correlated with one another, and their lack of independence may represent underlying latent variables. This possibility was investigated in a secondary analysis of the National Family Violence Survey (NFVS) (Straus et al., 1980). The data come from an area probability sample of 2143 families in which one adult family member was interviewed (960 men, 1183 women). An advantage of the NFVS data set is that the interview was very comprehensive allowing for measurement of 15 of the 18 risk markers in the preceding list. The NFVS did not include a measure of assertiveness and, because the sample comprised married and cohabiting couples only, marital status could not be examined. Also, verbal aggression was omitted as a risk marker because it was employed in the operationalization of the level of assaultive behavior.

In addition to its comprehensiveness, the NFVS offers two additional benefits for a thorough risk marker analysis. First, separate analyses can be conducted on male and female respondents. Thus, one can examine the causes of wife assault from both a victim and offender perspective. Second, these data provide a more refined measure of violent behavior than is usually found in studies of wife assault. Assaultive behavior was measured using the Conflict Tactics Scale (CTS) (Straus, 1979, 1989). The CTS assesses reports about the types of behaviors that people employ in resolving conflicts with intimate others. The behaviors range from the use of discussion, debate, and reasoning in resolving conflicts (Reasoning scale) to the employment of verbal acts that threaten or harm the partner (Verbal Aggression scale). It further includes behaviors that directly attempt to physically hurt the other

(Violence scale). Each of these tactics has a 7-point frequency scale associated with it, ranging from 0 ("never") to 6 ("more than 20 times").

Both men and women were divided into one of four groups, based on whether they ever employed or were the recipient of each of these tactics. For example, the *no-assault* group comprised males who reported that they never used any of the verbal or physical aggression tactics of the CTS. The *verbal assault* group reported using verbal aggression tactics but no physical assault tactics. The *minor assault* group reported that they, at least once, had pushed, grabbed, shoved, slapped, or threw something at their partners. The *severe assault* group reported that they kicked, bit, hit with a fist, threatened to use or used a knife or gun against their partner, or beat up their partners. Women were classified as *nonvictims, victims of verbal assaults, victims of minor assaults,* or *victims of severe assaults.* These group classifications for both victims and offenders are hierarchial in nature and mutually exclusive. Thus, respondents in the severe assault group may have also used less severe tactics, but would only be classified in the severe assault group.

Results for Victims

A factor analysis of 14 risk markers identified six latent variables for women in the survey: socioeconomic status, witnessing of violence as a child, experiencing of violence as a child, marital conflict, status incompatibility, and self-esteem.* A four-group analysis of variance was performed on each of the six factor scores using type of victimization (none, verbal assault, minor assault, severe assault) as the grouping factor. No significant between-group differences were found when the witnessing-violence-as-child factor, the experiencing-violence-as-child factor, self-esteem factor, or status incompatibility factor scores were analyzed. The two other factors (marital conflict and socioeconomic status) yielded significant findings.

Examination of the marital conflict factor scores revealed that both the minor and severely assaulted women reported significantly greater amounts

---

*Risk marker loadings and factor scores for the six latent variables for females are:

Factor 1: Socioeconomic Status. Family income, .93; husband's income, .83; husband's occupational prestige, .32

Factor 2: Experiencing Parental Violence as a Child. Frequency of mother's use of physical punishment, .82; frequency of father's use of physical punishment, .42

Factor 3: Self-esteem. Wife's self-esteem, .66; husband's self-esteem, .65

Factor 4: Witnessing Parental Violence as a Child. Frequency of respondent's mother hitting father, .71; frequency of respondent's father hitting mother, .47

Factor 5: Marital Conflict. Index of marital conflict, .45; frequency of husband's drunkenness, .55; traditional sex role division of labor, .30; husband's education relative to wife's education, .33

Factor 6: Status Incompatibility. Husband's religious participation relative to wife's participation, .51; husband's occupational prestige, .30

Figure 16.1. Factor scores of latent variables that differentiate responses of females classified by level of wife assault.

of marital conflict than the nonvictims and verbally assaulted women. Similarly, the verbally assaulted group had significantly higher marital conflict scores than nonassaulted women (see Figure 16.1). Severely assaulted women also had significantly lower socioeconomic scores than did the nonassaulted or verbally assaulted women. Victims of minor assault were not significantly different from these other three groups on the socioeconomic status factor.

Results for Offenders

The same procedure was applied to men in the NFVS data set. The factor analysis of 14 risk markers identified the same six factors as found using the responses of women.* No significant between-group differences were noted when the self-esteem factor scores and the status incompatibility factor scores were analyzed. The other four factors revealed significant findings. The marital conflict factor emerged as the most powerful discriminator of these four groups of male respondents. Men who used severe and minor assaultive behavior against their wives reported significantly greater amounts of marital conflict than nonassaultive or verbally assaultive males. Similarly, verbally assaultive men had higher marital conflict scores than men who did not use assaultive behavior of any kind. Also, severely assaultive men had significantly lower socioeconomic factor scores than the other three groups. The early exposure to violence in the family was related to wife assault, and the witnessing of parental violence exerted a more powerful discriminating effect on wife assault than the experiencing of violence as a child. Severely assaultive men had significantly higher scores on the witnessing-parental-violence factor than the other groups. A significant effect for experiencing violence as a child was yielded, in which the minor assault group scored higher on this factor than the other group of men in this sample (see Figure 16.2).

IMPLICATIONS FOR PRIMARY PREVENTION PROGRAMS

Several conclusions are apparent from this analysis, but none is more surprising than the finding that very few risk markers discriminate assaulted from nonassaulted women. After more than 15 years of empirical research on wife assault, relatively few markers have been found that identify women at risk for assault in close relationships. In fact, when these markers are

---

*Risk marker loadings and factor scores for the six latent variables for males are:

   Factor 1: Socioeconomic Status. Family income, .94; husband's income, .85; husband's occupational prestige, .36

   Factor 2: Self-esteem. Husband's self-esteem, .90; wife's self-esteem, .71

   Factor 3: Witnessing Parental Violence as Child. Frequency of respondent's father hitting mother, .81; frequency of respondent's mother hitting father, .70

   Factor 4: Experiencing Parental Violence as a Child. Frequency of father's use of physical punishment .70; frequency of mother's use of physical punishment, .75

   Factor 5: Marital Conflict. Index of marital conflict, .45; frequency of husband's drunkenness, .50: traditional sex-role division labor, .34

   Factor 6: Status Incompatibility. Husband's education relative to wife's education, .36; husband's religious participation relative to wife's participation, .32; husband's occupational prestige, .30

More detailed results of statistical analyses are available from the first author upon request.

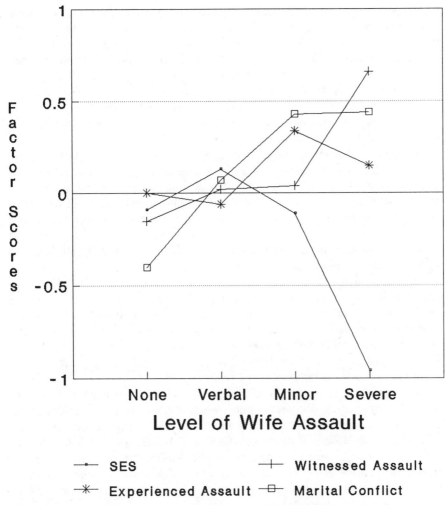

Figure 16.2. Factor scores of latent variables that differentiate responses of males classified by level of wife assault.

factor analyzed and subjected to multivariate statistical examination, only one factor discriminates violent relationships from others: high level of marital conflict. Certainly not all wife assault is due to high levels of marital conflict, but much of it is. Likewise, family sociologists are quick to point out that conflict is an inherent part of all intimate relationships (Coser, 1967; Hotaling & Straus, 1980) but does not always result in violence. What might separate wife-assaultive relationships from others are the particular issues over which conflicts arise and the ability to manage them. One interpretation for the finding that four risk markers (high marital conflict, traditional sex role expectations, frequent drinking by husband, wife having more education than husband) load on one factor is that issues concerning male drinking may be a major source of conflict, especially in relationships marked by sex-role traditionalism. The problems associated with heavy drinking by men are, plausibly, the focus of much marital conflict, and this conflict may be more likely to evolve into violence in relationships marked by traditional sex-role arrangements. The male may be more likely to use violence as a conflict resolution strategy if he feels that his wife has no right to comment or complain about his behavior.

A second important finding of this analysis is that two risk markers were found to discriminate victims of serious wife assault from nonvictims and from women victimized by minor physical violence and verbal aggression. Women with lower socioeconomic status and those with husbands who have witnessed parental violence as children are more likely to experience severe violence. Primary prevention programs geared to reducing the mortality and morbidity associated with wife assault should pay particular attention to these markers in planning and intervention.

Third, this analysis separately examined the responses of men and women, and it is important to note the unusually high level of agreement among victims and offenders about the risk markers associated with wife assault. Certainly, men and women will often provide different explanations to account for the occurrence of violent episodes, but when asked about the structure and processes that characterize assaultive relationships, the results point to the same underlying set of risk markers.

One can directly apply these three risk factors to primary prevention. Marital conflict, low socioeconomic status, and exposure to violence as a child have been found to be clearly related to wife assault even when controlling for the effects of other risk factors. Further, these risk factors are applicable to wife assault in the general population and, if modified, should have a preventive effect on the occurrence and severity of wife assault on a large scale. Implications of these findings for primary prevention are outlined in the following sections.

Marital Conflict

Close relationships are, by definition, characterized by total personality involvement and by a high frequency of interaction. It comes as no surprise that intense interaction ensures frequent occasions for conflict. A high level of conflict is inherent in intimate relationships because of, rather than in spite of, feelings of closeness, love, and support. As Hotaling and Straus (1980) point out, one of the ironies of marriage is that many of the same characteristics that contribute to intimacy and love also contribute to conflict. For example, because the family is concerned with "the whole person" rather than just specific roles in specific contexts, disagreements are possible over almost anything (Straus & Smith, 1989). Certainly not all wife assault involves conflict, but a great deal of it does (Straus et al., 1980). Conversely, not all conflict results in violence. In adequately functioning relationships, conflicts get resolved through negotiation and compromise. These are learned skills that people in distressed relationships do not possess. Teaching techniques of negotiation and compromise would seem to be a logical approach in the prevention of wife assault and, in fact, is used by many couples therapists (Blechman, Kotanchik, & Taylor, 1981; Patterson, 1982; Turkewitz & O'Leary, 1981). Attention directed toward learning these skills can also be found in treatment programs for male batterers. For example, these programs typically emphasize conflict management through teaching assertiveness training (Foy, Eisler, & Pinkston, 1975), communication training (Saunders, 1977), anger management (Deschner, 1984; Maiuro, Cahn, Vitaliano, & Zegree, 1987), and empathic listening (Douglas & Perrin, 1987). Evaluations of these strategies usually show an increase in conflict coping skills among the men (Saunders & Azar, 1989).

The teaching of the management of conflict in a nonviolent way is a major but not the only component of treatment programs for batterers. Many such programs attempt to reduce men's drinking (Douglas & Perrin, 1987), and almost all focus on changing sex-role attitudes. A recent survey of the characteristics of programs for men who batter found that between 80% and 90% of the programs attempted to change sex-role attitudes in addition to ending violent behavior (Pirog-Good & Stets, 1986). This combined emphasis on teaching nonviolent conflict resolution, confronting drinking behavior, and changing sex-role attitudes at the level of secondary prevention underscores the point that these factors support wife assault and should be the focus of primary prevention.

Skills training in conflict resolution must take place at a much earlier point in time. At the least, family problem-solving skills should be introduced as part of elementary and high school curricula. If conflict is an inevitable part of close relationships, information about nonviolent methods of dealing with conflict must be made widely available. The mass media could play an important role in this regard.

Teaching effective conflict resolution techniques would be good in and of itself even if it had no effect on reducing the occurrence of wife assault. Distressed, nonviolent couples who avoid conflict altogether, or those who are unable to resolve conflicts would directly benefit from information on conflict resolution. But what about relationships marked by wife assault? Are their conflicts the same as nonviolent couples? Surely, issues of money, sex, children, and housework are common, but other issues underscore much of the conflict in violent relationships. The previously cited factor analysis found that four risk markers loaded on the factor labeled "marital conflict." These included a marital conflict measure, frequency of husband's drinking, traditional expectations about division of labor in the relationship, and the wife having higher educational attainment than the husband. Much of the conflict that occurs in couples marked by wife assault may center on, or be

400 Prevention of Wife Assault

exacerbated by, the husband's drinking, his status insecurity, or frustration stemming from traditional sex-role expectations. Primary prevention strategies directed at wife assault must take this information into account either through efforts aimed at conflict resolution or more directly through education regarding alcohol use and sex-role expectations. Children need to be taught about issues of gender roles and male dominance.

That sexual equality issues may be a central focus of much marital conflict is consistent with some cross-cultural research on family violence. In a sample of 90 small-scale societies worldwide, Levinson (1988) found that, in 16 of these social systems, violence between family members occurs very rarely or not at all. What kinds of macrolevel risk markers differentiate societies with family violence from those in which it is essentially nonexistent? Levinson found four risk markers to be especially important. In addition to the presence of natural support systems, three other macrolevel risk markers are consistent with the findings reported here. First, societies free of family violence emphasize peaceful conflict resolution. Adult members of society resolve disagreements nonviolently through mediation, avoidance, and the use of techniques of disengagement. Second, there appears to be a high level of marital stability rather than of marital conflict and friction. Finally, in the family system spouses enjoy sexual equality that is reflected by joint decision making in household and financial matters, and the absence of a double standard in premarital sex and societal freedom.

Socioeconomic Status

There is no more controversial finding in the literature on wife assault than that concerning social class or socioeconomic status (SES). Several writers contend that wife assault occurs in all economic and social groups and that it is not limited to poor, disenfranchised sections of society (e.g., Pagelow, 1984). There is rich support for this point of view. Evidence from both clinical and general population surveys indicates that wife assault occurs in middle- and upper-class marriages. However, the bulk of empirical evidence points to a clear connection between wife assault and low family income. No one would deny that higher income groups are marked by all forms of family violence, but wife assault is more common and more severe in poorer families. In 9 of 11 case-comparison studies, family income has been found to be a consistent risk factor of wife assault (Hotaling & Sugarman, 1986). The evidence is even stronger in general population surveys. In the National Family Violence Survey, for example, it was found that families living at or below the poverty line had a rate of violence between husbands and wives that was 500% greater than the rate of spousal violence in the most well-to-do families (Straus et al., 1980).

In the analysis presented earlier, there is clear evidence from the perspectives of *both* victims and offenders that SES is strongly related to the severity of wife assault. One could conclude from Figures 16.1 and 16.2 that, when controlling for the effects of other known risk factors of wife assault, SES does not differentiate assaultive and nonassaultive relationships as well as it differentiates severely assaultive relationships from all others (nonassaultive, verbally assaultive, minor assaultive), especially for the males in the sample.

Three interpretations can be made of this finding. One possibility is that men who have a lower SES are exposed to greater stress and possess fewer resources (e.g., economic security, educational attainment) to cope with this stress. A second interpretation is that the relationship between lower SES and the increased likelihood of wife assault is due to the existence of a subculture of violence (Wolfgang & Ferracutti, 1967). Thus, individuals who have lower incomes and educational levels may hold values that condone assaultive behavior toward women. These two explanations are not mutually exclusive. A third viable interpretation of the link between SES and wife assault is that it is due to a reporting bias. It could be that higher SES men are more sensitive to the stigma concerning wife assault and, consequently, are less likely to admit such behavior to an interviewer. However, two findings from the present analysis do not support a reporting bias explanation. Higher SES men did report violence against their wives. In fact, they were just as likely to report verbal assaults and minor physical assaults as were lower SES men. The major difference between these two groups concerned the reporting of severe physical assault. In a comparison of men who completed the interview to those who "broke off" the interview without answering the questions about wife assault, lower SES men were less likely to answer the questions. This implies that lower SES men are just as sensitive as anyone else about responding to queries about their violent behavior. As a result, the present analysis may have actually underestimated the amount of severe wife assault in lower socioeconomic strata.

Witnessing Parental Violence as a Child

We found no evidence in the present analysis that victims of wife assault are any more likely than other women to have been exposed to family violence as children. This is the case for either the witnessing of or the direct experiencing of parental violence. On the other hand, severely assaultive males could be differentiated from the nonassault, verbally assaultive, and minor assaultive groups by their greater frequency of having witnessed violence between parents in their family of origin. It may be surprising to some, but the direct experience of parental violence did not discriminate the severely assaultive men from the other groups; rather, it only differentiated the verbally assaultive men from those who employed minor physical aggression. This finding supports prior research (see review by Pagelow, 1984) that suggests that witnessing violence as a child is a better predictor of the male use of severe assault than experiencing violence. One interpretation for this suggests that the use of physical punishment as a child-rearing technique is so common in this society that it loses some of its predictive utility (Sugarman & Hotaling, 1986).

The preventive implication that emerges from this finding appears tautological. In order to decrease the prevalence of severe wife assault in future generations of men, one needs to decrease their exposure to physically violent role models during childhood. To accomplish this, their parents must decrease their use of violent techniques of conflict resolution. This is the classic "violence-begets-violence" thesis: One may reduce the amount of violence in a younger generation by reducing it in an older generation. Consequently, secondary and tertiary prevention programs that attempt to limit intimate violence will have primary prevention consequences by limiting the exposure of younger generation members to violent role models. In addition, this risk marker can be used as a means of directing primary prevention programs to that sample of individuals who are exposed to parental violence.

SUMMARY AND FUTURE DIRECTIONS

This chapter has reviewed the state of existing knowledge on wife assault based on empirical research conducted over the past 15 years. Some writers feel confident about the state of knowledge on wife assault and its implications for prevention (Swift, 1988; Pagelow, 1984), and others feel that the causes of all forms of family violence have long been known but that there is resistance to implementing obvious changes (Gil, 1989). The present findings, however, point to a disturbing fact: we know very little about the causes of wife assault. The vast majority of studies on wife assault are cross-sectional and cannot address causality, whereas sampling and other research design problems impede explanation (see Hotaling & Sugarman, 1986). This state of affairs should not deter writers from suggesting strategies for the reduction of wife assault based on the current knowledge base. For example, reductions in poverty, gender inequality, and childhood socialization to violence are good in and of themselves and should be implemented (Gelles & Straus, 1988; Straus & Smith, 1989). The results of this chapter show that relationships marked by wife assault experience higher levels of conflict, and the conflicts involve more issues, than nonassaultive relationships. These results are consistent with findings at the macrolevel (see Levinson, 1988) revealing that societies with lower overall rates of family violence are those in which norms prescribe the use of mediation, compromise, negotiation, and disengagement to peacefully resolve conflicts.

The United States is a violent society. Children are exposed early and often to violent role models and often are trained to accept violence as a strategy for resolving conflict in interpersonal relationships. The results of two national studies of family violence underscore this aspect of child socialization. Each year in the United States between 30% and 32% of all children in families are either severely assaulted by one of their parents, witness one parent assaulting the other parent, or are exposed to both types of family assault (Hotaling, Straus, & Lincoln, 1989). Professionals must begin to ask why Americans choose, as a culture, to ill-equip children for nonviolent adult lives. No doubt the answer at least partly resides in this society's ideas about the type of adults children ought to become.

REFERENCES

Blechman, E., Kotanchik, N., & Taylor, C. (1981). Families and schools together: Early behavioral intervention with high risk children. *Behavior Therapy, 12,* 308–319.

Carmody, D. C., & Williams, K. R. (1987). Wife assault and perceptions of sanctions. *Violence and Victims, 2,* 25–38.

Coser, L. A. (1967). *Continuities in the study of social conflict.* New York: Free Press.

Deschner, J. (1984, July). *The results of anger control for violent couples.* Paper presented at the Second National Conference for Family Violence Researchers, Durham, NH.

Douglas, M. A., & Perrin, S. (1987, July). *Recidivism and accuracy of self-reported violence and arrest.* Paper presented at the Third National Conference for Family Violence Researchers, Durham, NH.

Foy, D. W., Eisler, R. M., & Pinkston, S. (1975). Modeled assertion in a case of explosive rage. *Journal of Behavior Therapy and Experimental Psychiatry, 6,* 135–137.

Frieze, I. H. (1979). *Power and influence in violent and nonviolent marriages.* Paper presented at the meeting of the Eastern Psychological Association, Philadelphia, PA.

Gelles, R. J., & Straus, M. A. (1979). Determinants of violence in the family: Toward a theoretical integration. In W. R. Burr, R. Hill, R. I. Nye, & I. L. Reiss (Eds.), *Contemporary theories about the family* (pp. 549–581). New York: Free Press.

Gelles, R. J., & Straus, M. A. (1988). *Intimate violence: The definitive study of the causes and consequences of abuse in the American family.* New York: Simon & Schuster.

Gentemann, K. M. (1980). *Attitudes of North Carolina women toward the acceptance and cause of wife beating.* Paper presented at the meeting of the Southwestern Women's Studies Association, Nashville, TN.

Gil, D. G. (1989). Exposing or concealing the roots of violence [Review of *Intimate violence*]. *Contemporary Sociology, 18,* 236–238.

Hotaling, G. T., & Straus, M. A. (1980). Culture, social organization, and irony in the study of family violence. In M. A. Straus & G. T. Hotaling (Eds.), *The social causes of husband–wife violence.* Minneapolis: University of Minnesota Press.

Hotaling, G. T., Straus, M. A., & Lincoln, A. (1989). Intra-family violence and crime and violence outside the family. In L. Ohlin & M. Tonry (Eds.), *Family Violence: Vol. 11. Crime and Justice: A review of research* (pp. 315–375). Chicago: University of Chicago Press.

Hotaling, G. T., & Sugarman, D. B. (1984). An identification of risk factors. In G. L. Bowen, M. A. Straus, A. J. Sedlak, G. T. Hotaling, & D. B. Sugarman, *Domestic violence surveillance system feasibility study: Phase I report. An identification of outcomes and risk factors* (pp. 3-1–3-66; D1-D28). Rockville, MD: Westat.

Hotaling, G. T., & Sugarman, D. B. (1986). An analysis of risk markers in husband to wife violence: The current state of knowledge. *Violence and Victims, 1,* 101–124.

Hudson, W. W., & McIntosh, S. R. (1981). The assessment of spouse abuse: Two quantifiable divisions. *Journal of Marriage and the Family, 43,* 872–885.

Kantor, G., & Straus, M. A. (in press). Response of victims and the police to assaults on wives. In M. A. Straus & R. J. Gelles (Eds.), *Physical violence in American families: Risk factors and adaptations to violence in 8,145 families.* New Brunswick, NJ: Transaction Books.

Last, J. M. (1983). *A dictionary of epidemiology.* New York: Oxford University Press.

Levinson, D. (1988). Family violence in cross-cultural perspective. In V. B. Van Hasselt, R. L. Morrison, A. S. Bellack, & M. Hersen (Eds.), *Handbook of family violence* (pp. 435–455). New York: Plenum.

Maiuro, R. D., Cahn, T. S., Vitaliano, P. P., & Zegree, J. B. (1987, August). *Treatment for domestically violent men: Outcome and follow-up data.* Paper presented at the annual meeting of the American Psychological Association, New York.

Marcus, P. (1983). Assault and Battery. In S. H. Kadish (Ed.), *Encyclopedia of Crime and Justice* (pp. 88–90). New York, The Free Press.

Mausner, J. S., & Bahn, A. K. (1974). *Epidemiology: An introductory text.* Philadelphia: W. B. Saunders.

Nisonoff, L., & Bitman, I. (1979). Spouse abuse: Incidence and relationship to selected demographic variables. *Victimology, 4,* 131–140.

Pagelow, M. D. (1984). *Family violence.* New York: Praeger.

Patterson, G. R. (1982). *A social learning approach: Vol. 3. Coercive family process.* Eugene, OR: Castalia.

Pirog-Good, M. A., & Stets-Kealey, J. (in press). Recidivism in programs for abusers. *Victimology: An International Journal 11,* 2 (Summer).

Rosenbaum, A., & O'Leary, K. D. (1981). Marital violence: Characteristics of abusive couples. *Journal of Consulting and Clinical Psychology, 49,* 63–71.

Saunders, D. G. (1977). Marital violence: Dimensions of the problem and modes of intervention. *Journal of Marriage and Family Counseling 3,* 43–52.

Saunders, D. G., & Azar, S. T. (1989). Treatment programs for family violence. In L. Ohlin & M. Tonry (Eds.), *Family violence: Vol. 11. Crime and justice: A review of research* (pp. 481–546). Chicago: University of Chicago Press.

Schulman, M. (1979). *A survey of spousal violence against women in Kentucky* (Study No. 792701 for the Kentucky Commission on Women). Washington, DC: U.S. Department of Justice—LEAR.

Sedlak, A. J. (1988). Prevention of wife abuse. In V. B. Van Hasselt, R. L. Morrison, A. S. Bellack, & M. Hersen (Eds.), *Handbook of family violence* (pp. 319–358). New York: Plenum.

Stark, E., Flitcraft, A., Zuckerman, D., Gray, A., Robinson, J., & Frazier, W. (1981). *Wife abuse in the medical setting: An introduction to health personnel*. Washington, DC: National Clearinghouse on Domestic Violence, Monograph Series No. 7.

Stets, J. E., & Straus, M. A. (in press). Gender differences in reporting marital violence and its medical and psychological consequences. In M. A. Straus & R. J. Gelles (Eds.), *Physical violence in American families: Risk factors and adaptations to violence in 8,145 families*. New Brunswick, NJ: Transaction Books.

Straus, M. A. (1979). Measuring intrafamily conflict and violence: The Conflict Tactic (CT) Scales. *Journal of Marriage and the Family, 41*, 75–86.

Straus, M. A. (in press). The Conflict Tactics Scale and its critics: An evaluation and new data on validity and reliability. In M. A. Straus & R. J. Gelles (Eds.), *Physical violence in American families: Risk factors and adaptations in 8,145 families*. New Brunswick, NJ: Transaction Books.

Straus, M. A., & Gelles, R. J. (1986). Societal change and change in family violence from 1975 to 1985 as revealed by two national surveys. *Journal of Marriage and the Family, 48*, 465–479.

Straus, M. A., Gelles, R. J., & Steinmetz, S. K. (1980). *Behind closed doors: Violence in the American family*. New York: Anchor/Doubleday.

Straus, M. A., & Smith, C. (in press). Family patterns and primary prevention of family violence. In M. A. Straus & R. J. Gelles, *Physical violence in American families: Risk factors and adaptations to violence in 8,145 families*. New Brunswick, NJ: Transaction Books.

Sugarman, D. B., & Hotaling, G. T. (1986, April). *Violent males in intimate relationships: An analysis of risk factors*. Paper presented at the meeting of the Eastern Psychological Association, New York.

Sugarman, D. B., & Hotaling, G. T. (1987, April). *Risk factor analysis of battered women*. Paper presented at the meeting of the Eastern Psychological Association, Arlington, VA.

Swift, C. F., (1988). Stopping the violence: Prevention strategies for families. In L. A. Bond & B. M. Wagner (Eds.), *Families in transition: Primary prevention programs that work* (pp. 252–285). Newbury Park, CA: Sage.

Telch, C. F., & Lindquist, C. U. (1984). Violent versus non-violent couples: A comparison of patterns. *Psychotherapy, 21*, 242–248.

Teske, R. H. C., & Parker, M. L. (1983). *Spouse abuse in Texas: A study of women's attitudes and experiences*. Huntsville, TX: Criminal Justice Center, Sam Houston State University.

Turkewitz, H., & O'Leary, K. D. (1981). A comparative outcome study of behavioral marital therapy communication therapy. *Journal of Marital and Family Therapy, 1*, 159–169.

U.S. Department of Justice. (1985). *FBI Uniform Crime Reports: Crime in the United States, 1984*. Washington, DC: U.S. Government Printing Office.

Wolfgang, M., & Ferracutti, F. (1967). *The sub-culture of violence*. London: Tavistock.

CHAPTER 17

Prevention of Elder Abuse

KARL A. PILLEMER AND J. JILL SUITOR

INTRODUCTION

The development of intervention programs to assist victims of elder abuse and neglect has been quite dramatic over the past decade. Since 1980, all states have passed mandatory reporting laws that cover maltreated elders. Task forces have sprung up in virtually all major cities, and in many smaller ones as well. Adult protective services programs have expanded their efforts to include the elderly, and some police departments now include an elder abuse component in officer training. In general, such intervention programs focus on treating elder abuse after it occurs. They attempt to reduce conflict and tension in the household by introducing services and, in some cases, by relocating the abuser or the victim (cf. Breckman & Adelman, 1988; Quinn & Tomita, 1986).

It is of critical importance to help elderly persons who are maltreated by their families. The need to help such persons, however, should not blind professionals to an equally great need: the development of programs that can *prevent* elder abuse. John McKinlay (1981) graphically demonstrates the need for prevention programs in the following anecdote. He quotes a physician friend, who describes the dilemmas of practicing medicine in American society:

> You know, sometimes it feels like this. There I am standing by the shore of a swiftly flowing river and I hear the cry of a drowning man. So I jump into the river, put my arms around him, pull him to shore and apply artificial respiration. Just when he begins to breathe, there is another cry for help. So back in the river again, reaching, pulling, applying, breathing and then another yell. Again

---

We are grateful to Karen E. Hayden, Research Assistant, Family Research Laboratory, for her contributions to this paper.

and again, without end, goes the sequence. You know, I am so busy jumping in, pulling them to shore, applying artificial respiration, that I have *no* time to see who the hell is upstream pushing them all in. (p. 613)

McKinlay holds that health care providers must "refocus upstream," that is, begin to combat the root causes of illness.

Although McKinlay used this parable to call for prevention of illness, the argument is equally applicable to elder abuse. The physician's intense frustration would most likely be shared by elder abuse workers across the country. In the present chapter, we attempt to create a framework for the development of programs designed to prevent domestic violence against the elderly.

First, we discuss obstacles to the development of prevention programs. A detailed analysis of risk factors for elder maltreatment follows, based on three bodies of research: the literature on family violence, research on the family relations of the aged, and the few reliable investigations of elder abuse and neglect. Based on this discussion, we propose a variety of options for programs to prevent elder abuse. Because very few elder abuse prevention programs exist, we employ examples from other forms of family violence and examine their applicability to elder abuse.

The discussion in this chapter primarily focuses on *physical* violence against the elderly. We employ the simple and clear definition of violence used by Straus, Gelles, and Steinmetz (1980): "An act carried out with the intention or perceived intention of causing physical pain or injury to another person" (p. 20). In this chapter, we use the terms *elder abuse* and *domestic violence against the elderly* interchangeably.

ISSUES IN PREVENTION

The designing of meaningful prevention programs is greatly handicapped by lack of knowledge. Despite major advances in research on spouse abuse, physical child abuse, and child sexual abuse in the past 10 years, very few scientifically valid studies of elder abuse have been conducted. Although the problems with studies of elder maltreatment have been catalogued frequently (cf. Callahan, 1981; Hudson, 1986; Pedrick-Cornell & Gelles, 1982; Pillemer & Suitor, 1988; Yin, 1985), they bear brief discussion here.

First, most studies have used imprecise definitions of elder abuse (Johnson, 1986). Researchers have failed to differentiate between various types of maltreatment in studies and have instead combined diverse types of abuse and neglect. Definitions have tended to be extremely broad and to include physical violence, verbal abuse, theft, and neglect by a caregiver. Many studies have also included cases in which an older person's care needs were not met, but in which there was no abuser or neglector (so-called self-neglect or self-abuse). As Callahan (1981) has correctly noted, "With some of these definitions there seems to be a drive to include all forms of troubled interpersonal relationships under the rubric of violence and abuse" (p. 2). This definitional confusion makes results from many studies nearly impossible to interpret.

Second, most studies have relied on case reports of abuse from professionals, rather than on direct interviews with victims or abusers, even though professionals' impressions of family situations are often quite different from those of the family members. In fact, there has been only one attempt to conduct a large-scale random sample of a community population regarding elder abuse (Pillemer & Finkelhor, 1988; Pillemer & Finkelhor, 1989).

Third, few studies have included comparison groups in their designs, thus reducing their generalizability. For example, some investigators have asserted that the abused and neglected elderly are likely to be physically and/or mentally impaired. However, without a comparison group, it is impossible to know if they are more or less impaired than other persons.

Fourth, widely varying criteria have been used to determine the population at risk for elder abuse. For example, some investigations have included only persons sharing a residence with the abusers or only caretakers of the elderly. Other researchers have included all potentially abused and neglected elders.

Thus, the attempt to detail possible prevention programs for elder abuse encounters a major obstacle at the outset: a dearth of reliable risk-factor analyses of elder abuse. This is compounded by the problem noted earlier: the shortage of existing elder abuse prevention programs. In contrast, a review of the child abuse and marital violence literatures demonstrates the existence of a variety of preventive options; this is not the case with elder mistreatment. Further, the few elder abuse prevention programs that exist have not been systematically evaluated; thus, the degree to which they are effective is unknown.

Taken together, these problems suggest that the ensuing discussion of risk factors and prevention programs cannot be derived from previous research or practice in the area of elder abuse. Therefore, throughout the remainder of this chapter, we draw upon other bodies of knowledge that may help to predict the occurrence of elder abuse. First, in the discussion of risk factors, we consider variables that have been found to be precipitants of other forms of family violence. This mirrors earlier attempts to identify risk factors for elder abuse by extending concepts relating to wife abuse and child abuse. However, in order to construct a more exhaustive model to explain elder abuse, we have included a second body of research as well: the more general literature on relations between spouses and between parents and their adult children. Of course, wherever possible, we also rely on research specifically on elder abuse.

Risk Factors*

A review of the literature suggests that four major factors† are likely to be related to elder abuse and have direct bearing on the planning of prevention programs. These are:

1. Intraindividual dynamics
2. Inequitable levels of dependency between abuser and abused
3. Social isolation
4. External stress

There is greater evidence that the first two factors may be related to elder abuse; they are, therefore, discussed in somewhat more detail than social isolation and external stress.

Intraindividual Dynamics

Intraindividual theories blame abuse on some pathological characteristic of the abuser, usually mental illness of some kind. Interestingly, family researchers have found that psychological well-being is related to the general quality of family relationships. Thus, various measures of psychological well-being have been consistently associated with marital satisfaction both in the general population (Andrews & Withey, 1979; Berry & Williams, 1987; Glenn & Weaver, 1981) and specifically among the elderly (Lee, 1978). Although the causal direction in these studies cannot be precisely determined, it seems persuasive that the psychological well-being of marriage partners affects the quality of relationships.

The existence of such a relationship has been widely held in the family violence literature. Although the use of intraindividual explanations has been criticized (Gelles, 1974), there is some evidence that intraindividual factors may play a part in elder abuse.

Douglass, Hickey, and Noel (1980) included, as one cause of abuse, the "flawed development" of the abuser that results from problems in his or her childhood. Similarly, Lau and Kosberg (1979) referred to the problem of the nonnormal child (e.g., mentally ill, retarded, or alcoholic) who has always been cared for by parents, yet may be expected to care for them if the parents become impaired. Further, research by Wolf, Strugnell, and Godkin (1982), Pillemer (1985a), and Pillemer and Finkelhor (1989) found a considerable degree of mental and physical illness among elder abusers.

One other intraindividual characteristic that has gained acceptance as a

---

*Material in this section is drawn from Pillemer and Suitor, 1988, and Wolf and Pillemer, 1989.
†In previous writings, we have presented a fifth risk factor: the intergenerational transmission of violent behavior (see Pillemer, 1986; Pillemer and Suitor, 1988). Data to support the existence of a "cycle of violence" in elder abuse, however, still do not exist. Therefore, although we believe that such a relationship exists, we cannot confidently include it as a risk factor.

partial explanation for the occurrence of child and spouse abuse is alcohol and drug abuse (cf. Colemen & Straus, 1981; Kantor & Straus, 1986). Preliminary evidence has indicated that a similar relationship between substance abuse and domestic violence may exist among the elderly (Pillemer, 1985b; Wolf, Godkin, & Pillemer, 1984).

Dependency and Exchange Relations

Interestingly, two competing theories have arisen that relate dependency to elder abuse. The first emphasizes the role of *caregiver stress* as a risk factor for maltreatment; abuse is seen as resulting from the resentment generated by the increased dependency of an older person on a caretaker. The second theory stresses the reverse configuration: the *continued dependency of the abuser* on his or her victim. These theories will be discussed in turn.

CAREGIVER STRESS.   The literature on the family relations of the elderly supports the notion that dependency of an old person leads to poor quality relationships with relatives. One of the most consistent findings is that parents' health is positively correlated with feelings of closeness and attachment between parents and their adult children (Baruch & Barnett, 1983; Cicirelli, 1981; Johnson & Bursk, 1977). A likely reason for this is the effects of a decline in a parent's health on the prior flow of support between the generations. Adult children may have to increase their support to the parent, and possibly to accept the cessation of assistance from the parent.

In fact, studies have documented the negative effects of parental dependency. Cicirelli (1983a, 1983b) found negative feelings on the part of adult children when both parental dependency and the amount of help from the child were high. Similarly, a study by Adams (1968) revealed that affectional ties to widowed parents were weaker when adult children's help was not reciprocated. Thus, it appears that when adult children feel that the support relationship with a parent is inequitable, the quality of the relationship declines.

Perhaps based on such findings, many students of elder abuse have also emphasized the dependency of elderly persons as a major cause of abuse (cf. Steinmetz, 1988; Steinmetz & Amsden, 1983). This view has developed in large part from gerontological research on the strains of family caregiving to elderly relatives. For example, Steinmetz (1983) argued that families undergo "generational inversion," in which the elderly person becomes dependent on his or her children for financial, physical, and/or emotional support, leading to severe stress on the part of the caregiver. As the costs of the relationship grow for the caregiver, and the rewards diminish, the exchange becomes perceived as unfair. According to this view, caregivers who do not have the ability to escape or ameliorate the situation may become abusive.

ABUSER DEPENDENCY.   Although the preceding theory appears plausible, there are few firm research findings to support it. It is clear from the gerontological literature that a substantial number of elderly persons are dependent on their spouses or other relatives (cf. Cantor, 1983; Kulys & Tobin, 1980). However, recent prevalence findings indicate that only a small minority of the elderly are abused (approximately 3%: see Pillemer & Finkelhor, 1988). The question therefore arises: Why are some of these dependent individuals abused and others not? Because abuse occurs in only a small proportion of families, no direct correlation between dependency of an older person and abuse can be assumed. In fact, Phillips (1983) failed to find any difference in level of impairment between a group of abused elderly and a control group. In addition, analyses presented elsewhere (Suitor & Pillemer, 1987, 1988) have shown that parents' health and dependency are not related to parent–child conflict when the generations share a residence.

Although it seems contradictory, preliminary research suggests that another cause of abuse may be the continued dependency of abuser or abused. Wolf, Strugnell, and Godkin (1982) found that in two thirds of their cases, the perpetrator was reported to be financially dependent on his or her victim. Hwalek, Sengstock, and Lawrence (1984), in a case-control study, also found that the financial dependency of the abuser on the elderly victim was an important risk factor in elder abuse.

Pillemer's (1985a, 1985b) results support this argument even more strongly. He found that the abusers in his sample were much more likely to be dependent on their victims financially and in a variety of other areas. In general, Pillemer found the abusers to be heavily dependent individuals, including disabled or cognitively impaired spouses and children. These findings have been replicated in a later study (Pillemer & Finkelhor, 1989).

Why should the dependency of an adult child or spouse on an elderly person result in physical abuse? A theoretical explanation of the phenomenon can be based on a concept from social exchange theory: that of power. Finkelhor (1983), in his attempt to identify common features of family abuse, observed that abuse can occur as a response to perceived powerlessness. Acts of abuse, he notes, "seem to be acts carried out by abusers to compensate for their perceived lack or loss of power" (p. 19). Thus, spouse abuse in younger populations has been found to be related to a sense of powerlessness, and the physical abuse of children "tends to start with a feeling of parental impotence" (p. 19). It may be that the feeling of powerlessness experienced by an adult child who is still dependent on an elderly parent is especially acute, because it goes so strongly against society's expectations for normal adult behavior. This perceived power deficit appears to be a better explanation for elder abuse than the notion that the abuser holds much power in the relationship (for a more complete discussion of the explanation, see Pillemer, 1985b).

In summary, dependency seems to play a critical role in elder abuse, but it is not yet clear who is depending on whom in these abusive relationships. Does an elderly person come to make excessive demands on caregivers? Are abusers persons who have remained dependent on the abused into later life, with unrealistic expectations of what the abused might provide? Or is the critical issue an imbalance of dependency, regardless of the direction it takes?* Future research must examine such factors as the need for assistance of the abused, feelings of caregiving burden on the part of the abuser, and dependency of the abuser. The following discussion of prevention programs will treat the two forms of dependency as separate risk factors.

Social Isolation

Social isolation has also been found to be characteristic of families in which other forms of domestic violence occur (Gelles, 1972; Gil, 1971; Justice & Justice, 1976; Stark et al., 1981). This is probably because behaviors that are considered illegitimate tend to be hidden. Detection of family violence can result in informal sanctions from friends, kin, and neighbors, and formal sanctions from police and the courts. Thus, all forms of family violence are likely to be less frequent in families with friends or relatives nearby (Nye, 1979). The presence of an active social network may be a particular strong deterrent to elder abuse, because it is viewed as a highly illegitimate behavior. Support for this argument has been provided by case-control studies by Phillips (1983) and Pillemer (1985c), which found abused elderly persons to have less social contact.

External Stress

A number of investigators have found a positive relationship between external stress (as differentiated from the stress that results from interpersonal relationships in the family) and child and wife abuse (Gil, 1971; Justice & Justice, 1976; Straus et al., 1980). A stress perspective on abuse can be seen as an alternative to the theories previously discussed. In Gelles and Straus's (1979a) terms, it is a sociocultural theory, rather than a social-psychological or intraindividual one, in that in emphasizes social structural and macrolevel variables, such as unemployment and economic conditions.

To date, no systematic exploration has been conducted of the relationship between stress and elder abuse, although Sengstock and Liang (1982) provided preliminary support for such a relationship.

The more general literature on family relations also appears to support this view. In particular, several studies have provided evidence that status transitions precipitated by negative life events are often associated with lower levels of marital adjustment. For example, Larson (1984) found lower levels of marital adjustment among blue-collar men following the loss of their jobs. Similarly, Simmons and Ball (1984) reported lower levels of marital adjustment among couples in which husbands had experienced spinal cord injuries during the marriage than among couples in which the injury had preceded the marriage. Suitor's (1987) panel study of married mothers' return

---

*Equity theory, a related perspective that has considerable empirical support, also suggests that perceptions of inequity play an important role in explaining marital conflict (see Suitor, 1989; Yogev and Brett, 1985).

to school suggests that status transitions may lead to declines in partners' satisfaction with one another's family role performance; this in turn can result in lowered marital adjustment.

Additional Factors

Research has uncovered two additional risk factors for elder abuse that do not fit neatly into these more general categories. First, it is clear that elderly persons are at substantially higher risk when they live with others, because the opportunities for interaction, and therefore conflict, are greater. Pillemer and Finkelhor (1988) found that persons who lived with a spouse or child were much more likely to be abused than elders who lived alone.

Second, recent studies have highlighted that a substantial proportion of elder abuse is perpetrated by spouses. Although many early investigators suggested that abuse was largely perpetrated by adult children, Pillemer and Finkelhor's (1988) random sample survey revealed that abuse by spouses is more common. In their study, 58% of the abusers were spouses of the victim, compared to only 24% who were children. Attempts to prevent elder abuse must therefore not ignore maltreatment that occurs in marital relationships.

In summary, the literature review points to four major factors that could lead to elder abuse: intraindividual dynamics, dependency of abuser and/or abused, social isolation, and external stress. In the framework proposed here, these factors may directly precipitate domestic violence against the elderly. That is, families that have one of these characteristics may be at greater risk of elder abuse. To the extent that a family has more of these characteristics, it will be more at risk. Further, the risk of elder abuse may be higher for persons who share a residence with others and who are married. Prevention programs, if they are to be effective, should therefore respond to the factors that increase the likelihood of abuse.

PREVENTION PROGRAMS: AN ANALYSIS OF THE OPTIONS

In the remainder of this chapter, we discuss a variety of interventions that may have potential to prevent elder abuse. We do so with the caveat, however, that both evaluation data and practical experience with elder abuse prevention are lacking. The discussion here, then, must be seen as somewhat speculative; careful evaluation studies are greatly needed to allow the recommendation of specific prevention options with more confidence.

In order to frame this discussion, we have relied on the work of several experts on child abuse. In particular, the presentation is organized along the lines specified by Cohn (1982), in her work on child abuse prevention. We emphasize, however, that we are not equating elder abuse with child abuse. In fact, as Pillemer and Finkelhor have argued elsewhere (1988), it is likely that the two types of abuse are quite different. However, much more work has been done in child abuse prevention than with other forms of family violence. It is therefore instructive to examine the degree to which the experience in child abuse prevention can be used to inform practice in elder abuse.

Screening

Perhaps the most widely researched prevention option in child abuse is screening. The premise behind such programs is that predicting the possibility of abusive child-rearing practices allows for intervention before maltreatment occurs. Screening programs often use interviews and/or direct observation of parents to identify problem families. Thus, for example, Gray, Cutler, Dean, and Kempe (1979) administered a prenatal interview and 72-item questionnaire, recorded observations by nurses in the hospital after the birth, and conducted a postpartum interview and observation.

There has been some discussion of screening programs among experts on elder abuse. Screening protocols have been developed most frequently in medical settings. Among the best known of these programs is the one employed by the Beth Israel Hospital Elder Assessment Team in Boston, Massachusetts (Fulmer & O'Malley, 1987). This multidisciplinary approach, which has been employed since 1981, involves a team of nurses, physicians, and social workers. The team evaluates cases referred to it and provides consultation on care plans for abused and neglected elderly patients.

Referrals made to the team are screened with an instrument developed for use in the hospital (Fulmer & O'Malley, 1987). This instrument assesses such areas as hygiene, nutrition, and clothing. The physical assessment includes symptoms of trauma such as unexplained bruises. Measures are also taken of the person's life-style and the degree of social contact. Finally, a medical assessment is conducted, which includes information about medications, possible malnutrition or dehydration, substance abuse, and other areas. Based on these data, the practitioner makes a summary assessment as to whether abuse has occurred. Similar protocols have been developed at Seattle's Harborview Medical Center, Mount Sinai Medical Center in New York City, and elsewhere.

The goal of such screening programs is the early identification of persons who may be at risk of elder abuse. As such, they could be extended to other settings besides hospitals, including senior centers, adult day-care centers, and meal sites. However, potential problems in screening for elder abuse must be taken into consideration.

The major difficulty should be clear from earlier sections of this chapter: the lack of firm risk factor data on elder abuse. In order to successfully screen for a phenomenon, it must be possible to specify subgroups of the population who are most likely to be affected. As Helfer (1976) points out, screening is based on a "serious disease model" in which clear early symptoms can be taken as warning signs of a condition. Thus, screening can take place for high blood pressure, as this is a generally accepted precursor of heart disease.

Such is not the case with elder abuse. Although there is reasonable likelihood that the four risk factors noted earlier are indeed related to elder abuse, much more research is necessary to establish such a relationship. Potential dangers thus exist in attempting to screen the elderly for abuse. As Helfer (1976) notes, one problem with all screening programs is threats to sensitivity and specificity: that is, their accuracy in identifying high-risk subjects on the one hand, and in correctly exempting low-risk subjects on the other.

If screening is carried out with unvalidated instruments, the reliability of which is unknown, then risks to subjects result. In particular, if the instrument inaccurately identifies someone as being at risk, he/she may be subject to an invasive investigation, and to being stigmatized as a "problem case." As desirable as early identification of potential elder abuse victims may be, then, it appears wise to await more definitive research findings before attempting screening programs on a wide scale.

Fulmer and O'Malley (1987) note two other problems with screening protocols. First, the lack of a generally accepted definition of elder abuse makes it difficult to develop an instrument that would be applicable in a variety of settings. Second, assessment of elder abuse invariably involves "professional judgment." That is, the experience of the health provider must be brought to bear on the case, in addition to the more structured instrument. As Fulmer and O'Malley (1987) suggest, perhaps the best role for the screening instruments available at present is to heighten professional awareness of the possibility of elder abuse and to alert clinicians to symptoms that might otherwise be missed. It is certainly difficult at present to recommend wide-scale screening for elder abuse; more limited goals appear appropriate.

Education Programs for Potential Victims

In a discussion of child sexual abuse, Finkelhor (1984) asserts that a substantial amount of such maltreatment could be prevented if children had basic information about the inappropriateness of sexual advances. Education of potential elder abuse victims could have a similar deterrent effect. One common finding of most protective services programs and elder abuse intervention projects is lack of self-referrals from victims; in fact, self-reports often constitute the smallest category of referrals (Wolf & Pillemer, 1989).

Numerous reasons are given for this unwillingness on the part of victims to seek help. Victims may be ashamed to admit that they have serious family problems. They may be unaware that services exist to aid them, or they may feel that their own situation is so hopeless that it would be futile to seek assistance. At least one study has found that elder abuse victims experience feelings of depression and helplessness similar to those experienced by victims of other forms of domestic violence (Pillemer & Prescott, 1989).

Public awareness campaigns directed toward elderly persons would begin to address these problems. Such programs can emphasize the right of elderly persons to live free of domestic violence as well as provide information on steps victims can take. Such a program was initiated by the Rhode Island Department of Elder Affairs. Using an acting troupe of elderly persons, the Department sponsored a program of skits that were performed to senior citizens' groups throughout the state. Many other states have conducted statewide public awareness campaigns, using television, radio, and print media to disseminate information about the rights of the elderly and to publicize available services.

Caregiver Training and Support Programs

Perhaps the most widely prescribed preventive programs for elder abuse have been those targeted toward family caregivers (cf. Steinmetz, 1988). For example, education and training for caregivers of the elderly have been proposed. Some of these programs are modeled on parent education programs designed to reduce child abuse, in which parents are offered education about child development and about nonabusive methods of discipline. In the same vein, training has been offered to family caregivers to the elderly, based on the idea that the stress of caregiving can be reduced with improved skills. Similarly, caregiver support groups sometimes have as a goal the prevention of elder abuse.

Many discussions of elder abuse also propose the provision of in-home health and social services as a method of preventing maltreatment. Services such as respite care, adult day care, and homemaker services are seen as ways of reducing caregiver stress, and therefore abuse.

Although no evaluation data are available, it seems plausible that such programs may reduce the likelihood of abuse in those cases where the victim is an impaired dependent person. As noted earlier, however, research indicates that caregiver stress is in general not a major risk factor for elder abuse, although it may precipitate abuse in a minority of cases. In fact, several studies indicate that elder abusers are frequently *not* caregivers to the victim (Bristowe, 1987; Pillemer, 1985b; Pillemer & Finkelhor, 1989). Unfortunately, elder abuse has in general been conceptualized as a problem of *caregiving,* rather than as domestic violence. Other programs that specifically address a more pressing problem—the impaired and dependent *abuser*—are more likely to prevent elder abuse.

Reducing Social Isolation

One of the most promising prevention strategies is to reduce social isolation by increasing the presence of outsiders in the home. Such programs are analogous to the use of home visitors in families at high risk of child abuse. A model program of this kind is that developed by the Alliance Elder Abuse

Project in Syracuse, New York (Wolf & Pillemer, 1989). Elder abuse aides spend approximately 2 to 4 hours a week in the homes of abuse victims. Their functions include providing socialization and advocacy for clients. They attempt to serve as a model for the abuser of more effective ways of communicating. In situations where the abuser is a caregiver, they also provide respite from assisting the elder. A systematic evaluation of the Syracuse program found it to be highly effective in preventing further victimization.

The Syracuse project, however, served already identified victims of abuse and neglect. Such services could also be offered to families who have been identified as at risk of maltreatment. For example, it would be possible to identify families in which an elderly person lives with a mentally impaired spouse or child, and in which stressful life events have occurred. If the family is also socially isolated, higher risk of abuse would be expected. The provision of an aide might help to prevent maltreatment in such a situation.

Increasing the Costs of Abusive Behavior

A final prevention is to enunciate more clearly social disapproval of elder abuse, by strengthening legal sanctions against maltreatment. The law enforcement system must play a key role in such efforts. As Gelles (1983) has convincingly argued, family violence is so widespread in part because of lack of effective social controls: people abuse each other because they *can*. Police intervention and arrest are used so infrequently in elder abuse cases that abusers are likely to feel that they have little to lose by engaging in violence.

Sherman and Berk (1984) have provided important (although controversial) evidence that police intervention may reduce the incidence of domestic violence. In one experiment, they found that arrest was the most effective method to prevent further episodes of wife abuse. If traditional police reluctance to become involved in domestic violence can be overcome, such law enforcement activity in elder abuse may also be effective. For many persons, the cost of being arrested would greatly outweigh the rewards obtained from abusive behavior. A variety of such attempts are now underway to increase police involvement in elder abuse (Police Executive Research Forum, 1988).

Community Organization

A final approach is larger in scope and less focused on specific risk factors. This involves the creation of task forces of service providers and other interested individuals in local communities. Many such efforts to raise the consciousness of professionals and lay people about elder abuse are underway throughout the country. Among the best known of these task forces is the San Francisco Consortium for Elder Abuse Prevention, which began in 1981. The task force has established goals and objectives for a service delivery program that includes outreach, training, coordination, service development, and advocacy. It serves the function of defining the roles and responsibilities of various service agencies. A task force like this can serve as a vehicle for public awareness and education as well as a location for screening and other prevention programs.

SUMMARY AND FUTURE DIRECTIONS

At the outset of this chapter, we, like McKinlay, attempted to make "a case for refocusing upstream." Many others have also argued that prevention of elder abuse should be a major goal of all those concerned with this problem. The remainder of our discussion, however, makes clear how daunting the development of elder abuse prevention programs actually is. Professionals must struggle against a weak knowledge base and a lack of practical experience in elder abuse prevention. The present chapter has only been able to offer a general, and somewhat speculative, treatment of possible ways to prevent domestic violence against the elderly.

It is therefore necessary to reiterate what is by now a familiar refrain: the need for more information. As a reading of review articles demonstrates, very little new knowledge has been acquired about elder abuse in the past 10 years: certainly less so than in other forms of family violence. As noted elsewhere (Pillemer & Suitor, 1988), a pressing need exists for scientifically valid studies of the phenomenon. In particular, large-scale, random sample surveys of the general population are needed, as are carefully conducted case-control studies. Further, systematic evaluation studies must be conducted to test various methods of preventing elder abuse. The results of new and better studies may suggest methods of "refocusing upstream" to help prevent elder abuse.

REFERENCES

Adams, B. (1968). *Kinship in an urban setting*. Chicago, IL: Markum.

Andrews, F. M., & S. B. Withey (1979). *Social indicators of well-being: Americans' perception of life quality*. New York: Plenum.

Baruch, G., & Barnett, R. C. (1983). Adult daughters' relationships with their mothers. *Journal of Marriage and the Family, 45,* 601–606.

Berry, R. E., & Williams, F. L. (1987). Assessing the relationship between quality of life and marital and income satisfaction: A path analytic approach. *Journal of Marriage and the Family, 49,* 107–116.

Breckman, R., & Adelman, R. (1988). *Strategies for helping victims of elder mistreatment*. Newbury Park, CA: Sage.

Bristowe, E. (1987, July). *Family mediated abuse of non-institutionalized frail elderly men and women living in British Columbia*. Paper presented at the Third National Conference for Family Violence Researchers, Durham, NH.

Callahan, J. L. (1981). *Elder abuse programming: Will it help the elderly?* Paper presented at the National Conference on the Abuse of Older Persons, Boston, MA.

Cantor, M. H. (1983). Strain among caregivers: A study of experience in the United States. *Gerontologist, 23,* 597–604.

Cicirelli, V. (1981). *Helping elderly parents: The role of adult children*. Boston MA: Auburn House.

Cicirelli, V. (1983a). Adult children and their elderly parents. In T. H. Bruabker (Eds.), *Family relationships in later life* (pp. 21–46). Newbury Park, CA: Sage.

Cicirelli, V. (1983b). Adult children's attachment and helping behavior to elderly parents: A path model. *Journal of Marriage and the Family, 45,* 815–826.

Cohn, A. H. (1982). Stopping abuse before it occurs: Different solutions for different populations. *Child Abuse and Neglect, 6,* 473–483.

Coleman, D., & Straus, M. A. (1981). *Alcohol abuse and family violence*. Durham: University of New Hampshire, Family Violence Research Program.

Douglass, R. L., Hickey, T., & Noel C. (1980). *A study of maltreatment of the elderly and other vulnerable adults*. Ann Arbor: University of Michigan.

Finkelhor, D. (1983). Common features of family abuse. In D. Finkelhor, R. J. Gelles, G. Hotaling, & M. Straus (Eds.), *The dark side of families: Current family violence research* (pp. 19–26). Newbury Park, CA: Sage.

Finkelhor, D. (1984). The prevention of child sexual abuse: An overview of needs and problems. *Siecus Report, 13,* 1.

Fulmer, T., & O'Malley, T. (1987). *Inadequate care of the elderly*. New York: Springer.

Gelles, R. J. (1972). *The violent home*. Newbury Park, CA: Sage.

Gelles, R. J. (1974). Child abuse as psychopathology: A sociological critique and reformulation. In S. Steinmetz & M. A. Straus (Eds.), *Violence in the family* (pp. 190–204). New York: Dodd, Mead.

Gelles, R. J. (1983). An exchange/social control theory. In D. Finkelhor, R. J. Gelles, G. T. Hotaling, & M. A. Straus (Eds.), *The dark side of families: Current family violence research* (pp. 151–165). Newbury Park, CA: Sage.

Gelles, R. J., & Straus, M. A. (1979a). Determinants of violence in the family: Toward a theoretical integration. In W. R. Burr, R. Hill, F. I. Nye, & I. L. Reiss (Eds.), *Contemporary theories about the family* (pp. 549–581). New York: Free Press.

Gelles, R. J., & Straus, M. A. (1979b). Violence in the American family. *Journal of Social Issues, 35,* 15–39.

Gil, D. (1971). *Violence against children: Physical child abuse in the United States*. Cambridge, MA: Harvard University Press.

Glenn, N., & Weaver, C. (1981). A multivariate, multisurvey study of marital happiness. *Journal of Marriage and the Family, 40*, 269–282.

Gray, J. D., Cutler, C. A., Dean, J. A., & Kempe, C. H. (1979). Prediction and prevention of child abuse and neglect. *Journal of Social Issues, 35*, 127–139.

Helfer, R. E. (1976). Basic issues concerning prediction. In C. H. Kempe & R. E. Helfer (Eds.), *Child abuse and neglect: The family and the community* (pp. 363–372). Cambridge, MA: Ballinger.

Hudson, M. F. (1986). Elder Mistreatment: Current research. In K. Pillemer & R. Wolf (Eds.), *Elder Abuse: Conflict in the family* (pp. 125–166). Dover MA: Auburn House.

Hwalek, M., Sengstock, M., & Lawrence, R. (1984, November). Assessing the probability of abuse of the elderly. Paper presented at the annual meeting of the Gerontological Society of America, San Antonio.

Johnson, E. S., & Bursk, B. J. (1977). Relationships between the elderly and their adult children. *Gerontologist, 17*, 90–96.

Johnson, T. (1986). Critical issues in the definition of elder mistreatment. In K. Pillemer & R. Wolf (Eds.), *Elder abuse: Conflict in the family* (pp. 167–195). Dover, MA: Auburn House.

Justice, B., & Justice, R. (1976). The abusing family. New York: Human Sciences Press.

Kantor, G. K., & Straus, M. (1986). The drunken bum theory of wife-beating. *Social Problems, 34*, 213–231.

Kulys, R., & Tobin, S. (1980). Older people and their responsible others. *Social Work, 25*, 138–145.

Larson, J. H. (1984). The effect of husband's unemployment on marital and family relations in blue-collar families. *Family Relations, 33*, 503–511.

Lau, E., & Kosberg, J. (1979). Abuse of the elderly by informal care providers. *Aging*, (Sept.–Oct), 10–15.

Lee, G. (1978). Marriage and morale in later life. *Journal of Marriage and the Family, 40*, 131–139.

McKinlay, J. (1981). A case for refocusing: The political economy of illness. In P. Conrad & M. Kern (Eds.), *The sociology of health and illness* (pp. 613–633). New York: St. Martin's Press.

Nye, I. (1979). Choice, exchange, and the family. In W. R. Burr, R. Hill, F. I. Nye, & I. L. Reiss (Eds.), *Contemporary theories about the family: Volume II* (pp. 1–41). New York: Free Press.

Pedrick-Cornell, C., & Gelles, R. (1982). Elderly abuse: The status of current knowledge. *Family Relations, 31*, 457–465.

Phillips, L. (1983). Abuse and neglect of the frail elderly at home: An exploration of theoretical relationships. *Journal of Advanced Nursing, 8*, 379–392.

Pillemer, K. (1985a). *Domestic violence against the elderly: A case-control study.* Unpublished doctoral dissertation, Department of Sociology, Brandeis University.

Pillemer, K. (1985b). The dangers of dependency: New findings on domestic violence against the elderly. *Social Problems, 33*, 146–158.

Pillemer, K. (1985c, Fall). Social isolation and elder abuse. *Response,* pp. 1–4.

Pillemer, K. (1986). Risk factors in Elder Abuse: Results from a case-control study. In K. Pillemer R. S. Wolf (Eds.), *Elder Abuse: Conflict in the Family* (pp. 239–263). Dover, MA: Auburn House.

Pillemer, K., & Finkelhor, D. (1988). Prevalence of elder abuse: A random sample survey. *Gerontologist, 28,* 51–57.

Pillemer, K., & Finkelhor, D. (1989). The causes of elder abuse: Caregiver stress versus problem relatives. *American Journal of Orthopsychiatry, 59,* 179–187.

Pillemer, K. & Prescott, D. (1989). Psychological effects of elder abuse. *Journal of Elder Abuse and Neglect, 1,* 65–73.

Pillemer, K., & Suitor, J. J. (1988). Elder abuse. In R. L. Morrison, V. B. Van Hasselt, A. S. Bellack, & M. Hersen (Eds.), *Handbook of family violence* (pp. 247–270). New York: Plenum.

Police Executive Research Forum (1988). *A time for dignity: Police and domestic abuse of the elderly.* Washington, DC: Author.

Quinn, M. J., & Tomita, S. (1986). *Elder abuse and neglect: Causes, diagnosis, and intervention strategies.* New York: Springer.

Sengstock, M. C., & Liang, J. (1982). *Identifying and characterizing elder abuse.* Detroit, MI: Wayne State University Institute of Gerontology.

Sherman, L. W., & Berk, R. A. (1984). The specific deterent effects of arrest for domestic assault. *American Sociological Review, 49,* 261–272.

Simmons, S., & Ball, S. E. (1984). Marital adjustment in couples married before and after spinal cord injury. *Journal of Marriage and the Family, 46,* 943–945.

Stark, E., Flitcraft, A., Zuckerman, D., Gray, A., Robinson, J., & Frazier, W. (1981). *Wife abuse in the medical setting: An introduction to health personnel.* Washington, DC: National Clearinghouse on Domestic Violence.

Steinmetz, S. (1983). Dependency, stress, and violence between middle-aged caregivers and their elderly parents. In J. I. Kosberg (Ed.), *Abuse and maltreatment of the elderly* (pp. 134–149). Littleton, MA: John Wright PSG.

Steinmetz, S. (1988). *Duty bound.* Newbury Park, CA: Sage.

Steinmetz, S., & Amsden, D. (1983). Dependency, family stress, and abuse. In T. H. Brubaker (Ed.), *Family relationships in later life* (pp. 173–192). Newbury Park, CA: Sage.

Straus, M., Gelles, R., & Steinmetz, S. (1980). *Behind closed doors: Violence in the American family.* New York: Doubleday.

Suitor, J. J. (1987). Marital happiness of returning women students and their husbands: Effects of part and full-time enrollment. *Research in Higher Education, 27,* 311–331.

Suitor, J. J. (1989). *Marital quality and satisfaction with the division of household labor: Variations across family life cycle.* Unpublished manuscript, Fordham University.

Suitor, J. J., & Pillemer, K. (1987). The presence of adult children: A source for elderly couples' marriages. *Journal of Marriage and the Family, 49,* 717–725.

Suitor, J. J., & Pillemer, K. (1988). Explaining intergenerational conflict when adult children and elderly parents live together. *Journal of Marriage and the Family,* *50,* 1037–1047.

Wolf, R., Godkin, M., & Pillemer, K. (1984). *Final Report from Three Model Projects on Elder Abuse.* Worcester, MA: University of Massachusetts, Center on Aging.

Wolf, R., & Pillemer, K. (1989). *Helping elderly victims: The reality of elder abuse.* New York: Columbia University Press.

Wolf, R., Strugnell, C., & Godkin, M. (1982, December). *Preliminary findings from three model projects on elderly abuse.* Paper presented at the University of Massachusetts Medical Center, Center on Aging, Worcester.

Yin, P. (1985). *Victimization and the aged.* Springfield, IL: Charles C Thomas.

Yogev, S., & Brett, J. (1985). Perceptions of the division of housework and child care and marital satisfaction. *Journal of Marriage and the Family, 47,* 609–618.

PART FIVE

Future Directions in Research

CHAPTER 18

Future Directions in Research

MICHEL HERSEN AND ROBERT T. AMMERMAN

INTRODUCTION

It is highly unlikely that a comprehensive book on the treatment of family violence could have emerged 10 years ago. Even if an enterprising editor were to have undertaken the task, the material would have been sketchy at best, and the research data supporting the effects of treatment would have been virtually nonexistent. Although the situation has markedly improved in the late 1980s (see Geffner, Rosenbaum, & Hughes, 1988; Rosenbaum, 1988), it is clear that much work will be required in this still nascent area to further improve the experimental rigor of treatment outcome studies. Indeed, as has been documented in the preceding chapters by the respective experts, there are some areas in the treatment of family violence where few research data are extant. Five areas in particular are the psychological mal-treatment of children (Brassard & Hart, in press), elder abuse (Pierce & Trotta, 1986), marital rape (Bidwell & White, 1986), the child witness of family violence (Fantuzzo & Lindquist, 1989), and adult survivors of incest (Browne & Finkelhor, 1986). More, of course, is known about the treatment of both the victims and perpetrators of child physical and sexual abuse (Ammerman & Hersen, in press) and battered wives (Gondolf, 1987a, 1987b), albeit only a research beachhead has been established in those areas.

CURRENT RESEARCH GAPS AND RECOMMENDATIONS

A number of reasons can be pinpointed for the research lags in the field of family violence. *First,* aside from the overall newness of the subject matter,

Preparation of this chapter was facilitated in part by a grant from the National Institute on Disabilities and Rehabilitation Research, U.S. Department of Education (No. G008720109) and a grant from the Vira I. Heinz Endowment. However, the opinions reflected herein do not necessarily reflect the position of policy of the U.S. Department of Education or the Vira I. Heinz Endowment, and no official endorsement should be inferred.

there are few areas of inquiry in the behavioral sciences where there is such a heterogeneity of professionals working concurrently. Indeed, in the study of family violence one finds pediatricians, endocrinologists, gerontologists, sociologists, social workers, psychologists, psychiatrists, lawyers, criminologists, and educators. Given the extremely varied backgrounds of such professionals and few commonalities in their inclinations and methodologies for carrying out research, the unevenness of the research quality of the work should not be surprising (see Rosenbaum, 1988).

Second, although obviously well intended, there has been a sampling bias in the actual populations that have been studied and reported on in the research literature. That is, in many instances the target population has been self-selected (e.g., battered women who reside in shelters), court remanded (e.g., perpetrators of child sexual abuse or battering husbands), or studied retrospectively on the basis of hospital charts (e.g., multihandicapped children who allegedly have been abused and/or neglected). The problem here is that only the proverbial "tip of the iceberg" is scrutinized. There is no doubt that the vast majority of perpetrators and victims remain undetected and understudied. It is quite likely that these individuals would differ on both major and minor characteristics if they were to be contrasted with their counterparts who already have been identified (either for legal or psychological reasons).

Third, again probably as a function of the newness of the area and the heterogeneity of the researchers involved, a standard system of assessment has not been established to evaluate perpetrators and victims or to uncover abuse and neglect in the first place. The field is replete with studies that were conducted retrospectively or that used measurement instruments of questionable reliability and validity. However, reliable and valid assessment tools (such as the ones currently used in the study of anxiety and depression) have not yet been developed to identify and uncover perpetrators and victims. Very much needed are standardized batteries of tests, such as those that appear in the research evaluating treatment techniques for anxiety and depression (see Bellack & Hersen, 1988; Hersen & Bellack, 1988; Hersen & Turner, 1985; Last & Hersen, 1988). It is necessary to improve the reliability and validity of existing measures and to develop viable behavioral assessment strategies, including those of the analogue variety. Establishment of semistructured interview schedules such as the Child Abuse and Neglect Interview Schedule (CANIS; Ammerman, Hersen, & Van Hasselt, 1987) to detect other abusive and neglectful practices should also prove invaluable. Certainly, in the realm of affective disorders, development of the Schedule for Affective Disorders and Schizophrenia (SADS) for adults (Spitzer & Endicott, 1977) and the Kiddie-Schedule for Affective Disorders and Schizophrenia for Children (Chambers et al., 1985) has yielded advancements in the field.

Development and validation of such semistructured interview schedules in the realm of family violence undoubtedly will sharpen the thinking of clinical researchers and will help to pinpoint and define classes of violent behavior that otherwise would remain vague and haphazardly documented.

A *fourth* research consideration involves the type of designs used by workers in the treatment of family violence. From the vantage point of treating child sexual abuse, Kolko (1987) underscores this issue:

> The absence of empirical data regarding treatment outcome and effectiveness . . . and the presence of various methodological limitations in the design and analysis of selected programs are of considerable import. . . . Many programs do not incorporate standardized instruments to assess those variables purported to change following treatment, and only rarely include needed control or comparison groups and statistical analyses to evaluate program impact. (p. 313)

Even in one of the better programs developed for the treatment and prevention of child abuse and neglect, the effects of Project 12-Ways were contrasted by including a post hoc control condition of families in the same geographic region who had received protective services that differed from those offered in the experimental treatment condition (Lutzker & Rice, 1987). Although admirable in intent and better than no control condition, a concurrent control condition carefully matched would represent a cleaner methodology.

It is undoubtedly true that carefully described clinical interventions and pre-post designs without adequate controls can lead to tantalizing conclusions about the treatments applied, but scientific rigor will best be served through the judicious use of single case designs (Barlow & Hersen, 1984) in pilot work. These designs should then be confirmed in large-scale group comparison designs that include appropriate control conditions. We fully agree with Rosenbaum (1988) that the time is ripe to move from a focus on epidemiology to one of controlled research on intervention.

A *fifth* recommendation that should improve research in the future is the precise documentation as to what takes place in treatment, be it for the perpetrator or victim. With the proliferation of new treatment programs a myriad of innovative intervention strategies have been developed (see Van Hasselt, Morrison, Bellack, & Hersen, 1988, for reviews). In some instances, as in Gondolf's (1985) "Men Who Batter," the treatment is thoroughly detailed on a session-by-session basis, with illustrative clinical examples and therapist–client dialogue. These kinds of descriptions allow for needed replication in the programs of colleagues, thus making interstudy comparisons feasible. However, in the field of family violence such is the exception rather than the rule.

It is clear, then, that clinical researchers need to present their therapeutic interventions in the form of comprehensive treatment manuals, as has been the case in the work with depressives (Bellack, Hersen, & Himmelhoch, 1980), chronic psychiatric patients such as schizophrenics (Beidel, Bellack, Turner, Hersen, & Luber, 1981), social skills training for visually handicapped children (Ammerman, Van Hasselt, & Hersen, 1985), and the behavioral treatment of families with an adolescent suffering from spina bifida (Rowley, Van Hasselt, & Hersen, 1986). Not only will the publication of manuals in the treatment of family violence foster meaningful interstudy comparisons, but the guides will prove to be invaluable for professionals and paraprofessionals working clinically with difficult cases.

A *sixth* issue that has affected how research is carried out in the area of family violence can best be labeled "emotionalism." Given the highly charged nature of family violence, it is quite understandable that even objectively trained social scientists will respond with bias to certain features of violent actions in the family setting. However, the excessive fervor exhibited by particular interest groups in the area of family violence has, at times, obfuscated both important clinical and research considerations. On the one hand, as a consequence of such fervor, the unfortunate tendency to blame the victim has diminished, and the authorities who must deal with the victims of sexual abuse, rape, and battering have learned to be more therapeutic. This is as it should be. But on the other hand, the almost total focus on the negative characteristics of the perpetrator has overshadowed the actions of the victim.

Clearly, victims can learn to protect themselves better and, in situations where they cannot avoid the perpetrator, there may be strategies that they can employ to diminish the further likelihood of victimization. For example, in some of the clinical work we have conducted with couples seeking marital therapy, one of the problems is the husband's aperiodic physical abuse of the wife. In those situations where the wife has decided to remain in the marital relationship despite the abuse, conjoint marital therapy is only one of several therapeutic modalities that will help to ameliorate the situation. Independent attention to the batterer naturally is recommended. However, in analyzing the interactions that culminate in physical altercations, we have found that the wife is not always attuned to the prodromal signs and may inadvertently escalate the conflict and reinforce her husband's violent proclivities. *Violence can never be condoned in the marital relationship. But, for those women who choose to remain, whatever their motivation, survival skills are crucial.* Teaching this subgroup of women how to prevent escalation of conflict (either by using extinction strategies or simply leaving the situation temporarily) is not only of clear clinical benefit but should be evaluated empirically. In the long run it is the victim who will benefit from such study.

Our *seventh* consideration and recommendation deals with the long-term follow-up of the treatment provided to perpetrators and victims of family violence. It is almost axiomatic that clinical researchers tackling a new therapeutic area are more concerned with the immediate efficacy of their strategies than with the long-term benefits of such application. We have found that therapeutics in family violence does not present an exception to the rule. For the most part, the longitudinal evaluation of perpetrators or victims has not been accomplished. In fact, less follow-up attention has been accorded to the victims of family violence (see Van Hasselt et al., 1988). Certainly, this situation will need to be redressed in future research evaluations. Indeed, we would hope that national funding agencies will be sufficiently perspicacious in highlighting the need for long-term undertakings. This also means the willingness to make 10-year commitments to clinical researchers who present viable designs for evaluating the long-term effects of treatment.

An additional consideration of the long-term follow-up of perpetrators and victims of family violence is the chronic course of the problems. Perpetrators, even after treatment, show marked patterns of recidivism, with the need for perpetual monitoring and frequent booster treatments. Victims of child abuse, especially sexual abuse, have been known to develop psychiatric symptoms even several decades after the original sexual violence was perpetrated. In light of what is known about posttraumatic stress disorder (PTSD), especially in cases where therapeutic intervention is especially delayed, the need to monitor the victim for protracted periods of time is warranted (see American Psychiatric Association, 1987).

The chronicity of the perpetrator's actions and the prolonged psychological sequelae evinced by victims suggest that the problem of family violence be reconceptualized as a chronic illness, wherein the patient is under consistent surveillance by medical authorities. It is only recently that the medical model of chronic illness as applied to psychological problems has regained some favor (cf. Hersen & Ammerman, 1989; Kazdin, 1987; Wolf, Braukmann, & Ramp, 1987). Pursuing this analogy a bit further, it is clear that future research efforts will have to incorporate (a) long-term follow-ups, (b) ethical methods for continued surveillance, (c) regular booster treatments, and (d) booster treatments on a crisis basis, as needed (i.e., PRN). In psychoanalytic parlance, the "analysis remains interminable."

Our *eighth* and final consideration in this section involves the importance of prevention in family violence. Nowhere is the old adage "An ounce of prevention is equal to a pound of cure" of greater applicability. We already have commented on the chronic nature of family violence, both for the perpetrator and victim. Moreover, despite Kaufman and Zigler's (1987) recent tempered conclusions on intergenerational transmission of violent and abusive behavior, it still is a documented fact that those who have been exposed to violence and abuse are at greater risk themselves to subsequently engage in such behavior (see Van Hasselt et al., 1988).

At this point in time a number of additional risk factors have been identified that can predict subsequent abusive behavior. Included are psychosocial factors (Lewis, 1987; Roberts, 1987); employment factors and observation of parental violence (Howell & Pugliesi, 1988); personality characteristics (Hamberger & Hastings, 1986); recent divorce (Bolton & MacEachron, 1986); early onset of sexual behavior, previous sexual victimization, and identified psychiatric disorder (Becker, Kaplan, Cunningham-Rathner, & Kovoussi, 1986); presence of handicapping conditions (Ammerman, Van Hasselt, & Hersen, 1988), and residential density in urban settings (Zuravin, 1986).

On the basis of such findings, a number of preventive programs have been developed, including a school-based sexual abuse program (Kolko, Moser, Litz, & Hughes, 1987), an ecobehavioral approach to the prevention of child abuse and neglect (Lutzker & Rice, 1987), and stress-management for teenage parents to prevent family violence (Schinke, Schilling, Barth, Gilchrist, & Maxwell, 1986). Although the indirect results of these programs are encouraging, with the exception of Lutzker and his colleagues' work, the follow-ups are very brief and the application of the programs is not widespread.

Much more work in the area will prove fruitful if precise predictive factors with high loadings can be identified through painstaking research efforts. We also believe that, although secondary and tertiary preventative efforts obviously are needed for remedial purposes, the greatest payoff will be in the realm of primary prevention. Further research evaluations of primary prevention efforts conducted statewide and nationally in school settings are required at this time. Perhaps schools should tackle in systematic fashion the problem of dealing effectively with the varied stresses of family living, in addition to alerting younger children about sexual abuse. Material on effective family living must be introduced in the early grades; in high school some of the attitudes of the students (possibly as a consequence of extensive modeling of faulty parental behavior) have solidified, and preventive efforts may be of little avail.

SPECIFIC RECOMMENDATIONS

This section provides a brief review of the specific recommendations for future research offered by the authors of Chapters 2 through 17, highlighting, in each instance, the most pressing needs facing the field.

Hansen, Conaway, and Christopher (Chapter 2), in discussing child physical abuse, make clear that insufficient attention has been accorded to the assessment of treatments for this population, either in terms of the short-term consequences of physical abuse or the more pervasive long-term consequences. Problems in the research to be rectified in the future involve the operational differences between abuse and neglect, determination of frequency, and severity of maltreatment. Matching groups in controlled studies on relevant demographic variables and controlling for recent separation or divorce in the family are additional concerns. Hansen et al., consistent with our earlier comments on the psychometric properties of assessment strategies, caution the reader to accept the current findings with a degree of

skepticism. There is no doubt that good treatment studies require good assessment tools. (Caveat emptor!)

In Chapter 3 on child sexual abuse, Conte echoes the need to refine existing measures of abuse and to develop new ones that are psychometrically sound. Then, he argues that it will be possible to link specific treatments with specific behavioral and emotional outcomes. The need for using viable comparison groups in outcome research is stressed. He also points out that it is quite likely that children in psychiatrically impaired comparison groups may in fact be undetected victims of abuse, thus yielding overlapping groups. There is a need to evaluate such possible overlap more carefully in future work.

In Chapter 4, Hart and Brassard have examined one of the most recent areas of inquiry in the field of family violence: the psychological maltreatment of children. Being especially new within a field that is itself new, the research, not surprisingly, is of an embryonic quality. Particularly needed are good operational definitions, careful assessment to uncover overlap with physical and sexual abuse, and the development and evaluation of corrective treatments.

Geffner and Pagelow, in Chapter 5 on the victims of spouse abuse, present clear guidelines for the direction that research should take. They seem most concerned with recent studies documenting the different subtypes of batterers. By deduction they argue that there probably are different subtypes of victims of spouse abuse as well. It therefore follows that once such subgroups are identified and labeled, the research goal will be to develop and test specific treatment strategies for each, thus maximizing therapeutic efficacy.

In Chapter 6, Marin and Morycz have lamented the absence of controlled outcome studies in the treatment of elder abuse and neglect. Unfortunately at this juncture, most of the extant data are anecdotal and of the clinical-speculative variety. In their recommendations for the future, Marin and Morycz stress the importance of looking at the interaction of a number of variables: demographic, subject dependency, functional ability of the subject, and the subject's psychiatric diagnosis. Contributing to the lack of direction in research is the apparent absence of consistent policy that would establish appropriate priorities in the field of elder abuse.

As is evident from Shields, Resick, and Hanneke, in Chapter 7 on marital rape, at this time very little is known about the efficacy of specific treatment strategies for this population. However, there is an increasingly large data base on the treatment of victims of nonmarital rape. But whether marital rape and "stranger" rape victims respond equally well to cognitive and behavioral treatment strategies is still an empirical question to be considered in formal study. So far, most of the research on marital rape has been adduced by comparing this population with marital rape victims who also are battered, battered women who have not been raped, or rape victims who are not married to the assaulter. Preliminary data would suggest that marital rape victims are most like nonmarital rape victims. But in the absence of sound methodology and carefully matched samples of sufficient size, no definitive statements can be made.

Yet another area in family violence that has been understudied is the child witness to marital violence. As noted by Rosenberg and Rossman in Chapter 8, contrary to parallel areas in the child abuse literature, basic incidence and prevalence data are absent here. Thus, the priority for future researchers is to gather such needed information, including the relationship of witnessing marital violence to child abuse and neglect. Then perhaps it will be possible to conduct systematic treatment outcome studies once the population has been carefully identified. Rosenberg and Rossman suggest that clinical researchers interested in the area be attuned to the kinds of treatments that currently are given when children who have observed marital violence partake in shelter programs.

Lundberg-Love, in Chapter 9, has outlined a clear research agenda to study the adult survivors of incest. She recommends, first, the development of reliable and valid instruments. Second, the need for treatment programs for male incest survivors is identified. Along these lines a comparison study of male and female survivors would be of great interest. Third, and especially crucial when working with adult survivors of childhood trauma, is the empirical evaluation of varied strategies for memory retrieval. And fourth is a comparative evaluation of those adult survivors who have received time-limited and long-term (i.e., continuous) treatment.

The current status of perpetrators of child physical abuse was tackled by Schilling in Chapter 10. On the basis of his evaluation, four research recommendations have emerged. First, he argues that a major priority is the identification of those perpetrators who are at the greatest risk for reabusing their victims. Second, and related to the first recommendation, is the determination of which abusers will benefit most from therapeutic intervention. Third is the obvious need to develop and test creative interventions. And fourth is the perennial call for longer term treatment studies and extended follow-up monitoring.

Perpetrators of child sexual abuse (Chapter 11, by Becker and Kaplan) represent complex cases, given that the development of sexual interest and arousal is a complicated and still relatively unstudied area. Becker and Kaplan point out that future research will need to identify why some perpetrators are involved in extrafamilial as well as intrafamilial sexual abuse, whereas some are only intrafamilial perpetrators. Given the high recidivism rates of child sexual abusers, research should carefully delineate when, if at all, a perpetrator should be reunited with the family. Finally, as in most of the family violence research literature, long-term follow-ups of perpetrators need to be conducted.

Although research data on the treatment of spouse abusers have accumulated at a fairly rapid rate, Rosenbaum and Maiuro (Chapter 12) identify several research gaps that need to be addressed. An important one concerns the issue as to whether batterers seen in treatment (i.e., volunteers) have the same characteristics as those abusers (i.e., nonvolunteers) described by battered women who have sought refuge in shelters. Also of interest is the evaluation of batterers' cognitions as contrasted to their nonbattering counterparts. Despite clinical evidence in support of such differences, no hard data have been offered in press. Further, the possible role of physiological variables in marital aggression has received scant attention. The following questions need to be evaluated in future research: What are the relative effects of clearly specified treatments? What are the effective components of treatment? Is treatment of couples in conjoint fashion effective and safe? What is the possibility of matching subtypes of batterers and relationships to specific treatments?

In considering future directions that research might take for the perpetrators of elder abuse, Wolf, in Chapter 13, argues convincingly that the problem be conceptualized as parallel to spouse abuse rather than child abuse. Also, Wolf makes the important point that research needs to focus more on the perpetrator than in the past, wherein most of the attention was accorded the victim. Such would be the case if clinical researchers examined the etiology and consequences of elder abuse from a family systems vantage point.

In Chapter 14 on the prevention of child physical abuse, Daro points out that the better evaluated strategies include home visitor programs, parenting education classes, and support groups. However, such programs are not widespread, and even in the more successful evaluative efforts, the research methodology is less than pristine. It is hoped that Daro's strong plea for a variety of preventive efforts in this area will be noted by both clinical researchers and funding agencies, who can bring such research evaluations to fruition. Moreover, she urges that efforts be directed toward altering the public's still positive view of physical punishment (i.e., spanking) to discipline children. Educational strategies to overturn this entrenched attitude definitely need to be evaluated.

Hazzard (Chapter 15) details the work that has been accomplished to date in the prevention of child sexual abuse. Although the school-based prevention programs for elementary schoolchildren appear to be effective on a short-term basis, at least on analogue measures, the long-term clinical viability of such interventions has not been established. On the other hand, with preschoolers it seems that the concepts involved in prevention training are too abstract; thus these very young children are given concrete rules about genital touching. Fewer prevention programs are directed to adolescents, and the area is not well researched. In addition to ascertaining the long-term clinical benefits of school-based programs, future research should evaluate potential disclosures as a result of such prevention training. Also, the impact of prevention training on the child's developing sexuality warrants careful examination. Finally, Hazzard rightfully argues that prevention education should be included in undergraduate and graduate curricula for teachers, mental health professionals, clergy, and pediatricians.

With respect to the primary prevention of wife assault, Hotaling and Sugarman (Chapter 16) underscore that very few risk factors can differentiate women who have been assaulted from those who have not. The obvious exception is a high level of marital conflict. In addition, women from a lower socioeconomic status and those with husbands who have witnessed parental violence are at greater risk. Thus, preventive efforts, according to Hotaling and Sugarman, should target the three aforementioned risk factors. From this analysis it is clear that research in this area is in its most elementary stage.

As one reads Chapter 17 on the prevention of elder abuse, by Pillemer and Suitor, it is apparent that even less is known here than in the prevention of wife assault. Very much needed are epidemiological studies, single case experimental design studies looking at the effects of new treatments, and then group controlled studies contrasting the best treatments available. The study of prevention is weakest in the area of family violence in general, but with respect to elder abuse the absence of evaluation stands out.

EPILOGUE

Family violence is a problem that has always plagued humankind, and obviously it will not be eradicated in our lifetime. However, it is important to acknowledge the strides that have been made in this field. It is easy to be critical; but it is infinitely more difficult to innovate and improve on the existing knowledge base. The researchers of the 1960s and 1970s have alerted professionals to the epidemiclike nature of the problem through their careful epidemiological surveys. More recently, it is the researchers of the 1980s who first developed treatment strategies to deal with the victims and perpetrators of family violence. But now and in the future, the researchers of the 1990s will be expected to develop and carefully evaluate the most promising treatments and preventive strategies in rigorous experimental fashion. We trust that the recommendations presented herein will challenge our colleagues in the field to study, test, innovate, and refine, doing so in scientific fashion.

REFERENCES

American Psychiatric Association. (1987). *Diagnostic and statistical manual of mental disorders* (DSM-III-R; 3rd ed.-Rev.). Washington, DC: Author.

Ammerman, R. T., & Hersen, M. (Eds.). (in press). *Children at risk: An evaluation of factors contributing to child abuse and neglect.* New York: Plenum.

Ammerman, R. T., Hersen, M., & Van Hasselt, V. B. (1987). *Child Abuse and Neglect Interview Schedule (CANIS)*. Unpublished instrument, Western Pennsylvania School for Blind Children, Pittsburgh.

Ammerman, R. T., Van Hasselt, V. B., & Hersen, M. (1985). Social skills training for visually handicapped children: A treatment manual. *Psychological Documents, 15*, 6 (Ms. no. 2684).

Ammerman, R. T., Van Hasselt, V. B., & Hersen, M. (1988). Maltreatment of handicapped children: A critical review. *Journal of Family Violence, 3*, 53–72.

Barlow, D. H., & Hersen, M. (1984). *Single-case experimental designs: Strategies for studying behavior change* (2nd ed.). New York: Pergamon.

Becker, J. V., Kaplan, M. S., Cunningham-Rathner, J., & Kovoussi, R. (1986). Characteristics of adolescent incest sexual perpetrators: Preliminary findings. *Journal of Family Violence, 1*, 85–97.

Beidel, D. C., Bellack, A. S., Turner, S. M., Hersen, M., & Luber, R. F. (1981). Social skills training for chronic psychiatric patients: A treatment manual. *JSAS Catalog of Selected Documents in Psychology, 11*, 36 (MS. no. 2257).

Bellack, A. S., & Hersen, M. (Eds.), (1988). *Behavioral assessment: A practical handbook* (3rd ed.). New York: Pergamon.

Bellack, A. S., Hersen, M., & Himmelhoch, J. M. (1980). Social skills training for depression: A treatment manual. *JSAS Catalog of Selected Documents in Psychology, 10*, 92 (MS. no. 2156).

Bidwell, L., & White, P. (1986). The family context of marital rape. *Journal of Family Violence, 1*, 277–287.

Bolton, F. G., & MacEachron, A. (1986). Assessing child maltreatment risk in the recently divorced parent–child relationship. *Journal of Family Violence, 1*, 259–275.

Brassard, M. R., & Hart, S. (in press). Psychological and emotional abuse of children. In R. T. Ammerman & M. Hersen (Eds.), *Case studies in family violence*. New York: Plenum.

Browne, A., & Finkelhor, D. (1986). Impact of child sexual abuse: A review of the research. *Psychological Bulletin, 99*, 66–77.

Chambers, W. J., Puig-Antich, J., Hirsch, M., Paez, P., Ambrosini, P. J., Tabrizi, M. A., & Davies, M. (1985). The assessment of affective disorders in children and adolescents by semistructured interview: Test-retest reliability of the K-SADS-P. *Archives of General Psychiatry, 42*, 696–702.

Fantuzzo, J. W., & Lindquist, C. U. (1989). The effects of observing conjugal violence on children: A review and analysis of research methodology. *Journal of Family Violence, 4*, 77–94.

Geffner, R., Rosenbaum, A., & Hughes, H. (1988). Research issues concerning family violence. In V. B. Van Hasselt, R. L. Morrison, A. S. Bellack, & M. Hersen (Eds.), *Handbook of family violence* (pp. 457–481). New York: Plenum.

Gondolf E. W. (1985). *Men who batter: An integrated approach for stopping wife abuse*. Holmes Beach, FL: Learning Publications.

Gondolf, E. W. (1987a). Evaluating programs for men who batter: Problems and prospects. *Journal of Family Violence, 2,* 95–108.

Gondolf, E. W. (1987b). Changing men who batter: A developmental model for integrated interventions. *Journal of Family Violence, 2,* 335–349.

Hamberger, L. K., & Hastings, J. E. (1986). Personality correlates of men who abuse their partners: A cross-validation study. *Journal of Family Violence, 1,* 323–241.

Hersen, M., & Ammerman, R. T. (1989). Overview of new developments in child behavior therapy. In M. Hersen (Ed.), *Innovations in child behavior therapy* (pp. 3–31). New York: Springer.

Hersen, M., & Bellack, A. S. (Eds.). (1988). *Dictionary of behavioral assessment techniques.* New York: Pergamon.

Hersen, M., & Turner, S. M. (Eds.). (1985). *Diagnostic interviewing.* New York: Plenum.

Howell, M. J., & Pugliesi, K. L. (1988). Husbands who harm: Predicting spousal violence by men. *Journal of Family Violence 3,* 15–27.

Kaufman, J., & Zigler, E. (1987). Do abused children become abusive parents? *American Journal of Orthopsychiatry, 57,* 186–192.

Kazdin, A. E. (1987). Treatment of antisocial behavior in children: Current status and future directions. *Psychological Bulletin, 102,* 187–203.

Kolko, D. J. (1987). Treatment of child sexual abuse: Programs, progress, and prospects. *Journal of Family Violence, 2,* 303–318.

Kolko, D. J., Moser, J. T., Litz, J., & Hughes, J. (1987). Promoting awareness and prevention of child sexual victimization using the red flag/green flag program: An evaluation with follow-up. *Journal of Family Violence, 2,* 11–35.

Last, C. G., & Hersen, M. (Eds.). (1988). *Handbook of anxiety disorders.* New York: Pergamon.

Lewis, B. Y. (1987). Psychosocial factors related to wife abuse. *Journal of Family Violence, 2,* 1–10.

Lutzker J. R., & Rice, J. M. (1987). Using recidivism data to evaluate Project 12-Ways: An ecobehavioral approach to the treatment and prevention of child abuse and neglect. *Journal of Family Violence, 2,* 283–290.

Pierce, R. L., & Trotta, R. (1986). Abused parents: A hidden family problem. *Journal of Family Violence, 1,* 99–110.

Roberts, A. R. (1987). Psychosocial characteristics of batterers: A study of 234 men charged with domestic violence offenses. *Journal of Family Violence, 2,* 81–93.

Rosenbaum, A. (1988). Methodological issues in marital violence research. *Journal of Family Violence, 3,* 91–104.

Rowley, F. L., Van Hasselt, V. B., & Hersen, M. (1986). Behavioral treatment of families with an adolescent with spina bifida: A treatment manual. *Social and Behavioral Science Documents, 16* (Ms. no. 2784).

Schinke, S. P., Schilling, R. F., Barth, R. P., Gilchrist, L. D., & Maxwell, J. S. (1986). Stress-management intervention to prevent family violence. *Journal of Family Violence, 1,* 13–26.

Spitzer, R. L., & Endicott, J. (1977). *Schedule for the affective disorders and schizo-phrenia*. New York: Biometrics Research, New York State Psychiatric Institute.

Van Hasselt, V. B., Morrison, R. L., Bellack, A. S., & Hersen, M. (Eds.). (1988). *Handbook of family violence*. New York: Plenum.

Wolf, M. M., Braukmann, C. J., & Ramp, K. A. (1987). Serious delinquent behavior as part of a significantly handicapping condition: Cures and supportive environments. *Journal of Applied Behavior Analysis, 20,* 347–359.

Zuravin, S. J. (1986). Residential density and urban child maltreatment: An aggregate analysis. *Journal of Family Violence, 1,* 307–322.

Author Index

Subject Index

DATE DUE

MAR 2 5 1999			
APR 0 3 2002			